WITHDRAWN-UNL

Adolescence

SECOND EDITION
Adolescence

ROBERT E. GRINDER
Arizona State University

JOHN WILEY & SONS
New York   Santa Barbara   London   Sydney   Toronto

Copyright © 1973, 1978, by John Wiley & Sons, Inc.

All rights reserved. Published simultaneously in Canada.

No part of this book may be reproduced by any means, nor transmitted, nor translated into a machine language without the written permission of the publisher.

Library of Congress Cataloging in Publication Data:

Grinder, Robert E
  Adolescence.

  Includes bibliographies and indexes.
  1. Adolescence.   I. Title.

HQ796.G737   1978   301.43′15   77-7239
ISBN 0-471-32767-0

Printed in the United States of America

10 9 8 7 6 5 4 3 2 1

For Jonathan, Timothy, and Elisabeth

Preface

Adolescence is a review of the current scientific literature pertaining to young people. I sought to accomplish four objectives in writing the book: (1) to integrate historical, contemporary, and futurist perspectives on adolescent development; (2) to describe the characteristic ways adolescents interact within the framework of social institutions—familial, peer-group, educational, and workforce; (3) to review essays and research studies that illustrate how adolescents learn role expectations, develop self-awareness and identity, and attain purpose in their lives; and (4) to analyze *why* adolescents are shaping new life style forms.

Adolescence is addressed to teachers and students of psychology, counseling, sociology, home economics, and to others who seek a comprehensive understanding of the adolescent stage of human development. The subject matter is reviewed topically, but special attention is given to interrelationships among the crucial factors in adolescent socialization. The book is divided into thirteen distinct chapters, each of which may be read separately or sequenced in any order without loss of continuity.

Learning aids are incorporated in each chapter to facilitate comprehension and to enhance retention. Each chapter opens with a listing of *Chapter Highlights* and *Issues*. The *Highlights* correspond to the table of contents and indicate how the chapter topics are organized; the *Issues* outline the substantive points underlying each of the main topics. *Review* and *Discussion Questions* follow the Summary section of each chapter. The *Review Questions* are keyed to the issues, and readers who answer them may be assured that they have become familiar with the significant points considered. The *Discussion Questions,* in contrast, are intended to stimulate reflective thought. Resolution of these questions call for integration of ideas presented in the text, data from other sources, insights from personal experiences, and viewpoints of colleagues. Detailed references are included, too, as study aids for students who may wish to make direct use of my primary sources. Finally, a glossary is presented at the end of the book for those who would like to check the meaning of a word used in the text.

This volume is the second edition of *Adolescence*. Since the publication of the first edition in 1973, perspectives have sharpened in respect to causes of social disaffection and ethnic prejudice, effects of sexism in socialization, facets of adolescent morality, and changes needed in educational practices to facilitate youth's entry into productive work. Attitudes toward drug usage, sexuality, and youth-culture styles also are more sophisticated today, and much of the idealism reflected in political activism has yielded to preoccupation with vocational and career issues. Changes clearly have been swift, and to keep pace, this new edition of *Adolescence* represents a thorough revision of the earlier version.

The book proceeds roughly from a broad consideration of the physical, biological, and hereditary influences that affect personality development to a focus on the interpersonal and social forces that influence socialization. Descriptions in Chapter 1 of G. Stanley Hall's recapitulation theory, Freud's storm and stress hypothesis, Erikson's epigenetic model of identity formation, and a current interpretation of self-concept development provide perspective for the book's central proposition—that adolescents develop life styles and acquire competencies through role-learning and interpersonal relationships, which occur cumulatively within the context of an expanding social environment. Chapters 2 to 4 cover a wide range of issues, including morphological aspects of physical growth, body image, maturation rate, physical fitness, sexism in sports, and such hazards to adolescents' physical well-being as automobile accidents, venereal diseases, suicide, alcohol, and cigarettes. Chapter 5 reviews the characteristics of psychoactive drugs and patterns of recreational and multiple drug usage, and Chapter 6 covers the meaning of intelligence and the acquisition of cognitive structures. Chapters 7 to 10 deal with dimensions of adolescent identity formation in contemporary society—motivation, role acquisition, sex-role stereotyping, parental role functions, parent-adolescent relations, runaways, birth order, maternal employment, father absence, and moral development, which is discussed in the context of both developmental-philosophic and social-learning theories. Youth-culture styles (conventional, hedonistic, and counter-cultural), patterns of peer interaction, and characteristics of interpersonal attraction, friendships, dating, and adolescent marriages are then considered. Chapter 11 documents recent changes in sexual attitudes and behavior and examines factors affecting sexual decision making. Chapter 12 focuses on the educational features of socialization, including student rights, interscholastic athletics, creativity, disciplinary controls, sex biases in curricula and programs, and compulsory education. Finally, Chapter 13 presents a summary of factors that affect career considerations, an overview of the conceptual bases of occupational decision making, an analysis of career education, and a discussion of ways in which schooling and experiential learning may be integrated.

I gratefully acknowledge the help of a number of persons in writing *Adolescence*. I am especially indebted to the researchers whose studies I have used in making my analyses. I have acknowledged their contributions via footnotes throughout the text. Quotations and permissions to report copyrighted material are individually acknowledged. I am also indebted to Edward A. Nelsen, my longtime friend and colleague, who helped me clarify portions of the manuscript, and to Christy A. Duff, whose invaluable secretarial assistance greatly expedited the book's development.

Robert E. Grinder

Contents

Adolescence

Chapter 1

Perspectives on Adolescent Development

CHAPTER HIGHLIGHTS

ISSUES

Many of the roles adolescents learn are unique to this period of life.

Self-examination, an instrumental work ethic, and upward mobility are important aspects of adolescent socialization.

Youth's hopes for self-realization through integrating occupational and personal goals are taking new forms.

Scientific inquiry in the field of adolescence involves sophisticated study of developmental, societal, and historical factors.

Compulsory education, child labor legislation, and legal procedures for delinquents provided the bases for the first social definition of adolescence.

The post-Darwinian consciousness of evolution and the theory of recapitulation provided a biological basis for the first scientific studies in adolescence.

Psychoanalytic theory has led to an interpretation of adolescence as a period of storm and stress.

Erikson's interactional model of human development, which integrates biological, social, and individual components, offers a widely accepted, comprehensive view of adolescent identity formation.

Self-concept theory provides a single, basic framework for understanding adolescent socialization.

ADOLESCENCE AND GROWING UP

Adolescence, as an area of scholarly study subject to scientific investigation, is one segment of the field of human development. Students of human development have separated the life span into stages such as infancy, childhood, adolescence, young adulthood, middle adulthood, and senior adulthood. The biological boundaries of the adolescent period often are simply and conveniently fixed by convention at the onset and end of the acceleration in physical growth that occurs during the second decade of life. If one were to use rapid development in height as a criterion, for example, adolescence for both sexes would range from age 11 or 12 until about 17 or 18. The biological limits can be specified rather easily, but reliance upon them leads to a narrow perspective of adolescence. Moreover, preoccupation with the biological reality of adolescence can lead to the belief that it is merely a stage in the life span through which individuals pass in their preparation for adulthood.

A comprehensive understanding of adolescence also requires knowledge of youth's consciousness or the personal factors—aspirations, attitudes, beliefs, dispositions—that enable young people to sustain intimate and lasting social relationships, accept vocational and economic responsibilities, and form ideological convictions.* It is necessary, too, to study the interaction between young people and social institutions—peer-group, familial, educational, economic, and political—to appreciate the cultural bases of their personal consciousness. A definition of adolescence based on social boundaries is necessarily abstract. When agrarianism and simple technology dominated life, social institutions served youth in much the same manner year after year, and the social boundaries were fairly easy to identify. Societal changes, however, have been swift in recent years. The outlook on drugs, sexual expression, and youth-culture styles is much more sophisticated today than a decade ago, and much of the idealism reflected in political activism has yielded to preoccupation with vocational and career issues. Satisfactory social definitions of adolescence, as a consequence, are now difficult to agree upon. The transition from elementary to middle-school or junior-high school (from sixth to seventh grade), which happens to coincide roughly with the beginning of rapid physical growth, is used by many researchers to mark the end of childhood and the beginning of early adolescence. Attainment of one or more of the characteristics of young adulthood

---

* Sometimes the term "youth" is employed to demarcate another stage of life between adolescence and adulthood. The distinction is said to be useful on the grounds that a particular group of young people (youth) are distinguishable from others (adolescents) in the twilight of adolescence by heightened self-awareness, and thus, capacity to bring about high levels of integration between personal and social values. The terms "adolescence" and "youth" are used interchangeably by most social scientists, however, since attempts to distinguish persons operationally on the basis of their effectiveness as change agents have not proven very useful. Consequently, no distinction is made between the two terms in this book.

Growing up in America means merging one's experiences with new assessments of the present, and thereby, acquiring one's personal view of destiny.

(marriage, parenthood, full-time employment, economic independence) often is regarded as the upper boundary.[1] These boundaries cast a net large enough to capture most aspects of adolescent development, including the biological, which can be viewed as one of the factors affecting the social reality of adolescence. Many personality characteristics acquired in preparation for adulthood are also integral to life as an adolescent, and the sociocultural approach lends credence to the belief that adolescence represents a unique period in the life span during which a variety of age-specific roles must be learned, skills developed, and tasks accomplished.

The process of growing up is an intricate undertaking. During adolescence, the capacity arises for achieving high levels of self-awareness. Self-examination lies at the heart of adolescence. Adolescents, in contrast to children, acquire the potential to merge the experiences of physical sexuality with the moral and social dimensions of sexual expression, to experiment with rewarding new forms of social interaction as the protective dependencies of childhood fade away, and to focus their intellects on understanding justice, equality, and respect for the rights of others. Since no two young people have exactly the same experiences or occupy identical positions in the social structure, each life must be developed in a unique setting in the context of a particular set of circumstances. Each adolescent has but one life to live, and the pattern it takes is always a compromise. Energies must be channeled, because consequences are cumulative, options are finite, and every choice reduces one's freedom. Adolescence evolves as young people encounter fresh dimensions of the past, make new assessments of the present, and acquire their own view of destiny.

Growing up in America has meant learning to view achievement as one of the dominant organizing principles of life and to invest one's pride and hope in the promise of realizing one's aspirations. Upward mobility, as classically expressed in the Horatio Alger myth, has long been held to be the promise of America. Whatever other meanings life has held—in the family, school, or work place— dreams engendered by the instrumental work ethic—a better tomorrow in return for sacrifice today—have dominated the personal consciousness of youth. This image, so strong historically, continues to dominate our moral systems. A recent study of the values of several hundred young people, for example, shows that instrumental values associated with "sense of accomplishment," "self-respect," and "wisdom," increased in strength for both boys and girls across grades 5, 7, 9, and 11. The boys' values reflected "a more unitary theme of increasing achievement orientation, while girls exhibited a dual theme of achievement and the stereotyped feminine sex role."[2] The buoyancy and resourcefulness of the job market up to the present time obviously has ensured the legitimacy of youth's demand for upward mobility. Young people have always aspired to attain work responsibilities different from those held by their parents, and it is their good fortune that the workforce has grown to satisfy their demands. A movement from agricultural to industrial work began long before the Revolutionary War. The nineteenth century witnessed a shift from blue-collar to white-collar work, and in recent years white-collar workers have become highly sophisticated professionals. Consequently, from the birth of the nation, the primary social institutions that engage youth—the family and the school—have been aligned to promote youth's attainment of adult privileges and statuses in the world of work.

But the situation today is not as it was in 1776. Upward mobility is less certain, and family and school are less relevant to youth. Modern society appears to have reached the end of the era in which technology can keep productivity climbing fast enough to yield a seemingly continuous rise in real, spendable income. It is difficult to imagine a limit to industrial growth being reached, but the signs of dramatic change are everywhere. Toffler[3] points out that our society is shifting away from industrialism; that is, a world system based on cheap raw materials, nonrenewable fossil fuel energy, a predominance of employment in the manufacturing sector, and materialistic values and growth ethics. Toffler says a new approach to the future is required, but what will the postindustrial economy be like? Bell[4] sees it principally as a communal society in which the production of goods and services are controlled more by public institutions than by the marketplace. It will probably be one in which supply and demand have leveled off, industrial output will fluctuate only slightly, and public choice rather than personal demand will determine the course of social progress.

The trends in society pointing to the rise of a postindustrial world have already led a sizeable proportion of the current generation to expect that work will have personal significance, provide opportunity for creative expression, and be a vehicle for making meaningful contributions to the wider society. But while young people's hopes for self-realization through integrating occupational and personal goals are beginning to take different and more pluralistic forms, the number of meaningful career opportunities available to them is decreasing in two important ways. First, the total quantity of career options is decreasing as the older methods of utilizing labor are being phased out. Second, the relative number of options available per person is declining because the youth segment of the population competing for them has soared. There were 27.1 million young persons between 14 and 24 years of age in America in 1960, for example, and they represented 15 percent of the population. As of July 1, 1975, the estimated population of young persons, 14 to 24 years of age, was 44.6 million, and these young people now represent approximately 20 percent of the total population. The United States Census Bureau projects that the number of persons 14 to 24 years old will peak in 1980 at 45.2 million and thereafter begin to decline, perhaps to about 42 million by 1985. Thus, the number of young people seeking careers will be very large in the near future, and will continue to be relatively large for the foreseeable future.

The contradictions between demands for upward mobility as we knew it and social reality as we are coming to know it are causing a vast number of young people to become underemployed, in the sense that tasks required of them are elementary relative to their skills, and they are tending to drive all but the well-trained into dead-end, low-paying jobs. The present situation constitutes a cancerous source of despair, cynicism, and alienation, and raises concern among many youth and adults alike about whether the future will complement or oppose the political, economic, and moral traditions of the past. The eventual resolution of the dilemmas posed by our transition from one kind of economy to another rests in part in the ways youth respond to the processes affecting change. Each successive generation experiments with new forms of roles and ideals. Adolescence is the stage of life when young people first begin to assert themselves as distinctly different human beings, and they have opportunity today to participate in the evolution of a new social order. The current generation of adolescents, both individually and collectively, must consider which aspects of society and which standards of adulthood should be reaffirmed and which should be challenged. Youth's attempt to cope with problems of identity, intimacy, and sexuality, for example, in the face of developments in birth control methods and equalization of career opportunities for the two sexes surely will lead to different expressions of marriage and family style. And as the significance given life through work and procreation shifts in meaning, new alignments of family, school, and workplace will evolve. To understand contemporary adolescents, therefore, as the ensuing discussion in this book implicitly emphasizes, it is necessary to study their physical, cognitive, and social development in the context of social change in America.

ADOLESCENCE AND SCIENTIFIC INQUIRY

The fundamental laws of logic have been well known since the time of Aristotle (384–322 B.C.). In a collection of treatises known as the *Organon*, Aristotle set forth the processes of logical inference necessary to prove the validity of rational conclusions. He described the fundamental technique for building a science of trustworthy knowledge. One must start, he said, with a few essential axioms or truths that intuition has shown to be correct. These become theorems or self-evident truths and are to be used with syllogisms. These are processes by which one may argue *deductively* from previously established premises or information to particular instances, or conversely, argue *inductively* from a collection of independently observed events toward generalizations. The deductive process results in a conclusion that contains no more information than in the premises; one might say that "all crows are birds; this is a crow; therefore, this is a bird." The inductive process, on the other hand, leads to a hypothesis that extends the information on which it is based; thus, "every crow seen so far has been black; hence, all crows are black." As a consequence of syllogistic reasoning, events and objects that prove reliable can be used as bases for hypotheses to predict new relationships, and information thus accumulated can inspire comprehensive generalizations, the formulation of explanatory principles and propositions, and, eventually, the systemization of knowledge. Aristotle warned those who might employ his methods to proceed cautiously, to be certain before applying them either that the premises were really relevant to the events deduced or that the generalizations actually represented the instances to which they applied.

Adolescence became the subject of scientific investigation late in the nineteenth century. During those heady, rustic days of psychological research, the significance of adolescence as a preparatory stage for adulthood was exaggerated out of proportion, and for a time several social scientists regarded the study of adolescence as "the focal point of all psychology."[5] Experimental and controlled procedures were unanticipated; youth were simply interrogated about their feelings or mailed questionnaires in which they could describe their sentiments. The problems of bias and lack of standardization and the influence of extraneous factors that might affect conclusions were naively ignored. Consequently, while hypotheses abounded, little momentum was gained in systematizing knowledge into a science of adolescence. Methods of studying adolescence have since improved, enabling social scientists to advance more objective and relevant interpretations of adolescent behavior. Aristotle's caveats, however, are as applicable today as ever. "Theories and research conclusions are to a degree the captives of the methods and raw data upon which they are based."[6] The empirical approaches now employed to investigate theories, assumptions, and generalizations about adolescent development have both strengths and weaknesses. These approaches usually take one of three general forms, and for illustrative purposes are labeled the *descriptive, designed,* and *retrospective* approaches.

Descriptive Approach

Data obtained by this approach are described either numerically or biographically. When the data are quantitative, they may be summarized by an arithmetic average, percentage figure, or simple frequency count. These quantitative measures (statistics) both describe the characteristics under study and provide standards for teachers and guidance counselors to determine whether adolescents are deviating too markedly from the "norms" of their group or class. The variables may range from precise measures of physical growth to rankings of academic performance and personality traits. The data can often be obtained quickly because counting and tabulating are relatively simple procedures. But the simplicity of obtaining such numerical data makes it difficult to explain relations among different variables since tabulation does not readily lend itself to such considerations. One lacks grounds for inferring whether separately observed events have any connection with each other. On the other hand, when the data are biographical, events are easily interrelated. The connections among the variables may be bridged intuitively by the chronicler who constructs the biography. Counselors, clinicians, and therapists, while treating adolescents, may develop protocols or word pictures of their life styles that describe their symptoms, problems, or advantages; that offers an interpretation of why their lives have developed as they have; and, perhaps, that forecasts how future events may unfold for them. Rich insights into the dynamics of adolescent behavior have been produced from such protocols, and the biographical method has probably contributed more to the development of such insights than any other research technique. The data, however, are derived from selective recall; despite the objectivity of the chronicler, the data may represent an unreliable mixture of actual events and conjectures. The record is organized to accord with one's views on human nature, which probably fall short of pure objectivity. The dynamics of the events one has observed may be unlike any others, greatly restricting the generality of one's interpretations. All too often, however, because a diagnosis is needed immediately, desire for insight overshadows problems of distortion and invalidation.

Designed Approach

The process of collecting data for reliable explanation and prediction of relationships among variables requires sophisticated techniques for controlling extraneous influences. There are two carefully designed procedures: the *naturalistic* and the *manipulative*. The naturalistic procedure constrains the researcher from disturbing the natural environment in making systematic observations. The manipulative procedure, on the other hand, sets forth special, contrived experimental conditions in the environment or laboratory to elicit specific behavior patterns. A significant proportion of the research on adolescence has been and is likely to continue to be naturalistic. Many significant ingredients of personality—aggressiveness, jealousy, enthusiasm, generosity—are seldom reflected reliably in experimentally devised situations. Further, the props for peer-group interaction and family byplay are difficult to manipulate or recreate artificially. Although naturalistic research is difficult, it is even more so with adolescents than with children. The latter are especially tractable; they are relatively naive, indiscriminate, trustful, and obliging. From middle childhood onward, however, children are reluctant to express themselves in the presence of an observer. The problem taxes the wits of every researcher. Hidden video cameras and long-range telescopes are often impractical, and it is hard for even an enterprising investigator to create the illusion that one and one's apparatus are like an isolated fly on the wall. Information is often obtained by watching from behind one-way-vision screens or by unobtrusive note-taking, but whether the protagonists express themselves in the presence of an intruder as they would in privacy is never known. In a naturalistic study of adolescent male peer groups, Sherif and Sherif[7] ingeniously collected data by creating a credible pretext for the presence of an interloper and by encouraging the boys to come to him. One trained observer, for example, began working out with a new ball at a play area in a poor neighborhood. When the boys sought to play with the ball, he graciously included them in his activity. To establish credibility, he informed them that he was attempting to lose weight and would be exercising at the playground regularly. Another observer obligingly ate charcoal-broiled hamburgers at a drive-in and spent many hours at a coffee-house listening to folk music. When members of the peer groups eventually admired his new and expensive car, he generously allowed some of them to drive it past the homes of girls whom they wanted to impress.

Sherif and Sherif's consummate approach to naturalistic research requires imagination and superior financial resources. But there is no assurance that a wide range of behavior patterns will be expressed. The alternative would be to design manipulative experiments in which special stimuli would help elicit given behaviors. Here extraneous influences would be controlled, and different responses could be subjected to analyses that would yield reliable, highly generalizable findings. The simulation of meaningful life settings, however, is often either impractical or prohibitively expensive. A traditional compromise adopted by some researchers has been to employ paper-and-pencil and projective "tests"—questionnaires, story-completions, drawings, ink-blots, and photographs. The "tests" may be administered in a classroom clinic, where adolescents are asked to respond as if they were in a hypothetical situation. The art of enticing adolescents to reveal themselves by responding to vignettes, pictures, props, and other artifacts may require highly technical, quasi-manipulative considerations, but the procedure is manageable, and it has become the most widespread method of collecting such data. It will probably continue to dominate the research scene until social scientists learn either to conduct naturalistic observations at more reasonable cost or to simulate social behavior more effectively in the laboratory.

Retrospective Approach

Researchers studying adolescence are led inevitably to retrospective data. The accrued effects of childhood socialization and physical growth profoundly influence behavior in adolescence. Questions bearing on the permanence of habits, the continuity of intelligence, the extent to which early experiences facilitate later learning, the way in which activity develops into mature behavior, and the consistency of parental attitudes and practices toward personality development in adolescence must be related to antecedent events.[8] Since retrospective study seeks to explain present behavior from past events, it requires at least two sets of data obtained at different points in developmental time.

The longitudinal method of collecting data (which measures the same person at periodic intervals) holds constant intraindividual differences in socioeconomic status, parental level of education, ethnic background, religious affiliation, and climatic conditions. This method enables the researcher to establish curves depicting physical growth and other dynamic characteristics of development since one can plot patterns across time for the same adolescents. Harold Jones, father of longitudinal studies in adolescence, adapted a principle of "organic relationship and adaptation" as the basis for his research.[9] Jones sought to study alterations across time in physiological equilibria, intraorganic stimulation, and growth in motor abilities. The longitudinal design suited Jones' purposes; however, this method is likely to be quite expensive, time-consuming, and troublesome to execute. The research program must be planned years in advance, and the investigators may have to wait a long time before the data can be interpreted and reported. The investigators who first design a study may inadvertently fail to anticipate many of the questions and problems that in succeeding years prove to be significant. And it is possible that the original data will be too ambiguously coded for subsequent analyses.[10] By the time a longitudinal study is a decade or two along, continuity may be disrupted as project investigators transfer to new positions or retire. New investigators introduce different values, skills, and interests, and data laboriously collected by the founding group may appear largely irrelevant to its successors. Bayley[11] illustrates how difficult it is to test every child at every scheduled testing session. They become sick, upset, or refuse to participate any more; their mothers forget appointments or refuse further cooperation; their families go on vacation or move away. It is difficult to obtain comparable measures unless identical tests are used; however, repeated measurements lead to familiarity with the instruments, memorization of items, and boredom—all of which reduce measurement reliability. Moreover, the instruments may become obsolete as newer and better ones are devised, and then the problem is whether to continue with the old, to sacrifice comparability by substituting the new, or to tax the time and tolerance of the participants by administering both the old and new.

A researcher may bypass the expense and time required for the longitudinal study by collecting current data on adolescents and asking them or their parents about earlier stages in their development. The same subjects thus are studied at different points in their development, but the data are collected simultaneously. The weakness in this hybrid technique, of course, lies in problems associated with recall. Parental reminiscences of child-rearing practices include what actually happened, what they have read about raising children, what they wished might have happened, and what they may want the investigator to think about them as parents. Parental practices also are often modified during a child's development, and parents may forget which practices they used with which child. They may be unaware of their attitudinal shifts and thus fail to report what actually happened. Although this technique has definitely expedited research on the antecedents of adolescent behavior, it is not precise, and so conclusions must be accepted cautiously.[12]

The cross-sectional method of collecting data overcomes the time-lag limitation of the longitudinal approach. Individuals of various ages are compared at the same point in real time. Since data are obtained simultaneously on individuals of different age groups, the moment in the culture is the same for each group. The enthusiasm and interest of the researchers usually holds for the length of the study, and the turnover in personnel is probably negligible. The short interval between the formulation of the hypotheses and the analyses of the data lessens the danger of obsolescence. The cross-sectional design of taking measurements on large groups of individuals of different ages is the most convenient and the least expensive procedure for gaining insight into developmental characteristics. But this method has serious limitations, too. Individuals cannot be matched precisely enough to approximate the kind of developmental comparisons that can be made in a longitudinal study of intraindividual patterns of growth.

The longitudinal and cross-sectional designs, unfortunately, do not enable us to understand how adolescent development is affected by societal changes and historical events as distinct from individual changes. The longitudinal design, by sampling only one group for a relatively brief time span, provides no point of reference for comparing the effects of societal change. The cross-sectional design, on the other hand, by comparing two or more age groups at the same point in time, tends to confound effects of societal change with maturational change because the subjects are at different ages when they encounter events like wars, economic depressions, and dramatic technological innovations such as radio and television. During the 1960s, for example, young people exhibited high levels of political activism, but one cannot determine solely from the data of the 1960s whether the degree of activism was a product of societal change or of conventional adolescent traits. But by comparing extent of activism in the late 1960s with that in the late 1970s, one might infer that the activism does indeed fluctuate with changes in societal factors. The logic of this comparison is reflected in a new, highly sophisticated sequential strategy that permits investigation of interactions between developmental aspects of adolescence and societal change as framed by historical periods.[13] This new strategy involves repeated applications of several cross-sectional studies at different points in time, a practice that creates, when the same persons are included in the investigations, an organized sequence of longitudinal studies. One can thereby study the interaction of individual and societal factors. The application of the sequential strategy probably will gain momentum in the next few years. Bengtson and Starr,[14] for example, have suggested five concepts by which the major aspects of the two types of change may be differentiated. The first relatively universal concept that the researchers have identified as reflecting change is chronological age. Individuals may be differentiated on the basis of personal and maturational characteristics, such as physical and cognitive development, and these individual characteristics will interact with the range and kind of statuses and roles open to them at both different ages and different historical periods. When economic conditions are stable, for example, a sudden increase in the birth rate would eventually lead to the availability of proportionately less workforce opportunities, and the keener competition for the openings would favor the youth of higher ability. The second concept, lineage, which refers to relationships between persons of different ages, is related to cultural transmission. Since tensions often exist between family, school, peer-group, and other agents of cultural transmission, lineage effects, or variations in the way values, knowledge, and skills are communicated to young people provide a useful concept for analyzing interaction between individual and societal changes. The third concept centers on life-cycle effects. Analyses are based on comparisons at successive points in time in terms of how much persons at similar ages are provided opportunity to participate responsibly in major areas of social life, such as marriage, family, work, and social activities. The assumption is that individuals of comparable ages will differ because of variations in the important developmental events that they have experienced. The fourth concept is labeled "period effect." The researchers suggest that dramatic economic, military, social and political events may be experienced at different ages, and once experienced, they may affect individuals throughout the rest of their lives. Thus, interaction between maturational and social changes may vary on the basis of events that tend to reorient individuals toward future activities. Finally, the researchers' fifth concept relates to the effect of ideological consciousness on interaction between individual and societal change. They say that during some historical periods, as when youth collectively see themselves threatened, youth-culture styles will lead young people to develop an awareness of themselves as a unique group with a distinctive ideological consciousness. This consciousness will interact with the personal consciousness that they are developing of themselves in respect to their physical, cognitive, and social attributes.[15]

TOWARD A SOCIAL DEFINITION OF ADOLESCENCE

The role of young people in Western society has undergone continuous transformation for several centuries. As cultural and economic forces have adapted to an increasingly technological world, changes in family relations, educational practices, and job opportunities have modified social definitions of adolescence. The pattern taken by the role transformations suggests three relatively distinct historical phases—recognition, social independence, and institutionalization, which correspond roughly with the preindustrial, early industrial, and industrial periods of society.

The recognition phase begins with the sociocultural revival that marks the beginning of modern society. Children in preindustrial Europe (especially in the lower class) mixed with adults, sharing work and play as early as they were able. Children became the companions of adults, and were indistinguishable from them in dress. As soon as a child abandoned the swaddling band—a band of cloth bound tightly around its body in babyhood—it was dressed like a man or woman, a miniature adult with all the external manifestations of masculinity or feminity.[16] Although children ostensibly belonged to adult society as soon as they could live without the constant solicitude of their mothers or guardians, preindustrial society in fact fostered a very long transitional period, beginning at the age youngsters could be somewhat independent of their families, usually about eight or nine, and ceasing with the independence attained at marriage, about mid-or late twenties.[17] By age 14, most young people were separated from their families largely for economic considerations, living as either servants in households, apprentices in their master's homes, or boarding students. This detachment of young people from their families led to the earliest recognition of a stage of adolescence. Life expectancy for both sexes in the seventeenth century was between 40 and 50 years of age. About one-half of the children died before they reached age 20, and the high mortality rate during the early years of life resulted in an average life expectancy of less than 30 years. Parents thus strived to attain several offspring in order to ensure that heirs would be on hand to care for them when they became too old to work. Many more children had to be born to offset the high mortality rate, a fact that led Gillis[18] to observe that we must imagine our ancestors in the perpetual presence of young offspring. High fertility meant that at some point the family was likely to be confronted with more labor than its resources could absorb. During the early years of marriage, even peasant families hired servants to help work the land, do household chores, or care for an abundance of young children. But as soon as children were physically able, they were put to work, and their labor was substituted for that of servants until they, too, became surplus. Younger children, therefore, forced

Adolescents found jobs caring for young children in abundance earlier in our nation's history.

out the older, who now began the transition from family dependence to adult independence by providing economic relief to their families in seeking their fortunes elsewhere. The eventual outcome of their servitude and with it the end of the transition, was governed by the laws of primogeniture; that is, societal norms dictated that the eldest living son should inherit the family estate on the death or retirement of the father, and acquisition of the farm or business enabled the son to marry and begin his own family. Final settlement might include dowries for daughters, to enhance their eligibility, and smaller grants for younger sons, who might become servants, craftsmen, artisans, or ministers.

The onset of industrialization initiated changes in inheritance practices and ushered in for young people an era of unprecedented social independence. The agricultural revolution of the eighteenth century led to the enclosure of large land holdings and a change in the status of peasants and artisans to that of landless laborers. The new economic order left them with neither wealth nor trade to leave to their children. Capitalism, however, enabled youth in the early-industrial period to turn their backs on roles associated with servitude. They attained their freedom because large land owners found it economically advantageous to create a class of laborers who would be sufficiently transient to work wherever they were needed. Migrations in the United States to industrial centers in search of higher wages and marriage opportunities led to large concentrations of young people free from adult supervision. The urban newcomers were characterized by striking age heterogeneity, and controls, to the extent that they existed at all, tended to be exerted by the older adolescents on the younger. The basic features of the American society that promoted adolescent independence also facilitated occupational mobility among young men. (The factory labor force was comprised primarily of young women in their teens or twenties, but the professions were denied to them.) Male talent was sought in agriculture, construction, marketing, and management. An absence of guilds, or feeble or nonexistent certification procedures in most professions and occupations, and loose and informal apprenticeship requirements ensured that upwardly mobile young men who left home at 18 or 20 to establish themselves faced relatively few institutional barriers to achievement.[19]

The tempo of industrialism increased during the second half of the nineteenth century, and the growth of an urban-technological society gave rise to a social context in which previous role patterns of young people's behavior were no longer applicable.[20] Cities were growing even more swiftly than before. More than half of the population living on the East Coast were in cities. The attraction of young people to the urban areas led inevitably to compromises in morality—drinking, sexual license, vagrancy, and delinquency—and growing insistence that the state intercede in controlling and educating the young. As humanitarian, economic, social, and political pressures maneuvered the state into a posture of *in loco parentis,* legislation evolved to institutionalize adolescence as a period associated with the ages specified in laws related to the following three areas: compulsory education, child labor legislation, and special legal procedures for juvenile delinquents.[21]

1. *Compulsory Schooling.* Compulsory attendance laws and public financing were an outgrowth of the belief that comprehensive public education could be an effective vehicle for socializing young people. "'The primary function of the public school . . . is not to confer benefits upon the individual as such.' Rather 'the school exists as a state institution because the very existence of civil society demands it.'"[22] English common law had assigned control of children's education to parents, and schools prior to the industrial era were organized more to enhance students' self-interests than to instill societal precepts of good citizenship.[23] Educational opportunities were available then in private academies, which ranged from one-teacher, family schools providing board and room for students in the family household to elaborate facilities offering comprehensive programs. The schools weighted the curricula toward the classics, mathematics, and composition. The middle and upper classes

seldom prolonged formal education to 21 or beyond, choosing instead a pattern of intensive schooling up to the age of 15 or 16 followed by entrance into merchant houses or professional apprenticeship. On the other hand, education in the academies among working-class young people was distinguished by seasonal attendance. A farm boy, for example, might attend school part of the year, perhaps during the winter, after harvesting and before planting, until his early twenties. Students at given achievement levels were thus likely to be anywhere from seven or eight to 25 years of age. The self-serving objectives, seasonal attendance patterns, and practice of mixing young people of all ages ended with the coming of factory labor, immigration, and public financing and control of schools. Public schools could not accomplish societal objectives of socialization on a casual basis, and therefore the development of standardized curricula, the training of certified teachers, the regularization of the annual cycles of promotion, the practice of insisting that all pupils go to a sequence of classes rather than to a few, and the requirement of teaching systems adapted to small, homogeneous classes resulted in an increasing correspondence between age and class.

Children of 7 to 13 or 14 were most affected at first by the standardization and bureaucratization of the schools. Most educators believed that the aims of literacy and moral training could be accomplished adequately with six or seven years of formal education, and high schools in the late nineteenth century were largely college-preparatory agencies for a select few. Moreover, unlike the earlier private academies, the high schools, although free, required attendance for nine or ten months, making schooling rather expensive especially for boys who could readily earn wages in farming or a trade. Coleman[24] has noted that few educators prior to the 1890s thought that the high school ever would be available to a high proportion of young people. Yet today every state except Mississippi, which has repealed its compulsion laws, requires compulsory attendance until age 16, and nine states require attendance until age 17 or 18. The dramatic growth of compulsory attendance laws occurred for several reasons. Child labor laws were enacted to keep young people out of the labor market, and the high school seemed to be the best alternative. An economic incentive evolved with the financing of secondary schools on the basis of average daily attendance. Parents began to entertain thoughts of upward mobility for their children and to recognize the economic value of a school diploma. The high school thus emerged in the twentieth century as a certifying agent to introduce young people to the marketplace, and by creating a bureaucratic barrier between schooling and the job market, compulsory education laws played a role in institutionalizing adolescence as a particular age group.

2. *Child Labor Legislation.* The movement to restrict child labor in the United States also contributed to the institutionalization of adolescence. In 1832 approximately 40 percent of the factory workers in New England were children. The economic value of displacing adults by children in the job market diminished, however, after the Civil War. The chronic labor shortage eased, demand for specialized workers grew with advancing technology, and a greater proportion of young women sought work in factories. The movement to constrain child labor was molded into legislation because of humanitarian objections to the exploitation of children for profit, awareness that industry was dependent on a literate and enlightened work force, and realization that young workers less than 14 years of age were inefficient, possessed a short work-span, and tended to have a disorganizing effect on the productivity of older workers.[25] Young workers are covered today by a federal law known as the Fair Labor and Standards Act, as amended in 1966.[26] The child labor provisions of the law require that young people be employed only in occupations in which their health and well-being is ensured. Children of any age may deliver newspapers to consumers, act in motion picture, theatrical, radio and television productions, or work for their parents either on the family farm or in occupations other than hazardous ones like manufacturing or mining. A 14- or 15-year-old minor may be employed in especially safe occupations providing that the work is *not* during school hours, before 7:00 a.m. or after 7:00 p.m. (9:00 p.m. from June 1 through Labor Day), more than three hours on school days, more than 18 hours during school weeks, more than eight hours on non-school days, or more than 40 hours on non-school weeks. A 16- or 17-year-old may work any hours at any job other than those declared by the Secretary of Labor as hazardous for minors between 16 and 18, for example, storing explosives, operating power-driven equipment, and butchering. Laws applicable to adults prevail after age 18.

3. *Special Legal Procedures for Juvenile Delinquents.* The juvenile courts contributed to the institutionalization of young people, too. According to Bakan,[27] "the great discrepancy between adult justice and juvenile justice and the legal vulnerability of juveniles has been one of the major factors associated with the conversion of the idea of adolescence into the social fact of adolescence." The researcher points to two basic reasons for the development of the notion of the juvenile delinquent. First, to remove young people from the jurisdiction of adult criminal laws, and second, to provide corrective rather than punitive treatment. A series of Juvenile Court Acts since the turn of the century have set the upper limit of "juvenile" delinquent between 16

and 21. About two-thirds of the states presently follow the recommendation of the United States Children's Bureau that the upper limit be age 19.[28]

ADOLESCENCE AND SIGNIFICANT VIEWPOINTS

As the twentieth century opened, the stage was set for new viewpoints about adolescence. The changes in society that were transforming the role of young people heightened social interest in the dynamics of individual growth. Scientific inquiry into the social sciences was beginning to take place, leading to new syntheses about human development. People of authority had long appreciated the unique nature of childhood, and the social and moral importance of educating children. For example, Jean Jacques Rousseau set forth in *Emile* (1762) a cogent developmental analysis of the biological and social aspects of children's growth. Written as a polemic against extremes in both secularism and religion, the book urged that *self-preservation* be viewed as the primary source of human activity. Reasoning, according to Rousseau, should be seen as a subsidiary faculty that imparts sentiment and higher meaning to emotions and feelings. Rousseau maintained that children should follow their instincts of self-preservation in acquiring enriching social experiences. In the developmental process emotional and reasoning functions interact with one another in relatively discrete, sequential stages. He saw the first stage, from birth until age five, as animalistic and prehuman. Self-consciousness dawns around middle childhood. At about age 12 rational faculties awaken, and by puberty, with the maturity of sexual capacities, social sentiments may be strong enough to control emotions. Since children are mainly innocent, if they could be sheltered from imperfections in the adult world, nature would ensure their healthy development. However, Rousseau's prophetic distinction between childhood and adolescence generated no systematic study. For centuries, facts, relationships, and theoretical propositions were unreliable, and most occurrences seemed unpredictable and capricious. Eventually, the study of human development merged with the natural sciences late in the nineteenth century as the theory of evolution gained widespread acceptance. The ferment and excitement of how the new science contributed to the study of adolescence is well documented in the early twentieth-century writings of G. Stanley Hall and Sigmund Freud. Hall and Freud were contemporaries. Both were profoundly affected by the post-Darwinian consciousness of evolution, and both emphasized the significance of hereditary determinants of personality. Hall and Freud ushered in the era of genetic psychology; both gave strong support to the *storm and stress (sturm und drang)* interpretation of adolescence. Hall studied socialization and the consequences of its failure from the viewpoint of recapitulation theory, which held that every individual repeated the history of his species in his own development. This theory acquired the force of an incantation in the hands of Hall. It was the first and thus far has been the last thorough integration of the literature from the philosophical and natural sciences into developmental psychology. His interest in linking ancestral evolution to individual development gave impetus to taxonomic, normative, and descriptive activities that, although far removed in purpose from his intent, have since accelerated in pediatrics, physical anthropology, and comparative psychology. Questions posed by Hall regarding the merits of psychical and physical traits in evolutionary progress are now curios of a forgotten era. Hall focused on the relationship between biological and psychological forces during adolescence, providing a rationale for limited interest in developmental events during infancy and childhood, but he overestimated the promise of adolescence and underestimated the significance of childhood. On the other hand, Freud held that personality growth was nearly complete by the end of the fifth year of life; thus neglecting adolescence as an important period in personality formation; however, insights from Freud's psychoanalytic theory have contributed immeasurably to the therapeutic treatment of adolescent personality deficiencies and to theoretical conceptualizations about personality development. His views have influenced therapists, clinicians, judges, probation officers, social workers, and teachers.

New research methods, new knowledge, and new interpretations of the ways young people interact with the social environment have rendered much of Hall's and major parts of Freud's viewpoint obsolescent. Nonetheless, significant vestiges of each are related to two important contemporary developmental interpretations that bear upon adolescence—Erik Erikson's epigenetic model and self-concept development. Let us, then, before turning to the two recent outlooks, consider respectively the contributions of Hall and Freud to the *genetic* and *storm and stress* viewpoints of adolescent development.

Genetic Viewpoint

Adolescence has always fascinated sages who have sought a better future for humanity—a transformed society—in the socialization of youth. The comingling of idealism, political reality, and scientific inquiry at different periods in history has produced distinctive viewpoints about adolescent development, and that of G. Stanley Hall has proven to be the most distinctive of all. Hall is considered to be the father of child study in America. He pioneered the questionnaire method in an era before controlled surveys and experimental procedures in the social sciences were anticipated, collated massive quantities of

Two pioneers in the field of adolescence, G. Stanley Hall and Sigmund
Freud are shown in this group photograph, which was taken at Clark
University in 1909 on the occasion of Freud's first visit to the United
States. Bottom, left to right: Freud, Hall, C. G. Jung, an early personality
theorist. Top, left to right: A. A. Brill, an American psychologist, E.
Jones, Freud's biographer, and S. Ferenczi, an early psychoanalyst.

research data, and reported them in *Adolescence* (1904), an enormously
comprehensive two-volume treatise, which has since been the foundation for discussions on adolescent development. Hall was the first at the threshold of
twentieth-century developmental psychology, but then he turned his back on the
future, preferring instead an outlook that expired with the nineteenth century.
More than any other leading psychologist of his time, Hall applied antiquated
principles of evolutionary theory to adolescent development.

Charles Darwin, in *The Origin of Species* (1859), was the first to muster sufficient evidence to sustain a theory of species mutability. His case for evolution
rested initially on the notion of natural selection, the belief that plants and animals possessing superior qualities for adaptation would survive and, by chance
variation, endow certain of their offspring with superior qualities, which, by
continued chance variation, might then be passed on to their progeny. Friends
in geology, however, pointed out to Darwin that life on earth simply had not
existed long enough for evolution to have occurred solely through random,
minute variations derived from natural selection. In countering their arguments
Darwin felt compelled to endorse Jean Lamarck's theory of acquired

characters.[29] A half century earlier Lamarck had advanced the notion that new habits and behaviors—acquired over time as adaptations to such events as climatic changes, migration, and geological upheaval—foist special shapes on organs and that these new structures, in turn, are inherited by offspring. For example, the body of a snake became elongated when its ancestors laid low in the grass to avoid predators, and the neck of the giraffe stretched out as its ancestors reached high into trees for sustenance. Although Lamarck's viewpoint was unconvincing to nineteenth-century scientists, Darwin and many of his followers vigorously incorporated Lamarckianism into the theory of evolution to complement the concept of natural selection. Two major schools of thought emerged, one insisting that hereditary changes occurred solely from the natural selection of mysterious chance variations, wholly immune to environmental pressures, and another holding that hereditary changes resulted from structural modifications brought about by adaptation. The conflict subsided with the discovery of genes and chromosomes and the reformulation of hereditary theory in 1900, based on Gregor Mendel's papers of 1865 on the hybridization of the sweet pea. Mendel's data revealed that hereditary changes occurred in large rather than imperceptibly small variations, reconciled the timing of mutability to the evidence of geologic time, and routed the Lamarckians, who never seemed to be able to demonstrate satisfactorily that experiences accumulated in one generation could be passed on to the next.

The tenuous theory of evolution was also bolstered in the nineteenth century by the advent of the theory of recapitulation, the idea that individuals retrace the historical record of their species development (phylogeny) in their own growth (ontogeny). Among Darwin's strongest supporters, Ernst Haeckel and Herbert Spencer believed that they possessed evidence showing recapitulatory stages among embryos and lower forms of life. Suddenly it seemed that all the missing links in the evolution of living species might eventually be reconstructed by recourse to the study of individual growth.

G. Stanley Hall's ingenuous faith in Lamarckianism and the theory of recapitulation led him to formulate five basic principles that became the basis of his science of human development. First and foremost was Hall's belief that any changes in the individual that would advance evolution had to occur in adolescence. Earlier speculation by Rousseau, who had suggested that moral and intellectual traits first appear at adolescence, corroborated his view. One early twentieth-century educator proclaimed that "the child is naturally successively animal, anthropoid, half-barbarian, and then civilized".[30] G. Stanley Hall[31] agreed: "The influence of the environment in producing acquired characters transmissible by heredity is greatest in the soma during adolescence. At any rate, for those prophetic souls interested in the future of our race and desirous of advancing it, the field of adolescence is the quarry in which they must seek to find both goals and means. If such a higher stage is ever added to our race, it will not be by increments at any later plateau of adult life, but it will come by increased development at the adolescent stage, which is the bud of promise for the race."

Second, Hall believed in the principle that *nature is right*. In postulating that individual growth is a retracing of the steps of species evolution, the recapitulation theorists held that human development must conform to a repetition of the ancestral record until adolescence, a time when the cessation of physical growth suggested that evolutionary momentum had subsided.

The notion that nature had preprogrammed recapitulation was strongly complemented by a third principle, *catharsis*. For example, if the intrinsically determined sequence of growth changes in an individual necessitates a retracing of racial evolution, each succeeding stage then becomes a vital link in the developmental chain. Every stage of growth, therefore, should be permitted full expression, since each serves as a stimulus to the one that follows. Should environmental pressures suppress a given stage, the course of development could become arrested or retarded. Indeed, traits thus lost might signify the onset of regressive evolution. It had been argued that many propensities, including avarice, disobedience, and aggression, were hardly "right"; but catharsis answered these objections to the nature is right principle. Catharsis required that an uncivilized trait characteristic of early racial history be expressed in childhood so that it would not be expressed in adult years. By allowing children, for example, to show mild cruelty, by kicking a dog or twisting a sibling's arm, presumably then they would not express cruelty in adolescence and adulthood. Hall always wavered between the direct and vicarious cathartic expression: "I incline to think that many children would be better and not worse for reading, providing it can be done in tender years, stories like those of Captain Kidd, Jack Sheppard, Dick Turpin, and other gory tales . . . on the principle of the Aristotelian catharsis to arouse betimes the higher faculties which develop later, and whose function it is to deplete the bad centers and suppress or inhibit their activity."[32]

Fourth, Hall thought physical growth was of more critical developmental significance than cognitive growth because the former appeared earlier in evolutionary history. Study of the evolution of animal forms had revealed that complex intellectual behavior appeared fairly late in phylogenetic history. Alfred R. Wallace, an English biologist who co-authored with Darwin a paper on natural selection prior to the publication of *Origin of Species*, suggested that the emergence of the human species had been preceded by occasions when natural selection worked on intellectual rather than physical processes. Wallace hypothesized that evolution had finally reached the stage at which intellectual variations were of more adaptive value than physical changes, and, therefore, the transition from the ape-like to the human condition was associated chiefly with changes in the mind and central nervous system. Hall agreed completely.

Fifth, Hall believed that developmental norms should be based on the concept of recapitulation and its corollary, the *nascent* period. Hall envisaged the sequential, invariant patterns inherent in development as a parade of distinct anthropoid forms, each of which represented a steplike progression in the corresponding history of evolution. A child or adolescent's growth would be at a plateau stage while passing through one of its ancestral forms, but then it would accelerate between stages. The plateau stages interested Hall, for they provided the norms needed to evaluate developmental progress, but the periods of transition, which he called the nascent, intrigued him. The recapitulatory momentum would be at a peak at these times, he believed, and hereditary energy would greatly facilitate proper growth. Hall and his students, therefore, searched for every clue to these wellsprings of developmental energy. Unadulterated recapitulation, nonetheless, was not to be interfered with by social forces. Hall felt that to encourage certain growth propensities too soon might induce precocity in one stage, thus overwhelming other nascent stages, and perhaps even contribute to their permanent arrest. On the other hand, he felt that by ignoring inhibiting influences, the nascent periods might be suppressed entirely.

G. Stanley Hall's concept of adolescence followed consistently from his basic principles of genetic psychology. He viewed the spontaneous activities of children as reminiscent of corresponding racial stages. When they climbed trees, they were reliving the stage of racial arboreal existence, and when they wandered and went camping, they were reliving the nomadic stage.[33] But he saw adolescents as infirm, hapless creatures. Recapitulatory instincts, so important in childhood, yielded to societal pressures in adolescence; Hall focused his attention, therefore, on the twin tasks of interpreting and suggesting changes in these new influences. A new, propitious environment for acquired characteristics would be of little avail, however, if parents and educators failed to adhere faithfully to the principles of nature is right and catharsis. Consequently, in *Adolescence,* Hall emphasized strongly that the child, so much older racially, was father of the adolescent, and that, to bring the adolescent to maturity, nascent periods at every stage of development must be carefully nurtured.

Hall, for example, reasoned that conscious thought and cognition were latecomers in evolutionary history. "Muscles are in a most intimate and peculiar sense the organs of the will. They have built all the roads, cities, and machines in the world, written all the books, spoken all the words, and in fact, done everything that man has accomplished with matter."[34] Although Hall assigned to the adolescent intellect a crucial role in his scheme to raise humanity to "superanthropoid" status, he thought it was detrimental to provide an enriched environment that might encourage children's creativity and originality. He felt that "staring, experimenting with sensation, surprise, active observation, the passion to touch, handle, taste everything" were associated with "the lust to know." "The question mania which may become a neurosis at about the earliest school age, anxiety to know the origin of life that is suppressed to stealthiness at about the same age when it really grows more intense, baffling theological queries, interest in death and in theological questions, in the *how* of mechanical processes that often motivates what seems destructiveness, desire to travel, the conquests of timidity by curiosity" lead to such problems as truancy and running away from home.[35] "All these expressions of a pure desire for knowledge are phenomena of the crepuscular dawn that precedes the sunrise of reason in adolescence."[36]

Hall's recapitulatory framework led him to conclude that parents and educators should respond differently to children's and adolescents' cognitive growth. The "only duty of young children is implicit obedience."[37] Children should express cathartically their boorish impulses, drill and exercise their minds, but avoid explanations and thinking. As difficult as inhibiting children's curiosity would be, harnessing the adolescent's blossoming intellect, checking precocity, preventing arrest, and simultaneously nurturing, guiding, and sustaining the budding powers seemed almost insuperable.

The recapitulation theory also convinced Hall that every person was born twice, once as an individual and again, in adolescence, as a member of the human race. Children were always self-centered, selfish, and aggressive, but adolescents could be altruistic and self-sacrificing. He recognized that hereditary impulses pushing toward a rebirth often failed to ascend and that in adolescence selfish actions might conquer altruistic inclinations permanently. To facilitate the new birth, Hall aimed to find the nascent periods of all the social instincts and hence maximize the salutary effects of intrinsic motivation. Hall commenced his search for social instincts with the assumption that the oldest racial instinct is sexuality—possession and reproduction. From this common denominator emerged the fundamental instincts of love and religiosity. He conceptualized love, for example, as a series of stages starting with a basic, animal-like, selfish love, and rising to friendship, romantic love, marital love, love of children, love of community, race, and, eventually, love for a deity. To show that love and religious instincts were derived from the same underlying impulse, Hall observed that young people in love were inclined to consider building houses in which they might live, think, talk, and write about death, and were exceedingly responsive to nature; likewise, religious persons have through the ages been preoccupied with building houses in which their gods could live and be worshipped, with death, immortality, and nature as sources of religious inspiration.[38]

Hall felt that as hereditary propensities waned at the end of recapitulation during adolescence, parents and other socializing agents should become nature's surrogates in serving the ends of evolution. They should foster and nurture adolescents' new but natural self-consciousness, bringing them to new choices and new experiences and continuing their hereditary momentum toward superanthropoid status. Hereditary impulses toward sex-role identity, however, were not too helpful to adolescents, whose racial instincts were weak and ineffectual. What might happen to them if they encountered an unfavorable social environment? There might be alienation, delinquency, and degenerate evolution:

. . . normal children often pass through stages of passionate cruelty, laziness, lying and thievery. . . . Their vanity, slang, obscenity, contagious imitativeness, their absence of moral sense, disregard of property, and violence to each other, constitute them criminals in all essential respects, lacking only the strength and insight to make their crime dangerous to the communities in which they live. We are told that to magnify the soul of the child before its more animal instincts are reduced to due proportion and controlled by conscience and reason, would give us the most truculent and menacing forms of criminality; just as to magnify all parts and organs of the infant's body in equal proportion would, as we have seen, produce deformity and monstrosity.[39]

Let us conclude our review of Hall's interpretation of human development by reiterating that it is largely discredited today. Behavioral scientists are no longer concerned about the primacy of physical growth, nature is right, or catharsis. They believe that children neither fight in order to be immune to "ethical mumps and measles" nor withdraw from intellectual stimulation. They also believe that "reasoning manias" are less likely to occur during adolescence if earlier social experiences have provided bases for cognitive learning. Because of Hall's enthusiasm for catharsis as a purging mechanism, as well as his fervor to harness the energy of nascent periods, he overlooked the degree to which childhood social experiences may resist extinction and subsequently influence adolescent development. Moreover, Hall's belief that fostering intellectual and creative precocity might arrest and pervert other areas of development appears today as more misleading than quaint.

Storm and Stress Viewpoint

The narrations of adolescent tribulations and deviance command rapt attention on television and in the popular press, greatly augmenting advertising revenues, which lead in turn to greater emphasis on adolescent escapades. The tradition of using the improprieties of youth to formulate a viewpoint on adolescent development is a long one. It is said that an Egyptian priest once carved on a stone: "Our earth is degenerate . . . children no longer obey their parents." Nearly eight centuries before Christ, the Greek poet Hesiod allegedly asserted: "I see no hope for the future of our people if they are dependent upon the frivolous youth of today, for certainly all youth are reckless beyond words. . . . When I was a boy, we were taught to be discreet and respectful of our elders, but the present youth are exceedingly wise and impatient of restraint . . . ." A few centuries later, Socrates complained: "Our youth now love luxury. They have bad manners, contempt for authority; they show disrespect for their elders, and love chatter in place of exercise. They no longer rise when others enter the room. They contradict their parents, chatter before company, gobble up their food, and tyrannize their teachers." Thus, by the turn of the twentieth century, Hall[40] had data from both evolution and folklore for his view of development in adolescence as "less gradual and more saltatory, suggestive of some ancient period of *storm and stress* when old moorings are broken and a higher level attained" (italics added).

Hall and his students came to accept storm and stress as the salient dimension of adolescent socialization; they perceived an unbridgeable gap between the potential of adolescence and its realization in contemporary society. The recapitulation theorists saw instincts dissipate in adolescence and become subject to environmental factors. "The momentum of heredity often seems insufficient to enable the child to achieve this great revolution and come to complete maturity, so that every step of the upward way is strewn with wreckage of body, mind, and morals. . . . Modern life is hard, and in many respects increasingly so, on youth."[41]

The recapitulationist interpretation of adolescent storm and stress was only superficially plausible; it became obsolete with new insight and knowledge. A comprehensive theory of human development was necessary in order to understand motives, aspirations, attitudes, values, and social relationships; theorists, therefore, began to draw on Sigmund Freud's psychoanalytic theory. Although successive interpretations of adolescence have been modified over the years, Freud's basic ideas continue to influence many contemporary analysts of adolescent behavior.

The psychoanalytic theorists generally agree that storm and stress is an inevitable trait of adolescence:

The inescapable fact is that this is everyone's dilemma at adolescence. No one is exempt—no matter how warm and understanding the family background. The comfort and security of having been loved may help sustain the adolescent in this moment of terror, but no parent, however devoted and well-intentioned, can spare his child this frenzied conflict. For this conflict follows the law of nature. It is the self-actualizing principle that provides the impetus toward growth; the dialectical development by which individual consciousness progresses from innocence to maturity; from boy to man, from girl to woman.[42]

The psychoanalytic view suggests that the pleasure-seeking, narcissistic child will be transformed during a stormy journey through adolescence into a reality-oriented, socialized adult. Although many people consider this outlook valid,[43] critics argue that when biological factors are so heavily weighted, especially during the first five years, many environmental influences are overlooked. And it is difficult to understand how the traumatic experiences of adolescence can melt away, enhancing personality development. How is it, then, that psychoanalytic theorists such as Gustin have come to view storm and stress as a "law of nature"? To explain this, let us summarize the developmental stages in the Freudian system:

Personality is divided into three major components in the Freudian system: the *id,* or biological component; the *ego,* or psychological component, and the *superego,* or social-conscience component. Each possesses distinct features. As Hall and Lindzey[44] explain psychoanalytic theory, the id obtains its strength from close association with bodily processes and is the source of psychic energy. Since the id largely experiences unpleasant tension, it is motivated to reduce this. The id is governed by a *pleasure principle.* A reflex like sneezing or blinking, for example, can reduce a specific tension instantly. But there are tensions that cannot be immediately discharged; for example, a hungry person may not be able to obtain food immediately. Therefore, through what is called a *primary process,* the id creates wish-fulfilling images to provide temporary satisfaction. Since the primary process does not actually reduce the tension, the hallucinations it creates may impede the individual's orientation to reality. Therefore, a secondary, reality-oriented psychological system, the ego, begins to form. As the ego evolves it mediates the pressures from the id and those of external reality. The ego is guided by a *reality principle*; it may suspend the pleasure principle temporarily, formulate plans of action, and test reality until there is satisfaction. To perform its role effectively, the ego must control all cognitive and intellectual functions.

The superego represents the ideal; it is the seat of internalized social standards and values. The superego takes shape as a child acts in accordance with the expectations of socializing agents. One incorporates into personality the capacity to praise, reward, rebuke, and punish oneself. The mature superego substitutes self-control for parental control, persuades the ego to strive for perfection, and inhibits such asocial id impulses as sex and aggression.

Freud divided the development of personality into three pregenital and two postgenital stages. The initial five years of life encompass the progressive differentiation of the first three stages, each of which is identified by reactions associated with a particular zone of the body. Then follows a five- or six-year period of relative stability or latency, which leads into adolescence, a time when anatomical and personality development once again engage in the dynamic process of differentiation. In the early days of genetic psychology, the physical and psychical onset of sexuality was presumed to occur at adolescence. However, as early as 1898, Freud insisted that sexual life begins in infancy. The small child is dominated by undifferentiated, loosely organized sexuality; that is, it is said to be *polymorphous perverse*.[45] First, it enters the *oral* stage which lasts until about the end of the first year. The mouth is a primary erogenous or tactile zone, and time is spent sucking, drinking, and eating. The helplessness of the infant engenders an emotional dependency on the mother or major caretaker, and in spite of subsequent ego-differentiation, persistent impulses toward dependency may influence behavior later in life, for example, in times of anxiety and uncertainty. In general, as impressions are differentiated by the individual, those bringing comfort are trusted and those arousing disquiet are mistrusted. The emergence of teeth introduces a new factor into the infant's social relationships; it can retaliate against frustration by biting, and it may become ambivalent toward those it loves, expressing its feelings in *oral sadism*. Its subsequent capacity for love and hate may depend on these early modes of oral functioning.[46]

From one to three years of age the child acquires mobility, goal-directed movements, and—most important—control of toilet functions. During the second pregenital stage, the *anal* stage, personality development centers on the surrender of uncontrolled expulsion of the feces and adoption of toilet regulations. Praise and reassurance may lead the child to believe it can please its parents, from which may emerge traits associated with autonomy and creativity. On the other hand, punitive and repressive experiences may cause the child to hold back feces, which may lead to later obstinacy and stinginess.[47]

The *phallic* stage is the third and last pregenital stage. Sexual and aggressive feelings are focused on the genital organs, and pleasures of masturbation and erotic fantasies lead the child to the Oedipal complex. Both sexes are initially attracted to the mother because she provides comforts and thereby satisfies needs. The boy's strong identification with his mother turns into a possessive, emotional attachment. He views his father eventually as a dominant rival; fearing the worse, the boy imagines that his father will castrate him. The anxiety thus engendered induces him to forsake his possessive desire for his mother and identify with his father, that is, take on the masculine characteristics of the father in order to become a comparable paramour.

The resolution of the complex is more complicated for a girl since she must exchange her mother, the original love object, for her father. This shift in affection is presumably facilitated because the girl holds her mother responsible for castrating her, an assumption that she supposedly makes when she compares her cavity with a boy's protruding organ, which she equates with pleasure. After developing this *penis envy* and resentment toward her mother, she shifts her affection to her father because he has the valued organ and she aspires to share it with him. The mother, however, is still a major source of comfort, and the girl experiences considerable ambivalence; this continuing attachment creates enough anxiety to orient her away from her father and toward her mother once again. A girl's oedipal conflict is unlikely to approach the intensity of that of a boy's and, lacking castration anxiety, she develops little motivation to identify with her mother. Nonetheless, orthodox analytic theorists generally assume that for both sexes the resolution of the oedipal conflict provides sufficient motivation for initial sex-role identification and the rise of the superego.

The first post-genital stage is called *latency*. Once the relatively narcissistic tribulations of early childhood are history, the child turns attention to school, work, play, and friends. At this moment in the child's development, the id appears to be acquiescent, leaving the ego in a fairly strong position. Sexuality is dormant, and the cognitive powers have the opportunity to develop. Processes of judgment, logic, and empathy seem stable; growth in physical stature permits greater independence and opportunity for environmental mastery.[48]

The calm and tranquility of latency is shattered by the onset of puberty or adolescence. The hormonal and psychic changes that initiate the reproductive period of life apparently create an imbalance that renews a war between the id and the ego that began in childhood:

The urgent necessity to cope with the novel conditions of puberty evokes all the modes of excitation, tension, gratification, and defense that ever played a role in previous years—that is, during the psychosexual development of infancy and early childhood. This infantile admixture is responsible for the bizarreness and the regressive character of adolescent behavior; it is the typical expression of the adolescent's struggle to regain or to retain a psychic equilibrium which has been jolted by the crisis of puberty. The significant emotional needs and conflicts of early childhood must be recapitulated before new solutions with qualitatively different instinctual aims and ego interests can be found. This is why adolescence has been called a second edition of childhood; both periods have in common the fact that 'a relatively strong id confronts a relatively weak ego'. . . .[49]

Picture an adolescent now poised at the brink of adulthood. Racked by sexual desire, frustrated by outer prohibitions and inner inhibitions; desperately longing for independence yet fearful of isolation; eager for responsibilities yet fraught with anxieties about inferiority; flooded by irrational impulses yet committed to rules of propriety, he is hopelessly and helplessly confused and an enigma to everyone and himself.[50]

Adolescents are said to pass through stages of "self-consciousness and fragmented existence." The process is accompanied by feelings of "isolation, loneliness, and confusion."[51] Their behavior encompasses inconsistency and unpredictability. They alternatively fight their impulses and accept them, love and hate their parents, rebel and affirm, and thrive on imitation or independence. They are more idealistic, artistic, generous, and unselfish than they will ever be again but they are also self-centered, egotistic, and calculating.[52] In the process of testing themselves, they find self-definition and attain identity.[53]

The cause of the storm-and-stress tension is sexual conflict.[54] Fear and anxiety associated with oedipal fantasies are displaced to masturbation, which may become extremely important if society's admonitions against premarital sex are taken seriously. Sexual development for the boy means a reawakening of infantile sexuality and a continuing interest in his penis. According to psychoanalytic theory, the girl becomes aware of her vagina as a source of pleasure, whereas previously, as a consequence of her desire to be boyish, she had been mainly interested in her clitoris. As Freudian theorists traditionally see it, the more passive feminine functions now must be accepted, but strong penis envy may inhibit the process. Her first menstruation may support fantasies about pregnancy and childbirth or lead to greater penis envy, a heightened castration complex, and rejection of femininity.[55]

Analytic theorists suggest that the male retains a high narcissitic interest in his penis throughout his life, but that the girl on reaching maturity values the beauty of face and figure.[56]

Fantasies triggered by inner genital tensions veer from ambitious plans to breed multitudes of animals to dressing up for dates, going to a wedding, becoming engaged and raising children in a manner superior to that of her mother. Sewing dresses and buying the right kind of brassiere or sweater may take up an inordinate amount of time and care. . . . Focusing on breasts is of course aided by localized mammal sensations and nipple erections, but this too spreads to articles of clothing, materials, costumes, and sketching of female bodies and dresses. The interest in pubic hair shifts to changing hair styles, which become expressive of changing moods and of trial identifications with idealized romantic figures.[57]

The metaphors psychoanalytic theorists employ to underscore their viewpoints obscure several useful insights contributed by them to understanding adolescence. Their emphases on such assumptions as (1) early experiences as being formative, (2) motivation for conscience or superego development as having predictable antecedents in childhood experiences, and (3) self-consciousness as being the dominant feature of the adolescent personality have proven to be exceedingly helpful. Nonetheless, the Freudian belief that biological factors are the major determinants of heterosexual behavior are difficult to sustain. The sexual behavior patterns among human beings have been shown to be highly variable across different cultures, and what is considered sexually stimulating in one society may be repulsive in another. Moreover, anthropological data suggest that the transition to sexual activity is relatively smooth in societies that permit and encourage early heterosexual exploration. Thus the extent to which heterosexual behavior may be increased at adolescence may be due less to a powerful biologically determined sexual drive than to cultural enticements to attain sexual gratification.[58] Other serious objections to psychoanalytic theory stem from the fact that its credibility is so often stretched to the limit. Every community possesses its share of adolescents who are rebellious, raucous, undisciplined, neurotic, and deviant, but are they typical? Adolescents who frighten senior citizens by their belligerence, violate our propriety by their uncouthness, or wantonly disregard property are highly newsworthy. The news media— literature, television, movies, national weekly magazines, and newspapers— portray the sensational because it elicits far more attention than the activity of the typical high school student. Adelson[59] also points out that visible, vocal, volatile youth have habituated adults to a conflict model of adolescence. He suggests that it is "appropriate for some adolescents most of the time and for most adolescents some of the time." But it does not provide a language or structure "for handling either the sluggish conformity or the effective adaptation" that characterizes most young people most of the time. The tendency to overgeneralize storm and stress from Freudian premises has led parents to expect young people to adopt rebellious and defiant roles. Although many parents may experience affectionate and rewarding relationships with their preadolescent children, they may inadvertently brace themselves for tensions during adolescence. The self-fulfilling prophesy may thus lead to expectations that in themselves can create unnecessary turbulances. Sometimes when the awaited storm and stress fails to materialize, the parents may wonder if the young people are socially normal.[60]

Erik Erikson's Epigenetic model of Identity Formation

Human development is held by many social scientists to be synonymous with *identity formation*. The foremost proponent of this view is the distinguished psychoanalyst, Erik H. Erikson, who considers adolescence a particularly critical period for identity formation. Erikson proposes an interactional view of development, which encompasses biological, social, and individual components and contains parallels to both recapitulation and psychoanalytic theories. He holds that our understanding of personality development derives from an *epigenetic principle:* "somewhat generalized, this principle states that anything that grows has a ground plan, and that out of this ground plan the parts arise, each part having its time of special ascendency, until all parts have arisen to form a functioning whole."[61] Furthermore, any part that fails to ascend on time is doomed as an entity and the hierarchy to which it belongs is likely to be defective. Erikson also accepts the psychoanalytic view that the human infant is born with instincts, drives, and impulses, and he acknowledges that the theory has contributed significantly to our understanding of the role of "inner conflicts" in personality development. But he sees development as more than a ground plan of idiosyncratic inner conflicts. Erikson says that the properly guided young person "can be trusted to obey inner laws of development," which create "a succession of potentialities" for significant social interaction. The specific characteristics of the interaction will vary from culture to culture, but Erikson believes, nonetheless, that each personality will develop "according to steps predetermined in the human organism's readiness to be driven toward, to be aware of, and to interact with a widening radius of significant individuals and institutions."[62] Erikson's description of the developmental process is shown in the "epigenetic diagram" depicted in Figure 1.[63] Each of the double-lined squares (I, 1; II, 2; III, 3; and so on) denotes one of eight stages in the life span; each is presumed to ascend in its proper developmental order. Every stage signifies a new shift in instinctual energy, which gives impetus to new growth and awareness as encounters with the environment ensue. Each stage also presents "a potential crisis" to the developing personality. But by crisis Erikson does not mean a threat or catastrophy, but a developmental turning point, a radical change in perspective, and simultaneously, "a crucial period of increased vulnerability and heightened potential. . . ."[64]

Each of the eight stages shown in Figure 1, four of which precede and three of which follow that of adolescence, unfolds in accordance with its own pre-

	1	2	3	4	5	6	7	8
VIII								INTEGRITY vs. DESPAIR
VII							GENERATIVITY vs. STAGNATION	
VI						INTIMACY vs. ISOLATION		
V	Temporal perspective vs. Time confusion	Self–certainty vs. Self–consciousness	Role experimentation vs. Role fixation	Apprenticeship vs. Work paralysis	IDENTITY vs. IDENTITY CONFUSION	Sexual polarization vs. Bisexual confusion	Leader–and followership vs. Authority confusion	Ideological commitment vs. Confusion of values
IV				INDUSTRY vs. INFERIORITY	Task identification vs. Sense of futility			
III			INITIATIVE vs. GUILT		Anticipation of roles vs. Role inhibition			
II		AUTONOMY vs. SHAME, DOUBT			Will to be oneself vs. Self–doubt			
I	TRUST vs. MISTRUST				Mutual recognition vs. Autistic isolation			

Figure 1

Erikson's epigenetic chart. (From Erikson, see text. Reprinted by permission.)

ordained plan, and hence, every individual faces the possibility of eight distinctive psychic challenges in his or her life span. A healthy, strong personality will acquire before the adolescent stage, for example, a basic sense of trust of persons and environment, a sense of autonomous will, a spirit of initiative, curiosity, and exploration, and a sense of pride and self-assurance in its ability to develop the skills and competence necessary for making its way in society; after adolescence, the strong personality will attain capacity relative to intimacy in social relationships, generativity—a desire to share one's experiences in guiding the coming generation, and integrity—an ability to look back and believe that life has been unique and worthwhile.

Problems faced at any given stage tend to thwart subsequent development, but even minor difficulties during adolescence may prove to have particularly serious consequences. Adolescence is an especially critical stage because attainment of a sense of identity strengthens the prospects for an enriched adulthood. On the other hand, drift into identity confusion endangers chances in the future of personality integration. Erikson thus firmly believes that identity formation is essential for "further and truly individual maturation."[65] At adolescence, he sees a crucial complementarity between life history and identity development: ". . . the body, now fully grown, grows together into an individual appearance; . . . . sexuality, matured, seeks partners in sensual play and, sooner or later, in parenthood; . . . the mind, fully developed, can begin to envisage a career for the individual within a historical perspective—all idiosyncratic developments which must fuse with each other in a new sense of sameness and continuity."[66] *Self-hood,* or *ego strength,* "emerges from the mutual confirmation of individual and community, in the sense that society recognizes the young individual as a bearer of fresh energy and that the individual so confirmed recognizes society as a living process which inspires loyalty as it receives it, maintains allegiance as it attracts it, honors confidence as it demands it."[67]

Identity formation carries with it a mastery of the four childhood stages and a readiness to face the challenges of intimacy, generativity, and integrity in adulthood. As the vertical axis in Figure 1 shows, the childhood stages may lay a strong foundation for adolescence by establishing the rudiments for positive social interaction, self-respect, and self-confidence. "The youth does *not* question *who he is* but rather what and in what context can he be *and* become."[68] Erikson sees the adolescent stage as a "psychosocial moratorium." The young person must integrate major maturational changes in physical self-image, new dimensions of sexuality, and enhanced intellectual powers in the context of the social reality that both is and will be. "In adolescence, the ego gradually establishes a synthesis of the past and future."[69]

The overall range of issues adolescents confront in meeting the "crisis" of identity formation is shown along the horizontal axis in Figure 1. A time perspective is necessary, for example, if the past is to be examined in the context of the future. Otherwise young people may either demand immediate action or develop an inability to prioritize decisions that will affect their future. Self-certainty is akin to self-confidence; it arises when self-impressions and impressions made upon others are brought into synchronization. The self-consciousness aroused in the process may be rather painful. Role experimentation minimizes doubts about the future for it is a means of sampling available opportunities and of entering into trial decisions before irrevocable commitments are required. Apprenticeship leads to feelings of competence, that is, to knowledge that one is adequate vocationally and can fulfill long-range career objectives. In respect to sexual polarization, Erikson holds to the traditional assumption that "heterosexual intimacy" is the primary goal of sexuality. Therefore, he says that adolescents must resolve their bisexual conflicts and achieve identification with their anatomical sex characteristics. This view is being questioned today, however, by a widening circle of young people (see

Chapter 11). Leader- and followership lead to harmony in social relationships. Adolescents should be ready either to assume leadership or submit to it when it is expected of them. Young people's capacity to deal with authority and their ability to adjust to situations is related in part to the ideological commitments that they make. Thus, the seventh issue adolescents face is attainment of a basic philosophy, ideology, or religion, which will provide a frame of reference, consistency, and stability for their moral and ethical decisions.

According to Erikson, every adolescent must deal with each of the seven issues in some fashion, and he believes that some degree of identity confusion is necessary if the strong identity is to be formed. He says the doubts and despairs aroused by identity crises may provide occasions for personality reorganization at higher levels of integration. Erikson[70] suggests, for example, that identity crises may not be too significant for youth who are able to invest their "fidelity" or "disciplined devotion" in activities that are relatively congruent with contemporary society. Adolescents who are committed to traditional middle-class definitions of success, oriented toward future goals, and who support conventional political and economic systems may find the transition into adulthood relatively effortless. By endorsing the standards, guidance, and authority of their elders and by pursuing traditional alternatives, they find that their choices are virtually made for them. Identity formed under such pristine conditions may, however, result in a weak character. How committed are such adolescents to their course of action? In his classic analysis of the "vanishing adolescent," Friedenberg,[71] who took a similar position, held that adolescents must differentiate themselves from their culture and must question it and themselves in order to learn who they are and what they really feel; in this way they become capable of deeply felt relationships with others. Friedenberg's analyses led him to conclude that adolescence, as a developmental process, was becoming obsolete, that the conflict between a growing human being and society, so necessary to personal integration—was not taking place in the generation of youth that he studied. Friedenberg's view may still apply to those adolescents who find growing up so easy that they fail to develop the motivation necessary to meet challenges and thus prematurely commit themselves to social roles that are beneath their capabilities. Erikson also insisted that adolescents must sample many different aspects of life, and he saw, too, that some degree of disequilibrium or instability of personality traits may indeed be beneficial for a time. Youth, he said, "must often test extremes before settling on a considered course. These extremes, particularly in times of ideological confusion and widespread marginality of identity, may include not only rebellious but also deviant, delinquent, and self-destructive tendencies. However, all this can be in the nature of a moratorium, a period of delay, in which to test the rock-bottom of some truth before commiting the powers of body and mind to a segment of the existing (or a coming) order."[72]

Development of Self-Concept and Social Competence

Every theory of adolescent development, whether it be Hall's genetic psychology, Freud's psychoanalytic interpretation, or Erikson's epigenetic model, sees the attainment of a stable sense of self as the primary developmental task. The effects of biological and physical changes, increases in sexual impulses, greater intellectual capacity, and social pressures to achieve independence contribute in some way to molding self-definition. The matter of self-concept development is so prominent a feature of adolescence that many social scientists prefer to make all of the developmental issues associated with identity formation subsidiary to this one basic concern. This approach also is exceedingly appealing because, relative to the genetic and quasi-genetic models of Hall, Freud, and Erikson, it involves the least amount of speculation. For these reasons, the general aspects of self-concept theory provide the basic framework for most of the chapters of this book.

Self-Concept. The notion of self-concept refers, in broad terms, to a person's perceptions of himself or herself.[73] These perceptions are formed largely through inferences drawn from experiences, and they are influenced especially by rewards and punishments bestowed by persons who are significant in the life of the individual (see Chapters 7 and 8). Perception of self influences actions, which, in turn, affect the ways in which the self is perceived; thus, an understanding of a person's self-concept provides a useful basis for explaining and predicting how that person will act.[74]

What constitutes the self-concept? Shavelson, Hubner, and Stanton[75] describe its main features as follows. First, the self-concept may be said to be organized or structured. The diverse experiences that impinge upon a person are recorded or generalized into simpler categories, which reflect the individual's particular culture, for example, school, family, or neighborhood. Because life is highly complex, the categories represent a way of organizing experiences to give them meaning. Second, the assumption that the self-concept is organized leads also to the belief that it is multifaceted. A young person's general self-concept, for example, will be comprised of several different categories (e.g., school, workplace, peer group, intellectual ability, social acceptance, and physical attractiveness). The foregoing assumptions lead to the third; that is, the categorical structure of the self-concept can be described hierarchically on a dimension of generality. Shavelson et al. say that the facets of self-concept form a hierarchy starting with individual experiences and particular situations at the base; these are successively integrated to form a general self-concept at the apex. An illustration of this formulation is shown in Figure 2.[76] The researchers depict the general self-concept of a high school student as divided into two main components: academic self-concept and nonacademic self-concept. The academic self-concept is divided into subject-matter areas, and then again, into more specific areas. The nonacademic self-concept first is divided into social, emotional, and physical categories; these are then divided into more specific facets in a manner similar to the way in which the academic self-concept is subdivided. A fourth aspect of self-concept, as one might infer from Figure 2, is that it is relatively stable at the general level but is relatively unstable in the context of specific situations. As one descends the self-concept hierarchy, the particular facets become increasingly dependent on specific situations, and at the base of the hierarchy, inconsistencies in respect to the general self-concept may arise as variations occur across situations. Shavelson et al. suggest that the process of modifying the general self-concept resembles that of inductive reasoning. Several situation-specific instances, for example, each of which is inconsistent with the general self-concept, would be required to bring about a different perspective. Fifth, Shavelson et al. view the self-concept as developmental. With increasing age and experience, as an individual coordinates and integrates the categories of his or her self-concept, its structure becomes more highly differentiated (see Chapter 6). Sixth, the self-concept may be said to be evaluative. An individual develops not only a description of himself or herself in a particular situation or in a class of situations, but also forms evaluations of himself or herself in these situations. These evaluations may be made against absolute standards, such as "ideals," relative standards such as those of peers, or "perceived" standards of "significant others." The importance a person assigns to evaluative dimensions depends in part on his or her past experience in particular social contexts (see Chapter 8).

Social Competence. A sense of social competence is an outgrowth of self-concept evaluation. The process stems from what is known in the social sciences as *socialization,* which is the sum total of past experiences individuals have had, that in turn, may be expected to play some role in shaping their future social behavior.[77] The concept of socialization refers to "the process whereby individuals acquire the personal system properties—the knowledge, skills, attitudes, values, needs and motivations . . . which shape their adaptation to the physical and sociocultural setting in which they live."[78] Effective socialization is marked by sophisticated comprehension of social expectations, skillful performance of appropriate role behavior, and efficient use of resources in the social system to achieve goals. In a very simple and stable society the process of socialization

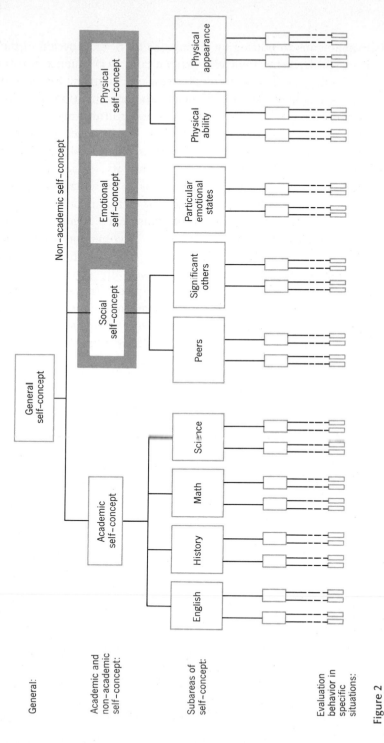

Figure 2

One possible representation of the hierarchic organization of self-concept. (From Shavelson *et al.*, see text. Reprinted by permission.)

would be analogous to putting on a play.[79] The roles expected of the actors are clearly prescribed; instructions are explicit and performances are preplanned. The actors interact easily and routinely with one another, and variations in role expectations are minor. In such a society the socialization of individuals into their appropriate roles would ensure social and cultural continuity and predictable self-concept development. The matter of competence would be foreordained. But socialization is not so simple in contemporary America. Traditionally stable roles associated with sex, ethnicity, social class, religion, and careers have become relatively unstructured. Whether young persons will become scientists or technicians, managers or clerks, marry or remain single, is largely indeterminant. But all adolescents must learn to cope with society and to participate effectively in some aspect of it. Acquisition of competence thus depends on continuous evaluation through interpersonal relationships. As important persons in young people's lives partially direct and prescribe their behavior, the ensuing censure or approval helps determine their emotional commitment to responsible behavior. Youth's sense of competence thus depends on whether they successfully meet the expectations of others. The specific dimensions of their competence will be a function of the standards of the persons who acquire significance in their lives.

SUMMARY

Adolescence is a stage in the life span through which individuals pass in their preparation for adulthood. It is an especially dynamic period because many of the roles adolescents learn are unique to this time of life. The capacity to achieve a high level of self-awareness arises during adolescence, and self-examination is the key to attaining maturity. Energies must be marshalled carefully, however, because consequences are cumulative, options are finite, and every choice reduces later freedom. Growing up in America has traditionally meant growing up in a context of upward mobility, viewing achievement as the dominant organizing principle of life, and investing one's pride and hope in the promise of realizing one's aspirations. But modern society appears to have reached the end of an era in which technology can keep productivity climbing fast enough to ensure the legitimacy of youth's drive for upward mobility. The signs of change are leading a sizeable proportion of the current generation to expect that work will have personal significance and be a vehicle for making meaningful contributions to the wider society. Many young people are beginning to integrate occupational and personal goals, and their aspirations are taking different and more pluralistic forms.

Adolescence was first investigated scientifically in the nineteenth century. Theories, assumptions, and generalizations about young people were derived initially simply by interrogating them about their knowledge, attitudes, and feelings. Three contemporary approaches to the study of adolescence have been developed in order to overcome problems of bias, lack of standardization, and effect of extraneous factors on drawing conclusions. The descriptive approach reports data either numerically or biographically. The designed approach tries to control extraneous factors; investigations are conducted systematically in either an ideal environment or a contrived, manipulated situation. The retrospective approach enables the researcher to assess the long-term effects of socialization either by the longitudinal method (investigating the same persons at periodic intervals) or by the cross-sectional method (investigating persons at different ages at the same time).

This chapter reviews the historical circumstances in America that gave rise to a social definition of adolescence—compulsory schooling, child labor legislation, and special legal procedures for juvenile delinquents—and provides a brief overview of classical and current theories of adolescent development. At the beginning of the twentieth century, for example, G. Stanley Hall (known as the father of adolescent study in America) offered a genetic viewpoint, in which adolescence was interpreted in the context of recapitulation—the idea that each individual in his or her own personal growth retraces the historical development of the species. Hall looked to evolutionary history, therefore, for clues about adolescent behavior. Sigmund Freud held that the hormonal and psychic changes that initiate the reproductive period of life create an imbalance in the personality structure that leads inevitably to storm and stress during adolescence. His view that turmoil during adolescence stems from biological bases has significantly influenced many contemporary analysts of adolescent behavior. The Freudian view is rather narrowly conceived, however, and to gain broader perspective, Erik Erikson has proposed an interactional model, which encompasses biological, social, and individual aspects of development. He describes life as unfolding in eight stages in accordance with a preordained plan. Each stage signifies a new shift in instinctual energy, which gives impetus to new growth and awareness as encounters with the environment ensue. Adolescents, for example, face a series of important decisions in choosing school programs, vocations, friends, and mates. Their choices are difficult to reverse; their sense of self-worth will be strengthened if they succeed in meeting each challenge constructively, but it may be diminished if their choices limit future options and opportunities.

It is generally recognized today that (1) socialization can best be understood in terms of the continuous interaction of physical development, cognitive growth, and cultural factors, and (2) the attainment of a stable sense of self is the primary developmental task of adolescents. The basic features of self-concept development thus are reviewed. Adolescents are described as attaining maturity by asserting themselves as distinct human beings; each individual's sense of competence and selfhood is described as depending upon the ways in which he or she responds to obligations and assimilates earlier experiences. Adolescents must anticipate and learn how to meet social expectations, perform appropriate role behaviors satisfactorily, and use the resources of society to achieve their goals. The process by which adolescents prepare themselves for the future by learning values, aptitudes, skills, and motivation is called *socialization*.

REVIEW QUESTIONS

1. What parameters might be used for establishing, respectively, biological and social definitions of adolescence?
2. Why is self-examination important in growing up?
3. Why are youth's personal goals beginning to take more pluralistic forms?
4. What kind of data about adolescence are collected by descriptive approaches?
5. What are the advantages and disadvantages of naturalistic and manipulative studies of adolescents?
6. Describe the contrasting features of cross-sectional and longitudinal designs.
7. What features of compulsory education, child labor legislation, and legal procedures for juveniles have influenced the social definition of adolescence?
8. How did G. Stanley Hall use the concepts of recapitulation and Lamarkianism to formulate his basic principles of human development?
9. Review the significance of the id, ego, and superego in psychoanalytic theory. How is each personality component formed?
10. How does psychoanalytic theory explain the relationship between storm-and-stress tension and sexual conflict?
11. What are Erikson's eight stages of development?
12. Describe the seven issues adolescents face during identity formation.
13. What are the main features of the self-concept?
14. How is social competence achieved?

DISCUSSION QUESTIONS

1. How might criteria for establishing the social definition of adolescence change if young people expect work in the future to have greater personal significance?
2. Name a few principles or facts about adolescent behavior that you would like to obtain. What research method would you use to obtain valid and reliable data about each of your interests?
3. What are the major differences between the circumstances of growing up in early industrial America and of becoming an adolescent today?
4. What are the most appealing features of G. Stanley Hall's theory of recapitulation?
5. What are the primary insights that psychoanalytic theory has contributed to our understanding of adolescence?
6. In what ways might Erikson's theory of identity formation be subjected to research?
7. What do you see as the most important aspects of adolescent self-concept development?

NOTES

1. G. H. Elder, Jr. Adolescence in the life cycle: an introduction In S. E. Dragastin and G. H. Elder, Jr. (Eds.). *Adolescence in the life cycle.* New York: John Wiley, 1975, pp. 1–22.

2. R. P. Beech and A. Schoeppe. Development of value systems in adolescents. *Developmental Psychology,* 1974, **10,** 644–656, p. 644.

3. A. Toffler. The American future is being bumbled away. *The Futurist,* 1976, **10,** 97–102, p. 97.

4. D. Bell. *The coming of post-industrial society.* New York: Basic Books, 1973.

5. E. G. Lancaster. The characteristics of adolescence. *Pedagogical Seminary,* 1897, **5,** 61–128.

6. M. Radke Yarrow, J. D. Campbell, and R. V. Burton. Recollections of childhood: a study of the retrospective method. *Monographs of the Society for Research in Child Development,* 1970, **35,** (5, Serial No. 138).

7. M. Sherif, and C. W. Sherif. *Reference groups.* New York: Harper, 1964.

8. E. S. Schaefer. An analysis of consensus in longitudinal research on personality consistency and change: discussion of papers by Bayley, Macfarlane, Moss and Kagan, and Murphy. *Vita Humana,* 1964, **7,** 143–146; L. J. Yarrow. Personality consistency and change: an overview of some conceptual and methodological issues. *Vita Humana,* 1964, **7,** 67–72.

9. H. E. Jones. The adolescent growth study: I. Principles and methods. *Journal of Consulting Psychology,* 1939, **3,** 157–159.

10. Radke Yarrow et al., *op. cit.*

11. N. Bayley. Research in child development: a longitudinal perspective. *Merrill-Palmer Quarterly of Behavior and Development,* 1965, **11,** 183–208.

12. Radke Yarrow et al., *op. cit.*

13. P. B. Baltes and J. R. Nesselroade. Cultural change in adolescent personality development:

An application of longitudinal sequences. *Developmental Psychology*, 1972, **7**, 244–256; J. R. Nesselroade and P. B. Baltes. Adolescent personality development and historical change: 1970–1972. *Monographs of the Society for Research in Child Development*, 1974, **39**, (1, Serial No. 154).

14. V. L. Bengtson and J. M. Starr, Contrast and consensus: A generational analysis of youth in the 1970s. In R. J. Havighurst and P. H. Dreyer (Eds.). *Youth—seventy-fourth year-book of the National Society for the Study of Education.* Chicago: University of Chicago Press, 1975, pp. 244–266.

15. Bengtson and Starr, *op. cit.*

16. P. Aries. *Centuries of childhood.* London: Jonathan Cape, 1962.

17. J. R. Gillis. *Youth and history.* New York: Academic Press, 1974.

18. Gillis, *op. cit.*

19. J. S. Coleman (Chairman). *Youth: Transition to adulthood.* Report of The Panel on Youth, President's Science Advisory Committee. Chicago: University of Chicago Press, 1974.

20. Coleman, *op. cit.*

21. D. Bakan. Adolescence in America: from idea to social fact. *Daedalus*, 1971, **100**, 979–995.

22. Bakan, *op. cit.*, p. 982.

23. Bakan, *op. cit.*

24. Coleman, *op. cit.*

25. Coleman, *op. cit.*

26. U.S. Department of Labor. *A Guide to Child Labor Provisions of the Fair Labor Standards Act.* Washington, D. C.: Child Labor Bulletin No. 101, 1973.

27. Bakan, *op. cit.*, p. 989.

28. Bakan, *op. cit.*

29. R. E. Grinder. *A history of genetic psychology.* New York: John Wiley, 1967.

30. J. M. Tyler. *Growth and education.* Boston: Houghton-Mifflin, 1907, p. 53.

31. G. S. Hall. *Adolescence.* New York: Appleton, 1904, Vol. I, p. 50.

32. Hall, *op. cit.*, I. p. 408.

33. Hall, *op. cit.*, I, pp. 202–204.

34. Hall, *op. cit.*, I, p. 131.

35. Hall, *op. cit.*, II, p. 450.

36. Ibid.

37. Hall, *op. cit.*, II, p. 451.

38. Hall, *op. cit.*, II, pp. 95–132.

39. Hall, *op. cit.*, I, pp. 334–335.

40. Hall, *op. cit.*, I, p. xiii.

41. Hall, *op. cit.*, I, p. xiv.

42. J. C. Gustin. The revolt of youth. *Psychoanalysis and the Psychoanalytic Review,* 1961, **98,** 78–90, p. 83.

43. C. S. Hall and G. Lindzey. *Theories of personality.* New York: John Wiley, 1970.

44. Hall and Lindzey, *op. cit.*

45. G. S. Blum. *Psychoanalytic theories of personality.* New York: McGraw-Hill, 1953.

46. Blum, *op. cit.*

47. Hall and Lindzey, *op. cit.*

48. P. Blos. *On adolescence.* New York: Free Press, 1962.

49. Blos, op. cit., p. 11.

50. Gustin, *op. cit.,* p. 83.

51. Blos, *op. cit.*

52. A. Freud. Adolescence. In J. F. Rosenblith and W. Allinsmith (Eds.). *The causes of behavior.* Boston: Allyn & Bacon, 1962, pp. 240–246.

53. Blos, *op. cit.*

54. Blum, *op. cit.*

55. Blum, *op. cit.*

56. Blum, *op. cit.*

57. J. S. Kestenberg. Phases of adolescence: with suggestions for a correlation of psychic and hormonal organizations. Part II. prepuberty defusion and reintegration. *Journal of the American Academy of Child Psychiatry,* 1967, **6,** 577–614.

58. C. S. Ford, and F. A. Beach. *Patterns of sexual behavior.* Harper and Row, 1951.

59. J. Adelson. The myths of adolescence: A polemic. Paper read at annual meeting of American Psychological Association, San Francisco, 1968.

60. A. Bandura. The stormy decade: fact or faction? *Psychology in the Schools.* 1964, **1,** 244–231.

61. E. Erikson. *Identity: youth and crisis.* New York: W. W. Norton, 1968, p. 92.

62. Erikson, *op. cit.,* p. 93.

63. Erikson, *op. cit.,* p. 94.

64. Erikson, *op. cit.,* p. 96.

65. Erikson, *op. cit.,* p. 89.

66. E. H. Erikson. The concept of identity in race relations: notes and queries. *Daedalus,* 1966, **95,** 145–170, p. 160.

67. Erikson, *Identity: youth and crisis, op. cit.,* p. 241.

68. H. W. Maier. *Three theories of child development.* New York: Harper, 1969, p. 57.

69. Maier, *op. cit.,* p. 58.

70. E. H. Erikson. Youth: fidelity and diversity. In E. H. Erikson (Ed.). *The challenge of youth.* New York: Anchor, 1965.

71. E. Z. Friedenberg, *The vanishing adolescent.* Boston: Beacon Press, 1959.

72. Erikson, Fidelity and diversity, *op. cit.,* p. 4.

73. R. J. Shavelson, J. J. Hubner, and G. C. Stanton. Self-concept: validation of construct interpretations. *Review of Educational Research,* 1976, **46,** 407–441.

74. Shavelson, et al., *op. cit.*

75. Shavelson, et al., *op. cit.*

76. Shavelson, et al., *op. cit.*

77. A. Inkeles. Social structure and socialization. In D. A. Goslin (Ed.). *Handbook of socialization theory and research.* Chicago: Rand McNally, 1969, 615–632, p. 615.

78. Inkeles, *op. cit.,* pp. 615–616.

79. Inkeles, *op. cit.*

Chapter 2
Physical Development During Adolescence

CHAPTER HIGHLIGHTS

ISSUES

Growth in height and weight provide excellent indices of overall physical maturation.

Statistics show that young people vary immensely as to the beginning, ending, and duration of the adolescent growth spurt.

Skeletal and muscular structures, primary and secondary sex characteristics, body proportions, and physiological characteristics change during the adolescent growth spurt and lead to sex differences in physique and strength.

Rate of growth can be affected by social factors.

The process of growing up has speeded up during the past 100 years.

Parents and teachers are expected to help the adolescent understand the physical and social aspects of growth. Growth standards have been derived from research, and a knowledge of these provides bases against which deviation from norms can be measured, thus setting the stage for such therapeutic measures as exercise and nutritional supplements. G. Stanley Hall[1] once declared that "growth upward out of the womb of nature is the one miracle of the world and its direction is the only clue to human destiny." And Tanner,[2] a leading contemporary analyst of children's development, holds that "self-stability," or "target-seeking," is the most striking feature of physical growth. "Children," he said, "no less than rockets, have their trajectories, governed by the control systems of their genetical constitution and powered by energy absorbed from the natural environment." Although a straight-forward process, physical growth is indeed complex and is affected by a number of hereditary and social factors. Heredity must be acknowledged as it relates to height and weight, spurt in growth, body proportions, the reproductive system, physique, and physiological and endocrinological growth; nutrition, climate, season, and social-class influence must also be discussed as they relate to physical development.

Adolescents must learn to live with their own physical endowments. The forces of growth are largely out of their control, but an expanding self-consciousness enables them as bystanders to watch every step of their development. For some the task is relatively easy because the physical images they project command respect and deference; for others, it is a major problem because their images arouse either indifference or disdain. Cultural valuation of physical attributes significantly affects how people will react to the adolescent. Klineberg describes how adolescent girls in Central Africa are segregated, fed with sweet and fattening foods, and carefully rubbed with oils, since corpulence is a desirable characteristic. In another society fashion dictates that the lower teeth be bent out, causing the underlip to protrude. This is achieved by knocking out the upper front teeth of both boys and girls.[3] There are enormous differences from one society to another, but few adolescents are free to move to one in which their particular attributes may be appreciated. America, although less brutal than other societies in its physical abuse of young people, has uncompromising expectations. Youths whose physiques are admired fare much better than others in attaining social rewards, and thus, to be perceived beautiful is a tremendous social asset. Dion, Berscheid, and Walster[4] reveal that physically attractive individuals of both sexes are seen by young people as possessing more socially desirable personalities. They are presumed to find more acceptable mates, marry earlier, enjoy happier marriages, and pursue more fulfilling professional lives. The researchers conclude that a what-is-beautiful-is-good stereotype plays an important part in governing the course of social interaction. As the characteristics of physical growth and the factors affecting physical well-being and

49

body image are discussed in this chapter, the physical traits that are valued in America also will be reviewed.

CHARACTERISTICS OF PHYSICAL GROWTH

Anthropometric Changes

Growth in Height and Weight. Standing height is the quickest and simplest comparative measure of physical growth, and weight, which may be determined by a scale, follows a close second. Growth curves for height and weight, respectively, have been usually prepared from the averages, at each age, of a large number of young people. Measurements may be taken of the same individual in a longitudinal study or of different person in a cross-sectional investigation. Tables 1 and 2 present the frequency distributions of height and weight, respectively, for youth, aged 12 to 17, in the United States. These data are from the Health Examination Survey, U.S. Public Health Service, which is based on a

Table 1

Height in Inches of Youths Aged 12–17 Years by Sex and Age at Last Birthday: Mean and Selected Percentiles, United States, 1966–70

| Sex and Age | $\bar{X}$ | Percentile | | | | | | |
		5th	10th	25th	50th	75th	90th	95th
Male								
12 years	60.0	54.6	55.7	57.8	60.0	61.9	64.0	65.2
13 years	62.9	57.2	58.3	60.4	62.8	65.4	68.0	68.7
14 years	65.6	59.9	60.9	63.2	66.1	68.1	69.8	70.7
15 years	67.5	62.4	63.7	65.7	67.8	69.3	71.0	72.1
16 years	68.6	64.1	65.2	67.0	68.7	70.4	72.1	73.1
17 years	69.1	64.1	65.7	67.2	69.2	70.9	72.6	73.7
Female								
12 years	61.1	55.8	57.4	59.5	61.2	63.0	64.6	65.9
13 years	62.5	57.8	58.9	60.7	62.6	64.4	66.0	66.9
14 years	63.5	59.6	60.5	61.9	63.5	65.2	66.7	67.4
15 years	63.9	59.6	60.3	62.0	63.9	65.8	67.2	68.1
16 years	64.0	59.7	60.7	62.4	64.2	65.6	67.2	68.1
17 years	64.1	60.0	60.9	62.3	64.3	65.9	67.4	68.1

Source: U.S. Public Health Service. *Vital and Health Statistics,* Series 11, No. 124, Height and weight of youths, 12–17 years, United States: January 1973. Reprinted by permission.

Table 2

Weight in Pounds of Youths Aged 12–17 Years by Sex and Age at Last Birthday: Mean and Selected Percentiles, United States, 1966–70

Sex and Age	$\bar{X}$	5th	10th	25th	50th	75th	90th	95th
					Percentile			
Male								
12 years	94.8	67.5	72.1	80.6	91.7	105.8	124.0	132.4
13 years	110.2	76.9	81.2	91.2	106.5	124.5	142.6	156.1
14 years	124.9	86.4	92.2	107.0	122.0	139.4	158.0	172.1
15 years	135.8	102.1	107.4	119.2	133.2	147.9	165.3	184.6
16 years	142.9	107.6	114.2	127.4	139.7	154.7	173.5	187.2
17 years	150.0	115.9	122.1	133.6	145.9	162.2	180.5	200.4
Female								
12 years	102.7	72.7	77.0	87.1	100.0	114.7	131.4	141.3
13 years	111.2	80.0	85.6	95.3	107.6	124.6	139.2	149.8
14 years	119.4	89.1	95.4	104.6	115.8	130.7	147.1	157.6
15 years	124.5	92.5	98.2	107.9	120.7	133.9	157.1	174.7
16 years	128.0	98.6	102.8	112.1	122.9	137.1	157.1	183.7
17 years	126.9	98.2	103.0	114.5	123.2	136.6	153.6	167.9

Source: U.S. Public Health Service. *Vital and Health Statistics,* Series 11, No. 124, Height and weight of youths 12–17 years, United States: January 1973. Reprinted by permission.

cross-sectional investigation of several thousand adolescents.[5] The data were collected at 40 pre-selected locations throughout the United States during an examination that lasted about three and one half hours. The noteworthy sample is highly representative of the millions of American young people in the 12 to 17 age range. The subjects are grouped in Tables 1 and 2 chronologically by one-year intervals. At each age their mean height and weight, respectively, is shown. Further, each table reports distributions by percentiles, which provide an indication of the ranges in height and weight that exist at the different ages. At age 16, for example, boys averaged nearly five feet, nine inches in height; however, 5 percent are less than five feet, four inches tall and 5 percent are more than six feet, one inch tall; similarly, the average 16-year-old girl is five feet, four inches in height, but 5 percent are shorter than five feet, and 5 percent are taller than five feet, eight inches. And, the 16-year-old boys average about 143 pounds in weight, with 5 percent weighing less than 108 pounds and 5 percent weighing more than 187 pounds; girls at age sixteen average 128 pounds, but 5 percent weigh less than 99 pounds and 5 percent weigh more than 183 pounds.

Growth in height and weight closely parallels the overall rate of physical maturation. The accrued increments, when presented graphically by age, illustrate over time the distance in growth attainment. Figures 1 to 4 present average height and weight curves, respectively, for white and black boys and girls, 6 to 18 years of age. (Comparable data are unavailable for such ethnic groups as native Americans and Mexican-Americans.) The curves of mean heights in Figure 1 indicate that black boys are slightly taller at ages 7 to 9 years, the white boys are slightly taller from 9 to 12 years, the two groups are virtually identical in mean heights from 12 to 14 years, and the white boys are consistently taller than their black counterparts from 15 to 17 years. Figure 2 reveals that the mean heights of black girls consistently surpass those of white

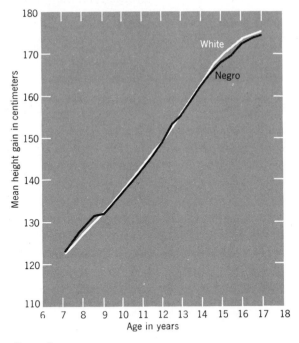

Figure 1
Distance curve of mean height attained by males 6–18 years of age, by half-year age group and race. (From U.S. Public Health Service. *Vital and Health Statistics,* Series 11, No. 126, Body weight, stature, and sitting height: white and negro youths 12–17 years, United States: August 1973. Reprinted by permission.)

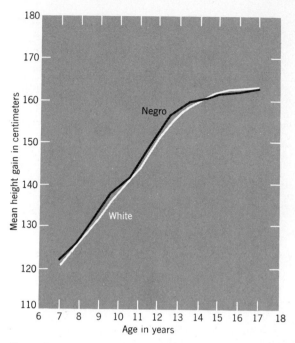

Figure 2
Distance curve of mean height attained by females 6–18 years of age, by half-year age group and race. (From U.S. Public Health Service. *Vital and Health Statistics,* Series 11, No. 126, Body weight, stature, and sitting height: white and negro youths 12–17 years, United States: August 1973. Reprinted by permission.)

girls from 7 to 14 years of age, but from 14 to 17 the mean heights of the white girls become slightly, but consistently, greater. Figure 3, which compares black and white boys by weight, shows that the mean weights of black boys are less than those of white boys from 7 to 13 years, about the same from 13 to 14 years, but relatively, a great deal less from 14 to 17 years. Figure 4, on the other hand, indicates that the mean weights of black girls are greater than those of white girls from ages 11 to 15, but after age 15 shows that there are no consistent differences between the mean weights of the two groups of girls.

The differences between the age-specific means in height of black and white boys and girls, respectively, are small. Figure 1 indicates that no significant differences appear during the longest part of the age span for boys, and the differences that do appear are in the order of one- or two-tenths of a centimeter (0.04 to 0.08 inches). The mean heights of black girls are consistently greater

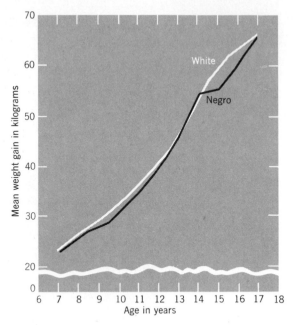

Figure 3
**Distance curve of mean weight attained by males 6–
18 years of age, by half-year age group and race.**
(From U.S. Public Health Service. *Vital and Health
Statistics,* Series 11, No. 126, Body weight, stature,
and sitting height: white and negro youths 12–17
years, United States: August 1973. Reprinted by permission.)

than those of white girls (Figure 2) until age 13½, after which the white girls'
averages are about one-half centimeter more (0.2 inches) for a few years, but
this difference tends to evaporate at maturity. Figures 3 and 4 reveal that differences between the two groups in mean weight curves are a function of sex.
The white boys surpass the black boys in mean weight consistently, except for
ages 13 to 14, and after age 14 the range in mean weights of the white boys are
approximately 1 to 6 kilograms (2 to 13 pounds) greater than the corresponding
means for the black boys. On the other hand, the only differences in the patterns
of mean weights for girls appear between 11½ and 13½ years, which may
simply be indicative of an earlier growth spurt in black girls.

The discrepancies between the height and weight growth patterns of white
and black youth may in part be accounted for by nutritional factors, but they
become more understandable in the context of comparisons of sitting height/sta-
ture ratios.[6] Stature (total standing height) is derived from sitting height and leg
length, and the sitting height/stature ratio describes the percentage of stature

accounted for by sitting height. Figure 5 reveals striking differences by both sex and ethnicity. White youth of both sexes have relatively longer trunks whereas black boys and girls tend to have longer legs. It is noteworthy, too, that the relative contribution of trunk length to stature shows for white girls a greater margin of difference over black girls than over white boys; similarly, differences between white and black boys' mean sitting height ratios are greater than differences in ratios between white boys and girls. The data presented in Figures 1, 2, and 5 suggest that white and black boys and girls, respectively, have arrived at similar standing heights through different ratios between the lengths of their trunks and legs. On the matter of weight (Figures 3 and 4), however, it appears that differences between white and black boys occur because white boys have longer trunks, which being thicker, weigh more per unit of length than do the longer legs of black boys. Girls apparently do not acquire trunk density, and thus their trunk and leg weights appear to be in equilibrium, which results in comparable mean weights for black and white girls.

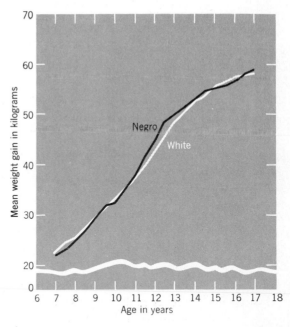

Figure 4
Distance curve of mean weight attained by females 6–18 years of age, by half-year age group and race. (From U.S. Public Health Services. *Vital and Health Statistics,* Series 11, No. 126, Body weight, stature, and sitting height: white and negro youths 12–17 years, United States: August 1973. Reprinted by permission.)

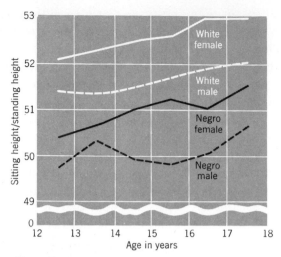

Figure 5
Mean sitting height/standing height ratio for youths 12–17 years of age by sex and race. (From U.S. Public Health Service. *Vital and Health Statistics*, Series 11, No. 126, Body weight, stature, and sitting height: white and negro youth 12–17 years, United States: August 1973. Reprinted by permission.)

Adolescent Growth Spurt. Physical growth during childhood and adolescence appears to manifest three distinct cycles.[7] The first extends from one month after fertilization until two years after birth; it is marked by a rapid rate of growth until the middle of pregnancy and then is followed by swift deceleration. During the second cycle, which ranges from about the age of two until the age of seven, the rate of growth peaks at about two and one half years of age. The third cycle begins gradually at about seven or eight years of age; between the ages of nine and fifteen nearly every child grows rapidly in almost every bodily dimension, giving rise to what is known as the "adolescent growth spurt."

Periods of slow and rapid growth may be identified by plotting annual increments of height and weight by age. These data are useful to researchers who want to relate variations in growth acceleration to physiological and endocrinological factors. The growth increment for each year can be determined by simple subtraction; then an individual's relative acceleration or retardation is revealed when the year at which he or she achieves maximum increment is compared with the pattern of maximum average increments of youth of the same age. These data, while demonstrating average patterns of growth rates, fail to reveal the speed and intensity of the adolescent growth spurt as it is experienced individually. In order to plot average growth curves, it is necessary to include persons who reach their peak velocity at different times; thus the "spurt" characteristics may be spread along the time axis. Tanner[8] accomplished this task by plotting increments every half year, from birth to 18 years of age, for white boys and girls whose peak growth velocity occurred during the year 12 to 13 for girls and 14 to 15 for boys. The magnitude of growth changes in height as they might occur in a typical boy and girl are shown in Figure 6. The velocity of growth during adolescence approximately doubles for a year or more, and both sexes are likely to be growing again at the rate they grew at about age two. The peak velocity of height averages about 10.5 centimeters (4 inches) a year in boys and 9.0 centimeters (3.5 inches) a year in girls.[9]

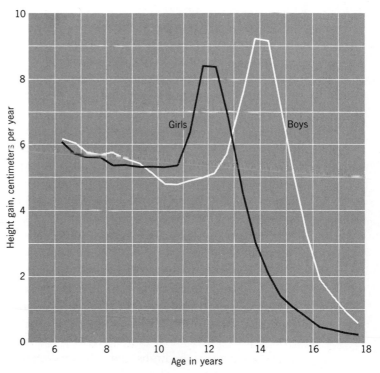

Figure 6
Adolescent spurt in height growth for girls and boys. The curves are from subjects who have their peak velocities during the modal years 12–13 for girls, and 14–15 for boys. Actual mean increments, each plotted at center of its half-year period. (From Tanner, see text. Reprinted by permission.)

Adolescents vary immensely as to the beginning, ending, and duration of the growth spurt. Boys may be anywhere from 10.5 to 16 years of age when they begin their rapid gain in height; they may be anywhere from 11 to nearly 17 before they attain their peak velocity. The typical boy may begin the velocity increase of body height about 12.5 years, reach a peak slightly after 14, and decelerate sharply by age 16. For girls the spurt occurs about two years earlier; thus they are taller and heavier than boys from about 10.5 to 13 years of age. The spurt rarely begins before age eight or after age 13. The typical girl begins her growth spurt shortly after age 10, reaches peak velocity at approximately age 12, and decelerates markedly by age 14. Figure 7 illustrates by sex how early- and late-developing boys and girls may differ. The three boys shown are all exactly 14.75 years in age and the three girls are exactly 12.75 years in age. All are normal and healthy, yet the young people in the first column could be mistaken easily for children and those in the third, as young adults. Thus, Tanner[10] points out that in most contexts statements about the maturity of a boy or girl who is 14 years of age are hopelessly vague. Whether the individual is pre-adolescent, midadolescent, or postadolescent depends on a host of morphological, physiological, and sociological factors.

Height and weight growth curves generally are closely correlated during the adolescent growth spurt. Deviations in achieving height are more likely to be significant than deviations in gaining weight. Failure to grow in height may reveal that a young person is off his or her "trajectory" and perhaps indicates a need for hormone supplements or some other form of therapeutic intervention.[11] Deviation in weight usually suggests the need for improved nutrition and exercise.[12] To obtain a clearer picture of the overall growth pattern in weight, Tanner[13] has advocated supplementing height and weight indices with that of subcutaneous fat, a measure that may be obtained by pinching together a double layer of subcutaneous tissue and measuring the thickness of the skinfold. This measure indicates the percentage of body weight that is fat. The thickness of subcutaneous fat all over the body decreases steadily from about age one to six or eight, when it begins to increase slowly. Then there is a marked increase in subcutaneous fat about a year before the height spurt in boys, and it lasts about two years. When the growth spurt is fully under way, there may be a thinning of the fat ring in the limbs and a loss rather than a gain in trunk fat. The thinning of the fat ring in the arms and legs may persist for several years after adolescence, resulting in a loss of fat in these areas, but toward the end of the growth spurt, fat is regained in the trunk.[14] Girls generally have more subcutaneous fat than boys at all ages, a distinction that is more apparent after the age of five or six. From that age on, the thickness of their subcutaneous fat increases steadily in both limbs and trunk. Girls continue to gain fat in their

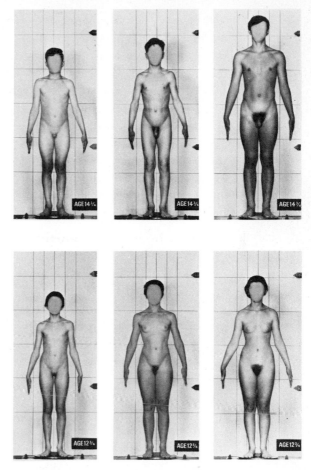

Figure 7
Differing degrees of pubertal development at the same chronological age. Upper row three boys all aged 14.75 years. Lower row three girls all aged 12.75 years. (From Tanner, "Growth and Endocrinology of the Adolescent,". Reprinted by permission.)

trunk during the adolescent growth spurt (as contrasted with boys), but there is a temporary check in fat gain in the limbs, which corresponds to that of boys.

It is noteworthy that following the growth spurt height and weight are more highly correlated among early- than late-developers. Adolescents who reach height maturity relatively early, in general, experience above-average annual increments in weight, whereas those who are late in respect to height acquire below-average increments in weight. The reason is that increments in height are more directly related to age than are increments in weight.[15] Late-developers will grow slowly in height while early-developers are in the midst of their high-velocity spurt. When their own spurt starts, the late-developers will grow more slowly at peak velocity, but as a consequence of the height they already have, they will attain the same average height at maturity as the early developers. However, in contrast to the differences in height, the mean weight of late- and early-developers is about the same at both the time of initiation of the adolescent growth spurt and at the start of the acceleration toward peak velocity in weight gain.[16] Since fastest weight gain occurs for the late-developer at the same mean weight as that of the early-developer, but at an older age, the late-developer will experience a shorter duration of weight accumulation before spurt deceleration, and will weigh less at maturity on the average than the early-developer. Thus, height and weight are more highly correlated among early- than late-developers.

Changes in Body Proportions.   Figures 1 to 4 present height and weight growth patterns, but they also implicitly illustrate growth in several skeletal and muscular dimensions; these appear to increase in size in a regular sequence.[17] In general, those parts of the limbs that are more peripheral to the trunk (for example, the far end of the leg) reach peak velocity first. The relatively early growth of hands and feet leads many adults to view younger adolescents as "all hands and feet." After the head, the foot is the first skeletal structure that ceases growing. The foot has a small acceleration about six months before the calf, which, in turn, accelerates shortly before the thigh. About four months after the leg has reached its peak velocity, the hips and the chest begin to widen. The hand grows almost as swiftly as the foot. The forearm reaches its peak velocity about six months before the upper arm. Shoulder width, at least for boys, follows hip width and chest breadth by a few months.[18]

Most skeletal and muscular structures follow the general pattern of the adolescent growth spurt. Notable exceptions are the brain and skull; the lymphoid tissues of the tonsils, adenoids, and intestines; and the reproductive organs.[19] Figure 8 shows the growth curves for each of these parts of the body. A general curve representing height is included for comparative purposes. As Figure 8 indicates, the lymphatic masses and tissues increase in size uniformly from birth to a maximum size between 11 and 15 years of age; thereafter, they decrease in size and weight. Tanner notes that children possessing large but otherwise normal tonsils and adenoids may expect "to lose their snuffles" at the start of adolescence. The head (including the brain, skull, eyes, and ears) on the other hand, develops the earliest and exhibits a relatively flat growth curve after middle childhood. The brain attains about 60 percent of its adult weight during the first year of life and 90 percent during the first five years. Head length and breadth achieve 96 percent of their adult size by age 10. Although the head

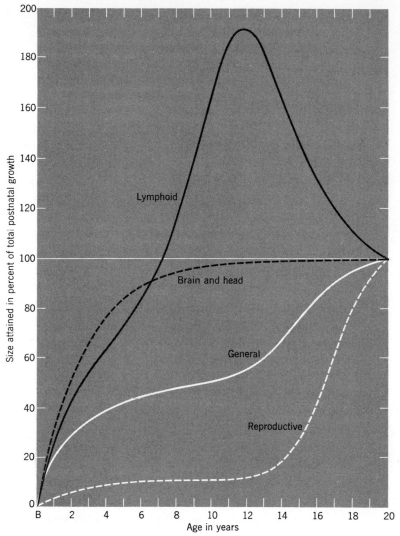

Figure 8
Growth curves of different parts and tissues of the body, showing the four chief types. All the curves are of size attained, and plotted as percent of total gain from birth to 20 years, so that size at age 20 is 100 on the vertical scale (From Tanner, see text. Reprinted by permission.)

Lymphoid type: thymus, lymph nodes, intestinal lymph masses.
Brain and head type: brain and its parts, dura, spinal cord, optic apparatus, cranial dimensions.
General type: Body as a whole, external dimensions (except head) respiratory and digestive organs, kidneys, aortic and pulmonary trunks, musculature, blood volume.
Reproductive type: Testis, ovary, epididymis, prostate, seminal vesicles, Fallopian tubes.

appears not to participate in the adolescent growth spurt, there is a slight increase in length and breadth due to a thickening of the skull over the eyebrows.[20] There are also relatively large skeletal changes in the face that parallel the growth in height and exhibit a considerable growth spurt. Krogman[21] suggests that white males acquire most of their facial depth or profile after 12 years of age, that white girls appear to experience equal amounts of facial growth before and after age 12, and that black youths of both sexes obtain most of their facial depth before age 12. The jawbone completes only 75 percent of its growth before adolescence. Then it becomes larger (in relation to the front of the face), thicker, and more projecting. The enlargements are more pronounced for boys than girls, but the profile for both sexes becomes straighter, the chin becomes more pointed, and the incisors of both jaws become more upright. There is acceleration in nose growth in both sexes; soft tissues change in the nose as well as in nasal bone structure, bringing the point of the nose further forward and downward in relation to the rest of the face. The eye may have a slight acceleration in growth; it seems to have a greater horizontal (rather than vertical) growth. Myopia (short-sightedness) increases continuously from about age six to maturity; there is a particularly rapid rate of change at about 11 or 12 for girls and 13 or 14 for boys, which would be expected if the axial rather than the vertical dimension of the eyeball accelerated in growth.[22]

Reproductive System. Figure 8 shows that both external and internal organs of the reproductive system grow spectacularly in adolescence. The growth spurt begins when pubic, axillary, and facial hair appear and when the testes and prostrate gland begin to function. The period when the reproductive system develops is often called puberty. The word is derived from *pubes* (meaning hair). Puberty was identified by the ancients as the stage of life when the genital region became covered with coarse, matted hair. In reference to boys, it sometimes implies the attainment of full reproductive capacity including production of gametes or spermatozoa; *nubility* often implies a girl's ability to ovulate, become pregnant, carry a fetus to full term, and manage childbirth.

There are two general kinds of change in the reproductive system at puberty. First, the genitalia and accessory organs (the primary sex characteristics) undergo major structural changes. Figures 9 and 10 diagram the developmental sequences for the primary sex characteristics of boys and girls, respectively.[23] Each figure depicts two significant sources of variance in the developmental pattern of the reproductive system: (1) The individual variations, which may be estimated by noting the point at which the maturity of the different organs are entered on the time axis. (2) The differences among individuals, which may be inferred from the range of ages inserted below each organ, indicating the

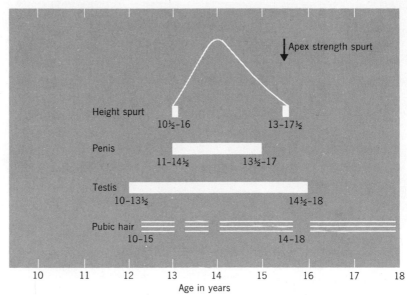

Figure 9
Diagram of sequence of events at adolescence in boys. An average boy is represented: the range of ages within which each event charted may begin and end is given by the figures placed directly below its start and finish. (From Tanner, see text. Reprinted by permission.)

average time when it begins and ceases its growth spurt. Second, there are striking body modifications, known as secondary sex characteristics. Although only indirectly associated with reproduction, these characteristics are responsible for conspicuous differences between the two sexes.

The development of the reproductive organs in boys begins before the height spurt (see Figure 9); the precise pattern differs among boys. The earliest observable pubertal change in boys is an acceleration in the growth of the testes and scrotum. Simultaneously there is often a change in the texture and reddening of the scrotum and pigmented pubic hairs appear near the base of the penis. The penis begins to lengthen about six months or a year later, when the cells of the testes begin to secrete male sex hormones. The increased size of the penis, the additional enlargement of the testes and scrotum, and the further darkening of the scrotal skin correspond closely to the general spurt in height and skeletal structure.[24]

Growth of the primary sex organs is paralleled by growth of the secondary sex characteristics. Axillary (armpit) hair usually appears two years after the pubic hair begins to grow; its appearance coincides with the peak in growth for

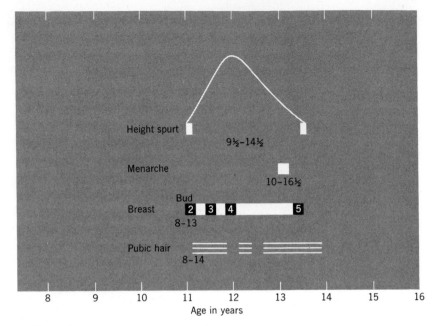

Figure 10
Diagram of sequence of events at adolescence in girls. An average girl is represented: the range of ages within which some of the events may occur is given by the figures placed directly below them. (From Tanner, see text. Reprinted by permission.)

body height. At about the same time, the sweat glands of the axilla enlarge and there is increased axillary sweating. Also facial hair begins to grow at the corners of the upper lip, spreads laterally across the upper lip to complete the moustache, then appears on the upper part of the cheeks (in the midline below the lower lip), and finally travels down into the neck region and along the sides and lower border of the chin. Pigmented hair on the thigh, calf, abdomen, and forearm usually appears before that on the chest and upper arms; it may appear anytime between the first axillary hair and well after the end of the growth spurt. There is a loss of hair above the forehead, causing a gradual indentation of the hairline on each side of the upper scalp above the eyebrows. About midway in the growth spurt, the male breast may enlarge moderately. The diameter of the areola, which is equal in both sexes before puberty, increases considerably in size. The skin darkens, and in some boys the breast develops a mound for a year or a year and a half, after which it usually disappears.[25] As the growth period draws to a close, the laryngeal (vocal system) muscles develop in size and strength causing vocal unevenness and huskiness and, eventually, perceptible deepening of the voice.

The events of puberty vary in the range of ages at which they occur. Consider the instance of boys. The pubertal enlargement of the testes often commences before 12 years of age; however, it could begin anywhere from 9.5 to 14.5 years. The typical period between the initial increase in velocity and the attainment of maximum size is about seven years, during which the testes may increase more than tenfold in size.[26] Acceleration in the growth of the penis generally begins around 12.5 years but could occur anywhere between 10 and 15 years of age. Penis growth always begins after and terminates before testical growth. The penis will double its prepuberal dimensions and may take up to five years to reach maximum size. Pigmented pubic hairs first appear about 13 years of age, and nearly all boys acquire noticeable hairs sometime between 10 and 16 years. Some boys take less than six months to reach maximum growth, but the average time is about three years.[27] Axillary hair typically appears around age 14, but a few boys have axillary hair by age 11 and some do not have any until after age 17. Consequently some boys between 13 and 15 are just starting their spurts in height and genitalia growth while others of the same age have nearly achieved their adult stature. The spurt in penis size, for example, may commence soon after the spurt in testical growth for one boy and fully two years later for another. Also, one boy may attain full penis size two years earlier than full testical growth and another boy may attain it only a few months earlier. About 25 percent of all boys acquire their first pigmented pubic hair before there is a noticeable growth in testical size.[28] A boy may reach the apex of his general growth spurt either without pubic hair or with very little. Occasionally boys may have some pigmented axillary hair before the appearance of pubic hair. The enlargement of the larynx may occur before penis growth acceleration or the presence of any pubic or axillary hair, but this enlargment is more likely to take place at a later time. At the time spermatozoa are first discharged in the urine, a boy may be at any stage of pubic and axillary hair development.

Figure 10 shows for girls the average individual sequence and ranges in timing of growth spurts for pubic hair, enlargement of the breasts, and menarche. The appearance of pubic and axillary hair for girls parallels that of boys. A few pigmented hairs appear in the pubic region about age 11, at least for most Caucasian girls. Axillary hair appears shortly after age 12; however, axillary hair could precede pubic hair. It takes about three years from the time either pubic or axillary hair first appears until it reaches full density.[29] The beginning of breast growth is usually the first external sign of impending puberty in an adolescent girl. It may occur as much as two years before pubic hair appears; however, sometimes it occurs simultaneously, or even two years afterward. Breast development follows a definite pattern in most girls. Tanner[30] has identified five separate stages; in Figure 10, the numbers in the bar depicting breast growth indicate the average age of each stage. During preadolescence (1), which is not shown, only the papilla is elevated; in the breast bud stage (2), the areola enlarges and the breast and papilla elevate. The enlargement and elevation continue without relative contour change (3) until the areola and papilla project (toward the end of breast development) to form a secondary mound (4). Eventually, due to recession of the areola and the general contour of the breast (5), the papilla becomes projected.

The age of menarche (occurrence of first menstrual cycle) has been investigated far more thoroughly than pubescent hair growth or breast development;[31] it is easier to investigate because women generally recall their menarcheal age quite accurately.[32] Contemporary data suggest that about half the Caucasian girls in the United States reach menarche between ages 12 and 14, 80 percent between 11.5 and 14.5, over 95 percent between 10 and 16, and fewer than 2 percent before age 10 or after age 16. The ovaries have a relatively limited adolescent growth spurt, but the uterus, vagina, labia, and clitoris are likely to have begun enlarging simultaneously with the appearance of the breast buds. Although menarche signifies a degree of maturity in uterine development, full reproductive capacity is not achieved immediately. The early menstrual cycles are often irregular, and commonly there is a pubertal sterility interval of one year to 18 months after the first menstruation, for the early menstrual cycles may be anovulatory, that is, unaccompanied by the shedding of an egg.[33] Data on the lack of fertility in females are highly unreliable; however, Tanner[34] speculates that maximum fertility may not be reached until the early or mid-twenties.

The maturity of the sexual organs is also variable, and there are different patterns in the sequence.[35] Menarche may occur anywhere from one year before to three years after the crest of height velocity. A typical girl will grow 2.5 inches more in height after menarche, and one girl in seven will grow 4 inches or more. Pubic hair may appear anywhere from three years before to six months after the peak in height. Axillary hair may appear from two years before to three years after the maximum velocity in trunk and limb dimensions. Breast and pubic hair growth may begin as early as three years before to as late as six months after menarche. Axillary hair may appear from four years before to two years after menarche. Pubic and axillary hair may appear anywhere from about 8 to 14 years of age.[36]

Sex Differences in Physique. At birth the male is slightly larger than the female—about 1 to 3 percent in length and 4 percent in weight. At first boys grow slightly faster than girls, but growth velocities are virtually identical from about one to nine years of age; except for the size of the head, sex differences are small.[37] Girls reach the adolescent growth spurt before boys on nearly all measurements; from about 10.5 to 13 years they are generally larger than boys. Although the male spurt occurs later, it persists longer, and the body, especially in leg and arm length in relation to the trunk, has a long period of growth. Boys are about 10 percent larger than girls after the termination of the spurt. The magnitude of their growth appears to be due more to prolongation than to greater peak velocity.[38]

An "androgynic," meaning man-woman, profile of sexual differentiation is presented in Figure 11.[39] The development of masculine and feminine characteristics is portrayed as comparable to a fan opening; it proceeds from undifferentiation to specific sex traits. In Bayer and Bayley's scheme there are eight distinct body measurements: (1) surface modeling—muscle, subcutaneous fat, bony protuberances, veins, and tendons; (2) shoulder girdle; (3) waistline; (4) hip flare; (5) buttocks; (6) thigh form; (7) space between the legs; (8) muscle bulge (lower legs). A total "androgny" score is obtained by totaling the scale values. Using this scale Bayer and Bayley present relatively ideal masculine and feminine profiles; a person possessing one of these profiles presumably projects the perfect body image. Bayer and Bayley say that preadolescents are largely indistinguishable in terms of surface modeling because they are covered by a

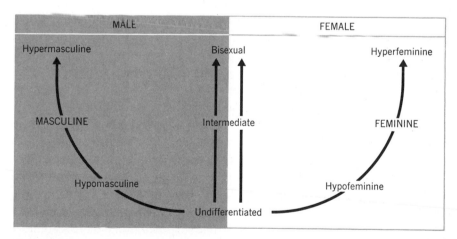

Figure 11
Diagrammatic representation of somatic sexual differentiation from relatively neutral childhood forms into masculine and feminine forms. Each of these adult forms varies in degree and direction of differentiation. An individual may be average, exaggerated, or muted in masculinity or femininity; may remain undifferentiated or may show a combination of masculine and feminine characteristics. (From Bayer and Bayley, see text. Reprinted by permission.)

relatively uniform layer of subcutaneous fat. Toward maturity, masculine modeling produces larger muscle masses, and veins and tendons stand out on the arm. On the other hand, feminine modeling is marked by fat deposits in the arm, and veins and tendons tend to fade into its contours. These differences seem to be due more to an absence of subcutaneous fat in males than to specific fat accumulation in the female arm.[40] In childhood the shoulder girdle, waistline indentation, and hip width are parallel to trunk size. But in adolescence the masculine shoulder appears wide, heavy, and muscular; its massiveness is accentuated by the fact that the hip widens only slightly from the waist, while the waistline has lowered, presumably because of trunk growth. The major growth of trunk breadth in the male is in the shoulder, but in the female it is in the pelvis. The feminine shoulder is slight, narrow, and poorly muscled, but the feminine waistline is marked by indentation below the ribs, primarily because of a flaring of the hips that produces a narrow, high waisted effect. Preadolescent boys and girls have knobby, spindly legs because childhood fat and muscle are only moderately developed. The adolescent boy's legs become muscular and large boned, resulting in cylindrical, fatless thighs, spaced relatively widely apart, and knobby, uneven lower legs. The girl's legs, in contrast, deviate more from the preadolescent pattern, becoming more rounded with fat. As a result, the thighs are relatively funnel-shaped, providing for little interspace, and the lower-leg contours are smooth.

Although body form is relatively undifferentiated before the adolescent growth spurt, the androgynic differentiation that takes place appears to be closely related to childhood characteristics. Preadolescents who are relatively tall, small-hipped, and long-legged appear to grow predominantly in height, leg length, and shoulder breadth; those who are relatively short, wide-hipped, and short-legged tend to grow in strength, circumference of thigh, and subcutaneous tissue. Children who are relatively linear or skinny seem to mature physically later and grow more slowly during adolescence than those who are curvilinear, as a consequence of fat deposits, and have a short growth period.[41] Apparently, individuals do not change their basic body types during the adolescent growth spurt.[42] Broverman et al.[43] believe that the growth spurt per se contributes little, in absolute terms, to postadolescent skeletal dimensions, and only moderately to weight and strength. It is not surprising that the preadolescent body shape correlates highly with the mature one since preadolescence may last 11 to 15 years while the adolescent spurt spans only two to four years.

Prediction of Adult Size.   Is it possible to predict whether a given child in a group would hold the same rank in height if his group position were assessed again in adolescence and in adulthood? Is it possible to predict relative standing from adolescence to adulthood? Such predictions are of intrinsic value to parents, teachers, and counselors who can counsel youths regarding activities and attitudes that are appropriate to their physical size. Will the large, powerful boy have a good chance of being accepted by the football team? Is the tall, conspicuous girl likely to have a permanent social disadvantage? The answer is that it is usually possible to predict from one age to another because there is a close correlation between the adult height of a person and his or her growth during childhood and adolescence. The vertical scale in Figure 12 shows the correlations between mature height and the height of those same individuals from birth through age 17.[44] As the curve suggests, the height at birth reveals nothing about adult height, but the curve rises steeply during the first year until it reaches a correlation of .65. It continues to rise rapidly until age three and then slows down until—at the beginning of adolescence—it reaches .85. Individual differences in timing and velocity during the adolescent growth spurt substantially alter the magnitude of the preadolescent correlations. During adolescence there is only a weak relationship between chronological age and biological age; two persons of the same sex who might have been the same height at age 8 may be widely separated at age 13; however, they will probably be near

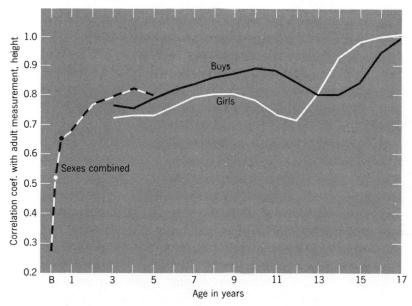

Figure 12
Correlations between adult height and heights of same individuals as children. Sexes combined lines (0–5). All data pure longitudinal. (From Tanner, see text. Reprinted by permission.)

each other in height again at age 18. The difficulty of predicting adult height during adolescence can be overcome by employing measures of skeletal age or degree of bone maturity.[45] While the bone epiphyses (the ends of a bone that separately ossify and become part of the bone) are uncalcified or open, the skeleton is still immature; but when they become fully calcified, the skeletal growth potential has been reached. These changes may be discerned on X-ray pictures, which distinguish the translucent areas of cartilage (the uncalcified parts) from the opaque areas (the calcified parts). Although any portion of the skeleton can be used to assess bone age, the hand and wrist are most frequently used. In the hand many bones and epiphyses are developing, and it may be X-rayed with minimal equipment and danger of spreading radiation to other parts of the body.[46] The skeletal age may then be determined by comparing the X-ray with established norms.[47]

Physiological and Endocrinological Change

Physiological Growth. Several physiological changes occur at adolescence that augment the growing differences between the two sexes and help explain why boys acquire greater capacity for physical output than girls.[48] First, girls experience an earlier rise in systolic blood pressure but boys have a greater rise, perhaps because of their more extensive increase in heart size and blood volume. Diastolic blood pressure, on the other hand, remains about the same for both sexes. Second, the basal heart rate falls gradually throughout adolescence, except for a slight rise at the time of peak velocity in growth. The heart rate for both sexes varies little until age 11; thereafter, the girls' rate decreases less than that of boys. About age 12, the resting heartbeat of girls is established for adulthood as approximately 10 percent greater than that of boys. Third, in boys the number of red blood corpuscles rises and the hemoglobin in the blood increases. Girls do not experience an increase in red blood cells or hemoglobin. Tanner[49] suggests that the hemoglobin ratio to body weight and the corresponding effect of red cells on blood volume increase may be related to the extent of muscle growth. Fourth, the increase in red blood cells and hemoglobin is related to sex differences in respiratory functions. The respiratory rate decreases steadily throughout childhood and adolescence for both sexes. However, (1) the resting respiratory volume—both per minute and per breath, (2) the vital capacity—maximum expiration following a maximal inspiration, and (3) the maximum breath capacity—volume breathed during a 15-second period in which the individual breathes as deeply and rapidly as possible—show a much greater increase in boys than in girls. Adolescent boys also possess a greater

vital capacity per size of body surface, a difference that may be due to boys'
greater lung growth and their corresponding increases in shoulder and chest
width. Fifth, boys have an increased alkali reserve, which is apparently
associated with the fact that their blood is able to absorb greater quantities of
lactic acid and other muscular metabolites during exercise than can girls' blood
without a change of pH in the blood. Probably the relatively greater development of muscular bulk in males makes the new ability a necessity.[50] Sixth, the
fact that boys have a larger respiratory volume and a smaller percentage of
oxygen in their expired air (reflecting their increased oxygen consumption) is
demonstrated in their basal metabolism rate. This rate (which is the amount of
heat produced per square meter of body surface during rest) falls continuously
from birth. The metabolic rate of boys is greater than that of girls in relation to
the surface area; in adolescence it tends to level off rather than decline whereas
the girls' rate continues to decline steadily. The slowing down, especially for
boys, coincides with the adolescent growth spurt and may be related to the extra
heat production that is necessary to build new tissue. None of these rather dramatic changes seems to create physiological instability or produce day-to-day
variability in blood pressure, heart rate, or metabolic rate. Although G. Stanley
Hall[51] argued that transitory physiological variability stimulated psychological
instability during adolescence, there has been no evidence to support this
hypothesis.[52]

Endocrinological Growth.   The initiation of the adolescent growth spurt,
and its attendant changes, begins with the secretion of hormones from the
ovaries, testes, and adrenal glands into the bloodstream and tissues. These
glands, in their turn, have been stimulated by hormones from the pituitary
gland. This little gland is located underneath the base of the brain near the
center of the head, and is itself biochemically energized by a small area in the
brain known as the hypothalamus.[53]

Growth at adolescence is due to the combination of several hormones. The
secretion of gonadotrophins begins about the time pubic hair appears in both
sexes, and it reaches adult levels with the maturity of secondary sex characteristics. Estrogens and androgens, which are produced by the ovaries, the testes,
and the adrenal cortices, are secreted at a low but constant rate in both boys and
girls from age 3 to 7. At about age 7 these secretions gradually rise equally in
both sexes until about age 10. At adolescence the estrogen secretion in girls rises
sharply and begins to be cyclical, but even the monthly low is much greater than
the level in boys. There is a sharp rise in androgenic substances in adolescent
boys; within a 24-hour period, the secretion for boys is likely to be twice that for
girls.[54]

FACTORS AFFECTING PHYSICAL GROWTH

Cultural and Class Differences

Cultural differences and related social-class distinctions account for some discrepancies in the rate of growth; those of higher status seem to grow more rapidly.[55] Tanner[56] reports that children whose parents are in the professional and managerial classes are about an inch taller at three years of age and one and one-half to two inches taller at adolescence than children whose parents are unskilled laborers. Young people from affluent homes also seem to be more linear, less squat, and less muscular; when equated in height, they weigh relatively less. Also menarche occurs earlier in girls from higher socioeconomic classes; in southern England and Denmark, for example, these girls reached menarche about two to three months before girls from lower socioeconomic groups.[57] In a study of 47,420 African Bantu girls, Burrell et al. found that there was a four-month difference between the "poor" and the "not-so-poor" groups; these groups differed mainly in the amount of animal protein in their diet. The researchers also found that girls born early in the calendar year (when malnutrition is greatest in Africa) tended to begin menstruation four months later than girls born at other times. Likewise, Israel[58] reported that girls from higher social classes in India menstruated earlier than girls from the lower classes. Tanner and O'Keefe[59] found that the average age of menarche for a group of Nigerian girls was 14.07, which was the average menarcheal age in Great Britain over a generation ago. Another group of girls from prosperous homes in Uganda reached the menarche at about 13.4 years of age.[60] Similarly, in a Rumanian seaport it was learned that the average age of menarche was 13.3; however, because a family's socioeconomic status decreased proportionately with each child, each successive daughter (up to a total of four) increased the average age of menarche in the family about 2.1 months.[61] Tanner[62] reported that in general young people who have more (rather than fewer) siblings are shorter in height, weigh less is comparison with others of their age, and experience a later growth spurt. Apparently the larger the number of children to feed and care for in a not-too-prosperous family results in less than optimal nutrition and care. Good nutrition, together with regular meals, sufficient sleep and exercise (which characterize relatively affluent households), may be the major factors accounting for class differences in rates of growth.[63] However, other evidence shows that rather astonishing circumstances may contribute to growth in stature. For example, Landauer and Whiting[64] reported a positive relationship between physiological stress in infancy and adult height. In a cross-cultural study, they found that male children under age of two who had had their heads or limbs repeatedly molded or stretched; their ears, nose, or lips pierced; their bodies circumcised, vaccinated, or inoculated; or their skin burned for tribal marks or cuts were about two and one-half inches taller in adulthood than other males who had not been subjected to these practices. Another (longitudinal) study, which employed immunization before age two as a measure of stress in infancy, found also that stress was related to greater stature at age 18.[65]

Earlier Maturation Today

Tanner[66] has presented convincing evidence that the process of growing up has increased in speed during the past 100 years. At the turn of the century men failed to reach their adult height until age 26;[67] today, boys achieve their maximum stature at about 18 (only rarely does a male grow more than a fraction of an inch after he is 19), and girls achieve theirs between 16 and 17.[68] Children, adolescents, and adults are also all growing proportionately larger than their earlier counterparts. A contemporary Polish child is morphologically two years older than a child of the same age in the nineteenth century.[69] Tanner[70] reports that in Europe and North America, beginning about 1900, all children between 5 and 7 years of age have increased in height between ½ and ¾ an inch per decade. Those between 10 and 14 have increased in height between one and one and one-half inches per decade. The increase for white adults in the United States was about ½ inch per decade from 1915 to 1940 and about ⅛ inch per decade from 1940 to 1960. For black adults it was ¼ inch per decade from 1940 to 1960. Similarly, Espenschade and Meleney[71] report that boys are one inch taller and 10 pounds heavier and girls one inch taller and six pounds heavier than boys and girls of the same age a generation earlier.

The onset of the adolescent growth spurt and the age of menarche are both occurring earlier. Tanner[72] has reported that children in much of North America, Europe, Japan, and China are reaching the growth spurt three to five years sooner than they did 100 years ago. Milicer[73] has pointed out that Polish youth are entering the growth spurt two years sooner than they did a century ago. This trend toward earlier maturation is illustrated by changes in the age of menarche presented in Figure 13.[74] The main conclusion to be drawn is that menarche for American girls and West European girls has generally been occurring at a progressively earlier age for the past 100 years by about three or four months per decade. Thus girls in these countries today may begin menstruation by as much as two and one-half to three and one-half years earlier than they did a century ago. Tanner[75] believes that the trend toward earlier menarche may continue for another decade or two, but Poppleton and Brown[76] feel that the trend may have already stopped in Great Britain. Frisch and

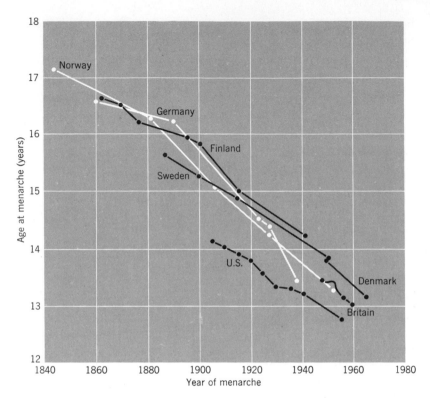

Figure 13
**Age at menarche, or first menstrual period, has declined in the U.S.,
Britain and Europe. Girls are estimated to begin menstruation between
2.5 and 3.3 years earlier on the average than a century ago. The age of
menarche is an index of of the rate of physical maturation.** (From *Earlier
Maturation in Man.* J. M. Tanner. Copyright © (1968) by Scientific
American, Inc. All rights reserved. Reprinted by permission.)

Revelle[77] suggest that today's earlier menarche may be due to the fact that it is
related to the attainment of a critical weight, which is being reached by girls at an
earlier age today.

SUMMARY

Descriptions of adolescent physical development are usually based on averages taken
from the study of a number of persons. Height and weight curves indicate that girls
attain average adult height somewhere between two years earlier and about the same
age as boys and that they may be from five or six inches shorter to about the same
height. Between the ages of 9 and 15 nearly every adolescent grows rapidly in almost

every body dimension. This phenomenon of accelerated growth is known as the *adolescent growth spurt*. The period during the spurt when the reproductive system develops is called puberty. The genitalia and accessory organs (the primary sex characteristics) undergo major structural changes. Menarche usually occurs after the peak in the height spurt and well after the beginning of breast development. In terms of body-surface characteristics, pre-adolescents are largely indistinguishable by sex; both are covered by a relatively uniform layer of subcutaneous fat. Physical maturity in the male produces larger muscle masses; in the female muscles tend to be incorporated in body contours.

Researchers have shown that it is possible to predict adult height from childhood and adolescent growth patterns. The most accurate measures are those based on skeletal age or degree of bone maturity.

Physiological changes in blood pressure, heart rate, red blood cells, respiratory rate, and metabolic rate occur at adolescence, which augment the growing differences between boys and girls. The initiation of many features of the adolescent growth spurt is due to the secretion of several different hormones. At adolescence, for example, the estrogen secretion rises sharply in girls while the androgen secretion rises markedly in boys.

Factors associated with social class seem to affect physical growth. Research indicates that children whose parents are in the professional and managerial classes are about an inch taller at three years of age and one and one-half to two inches taller at adolescence than children whose parents are unskilled laborers. Good nutrition, regular meals, and sufficient sleep and exercise (which are often found in more affluent households) may be the major factors accounting for class differences in rates of growth. These same factors appear to be responsible for increasing the speed of growing up during the past 100 years. At the turn of the century men reached adult height around age 26; today, boys achieve their maximum stature at about age 18 and girls at about 16 or 17. Young people today are also growing proportionately larger than their earlier counterparts. Youth between 10 and 14 have increased in height on the average between one and one-half inches per decade over the past several decades.

REVIEW QUESTIONS

1. What is the height and weight, respectively, of the average American adolescent boy and girl?
2. What are the major growth differences between black and white adolescents?
3. What are the average ages at which boys and girls, respectively, begin and end the adolescent growth spurt?
4. What parts of the body increase in size in a regular sequence during the growth spurt?
5. Name the parts of the body that reveal relatively independent growth spurts.
6. What changes occur during adolescence in primary and secondary sex characteristics?

7. In what ways do the events of puberty vary in the ages at which they occur?

8. What changes during adolescence sharpen distinctions between the physical appearances of men and women?

9. Is there a close correlation between the adult height of a person and his or her growth during childhood and adolescence?

10. Name the physiological and endocrinological changes that occur at adolescence.

11. What social factors affect adolescent growth?

12. What are the characteristics of the trend toward earlier maturation?

DISCUSSION QUESTIONS

1. What are some of the nonhereditary factors that cause young people of the same age to vary in average height and weight (see Tables 1 and 2)?

2. Do you think that social circumstances can affect whether adolescents are awkward and clumsy during the growth spurt?

3. What would you judge to be the current status of the trend toward earlier maturation?

NOTES

1. G. S. Hall. *Adolescence*. New York: Appleton, 1904, 2 vols.

2. J. M. Tanner. The regulation of human growth. *Child Development*, 1963, **34,** 817–847.

3. O. Klineberg. *Social psychology*. New York: Holt, 1954.

4. K. Dion, E. Berscheid, and E. Walster. What is beautiful is good. *Journal of Personality and Social Psychology*, 1972, **24,** 285–290.

5. National Center for Health Statistics. *Height and weight of youths 12–16 years, United States*. (DHEW, Pub. No. [HSM] 73-1606.) Series 11, No. 124, 1973.

6. National Center for Health Statistics. *Body weight, stature, and sitting height: white and negro youths 12–17 years, United States*. (DHEW, Pub. No. [HRA] 74-1608.) Series 11, No. 126, 1973.

7. J. M. Tanner. *Growth at adolescence* (2nd ed.). Oxford: Blackwell Scientific Publications, 1962.

8. J. M. Tanner. Twelve to sixteen: early adolescence. *Daedalus*, 1971, **100,** 907–930; J. M. Tanner. *Sequence and tempo in the somatic changes in puberty*. In M. M. Grumbach, G. D. Grave, and F. E. Mayer (Eds.). *Control of the onset of puberty*. New York: John Wiley, 1974, pp. 448–470.

9. Tanner, Twelve to sixteen, *op. cit.*

10. Tanner, Twelve to sixteen, *op. cit.*, p. 914.

11. J. M. Tanner. *Education and physical growth*. London: University of London Press, 1961.

12. W. M. Krogman. Growth of head, face, trunk, and limbs in Philadelphia white and negro children of elementary and high school age. *Monographs of the Society for Research in Child Development*, 1970, **35,** (5, Serial No. 136).

13. Tanner, Education and physical growth, *op. cit.*; Tanner, Growth at adolescence, *op. cit.*

14. Tanner, Growth at adolescence, *op. cit.*

15. R. E. Frisch. Critical weight at menarche, initiation of the adolescent growth spurt, and control of puberty. In M. M. Grumbach, G. D. Grave, and F. E. Mayer (Eds.). *Control of the onset of puberty.* New York: John Wiley, 1974, pp. 403–423.

16. Ibid.

17. Tanner, Physical growth, *op. cit.*; Tanner, Growth at adolescence, *op. cit.*

18. Tanner, Physical growth, *op. cit.*

19. Tanner, Physical growth, *op. cit.*; Tanner, Growth at adolescence, *op. cit.*

20. Tanner, Physical growth, *op. cit.*

21. Krogman, *op. cit.*

22. Tanner, Physical growth, *op. cit.*

23. Tanner, Growth at adolescence, *op. cit.*

24. Ibid.

25. Ibid.

26. H. V. Meredith. A synopsis of puberal changes in youth. *Journal of School Health,* 1967, **37,** 171–176.

27. Ibid.

28. Ibid.

29. Ibid.

30. Tanner, Growth at adolescence, *op. cit.*

31. Meredith, *op. cit.*

32. N. Livson, and D. McNeill. The accuracy of recalled age of menarche. *Human Biology,* 1962, **34,** 218–221.

33. Tanner, Twelve to sixteen, *op. cit.*

34. Tanner, Growth at adolescence, *op. cit.*

35. Meredith, *op. cit.*

36. Ibid.

37. Tanner, Growth at adolescence, *op. cit.*

38. Ibid.

39. L. M. Bayer and N. Bayley. *Growth diagnosis.* Chicago: The University of Chicago Press, 1959.

40. R. M. Malina and F. E. Johnston. Significance of age, sex, and maturity differences in upper arm composition. *Research Quarterly,* 1967, **38,** 219–230; S. M. Garn and J. A. Haskell. Fat changes during adolescence. *Science,* 1959, **129,** 1615–1616.

41. D. M. Broverman, I. K. Broverman, W. Vogel, R. D. Palmer, and E. L. Klaiber. Physique and growth in adolescence. *Child Development,* 1964, **35,** 857–870; D. McNeill and N. Livson. Maturation rate and body build in women. *Child Development,* 1963, **34,** 25–32; Tanner, Growth at adolescence, *op. cit.*

42. Zuk, G. H. The plasticity of the physique from early-adolescence through adulthood. *Journal of Genetic Psychology,* 1958, **92,** 205–214.

43. Broverman, et al., *op. cit.*

44. Tanner, Physical growth, *op. cit.*

45. F. E. Johnston. The concept of skeletal age. *Clinical Pediatrics,* 1962, **1,** 133–144; F. E. Johnston. Individual variation in the rate of skeletal maturation between five and eighteen years. *Child Development,* 1964, **35,** 75–80; Tanner, Physical growth, *op. cit.*

46. Tanner, Physical growth, *op. cit.*

47. Bayer and Bayley, *op. cit.*; Johnston, Skeletal age, *op. cit.*; Johnston, Rate of skeletal maturation, *op. cit.*

48. Tanner, Growth at adolescence, *op. cit.*

49. Ibid.

50. Ibid.

51. Hall, *op. cit.*

52. D. H. Eichorn and J. P. McKee. Physiological instability during adolescence. *Child Development,* 1958, **29,** 255–268; Tanner, Growth at adolescence, *op. cit.*

53. Tanner, Physical growth, *op. cit.*

54. Tanner, Growth at adolescence, *op. cit.*

55. E. Takahashi. Growth and environmental factors in Japan. *Human Biology,* 1966, **38,** 112–130; Tanner, Growth at adolescence, *op. cit.*; J. M. Tanner. Growth and physique in different populations of mankind. In P. T. Baker and J. J. Weiner (Eds.). *The biology of human adaptability.* Oxford: Clarendon Press, 1966, pp. 45–66; J. Whitacre and E. T. Grimes. Some body measurements of native-born white children seven to fourteen years in different climactic regions of Texas. *Child Development,* 1959, **30,** 177–209.

56. Tanner, Physical growth, *op. cit.*

57. R. J. W. Burrell, M. J. R. Healy, and J. M. Tanner. Age at menarche in South African Bantu school girls living in the Transkei Reserve. *Human Biology,* 1961, **33,** 250–261.

58. S. Israel. The onset of menstruation in Indian women. *Journal of Obstetrics and Gynecology of the British Empire,* 1959, **66,** 311–316.

59. J. M. Tanner and B. O'Keefe. Age at menarche in Nigerian school girls, with a note on their heights and weights from 12 to 19. *Human Biology,* 1962, **34,** 187–196.

60. A. P. Burgess and H. J. L. Burgess. The growth pattern of East African school girls. *Human Biology,* 1964, **36,** 177–193.

61. R. Stukovsky, J. A. Valsik, and M. Bulai-Stirbu. Family size and menarcheal age in Constanza, Roumania. *Human Biology,* 1967, **39,** 277–283.

62. Tanner, Growth and physique, *op. cit.*

63. Tanner, Physical growth, *op. cit.*

64. T. K. Landauer and J. W. M. Whiting. Infantile stimulation and adult stature of human males. *American Anthropologist,* 1964, **66,** 1007–1028.

65. J. W. M. Whiting, T. K. Landauer, and T. M. Jones. Infantile immunization and adult stature. *Child Development,* 1968, **39,** 59–67.

66. Tanner, Physical growth, *op. cit.*; Tanner, Growth at adolescence, *op. cit.*; J. M. Tanner. Earlier maturation in man. *Scientific American,* 1968, **218,** 21–26.

67. Hall, *op. cit.*

68. Tanner, Earlier maturation in man, *op. cit.*

69. H. Milicer. The secular trend in growth and maturation as revealed by Polish data. *T. soc. Geneesk,* 1966, **44,** 562–568.

70. Tanner, Earlier maturation in man, *op. cit.*

71. A. S. Espenschade and H. E. Meleney. Motor performances of adolescent boys and girls of today in comparison with those of twenty-four years ago. *Research Quarterly,* 1961, **32,** 186–189.

72. Tanner, Earlier maturation in man, *op. cit.*

73. Milicer, *op. cit.*

74. Tanner, Earlier maturation in man, *op. cit.*

75. Ibid.

76. P. K. Poppleton and P. E. Brown. The secular trend in puberty: has stability been achieved? *The British Journal of Educational Psychology,* 1966, **36,** 97–101.

77. R. E. Frisch and R. Revelle. Variation in body weights and the age of the adolescent growth spurt among Latin American and Asian populations, in relation to calorie supplies. *Human Biology,* 1969, **41,** 185–212; R. E. Frisch and R. Revelle. Height and weight at menarche and a hypothesis of critical body weights and adolescent events. *Science,* 1970, **169,** 397–398.

Chapter 3

Body Image and Personality Development

CHAPTER HIGHLIGHTS

BODY IMAGE
EARLY AND LATE MATURATION
PHYSICAL FITNESS, ATHLETIC PARTICI-
    PATION, AND SEXISM IN SPORTS
    PHYSICAL FITNESS

ATHLETIC PARTICIPATION
  SEXISM IN SPORTS
SUMMARY
REVIEW QUESTIONS
DISCUSSION QUESTIONS

ISSUES

Body image is an important aspect of self-concept development.

Ideal standards of physical attractiveness influence the images young people develop of their social worth.

The timing of the adolescent growth spurt may affect development of body image.

Rate of physical maturation has more impact on the personality integration of boys than of girls.

Physical fitness, body image, and physical strength, respectively, are correlated with rate of maturation.

Athletics provides a strong network of social relationships, which may affect socialization in positive ways, but young people do not generally enjoy a broad-based sports program.

Cultural circumstances have tended to depress the skill performance levels of adolescent girls.

BODY IMAGE

The image presented by the human body has been an object of interest since the time of Hippocrates. We had long been led to believe that temperament and character—the major ingredients of body image—were biologically determined and were based on the general body shape. It was felt that a male who possessed a large body, especially if he was tall, must surely be a dominant, self-confident, strong leader. And it was believed that persons who tended to have a lot of subcutaneous fat and tended to be round in shape were phlegmatic, passive and relaxed, gluttonous and insensitive, but also warm and soft-hearted. Men with well-developed muscles and ideal proportions were considered to be self-confident, energetic, adventurous, enterprising, and extroverted. And those who tended to be tall and thin and have small muscles were though to be active, tense, excitable, intelligent and reserved. With respect to specific characteristics, it was thought that red hair signified a fiery temper; a mustache, evil and villainy; blond hair, seductiveness; short hair, heroic and reactionary interests; and long hair, an inclination toward martyrdom and revolutionary endeavor. Lerner[1] argues that certain stereotypes prevail regardless of age, sex, race, or geographical location within the U.S. For example, American males from 10 to 20 and females from about 16 to 40 believe that the muscular, well-proportioned male is the best leader, athlete, and desirable friend.[2] Cross and Cross[3] asked black and white members of both sexes in age groups of 7, 12, 17, and about 36 years, who were living in the midwest, to rate the physical attractiveness of facial features of persons who were comparable to themselves in age, sex, and ethnicity. The overall beauty ratings were nearly the same for all of the age groups, which suggests that prevailing standards of physical attractiveness are learned very early in life and very uniformly. Kurtz[4] also reported that men who were neither fat nor thin but well-muscled regarded themselves as more active, "he-man" types and liked their own bodies better than did less well-proportioned males. He reported, too, that thin women considered themselves to be more desirable than heavy women.

In the social sciences today, body image is thought to arise from social interaction. Cavior and Lombardi[5] asked boys and girls individually at four age levels, from five to eight, to rate the physical attractiveness of full-length photographs of white, middle-class, male and female, 11- and 17-year-olds. These findings were compared to rankings made by peers who were the same ages as those in the photographs. The results indicated that judgments of physical attractiveness become relatively consistent among age groups around age six and that boys and girls by age eight use the same cultural standards for judging physical attractiveness as older persons. One might expect that the processes of learning to judge physical attractiveness and acquiring a body image are comparable. For example, body image seems to be the product of real and fantasied experiences, which stem in part from one's own physical development, from peer emphasis on physical attributes, and from increasing awareness of cultural expectations. Adolescents derive concepts of their body through interpreting their status in the eyes of others. Their assessment of their bodies, therefore, depends on such matters as their relationships with others, assimilation of new roles, capacity to accomplish goals and meet expectations, and feelings of self-esteem, security, and frustration. If a family overvalues a beautiful body, an adolescent may find it difficult to accept any deviation from the ideal body configuration. Parents may foster anxiety by making deprecating remarks about such physical features as a son's short height, lack of muscles, or small penis, or a daughter' delayed menarche, small breasts, or excessive weight.

Cabot[6] advanced a theory of "socio-biological advantage," in which he suggested that adolescents whose body types resembled the "athletosome" (or ideal) enjoyed special advantages and opportunities because of the favorable images they projected. The adolescent with "athletosome" physical characteristics is indeed fortunate, for other persons will have favorable impressions based on old cultural stereotypes and contemporary standards of attractiveness. The competition for peer status, popularity with the opposite sex, and adult privileges is often keen; unfortunately, the adolescent whose body creates an unfavorable image may be discriminated against, ostracized, rejected by the opposite sex, and even treated with contempt and hostility. Advertising, magazines, movies, television, and hero worship of athletes all contribute to glorification of the ideal body and disparagement of the deviant.[7]

Many studies support the idea that adolescents' attitudes toward their own bodies influence their self-concepts and that the attitudes of others toward their bodies affect their responses to the others' expectations. Cortes and Gatti,[8] for example, reported that adolescent boys with admired physiques had a strong need to achieve, were concerned about their accomplishments, wanted to do well, and were willing to take risks. Broverman, Broverman, Vogel, Palmer, and Klaiber[9] found that well-coordinated, mature-looking youths demonstrated more task persistence than other youths. And Gunderson[10] has shown that dissatisfaction with height and weight, respectively, increases with magnitude of deviation from ideal images. His study was derived from reports of young enlisted navy men who were asked to rate the degree to which they were satisfied with their height and weight. Most of the young men wanted to be 72 inches tall, about two inches more than their average mean height of 70 inches. The optimum amount they wanted to weigh was 171 to 180 pounds, whereas their actual mean weight was 159. The study revealed that the extent of satisfaction formed a curvilinear relationship with each ideal. Deviation from the generally preferred height of 72 inches and weight of 171 to 180 pounds in either direction resulted in increased dissatisfaction. These findings have been confirmed for boys in a recent national health examination survey;[11] however, the national survey reveals that patterns of relationships between perceived and preferred body weight are distinctively different among boys and girls 12 to 17 years of age. Almost all of the girls who thought that they were heavier than most others, for example, stated that they would like to be thinner; further, girls who considered themselves thin preferred to remain thin or to be even thinner. The national survey also showed that girls are more likely than boys to express satisfaction with existing height, whether they are short or tall. In demonstrating the importance of body image to adolescents, Arnhoff and Damianopoulos[12] found that 20-year-old males could easily identify their own photo from among six others ranging from high to low similarity, but that men in their early forties could not. Each photo was taken against a black background, and the individual was clad only in a pair of white jockey shorts—legs slightly spread, head facing front, arms slightly spread away from the body. Comparative height cues, head shape, and outline of hair were omitted, and faces were covered. The researchers concluded that the older participants were less interested in their body image, failed to keep it up-to-date, and thus, were unable to recognize themselves. It has also been demonstrated that adolescents see others as they see themselves. Ward[13] showed that tall college students tended to estimate the height of the average American male and female as relatively tall. Each sex was more consistent in judging the height of the same sex than that of the opposite sex.

Body image is generally of more critical significance to the adolescent girl than it is to the boy. Sexism dominates many quarters of American society, and to the extent that the female form receives more emphasis than the male, women are more inclined then men to try to capitalize on their body appearance. Traditional forms of sexism demand that women stress their attractiveness by use of sexually arousing clothing and jewelry and presume that men take less active interest in their body appearance. Cross and Cross[14] report that female and male young people tend to rate male facial beauty about the same, but that females rate female faces more highly than do males. Kurtz[15] reports that girls are expected to focus attention on the details of their bodies and therefore are likely to develop a more differentiated body concept then boys. But Kurtz[16] suggests, too, that a girl who is oriented toward a career in engineering or physics may have a body image of herself closely resembling that of the typical male. He also says that youth possessing limited opportunity to achieve in school and the workplace, for example, might rely on "good physiques" to define and support the adequacy of their sex-role identities.

EARLY AND LATE MATURATION

Whether an adolescent enters the growth spurt relatively early or late may affect his or her body image. A muscular boy who matures early may continue to dominate athletics.[17] Adults and his peers, responding to his size, may offer him tasks and privileges that are ordinarily reserved for older boys. If he meets the challenge, thus confirming their impression, he both increases his skills and widens the number of adult-oriented opportunities that are open to him.[18] He may also be thrust into heterosexual relationships and thereby develop at an early age sexual prowess and various social amenities.[19] A boy who does not enter the growth spurt until later may be disadvantaged in the march toward adulthood. Those whom he formerly beat in competitive sports may suddenly surpass him, and even younger boys may loom as new threats. Family members and friends may still consider him a child and therefore restrict his opportunities for demonstrating adult behavior. Girls are not likely to consider him as a desirable date.

A girl who matures early is often confronted with social situations that (because of her inexperience) may intensify her sexual anxieties. The late-maturer, in relation to the stocky and muscular early-maturer, tends to develop a more slender, feminine body. Her physical growth takes place at about the same time as boys her age; since her figure is relatively inconspicuous until somewhat later, she attracts less predatory attention from older boys.

Researchers associated with the Adolescent Growth Study in California have studied longitudinally the timing of the adolescent growth spurt and its relationship to various aspects of personality development.[20] Each researcher has employed the same general approach.[21] Assessments of physical maturity, based on skeletal X-rays of the wrists and hands, were made initially on 90 boys and 87 girls beginning at an average chronological age of 14 years. Those chosen for each of the ensuing studies, however, were the 16 most consistently retarded and the 16 most consistently accelerated boys from 14 to 18.5 years[22] and the 17 most consistently retarded and 17 most consistently accelerated girls from 14 to 18 years.[23] Each investigator studied these boys and girls with respect to behavioral, behavior-inferred, and projective measures of personality. The fact that average adolescents were excluded suggests that the conclusions drawn from the findings pertain only to adolescents who are either *very* early or *very* late in their growth spurt. Moreover, since the subjects were drawn from urban, middle-class, western homes, it is not known to what extent the findings might be affected by nutrition, disease, and socioeconomic status. Also it is not known to what extent the findings are still applicable since the data were collected a generation ago. The conclusions are significant, however, because they were well conceptualized and are a provocative today as ever.

The first of the studies[24] focused on the effects on personality development of different maturation rates in boys. The boys' personality attributes were rated by adult observers while the boys participated in sports, waited for physical examinations, and talked with girls at a dance. Peer reputation scores were also obtained from classmates who matched the names of individuals with descriptions of personality traits. The findings of both the adult ratings and the peer descriptions supported the assumption that physically accelerated boys are more often accepted and treated as mature adults than other children.[25] Both adults and peers felt that the athletic, muscular early-maturers were most attractive, especially at about age 15. The early-maturers (in relation to the late-maturers) were also regarded as less childish—less talkative, active, busy, peppy, laughing—particularly at age 16. The early-maturers showed more interest in girls, whereas the late-maturers seemed to be more attention-oriented, restless, talkative, and less grown-up. And peers usually gave greater social recognition—school offices, committee chairmanships, mention in the school newspaper, athletic popularity—to the early-maturers.[26]

When the boys were 17 years of age, projective personality tests indicated that those who had matured early were more self-confident, less dependent, and more capable of fulfilling adult expectations in interpersonal relations. By contrast, those who had matured late had negative self-concepts—profound feelings of rejection by others, strong heterosexual affiliative needs, prolonged dependency needs, and rebellious attitudes toward their parents.[27] About a year after high school graduation, adults rated the boys on nine separate motivational drives. The late-maturers were found to have higher drives for social affiliation (to be accepted and liked) and aggression (to deprive others by belittling, attacking, ridiculing). It was believed that this was due to the "basic insecurities, feelings of rejection, and intense dependency needs" of the late-maturers; these findings were felt to be congruent with those of the earlier Jones and Bayley study.[28] Subsequent follow-up studies showed that personality differences between the early- and late-maturers persisted long after the physical distinctions had passed. When the two groups were 33 years of age, the early-maturers seemed to be men whose advice was sought, who made good impressions, and who were cooperative, enterprising, persistent, goal-directed, sociable, warm, conforming, and somewhat overcontrolled. The late-maturers seemed to be men who sought the aid and encouragement of others; they also appeared to be more insightful and flexible, but were more impulsive, rebellious, touchy, self-assertive, and indulgent.[29] These findings were confirmed again when the subjects were 38 years old.[30]

In an independent investigation, Weatherly[31] compared the self-reports of relative maturation of 19-year-old boys and girls with their scores on several standardized personality tests and with self-ratings of perceived similarity to parents and peers. The late-maturing boys were more likely to seek attention and affection, resist leadership roles, and participate in unconventional behavior. Weatherly also reported that the early- and average-maturing groups in his study resembled one another in personality attributes, but that the late-maturers were distinctly different. His findings suggest that only the visible, obvious late-maturers are socially handicapped; in fact, to mature at an average age may be as much of a relative advantage as to mature early.

Although it might appear that the prospects for late-maturing boys are fairly dismal, it should be emphasized that the two groups of boys in the Growth Study were similar in intelligence, grade placement, and peer status; as adults, they were similar in educational attainment, socioeconomic status, incidence of marriage, and number of children.[32] The initial investigation[33] revealed that the two groups, while different in many respects, were surprisingly similar in such traits as popularity, leadership, prestige, poise, assurance, cheerfulness, and group behavior. A year after high school, although the two groups differed on two of the nine motivational drives, they were approximately the same on autonomy, achievement, recognition, abasement, help-from-others, dominance, and avoidance of unpleasant situations.[34] Jones[35] said that late-maturers may have greater advantages as they become older. It is possible, for example, that the trauma of having been late-maturers in adolescence is related to having more insight, tolerance of ambiguity, selective awareness, and flexibility 15 or 20 years later; the late-maturer thus may become more liberal and more adaptive. Furthermore, as Jones[36] has wryly observed, late-maturers may not be looked upon unfavorably anymore; they have read many of the published reports about themselves and are unhappy about the image that has been presented.

The Growth Study investigations have consistently reported that early-maturing boys have a relative social advantage during adolescence. Although initially it had been assumed that early-maturing girls would experience greater conflicts, the investigations did not bear this out. Early-maturing girls were first seen as towering in stature over both boys and girls of the same chronological age. They were presumed to be relatively submissive, listless, without poise, and indifferent in social situations.[37] But personality analyses made when the girls were 17 showed that the early-maturers were at that time better adjusted, in terms of positive self-concepts and personal relations, than the late-maturers.[38] The discrepancy may be due to the problems of making social adjustments at different times during adolescence. A girl with an early growth spurt may have fairly stressful relations with her peers and parents, but she is also being exposed to situations in which she can learn adult-like behavior. If the stress is not crippling and if she can cope with the problems, she will probably enhance her self-esteem and feelings of adequacy. By the time she is 17, when there are fewer physical differences and environmental stresses, the fact that she had enjoyed easier access to mature roles may contribute significantly to her adjustment. Weatherly[39] found "absolutely no support for the proposition that the effect of rate of physical maturation on the adequacy of personality integration in girls is the reverse of that operating in boys." He pointed out that the discrepancies between early- and late-maturers are much less for girls than for boys: "for girls as opposed to boys rate of physical maturation is a much less influential variable mediating personality development." This is partly because of the high value society places on physical strength and athletic prowess, which may cause a late-maturing boy to encounter social disadvantages.[40]

PHYSICAL FITNESS, ATHLETIC PARTICIPATION, AND SEXISM IN SPORTS
Physical Fitness

Physical fitness means more than just good health or freedom from disease; it means having reserve physical energy, a greater capacity for work and exertion, a lower resting pulse rate, and a faster return to normal blood pressure and pulse rate after exercise. In other words, it is the ability to maintain internal equilibria as closely as possible to the resting state during strenuous exertion and to restore the equilibria promptly after exercise.[41] Physical fitness is a relative condition that ranges from good health to athletic stardom. To become physically fit requires activity that expends energy, and fitness is transitory, particularly with respect to endurance and cardiorespiratory efficiency. Tanner,[42] for example, has noted that muscles enlarged by heavy weight-lifting soon regress to their former size when the exercise is stopped. Physical fitness is a lifelong objective; although it is especially significant during adolescence; it cannot be attained at any age without sufficient sleep, good nutrition, and adequate exercise.[43]

In adolescence, there is a relationship between physical fitness and both body build and rate of growth. After making a comprehensive longitudinal investigation, Clark,[44] Clarke, Irving, and Heath,[45] and Clarke and Petersen[46] reported that boys who actively participated on athletic teams in both elementary and junior high school were superior to their peers in skeletal maturity, body size, muscular strength, endurance, and power. The size discrepancy between participants and nonparticipants was greater for youth in junior high school than at the elementary level. A larger percentage of the boys with muscular body builds was found among the athletes, who differed from the nonparticipants on such anthropomorphic measures as body weight, height, and lung capacity; at the junior high school level, they also differed on arm girth, chest girth, and calf girth. The athletes also excelled in arm-strength and cable-tension tests and were superior in the standing broad jump, pull-ups, and push-ups. Ruffer[47] studied boys in grades 7 to 12 and found that the athletes tended to be taller, performed motor tasks more effectively, and made better cardiovascular adaptation to moderate exercise. Carron and Bailey[48] also report, as one might expect, that early-maturers possess significantly greater strength than late-maturers. It appears that the superiority of the early-maturers may be attributable to their greater body weight. The researchers tested 99 boys annually on seven strength tests from 10 through 16 years of age. The data showed that variations in height were unrelated to strength whereas those in weight were relatively highly correlated with it. They also revealed considerable growth in strength from 10 to 16, and high stability of the relative standings among the boys from year to year.

The relationship between physical growth and strength, however, is more than simply one-to-one. Strength development in early-maturers tends to lag behind their growth in height and weight. Tanner[49] described how growth in muscle strength follows growth in muscle size and suggested that with maturation there is a qualitative change in muscular tissue. Large amounts of subcutaneous fat also may affect size-strength relationships. Malina and Johnston[50] found that relatively large boys from 6 to 12 years of age with a low muscle/fat ratio performed strength and motor tasks less efficiently per unit of body weight than smaller boys. Clarke et al.[51] show that, in comparison with tall and linear or muscular boys, relatively obese boys perform fewer pull-ups and push-ups and have lower arm-strength scores. Garrity[52] reports similar results using college girls as subjects. Rarick and Smoll[53] have shown, too, that the growth in strength of the arms and hands from childhood to adolescence for both boys and girls is more variable than motor performance. Rarick and Smoll studied 25 boys and 24 girls living in an upper-middle-class community each year from age 7 through 12 and again at age 17. The between-age correlations of height and weight were high and relatively stable over the 10-year period. The correlations among the aspects of muscular strength were substantially lower, especially from childhood to adolescence. Growth in strength in the arms and hands was shown to be highly unstable over a time span of more than two years. By contrast, motor performance measures showed more stability of growth in both sexes but substantially less stability than height or weight. Performance in the standing broad jump, for example, showed stability of growth for both sexes, running performance was stable for girls, but throwing performance, which utilizes arm strength, showed considerable between-age variability for both sexes from childhood to adolescence. The researchers suggest that because the weight-bearing muscles used in locomotion are exercised daily, their growth in strength tends to be correlated primarily with increases in body weight. However, the muscles of the upper extremities are not widely used, and so their growth in strength probably varies considerably from child to child as a function of work and exercise.

Athletic Participation

Athletic participation in general exerts a salutary effect on adolescent socialization. Ruffer[54] found that active junior and senior high school male athletes maintained better academic averages than nonactive youth. Schafer[55] compared boys who participated one full semester in any interscholastic sport during the last three years of high school with their academic performance during the second semester of the ninth grade. Forty percent of the boys who later completed a season of sports had been in the top half of their class. Also boys from 9 to 14 years of age with athletic skills enjoyed greater peer status and were judged by administrators and teachers as having desirable personality traits,[56] scored higher on measures of level of aspiration,[57] scored higher on measures of scholastic achievement, and attained higher grade point averages.[58] High school boys in contact sports (football and wrestling) also may acquire greater capacity to tolerate physical pain than either those in noncontact athletic activities (tennis and golf) or those who avoid such activities.[59]

The evidence, however, shows that the athlete does not have all of the personality advantages. Slusher[60] compared junior and senior lettermen in high school baseball, basketball, football, swimming, and wrestling with nonathletes, and found that athletes scored lower on measures of intelligence. The lettermen also had more unusual fears, worries, and difficulties in concentration. Most problems were found among basketball players, followed in order by football players, wrestlers, baseball players, and swimmers. Schendel[61] found that although ninth and twelfth grade male athletes had more positive personality characteristics than nonathletes, at the college level, the situation was reversed. The nonathletes had more of the qualities associated with status, were more conscientious and responsible, expressed greater tolerance, were more capable of independent achievement, had greater intellectual efficiency, were more concerned with the needs of others, and had more interest in heterosexual activities.

Athletics may be correlated positively with personality characteristics to the extent that it facilitates socialization. In a study of 585 high school students in moderate-size cities, Schafer[62] found that fewer athletes, particularly those from blue-collar homes and low achievers in school, were entered in the juvenile court records for delinquent behavior. Schafer suggested that athletics may inhibit delinquency for the following reasons: greater exposure to nondelinquent influences, stronger social controls, less pressure toward rebellion, less boredom, less need to assert masculinity through deviant behavior, and less chance of being labeled delinquent.

It appears that athletic participation provides a strong support network of social relationships. The junior high athlete belongs to a team, is observed and lauded, and adapts role behaviors in accordance with the expectations of parents and teachers. During this period, academic pressures are light, there are no significant vocational decisions to make, and the competition of high school and college are still in the future. Consequently, athletics supports interpersonal and academic growth. However, in high school, both athletics and academic pursuits become increasingly selective and incompatible. Both require an inordinate amount of time, and the adolescent's personality will be molded in part by the choices made. Moreover, athletics may introduce a "two-edged sword effect" in that it may serve as an avenue for raising aspirations without providing ways of learning the academic and social skills necessary for achieving them.[63]

How would sports contribute to the physical fitness of young people if all could participate? Swimming, baseball, basketball, bowling, and ice skating are among the most preferred sports, but, unfortunately, many young people do not participate in these activities, or, if they do, they are clumsy. Hunsicker[64] believes that systematic instruction should be given, starting with preadolescents of both sexes, in swimming, skiing, handball, gymnastics, tennis, badminton, soccer, softball, speedball, touch football, volleyball, wrestling, and track and field. The preadolescent, he feels, is highly receptive to such activities and is capable of mastering highly complex motor skills.

Prior to 1950 it was generally held that young people should not participate in strenuous athletics. But in the late 1950s, after several athletic programs had been assessed by qualified researchers, the earlier view began to change.[65] Orthopedic experts, however, are divided on the question of significance of bone injuries to young people. About 6 percent of the athletic injuries among 9- to 15-year-olds cause bone and cartilage separation, but the danger of such injuries apparently is not as great as had been supposed. The hazard is in the failure to recognize an injury and provide proper treatment.[66] Also, adolescents in the midst of the growth spurt may find that their bones are temporarily growing faster than their muscles and that they are not well suited for bruising, fatiguing activities that may cause injury. Moreover, certain dangers are possible because of the general anatomical immaturity of elementary school children. They may be injured by heavy weight-bearing and shearing stresses near their body joints, especially knees and arms.

To avoid possible athletic injuries, the school should offer sports that are appropriate for the psychological and physiological maturity level of the young person. Although the rules and the equipment may have to be altered to suit the age level, the excitement of participation can still be there. "The teacher should know that most children, by ten years of age, have the neuromuscular potential to master the skills required in practically any physical education course currently offered at the college level."[67] Hunsicker also points out that practice is indispensable in mastering motor skills. If skills are learned early in adolescence they can be practiced later. When adolescents master a motor skill, it becomes part of their neuromuscular structure and they retain it for nearly the rest of their lives, even though they lose their physical fitness. Rarick and Smoll[68] observed that boys or girls who perform well in selected motor activities in childhood, while perhaps relinquishing their superiority in adolescence, will still retain their competitive position. A child who is both strong and well versed in the basic skills of running and jumping will, as an adolescent, rank high among his or her peers in these skills. The child who has learned to swim will never be a nonswimmer.

Young people do not generally enjoy a broad-based sports program. All too often a broad intramural program that provides games, sports, and participation for all students becomes subverted into a competitive sports program for the few. Every school's physical education program should begin by teaching the funda-

A Road Ralley of Feet is a sports activity in which persons of all ages may participate. Following a course by map and compass, the runners pound the pavement to make the best possible time from one "control point" to the next.

mental skills of a sport. In team sports, each student should be regarded as having distinctive strengths and growth propensities. Young people should be able to discover themselves and develop confidence in their skills. And all children, no matter what their skill (or lack of it), should have the opportunity to participate if they desire. Unfortunately, however, many well-meaning but naive adult coaches of volunteer, neighborhood, or after-school intramural teams sift through their players for the "best," hoping to find a winning combination that will lead to a league championship and acclaim for their coaching skills. And elementary and junior high school teams are usually segregated into first and second strings and players and substitutes; the latter play only after the game has been assured for the coach. A good sports program, however, can provide youngsters with an exhilarating experience that will motivate them to participate in athletics and develop proficiency. But when there is excessive parental interest, adult direction, and pressure to win, the activity becomes a degrading experience for all, inculcating not team spirit but harsh competitiveness.

Sexism in Sports

Espenchade,[69] a pioneer in the study of motor skills, showed several years ago that sex differences in athletic performances are considerable during adolescence. Her performance curves revealed that skills rose sharply for boys throughout adolescence and into young adulthood, whereas the slopes for girls reached a plateau at about age 14. Figure 1 illustrates the differences she reported between the two sexes in six motor tasks requiring power, speed, agility, coordination, and balance.[70] The boys and girls at the outset of adolescence have approximately the same performance levels in all tasks except throwing. Boys swiftly improve all of their performances thereafter, but girls reveal no improvement on any of the tasks. The significance of the discrepancy between the two sexes on each of the performance curves presented in Figure 1 lies not in demonstrating that adolescent boys consistently show greater physical strength than girls but that girls' performance curves fail to show increases corresponding to those of boys. Are the differences between the two sexes in the skill performances a product of physical maturation or cultural factors? Malina[71] notes that current cross-sectional studies employing physical fitness tests involving skills similar to those identified in Figure 1 are starting to indicate slight but continual improvement in the performances of girls through age 17. His data suggest that cultural circumstances are the cause of the differences; certainly, cultural impediments have traditionally curtailed the participation of girls in high school athletic programs.

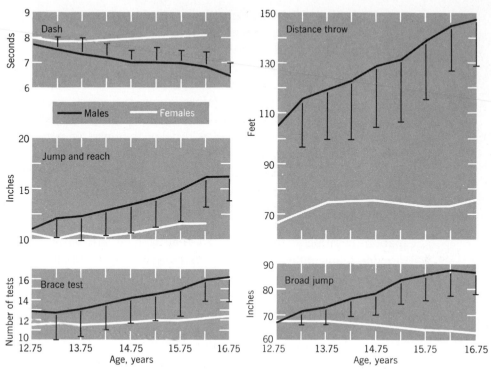

Figure 1

Motor performance (mean plus or minus one standard deviation) during adolescence. (Drawn from the data of Espenschade.) Adapted from Malina, see text. Reprinted by permission.)

Policies toward athletics in most American high schools and colleges have long been both sexist and hypocritical. They have proclaimed that athletics develops strong bodies and minds, fosters citizenship, and promotes a better society, but since its inception, participation has been largely restricted to boys. Funds, facilities, equipment, coaching, rewards, and honors allocated to boys have been uniformly superior to those granted to girls. Boys have enjoyed the best facilities available and have practiced in the gymnasium during the most convenient hours. They have taken long trips on which they have been driven by commercial carriers, enjoyed well-balanced dinners and excellent sleeping quarters, and have been provided laundered "at home" and "away" uniforms. Their varsity teams are usually supplied trainers and waterboys, and their exploits, both team and individual, are lauded in the local press. The girls, on the other hand, have often been assigned cast-off field space and the least favorable hours for gymnasium practice. Their teams usually have faced nearby opponents, and on the rare occasions when they have traveled, they have raised the funds themselves through "bake sales" and "car washes." Their coaches have served for less compensation than that paid the boys' coaches, and few of their teams have had trainers. The press has generally paid less attention to their athletic accomplishments than to those of the boys.[72]

The rationale for extensive sex discrimination in athletics is partly a product of several stereotypical assumptions about the effects of physical activity on women.[73] First, it is said that vigorous athletic participation will injure the female reproductive system and will delay the onset or regularity of menstruation. The available evidence indicates, on the other hand, that the uterus is one of the most shock-resistant of all internal organs. The external genitalia of females is less exposed than those of males and can easily be protected. And surveys conducted at Olympic games reveal that women have set world records at all stages of the menstrual cycle.[74] Second, antagonists toward womens' participation in athletics have asserted that women are more prone than men to accidents and injuries, but there is no evidence to support the claim that any sport is more harmful for girls than it is for boys. Nonetheless, dance, tennis, gymnastics, badminton, golf, and archery have been traditionally the only athletic activities open to high school girls. Organized extracurricular team sports involving struggle and endurance—baseball, basketball, field hockey, soccer, and lacrosse—are less likely today to be denied girls, but they are gender-segregated nearly everywhere that they are available to them. Proponents of women's rights contend, however, that a girl should be as free as a boy to subject her body to the stress and dangers of mixed-athletic competition. Lacerations, sprains, and broken bones are treated and healed in the same way for both sexes, and why, they say, should girls be any more "protected" from injury than boys? Third, the insinuation has circulated that girls who engage in athletic activities will develop bulging muscles, but even if this were true, the loss of fatty tissue during adolescence would camouflage muscle prominence.[75]

Sexist attitudes toward female athletic participation became one of the targets of the Civil Rights movement early in the 1970s. As a consequence of Title IX of the Education Amendments of 1972, and of Title IX guidelines of 1975, all educational programs receiving federal financial assistance are required today to maintain equal athletic opportunities and facilities for boys and girls. But major questions have arisen regarding the meaning of equality. It may be measured in terms of opportunity for participation in major and minor interscholastic and intramural sports, redistribution of sports revenues to women's athletic activities, and provision for equal access to scholarships and facilities. The resolution of such issues will take years, however, and real extinction of sexism in sports will occur only when the old-wives tales about the physical dangers of athletics to young women are laid to rest, when female athletes and coaches

Called out in a State softball tournament. Scenes like this were less common before the passage of Title IX regulations.

"make it" in the system, becoming models for new patterns of self-expression through physical activity for up-coming young aspirants, and when less attention is paid to anatomical and physiological differences and more to the significance to both sexes of the healthful, life-long benefits of developing physical prowess and skill during adolescence.

SUMMARY

Adolescents develop their body images through social interaction. They acquire a perception of their own physical development, an understanding of the way their peers evaluate physical attributes, and an awareness of standards held in society at large. Adolescents may find it difficult to accept deviations from ideal body configurations since society tends to overvalue beautiful bodies. Advertising, magazines, movies, television, and hero worship of athletics and glamour contribute to the glorification of the ideal body and the disparagement of the deviant. Whether adolescents enter the growth spurt relatively early or late may affect their body image. A muscular boy who matures early may excel in athletics and be given the privilges of an older youth; a late-maturing boy may be surpassed in athletics by younger boys and be treated as a child by others. An early-maturing girl may be confronted by threatening heterosexual relationships because she is socially immature, while a late-maturing girl presumably matures at the same time as boys her age. Thus, it has been believed that early-maturing boys and late-maturing girls enjoy certain advantages during socialization; however, recent evidence suggests that early-maturing girls have greater opportunity to participate in adult-like behavior. Hence, it seems that only late-maturing boys encounter social disadvantages as a consequence of their slower maturation.

Physical fitness is related to the socialization of adolescents in two major ways. First, there is a positive relationship between physical fitness and both body build and rate of growth. Second, there is generally a positive correlation between athletic participation and possession of desirable personality characteristics, perhaps because high school athletics often leads to positive social relationships. Cultural impediments, however, have traditionally curtailed the participation of girls in athletic programs. The rationale for extensive sex discrimination in athletics has been the product of several old-wives tales about the dangers of physical activities to young women. These sexist views are being dispelled as more is being learned about the significance of athletics during adolescence to the development of healthful skills and life-long interests in physical activity.

REVIEW QUESTIONS

1. What experiences foster development of body image?
2. Why is an attractive body image of more critical significance to adolescent girls than to boys?
3. What is the meaning of early- and late-maturation?
4. What are the advantages and disadvantages boys and girls, respectively, encounter in being early- or late-maturers?
5. Why is physical fitness especially significant during adolescence?
6. Which aspects of physical strength are relatively stable (highly correlated with each other) during adolescence?
7. What is the significance of physical fitness to adolescent socialization?
8. What advantages does athletic participation offer young people?
9. What are the optimal features of a broad-based sports program in a school serving adolescents?
10. What has been the rationale for sex discrimination in high school athletics?

DISCUSSION QUESTIONS

1. Given the fact that advertisements, movies, and television glorify the ideal body, what might one do to assist in the socialization of young people who fall short of the ideal?
2. Do you think it is true that sex differences in emphases on physical attractiveness are partly products of sexism?
3. Consider adolescents with whom you are familiar who are early- and late-maturers. Would you say that their personality traits correspond with those of the youth who are described in the Adolescent Growth Study?

4. What factors impede development of broad-based athletic programs in most neighborhoods and schools?

5. All educational programs that receive federal financial assistance are required today to maintain equal athletic opportunities and facilities for boys and girls. How are the federal laws being interpreted in the high schools with which you are acquainted? In what areas has equality clearly been established?

NOTES

1. R. M. Lerner. Some female stereotypes of male body build-behavior relations. *Perceptual and Motor Skills,* 1969, **28,** 363–366; R. M. Lerner. The development of stereotyped expectancies of body build-behavior relations. *Child Development,* 1969, **40,** 137–141.

2. Lerner, Female stereotypes, *op. cit.;* Lerner, Stereotyped expectancies, *op. cit.*

3. J. F. Cross, and J. Cross. Age, sex, race, and the perception of facial beauty. *Developmental Psychology,* 1971, **5,** 433–439.

4. R. M. Kurtz. Body image—male and female. *Trans-action,* 1968, 25–27.

5. N. Cavior and D. A. Lombardi. Developmental aspects of judgment of physical attractiveness in children. *Developmental Psychology,* 1973, **8,** 67–71.

6. P. S. de Q. Cabot. The relationship between characteristics of personality and physique in adolescents. *Genetic Psychology Monographs,* 1938, **20,** 3–120.

7. W. A. Schonfeld. Body-image in adolescents: a psychiatric concept for the pediatrician. *Pediatrics,* 1963, **31,** 845–855.

8. J. B. Cortes and F. M. Gatti. Physique and motivation. *Journal of Consulting Psychology,* 1966, **30,** 408–414.

9. D. M. Broverman, I. K. Broverman, W. Vogel, R. D., Palmer, and E. L. Klaiber, The automatization cognitive style and physical development. *Child Development,* 1964, **35,** 1343–1359.

10. E. K. E. Gunderson, Body size, self-evaluation, and military effectiveness. *Journal of Personality and Social Psychology,* 1965, **2,** 902–906.

11. U.S. Public Health Service. *Vital and health statistics,* Series 11, No. 147. Self-reported health behavior and attitudes of youth 12–17 years. Rockville, Md. National Center for Health Statistics, April 1975, p. 5.

12. F. N. Arnhoff and E. N. Damianopoulos. Self-body recognition: an empirical approach to the body image. *Merrill-Palmer Quarterly,* 1962, **8,** 143–148.

13. C. D. Ward. Own height, sex, and liking in the judgment of the heights of others. *Journal of Personality,* 1967, **35,** 381–401.

14. Cross and Cross, *op. cit.*

15. R. M. Kurtz. Sex differences and variations in body attitudes. *Journal of Consulting and Clinical Psychology,* 1969, **33,** 625–629.

16. Ibid.

17. Tanner, Physical growth, *op. cit.*

18. D. H. Eichorn. Biological correlates of behavior. In H. W. Stevenson (Ed.) *Child Psychology—sixty-second yearbook of the National Society for the Study of Education.* Chicago: University of Chicago Press, 1963, 4–61.

19. A. C. Kinsey, W. B. Pomeroy, and C. E. Martin. *Sexual behavior in the human male.* Philadelphia: Saunders, 1948.

20. Eichorn, *op. cit.;* M. C. Jones. The later careers of boys who were early- or late-maturing. *Child Development,* 1957, **28,** 113–128; M. C. Jones. A study of socialization patterns at the high-school level. *Journal of Genetic Psychology,* 1958, **93,** 87–111; M. C. Jones. Psychological correlates of somatic development. *Newsletter,* Division Seven, American Psychological Association, Fall 1964; M. C. Jones, Psychological correlates of somatic development. *Child Development,* 1965, **36,** 899–911; M. C. Jones, and N. Bayley. Physical maturing among boys as related to behavior. *Journal of Educational Psychology,* 1950, **41,** 129–148; M. C. Jones and P. H. Mussen. Self-conceptions, motivations, and interpersonal attitudes of early- and late-maturing girls. *Child Development,* 1958, **29,** 492–500; P. H. Mussen and M. C. Jones. Self-conceptions, motivations, and interpersonal attitudes of late- and early-maturing boys. *Child Development,* 1957, **28,** 243–256; P. H. Mussen and M. C. Jones. The behavior-inferred motivations of late- and early-maturing boys. *Child Development,* 1958, **29,** 61–67.

21. Eichorn, *op. cit.*

22. Jones and Bayley, *op. cit.*

23. Jones and Mussen, *op. cit.*

24. Jones and Bayley, *op. cit.*

25. Jones and Bayley, *op. cit.*

26. Jones and Bayley, *op. cit.;* Jones, Socialization patterns, *op. cit.*

27. Mussen and Jones, Behavior-inferred motivations, *op. cit.*

28. Ibid.

29. Eichorn, *op. cit.*

30. Jones, Somatic development, *op. cit.*

31. D. Weatherly. Self-perceived rate of physical maturation and personality in late adolescence. *Child Development,* 1964, **35,** 1197–1210.

32. Eichorn, *op. cit.*

33. Jones and Bayley, *op. cit.*

34. Mussen and Jones, Behavior-inferred motivations, *op. cit.*

35. Jones, Later careers, *op. cit.;* Jones, Psychological correlates (1964), *op. cit.;* Jones, Psychological correlates (1965), *op. cit.*

36. Jones, Psychological correlates (1964), *op. cit.*

37. Jones and Mussen, *op. cit.*

38. Mussen and Jones, Behavior-inferred motivations, *op. cit.*

39. Weatherly, *op. cit.,* p. 1209.

40. Jones and Mussen, *op. cit.;* M. Frisk, T. Tenhunen, O. Widholm, and H. Hortling.

Psychological problems in adolescents showing advanced or delayed physical maturation. *Adolescence,* 1966, **1,** 126–140; Weatherly, *op. cit.*

41. P. Hunsicker. *Physical Fitness: What Research Says to the Teacher.* No. 26. Washington, D.C.: National Education Association, 1963.

42. Tanner, *op. cit.*

43. Hunsicker, *op. cit.*

44. H. H. Clarke. Characteristics of the young athlete: A longitudinal look. *Kinesiology Review,* Washington, D.C.: AAHPER, 1968.

45. H. H., Clarke, R. N., Irving, and B. H. Heath. Relation of maturity, structural, and strength measures to the somatotypes of boys 9 through 15 years of age. *Research Quarterly,* 1961, **32,** 449–460.

46. H. H. Clarke and K. H. Petersen. Contrast of maturational, structural, and strength characteristics of athletes and nonathletes 10 to 15 years of age. *Research Quarterly,* 1961, **32,** 163–176.

47. W. A. Ruffer. A study of extreme physical activity groups of young men. *Research Quarterly,* 1965, **36,** 183–196.

48. A. V. Carron and D. A. Bailey. Strength development in boys from 10 through 16 years. *Monographs of the Society for Research in Child Development,* 1974, **39** (4, Serial No. 157).

49. Tanner, Growth at adolescence, *op. cit.*

50. R. M. Malina and F. E. Johnston. Significance of age, sex, and maturity differences in upper arm composition. *Research Quarterly,* 1967, **38,** 219–230.

51. Clarke et al., Somatotypes *op. cit.*

52. H. M. Garrity. Relationship of somatotypes of college women to physical fitness performance. *Research Quarterly,* 1966, **37,** 340–352.

53. G. L. Rarick and F. L. Smoll. Stability of growth in strength and motor performance from childhood to adolescence. *Human Biology,* 1967, **39,** 296–306.

54. Ruffer, *op. cit.*

55. W. E. Schafer. Participation in interscholastic athletics and delinquency: a preliminary study. *Social Problems,* 1969, **17,** 40–47.

56. H. H. Clarke and D. H. Clarke. Social status and mental health of boys as related to their maturity, structural, and strength characteristics. *Research Quarterly,* 1961, **32,** 326–334.

57. H. H. Clarke and D. H. Clarke. Relationship between level of aspiration and selected physical factors of boys aged nine years. *Research Quarterly,* 1961, **32,** 12–19.

58. H. H. Clarke and B. O. Jarman. Scholastic achievement of boys 9, 12, and 15 years of age as related to various strength and growth measures. *Research Quarterly,* 1961, **32,** 155–162.

59. E. D. Ryan and R. Foster. Athletic participation and perceptual augmentation and reduction. *Journal of Personality and Social Psychology,* 1967, **6,** 472–476.

60. H. S. Slusher. Personality and intelligence characteristics of selected high school athletes and nonathletes. *Research Quarterly,* 1964, **35,** 539–545.

61. J. Schendel. Psychological differences between athletes and nonparticipants in athletics at three educational levels. *Research Quarterly,* 1965, **36,** 52–67.

62. Schafer, *op. cit.*

63. E. E. Snyder and E. Spreitzer. Sociology of sport, an overview. *The Sociological Quarterly,* 1974, **15,** 467–487.

64. Hunsicker, *op. cit.*

65. J. W. Dellastatious, and W. Cooper. The physiological aspects of competitive sports. *South Carolina Journal of Health, Physical Education, and Recreation,* 1969, **1,** 8–10.

66. Dellastatious and Cooper, *op. cit.*

67. Hunsicker, *op. cit.*, p. 25.

68. Rarick and Smoll, *op. cit.*

69. A. S. Espenschade. Motor performance in adolescence. *Monographs of the Society for Research and Child Development,* 1940, (**5,** Serial No. 24).

70. R. M. Malina. Adolescent changes in size, build, composition and performance. *Human Biology,* 1974, **46,** 117–131.

71. Ibid.

72. C. Ulrich. She can play as good as any boy. *Phi Delta Kappan,* 1973, **55,** 113–117.

73. B. Gilbert and N. Williamson. Sport is unfair to women. *Sports Illustrated,* 1973, **38,** No. 21, 88–98; No. 22, 45–54.

74. Ibid.

75. Ibid.

Chapter 4

Hazards to Adolescent Physical Well-Being—Automobile Accidents, Venereal Diseases, Suicide, Alcoholic Beverages, and Cigarettes

CHAPTER HIGHLIGHTS

AUTOMOBILE ACCIDENTS
VENEREAL DISEASES
SUICIDE
ALCOHOLIC BEVERAGES
   THE PHYSICAL AND PSYCHOLOGICAL
      CONSEQUENCES OF DRINKING
   ALCOHOL EDUCATION

CIGARETTES
   THE PHYSICAL AND PSYCHOLOGICAL
      CONSEQUENCES OF SMOKING
   ADOLESCENT CIGARETTE SMOKING
     PATTERNS
SUMMARY
REVIEW QUESTIONS
DISCUSSION QUESTIONS

ISSUES

Driver-education courses might stress development of emotional control as well as skill coordination.

Venereal diseases have become a critical national health problem because the infections have become more resistant to treatment, sexual activity among young people has increased, and mechanical birth control devices are being ignored.

More boys than girls are victims of suicide, but more girls attempt suicide.

Absence of meaningful relationships with significant persons characterizes the life style of suicide-prone adolescents.

An unprecedented boom in adolescent drinking, especially beer, has occurred during the past decade.

Adolescent drinking habits develop in the context of socialization.

Adolescent drinking usually starts at home and shifts later to the company of peers.

Young people generally perceive alcohol as a social beverage.

Educational programs regarding alcohol usage today stress development of responsible attitudes toward drinking.

Cigarette smoking may result in several different physical ailments during adolescence.

Cigarette smoking is correlated in adolescence with several personality characteristics.

Fifteen percent of the adolescent population, 12 through 17 years of age, regards itself as regular smokers; the percentage of boys who smoke exceeds that of girls at every age.

Adolescent smoking appears to stem more from efforts to conform than to be rebellious.

Peer pressure to smoke often is intense in the later years of high school.

Antismoking campaigns appear to be most effective among youth when they are realistic and when youth themselves conduct them.

Adolescents in general know very little about the serious hazards to their physical well-being. Young people are only dimly aware, for example, of the dangers inherent in automobile accidents, venereal diseases, suicide, alcohol, cigarettes, and drugs. For too long adults have expected adolescents to learn about these dangers mainly by talking with their friends and by exploration. This chapter, therefore, is divided into five major parts in order to review issues associated with each of these dangers (except drugs) separately. Drug usage, and its implications for adolescent socialization, is covered in detail in Chapter 5.

AUTOMOBILE ACCIDENTS

Among young people between 15 and 24 years of age, accidents are the leading cause of death (boys outnumbering girls by about five to one). Motor vehicle mishaps exceed, in the youthful population, all other causes of accidental death combined, including drownings, firearms, fires, explosives, and falls.[1] In many states, young people may begin driving on public roads and highways at age 16. In other states youth may begin driving much earlier on private roads and farms, especially with snowmobiles, go-carts, dune buggies, and motor-driven cycles. Whether young people can find a way to drive before they are legally sanctioned, few parents escape pressure to find ways in which they might. Any motor-driven vehicle means an extension of mobility to adolescents. Their options are multiplied because they can go to more places and get where they want to go more rapidly. The automobile facilitates peer contact and opens new possibilities for heterosexual relationships.

The National Safety Council has provided statistics showing that drivers under 25 years of age hold only 21 percent of the drivers' licenses in the United States but are involved in 35 percent of all traffic accidents.[2] One may not assume, however, that because drivers under 25 hold 21 percent of the drivers' licenses, that they also represent 21 percent of the driving activity in America.[3] Perhaps young people drive more frequently than older persons and thus expose themselves to greater risk of collision? Zylman,[4] in a study of collision rates as a function of age, controlled for exposure to traffic accidents by randomly selecting and interviewing drivers who were using roads at the time and places when collisions often occurred. His study compared the age characteristics of drivers who had managed to escape accidents with the characteristics of drivers who had been involved in collisions. Zylman's results indicated that drivers under 20 years of age did indeed appear in accidents 22 percent more often than would be expected relative to their exposure to accidents. Moreover, drivers between 20 and 24 years of age appeared in collisions nearly 13 percent more often; however, drivers 75 years of age and older possessed collision rates relative to exposure about equal to the 20 to 24 year olds and higher than the 15- to 19-year-old group. Thus, it appears that it would be unwarranted to assume that young drivers constitute the most dangerous age group of drivers even though they are involved in accidents disproportionate to their numbers.

What are the characteristics of the young people who are involved in relatively more automobile collisions? In an analysis of 288 unmarried male drivers between 16 and 24 years of age, Schuman et al.[5] found that the younger drivers (under age 21) had more accidents, but they were less serious; the older drivers had fewer accidents, but they were more serious. Those between 16 and 18 were more likely to engage in such "dare-devil" practices as racing and accepting dares to accelerate rapidly. Twice as many in the 16 to 18 bracket as in the 23 to 24 age range reported that they had recently taken chances in their cars with one or more friends. The 16 to 20 year old was also more likely to drive to "blow off steam" after an argument with his family or friends, financial problems, and so forth. Overall, the study suggested that youth from 16 to 21 tended to be highly impulsive in their driving. With increased age, there was less impulsive expression through use of the automobile, less anxiety about driving, and less preoccupation with possible injury and death to the driver, passengers, or other drivers. Schuman et al. found that drivers with high accident rates were more likely to own their own car, be employed (rather than in school), and be school dropouts. Asher and Dodson[6] also report that sloppy attention to class assignments and inattention in school increases the probability of automobile accidents. Drivers with high accident rates did not, however, receive more traffic-violation tickets than less accident-prone youth. Further, Schuman et al.[7] report that alcohol was a factor in only about 5 percent of the first accidents and 12 percent of all subsequent accidents. Zylman[8] notes that driving-after-drinking is rare under age 18, increases rapidly among 18 and 19 year olds, and reaches adult proportions in the 20 to 25 age group. Although Zylman asserts that driving-after-drinking by young people is less widespread than generally believed, he points out, nonetheless, that adolescents are more susceptible to the influence of concentrations of alcohol in their blood than are adults. On the average, an adolescent's driving becomes impaired after consumption of four 12-ounce cans of beer within a two-hour period. Drivers under 18 years of age who possess poor collision records, therefore, may greatly increase their vulnerability to traffic accidents after only a little drinking.[9]

What can be done about the juvenile traffic violator and accident-prone adolescent? Shapiro and Asher[10] report that adolescent drivers have a disproportionate number of single-car accidents. As a consequence of excessive speed, they tend to run off the road, overturn, and collide with fixed objects. The researchers believe that the skilled coordination essential to successful vehicle operation is easily learned in driver-education courses and, therefore, that safe driving is less a matter of learning skills than acquiring control of strong emotions such as anger, elation, and depression, which may incite reckless or high-speed driving. They argue that young people should be taught "*not* to drive when under the influence of strong emotions." Mecham[11] sees the question of safe driving similarly and stresses that it is important to use constructive, insightful, rehabilitative education with adolescents involved in accidents and that, above all, the young victims should not be treated as if they committed a crime. He studied 50 boys and 15 girls who had been referred to a Utah juvenile court for traffic violations, and who had been randomly assigned (1) to be fined, (2) to be restrained from driving, (3) to attend traffic schools, and (4) to write a paper on traffic safety. The court file for each adolescent was examined after one full year to determine whether the violator had committed any subsequent infractions. Mecham found that both boys and girls who had been ordered to write a paper on traffic safety, and thus to justify and analyze their actions and emotions, committed fewer violations during the year than those who had been fined, restrained from driving, or required to attend traffic school. Only 16 percent of the boys who wrote papers on safety committed another violation during that year, whereas 52 percent who paid fines did so. Those assigned to write papers also drove for a longer period before committing another violation. The boys who wrote papers averaged 22 weeks between their initial court appearances and the time they committed their next violation; the comparable period for fined boys was two weeks. For girls, the difference was 23 weeks and three weeks respectively. Next to fines, the traffic school seemed to be least effective in reducing recidivism. But restraints on driving proved to be fairly effective; only 36 percent of the boys and 20 percent of the girls who were restrained committed additional violations during the year. Yet these figures may be deceptive in that restraint keeps the adolescent out of a car, thus precluding opportunity to commit a traffic violation. Mecham[12] also points out that the indiscriminate use of restraint may deprive adolescents of their livelihood if they have to use a car to get to a job. When driving privileges are taken away without adequate justification, the youth may be more severely punished than if they were required to pay a heavy fine. They may become resentful, decide to drive in spite of the court order, and attempt to avoid arrest for an otherwise insignificant violation; this can lead to a reckless chase and eventual disaster.

VENEREAL DISEASES

Venereal diseases have always cursed mankind, except for perhaps two brief decades—1940–1960. When penicillin was found to be effective in combating venereal diseases in the mid-1940s, reported cases began to drop steadily, until in 1957, there were only 3.8 cases reported for every 100,000 persons in the United States. The dramatic arrest was hailed as one of the great triumphs of science, but it was short-lived. The frequency of reported cases of gonorrhea and syphilis, the two major venereal infections, which seemed to be fairly well controlled in the 1950s, has risen at a steep rate ever since. Today we are in the midst of a critical national public health and educational problem, especially in respect to the youthful population, since venereal diseases are most likely to be contracted by 20 to 24 year olds, and almost as likely to occur in 15 to 19 year olds. The incidence of reported cases presently exceeds more than 600,000 each year or, roughly, 300 per 100,000 members of the population. Since it is estimated that from three to four infections occur for every reported incident, it is probable that as many as two and a half million cases appear each year in the United States.[13]

Gonorrhea, the most common of the venereal diseases has been known for thousands of years. A description of a man with "an issue" as "unclean" in the Old Testament book of Leviticus is believed to refer to gonorrhea.[14] This infection affects primarily the genito-urinary organs; the parasite (neisseria gonococcus) is exceedingly delicate, very susceptible to variations in temperature, and dies swiftly when deprived of body warmth. The requirements for the parasite's survival means that the disease is virtually always transmitted by sexual contact and hardly ever by water, food, air, or contact with toilet seats, door handles, drinking fountains, or eating utensils. Gonorrhea is much more difficult to detect in the female than the male. A female who contracts the disease usually has an incubation period from 2 to 5 days; however, she may not initially experience any uncomfortable symptoms or even know that she has gonorrhea until advised of it by a male whom she has infected. Without treatment, a female will eventually experience signs of discomfort during urination; later there will be a discharge followed by menstrual disturbances and abdominal discomfort. A male also undergoes an incubation period of about 2 to five days, but (unlike the female) he probably will experience immediate symptoms. There is a burning sensation during urination, followed shortly thereafter by a continuous flow of yellow pus. Delay in treatment will result in extreme discomfort. However, in the case of rectal gonorrhea (which can happen to a passive male homosexual), the symptoms will appear as slowly as in a female.[15] Moreover, in perhaps as many as 10 to 15 percent of the males who contact the disease via their penises, the symptoms may be as difficult to detect as in females.[16]

Syphilis, less common, but more deadly than gonorrhea, has been said to have existed in very early Paleolithic times, possibly in Africa or the Near East, and to have reached the New World only after Columbus and his sailors transmitted it to the natives of the West Indies or (2) to have been endemic to the New World and to have spread in Europe after Columbus' expedition returned from Haiti. Records of the disease are too poor to affirm or refute either of these beliefs; however, recent archeological excavations suggest that the disease has existed in both hemispheres of the world since prehistoric times.[17]

The syphilis parasite cannot survive in a dry environment or at a temperature higher than that of the human body; therefore, it flourishes in such areas as the mouth, genitals, and anus. Syphilitic sores in these areas are especially infectious. Syphilis appears in three or four stages that are similar in both men and women. First, there is a painless ulceration or sore that is most likely to appear on a sex organ because the contact is usually sexual. This lesion may develop between 10 and 90 days after the infectious contact; in the case of a female or passive male homosexual, the infection may be internal and remain undetected. The initial chancre will disappear, but then the second stage will emerge one to six months later; there may be (in varying combinations) spotty but temporary baldness, headaches, fever, sore throat, small flat sores in the moist areas of the body, a loss of weight, and aches in the bones and joints.[18] Syphilis is most contagious during this second stage, and it may be contracted through kissing and hand contact. Without treatment, this second stage may come and go in varying intensity for four or five years until eventually it seems to disappear. When host and parasite reach an equilibrium,[19] there is a latent stage during which the disease is dormant, perhaps for many years. When it appears in its last stage, syphilis may cause intellectual impairment, blindness, skin and bone problems, cardiovascular disturbances, nervous disorders, and death.

Venereal diseases are communicated from one person to another through physical contact, and are spread through homosexual as well as heterosexual relations. Increased sexual activity among young people provides an obvious positive correlation with the rise in cases of venereal diseases, but a major secondary factor is the changes that have occurred in young people's attitudes toward contraception, especially toward mechanical devices that actually prevent physical contact between genitalia. Mechanical devices such as the condom have fallen into disrepute because it is believed that interference with the "natural-ness" of the act will deplete some of its pleasure. Unfortunately, reduction in the use of mechanical devices, and perhaps greater reliance on other birth control methods like the "pill" or intrauterine devices, is perhaps the most significant of the factors associated with the current epidemic in venereal diseases.[20]

The traditional method used to control venereal diseases in the United States is that of seeking out and treating each sexual contact of newly reported cases. Private physicians see about three-fourths of all venereal disease patients, and to avoid any possibility of compromising confidentiality, many of the cases, especially those incurred in the higher social strata, are never reported. Consequently, the sexual contacts of these patients are free to continue transmitting the infection. Even when a report is filed, the chain of sexual promiscuousness with which the patient is linked may be impossible to trace. Pfrender[21] argues that the best alternative to the reporting system is a massive educational campaign through newspapers, radio, and television, to advertise the prevalence, signs and symptoms, and need for immediate treatment of venereal diseases. He asserts that emphasis must be placed on "the unsymptomatic infection and the need for examination following any casual sexual experience." He would accompany advertising campaigns with school programs starting in the seventh grade and wherever adolescents and adults congregate—adult education classes, family planning groups, pregnancy classes, Sunday school, women's Lib and Gay Liberation meetings, and street clinics.

SUICIDE

Suicide-prone behavior among adolescents is today a serious health problem. Suicide follows automobile accidents and homicides as the third leading cause of death among young people. Table 1 reveals that since 1945–1949 rates of suicide for youth, by ethnicity and sex, have about doubled. The increase in rates of adolescent suicide are not accompanied, for the most part, by corresponding increases in adult age groups. Moreover, the attempted suicide rates probably exceed those of completed suicides by eight or ten to one,[22] and the psychic toll extracted from both the adolescents and their parents is incalculable. Table 1 also indicates that more boys than girls are victims of suicide. On the other hand, it has been estimated that by a rate of about three to one, more adolescent girls than boys attempt suicide. The majority of boys use firearms or explosives, hanging or strangulation, and poisons as suicide methods whereas girls seldom consider hanging or strangulation and resort less to firearms and explosives than to poisons. Perhaps more boys die by suicide because their methods are more

Table 1
Death Rates for Suicide in the United States per 100,000 in Given Birth Groups

Period	White, male 15–19	White, male 20–24	All other, male 15–19	All other, male 20–24	White, female 15–19	White, female 20–24	All other, female 15–19	All other, female 20–24
1965–69	9.0	17.0	5.8	15.4	2.6	5.0	3.2	5.2
1960–64	6.6	12.8	4.0	13.5	1.7	4.5	1.8	2.3
1955–59	5.4	11.0	3.4	10.6	1.6	2.8	1.7	2.9
1950–54	3.8	10.3	1.7	10.1	1.2	2.4	1.8	1.3
1945–49	3.8	9.9	2.4	7.0	1.5	3.7	.9	2.4

Source: National Center for Health Statistics, Adapted from Table S, Series P-20, No. 16, DHEW Pub. No. (HRA) 74-1853. Mortality trends for leading causes of death: March 1974. Reprinted by permission.

violent and lethal. The number of completed suicides among girls might surpass the number among boys except for the fact that girls' choice of ingestion ensures them reasonable likelihood of survival.

The suicidal victim's life style is a product of a long history of unsatisfying interpersonal experiences, feelings of social rejection, and loss of significant social relationships. Mental illness has been shown to be associated with about half the instances of adult suicidal behavior; alcoholism in about 30 percent, homicide (murder immediately preceding suicide) in nearly 9 percent, and economic failure—unemployment and financial collapse—in approximately 20 percent.[23] Although adolescent suicides often ensue in psychiatric or general hospitals, studies of noninstitutionalized young people who look to suicide as a resolution to their stresses show that only a small proportion had ever received psychiatric treatment. Moreover, alcohol, homicide, and economic failure are relatively insignificant factors in adolescent suicidal behavior.[24] In contrast, the major characteristic of suicide-prone adolescents' life styles is absence of meaningful identification with significant persons. Adolescent suicide attempters, for example, frequently assert that they fail to feel close to any adult and that they are unable to remember when they ever felt warmth toward an adult.[25] Jacobs[26] holds that adolescent suicidal behavior acquires its antecedents in childhood problems and pathology. He organized his viewpoint in terms of five complementary hypotheses, each of which helps to account for the progressive social isolation that epitomizes adolescent suicidal behavior: (1) a long-standing history of problems from early childhood; (2) an escalation or intensification of problems above and beyond those that typically occur during adolescence; (3) a

Adolescent suicide behavior may be precipitated when social relationships break down.

progressive failure of available adaptive techniques for coping with difficult experiences; (4) a chain reaction dissolving any remaining meaningful social relationships in the days and weeks preceding the suicidal attempt, leading the adolescent to believe that "the end of hope" has been reached; and (5) an internal process of rationalization that enables the adolescent to justify suicidal behavior and thus to bridge the gap between thought and action. The stresses indicated by the hypotheses probably converge, and then, culminate in "a complete breakdown of meaningful social relationships."[27]

One might hope that studies of suicidal behavior among adolescents would yield signs indicative of impending suicide attempts, but all the careful psychological autopsies of victims (based on data obtained from death certificates, court records, diaries, suicide notes, and reminiscences of relatives and peers) and the analyses of life-histories of attempters, have failed to provide useful diagnostic data.[28] Researchers are aware, however, that the school and family constitute the two major sources of tension that lead to suicide-prone behavior. Academic and social failures at high school, for example, exact several adolescent suicides each year. Consider the following event that preceded recent graduation exercises in an Arizona high school:

Rowele . . . picked up her 18-year-old daughter, Joyce Ann, from . . . high school early Tuesday afternoon. While in the car, Joyce Ann told her mother she was not going to graduate with her classmates May 29 because she had written an economics class final paper in longhand rather than typing it. Her mother could sense the student's depression.

When they arrived home, Rowele . . . went to the bathroom while her daughter walked to her parents' bedroom. While washing her hands, the woman heard a loud noise—a shot. She rushed to the bedroom.

Joyce Ann had taken a .22 caliber Ruger revolver, pointed it at her nose, and killed herself. . . .

The girl was declared dead at Scottsdale Memorial Hospital within 45 minutes after she had told her mother about the economics paper, a paper which would not have affected her grades. The police investigator said this morning that he talked to the economics instructor and learned that it was not mandatory that the final paper be typed, that longhand was fine, and the victim would have graduated. (Scottsdale Daily Progress, May 21, 1975)

Peck[29] believes that close examination of school-related suicides usually reveals that the precipitating pressures are derived more from a young person's efforts to satisfy parental expectations than to meet classroom requirements. Peck also points out that the boys in these instances are often involved with successful, demanding fathers who relentlessly stress school success and masculinity. A father may fail to appreciate his son's efforts to achieve masculinity, and his expectations may have the effect of pushing the boy toward suicide to escape them. The father who advised his 19-year-old son: "If you can't cut it in this world, you might as well take a gun to your head," was in fact encouraging his son to follow his suggestion, and perhaps was the only one who was surprised when the boy borrowed his gun and followed the advice.[30]

Growing up in a hostile and disorganized family environment, where economic and emotional deprivation, neglect, rejection, and parental marital conflicts are the rule, also contributes to suicide proneness.[31] Such an environment deprives adolescents of significant models, fosters feelings of hopelessness and depression, impedes development of future perspective, and, importantly, restricts meaningful development of social relationships. The despair emanating from family disorganization may be heightened by role reversal in one-parent families. Kreider and Motto[32] point out that when a parent expects an adolescent to fulfill the role of the other parent, the adolescent is deprived of nurturance, restricted in age-appropriate behaviors, and forced to carry unwarranted responsibilities. The expectations may be so great that the parental role cannot be filled adequately, and to escape the intolerable burdens, the adolescent may resort to a suicidal act.

The loss of a loved one, perhaps through death, separation, or a broken romance, may constitute an important component of adolescent suicidal behavior. An adolescent's suicide attempt, for example, sometimes follows a breakup with a girlfriend or boyfriend.[33] Romantic dissolutions in the lives of suicide-prone adolescents, who have been deprived of meaningful relationships in their families, may represent severe, irreplaceable losses of dependency gratification. Jacobs and Teicher[34] insist, however, that it is not the loss of a loved one per se that predisposes the suicidal act, but the loss of love itself; that is, the absence of the reciprocal intimacy, spontaneity, and closeness that one experiences in a romantic or loving relationship.

Adolescent suicidal behavior thus appears to stem from a series of debilitating real-life experiences. Since adverse experiences are common to everyone, there is little to distinguish the suicide-prone adolescent from others who are encountering "normal" difficulties in school and at home. Unless an adolescent explicitly threatens to commit suicide, the individual's intentions are likely to escape notice. However, if the seeds of adolescent suicidal behavior do indeed grow when social relationships are impoverished, one might presume that school personnel could effectively neutralize them by assisting adolescents in their search for meaningful relationships, perhaps by helping them build a network of planned extracurricular activities, intramural sports, and peer relationships.

ALCOHOLIC BEVERAGES

The "drug" that adolescents are most likely to abuse during the late 1970s is alcohol. Hard drug use reached epic proportions among youth as the decade began, and heightened apprehension led parents and school authorities to hope wistfully that young people would turn to beer rather than pot. The majority of adults drink themselves and see drinking among their children as a safe alternative to the much advertised evils of hard drugs and marijuana. Thus in contrast to the 1950s and early 1960s, when the adult society tended to view adolescent drinking as morally reprehensible, believing that youth should not drink at all, many adults today tolerate and even sanction drinking among young people. The permissive atmosphere has promoted an unprecedented boom in adolescent drinking. Hardly 10 percent of the young people presently entering adolescence will pass through this period of life in abstenance from alcoholic beverages. The highest proportion of heavy drinkers among men exists in the 18 to 20 age group, and among women, in the 21 to 24 age group.[35] It is estimated that there are today approximately one-half million young people who have serious problems involving alcohol.[36] Indeed, the American Medical Association has declared that one out of 15 youth in the United States may become an alcoholic in the near future unless radical changes occur in patterns of current alcoholic usage.[37]

Figure 1 provides a comprehensive overview of the status of adolescent

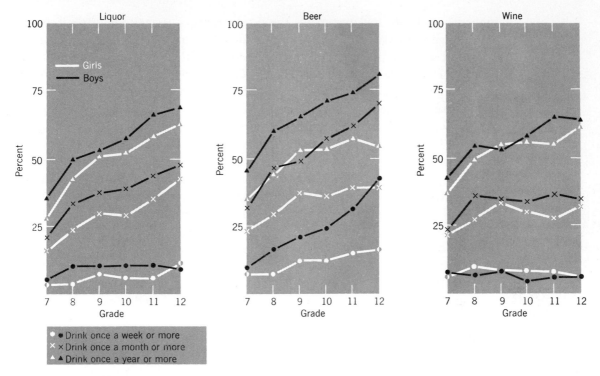

Figure 1
Percent of drinkers among teenagers by sex, grade, frequency of drinking and type of beverage, 1974. (From U.S. Public Health Service. *Alcohol and Health.* Rockville, Md. National Institute on Alcohol Abuse and Alcoholism, 1974. Reprinted with permission.)

drinkers by frequency of drinking, school grade, sex, and beverage. The data are derived from a special report to Congress by the National Institute on Alcohol Abuse and Alcoholism.[38] Figure 1 indicates that the quantity of alcohol consumed by both boys and girls increases with school age for all beverage types. The weekly beer consumption of boys shows the most dramatic age change, rising from 10 percent in the seventh grade to 43 percent among twelfth graders. As may be seen in Figure 1, beer is clearly the most preferred beverage of adolescents, especially among boys. Sixty percent of the twelfth-grade boys and 35 percent of the twelfth-grade girls drink beer once a month or more. Figure 1 also shows that frequency of drinking liquor and wine, respectively, is relatively comparable for both sexes. Note that about 70 percent of the twelfth-grade boys and girls are shown to drink these beverages about once a year or more whereas about 10 percent drink them once a week or more. The sale of sweet pop wines, primarily to youth, has risen from three million bottles in 1968 to over 33 million today;[39] thus the extent of wine consumption shown in

Figure 1 probably underestimates the actual rates of usage. The magnitude of the difference between the proportions of youth who report drinking wine once a week and once a year may be narrowing rather swiftly.

Adolescents are motivated to begin drinking largely according to their parents' interest in drinking.[40] Parents often permit drinking at home and in their presence. Indeed, most adolescents begin drinking at home under parental supervision. The initial drink usually occurs on a holiday or special occasion. Maddox[41] has observed that adolescents who drink usually report that at least one parent also drinks. The probability that adolescents will drink is increased if both of their parents drink. Their chances of drinking are less if the parents abstain. Riester and Zuker point out that by their senior year in high school nearly all adolescents whose parents drink have begun to drink themselves. Maddox also said that adolescents who feel that their parents approve are most likely to do their own drinking at home. But if the parents differ on the matter of drinking, adolescents have difficulty developing a well-integrated attitude toward alcohol.[42] Parents who drink moderately tend to communicate moderation to adolescents about when and how to drink, and those who drink excessively tend to foster unrestraint in their children.[43]

The contexts in which adolescents consume alcoholic beverages varies with age. Figure 2 highlights school grade differences in four settings: special occasions at home, at teenage parties with no adults present, family dinners at home, and driving or sitting in a car at night. The data reveal that most adolescent drinking occurs at home on special occasions until the tenth grade. As adolescents grow older drinking takes place more in the company of peers than under adult supervision at home. The family dinner scores as the least likely occasion on which adolescents participate in drinking after grade nine. Their preference for drinking is at teenage parties. Seventy-five percent of twelfth-grade adolescents who drink indicate that they prefer to drink when no adults are present. Most of their drinking occurs in homes when parents are out for an evening or away for a weekend. Drinking parties in the woods or open fields—known as "grassers" or "boomers" are also highly popular sites, as are cars, trucks, vans, local vacant estates, unoccupied new homes, barns, school parking lots, vacant lots, and gravel pits.[44]

Adolescents' drinking habits appear to reflect their efforts to relate to the adult world. By drinking, an adolescent boy can say to himself "I am a man" or "I am one of the crowd."[45] Drinking among younger adolescents, however, may meet with peer disapproval; an adolescent who drinks may be viewed as "show-off" or as "acting smart." Disapproving attitudes decrease with age and a majority of nondrinkers will approve of some social drinking by others by the

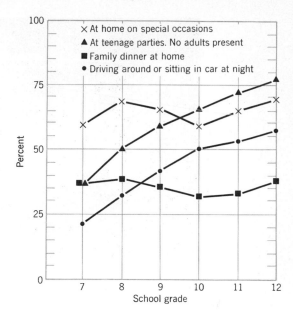

Figure 2
Percent of teenage drinkers by school grade and setting. (From U.S. Public Health Service. *Alcohol and Health.* Rockville, Md. National Institute on Alcohol Abuse and Alcoholism, 1974. Reprinted by permission.

senior year in high school.[46] Riester and Zucker[47] explored alcoholic consumption in several informal peer groups within a high school social system, and found that those who were classified as either "collegiate" (oriented toward social aspects of school extracurricular activities) or "leathers" (oriented toward social activities not sanctioned by the school) were more likely to become drinkers than those who: (1) seldom dated and seldom attended parties or dances, (2) belonged to a clique that was interested in the performing arts and spent a lot of time attending concerts and visiting museums, (3) were immersed in competition for good grades, (4) participated in extracurricular activities requiring verbal skills such as the school newspaper or yearbook, or (5) went steady or were intensely involved with a member of the opposite sex. The researchers found that the collegiate and leather groups accounted for about 90 percent of those who drank regularly. These youth reported overwhelmingly that they preferred to drink alcoholic beverages socially; they disliked drinking alone or in the company of only one friend, especially one of the opposite sex. The boys in the collegiate and leather groups most preferred to drink in the

Adolescent drinking patterns are shaped largely by peers.

company of male friends exclusively. But secondly they liked to drink at a party that included both sexes. The girls seldom ever drank in an exclusively girls' group; they preferred to drink in mixed company.

Although parental sanction is a critical variable in adolescent drinking, young people generally assert that they "learned" their drinking habits from peers.[48] Tobias and Wax[49] report that friends usually supply each other with the booze. Many adolescents regularly steal a shot or two from the family liquor cabinet and stash it away for future parties. Others obtain it through "garaging," that is, stealing beer and hard liquor from unlocked neighborhood garages. Often it is not too difficult to find suppliers who either are over 21 or possess false identification to certify that they are. And there are stores that sell directly over the counter to minors and never ask for proof of age.

The Physical and Psychological Consequences of Drinking

According to Harger,[50] alcoholic beverages contain ethyl alcohol, which is produced by fermenting sugar and yeast. Table 2 compares the caloric value of several beverages to that of milk and indicates the percentage of alcohol by volume.[51] It can be seen that wine is made from grape juice and contains 15 to 30 percent sugar (except for the drier varieties) and 10 to 22 percent alcohol.

Cider is made from apple juice and contains 8 to 12 percent alcohol. Beer is produced by malting (a process that converts the starch in cereals into a sugar and usually contains 4 to 6 percent alcohol). Ale is also a malted beverage and contains 6 to 8 percent alcohol. Distillation, a process known to the Chinese as early as 2,000 B.C., is required to produce a more potent beverage. The alcoholic content of distilled liquors is called "proof." This expression originated with an old English test in which gunpowder was moistened with a whiskey and lighted; the ensuing explosion provided "proof" that the whiskey contained a satisfactory amount of alcohol. Proof in the United States today is designated by a number which indicates twice the alcoholic content by volume. For example, most whiskey ranges from 80 to 100 proof (40 to 50 percent alcohol).[52]

Intoxication begins when alcohol enters the brain. Alcohol has a low molecular weight and is highly soluble in water; thus it can be absorbed rapidly into the bloodstream. It can be detected in the blood only a few moments after a few sips of whiskey reach the stomach, unless a large quantity of food is present to slow the absorption rate. Alcohol affects the higher brain functions, impairing

Table 2

Manufacturing Process, Percent Alcohol, and Caloric Content of Different Alcoholic Beverages, Compared With Milk

Beverage	Made From	Malting	Distillation	Percent Alcohol By Volume	Calories Per Fl Oz
Wine	Grape juice	No	No	10–22	18–50
Hard cider	Apple juice	No	No	8–12	10–20
Beer	Cereals	Yes	No	4–6	10–18
Ale	Cereals	Yes	No	6–8	16–21
Whisky	Cereals	Yes	Yes	40–55	60–90
Brandy	Wine	No	Yes	40–55	60–90
Rum	Molasses	No	Yes	40–55	60–90
Gin	Neutral spirits plus juniper berries, orange peel, etc.	No	Usually	40–55	60–90
Vodka	Neutral spirits	No	No	40–55	60–90
Milk	—	—	—	·—	18–24

Copyright (1964) by McGraw-Hill, Inc. Used by permission.

concentration, judgment, and self-control, according to the amount present in the body. There may be changes in vision, hearing, and muscular control, ranging from slight impairment in the performance of coordinated tasks to a staggering gait, thick speech, and paralysis of the voluntary muscles of the lungs and heart (which could result in death from respiratory failure).[53] Two of the common reactions to alcohol are longer reaction times (or lowered muscular efficiency) and euphoria (or lessened judgmental capacity). A longer reaction time can be dangerous to automobile driving. When a person is in a state of euphoria (a popular reason given for drinking), jokes seem to sound funnier, companions seem to be more congenial, and risks appear to be less hazardous. Teger, Katkin, and Pruitt,[54] for example, tested 36 male graduate students over 21 years of age for risk-taking behavior under different conditions of sobriety using bourbon, vodka, and synthetic alcohol. They found that the inebriated subjects accepted greater objective risks than the sober subjects. Those who are inebriated apparently distort the probability of success, perceiving certain alternatives as being less risky than they actually are.

Depending on the external conditions, dosage, and personal characteristics, alcohol may have a stimulating or depressing effect on behavior.[55] An individual drinks wine, beer, gin, or whiskey in small amounts at cocktail parties, in bars and saloons, and at home to feel different—to increase one's pep or to relax.[56] An adolescent boy, for example, may drink either to feel more confident or to overcome shyness and apprehension on a date. Another may drink to feel more comfortable in coping with work, to feel less lonely, or to free himself from thinking about burdensome responsibilities. An adolescent girl may feel she must drink on dates in order to be popular. A small amount of alcohol probably does heighten effectiveness, but a large amount will reduce efficiency. By and large, youth who drink excessively also tend to be more belligerent—they get into more fights, destroy more property, and lose more friendships than moderate drinkers or non-drinkers.[57] Adolescents who continue to drink are likely to be trying to escape from the daily frustrations of an unsatisfactory family, job, or peer group.[58] Williams[59] found that problem drinkers scored higher than nonproblem drinkers on measures of anxiety and depression. He suggested that those who have a high amount of anxiety and depression appreciate the relief offered by alcohol; indeed, they may drink primarily to obtain temporary relief. The motivation to drink thus becomes stronger and more insistent among problem drinkers, creating a reinforcing pattern that may precipitate alcoholism.

An analysis was made of the drinking patterns of the males in the Oakland Growth Study to determine whether personality and drinking habits were related over a 25-year period, from adolescence to the mid-forties.[60] They were classified according to their adult drinking patterns and compared in terms of personality ratings made when they were in junior high school (ages 12, 13, and 14), senior high school (ages 15, 16, and 17), and as adults (ages 33 and 34). In junior and senior high school the future moderate drinkers and abstainers were rated higher on such attributes as being overcontrolled, conservative, objective, dependable, and considerate. Some were also seen as being more introspective and analytical in their relationships with others. Others appeared to be more thin-skinned, sensitive to criticism, aesthetically reactive, and preoccupied. Moreover, a certain percentage tended to behave dependently, to be submissive, and to seek reassurance. The future problem drinkers, who were also overly dependent in junior high school, were more rebellious and less able to maintain adequate interpersonal relationships. In senior high school they seemed oblivious of the impressions that they made, performed less productively, were less calm, and appeared to be less socially perceptive. Jones[61] reported that in adulthood the nondrinkers were still rated as overcontrolled and emotionally bland, but the problem-drinkers emerged as "expressive with a rapid lively tempo;" they were also disorganized under stress, moody, rebellious, prone to direct expression of hostility, and sensuous and erotic. Jones[62] and Rosenberg[63] both believe that problem drinkers place a high value on masculine behavior, which may relate to their dependency conflicts and interpersonal difficulties during adolescence. Zucker[64] also reports that regular drinkers among adolescent boys (as compared with nondrinkers) tend to express sex-role conflict by developing a hypermasculine facade. Wilsnack[65] has observed, too, that in young men aspects of their power or "masculine" needs may increase in intensity after drinking. Small to moderate amounts of alcohol may enhance thoughts of social power—about helping others or promoting causes—whereas heavy drinking may stimulate fantasies of personal power—about self-aggrandizement and disregard for others. In young women, on the other hand, Wilsnack notes that power needs, as they are reflected in images of masculinity, tend to decrease. Light to moderate drinking appears to have no effect on their needs for social power and heavy drinking seems to reduce interest in power and assertiveness. Wilsnack thus suggests that drinking may enhance feelings of manliness among men and those of "womanliness" among women.

Alcohol Education

The implementation of effective alcohol education programs for adolescents has long been impeded by bitter emotionalism in the United States. The legacy of the Temperance and Prohibition Movements has stressed an either-or interpretation of drinking—abstinence or alcoholism. Most drinkers have been described as persons whose intake of alcohol results in becoming "tight," "smashed," or "bombed." Obviously, not all drinkers are alike. Although many alcoholics get drunk, not all persons who get drunk are alcoholics, and not all persons who drink get drunk. The vast majority of persons use alcohol without problems.

Drinking habits develop in the context of socialization; they are not necessarily related to the availability of alcohol or an individual's weaknesses. Adolescent drinking can most easily be understood in the context of attitudes toward self, parents, peers, and community. How adolescents feel about liquor and why they choose to drink constitute the critical questions that must be faced in determining whether they become either responsible or problem drinkers. Today, more than at any other point in American history, adolescents must make the decision for themselves; if they decide to drink, they must decide what, how much, and under what circumstances, and with whom to drink. The Prohibition Era, for example, had led to the enactment of laws to control the sale of alcoholic beverages to minors. It was assumed that young people were not yet mature enough to exercise moderation and restraint in using alcohol, and the minimum age at which alcoholic beverages could be purchased in most states was set at 21 years of age. The impossibility of enforcing the laws and the recognition that most youth are indeed capable of making mature decisions at a younger age has led to a trend, widespread among the states, to reduce to 18 the legal minimum age below which purchases of liquor are illegal. In some states, adolescents may purchase beer and wine at age 18, but must wait until they are older to buy distilled spirits. Whatever the specific minimum requirements in each state, the emphasis on individual responsibility rather than social legislation to control liquor purchases marks an important trend, and it makes imperative the development of effective elementary and high school programs in alcohol education.

Responsible use of alcohol by adolescents cannot be achieved by "crack-down, by law, by regulation, by moralizing, or by scare tactics."[66] Teaching about alcohol in the public schools has stressed traditionally, however, its harmful effects on the body.[67] Unfortunately, educational programs that mainly emphasize the evil aspects of drinking with solemn pronouncements and admonitions may simply distract adolescents. Adolescents may be pursuaded that their drinking is inconsistent with achieving certain goals, but it is unlikely that they can be pursuaded that all drinking is "illegitimate, physically harmful, or immoral."[68] More importantly, adolescents are inhibited from developing a mature understanding of the physical and emotional aspects of the use and the nonuse of alcohol.[69]

DiCicco and Unterberger[70] assert that the basic goal of alcohol education should be "to allow young people to make mature and responsible decisions about their own drinking, which may include responsible use or non-use of alcohol . . . to prevent irresponsible drinking or drunkenness." The researchers suggest that teachers must be trained to differentiate between moderate levels of drinking and drunkenness and to deal realistically with the issues adolescents raise. Chafetz[71] suggests that alcohol education and drug education programs might be viewed as synonymous. Chafetz holds that the "colossal failure" of education programs in these areas has revealed that "the answer lies only in full awareness and understanding of the entire problem; in the human compassion that is nurtured by actual knowledge; in people-oriented programs which reflect that compassion and respond to individual human needs and differences; and finally, in the long-term, slow, persistent cultivation of a sense of responsibility to self and to society."[72]

CIGARETTES

For several centuries tobacco has largely been consumed in pipes and cigars and in the form of chewing tobacco and snuff. Awareness of the effects of tobacco on health grew slowly. Heavy users experienced unpleasant withdrawal symptoms when they tried to stop, indicating some degree of nicotine habituation. But most of the opposition to tobacco rested on moral grounds. Smoking was said to be a "filthy" habit, and religious groups held that it was sinful. From about 1920 to 1960, however, the consumption of manufactured cigarettes rose dramatically while the consumption of tobacco in other forms declined 70 percent.[73] This increase in cigarette smoking eventually led to the question of the relationship between cigarette tobacco and health.

In the early 1960s the advertising industry was linking cigarette smoking with athletic prowess, beauty, masculinity, youth, and intellect. Smoking was widespread among the youth's adult models. They saw their parents smoke, saw their teachers excuse themselves during recess to enjoy a cigarette, and saw heroes of the movie and television screen smoke. They were irresistibly tempted to follow their example. Then convincing scientific evidence began to be revealed, indicating that there was a definite association between heavy smoking and lung cancer, chronic bronchitis, emphysema, and coronary heart disease. Cigarette manufacturers have since invested millions of dollars in developing filters to remove the carcinogenic ingredients from cigarettes, but their efforts have only been of questionable value.

Counter efforts to stem the quantity of cigarettes smoked began in the early 1960s when United States Post Office delivery trucks began to carry the simple message in bold print "100,000 doctors have quit smoking cigarettes," and in small print "Maybe they know something you don't."[74] Then in 1964 the Advisory Committee of the Surgeon General issued a report entitled *Smoking and Health* that implicated cigarettes in the etiology of lung cancer and other diseases. The report stated: "cigarette smoking is a health hazard of sufficient importance to warrant appropriate remedial action."[75] Since then there have been concerted public campaigns to dissuade young people from smoking. Cigarette advertisements have been banned from television, and a few television commercials even decry cigarette smoking. Adolescents are no longer employed as models to promote cigarettes in advertising; however, the attractive, worldly young adults who are portrayed probably are much more effective in selling to adolescents than their own peers would be. Schools also have joined the effort to curb cigarette smoking, and are using materials and programs provided by such associations as the American Cancer Society, American Heart Association, and the National Tuberculosis and Respiratory Diseases Association. School programs may have some effect, but the number of adolescents who take up smoking each year exceeds the number of adults who stop; thus, the quantity of persons who are smoking is growing.

The Physical and Psychological Consequences of Smoking

The physically disabling effects of cigarette smoking are well documented. One-third of the deaths of men between 35 and 60 years of age are partly attributable to smoking.[76] Deaths from lung cancer equal those from traffic accidents, the rate having jumped from about three deaths per 10,000 in 1930 to about 30 per 100,000 in the late 1960s. The death rate from coronary heart disease is approximately 70 percent greater among men who smoke, and is about 200 percent greater when it is associated with high blood pressure and high serum cholesterol.[77] Approximately 77 million work days (about 20 percent of the annual work loss) in the United States are lost each year due to illnesses associated with smoking. Nearly one out of every 14 wage earners over 45 years of age is disabled by chronic bronchitis or emphysema, and the number of women afflicted with these diseases has quadrupled since the mid-1950s.[78] Also there is a high correlation between cigarette smoking and gastric ulcers, pneumonia, bladder cancer, cirrhosis of the liver, and cancer of other tissues— mouth, tongue, lip, larynx, pharynx, and esophagus. The degree of inhalation has been shown to be related to coughing, shortness of breath, loss of appetite, and loss of weight.[79] Although these ailments typically affect adults, Peters and Ferris[80] found that among college students, there is a strong correlation between respiratory disease and the number of years one has smoked and the number of packs smoked daily. Students who smoke have more coughing, phlegm, breathlessness, wheezing, and chest affliction with colds.

The psychological consequences of cigarette smoking are more vague and difficult to assess than the physiological. Most habituated smokers inhale regularly, and the amount of chemically active materials absorbed into their body tissue is fairly large. When nicotine is injected directly into the bloodstream, many individuals report that they prefer pure nicotine to smoking, which suggests that some of the pleasure obtained from smoking is due to nicotine.[81] Is the cigarette smoker's habit, then, maintained by the addictive properties of nicotine? Bernstein[82] believes that too many persons are prone to answer this question affirmatively. He distinguishes between addiction and habituation, as conceptualized by the World Health Organization. Addiction is seen "as a state of periodic or chronic intoxication produced by the repeated consumption of a drug, accompanied by a compulsion to continue taking it (in increasing doses) and by psychological and physical dependence. . . . Habituation is described as a condition resulting from repeated drug use involving a desire to continue taking the drug (at a relatively constant dose), which results in psychological but not physical dependence, that is, no consistent and reproducible withdrawal syndrome appears."[83] Bernstein sees cigarette smoking as more habituating than addicting. Heavy smokers may have a strong desire to quit smoking, for example, but will not seek cigarettes of stronger nicotine content as a morphine addict might do under comparable circumstances. Stopping or drastically reducing smoking may produce somatic complaints, but there will be no spontaneous and inevitable withdrawal symptoms. Any withdrawal symptoms resemble the emotional reactions of being deprived of other desired objects or habituating experiences. Bernstein,[84] therefore, argues that the habituation of smoking "is the result of a very complex system of physiological, social, and other environmental stimuli, and for any one individual, some particular combination of them is relevant (i.e., functional)."

During the initial period, smoking may either arouse a positive affect or reduce a negative affect.[85] Smoking may make situations more enjoyable or exciting: youth may smoke "to gain direct oral or gustatory arousal, to watch smoke leave their lips, or to have something to do with their hands."[86] It may also help to relax them, as at the end of a meal or during a pleasant conversation. In reducing negative feelings, smoking may help individuals relieve fear, shame, or disgust. It may also serve as a partial sedative, enabling persons to react effectively to a problem or to avoid it entirely.[87] But after persons have become habituated they can smoke without any affect at all. Davis[88] holds that much habituated smoking occurs almost without awareness. Persons light cigarettes on certain occasions because that is what they are accustomed to doing. Eventually, when smoking becomes relatively habitual, the positive affect or reduction in negative affect may be focused on the cigarette itself. The smokers sense pleasure when they are smoking and become anxious when they are not. The cigarette has become a "crutch," which is needed to cope with an everlasting series of events and crises.

Because it is difficult to determine the psychological effects of smoking, researchers cannot easily distinguish smokers from nonsmokers on the basis of personality attributes. As Wohlford and Giammona[89] point out, most studies focus on concurrent relationships between smoking behavior and personality variables. There have been few longitudinal investigations of individuals' personality traits before they began smoking and after habituation. Nevertheless, some investigators have differentiated smokers and nonsmokers on several characteristics; they have utilized psychoanalytic theory, which holds that smoking is an attempt to reinstitute the passive pleasures of infantile nursing. Thus, smokers are held to possess relatively greater dependency needs, which lead them to seek nurturance. Lawton[90] referred to a study of college students which reported that those who were able to give up smoking more easily also had been breast-fed for a longer time in infancy. Moreover, many of those who quit smoking substituted candy, gum, food, and alcohol for cigarettes. The unresolved oral needs of the male smoker are sometimes thought to be expressed in outgoing, happy-go-lucky, extroverted, masculine roles.[91] At least hypermasculinity appears to be associated with smoking among males. McKennell and Bynner[92] reported that among adolescent boys, aged 11 to 15, smokers tended to attain status in the eyes of their peers with respect to "toughness" and "sexual precocity." Toughness meant being good at sports, a good fighter, strong and rough, and a team or group member with many friends; the boys who smoked believed that they were fairly close to being tough, but those who did not smoke felt that they had a long way to go. The boys also perceived the smokers as being more interested in girls and more attractive to them. As the boys grew older, they increasingly valued these aspects of personality, which provided the older smokers with an enviable position among their peers.[93] On the other hand, McKennell and Bynner[94] found that most boys, including those who smoked, regarded the typical smoker as an academic failure and the nonsmoker as a success in school. This finding has been confirmed by other investigations. Horn;[95] Salber, Welsh, and Taylor;[96] Peters and Ferris;[97] and Horowitz;[98] for example, reported that highschool smokers are less studious, less successful, and more prone to fall behind in school than are the nonsmokers. Newman[99] found that nonsmoking ninth graders scored higher marks in school than the smokers and that both male and female smokers were much more likely than nonsmokers to perceive themselves as failing to meet the expectations of their parents, peers, and teachers. Dvorak[100] studied 860 males and 563 female college freshman, and reported that those who did not smoke had achieved a higher high school rank, earned better grades in college, and were more apt to complete the entire freshman year than those who smoked. Dunn[101] showed that among freshmen only 16.7 percent of those with an "A" average smoked whereas 59.1 percent of those with a failing average smoked. Furthermore, over one-half of the students who dropped out of school in the fall of their sophomore year were smokers. One might expect, then, that adolescent smokers will rebel against traditional objectives of socialization. However, the evidence for this expectation is contradictory. McKennell and Bynner[102] found that high school smokers were conscious of their limitations in school and valued educational success. The 1964 report of the Surgeon General indicated that rebelliousness was probably a minor reason for smoking. Lawton[103] has insisted that smoking is overwhelmingly a conforming rather than a rebellious act, since the proportion of high school youth who smoke against their parents' wishes is small. Horowitz[104] argued that while youths may appear to rebel against their parents by taking up smoking, actually they are emulating a model and are trying to be liked by someone. Parents may allow adolescents to smoke occasional cigarettes at age 13 but become angry later when they are smoking regularly; under such circumstances, adolescents may become rebellious. On the other hand, some evidence shows that rebellious adolescents are attracted to smoking. Stewart and Livson[105] compared retrospectively smokers and nonsmokers of both sexes at age 30 on several measures of rebelliousness from kingergarten through high school and into adulthood. Measures derived from both teacher ratings and personality tests revealed that members of both sexes who later took up smoking were more rebellious. The researchers suggested that the most rebellious may pursue openly and vigorously, and at an earlier age, an activity such as smoking which they see as a pleasurable prerogative of adults.

Adolescent Cigarette Smoking Patterns

Michelson[106] tells the story of a five-year-old girl who repeatedly came late to nursery school because her mother, believing that cigarettes prevented nervousness, gave her daughter a cigarette after each meal. The child was unable to finish her morning cigarette quickly enough to get to school on time. This extraordinary incident is not typical, but surveys disseminated by the U.S. Public Health Service and the National Clearing House for Smoking and Health suggest that cigarette smoking among young people is fairly prevalent. A National Health Examination Survey[107] of several thousand youth 12 through 17 years of age, which was conducted by the Health Service between 1966 and 1970, indicate that 54 percent of them had never tried smoking. Another 31

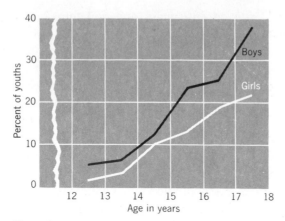

Figure 3
Percent of U.S. youths reporting themselves as regular smokers, by age and sex. (From U.S. Public Health Service. *Vital and Health Statistics,* Series 11, No. 147, Self-reported health behavior and attitudes of youth 12–17 years: April 1975. Reprinted by permission.)

percent reported that they had tried smoking and had stopped. The remainder, about 15 percent, regarded themselves as regular smokers. The 12-year-olds constituted about 4 percent of the regular smokers and the 17-year-olds about 31 percent. Approximately 61 percent smoke less than a half a pack of cigarettes per day, 25 percent smoke better than one-half to one pack per day, and 14 percent smoke one or more packs each day. Figure 3, which is based on the Health Service data, shows that sex differences as well as age differences are related to magnitude of regular smoking among adolescents. The percentage of boys who smoke regularly exceeds that of girls at every age. At age 17, for example, 41 percent of the boys but only 22 percent of the girls report themselves as being regular smokers. When the 12- to 17-year-olds are considered as an age group, 18 percent of the boys versus 11 percent of the girls see themselves as regular cigarette smokers. The survey also indicates that adolescents usually start exploring smoking in the upper elementary grades and that regular smoking habits take hold in the eighth or ninth grade among those who pursue smoking. These data are augmented by a recent National Clearing House Survey that demonstrated the proportion of regular smokers in the adolescent age group jumped 4 percent for boys and 3.5 percent for girls (particularly the 15 to 16 age group) between 1968 and 1972. This survey shows that about 4 million adolescents in the 12- to 18-year-old group smoke on a regular basis in the United States.[108]

When asked why they smoke, curiosity—a highly superficial answer—is the reason adolescents most often give. By watching parents, older siblings, friends, and public figures smoking, adolescents are often intrigued by the prospects of sharing in the enjoyment; thus they smoke a few cigarettes and then decide whether or not to continue. They may justify their decision to continue smoking by saying that they like the taste and smell of cigarettes, that it is a pleasant experience in the company of others, that it is relaxing, or that it gives them something to do with their hands. And they may think that smoking is better than munching or nibbling on food.[109] Occasionally adolescents will continue smoking even though they dislike it. Michelson[110] found that some youth drink a Coke or chew peppermint gum while smoking to dilute the taste. Others asserted that they smoked because they lacked the willpower to stop. They blamed their parents, the easy accessibility of vending machines, or enticing advertisements. Adolescents who smoke heavily are prone to report dissatisfaction with their habit, to believe their smoking is an automatic act, and to think that they lack willpower to stop.[111]

There are two major sources of incentives for continuing smoking—peers and parents. Levitt and Edwards's[112] study of 493 pupils in grades 5 to 13 in a suburban, middle-class community showed that "a smoking best friend" and "a smoking group" significantly influenced an adolescent's smoking habits. The majority of adolescent smokers report that they smoked most often in small

Sometimes smoking is a matter of making an impression.

groups, at parties, and large casual gatherings. Several studies confirm the general impression that an adolescent smokes in order to belong or conform to a peer group, to avoid being called "chicken," or to impress a friend.[113] Investigators unanimously report that at all ages boys smoke more than girls and begin to smoke earlier.[114] Boys are likely to feel that others expect them to be tough and masculine and thus they are inclined to smoke in order to conform.[115] As Newman[116] indicated, there are different peer standards for the two sexes in terms of status and smoking. Newman's investigation of ninth-grade boys and girls in an urban high school showed that girls who smoked (openly or secretly) did not achieve status in the eyes of their peers. Boys who smoked openly also had little status and were characterized as "hoods," but those who concealed their smoking from school authorities were well regarded. It was also found that boys preferred to be with girls who did not smoke.[117] The low regard for adolescent girls who smoke may explain why Horn et al.[118] found that among high school youths who smoked less than five cigarettes a day solitary smoking was twice as common among girls as boys.

The parental model appears to be a powerful influence on adolescent smoking; it is part of the socialization process when it is accepted in the family as normal and expected. Socioeconomic status also seems to be significant, especially when young people are in the sixth, seventh, and eighth grades. At these ages boys and girls from lower socioeconomic groups tend to smoke more than those from higher groups. Socioeconomic status appears to lose its importance during the later years of high school.[119] Horn[120] also reported that an adolescent is more likely to smoke when both parents or an older sibling smokes. Dunn[121] has suggested that when one parent smokes, especially the father, it influences the adolescent as much as if both parents smoke. Levitt and Edwards[122] indicated that smokers of both sexes are likely to have a smoking father; there was only a slight tendency for smokers to have smoking mothers, but girls (more than boys) were likely to have a smoking mother. Indeed, Williams[123] reports that the smoking behavior of mothers is the most significant influence on their daughters' smoking habits. Horn et al.[124] have argued that the smoking habits of boys are likely to resemble those of their fathers whereas those of girls follow the pattern of their mothers. Additional evidence,[125] confirms that both sons and daughters tend to follow the smoking pattern of their same-sex parent more than that of the opposite sex, and the relation between the father's and son's smoking is relatively stronger than between the mother's and daughter's, especially when the family is intact.

Knowledge of the effects of smoking on health has generally failed to deter adolescents from taking it up. Forrest[126] reported that several smokers saw minimal risk with "what little I smoke" or "the findings do not apply to me."

Some smokers took a fatalistic attitude: "I am not worried with H bombs on all sides"; "As I believe I am fated to die one day, I am not worried about the smoking"; "Let's live for the present."[127] And adolescents may view the risk as remote and improbable.[128] One boy said, "It's hard to believe that you can die."[129]

Programs designed to curtail the smoking of adolescents have varied in subtlety and effectiveness.[130] Higher tobacco taxes and the prohibition of smoking in certain school areas apparently have not reduced the incidence of smoking.[131] Antismoking drugs and withdrawal clinics are attempts to provide alternatives for the smoker, but they are only successful to the extent that these alternatives are adopted. Some of the activities that have been encouraged include: chewing one's food a certain number of times before swallowing, keeping especially clean, avoiding profane language, changing one's diet, rising early, taking hot baths, taking cold showers, sending one's clothes to be cleaned, and performing deep breathing exercises. Bernstein[132] suggested that placebos are about as effective as antismoking drugs and that most clinics achieve an immediate quitting rate of 30 percent to 85 percent, but these figures fall off substantially as soon as the formal meetings are over. Campaigns against smoking are often highly imaginative, but may not be of much value. Arnett[133] showed posters, displayed flip cards, and handed out fliers telling of the relationship between smoking and diseases to more than 300 graduating college seniors, but only two reported that they stopped smoking as a result of the campaign. Sixteen youth gave up smoking for other reasons, and 49 became smokers during the campaign. Arnett[134] concluded that the youth were unimpressed by the fact that fewer physicians smoked or that many smokers die of cancer. Michelson[135] noted that advertising has contributed substantially to changing attitudes since the 1920s, when the average male cigarette-smoker was regarded as effeminate and the female cigarette-smoker as immoral. He suggests that a massive advertising campaign might be able to alter images of smokers again if the effort were made.

The development of school programs to deal with cigarette smoking has raised several issues. Adolescents who smoke constitute a population with relatively poor health habits in general.[136] Many researchers, therefore, believe that cigarette education should be included as an integral part of health education. Antismoking campaigns that convey to adolescents the immediate disadvantages of cigarette smoking have proven to be ineffectual because too many circumstances are involved in supporting the cigarette habit.[137] These campaigns, known as the "contemporary approach," emphasize that cigarettes are costly; start forest fires; burn holes in clothing, carpets, furniture, and woodwork; impart a disagreeable odor to the smoker's clothing and breath; stain one's fingers; and impair one's senses, preventing one from smelling and tasting as nonsmokers do. According to National Clearing House experts, the approaches recognized as the most promising today are those in which adolescents themselves run their own antismoking campaigns. Educational models have been devised to assist youth shape their smoking destiny, and in general, attention is centered on the prevention of disease and the effects of cigarettes on the heart, respiratory, and nervous systems. The results have been noteworthy.[138] One of the more striking findings is that young people become so personally convinced of the deleterious effects of cigarettes that they often compel their parents to cease smoking. As one mother put it, "every time I picked up a cigarette, my child bugged me. I finally felt so self-conscious, I quit." Teachers may also be affected by the antismoking stance of young people. Edson[139] recounts the story of a teacher, a heavy smoker, who was unable to cut down his consumption. The students placed a gravestone at the front of the teacher's desk, and marked on it the teacher's life expectancy. Each time the teacher admitted to lighting up a cigarette (outside the class) a student representative reduced the life expectancy figure by a few moments. Although earlier investigators have cautioned against the use of such fear stimuli, on the grounds that they will seem remote to adolescents, Edson's review suggests that fear stimuli can be persuasive when presented in a believable, meaningful context.

SUMMARY

Adolescents tend to have little awareness of the potential hazards to their physical well-being from automobile accidents, veneral diseases, suicide, alcoholic beverages, and cigarettes.

Automobiles are the major cause of death and disability among youth from 15 to 24 years of age. Young drivers with high accident rates tend to own their own cars, be employed, and be uninterested in attending school. Research suggests that among adolescents who have committed one traffic violation, those who are required to write a reflective essay on traffic safety are less likely to commit another violation than those who are assigned to traffic school or assessed fines.

The number of youth who contract a venereal disease is growing precipitously. Today we are in the midst of a critical national public health and educational problem. Gonorrhea, the more common of the diseases, is almost always transmitted by sexual contact; in males, it produces a discharge and causes discomfort during urination. It is more difficult to detect in females. Syphilis is less common than gonorrhea but more deadly. It is usually acquired by sexual contact and is likely to appear in three or four stages, each of which is successively more serious. In its last stage, syphilis may cause intellectual impairment, blindness, and sometimes even death.

Suicide follows automobile accidents and homicides as the third leading cause of death among young people. More boys than girls are victims of suicide, but more girls attempt suicide. Lack of meaningful identification with significant persons characterizes the life styles of suicide-prone adolescents. The two major sources of tension that lead to suicide-prone behavior are school and family. Close examination of school-related suicides, however, suggests that many stem from young people's efforts to satisfy parental achievement expectations.

An unprecedented boom in adolescent drinking occurred during the past decade. Beer is the most preferred beverage of young people, especially among boys. Approximately 70 percent of the twelfth-grade boys and 35 percent of twelfth-grade girls, for example, drink beer once a month or more. Adolescent drinking habits develop in the context of socialization. Youth's first drinking experiences are likely to be at home and to be encouraged by parents. Drinking later shifts to the company of peers. Young people are inclined to perceive alcohol as a social beverage, but sex-role conflicts and other forms of tension and anxiety may be related to why some young people drink immoderately. The development in school of functional attitudes toward alcohol usage depends on educational programs that emphasize individual responsibility rather than those that stress social legislation to control purchases, scare tactics, or the evil aspects of drinking.

For many years, concerted efforts have been made to curb adolescent cigarette smoking by emphasizing its threat to physical well-being and playing down the advertisements that associate smoking with athletic prowess, beauty, masculinity, youthfulness, and intellect. Prolonged smoking is generally believed to cause coughing and shortness of breath. It may also lead to chronic bronchitis and emphysema and is correlated with a variety of cancers. In general, smoking appears to stem more from efforts to conform than to be rebellious. The proportion of youth who smoke against their parents' wishes is small and consists largely of girls. Parents who smoke may influence their children to smoke. Young people are likely to smoke for reasons of curiosity, enjoyment, peer acceptance, and emulation of adult models. Young people start exploring smoking in the upper elementary grades and regular smoking habits take hold in the eighth or ninth grade among those who pursue smoking. Peer pressure to smoke is often quite intense in the later years of high school. Although young people usually know that cigarette smoking is habit forming, tends to cause lung cancer and other ailments, and reduces one's life expectancy, they seldom believe that these risks apply to them. Antismoking educational programs, however, have proven to be effective when attention is centered realistically on the long-term physical effects of cigarettes.

REVIEW QUESTIONS

1. What are the characteristics of the young people who are involved in automobile accidents?
2. What appears to be an effective educational technique for reducing traffic violations among adolescents?
3. What are the characteristics of gonorrhea?
4. What are the symptoms of syphilis?
5. How are venereal diseases communicated?

6. What are the various ways in which young people attempt suicide?
7. What are the antecedents of adolescent suicidal behavior?
8. What two major sources of tension among adolescents lead to suicide-prone behavior?
9. What is the general pattern of adolescent drinking in the United States?
10. How do adolescents obtain liquor?
11. What are the physical and psychological consequences of immoderate drinking?
12. How do adolescent drinking habits develop?
13. What is the basic goal of contemporary alcohol education programs?
14. What physical ailments may arise in adolescents as a consequence of smoking?
15. What personality characteristics during adolescence are correlated with cigarette smoking?
16. What circumstances give rise to adolescent cigarette smoking?
17. What are the characteristics of programs designed to control cigarette smoking among adolescents?

DISCUSSION QUESTIONS

1. Why should asking adolescents to write a paper on traffic safety, in which they must justify their actions and emotions, help them develop good driving habits?
2. If you were asked to design a campaign to reduce the prevalence of venereal diseases in your community, what would you do?
3. What specific steps might school personnel take to neutralize suicide-prone behavior among adolescents?
4. What signs in young people's behavior might be identified as early symptoms of suicidal tendencies?
5. Give several reasons for the marked increase in adolescent drinking during the past few years.
6. What do you think of the following social techniques for controlling alcoholic consumption among adolescents: educational programs that stress responsible usage, legislation to control purchases, and educational programs centered on scare tactics?
7. To what extent do you believe that adolescents are the target of advertising efforts to market cigarettes?
8. Why is cigarette smoking appealing to young people in contemporary society?
9. How would you approach the design of an antismoking campaign for the high schools in your community?

NOTES

1. S. H. Schuman, D. C. Pelz, N. J. Ehrlich, and M. L. Selzer. Young male drivers: impulse expression, accidents, and violations. *The Journal of the American Medical Association,* 1967, **200**, 1026–1030; M. K. Shapiro and W. Asher. Teaching the driver education student to cope with dangerous emotions. *Traffic Safety,* 1972, **72**, 20–21.

2. Shapiro and Asher, *op. cit.*; R. Zylman. Youth, alcohol, and collision involvement. *Journal of Safety Research,* 1973, **5,** 58–72.

3. Zylman, *op. cit.*

4. Ibid.

5. Schuman, et al., *op. cit.*

6. W. Asher and B. Dodson. Automobile accidents in the year following high school: The predictive value of 377 unobtrusive variables. *Behavioral Research in Highway Safety,* 1971, **2,** 107–122.

7. Schuman, et al., *op. cit.*

8. Zylman, *op. cit.*

9. Ibid.

10. Shapiro and Asher, *op. cit.*

11. G. D. Mecham. Proceed with caution: which penalties slow down the juvenile traffic violator? *Crime and Delinquency,* 1968, **5,** 142–150.

12. Ibid.

13. R. E. Pfrender. VD case reporting: why waste the time when it doesn't work? *Medical Opinion,* 1973, **2,** 36–39; R. Shenker and M. Schildkrout. Physical and emotional health of youth. In R. J. Havighurst and P. H. Dreyer (Eds.). *Youth—Seventy-Fourth Yearbook of the National Society for the Study of Education.* Chicago: University of Chicago Press, 1975, pp. 61–86.

14. R. S. Morton. *Venereal diseases.* Baltimore: Penquin Books, 1966.

15. Ibid.

16. Shenker and Schildkrout, *op. cit.*

17. J. E. Lobdell and D. Owsley. The origin of syphilis. *Journal of Sex Research,* 1974, **10,** 76–79.

18. J. L. Breen. Venereal disease. *Journal Newark City Hospital,* 1967, **4,** 25–37; Morton, *op. cit.*

19. Morton, *op. cit.*

20. Shenker and Schildkrout, *op. cit.*

21. Pfrender, *op. cit.*

22. Shenker and Schildkrout, *op. cit.*

23. W. A. Rushing. Deviance, interpersonal relations and suicide, *Human Relations,* 1969, **22,** 61–76.

24. D. E. Sanborn, C. J. Sanborn, and P. Cimbolic. Two years of suicide: a study of adolescent suicide in New Hampshire. *Child Psychiatry and Human Development,* 1973, **3,** 234–242.

25. B. F. Corder, W. Shorr, and R. F. Corder. A study of social and psychological characteristics of adolescent suicide attempters in an urban disadvantaged area. *Adolescence,* 1974, **9,** 1–5.

26. J. Jacobs. *Adolescent sucide.* New York: John Wiley, 1971.

27. Jacobs, *op. cit.,* p. 107.

28. Sanborn, et al., *op. cit.*

29. M. L. Peck. Suicide motivations in adolescents. *Adolescence,* 1968, **3,** 109–118.

30. Ibid.

31. J. Tuckman, W. F. Youngman, and B. Leifer. Suicide and family disorganization. *International Journal of Social Psychiatry,* 1966, **12,** 188–191.

32. D. G. Kreider and J. A. Motto. Parent-child role reversal and suicidal states in adolescence. *Adolescence,* 1974, **9,** 365–370.

33. Peck, *op. cit.*

34. J. Jacobs and J. D. Teicher. Broken homes and social isolation in attempted suicides of adolescents. *International Journal of Social Psychiatry,* 1967, **13,** 140–149.

35. U.S. Public Health Service. *Alcohol and Health*: Second special report to the U.S. Congress. Rockville, Md.: National Institute on Alcohol Abuse and Alcoholism, 1974.

36. M. E. Chafetz. Alcoholism: Drug dependency problem number one. *Journal of Drug Issues,* 1974, **4,** 64–68.

37. *Boston Globe,* Saturday, January 26, 1974.

38. U.S. Public Health Service, Alcohol and health, *op. cit.*

39. *Boston Globe, op. cit.*

40. G. L. Maddox. Adolescence and alcohol, chapter 2; Teenage drinking in the United States, chapter 12. In R. G. McCarthy (Ed.). *Alcohol education for classroom and community.* New York: McGraw-Hill, 1964; A. E. Riester and R. A. Zucker. Adolescent social structure and drinking behavior. *Personnel and Guidance Journal,* 1968, **47,** 304–312; U.S. Public Health Service, alcohol and health, *op. cit.*

41. Maddox, *op. cit.*

42. Riester and Zucker, *op. cit.*; A. F. Williams. Validation of a college problem-drinking scale. *Journal of Projective Techniques and Personality Assessment,* 1967, **31,** 33–40.

43. Riester and Zucker, *op. cit.*; C. M. Rosenberg. Young alcoholics. *The British Journal of Psychiatry,* 1969, **115,** 181–188.

44. J. J. Tobias and J. Wax. Youthful drinking patterns in the suburbs. *Adolescence,* 1973, **8,** 113–118.

45. Maddox, *op. cit.*

46. Ibid.

47. Riester and Zucker, *op. cit.*

48. Tobias and Wax, *op. cit.*

49. Ibid.

50. R. N. Harger. Alcohol and the alcoholic beverages. In R. G. McCarthy (Ed.). *Alcohol education for classroom and community.* New York: McGraw-Hill, 1964.

51. Harger, *op. cit.,* p. 75.

52. Harger, *op. cit.*

53. R. N. Harger. The sojourn of alcohol in the body. In R. G. McCarthy (Ed.). *Alcohol education for classroom and community.* New York: McGraw-Hill, 1964.

54. A. I. Teger, E. S. Katkin, and D. E. Pruitt. Effects of alcoholic beverages and their congener content on level and style of risk taking. *Journal of Personality and Social Psychology,* 1969, **11,** 170–176.

55. E. S. Lisansky. The psychological effects of alcohol. In R. G. McCarthy (Ed.). *Alcohol education for classroom and community.* New York: McGraw-Hill, 1964.

56. Lisansky, *op. cit.*

57. G. Globetti. The use of beverage alcohol by youth in an abstinence setting. *The Journal of School Health,* 1969, **39,** 179–183.

58. G. L. Maddox. Drinking among negroes: inferences from the drinking patterns of selected negro male collegians. *Journal of Health and Social Behavior,* 1968, **9,** 114–120.

59. A. F. Williams. Social drinking, anxiety, and depression. *Journal of Personality and Social Psychology,* 1966, **3,** 689–693.

60. M. C. Jones. Personality correlates and antecedents of drinking patterns in adult males. *Journal of Consulting and Clinical Psychology,* 1968, **32,** 2–12.

61. Jones, *op. cit.*

62. Jones, *op. cit.*

63. C. M. Rosenberg. Determinants of psychiatric illness in young people. *The British Journal of Psychiatry,* 1969, **115,** 907–915.

64. R. A. Zucker. Sex role identity patterns and drinking behavior in adolescents. Center for Alcohol Studies, Rutgers University, 1967.

65. S. C. Wilsnack. The effects of social drinking on women's fantasy. *Journal of Personality,* 1974, **42,** 43–61.

66. Chafetz, *op. cit.*

67. L. M. DiCicco and H. Unterberger. Does alcohol follow drugs? *Bulletin of the National Association of Secondary School Principals,* 1973, **57,** 85–91.

68. Maddox, *op. cit.*

69. G. Globetti. Parents favor alcohol education. *Mississippi Educational Advance,* 1968, 18–19.

70. DiCicco and Unterberger, *op. cit.,* p. 88.

71. Chafetz, *op. cit.*

72. Chafetz, *op. cit.,* p. 67.

73. E. C. Hammond. The effects of smoking. *Scientific American,* 1962, **207,** 39–51.

74. R. L. Davis. Smoking: are we progressing in its curtailment? Unpublished Manuscript. Presented at the Convention of the American Association for Health, Physical Education, and Recreation, St. Louis, 1968.

75. J. H. Arnett and M. W. Black. Smoking habits at Drexel Institute of Technology. *The Journal of the American College Health Association,* 1967, **15,** 375–376.

76. R. L. Davis. Smoking: PTA steps out in a new field. Unpublished manuscript. Presented at the Convention of the Colorado Congress of Parents and Teachers, La Junta, Colorado, 1968.

77. Davis, Smoking curtailment, *op. cit.*

78. Davis, PTA in a new field, *op. cit.*

79. Hammond, *op. cit.*

80. J. M. Peters and B. G. Ferris, Jr. Smoking, pulmonary function and respiratory symptoms in a college-age group. *American Review of Respiratory Disease,* 1967, **95,** 774–782; J. M. Peters and B. G. Ferris, Jr. Smoking and morbidity in a college-age group. *American Review of Respiratory Disease,* 1967, **95,** 783–789.

81. M. P. Lawton. The psychology of adolescent anti-smoking education. *The Journal of School Health,* 1963, **33,** 1–8.

82. D. A. Bernstein. Modification of smoking behavior. *Psychological Bulletin,* 1969, **71,** 418–440.

83. Bernstein, *op. cit.,* p. 419.

84. Bernstein, *op. cit.,* p. 420.

85. R. L. Davis. Research and health problems: status of smoking education research. Unpublished Manuscript. Presented at the Conference of the American Medical Association, Chicago, 1967; P. Wohlford and S. T. Giammona. Personality and social variables related to the initiation of smoking cigarettes. *The Journal of School Health,* 1969, **39,** 544–552.

86. Wohlford and Giammona, *op. cit.,* p. 550.

87. Wohlford and Giammona, *op. cit.*

88. Davis, Research and health problems, *op. cit.*

89. Wohlford and Giammona, *op. cit.*

90. Lawton, *op. cit.*

91. R. B. Cattell and S. Krug. Personality factor profile peculiar to the student smoker. *Journal of Counseling psychology,* 1967, **14,** 116–121; R. R. Evans, E. F. Borgatta, and G. W. Bohrnstedt. Smoking and MMPI scores among entering freshmen. *Journal of Social Psychology,* 1967, **73,** 137–140; J. T. Fodor, L. M. Glass, and J. M. Weiner. Smoking behavior, cognitive skills and educational implications. *The Journal of School Health,* 1968, **38,** 94–98.

92. A. C. McKennell and J. M. Bynner. Self images and smoking behavior among school boys. *The British Journal of Educational Psychology,* 1969, **39,** 27–39.

93. Ibid.

94. Ibid.

95. D. Horn. Modifying smoking habits in high school students. *Children,* 1960, **7,** 63–65.

96. E. J. Salber, B. Welsh, and S. V. Taylor. Reasons for smoking given by secondary school children. *Journal of Health and Human Behavior,* 1963, **4,** 118–129.

97. J. M. Peters and B. G. Ferris, Jr. Association of smoking with certain descriptive variables

in a college-age group. *The Journal of the American College Health Association,* 1967, **16,** 165–173.

98. M. J. Horowitz. Psychological aspects of education related to smoking. *Journal of School Health,* 1966, **36,** 281–288.

99. I. M. Newman. Adolescent cigarette smoking as compensatory behavior. Unpublished manuscript. Presented to the Research Council of the American School Health Association, Philadelphia, 1969.

100. E. J. Dvorak. Educational and personality characteristics of smokers and nonsmokers among university freshmen. *Journal of the American College Health Association,* 1967, **16,** 80–84.

101. D. F. Dunn. Cigarettes and the college freshman. *Journal of the American Medical Association,* 1967, **199,** 19–22.

102. McKennell and Bynner, *op. cit.*

103. Lawton, *op. cit.*

104. Horowitz, *op. cit.*

105. L. Stewart and N. Livson. Smoking and rebelliousness: a longitudinal study from childhood to maturity. *Journal of Consulting Psychology,* 1966, **30,** 225–229.

106. E. Michelson. Adolescent smoking withdrawal clinic. *The Journal of School Health,* 1966, **36,** 364–367.

107. U.S. Public Health Service. *Vital and Health Statistics,* Series 11, No. 147, Self-reported health behavior and attitudes of youth 12–17 years. Rockville, Md. National Center for Health Statistics, April 1975.

108. National Clearing House for Smoking and Health: *Patterns and Prevalence of Teenage Cigarette Smoking: 1968, 1970 and 1972.* DHEW Pub. No. (HSM) 73-8701. Public Health Service. Washington. U.S. Government Printing Office, August 1972.

109. Dunn, *op. cit.*

110. Michelson, *op. cit.*

111. D. J. Baer. Smoking attitude behavior, and beliefs of college males. *The Journal of Social Psychology,* 1966, **68,** 65–78; D. W. Forrest. Attitudes of undergraduate women to smoking. *Psychological Reports,* 1966, **19,** 83–87.

112. E. E. Levitt and J. A. Edwards. A multivariate study of correlative factors in youthful cigarette smoking. *Developmental Psychology,* 1969, **2,** 5–11.

113. K. J. Lampert, P. K-M. New, and M. L. New. The effectiveness of anti-smoking campaigns: moralistic or scientific approach? *Journal of School Health,* 1966, **36,** 34–40; Michelson, *op. cit.*; Salber et al., *op. cit.*

114. Levitt and Edwards, *op. cit.*

115. McKennell and Bynner, *op. cit.*; Salber et al., *op. cit.*

116. Newman, *op. cit.*

117. Michelson, *op. cit.*

118. D. Horn, F. A. Courts, R. M. Taylor, and E. S. Solomon. Cigarette smoking among high school students. *American Journal of Public Health,* 1959, **49,** 1497–1511.

119. Horn, et al., *op. cit.*; Lampert, et al., *op. cit.*

120. D. Horn. Smoking habits of high school students. Unpublished Manuscript. Presented at New York Academy of Medicine Symposium on Smoking and Health, New York, 1960.

121. Dunn, *op. cit.*

122. Levitt and Edwards, *op. cit.*

123. A. F. Williams. Personality and other characteristics associated with cigarette smoking among young teenagers. *Journal of Health and Social Behavior,* 1973, **14,** 374–380.

124. Horn, et al., *op. cit.*

125. P. Wohlford. Initiation of cigarette smoking: is it related to parental smoking behavior? *Journal of Consulting and Clinical Psychology,* 1970, **34,** 148–151.

126. Forrest, *op. cit.*

127. Ibid.

128. J. H. Arnett. Youth confronts the cigarette. *College Health,* 1962, **11,** 159–161.

129. Michelson, *op. cit.*

130. Bernstein, *op. cit.*; Horn, Modifying smoking habits, *op. cit.*

131. Bernstein, *op. cit.*

132. Ibid.

133. Arnett, *op. cit.*

134. Ibid.

135. Michelson, *op. cit.*

136. Williams, *op. cit.*

137. L. Edson. Schools attack the smoking problem. *American Education,* 1973, **9,** 10–14.

138. Ibid.

139. Ibid.

Chapter 5

Contemporary Adolescent Drug Usage

CHAPTER HIGHLIGHTS

PSYCHOACTIVE DRUGS
  DEPRESSANTS
    BARBITURATES AND RELATED SEDATIVES
    INHALANTS: GLUE AND PAINT SNIFFING
    OPIATE NARCOTICS
  STIMULANTS
    AMPHETAMINES
    COCAINE
  PSYCHEDELICS
    HALLUCINOGENS
    MARIJUANA

REASONS FOR DRUG USE AND NONUSE
PATTERNS OF ADOLESCENT DRUG USAGE
  PERSONALITY AND SOCIAL
    CHARACTERISTICS
  PATTERNS OF MARIJUANA USE AMONG
    ADOLESCENTS
  PATTERNS OF MULTIPLE DRUG USAGE
SUMMARY
REVIEW QUESTIONS
DISCUSSION QUESTIONS

ISSUES

Young people are experimenting increasingly with drugs for recreational purposes.

Psychoactive drugs affect mood, perception, and level of consciousness.

A myriad variety of psychoactive drugs are available on the street.

The effects of drugs used for recreational purposes vary immensely.

Drug advocates do not look upon their behavior as an escape from reality.

Young people say they avoid drugs more for practical than moral reasons.

Light drug users may have only one or two reasons for drug use, but heavy users are likely to have several reasons.

Young people who use drugs may be classified as experimental, depressive, and characterological users.

Most youth who have experimented with marijuana were introduced to it by peers.

Marijuana appears to facilitate the transition of young people to other recreational drugs.

Most young people who experiment with drugs are multiple drug users.

In Civilization and Its Discontents, Sigmund Freud[1] observed the beneficient effect of drugs in helping individuals find happiness and ward off misery. He said that they enable people to "slip away from the oppression of reality and find a refuge in a world of their own where painful feelings do not enter." The expression of these longings through the ages has been abetted by drugs, whether for medicinal, health, or religious purposes. For example, the Indians of Bolivia and Peru chewed coca leaves to ease their hunger pangs and to enhance their capacity for physical output. Opiates have been widely used for centuries to reduce pain. The satisfactions to be derived from marijuana were discovered in China around 2800 B.C. Amphetamines were produced in the 1920s for medicinal purposes, and because they are effective stimulants of the central nervous system, they have been widely used to combat fatigue.

Public pressure exerts a powerful influence on the course of drug usage. When distilled spirits were first introduced in Europe, a period of initial enthusiasm was soon followed by widespread oppression on the part of those who saw them as evil. For a time it was a capital offense in the Middle East to drink coffee, and in Europe, a tobacco user could be mutilated or put to death. In the United States the Temperance Movement arose because alcoholic beverages became a source of concern to many people. Like many opponents of drugs today, the Temperance protagonists considered the use of alcohol a religious sin and a moral transgression. Passage of the Eighteenth Amendment to the Constitution and the Volstead Act represented the zenith in oppression. The fact that the Volstead Act was flagrantly violated and the Eighteenth Amendment was eventually repealed indicates that a socially appealing practice cannot easily be forbidden by decree. Nonetheless, alcohol and tobacco are today the only nonmedical drugs that are legally permitted widespread use in our society. The prevailing opinion is that drugs should be used only under the guidance of a physician for the purpose of facilitating proper body functioning.[2]

The contemporary "drug problem" stems from the fact that more and more persons are straying from "prevailing opinion" and are using various drugs either without appropriate medical supervision or for nonmedical purposes.[3] Socialization has taught young people to affirm drug usage. The relief from pain that they obtained as children when their mothers judiciously administered drugs has predisposed youth to look favorably upon using them. Advertisements have been exhorting young people all of their lives to try new drugs as they come along—cold tablets, gastrointestinal pills, and so forth. As a source of information about drugs, the news media probably is more important than all other sources combined, including friends, family, church, school, and one's own experience.[4] Further, a huge variety of "over-the-counter" substances may be obtained today without prescription in neighborhood pharmacies, supermarkets,

Buying a joint, perhaps for a smoke during the lunch hour.

and "discount" stores. These medications are primarily antacids for upset stomach, sleep-aids for sedation, laxative preparations for bowel functions, and analgesics (aspirins) for headaches and skeletal muscle pain.[5] Circumstances such as these have led young people to the widespread conviction that the magic of chemistry can solve any physical or psychological concern. Why should anyone be sad, anxious, or depressed when drugs can modify moods, create euphoria, and demolish tension?

The positive, pleasurable effects of drugs have led many users to insist that the right to take them for the purpose of experimenting with their own inner world is a private matter. The history of federal and state legislation on drug usage up to the present time, however, has complemented "prevailing opinion" and has looked upon drug usage, on the one hand, as a sign of moral degeneration, and on the other, as a manifestation of illness calling for medical treatment. The dominant viewpoint was established with the passage of the Harrison Narcotic Act of 1914, which established the still prevalent belief that the nonmedical use of drugs is criminally illegal. Users of drugs for nonmedical purposes, as a consequence, have had, for the most part, to obtain drugs from shadowy, often unreliable sources on the "street." The Harrison Act was intended to control the dispensing of opium and cocaine by physicians; it required them to maintain special records of prescriptions and prohibited them from providing narcotics to drug users who had come to rely upon them for maintenance of physical balance. Indeed, the Supreme Court ruled in 1919 that physicians could not even prescribe narcotics to keep habitual users comfortable when they were en route to a hospital. Following passage of the Harrison Narcotics Act, addicts were treated not as patients but as criminals, and their care was removed from the hands of physicians and placed in the hands of law enforcement officers and the court. After the Federal Bureau of Narcotics was established following an amendment to the Harrison Act in 1930, the public also began to view the nonmedical use of most drugs as criminal behavior. The Federal Bureau of Narcotics functioned as a highly moralistic agency, and repeatedly pointed out that death or moral deterioration might result from just one single dose of any of the drugs on its list of dangerous drugs, which expanded markedly with the passing years. In 1937, the Marijuana Tax Act (covering marijuana as a narcotic) was passed, placing similarly stringent taxes and control on its import, sale, and manufacture. Then, in 1965 (as amended in 1968) the federal dangerous drug laws were extended to barbiturates, amphetamines, and any other drug, which "after investigation, is designated by the FDA as having a potential for abuse because of its depressant or stimulant effect on the central nervous system or because of its hallucinogenic effect."[6] Also in 1968, the Federal Bureau of Narcotics and the Bureau of Drug Abuse Control were merged to establish the Bureau of Narcotics and Dangerous Drugs, which was placed under the auspices of the Department of Justice for purposes of law enforcement and drug control. The Comprehensive Drug Abuse Prevention and Control Act of 1970, however, moved authority for drug control to the Department of Health, Education, and Welfare. Although the Attorney General retained authority to control drugs, he or she must now obtain the advice of the Secretary of Health, Education, and Welfare before a drug is either placed under control or released from control. The 1970 bill also consolidated many of the different earlier laws, and substantially reduced the penalties for possession of marijuana, heroin, and other drugs. The legalistic approach was strengthened between 1914 and 1970 to provide increasingly stiff penalties for possession and sale of dangerous drugs, but after 1970 possession of marijuana, for example, was classified as a misdemeanor rather than a felony, thus revealing that a more humane approach to the problem of the drug user was evolving.[7] And the new law gave judges more discretion in sentencing offenders, because it provides for suspended sentences, probation, parole for violators, and permits police records to be eradicated for persons who are deemed to be rehabilitated. But the new legislation continued to be punitive toward those who manufactured, distributed, peddled, or pushed drugs. A first offense for selling heroin, for example, may lead to a minimum sentence of 15 years or a maximum sentence of life imprisonment and a fine of $25,000; these penalties may be doubled for the second offense.

The new emphases in the courts on leniency for drug users, especially in respect to marijuana, has received impetus from a series of reports issued each year since 1972 by the National Commission on Marijuana and Drug Abuse.[8] The reports imply that stiff penalties for the possession of marijuana have been ineffective if not counterproductive in the reduction of marijuana consumption in the United States. Further, they affirm the trend toward heavy criminal penalties for the production and sale of marijuana and light penalties, if any, for its possession and use in small amounts.

PSYCHOACTIVE DRUGS

Kalant and Kalant suggest that a drug is "any substance, other than those required for maintenance of normal health . . . which by its chemical nature alters the structure or function of a living organism."[9] This definition excludes food and other nutriments, but it encompasses caffeine, nicotine, and alcohol, which appear in such forms as coffee, tea, cigarettes, and beverages. Most persons use these substances in moderation, and they suffer no ill effects from them. The psychoactive drugs, on the other hand, constitute a particular category of drug, and they are primarily used for "their effects on mood, perception, and consciousness, regardless of what the normal medical use of such substances may be."[10] Kalant and Kalant classify the mood-altering drugs into three major groups on the basis of their effects on alertness and awareness of external reality. The first group encompasses the depressants, which decrease alertness and diminish impact of the outer environment on thoughts and feelings. The depressants include all drugs that normally are used as sedatives or sleeping pills, tranquilizers, and agents for relief of pain. They also include inhalants (glue, paint, and gasoline) and narcotics (opium, heroin, and morphine). The second classification includes the stimulants, amphetamines and cocaine, that heighten mental activities, enabling large inputs of environmental information to be processed. The third category comprises the psychedelics, which possess varying degrees of depressant and stimulant action. These substances are used primarily to alter the quality rather than the intensity of perceptions. They include the hallucinogens (LSD, mescalene or peyote, psilocybin, etc.) and marijuana, which may affect the central nervous system both as a depressant and stimulant.

Let us now consider the general properties and effects of these psychoactive substances.

Depressants

Barbiturates and Related Sedatives. Barbiturates are highly beneficial central nervous system depressants for treating insomnia, high blood pressure, epilepsy, and various forms of anxiety. When taken in appropriate, supervised amounts, barbiturates slow the breathing rate, lower the blood pressure, and tranquilize the action of the heart, nervous system, and skeletal muscles. The first barbiturate sedatives were invented around the turn of the century, and thousands, each with slightly different characteristics, have been synthesized in the years since then.[11] The barbiturates are known commonly as "downer" drugs, and individually they are called barbs, goof-balls, yellow-jackets, dolls, reds, devils, rainbows, and other names that represent the odor or shape of the capsule in which they are enclosed. Since the drugs are distributed to consumers through an enormous prescription market, to hospitals for anesthesiology, and to laboratories for animal experimental work, a sizeable number of them is channeled easily into the street market.

The effects of barbiturates parallel those of alcohol, and the influence of higher doses characteristically resembles alcoholic intoxication. A user will become relaxed and drowsy, muscular coordination may deteriorate, and emotional control may be less stable. Since downers and alcohol are exceedingly popular recreational substances among young people, they are often combined; for example, a user may take a pill, and then take alcohol to heighten the experience. The user, however, may become intoxicated and confused as the alcohol augments the effect of the barbiturate, and not realizing what quantities he or she has already ingested, take another dose of pills or more alcohol. Such combinations may be lethal.[12] An individual may also inadvertently ingest drugs not recognized as being depressants. Antihistamines for cold and hay fever carry enough depressant action when combined with alcohol and other downers to produce dangerous levels of drowsiness. Serious accidents, especially those involving automobiles, may then occur.[13] Another problem is that tolerance develops swiftly to the psychoactive effects of barbiturates, but not to the amount that will produce a lethal dose. Consequently, when usage of barbiturates is escalated to attain a given effect, a dangerous overdose may ensue.[14]

Barbiturates and other sedatives differ from one another in the "rapidity, intensity, and duration" of their effects.[15] Phenobarbital and barbital are slow-acting, but long-duration drugs, making them useful for prolonged sedation and control of epilepsy. But pentobarbital, secobarbital, and amobarbital are swift-acting, moderate-duration drugs that will induce an intensely satisfying experience in doses that do not also induce sleep, and it is this family of sedatives that is exceedingly popular for recreational uses.

Several sedative compounds have been promoted in recent years as nonbarbiturates, and until the mid-1970s, these substances were controlled much less stringently than the barbiturates themselves. Methaqualone has emerged on the street as the most popular of the sedative compounds. It was first developed in

1951, and after early clinical testing, it was promoted as "a safe, non-addicting, non-barbiturate, sedative-hypnotic" drug.[16] Methaqualone, patented under more than 30 trade names, is known to street users as Quads, Soapers, Paris 400s, Canadian Blues, Quas, Ludes, and Qs. It has sometimes been called the "love drug" and its effects have been described as "aphrodisiac" because of its long duration and capacity to relax muscles. Methaqualone was first marketed in the United States in 1965 as a prescription drug, and it was presumed then that its use would lead to neither physical nor psychological dependence, in spite of investigations in Great Britain and Japan that indicated both forms of dependence might result from extended use.[17] Methaqualone thus was exempt for a time from the criminal penalties associated with barbiturates, and thousands of pills were distributed on the street and on college and high school campuses. As a consequence, by the early 1970s, the nonmedical or recreational use of methaqualone had reached epidemic proportions among young people, and for a time, students "'Luding Out' on Quaaludes, whether roaming the halls in stupors or sitting 'high' in classes," became a serious problem.[18] Methaqualone use today, however, is under strict legal control, and its availability on the street has been greatly reduced.[19]

Inhalants: Glue and Paint Sniffing.   The inhalation of solvent vapors from gasoline, kerosene, lacquer, paint thinner, and lighter and cleaning fluids depresses central nervous system activity. Inhalation has been practiced for decades by industrial workers and others with access to these substances. The advent of plastic cement in the 1960s led younger adolescents, between the ages of 13 and 16, to begin sniffing the fumes of various glues for depressant effects. The problem of abuse became so severe that the Toxic Glue Law was passed to prohibit the sale of glue products to minors, and at the same time an offensive odor, something like that of horseradish, was added to the glue. But curtailment in the availability of glue was paralleled by a rise in the widespread distribution of aerosol sprays, whose propellant gas produces a sweet, highly appealing smell, something like candy cane or mint, and when inhaled along with paint (from a spray can) can induce a potent intoxicating effect.

The art of smelling paint and propellant gas requires some practice before it is mastered. A soft rag, perhaps a diaper, handkerchief, or sock, and a spray can of paint are basic necessities. The cloth usually is sprayed at a distance of about 12 inches. A greater distance leads to the escape of fumes into the atmosphere; a closer distance leads to saturation of the cloth with paint, and a messy outcome. Generally, the rag is sprayed and folded over again and again until it is about the size that can be held in a clenched fist, which is then held to the mouth while the fumes are slowly inhaled. The exhilaration and excitement of a "high" lasts for one-half hour to one hour after inhalation. Sniffers are likely to feel dizzy and to stagger about with slurred speech, double vision, watery eyes, and glassy stares. They are also likely to experience forgetfulness, poor concentration, and lethargy. Their reflex action is decreased, and muscular tremors may occur. Sniffers may have hallucinations during a euphoric state and may lose control of their senses, misjudging heights, distances, and so forth. Often there is direct irritation of the respiratory membranes, resulting in sneezing, coughing, and chest pains. The "high" usually dissipates after several hours of sleep, but headaches may follow. Some researchers hold, too, that habitual sniffing may result in pulmonary injury, kidney and brain damage, liver enlargement, and irritation of the eyes.[20]

A majority of paint sniffers report feeling a "buzz" that they associate with the crackling sound of electricity a live wire makes when it contacts metal. Montiel provides the following two accounts of how young sniffers perceive the "buzz:"

After sniffing, you get a buzz. It felt kind of good the first time; it's a nice feeling. It seems like you're in another world. Everything is different, but then the hangover is something else. Your fingers and hands all get full of paint.

Sometimes the buzz comes to me, too. It comes up my legs and when we were sniffing the last time, I felt it and I tried to put my feet up but it still kept on coming up. You can hear it, too. I can see the buzz, just like little wires, pure white; you can see it easily at night. You just look at the buzz and it just stays right in front of you. Like when we were walking, the streets and cars would go by; you would just walk all crooked.[21]

Opiate Narcotics. The terms "opiate" and "narcotic" are synonyms for opium and drugs derived from opium—codeine, morphine, and heroin. These drugs are depressants and sedatives which are produced from juice at the base of the poppy flower. Opium, which may be smoked in a special pipe or eaten as snuff, was introduced in the United States by Chinese laborers who worked on railroad construction gangs in the late 1800s. Codeine, although relatively weak, is an effective cough suppressant and a reasonably good pain-killer. It has been a popular ingredient in patent cough medicine and, because of its weakness, has been relatively exempt from legal control. Codeine thus has been available to young people in cough syrups and is often swigged with beer, wine, or hard liquor to achieve fairly substantial highs. Morphine, a valuable pain-killer, is widely used by physicians to relieve short-term acute suffering and to reduce pain from bone fractures, cancer, and so forth. Morphine is a fine, feathery powder that was first used in the United States during the Civil War, shortly after the invention of the hypodermic needle. Heroin, a white crystalline powder resembling morphine (from which it is extracted) possesses, grain for grain, ten times the potency of morphine, and it is regarded by drug authorities and street users alike as one of the "hardest" drugs. It is sold by pushers in the form of a powder in "caps" or "decks"; it is always cut or diluted by the trafficker with substances like milk sugar or quinine. The user, whose bulk powder may contain from 3 percent to 10 percent heroin, usually mixes it with a small amount of liquid and heats it. When the drug is dissolved in the liquid, the substance is drawn with a hypodermic syringe and injected or "mainlined" into a vein. Although heroin may be taken by inhalation or swallowing, "mainlining" produces the most pronounced and rapid effect; however, because it is often done crudely, scars and hepatitis commonly result.

Typically, the first reaction produced by heroin is an easing of fear and a relief from worry. Users are likely to feel drowsy and lethargic; to be indifferent to their environment; to feel euphoric and confident that everything will be all right. When users first begin to take the drug, they may experience loss of appetite, constipation, vomiting, itching, and constriction of pupils. One injection provides a high for about four hours. After the effects of their first injection wear off, they feel no pain and are relaxed and steady. After about three injections, users may begin to feel slight withdrawal pains about 12 to 18 hours after each injection. After five or six injections, withdrawal becomes even more painful, and after ten injections, users are likely to become physically dependent. At this time users must have narcotics to maintain their physical composure. And once they are hooked, stronger and stronger doses are required to reach comparable highs because their bodies readily develop tolerance for the drug. The withdrawal symptoms may be terrifying and painful; they may include chills, nausea, cramps, diarrhea, severe aches in back and leg muscles, and an obsession to obtain a fix. The intensity of the symptoms vary with the degree of physical dependence, but they usually reach a peak within 36 to 72 hours. Then they diminish gradually for the next five to ten days, but insomnia, nervousness, aches, and pains may persist for many days or even years afterward.

Physical dependence on the opiates may be treated medically rather easily, but successful rehabilitation usually requires establishing the user in a strong, supportive environment. To be effective, "successful programs must include checks to avoid cheating, vocational training, counseling, and group work to help individuals learn new life-style patterns apart from their drug sub-culture to be effective."[22] Methadone maintenance programs have evolved in recent years to assist heroin users make their way in the environment. Methadone is a long-acting opiate that will block withdrawal and craving symptoms for about 24 hours when properly administered. Research in England suggests that when legitimate medical care replaces the hazards of using impure drugs, unsanitary injection techniques, and a criminal life style, good health and productive work may be compatible with opiate dependence.[23]

Stimulants

Amphetamines.   The amphetamines act on the brain's arousal system. Their effects suppress sleep and appetite, but importantly for the purpose of effecting mood changes, they push individuals to substantial expenditures of energy, check fatigue, and produce feelings of alertness, self-confidence, and well-being. "Thinking is faster and learning proceeds more rapidly."[24] Persons under the influence of amphetamines enhance their reaction to stimuli and are able to process information more swiftly. Because they feel better able to cope with the environment, they may also experience a sense of exhilaration, euphoria, and power.[25]

Amphetamines are available in a variety of forms. Benzedrine (bennies, peaches, cross tops) and Dexedrine (dexies, Xmas trees) are available in many kinds of orally administered tablets and capsules. Methedrine (speed, crystal, meth) comes in a powderlike form (known as crystals) and is usually sold in capsules, which are then mixed with water and taken intravenously. The recreational use of amphetamines began when users started taking them for their side effects. In the 1930s, amphetamine pellets were put in commercial inhalators to produce vapors for shrinking nasal membranes to relieve headcold stuffiness. Users would soak the pellets in a liquid and drink it to obtain a kick. Dieters sometimes consumed extra diet pills, not to curb their appetites, but to achieve euphoria. During the late 1940s students began to use amphetamines at examination time to help them cram all night. Most of the amphetamine preparations were distributed loosely and were readily available on the street until 1972, when stringent federal legislation reduced their general availability.[26] Moreover, because tolerance develops rapidly with the daily use of amphetamines, especially in respect to their ability "to produce euphoria, arousal, and decreased appetite," the Federal Food and Drug Administration has required that diet preparations based on these drugs be removed from the market. "In this respect, the only uniformly agreed-upon medical uses for amphetamines today are in the treatment of hyperactive children and in treating a pathological sleeping condition known as narcolepsy."[27]

Sophisticated participants in the drug culture will typically turn to amphetamines when they want a swift, jolting kick followed by euphoria, and they will particularly prefer methedrine for this purpose. An amphetamine high is achieved rather dramatically when methedrine is injected directly into a vein, but the toxic dangers also increase—hence the phrase "speed kills." The full impact of speed can be felt even before the needle is withdrawn.[28] Shooting speed has been compared to the jolt of electric shock or the sensation of having ice water splashed on one's face.[29] As the effect "rushes" through the blood stream, there is an intense feeling akin to sexual orgasm. The appetite is depressed, but the action of the heart and the metabolic processes are stepped up: there is a dryness of the mouth, a dilation of the pupils, blurred vision, and profuse perspiration which accompany increases in the heart rate, blood pressure, palpitation, and breathing. During a speed high, it is reported that male and female orgasms can be delayed so that sexual activity may continue at a highly pleasurable level for hours.[30] Concentration on any one idea becomes difficult and relaxation is almost impossible; users become preoccupied with their own thoughts and they may engage in meaningless, compulsive behavior, such as the stringing of beads for hours.[31] Users also may experience vivid hallucinations and under slight provocation may engage in physically violent behavior. Minor noises, for example, "may be misinterpreted as voices talking behind the person's back, and out of these he may construct paranoid delusions that people are talking about him or plotting against him. He may even commit violent acts in response to these imaginary events or people." Further, sensory information may be misinterpreted; for example, sensations from the skin may give rise to hallucinations in which worms seem to be crawling beneath the skin, and the user may severely scratch and injure himself or herself by trying to dig them out.[32]

After about 8 hours, a light user will crash (come down from the effects) and is likely to be sleepy and hungry, and perhaps somewhat jittery. A high may be heightened for habitual users who might extend it for as many as three or four days. During this period users may "shoot up" from one to ten times a day, always striving for a peak experience. They are unlikely to eat or sleep. Eventually, fatigue overcomes them, and as they terminate the high they are likely to lapse into a deep sleep, ranging from 24 to 48 hours, and eat ravenously upon awakening.[33] The crash at the end of an intense high may bring extreme depression as well as strong anxiety, irritableness, violent behavior, and suicidal tendencies.[34] The intensity of the depression period is painful, and many habitual users shoot speed again, thus initiating another cycle. "Experienced users have learned to circumvent this problem by injecting depressants or opiates, especially heroin, to smooth out the post-run letdown."[35]

Cocaine.   Cocaine, one of the more powerful natural stimulants, has become today the new "in" drug in America for the affluent. Cocaine is a white crystalline powder extracted from the leaves of the coca bush and is known to its users as coke, snow, white girl, blow, and candy. Most of it it smuggled into the United States from South America via "couriers" or "mules" who carry it in the false bottoms of suitcases or hidden on their bodies. It has a reputation as the "champagne" of drugs, mainly because of its street price, which ranges today between $40 and $100 for one gram (or $1000 to $2000 per ounce). Its status as a prestige drug is enhanced by jewelers who hammer silver and mold gold into fashionable "coke" spoons, which persons wear ornamentally around their necks.

Cocaine generally is inhaled by snorting or sniffing, and the spoons are used to convey the powder to the nostrils. The effects of cocaine are felt immediately, but it is necessary to repeat the inhalation approximately every 15 to 30 minutes to maintain intense arousal and euphoria. Approximately 40 "administrations" or "hits" may be obtained from a single gram. Its use produces a strong, local anesthetic action that numbs the mucous membranes. Repeated and heavy use may destroy the membranes lining the nasal passages, causing the user to have a perpetual and painful running nose. Heavy use, while apparently not physiologically addicting, may also lead to serious psychological disorientation.

Psychedelics

Hallucinogens. The hallucinogens produce perceptions of objects that do not actually exist or sensory impressions that have no direct environmental basis. Mescaline, one of the hallucinogens, has been used for thousands of years. It is derived from the buttons or tops of a cactus known as mescal and has long been used in religious rituals. Indeed, several Indian groups in the Southwest have been given exemption from federal laws to use mescaline. Hallucinogens first came under government regulation in 1965 when it was realized that they could be synthesized in simple kitchen-chemistry laboratories and that the manufactured varieties were far more powerful in their capacity to alter the senses than were those derived from the cactus plant. The most widely used of these drugs is LSD (lysergic acid diethylamide), popularly known as "acid." LSD was first synthesized by Dr. Albert Hofmann in Switzerland, in 1938, from ergot alkaloids, a fungus that grows as rust on rye grain. In 1943, Hofmann discovered the hallucinating effects of the drug accidentally. His initial impression led him to believe that LSD simulated psychoses and that it would be useful in doing research on mental disorders. As William Jenner had evoked cowpox to study smallpox, psychiatrists initially thought that researchers could evoke psychosis to study schizophrenia. But later it was found that the effects of LSD differed too much from those of real psychoses for it to be of much therapeutic value.

LSD is odorless, tasteless, and effective in exceedingly high dilutions. A single ounce of LSD is sufficient to provide about 300,000 average doses. A typical dose—enough for a trip—is hardly more than a speck. LSD may be distributed as a powder in a capsule, as a small white pill, as a liquid that can be dropped onto sugar cubes or crackers, or as a mixture ready for injection into the body. Visual identification of the drug is impossible, and it can easily be disguised and transported on sugar cubes, chewing gum, hard candy, mints, crackers, blotter paper, postage stamps, handkerchiefs, aspirins, vitamins, antacid pills, and so forth. Most users face the common problem of not knowing exactly what they are ingesting. A user is likely to obtain acid from an unknown source, in an unknown amount, and of unknown purity. "Drug analysis services have reported on the extremely poor quality and credibility of hallucinogens sold on the street, pointing out the difficulties associated with trying to evaluate adverse reactions reported with these preparations."[36]

A dose of 50 to 200 micrograms, about the size of a speck of dust, usually initiates a trip of approximately 8 to 16 hours. The effects of LSD vary, depending on the user's mood, expectations, and previous experience with the drug. However, several unpleasant physical reactions generally occur within a few moments after ingestion. "Very low doses produce only the body and perceptual effects and are similar to those seen with amphetamines."[37] The sensations derived from higher doses are like those of intense fear—blood pressure rises, pupils dilate, pulse quickens, heart-rate increases, hands and feet shake, palms grow cold and sweaty, and facial paleness, shivering, chills and goose pimples, irregular breathing, nausea, and loss of appetite occurs. But psychological effects supersede biochemical ones within an hour, and during the next several hours striking changes in reality perception may evolve. The walls of a room may pulse in and out; colors may seem saturated and brilliant. Users may see flat objects stand out in three dimensions; taste, smell, hearing, and touch may seem more acute. One sensory impression may merge into another—music may, for example, appear as colors and colors may acquire taste. Actually, the ability of users to perceive objects and to make practical judgments may be severely impaired. They are likely to find concentration difficult, and objectively trivial issues, such as the way a cup is placed on a saucer, may take on a great deal of importance. Or they may become fascinated and absorbed by a nearby object, like a chair or vase. Detachment from reality may lead users to think that they can fly or float, and they might try to leap out of a high window or try to walk on a body of water. They might even step in front of a moving car, train, or bus believing that they would not be harmed. While driving they might see a red light and become enamored with the hue of the light rather than realize that they should stop.[38] But users may also begin to feel that the drug has them in its power and, sensing that they can no longer control what is happening, they may panic, become frightened, and feel that they are losing their minds. They may become increasingly suspicious, fearing that someone is trying to harm them or control their thinking—a feeling that may last for about three days. Eventually, after about 12 to 24 hours, the trip comes to a close with the letdown accompanied by mild fatigue and a period of insomnia.

Tolerance develops rapidly to LSD: the same dose taken repeatedly several days in a row will lose its sensation-evoking power. The swift development of tolerance and the capriciousness of the experience have greatly reduced the popularity of LSD over the past decade, and many street users have switched their preferences to other hallucinogens thought to be safer. "In particular, mescaline and psilocybin are in great demand on the street, although analysis results indicate that these substances are rare and that LSD is usually what is sold under these names. Consequently, although the intentional use of LSD is definitely on the decline in this country, its unintentional use is still prevalent."[39]

Marijuana. Marijuana is derived from the Indian hemp plant, *Cannabis sativa*. Cannabis has been known to man for thousands of years as a healing drug. In the fifteenth century B.C. it was used in China as a source of textile fibers, a means of relieving pain during surgery, a ritual potion, and an intoxicating agent. Eventually its use spread to India, the Middle East, and to every corner of the world. Today the stocks and stems of the cannabis plant are used in the manufacture of rope, fiber, and paper; its seeds, after sterilization, are used occasionally for birdseed. However, marijuana's biggest appeal is in its ability to induce intoxication. Surprisingly, Americans had little interest in it until it became popular in Hollywood and among the artistic circles of New York and Chicago in the late 1930s and early 1940s. Marijuana was declared a dangerous narcotic in 1937, which forced recreational users to become secretive. The extent of secretiveness associated with marijuana use has changed markedly, however, during the past decade. Whereas in the late 1960s marijuana popularity was concentrated among youth who opposed traditional values and the prevailing political ideology, its use has spread today to involve more than half of the 18- to 25-year-old age group, and it has now lost much of its antiestablishment symbolism.[40]

The cannabis plant is a tall annual, reaching a mature height of four 4 to 16 feet. It is adaptable to a wide variety of climates, needs little cultivation, and thrives in mild temperate zones throughout the world. The plant is chemically very complex. The major psychoactive ingredient is known as "delta-9-tetrahydrocanniabinol," but the part played by several other ingredients may also be important in producing other cannabis effects. How these ingredients function alone or in combination has yet to be determined. Research into the effects of marijuana is much more difficult, for example, than that into the effects of alcohol. Marijuana is used in much smaller quantities than alcohol, and it is very rapidly transformed into different body chemicals. Detection techniques have improved recently, however, and significant advances in isolating the effects of cannabis constituents are likely to occur in the near future.

The THC ingredient is known to be in the resin of the plant, which appears in the flowering, stringy-white tops of the female plant and in the odd-numbered leaves of both the male and the female plants. A major botanical feature of the hemp plant is its astonishing number of varieties; in an earlier age, they were thought to constitute different species. When the climate of the growing area is warm and moist, the plant will produce a strong trunk and fibrous stems that are suitable for textiles but have little intoxicating potency; when the climate is hot, dry, and sunny, the plant will have poorer textile properties but greater intoxicating potentialities, presumably due to the resin secreted by the plant as a defense against heat.[41] Moreover, the unfertilized female flower yields the largest quantities of resin, and they must be carefully pruned and culled to ensure a high THC yield. The plants must be harvested just before the flowers blossom, or the potency inherent in the resin will be lost.

The marijuana as purchased is a mixture of leaves and flowering tops (containing resin) and superfluous parts of the plant such as stems, stalks, and seeds (which have no resin). Further, adulterants such as tobacco, oregano, grass, and so forth are often added to increase the bulk and thus the profit to the seller.[42]

The THC content, and thus the capacity to intoxicate, varies enormously across mixtures of marijuana. "This variability results from differences in plant genetic origin, conditions of cultivation and preparation of the material including the degree of concentration of leaves and flowering tops."[43] The weakest mixture, known as "bhange" or "grass" is composed of the dried matured leaves and flowering chutes of the female plant, and contains about 5 to 8 percent resin. A stronger mixture is prepared by "manicuring" or finely grinding the leaves and flowers, and then alternatively drying and pressing them, a process that compresses the marijuana, yielding a resin content of about 40 percent. Since the resin is soluble in oil or alcohol, sometimes the marijuana is placed in one of these agents; later the bulk is strained, and the oil or alcohol cooked out. The two most common names for the resulting product are "ganja" and "hashish," both of which are fairly high in resin content. Although formerly a rare product, hashish oil has become a relatively recent addition on the street market.[44]

Marijuana is usually prepared in a form that can be smoked in either a pipe or cigarette, although many people prefer to drink marijuana tea, eat grass brownies, or sniff it. It is often smoked in a group, where the pipe or cigarette is passed from one person to another. The burning substance produces a heavy, acrid odor, like burning rope or hay; thus, for aesthetic reasons, the odor often is masked by the simultaneous burning of incense. When users purchase marijuana in bulk, they must strain out the twigs and seeds, and they are almost certain to roll their own joints. Consequently, most of the marijuana sold in the United States, especially that which is sold to high school students, is usually of poor quality, grown under adverse conditions, and diluted with common garden grass. Given the variations and the quality of marijuana harvests, the quality of THC in the different preparations, and the dilution that occurs as it passes from hand to hand in marketing, inexperienced adolescent users may literally smoke "weed" or "grass."

Most smokers will use marijuana or hashish interchangeably, depending on availability, how intoxicated they want to be, how fast they want to reach a given high, and how long they want to remain high. The fifth annual Marijuana and Health Report to the Congress of the United States divides the effects of marijuana into two groups: (1) The acute consequences of cannabis intoxication and (2) the long-range consequences of regular or chronic use.[45] Let us consider the circumstances described in each category:

1. *Effects of intoxication.* The most consistently reported physiological effects of marijuana include increase in heart rate and a reddening of the eyes, but impairment of memory, arm-and-leg coordination, reflex action, and time-and-space judgment also frequently occurs. Experimental studies clearly indicate, for example, that driving under the influence of marijuana is hazardous. Apparently, there is a dose-related impairment in the ability to attend to peripheral stimuli while driving, which might interfere with a driver's response to a car suddenly emerging from a side street or a pedestrian stepping off of the curb near the car.[46] Tasks that are relatively simple and with which the user is familiar are influenced less than complex tasks. At lower doses research evidence shows that when the situation so demands, users are often able to "suppress the marijuana high."[47] Further, many users have reported enhanced auditory, visual, and tactual awareness and sensitivity, but experimental research has not confirmed these reports.[48] And adequate data elucidating the effect of marijuana use on sexual functioning are not yet available. Small to moderate doses appear to facilitate release of inhibitions, but larger doses and/or chronic use of marijuana may actually diminish sexual interest and potency in males. Koff[49] has reported that males

who smoke one joint or less claimed more of an increase in sexual enjoyment than those who smoked two or more joints per sitting. Koff suggests that mild dosages of marijuana, relative to strong dosages that result in intoxication, may enhance both sexual desire and enjoyment of sexual activity.

2. *Effects of chronic use.*   Systematic, controlled studies in which known doses of marijuana have been administered over extended periods have confirmed that users may develop a tolerance to cannabis. Further, irritability, restlessness, decreased appetite, sleep disturbance, sweating, tremor, nausea, vomiting and diarrhea may occur as aftereffects following unusually high doses, but such changes are not commonly observed among typical users. Chronic cannabis smokers, nonetheless, may develop bronchitis, obstructive pulmonary defects, and chronic cough.[50]

A variety of psychological disorders also are associated with the use of cannabis; however, whether the psychopathology is an antecedent to use, a consequence, or a mere coincidence is still very much open to question. A best guess is that cannabis use, like that of many other psychoactive drugs, will sometimes be an antecedent, a consequence, or coincidental to psychopathology, depending on the overall vulnerability of the users to psychological disturbance.[51]

REASONS FOR DRUG USE AND NONUSE

Countless young persons have investigated mood-modifying, psychoactive drugs as a means of finding avenues to more satisfying and self-fulfilling life styles. Drug advocates themselves do not look upon their behavior as "escape from reality" or a "false reality." Farnsworth[52] points out that drug users believe that drugs will aid them in expanding their consciousness, that is, in exploring new areas of the mind or in opening up areas that are usually not consciously functioning. They feel that they can search for new values, enjoy heightened aesthetic responses, acquire self-knowledge and understanding of others, and experience pleasure and creativity "in a way that is quick, reliable, and reasonably safe." In contrast, persons who oppose drug usage for nonmedical purposes may view seeking to expand one's consciousness via drugs as an instance of personality pathology or social deviance.[53]

The number of reasons persons may offer for either integrating drugs into their life styles or avoiding them entirely is extensive. Fortunately, considerable insight into these reasons is provided by a recent preliminary report based on a study of the nonmedical use of psychoactive drugs among young men in the United States.[54] The investigation shows how the young men ranked several representative reasons for both discontinued and continued use. The sample of 2,510 young men was selected to be representative of all males in the general population who were 20 to 30 years old in 1974. The pattern of reasons for avoiding drugs appears to be similar across eight psychoactive substances—alcohol, marijuana, psychedelics, stimulants, sedatives, heroin, opiates, and cocaine—for both those who had never used any drugs and those who had tried them only a few times. The two most common reasons for general drug avoidance included "possible bad effects on health" and "dislike or expectation of undesirable effects." In contrast, the least frequently reported reason for avoiding use was "because you couldn't get it, or it costs too much," except for heroin and cocaine, where "because family or friends would not approve" proved to be an even less significant reason for using these drugs. Reasons ranked in the middle-range as a basis for drug-avoidance included "fear of developing dependency," "fear of trouble with police," and "fear of loss of self-control." The pattern of reasons revealed by the investigation suggests that young men look more to practical than to moral values in explaining why they hold negative attitudes toward drug usage. The most frequently stated reasons for not using drugs, for example, were practical and expedient—effect on health, did not like it, might cause trouble with police, loss of self-control—rather than either expressions of moral or religious convictions or of commitment to the ethical standards of one's family or friends.

Table 1 provides nine reasons given by users for their interest in the same eight drugs—alcohol, marijuana, psychedelics, stimulants, sedatives, heroin, opiates, and cocaine. The "experimental users" shown in Table 1 are those who used each drug less than 10 times; the "other users" are those who used it 10 times or more. As the data indicate, the most important reason given by both experimental and regular users for use of all drugs except alcohol and stimulants is "to get high, or stoned." For example, nearly 100 percent of the regular users of psychedelics, heroin, and cocaine, 93 percent of the users of marijuana, 80 percent of the users of opiates, and over 70 percent of the users of sedatives sought a "high" from the drugs. The users of alcohol, on the one hand, said that they used it primarily because it was expected of them, and users of stimulants, on the other, sought largely to find help staying awake or alert. The second and third ranked general reasons for drug usage were "because you are bored" and "because it was expected in the situation," except for psychedelics and cocaine, where "to heighten the senses," ranked second. It is noteworthy that "to heighten the senses" was ranked less significant in general as a reason for drug usage than was "to get high, or stoned." The former reason was ranked fourth for marijuana and stimulants, and sixth to eighth for all other drugs by both experimental and regular users. "From force of habit" is shown

Table 1
Reasons for Drug Use, for Experimenters and Other Users of Each Drug (Percentages)

		Alco-hol	Mari-juana	Psyche-delics	Stimu-lants	Seda-tives	Her-oin	Opi-ates	Co-caine
Experimental Users[a] (n)		(93)	(423)	(291)	(207)	(177)	(72)	(300)	(214)
Other Users[a] (n)		(2341)	(959)	(259)	(374)	(232)	(76)	(193)	(138)
To help you get to sleep or relax?	Experimental users	10	8	3	5	50	13	27	10
	Other users	37	47	4	4	68	50	51	12
To help you forget your worries or troubles?	Experimental users	8	7	9	9	24	14	16	11
	Other users	36	32	19	18	50	54	36	28
Because it was expected of you in the situation?	Experimental users	40	43	23	19	18	18	21	21
	Other users	49	40	23	19	21	29	23	19
To help you stay awake, or alert?	Experimental users	1	1	7	75	2	0	4	13
	Other users	2	6	24	90	3	11	4	34
To get high, or stoned?	Experimental users	12	53	82	48	72	75	75	87
	Other users	65	93	97	73	72	99	79	97
From force of habit, or because you were *used* to using it?	Experimental users	0	1	3	2	3	4	4	4
	Other users	28	26	13	21	21	55	17	15
To heighten your senses—like taste, touch, or hearing?	Experimental users	0	11	39	31	4	8	12	35
	Other users	6	46	56	42	8	22	22	47
Because you were bored, and it helped pass the time?	Experimental users	17	14	23	18	24	21	26	26
	Other users	48	56	41	33	36	46	40	42
To enable you to get through the work day?	Experimental users	0	1	2	39	3	3	5	5
	Other users	5	14	5	59	9	33	14	17

Source: J. A. O'Donnell, H. L. Voss, R. R. Clayton, G. T. Slatin, and R. G. W. Room, *Young Men and Drugs—A Nation-wide Survey*, Rockville, Maryland: National Institute on Drug Abuse, 1976. Reprinted by permission.
[a] Quasi-medical users are excluded, for stimulants, sedatives and opiates.

in Table 1 to be of less value to both experimental and regular drug users, except for those who used heroin, where it was the second most frequently cited reason for use. "To get through the day" is shown to be of very low value for every drug except the stimulants, where it was ranked third. The other reasons shown in Table 1 varied immensely in their significance across the different drugs. For example, "to sleep or relax" ranked high for sedatives and opiates, in the high to middle range for alcohol, marijuana, and heroin, but low for psychedelics, cocaine, and, of course, stimulants. "To forget worries or troubles" ranked as high as third for regular users of heroin and sedatives, as low as eighth for regular users of stimulants, and fluctuated between these extremes among users of the other drugs.

The data reported in Table 1 indicate that several reasons account for the popularity of each street drug. Indeed, any reason at all seems to serve those who have used heroin and cocaine ten or more times, and this is almost as true for several other drugs. For marijuana, stimulants, and opiates, eight of the nine reasons were endorsed by at least 10 percent of those who were regular users. And some drug use, especially of the stimulants, sedatives, and opiates, appears to have been quasi-medical, that is, instrumental in facilitating work or rest. On the whole, however, the reasons for drug use shown in Table 1 appear to be largely recreational; namely, the salient reasons relate to the power of given drugs to generate psychoactive effects.[55]

PATTERNS OF ADOLESCENT DRUG USAGE

Personality and Social Characteristics

Young people reflect their personality styles in the myriad nonmedical and recreational uses to which they put drugs. For purpose of rough classification, Zinberg[56] has distinguished two basic styles: the "oblivion-seekers" (who move away from life) and the "experience-seekers" (who move toward life). He describes oblivion-seekers as being casualties of society. They may turn to drugs to escape from pressures and worries, achieve uninhibited enjoyment and relaxation, or attain a state of boredom in which nothing much happens—in other words, to escape from life styles that have become relatively hopeless for them. The experience-seekers, in contrast, use drugs to embrace life. They aim to gain psychological insight and to heighten their aesthetic appreciation through the vividness of color, visual harmonies, sharper definition of details, shifts in sense of time, and greater depth perception.

Proskauer and Rolland[57] suggest that the personality styles of drug users fall into three rather than two patterns. The researchers see drug usage for some

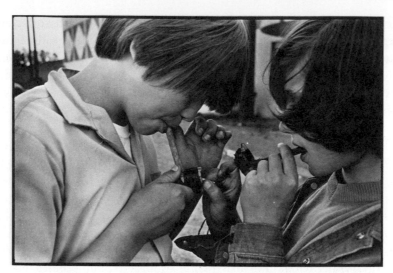

Young people are introduced to marijuana mainly through their peers.

youth as representing a "'moving in' on society in a way that is often ethical and courageous;" for other youth they view it as leading to "a lifetime of dereliction." Because drug usage may become part of young people's "adaptive and defensive" choices to life, "for a combination of intrapsychic, familial, and social reasons," Proskauer and Rolland contend that a broad range of personality antecedents lie behind drug usage, and argue, therefore, for a classifying system based on three categories. Youth who fall into the first group, *the experimental drug users,* comprise those who use drugs at one time or another perhaps out of desire for new sources of aesthetic or sensual experience, in defiance of adult authority, or as a consequence of peer pressure. The young people in this group cannot be said to have a "drug problem" as such; moreover, the researchers say, it is crucial to distinguish the youth who are simply experimenting with drugs from other drug users for two important reasons. First, casual experimentation is unlikely to lead to physical, psychological, or social damage; two, labeling mere experimenters as confirmed "drug abusers" and subjecting them to legal or disciplinary action and social rejection may lead them to view themselves as heavy drug users and to act accordingly. Youth who fall into the second classification, *the depressive drug users,* comprise those young people "who are seeking adaptive and defensive solutions primarily to feelings of emptiness, hopelessness, loneliness, and worthlessness through drug experience."[58] These youth use drugs as an attractive way of avoiding pain and bypassing the active work needed to establish mature relationships. The researchers note that expression of their feelings may manifest itself in complex forms, for example, somatic complaints, irritability, poor school performance, frantic pleasure-seeking, and self-punishment. When young people have difficulty meeting expectations regarding achievement in school and work, or when their intrafamilial relationships are strained, their feelings of depression may become intensified and as an alternative, drugs may produce a "passive, self-absorbed state, accompanied by motor quiescence," which "serves to relieve young people for a time of anxieties about the emptiness, conflict, or violence within."[59] The youth in the third group, *the characterological drug users,* comprise a relatively small group of young people who, perhaps as a result of deprivation, inconsistency, and rejection early in life, attained major personality deficits, and now seek to escape through drugs from tensions produced by developmental and environmental stresses. These young people had developed serious personality difficulties before they started using drugs, and as adolescents and adults, very likely contended with "low tolerance for frustration, poor impulse control, a relatively poor capacity to bear anxiety and depression, trouble relating to others in a mutual way, and unreliable reality testing, especially under internal or external stress."[60] Proskauer and Rolland suggest that for them, "a reliable source of satisfaction, such as a drug, becomes mandatory in order to achieve transient contentment in an otherwise unstable and ungratifying existence."[61] Geist[62] has described adolescent drug users who resemble those with characterological disorders as ascribing to a "philosophy of non-existence." He says that these adolescents mainly use hard drugs. They live in "a state of animated death—a world of being high, stoned, freaked out, tripping, getting off—a partial suspension of worldly participation in order to cope with early dilemmas which seem unresolvable when approached with humanly psychic efforts."

Patterns of Marijuana Use Among Adolescents

The number of young people who may be classified as depressive or characterological drug users is miniscule relative to the quantity of youth who are experimenters, especially in respect to marijuana. Nearly one adult in five (19 percent) and nearly one adolescent in four between 12 and 17 years of age (23 percent) has experimented at least once with marijuana. Moreover, "virtually everyone," adult and adolescent alike, who has recently used marijuana indicates an intention to use it again.[63]

How, then, are young people introduced to marijuana? The research evidence overwhelmingly affirms that peers play a more significant role than anyone else in affecting the pattern of young people's marijuana use. Since we live in a "pill-oriented" society dominated by adult consumption of tranquilizers, barbiturates, and stimulants, one might reasonably expect that young people, sharing the cultural ethos of their parents, would become initiated into drug use via parental modeling.[64] The highest rates of adolescent marijuana use indeed belong to youth whose parents regularly consume over-the-counter drugs. But as Kandel[65] observes, the crucial factor in determining whether young people will use marijuana is whether their peers also use it; the researcher shows convincingly that parental behavior exerts little more than a "modulating" effect on peer influence. Peer support *and* parental tolerance, for example, may give young people considerable encouragement as they experiment with drugs. Kandel's investigation contrasted peer and parental influence on adolescent marijuana use. It included over 8,000 young people who were representative of public secondary school students living in the state of New York. The researcher found that only 2 percent of the adolescents who reported that none of their close friends were marijuana users had used it themselves. Seventeen percent were users, however, if they perceived a "few" of their close friends as users. And the percentage of youth who were users continued to rise as the proportion of friends whom they saw as users also rose. Fifty percent of the adolescents reported themselves as users, for example, when they perceived "some" of their friends as users, 80 percent were users when they saw "most" of their friends involved with marijuana, and all of them were users when they perceived over 90 percent of their friends using it. Further, adolescent marijuana use among adolescents was especially highly correlated with the use patterns of a friend. Only 15 percent of those adolescents, for example, whose friends reported never having used marijuana also used it, but of those whose friends reported having smoked marijuana 60 times or more, 79 percent also had used it. Although the likelihood that adolescents will themselves be users increases with the frequency with which marijuana is used by friends, the impact of friends' use levels off rather swiftly. If one or two friends of an adolescent had tried marijuana even only once, he or she was very likely to have tried it, too, but heavy usage relative to light usage by a friend does not appreciably increase the likelihood that the adolescent also will be a user. Kandel also notes that drug users are more likely to be found among youth who visit daily with their friends who use marijuana, see them even over their parents' objections, and when faced with a problem, respect their friends' opinions more highly than those of their parents.[66]

Several independent studies corroborate Kandel's findings. Fisher and Steckler[67] report that from 70 to 90 percent of the young persons who use marijuana, whether rarely or daily, were introduced to the drug by friends. And Clark et al.[68] indicate that high school youth who have tried marijuana report that their friends who used marijuana were their primary sources of information about it. Weis[69] points out that marijuana generally is unavailable to adolescents until they gain access to a social group in their peer culture that uses it. The researcher thus insists that there is a differential probability of becoming an adolescent drug user, which is determined by an adolescent's "social-type identity and position within the peer culture." And "it is exclusion from these social-type groups which restricts access to drugs and certain styles of drug use."[70]

Personality style appears also to be a central factor in explaining adolescent marijuana use. Burkett and Jensen[71] suggest that marijuana use is based principally within a sector of youth who have at least temporarily withdrawn from "conventional" adult-sponsored and youth-supported activities. But the researchers also point out that youth who have withdrawn to the extent that they have low attachments to their family and have few, if any, friends in school who use marijuana, are no more likely to use it than are those with strong conventional ties. Jessor, Jessor, and Finney[72] also emphasize the significance of personality styles. The researchers compared marijuana use among male and female junior high, senior high, and college students. They found that across all ages marijuana use was related to instances of problem-prone behavior involving alcohol, sex, activism, and general deviance. In contrast, conventional behaviors involving church, school, and clubs and organizations tended to vary inversely with its use. Relative to nonusers, the users tended to value independence, decry school achievement, be tolerant of deviance, manifest little traditional religiosity, perceive themselves as having limited compatability with their peers and parents, and acknowledge greater peer relative to parent influence on their views. Victor et al.[73] found, similarly, that "openness to experience"—high creativity, adventuresomeness, novelty seeking, and low authoritarianism—was descriptive of marijuana users in a college-oriented high school. Blake et al.[74] also reported that relatively bold but less conscientious adolescents—youth who seemed ready to disregard rules in seeking adventure and to perceive themselves as somewhat unique and innovative—more frequently used marijuana. Finally, Knight et al.[75] found, too, that in a college-age population, disaffection with the institutions of law, government, marriage, and the work ethic were related to marijuana usage.

Patterns of Multiple Drug Usage

Two recent research investigations clearly reveal that young people who use "street" drugs engage in multiple drug usage.[76] The data presented in Table 2 are drawn from the preliminary report of the nonmedical use of psychoactive drugs among young men in the United States who are between 20 and 30 years

Table 2
Percent of Users and Nonusers of Each Drug Who Have Used the Other Drugs[a]

	Tobacco		Alcohol		Marijuana		Psychedelics		Stimulants		Sedatives		Heroin		Opiates		Cocaine	
	Yes	No	Yes	No	Yes	No	Yes	No	Yes	No	Yes	No	Yes	No	Yes	No	Yes	No
n	2211	299	2434	76	1382	1128	550	1960	581	1929	409	2101	148	2362	493	2017	352	2158
Tobacco	—	—	90	41	94	81	95	86	96	86	95	87	99	87	96	86	96	87
Alcohol	99	85	—	—	100	94	100	96	100	96	100	96	100	97	100	96	100	96
Marijuana	59	27	57	4	—	*b*	100	43	97	42	97	47	99	52	91	46	100	48
Psychedelics	24	9	23	0	40	1	—	—	71	7	80	11	92	18	72	10	89	11
Stimulants	25	7	24	0	41	*b*	75	9	—	—	82	12	86	19	71	21	86	13
Sedatives	18	6	17	1	29	1	60	4	58	4	—	—	80	12	60	6	72	7
Heroin	7	*b*	6	0	11	0	25	1	22	1	29	1	—	—	27	1	38	1
Opiates	21	7	20	0	33	4	65	7	60	7	73	9	91	15	—	—	79	10
Cocaine	15	5	14	0	25	*b*	57	2	52	3	62	5	90	9	56	4	—	—

Source: J. A. O'Donnell, H. L. Voss, R. R. Clayton, G. T. Slatin, and R. G. W. Room, *Young Men and Drugs—A Nationwide Survey*, Rockville, Maryland: National Institute of Drug Abuse, 1976. Reprinted by permission.

[a] For stimulants, sedatives, and opiates, quasi-medical use was defined as no use.

[b] Less than half of 1 percent.

of age, and these data provide the basis for the first of the investigations to be discussed.[77] Table 2 describes the percentages of users and nonusers of nine different drugs. An examination of the pairs of columns for each drug, in which users of the drug are compared with nonusers, shows that use of any drug was associated with use of all other drugs. Alcohol especially was associated with use of the other drugs: 57 percent of the alcohol users have also used marijuana; 23 percent have used psychedelics; 24 percent stimulants; 17 percent, sedatives; 6 percent, heroin; 20 percent, opiates; and 14 percent, cocaine. On the other hand, nonusers of alcohol rarely used any other drug, except tobacco. Table 2 also suggests on two counts that marijuana may be the key to predicting multiple drug use. First, the column indicating the percentages of users and nonusers of marijuana shows that 40 percent of those who had used marijuana had also used psychedelics while virtually none of the nonusers reported using psychedelics. A rather extensive discrepancy between users and nonusers is reported for each of the other drugs: stimulants, 41 percent to 1 percent; sedatives, 29 percent to 1 percent; heroin, 11 percent to less than 1 percent; opiates, 33 to 4 percent; cocaine, 25 percent to less than 1 percent. Second, the data in Row 3 of Table 2 show that of those who had ever used psychedelics or cocaine, 100 percent had also used marijuana; of those who had used stimulants or sedatives, 90 percent had tried marijuana, of those who had used opiates, 91 percent were involved with marijuana, and of those who had used heroin, 99 percent had used marijuana. On the likely assumption that use of marijuana may predate use of the other drugs, it would appear that marijuana facilitates movement of an individual into use of other substances.[78] The preliminary report suggests, too, why marijuana rather than alcohol may be the best key to predicting multiple drug use. All users of marijuana used alcohol and nearly all of them also used tobacco. Consequently, to know that persons had used marijuana is to know that they used alcohol and probably tobacco; in contrast, to know that they used alcohol and tobacco tells us much less about their marijuana usage.

The data in Table 2 also show that use of heroin signifies the deepest involvement in the drug milieu. Persons who had ever used heroin were very likely to have used most of the other drugs. At least 99 percent of those who had used heroin had used tobacco, alcohol, and marijuana, and at least 80 percent had used psychedelics, stimulants, sedatives, opiates, and cocaine. Two-thirds of the young men who had ever used heroin had used *all* of the other drugs studied.[79] Further, the data shown in the last two columns and the last row of Table 2 indicate that those who had used cocaine were likely to have used all the other drugs, except heroin. One hundred percent of the users of cocaine had also used marijuana, 89 percent had tried psychedelics, and 70 percent had used stimu-

Table 3
Product Moment Correlations[a] Among Adolescent Use of 15 Legal and Illegal Drugs

	1	2	3	4	5	6	7	8	9	10	11	12	13	14	15
1. Beer or Wine		299	464	214	180	106	115	090	128	122	097	074	046	101	116
2. Cigarettes			400	433	378	283	232	239	328	334	212	182	148	267	259
3. Hard Liquor				368	300	185	180	160	235	215	157	119	094	171	169
4. Marijuana					776	471	435	382	536	534	293	300	252	397	336
5. Hashish						560	528	446	570	598	327	356	273	444	329
6. LSD							674	624	550	584	354	467	391	526	374
7. Other Psychedelics								588	528	535	370	469	327	513	349
8. Methedrine									509	541	361	509	373	536	380
9. Other Amphetamines										696	408	390	295	484	397
10. Barbiturates											432	427	361	509	417
11. Tranquilizers												277	220	419	318
12. Cocaine													476	450	285
13. Heroin														370	248
14. Other Narcotics															248
15. Inhalants															
Total $N \geq$	7517	7534	7658	7581	7517	7671	7663	7647	7661	7676	7667	7671	7654	7606	7630

Source: E. Single, D. Kandel, and R. Faust, Patterns of multiple drug use in high school, *Journal of Health and Social Behavior,* 1974, **15**, 344–357. Reprinted by permission.
[a] All significant at .001 level; decimal points omitted.

lants, sedatives, and opiates. It is noteworthy that only 39 percent of the men who had used cocaine had also used heroin, but 90 percent of those who used heroin reported using cocaine.

Single et al.[80] studied the patterns of multiple drug use in a representative sample of over 8,000 New York public secondary school students from 18 different high schools, and their data constitute the second of the investigations referred to above. Their findings generally corroborate those cited in Table 2. The majority (70 percent) of the adolescents who used "street" or illicit drugs were multiple drug users. The overwhelming majority of the drug users had used beer or wine (94 percent), hard liquor (90 percent), or tobacco (89 percent). The correlations among the use of 15 legal and illegal drugs are shown in Table 3. Smoking cigarettes or drinking hard liquor, beer, or wine are shown to be highly associated with use of illicit drugs. Correlations are highest in Table 3 between pairs of drugs that are similar in that both are either legal or illegal. For example, use of "hard liquor" is correlated most highly with "beer or wine" ($r = .464$); marijuana, with hashish ($r = .776$); heroin, with cocaine

Table 4
Percent of Adolescents Using Other Illegal Drugs by the Use of Marijuana

Percent using:	Among Those Who Use Marijuana	Among Those Who Do Not Use Marijuana
Hashish	71%	1%
LSD	29%	a
Other psychedelics	23%	1%
Methedrine	21%	a
Other amphetamines	44%	2%
Barbiturates	40%	1%
Tranquilizers	20%	3%
Cocaine	13%	a
Heroin	9%	a
Other narcotics	24%	1%
Inhalants	20%	2%
Total $N \geq$	2225	5446

Source: E. Single, D, Kandel, and R. Faust, Patterns of multiple drug use in high school, *Journal of Health and Social Behavior,* 1974, **15,** 344–357. Reprinted by permission.

a Less than one half of one percent.

($r = .476$). The one exception to this pattern is tobacco, which is highly correlated with a wide variety of legal and illegal drugs. The analyses of Single et al. also indicate that marijuana, following tobacco and alcohol, was by far the drug most frequently used by the adolescents, and among the illicit drugs, it is the drug most frequently involved in patterns of multiple drug use. Their data reveal that adolescents are very unlikely to try other illicit drugs unless they have also used marijuana. Adolescents who do not use marijuana generally appear not to use any of the other drugs, and only a small proportion of the adolescents who have used marijuana once or twice report using any of the other drugs. An indication of extent of young people's drug use by whether or not they have used marijuana is presented in Table 4. Clearly, the data show that it is within the marijuana users that usage of other drugs emerges. For example, 40 percent of those who report that they have used marijuana are also barbiturate users whereas only 1 percent of the nonusers are also involved with barbiturates; similarly, 44 percent of the marijuana users also use amphetamines but only 2 percent of the nonusers have tried amphetamines, and so forth.

SUMMARY

Many young people experiment with drugs for recreational purposes—to modify moods, create euphoria, and reduce tension. The contemporary "drug problem" stems from the fact that more and more persons are using various drugs with or without appropriate medical supervision or for nonmedical purposes. Federal and state legislation on drug usage up to the end of the 1960s was exceedingly restrictive. Penalties for the possession of all drugs were equally harsh. The Comprehensive Drug Abuse Prevention and Control Act of 1970, however, consolidated many earlier laws and substantially reduced penalties for possession of marijuana. Many adults and adolescents today believe that the right to take drugs for the purpose of experimenting with one's own inner world is a private matter, and few young people believe that smoking marijuana once in a while constitutes drug misuse.

This chapter describes the general properties and characteristic effects of three classes of psychoactive drugs—those drugs that affect moods, perceptions, and levels of consciousness. The first group encompasses the depressants (barbiturates and related sedatives, inhalants like glue and paint, and opiate narcotics including heroin), which decrease alertness and diminish impact of the outer environment on thoughts and feelings. The second classification includes the stimulants (amphetamines and cocaine), which heighten mental activities, enabling larger inputs of environmental information to be processed. The third category comprises the psychedelics (hallucinogens, such as LSD and psilocybin, and marijuana), which are used primarily to alter the quality rather than the intensity of perceptions.

A study of the reasons for drug avoidance, involving a national sample of young men, shows that the most frequently stated reasons have to do more with practicality and expedience—effect on health, did not like drugs, might cause trouble with police, or loss of self-control—than with moral standards or religious convictions. The most common reason for using drugs given by the sample of young men, which included users of all types, was to get high or stoned. Drug users reflect their personality styles in the myriad recreational uses to which they put drugs, and for purposes of rough classification, they may be described as *experimental users,* who look to drugs for new sources of aesthetic or sensual experiences, as *depressive users,* who seek through drugs to make adaptive solutions to complex interpersonal problems, and as *characterological users,* who seek via drugs to relieve tension resulting from major personality deficiencies. By and large, most adolescents who are involved in drugs are experimental users.

Experimental drug use is relatively widespread. Nearly one adult in five and nearly one adolescent in four between 12 and 17 years of age has experimented at least once with marijuana. Most young people are introduced to marijuana and other drugs through their peers. On the whole, marijuana appears to predate use of other drugs and to facilitate movement of young people into using other substances. Users of heroin, on the other hand, are usually deeply involved in the drug milieu; persons who have used heroin are likely to have also used most other drugs.

REVIEW QUESTIONS

1. What circumstances have led to widespread use of recreational drugs?
2. What are the trends in federal and state legislation regarding both drug possession and drug usage?
3. Describe the general characteristics of depressants, stimulants, and psychedelics, respectively.
4. How are barbiturates and alcoholic beverages related?
5. Why are inhalants popular among younger adolescents?
6. Which of the recreational drugs is regarded as the "hardest"?
7. Which is the most popular recreational drug for obtaining a swift, jolting kick followed by euphoria?
8. Which drug is known as the "champagne" of drugs?
9. Why is LSD less popular today than during the late 1960s?
10. What are the general effects of marijuana intoxication?
11. What reasons do young people most often give for not getting into drugs?
12. Why do young people say that they use drugs?
13. What are the personality differences among, respectively, experimental, depressive, and characterological drug users?
14. In what way is adolescent marijuana use related to problem-prone behavior?
15. How is marijuana, alcohol, and tobacco use interrelated?
16. What is the basis for asserting that most recreational drugs users are multiple users?

DISCUSSION QUESTIONS

1. Do you agree with the assertion that experimenting with recreational drugs is a private matter?
2. Which of the recreational drugs do you hold to be the most injurious to the health of young people? If given an opportunity, what effects would you concentrate on warning them about?
3. Why should peers be so important in determining whether young people experiment with marijuana?
4. How are young persons likely to progress to the stage of heroin use?
5. If you were asked to counsel young people regarding recreational drug usage, what would you tell them?

NOTES

1. S. Freud. *Civilization and its discontent.* Garden City, N.Y.: Doubleday, Anchor Books, 1958.

2. D. L. Farnsworth. Drug use and young people: their reasons, our reactions. *Resource Book for Drug Abuse Education* (2nd ed.). Washington, D.C.: National Clearing House for Drug Abuse Information, 1972.

3. Farnsworth, *op. cit.*

4. D. Fejer, R. G. Smart, P. C. Whitehead, and L. Laforest. Sources of information about drugs among high school students. *The Public Opinion Quarterly,* 1971, **35,** 235–241.

5. D. M. Serrone. Over-the-counter drugs: a challenge for drug education. *Journal of Drug Education,* 1973, **3,** 101–110.

6. H. B. Bruyn. Control of dangerous drugs on university campuses. *Journal of the American College Health Association,* 1967, **16,** 13–18, p. 16.

7. R. E. Muuss. Legal and social aspects of drug abuse in historical perspective. *Adolescence,* 1974, **9,** 495–506.

8. R. L. DuPont, *Marihuana and Health: Fifth Annual Report to the U.S. Congress.* Rockville, Maryland: National Institute on Drug Abuse, 1975.

9. H. Kalant and O. J. Kalant, *Drugs, society and personal choice.* Toronto: Paperjacks, 1971.

10. Kalant and Kalant, *op. cit.,* p. 15.

11. Kalant and Kalant, *op. cit.*

12. R. R. Kleinhesselink, C. St. Dennis, and H. J. Cross. Contemporary drug issues involving youth. In J. F. Adams (Ed.). *Understanding Adolescence* (3rd ed.). Boston: Allyn & Bacon, 1976.

13. Kleinhesselink et al., *op. cit.,* p. 392.

14. Kleinhesselink et al., *op. cit.,* p. 393.

15. Kalant and Kalant, *op. cit.,* p. 26.

16. R. J. Kempton and T. Kempton. Methaqualone abuse: an epidemic for the seventies. *Journal of Drug Education,* 1973, **3,** 403–413.

17. Kempton and Kempton, *op. cit.*

18. Kempton and Kempton, *op. cit.*

19. Kleinhesselink et al., *op. cit.*

20. R. G. Smart. Education and the drug question. *Manitoba Medical Review,* 1969, **49,** No. 2.

21. M. Montiel. *Paint inhalation among chicano barrio youth.* Phoenix: Valle del Sol, 1976, pp. 96–97.

22. Kleinhesselink et al., *op. cit.,* p. 396.

23. Ibid.

24. Kalant and Kalant, *op. cit.,* p. 31.

25. Kalant and Kalant, *op. cit.*

26. Kleinhesselink et al., *op. cit.*

27. Kleinhesselink et al., *op. cit.,* p. 399.

28. C. Cox and R. G. Smart, The nature and extent of speed use in North America. *Canadian Medical Association Journal,* 1970, **102,** 724–729.

29. Cox and Smart, *op. cit.;* Smart, *op. cit.*

30. Cox and Smart, *op. cit.*

31. Cox and Smart, *op. cit.*

32. Kalant and Kalant, *op. cit.,* p. 32.

33. B. E. Smith. "Speed freaks" vs. "acid heads." A conflict between drug subcultures. Unpublished manuscript. Haight-Ashbury Medical Clinic, San Francisco, 1969.

34. Cox and Smart, *op. cit.*

35. Kleinhesselink et al., *op. cit.,* p. 400.

36. Kleinhesselink et al., *op. cit.,* p. 401.

37. Ibid.

38. Smith, *op. cit.*

39. Kleinhesselink et al., *op. cit.,* p. 401.

40. DuPont, *op. cit.*

41. C. J. Schwartz. Toward a medical understanding of marijuana. *Canadian Psychiatric Association Journal,* 1969, **14,** 591–600.

42. R. Snedeker. Hash, pot and heads. *Signal One,* 1968, 7–11.

43. DuPont, *op. cit.,* p. 4.

44. DuPont, *op. cit.*

45. DuPont, *op. cit.*

46. DuPont, *op. cit.*

47. DuPont, *op. cit.,* p. 5.

48. DuPont, *op. cit.*

49. W. C. Koff. Marijuana and sexual activity. *Journal of Sex Research,* 1974, **10,** 194–204.

50. DuPont, *op. cit.,* p. 80.

51. DuPont, *op. cit.*, p. 87.

52. Farnsworth, *op. cit.*

53. M. R. McKee. Main Street, U.S.A.: Fact and fiction about drug abuse. *Journal of Drug Education,* 1973, **3,** 275–295.

54. J. A. O'Donnell, H. L. Voss, R. R., Clayton, G. T. Slatin, and R. G. W. Room. *Young men and drugs—a nationwide survey.* Rockville, Maryland: National Institute on Drug Abuse, 1976.

55. O'Donnell et al., *op. cit.*, p. 71.

56. N. E. Zinberg. Facts and fancies about drug addiction. *The Public Interest,* 1967, **6,** 75–90.

57. S. Proskauer and R. S. Rolland. Youth who use drugs: psychodynamic diagnosis and treatment planning. *Journal of the American Academy of Child Psychiatry,* 1973, **12,** 32–47, p. 33.

58. Proskauer and Rolland, *op. cit.*, p. 34.

59. Proskauer and Rolland, *op. cit.*, p. 40.

60. Ibid.

61. Proskauer and Rolland, *op. cit.*, pp. 40–41.

62. R. A. Geist. Some observations on adolescent drug use. *Journal of the American Academy of Child Psychiatry,* 1974, **13,** 54–71.

63. H. I. Abelson and R. B. Atkinson. *Public experience with psychoactive substances: a nationwide study among adults and youth.* Princeton, New Jersey: Response Analysis Corporation, 1975.

64. D. Kandel. Inter- and intragenerational influences on adolescent marijuana use. *Journal of Social Issues,* 1974, **30,** 107–135.

65. Kandel, *op. cit.*

66. Kandel, *op. cit.*

67. G. Fisher and A. Steckler. On being introduced to marijuana: expectations, effects, and experiences of past and current users. *Journal of Drug Education,* 1974, **4,** 85–95.

68. R. E. Clark, A. Kowitz, and D. Duckworth. The influence of information sources and grade level on the diffusion and adoption of marijuana. *Journal of Drug Issues,* 1975, **6,** 177–188.

69. J. G. Weis. Styles of middle-class adolescent drug use. *Pacific Sociological Review,* 1974, **17,** 251–285.

70. Weis, *op. cit.*

71. S. R. Burkett and E. L. Jensen. Conventional ties, peer influence, and the fear of apprehension: a study of adolescent marijuana use. *Sociological Quarterly,* 1975, **16,** 522–533.

72. R. Jessor, S. L. Jessor, and J. Finney. A social psychology of marijuana use: longitudinal studies of high school and college youth. *Journal of Personality and Social Psychology,* 1973, **26,** 1–15.

73. H. R. Victor, J. C. Grossman, and R. Eisenman. Openness to experience and marijuana

use in high school students. *Journal of Consulting and Clinical Psychology,* 1973, **41,** 78–85.

74. B. F. Blake, E. Wick, W. Burke, and A. Sanesino. The early adolescent's personality and his style of marijuana usage. Paper presented at the meeting of the American Psychological Association, New Orleans, 1974.

75. R. C. Knight, J. P. Sheposh, and J. B. Bryson. College student marijuana use and societal alienation. *Journal of Health and Social Behavior,* 1974, **15,** 28–35.

76. O'Donnell et al., *op. cit.;* E. Single, D, Kandel, and R. Faust. Patterns of multiple drug use in high school. *Journal of Health and Social Behavior,* 1974, **15,** 344–357.

77. O'Donnell et al., *op. cit.*

78. O'Donnell et al., *op. cit.*

79. O'Donnell et al., *op. cit.*

80. Single et al., *op. cit.*

Chapter 6

Cognitive Development and Adolescence

CHAPTER HIGHLIGHTS

ISSUES

The value of intelligence and other ability tests is determined by their social usefulness.

Tests of intelligence, achievement, and aptitude are distinguishable in respect to purpose, breadth, specificity, and recency.

Alternatives to competitive ability tests, for purposes of classification and selection, range from lotteries to mastery tests.

Intellectual growth is fostered in family environments where parents attempt to accelerate intellectual behavior in the context of moderate structure and discipline.

Variations in parental child-rearing practices produce different patterns in youth's intellectual growth.

Adolescent thought is characterized by capacity to reason without reference to direct experience.

Peel believes that cognitive maturity (the ability to explain, judge, and consider alternatives realistically) is attained by a minority of adolescents.

Piaget says that cognitive operations are constructed as the individual interacts with his or her environment.

The dynamics of cognitive knowing in the Piagetian system are based on assimilation and accommodation.

Equilibration, according to Piaget, provides the motivation for intellectual growth.

Formal operational thinking is based on incorporating, extending, and unifying cognitive structures achieved earlier.

Cognitive growth requires that adolescents continue the decentering process.

Development of formal operational thought varies as a function of cultural demand for it.

The manner in which individuals interpret the events around them, act in relation to expectations of others, understand their role in society, and communicate their insights and aspirations to others are aspects of their cognitive or intellectual abilities. Ever since scientists and philosophers began to examine intelligence, the effectiveness of behavior has been considered a crucial factor. In the nineteenth century Herbert Spencer was the chief architect of a theory of intelligence. He recognized that cognitive abilities were crucial in enabling individuals to adjust themselves effectively to the complexities of living. He thought that during the course of evolution intelligence differentiated itself into a hierarchy of cognitive skills. Animals lower on the evolutionary scale managed their behavior through instincts or "lapsed intelligence." But in humans, intelligence was flexible, requiring "the mental adjustment of internal relations to external relations." Spencer drew heavily on the earlier work of the eminent Harvard philosopher and historian, John Fiske. Fiske had attempted to explain, in evolutionary terms, the relatively long duration of infancy in humans. He reasoned that lower animals experience a short infancy because their "reflective" behavior is impressed on a fairly small brain during fetal development. A lower animal, "when he comes to be born, comes all ready to go to work."[1] On the other hand, higher vertebrates have a number of potentialities which have to be aroused according to their own individual experiences."[2]

Spencer and Fiske are the forerunners of contemporary studies of adolescent cognitive or intellectual functioning, which may be divided into two distinct traditions. The first offers a comparative evaluation of intellectual functioning. For three-quarters of a century efforts have been made to transform assumptions about intelligence into performance tests to determine the relative cognitive strengths of individuals. In general, a systematic effort is made to derive numerical values with respect to a reference group, for example, other school-age children or the population at large, and to attach these values to whatever is measured. Intellectual functioning is conceptualized largely in psychometric or quantitative terms, and persons are evaluated as having "more or less" of the attributes on which they have been compared. The second tradition in studying adolescent cognition focuses on changes in mode of functioning from infancy through adolescence and into adulthood. Cognitive development is viewed as progressing through an invariant series of stages, each of which provides an essential foundation for the next. Social scientists have long struggled to characterize the development of the structures of the mind that are common to all persons, and as they analyze each sequence in the order, differences from one individual to another are largely ignored.

The meaning of intelligence as it pertains to adolescence and the significance of factors that may influence intellectual behavior, as measured by tests of intellectual abilities, are still not completely understood. These issues are given special emphasis in the first section of this chapter. Further, cognitive structures are exceedingly complex, and the adolescent's thought processes are much more intricate than those of the child. A great deal of theoretical speculation and research have ensued, nonetheless, and theorists have had opportunity to develop a comprehensive developmental outlook on cognitive growth. The outlook is among the more provocative in psychology today, and expressions of it are dealt with in detail in the second section of the chapter.

INTERPRETATION OF DEVELOPED ABILITIES

The Meaning of Intelligence

Intelligence, unlike relatively fixed attributes in the physical world such as height and weight, must be inferred from various patterns of behavior. It is not surprising, therefore, that there have been many different definitions of intelligence. Early definitions focused on thought processes. Alfred Binet, founder of modern intelligence testing, asserted that "in intelligence there is a fundamental faculty, . . . this faculty is *judgment,* otherwise called good sense, practical sense, initiative, the faculty of adapting oneself to circumstances. To judge well, to comprehend well, to reason well, these are the essential activities of intelligence."[3] Binet emphasized the ability to adjust to new situations, but his successors stressed the ability to learn. Terman,[4] the major author of the famed Stanford-Binet intelligence test, held that individual intelligence was based on ability to carry on abstract thinking. Ausubel and Ausubel[5] said that during adolescence and adulthood, intelligence represents "a general capacity for processing information and for utilizing abstract symbols in the solution of abstract problems." Wechsler,[6] author of the Wechsler Intelligence Scales, once defined intelligence as the "aggregate or global capacity of the individual to act purposefully, to think rationally, and to deal effectively with his environment." Intelligent behavior today, however, is acknowledged to be a product of many factors. According to Wechsler, such "behavior must not only be rational and purposeful; it must not only have meaning but it must also have value, it must be esteemed."[7] Wechsler thus suggests that an effective intelligence test will assess "the capacity of an individual to understand the world about him and his resourcefulness to cope with its challenges."[8]

Cleary et al.[9] stress that the usefulness of an intelligence test lies in its capacity to assess whether the performance it taps is representative of intellectual behavior. In a review of the educational uses of tests, they appear to agree with Wechsler in that they point out that intelligence and other ability tests have value only to the extent that the tests are deemed "socially relevant and important."

Cleary et al.[10] emphasize that the usefulness of an intelligence test lies not in its capacity to determine whether heredity or environment contribute to performance, but in its capacity to discriminate individuals on the basis of socially important criteria. Early genetic theorists, however, concentrated on trying to determine the relative effects of heredity and environment on intelligence. In *Hereditary Genius* (1869), for example, Francis Galton, a cousin of Darwin, compared the professional careers of the sons of men of genius and men of average ability. The two groups of men were matched for social rank, and Galton reasoned that if heredity exerted greater influence than environment, he would find a larger proportion of eminent men among the sons of geniuses. His hypothesis was supported, for the genius group had many more eminent relatives than the average group. Galton's critics argued, however, that the environment of a child in the family of a gifted man would be different from that in the family of an average man, even of similar social rank. Galton then compared the adopted sons of Popes. Although these boys were presumably reared in an atmosphere of intellectual and cultural attainment, Galton again confirmed his hypothesis—he found no evidence that any had achieved the degree of eminence reached by the real sons of gifted men. Since both the early definitions and the early evidence of intelligence stressed the role of heredity, researchers at first believed that the results of intelligence tests were free of cultural influences. During the 1930s research accumulated showing that no test could be completely culture-free, and by 1950, the hope of constructing such a test had been abandoned.[11]

Jensen[12] advanced the concept of heritability to explain how cultural and biological forces interact to influence performance on intelligence tests. He described heritability as the extent to which variability is controlled by internal biological rather than external social-psychological influences. He argues that heritability (or innate traits) will have a greater influence on individual differences in intellectual functioning among members of a group when all have shared a common environment, such as excellent schooling. A decrease in the environmental sources of variation will increase the relative influence of the heritability of intelligence; conversely, when social advantages are unequally distributed, the relative effect of the environment will be greater and the influence of heritability will be lowered. Thus, in an inbred population with diverse living conditions, environmental more than hereditary conditions will affect the course of intellectual growth; if the environmental circumstances should be uniform, magnitude of genetic diversity would account for differences in the growth of intelligence.

Contemporary tests of intelligence, achievement, and aptitude are comprised of similar items; however, they are distinguishable on the basis of four dimensions—purpose, breadth, specificity, and recency.[13] First, the purpose for which a test is intended differentiates the three types of test. The "intelligence" test seeks to predict a young person's future success in a wide variety of situations, the "achievement" test aims to determine how much a person has learned in a particular area or school subject, and the "aptitude" test aims to predict how well a young person might learn a new subject, skill, or task. Second, an intelligence test is much broader in coverage than the average achievement test. The Stanford-Binet, for example, a general intelligence test, is the standard against which most other tests are compared. It was pioneered by Lewis M. Terman, a student of G. Stanley Hall, and has been revised successively since 1916. It has achieved unrivaled popularity in clinics, schools, and hospitals. Its intelligence quotient, (obtained in part by summarizing scores from a variety of subtests) provides a convenient quantitative indication of a young person's relative intelligence. The intelligence test taps learning both inside and outside the school. As a consequence of its breadth, high school students' performances on the test are likely to be unaffected by what is taught in their particular schools at given periods in time. Third, achievement and aptitude tests are much more specific than an intelligence test. They are based on a particular curricula area—reading, mathematics, history. Achievement tests are the more specific of the two and usually must be revised whenever the curriculum changes. Fourth, intelligence, achievement, and aptitude tests may be differentiated on the basis of recency. Achievement tests generally measure current learning whereas intelligence and aptitude tests sample older learning. Cleary et al.[14] note that questions administered in junior high school as achievement items will appear again as part of the "aptitude" section of the College Board Examination, and elements of high school achievement tests will be covered again by the "aptitude" section of the Graduate Record Examination.

Proposals to eliminate all forms of testing from public educational institutions reached the stage of vigorous public controversy within the past decade.[15] The opponents of testing generally object to tests on the grounds that minority and economically disadvantaged young people may be misclassified. The testing movement, it is argued, by reinforcing homogeneous grouping in elementary schools, classification and assignment of "retarded" children to special classes, and selective college admission policies, limits educational opportunities available to black, chicano, and other minority young people.[16] What are the alternatives? If the educational community is to conduct an effective placement program at optimal social cost, what alternative procedures are available for classification, selection, diagnosis, and assignment? Cleary et al.[17] have reviewed several practical procedures; let us briefly consider three of these.

1. *Measures other than tests:* Cleary et al.[18] mention lotteries, use of prior experience, demographic data, subjective evaluations, and academic grades as possible alternative selection procedures to intellectual tests. Each possesses distinct strengths and weaknesses. (a) The lottery is fair in that everyone has an equal chance to attain access to educational opportunity, but in eliminating "feedback," it destroys "institutional influence on self-selection" and creates "serious problems in individual guidance and planning." (b) Evaluation of prior experience is easiest when individuals are from small, homogeneous systems, but when variations are large, interpretation of differences in prior experience may be difficult. (c) Selection based on demographic data creates a quota system. It ensures that ethnic and socioeconomic groupings will be represented in a student body, but it also raises serious questions about who should be excluded. Indeed, in the context of current civil rights legislation, school admission policies based on quotas are illegal. (d) Subjective evaluations, on the other hand, derived from interviews, application form essays, letters of recommendation, and submission of artistic, literary, or scientific products, are often used to differentiate individuals. Cleary et al.[19] observe that subjective measures could provide an alternative to tests, "except that their predictive efficiency is usually low and they are enormously expensive to use." (e) Cleary et al.[20] note, too, that records of academic performance represent, perhaps, the best alternative to tests. Academic grades, however, are notoriously difficult to compare on individual bases across schools, especially when region and ethnic composition are significant characteristics. Tests, in contrast, may be standardized with regional and national norms, and thus can provide an independent appraisal of youth's performance.

2. *Tests of important qualities other than intelligence.* Cleary et al.[21] question whether intellectual test performance provides an adequate basis for selecting and classifying musicians, athletes, mechanics, and so forth. Qualities of temperament, interests, physical skills, and motivation may be more important than attributes tapped by conventional intelligence tests in differentiating high school students for such roles. Unfortunately, however, these qualities are difficult to differentiate via tests of any sort. Both interest inventories, which are effective in differentiating choices among educational and occupational opportunities, and personality tests have been unsuccessful in predicting specific kinds of role proficiencies. Cleary et al.[22] suggest, therefore, that noncognitive qualities may be best assessed through subjective evaluations made by informed persons.

3. *Variants of commonly used intellectual tests.* Cleary et al.[23] classify the

variants into two major types—"diagnostic" and "mastery" tests. Programs of remedial education generally employ diagnostic tests. They are designed to identify specific deficiencies and to indicate areas that require improvement. The need for good diagnostic tests is great; however, they are enormously difficult to develop, for detailed analyses of the specific components must be made. Furthermore, diagnostic tests must provide reliable measurement of each component, and if several components are involved, the test or subtests needed may prove too expensive to construct. Finally, diagnostic tests should be part of a total diagnostic program that will provide a trained specialist with data about maturation and personality as well as analyses of skill deficiencies. Mastery tests are comparable to diagnostic tests in that role deficits and need for remediation are revealed. Mastery tests, however, also uncover how much students know or to what extent they can do something. Whereas traditional intelligence tests are designed to sample a broad field of intellectual activity and to determine how students compare with one another, items in a mastery test measure knowledge that students should have. When students answer items in a history test inaccurately, the teacher is alerted to focus on the specific deficiencies. Mastery tests can be designed to provide experiences of success rather than failure during learning activities, and are admirably suited for evaluating progress in educational settings.

Family Background and Intellectual Growth

The more significant environmental factors that influence intelligence include family cultural interests, parental educational level, parental encouragement, home reading facilities, and parental speech. The accumulated records of the Berkeley Growth Study, one of the longitudinal studies initiated at the University of California about 40 years ago, provide a well-documented analysis of the relationship between family background and intellectual growth. The study began with full-term, healthy, hospital-born babies of white, English-speaking parents. The full sample of 74 babies remained in the study through 7 months; 63 remained through 3 years; and 48 remained until they reached 18 years of age.[24] The study reveals several consistent correlations that extend from birth through adolescence. Starting at about two years of age and continuing through age 18, the correlation between intelligence scores and such measures, respectively, as parental education, occupation, and social class grew increasingly stronger for both sexes. Later in childhood, verbal skills, associated with good linguistic models and stimulation, became important; the researchers suggested that the primary differentiating factors may have to do with child-rearing practices of different socioeconomic groups. Higher class mothers, for example, were rated as more "cooperative, equalitarian, and affectionate" toward children; lower class mothers appeared more "irritable, punitive, and ignoring." Honzik[25] reported that parental concern over educational achievement was positively correlated with intelligence test scores of both boys and girls from 3 to 30 years of age. "When parents are *concerned,* children are likely to accelerate in test performance; and when the concern is with *achievement,* the acceleration is likely to be more marked." Honzik's[26] data also suggest that parental concern exerts a greater impact on boys than on girls. The closeness of the mother-son relationship was highly predictive of boys' scores from ages 8 to 18. For optimal intellectual growth in boys, there appeared to be a need for "a warm, close relation with a mother or caretaker, followed by a masculine model who not only achieves but is concerned about his son's achievement."[27] Moss and Kagan[28] reported that "when a close symbiotic relationship exists between mother and son (as judged by her 'protectiveness,' 'lack of hostility,' 'preference over sibs,' and 'acceleration'), the mother's efficacy as a reinforcing agent of developmental skills is maximized." On the other hand, according to Honzik,[29] a close, friendly mother-daughter relationship was related to a girl's preschool scores, but was negligibly related to her scores at later ages. Her intellectual growth "is accelerated when she has *compatible parents,* a father who is *friendly to the mother and daughter* but who is *not very expressive of his affection* for his daughter."[30] As Moss and Kagan[31] see it, "when the female child is given sufficient latitude (in terms of being non-restricted) . . . she is able to exhibit greater developmental progress as measured by the Stanford-Binet."

The findings reported by the above studies, relating child-rearing to intellectual growth, have been corroborated by the recent National Health Examination Survey, a section of which compared intelligence and selected aspects of family background.[32] First, a strong association was found between children's intellectual development and intellectual maturity, respectively, and parental educational attainment and family income. Second, children who lived with either their mother only or their mother and father (or stepfather) generally obtained higher intellectual test scores than children who lived with grandparents, other relatives, or foster parents. Third, intelligence test scores increased consistently as a function of mother's age at the time the children were born until about age 25, remained stable for mothers between 26 and 39, and declined after age 39. Fourth, children's intelligence increased as the number of children in the household decreased. Children from families of no more than three children obtained the higher test scores. Fifth, small family size, especially among highly educated parents, was related more to verbal than to performance aspects of young people's intelligence.

McCall et al.[33] have distinguished five different patterns of IQ change over time. The young people within each group or cluster are relatively homogeneous in respect to IQ development. Figure 1 displays the average IQ in each cluster for ages between 2½ and 17 years. The subjects, drawn from the Fels Longitudinal Study, Yellow Springs, Ohio, were tested every six months through age six and every year thereafter with the Stanford-Binet individual IQ test. Eighty young persons participated in the study, and clusters ranged in size from 36 (#1) to five (#5). Their parents were predominantly white, middle-class citizens living in medium-sized Ohio towns. As Figure 1 illustrates, Cluster 1 young people show minimal deviation from a slightly rising pattern throughout childhood. Cluster 2 youth are characterized by a sharp decline in IQ performance between the ages of four and six, followed by a slight recovery, and then, a sharp downward trend after age 14. The Cluster 3 group reveals a preschool decline, but relatively level performance between 6 and 14 years, which is followed by an upswing. Cluster 4 young people display an inverted-U trend of considerable magnitude, which peaks between eight and ten years of age. Cluster 5 youth also show a strong and steady rise in IQ until ages eight to ten and a decline thereafter until age 17, but both their peak and subsequent decline are less marked than for the youth in Cluster 4.

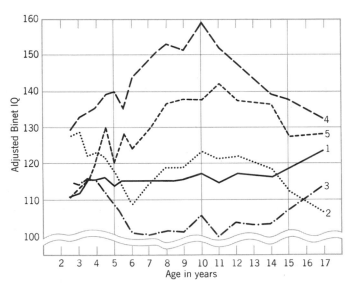

Figure 1
Mean IQ (adjusted for differences between Binet revision) over age for the five IQ clusters. (From McCall et al., see text. Reprinted by permission.)

McCall et al.[34] also sent a trained observer to the young people's homes every six months for the first six years and once every year thereafter to make global assessments of parental behavior. Ten parental behavior ratings were made— *adjustment of the home, restrictiveness of the regulations, severity of actual penalties, clarity of the policy of regulations and enforcement, coerciveness of suggestion, accelerational attempt, general babying, general protectiveness, direction of criticism,* and *affectionateness.* The researchers found that the patterns of IQ change could be distinguished from one another by the ratings of parental behavior. Children who evidenced early increases in IQ and whose performance levels were highest had parents who attempted frequently to accelerate their children in intellectual tasks. These parents tended to adopt a middle-of-the-road policy regarding severity of discipline. On the other hand, parents of children whose IQ declined during the preschool period, and who showed the lowest levels of performance, seldom attempted to stimulate the children's intellectual behavior. Moreover, among the latter parents, the children of those most punitive attained the most depressed IQ records, while the children of those most lax in their penalties showed some recovery in IQ during the middle school years. Thus, according to McCall et al.,[35] "the environment associated with optimum IQ profiles seemed to be one in which the parent encouraged and attempted to accelerate intellectual behavior, but in a context of moderate structure and discipline."

The parents of Clusters 4 and 5 youngsters appeared to provide the more ideal homes for intellectual stimulation. Cluster 4 youngsters displayed the highest levels of IQ performance of any group at every age, with an average IQ peak of 159 at about ten years of age. The children of Cluster 5 were next highest, peaking also at ten years of age with an average IQ of 145. Cluster 5 parents were less extreme than those in Cluster 4, but both sets of parents had "the highest ratings of adjustment, clarity of policies, accelerational attempt, protectiveness, education, and parental Otis IQ, and they were relatively rewarding and minimally coercive."[36]

McCall et al.[37] describe two child-rearing patterns to account for why the youngsters lost the impressive gains that they had made in IQ during the preschool years. First, parents who want to accelerate their children's IQ have the opportunity during the preschool years when their control over the children's intellectual activities and social experiences is relatively pervasive. Parents may uphold high standards for the children and expect them to evaluate their intellectual accomplishments against them. When school starts, however, parents must relinquish much of this control. Parental acceleration may now become threatening, frustrating, and disruptive. Children may interpret continued accelerational attempts as "pushiness," and they may rebel against parental pressures. The effects of the children's reactions on test performance may be delayed until age 10, partly because early reading and mathematical learning may be challenging and partly because serious striving for independence from parental authority and values usually is delayed until early adolescence. Second, the youngsters may have been "turned off" toward intellectual activities. Perhaps school became uninteresting following mastery of basic reading and mathematical skills. Given their high IQ and the momentum provided by accelerating parents, the school environment, by comparison, may have appeared "cold, impersonal, non-rewarding, restrictive, and regimented."[38] Maybe the two patterns complement one another? Children may be particularly inclined to withdraw from intellectual activity when they find themselves both unable to meet the pressure of parental standards and repulsed by the school environment. Fortunately, not all parents are "disruptively 'pushy,'" not all school environments are uninteresting, and in fact, only a few able youngsters forsake their relatively high intellectual standing.

Prospects for Intellectual Growth

The early pioneers of mental tests, Binet and Terman, assumed that the abilities reflecting intellectual competence declined with age and that performance of these abilities reached a peak either in late adolescence or in the early twenties. The "decline" assumption[39] was firmly embedded in the lore of genetic psychology. It was long believed that intelligence emerged as a function of neurological growth;[40] those who developed the traditional intelligence tests overlooked the possibility that education and cultural stimulation after adolescence might affect intelligence.[41] But research for the past quarter-century has uniformly supported the conclusion that postadolescent intellectual performance is strongly affected by sociocultural factors.

Whether intelligence test scores increase, remain stationary, or decrease later in life may be a function of the quality of one's education. Green[42] holds that "the level of formal education received tends to set the level of cognitive functioning of an individual for life." For example, Owens[43] compared the Army Alpha intelligence test scores of 96 men, 61 years of age, who had first taken the test 42 years earlier. His findings showed that the men whose scores increased over the years had pursued educational interests, cultural activities, and physically vigorous activities. Nisbet[44] studied 141 persons, divided about equally by sex, on a group intelligence test when they were 22½ years of age and again when they were 47 years of age. He found that those who had attained more educational training and had stimulating experiences in life improved the most in their test scores.

Bloom[45] has described how certain patterns of parent-child interaction provide models for language development, which, in turn, stimulate the growth of general intelligence. An ideal environment should offer children occasions for direct contact with the world around them and for vicarious experiences through books, pictures, films, television, and so forth. Children should have opportunities to solve problems and be encouraged to think clearly about issues in and out of school. Bloom also contends that the environment of people after the age of 18 influences their intellectual development. Leaving school at 18 and working at a job that makes minimal demands on verbal skills and problem solving may deter intellectual growth. On the other hand, certain occupations that require higher education and emphasize verbal skills and problem solving (such as law and teaching) probably facilitate the continued development of intelligence.

Recent investigations have shown that cognitive functioning assumes a characteristic pattern prior to adolescence and becomes relatively stable thereafter. For example, Fitzgerald et al.[46] divided nearly 2,000 adolescents into three groups, Grades 7–8, 9–10, and 11–12, for purposes of comparison in a cross-sectional study. The researchers employed an adult model of intelligence based on four primary factors or abilities—verbal, number, reasoning, and spatial—as a frame of reference. Their analyses of the factor intercorrelations revealed a constancy of intellectual structure across the age groups. Further, at all levels, the structure of youth's intelligence resembled that of the adults. Schaie[47] studied the impact of sociocultural change on age differences in adult cognitive behavior by comparing findings from three independent, cross-sectional studies conducted in 1956, 1963, and 1970. Subjects ranged from 21 to 84 years of age. The design of the studies permitted both cross-sectional and time-sequential comparisons of their performance on verbal, number, reasoning, and spatial measures of intellectual activity. The data analyses showed that younger persons performed more effectively on the tests than older persons when persons of different age were compared. However, the time-sequential data revealed (when persons of the same age but of different generations were compared) that each successive generational cohort achieved somewhat higher performance scores, especially in respect to verbal and reasoning measures. Thus, the data indicate that apparent losses in intellectual performance across age may be less a matter of loss of cognitive powers in older persons than the fact that cultural factors produce higher and higher intellectual test scores in upcoming generations. The data have led Schaie[48] to suggest that cognitive functioning is stable "throughout most of the adulthood range." Storck and Looft[49] also report that little change occurs in the pattern of intellectual activity following adolescence.

They asked subjects of both sexes, ranging in age from six years to advanced old age, to define each of the 45 words contained in the vocabulary subtest of the Stanford-Binet Intelligence Scale. No sex differences appeared, but error rate decreased throughout the childhood and adolescent years, stabilized in adulthood, and increased again after age 60. The researchers found that definitions based on description, demonstration, and illustration were rare at all ages. The definitions based on explanation were slightly more common among adults; however, those based on synonyms rose sharply after childhood to predominate as the adult form of response. Storck and Looft[50] concluded that individuals progress in their structuring of word definitions from concrete and action-oriented definitions in early childhood to more abstract and conceptual formulizations in later childhood, adolescence, and adulthood.

DEVELOPMENTAL ANALYSES OF COGNITION

The broad developmental guidelines of cognitive growth were anticipated in philosophy before psychology became an empirical science.[51] It was assumed that children's thought processes became increasingly complex as they advanced in age through adolescence. Whether intelligence was a product of unfolding genetic structures or of experience (interaction with the environment), successively more advanced modes of function were believed to be predicated on mastery of earlier modes. The venerable assumption that cognitive growth advanced from elementary to complex thought processes is today a major cornerstone of psychological theory.

Cognitive growth appears to take place in invariant sequences; for purposes of contrast, the child's cognitive-developmental status has usually been designated as *concrete* and the adolescent's as *abstract*. Elkind, Barocas, and Johnsen[52] have suggested three criteria by which the intellectual processes of the child and the adolescent may be distinguished: (1) quantitative—the logic of the child is restricted to simple combinations of one or two classes or relations, whereas that of the adolescent is open to a synthesis of several factors; (2) qualitative—the child is bound to a single, concrete level of symbolic representation of the perception and function of things, but the adolescent possesses a sophisticated reasoning capacity that permits manipulation of symbols in novel ways; (3) affective—the child is less certain than the adolescent of the efficacy of thought processes and, being less able to assimilate facts, is more susceptible to suggestion. The essence of these distinctions lie in an adolescent's greater capacity to reason without reference to direct experience. A child is not entirely dependent on concrete experiences for the substance of thought, but the level of a child's generalizations is likely to be relatively simple. An adolescent, in

Intellectual development is essentially a process of coming to terms with one's world.

contrast, can manipulate hypothetical relations among ideas and can formulate general laws that relate to categories far removed from immediate (concrete-empirical) reality.

The Acquisition of Cognitive Structures

Every phase of a high school program stresses intellectual standards, whether in history, electronics, or athletics. The necessity of efficient judgment and effective action dominates every phase of the curricula. Adolescents are required to master factual and conceptual content, and their thought processes are expected to be clear and precise.[53] How, then, do adolescents acquire powers of analysis and judgment? How does one enter the world of abstractions and ideas? Two explanations are discussed here. The first, that of E. A. Peel, concentrates on the judgmental factors that lead to mature intellectual behavior. The second, that of Jean Piaget, centers on young people's use of propositional logic. The two viewpoints are highly complementary, and considering them together provides a comprehensive review of the logical operations by which adolescents structure information.

E. A. Peel's Explanation of Cognitive Growth. Peel[54] holds that "the urge to come to intellectual terms with one's world provides the mainspring of intellectual development." Intellectual effort prior to adolescence is dominated by descriptive content, which is seldom integrated in the wider context of ongoing knowledge. It is limited to the here-and-now. Adolescent thought, on the other hand, is marked by efforts to explain, judge, and invoke the possible, setting it against the actual. Cognitive growth during adolescence thus signifies transition from "content-dominated to possibility-invoking" analyses.[55] A rational outlook requires, however, that the elements in every new situation be brought into equilibrium. The necessity of equilibrium operates in the realm of cognitive activity just as it does in the world of nature, where climate, terrain, organic life, and human intervention constantly upset ecological balances.[56] Childhood forms of cognitive equilibrium may occur, for example, when events are simply described. Adolescent equilibrium may require sophisticated hypotheses and analyses.

Peel uses simple reasoning tests to illustrate the wide range found among adolescents in their capacity for setting the possible against the actual. Young people may be given a proposition and be asked to examine it against information also provided them. One proposition put to youth pertained to Crofter [small field] farmers in Scotland: "Are the Crofters making the best use of their land by growing crops over such a small area?" The adolescents were supplied with surveyor, climactic, demographic, and geographical data, all of which brought out the poor quality of the land. And they were provided charts showing both the kind of crops that might grow on the land and the number of sheep and cattle that might be pastured on it. The adolescents were required to use deductive reasoning in analyzing the proposition. The following statements reveal the breadth in their logical powers:[57]

1. Egocentric:
   "'Yes, because they've got the beauty of the deer in the forest.'"
   "'They're making good use of their land.'"
2. Content-dominated—seizure of *one* piece of visual evidence:
   "'If they didn't have so many animals, they could have more crops.'"
3. Consideration of more than one factor:
   "'Yes, because he does not need too many crops. The more pasture he has the better his sheep and cattle are fed.'"

4. Systematic appraisal:

"'The crofters are sensible in growing only a few crops over a little area because the ground is mainly mountains and very rough. It would be hard to get the necessary amount of crops needed to feed the crofters, the only crops which they have cultivated with a little success are the hardier, tougher crops, oats and potatoes. The land can be made better use of by rough grazing with sheep on the hills and mountains.'''

The quality of adolescent explanations and judgments obviously varies considerably among youth. Adolescent thought reveals itself "chiefly in the range of circumstantial and imaginative-comprehensive judgments" that youth make, and Peel has identified three basic criteria against which the quality of their judgments may be assessed:[58]

1. *Restricted*—adolescent denies premise or other conditions of problem, or is put off by irrelevancies.
2. *Circumstantial*—adolescent is dominated by the content of material, often fails to look beyond it, and may take account at first of only one element.
3. *Imaginative-Comprehensive*—adolescent considers material in terms of hypotheses from previous experience and invokes independent ideas.

Peel's data also suggest that the power to maintain a sustained argument, to reason deductively, to hold more than one hypothesis in mind, and to discuss a problem situation comprehensively in terms of all possibilities, appears only in a minority of young persons before 13 to 15 years of age. Moreover, Peel contends that "selecting and rejecting hypotheses provides a severe test of thinking for all but the most able and mature adolescent thinkers."[59] Although a rapid acceleration of power to offer explanation and make judgments occurs during adolescence, many youth and adults, he says, never acquire the capacity to make satisfactory explanations, and hence, cannot arrive at sound judgments. What then, are the cognitive elements that affect intellectual judgment and the developmental factors that contribute to individual differences in maturity of judgment? Let us turn now to Piaget's outlook for consideration of these issues.

Jean Piaget's Explanation of Cognitive Growth. Since his book, *Language and Thought of the Child,* appeared in 1923, Piaget, a Swiss psychologist, and his collaborators have published more than 30 books and hundreds of research studies. Elkind[60] divides the substance of this output into three chronological periods: exploration of children's mental processes and spontaneous ideas about the physical world, search for the origin of children's intellect in infant behavior, and study of how children cope conceptually with alterations either in aspects of reality or in their own movements relative to aspects of reality.

Piaget has concentrated his attention, throughout his long and productive career, on one basic, epistemological question: How does an individual become progressively able to interpret and understand experiences objectively? The question of knowledge acquisition is synonymous in the Piagetian system with the question of the development of intelligence. Piaget, moreover, is more interested in the adaptive aspects of intellectual activity than in the range of variations that may appear across individuals. Cognitive functions, he says, extend biological organization and adaptation. As Furth[61] suggests, Piaget's theoretical outlook should be interpreted in the wider context of evolutionary theory.

Cognitive knowledge, and hence, intellectual growth, is acquired as an individual learns to coordinate actions and interrelate experiences. It is *constructed* via actions as an indivisible subject-object relation; knowledge originates neither as preformed structures in the subject nor as external configurations in the environment. It is a product of *interaction* between subject and environment. Piaget thus rejects the implication found in several current learning theories that knowledge is a body of content apart from the individual and that intelligence is acquired by filing perceptions and associations in the mind. On the contrary, objective knowledge is linked with action—"in order to know objects, the subject must act upon them, and therefore transform them: he must displace, connect, combine, take apart, and reassemble them."[62]

Piaget's explanation of cognitive growth begins with the assumption that motor behavior is the basis for cognitive activity. Although the infant is largely unable to differentiate the external world from the subjective world, its primitive interactions lay the basis for knowledge acquisition. At birth the individual has a few unmodifiable innate reflexes, like yawning, sucking, and sneezing, and a variety of initial reflexes that will begin to stabilize with experience. These early, flexible mental structures are called *schemas*. In the Piagetian system the schema is the primary unit of cognitive organization, and it is viewed as the product of both experience and maturation. It is never static, but is continuously changing. A schema is modified as new experiences are incorporated into it. The concept of schema thus is advanced to describe how changes in perception and motor behavior are coordinated in the course of learning. When the level of coordination develops to the point that interrelationships among experiences occur, the primitive actions yield to logical systems and cognitive activity is transformed into "operations." The operations are "interiorized actions." An active operation, for example, might involve addition, which may be reversed through subtraction. Operations lead eventually to the generalizable aspects of action. The general content of knowledge is disassociated from specific instances, and thus, more abstractions are acquired and greater internalization of knowledge occurs.

The dynamics of cognitive knowing in Piagetian terms may be illustrated by two major psychological processes: *assimilation*—whereby incoming information is integrated into evolving or completed structures; *accommodation*—whereby existing schemas or structures are modified on the basis of incoming information. Assimilation and accommodation function simultaneously at all age levels to facilitate cognitive adaptation and intellectual growth. Assimilation ensures "the continuity of structures and the integration of new elements to these structures."[63] When assimilation "outweighs" accommodation thought may become egocentric or autistic, for then, the reality at hand is construed to represent whatever the individual is imagining. Accommodation services knowledge acquisition by subordinating assimilation to the objective properties of external reality. Accommodation, nonetheless, must also be subordinated to existing cognitive structures, for otherwise, the representation of reality may be accepted so uncritically that cognitive activity will fail to rise above imitative levels of thought.

Cognitive adaptation consists of achieving equilibrium between assimilation and accommodation. Intellectual growth may be seen as "a progressive series of attempted assimilations, necessary accommodations, and new equilibriated assimilations at a higher level."[64] Piaget points out that equilibrium between the two processes is difficult to attain and to maintain, but it exists at all levels, whether in the early intellectual development of a child or in the advanced scientific thought of an adult. Progressive equilibration between assimilation and accommodation involves a process that Piaget describes in terms of "*centration*" and "*decentration*." When assimilations are distorted because adequate accommodations are lacking, individuals remain "centered" on their own actions and their own viewpoint. On the other hand, appropriate accommodation is marked by "decentration," whereby individuals take the point of view of other persons or of things and elements, which leads gradually to successful equilibrium. Piaget[65] says that systematic decentration is required for cognitive progress, for it is a necessary prerequisite of objectivity.

Equilibriation provides the dynamic motivation for intellectual growth. Most individuals will avoid investing cognitive energy in situations that are either too elementary or too complex. Individuals are mainly interested, for example, in events occurring around them that are novel enough to warrant assimilation and familiar enough to justify accommodation. But a stream of new information usually disturbs that which is incomplete or incorrect, and new equilibria often falter, resulting in further efforts toward assimilation and accommodation. Furth[66] suggests that seeking a state of equilibrium is like looking for a pot of gold at the end of a rainbow. Equilibration is self-regulatory, however, not in the sense of balancing opposite forces, but in the sense that it facilitates cognitive organization as it seeks out more advanced structures. It holds external disturbances aroused by assimilation and accommodation reciprocal to one another. Its processes are constantly at work, correcting and self-regulating the coordination of actions and constructing structures, and Piaget regards this work as the basis of intelligence.

Equilibriation is viewed in the Piagetian system as being a function simultaneously of neurological maturation, interaction with the physical world, and feedback from social experiences. First, the course of intellectual growth is regarded as essentially gradual and continuous, unfolding in an invariant, lawful sequence, which attests to its partly biological origins. Second, interaction with the physical environment fosters cognitive development in two major modes. On the one hand, Piaget has identified *physical experience,* which consists of extracting information from external reality through simple abstraction. Physical experience involves discovery of such characteristics, qualities, and properties as shape, color, and form. A child, for example, may discover weight while disregarding color, or discover among similar objects that weight is greater as volume increases, and so forth. Such abstractions are arbitrary in the sense that they may be derived solely from physical properties and are largely devoid of logical necessity.[67] On the other hand, Piaget has also identified *logicomathematical experience* as another interactive experience with the physical world. It consists of discovering knowledge through action exerted on things that otherwise would lack the knowledge. This kind of interaction extends perception beyond simple awareness of physical properties, and it possesses a logical necessity. Let us say, for example, that a child who is counting marbles happens to put them in a row. The child may discover that the number remains the same by counting either to the left or to the right, and should the marbles be arranged in a circle, the child may find that the sum is independent of order. Piaget views such behavior as a logicomathematical experiment and not a physical one because neither the sum nor the order was innate to the marbles before the child's action upon them. Third, feedback from social experience is important because cognitive growth may be accelerated or retarded in respect to average chronological age by the child's cultural and educational environment. Although

Piaget insists that intellectual growth follows the same sequential order in any environment, he also acknowledges that differences among young people in their intellectual maturity may be attributed in part to the influence of the social environment. Equilibriation, then, in dealing with assimilation and accommodation, must also coordinate these three factors "in a consistent, non-contradictory totality."

Jean Piaget's Stages in Cognitive Growth. Since the progression to sophisticated operational thought is continuous, its division into stages is fairly arbitrary. The concept of stages, however, enables one to distinguish aspects of children's thinking from those of adolescents and adults. Piaget has identified a succession of relatively stable stages; the later ones incorporating and extending what has been achieved by the earlier ones. But Piaget has been imprecise in designating the number and the names of the stages in his hierarchical model. Tuddenham[68] noted that the later writings of Piaget and his followers discuss four stages: the *sensorimotor,* from birth until two or three years of age; the *preoperational,* between two and seven years of age; *concrete operations,* between seven and 11 or 12 years of age; and *formal operations,* from 12 years of age onward, when full cognitive capacity has been attained. Each of these stages may be further subdivided. As many as six substages have been identified within the sensorimotor period, for example, where fine distinctions can be made in the coordinations between internal thought and external action. Since internalized operations become increasingly significant with age, detailed subdivisions tend to lose their meaning at adolescence; at that time age appears to be very loosely correlated with specific points in the sequence of cognitive growth.

 1. During the *sensorimotor stage,* the child comes to understand mean-ends relations. At first, innate reflexes are merely exercised, but later they are coordinated into elementary habits. At this stage, concepts of objects develop gradually from the coordination of several schemas. The infant initially is unaware of the boundaries even of its own body; it responds reflexively to objects in its perceptual field, including parts of its own body. The growth of infant thought during this period poses a series of unique problems and solutions, each of which adds new dimensions to equilibriation. If an infant looks on while a bright object, such as a watch, is slipped under a handkerchief, it will ignore the object after is has disappeared if it is only a few months old. When the infant is a little older, it will search randomly for the watch when it disappears, but gradually, with advancing age, it will learn to search for the shiny object with increasing purpose and insight. The child progresses from simply

reacting to things to knowing things; it moves toward internalized coordination of action and develops the capacity to distinguish between its symbolic representation of things and events and the referents themselves. Thus the child starts to use symbols to evoke and reconstruct past and future events. The symbol becomes more than an appendage to its actions; it becomes a significant resource for conceptualizing the action in memory. It enables the child to perceive objects as permanent, with a constant size, shape, and color. During this stage, the child acquires the cognitive capacity to consider simultaneously events that actually occurred separately in time. It begins to integrate events comprehensively. Its memory of past events and its anticipation of future contingencies enables it to consider symbolically events in other time sequences than those that have happened or might occur. The child acquires the capacity to elaborate new means to ends "not merely by external differentiation and combination with trial and error, but by internal coordination that manifests itself in new and sudden insights."[69] When the child realizes that things are distinguishable and have relationships with one another, it has finally achieved its earliest form of symbolic behavior. This start of internal coordination will take more than 12 years to complete.

The initial momentum necessary for the transition from sensorimotor acts to mental operations happens when the child takes an active interest in its cognitive activity as well as in the results of its actions, and when its capacity for subject-object differentiation trancends the spatial and temporal bounds of immediate experience. However, at this stage, the young child's interaction with its environment is marked by certain aspects of egocentrism. It lacks the capacity, for example, to differentiate between the reality of an object and its sense impression of it. By one year of age, the infant can show that it knows how to differentiate between an object and its experience of it. Although object *permanence* occurs fairly early, the young child will still have difficulty understanding that objects have more than a temporal identity. For example, it will insist that the shape of a mountain changes as it passes by it. The child's concept of spatial relations will shift with changes in its perspective; the concept appears to be limited by the extent to which the child has explored its environment and its capacity to recall familiar places.

2. During the *preoperational stage,* from two until around seven years of age, children make a "conquest of the symbol."[70] Their mental imagery grows out of sensorimotor activity. Flavell[71] describes the preoperational child as "a cognizer for whom the world is beginning to stand still and stay put—a world which, like the child himself, knows something of law and order, and above all a world in which thought really counts for something, in which thought can be a more trustworthy guide to action than perception is." At this stage, children acquire language and symbolic functions. At first, preoperational children are wholly egocentric in their representations; they will interpret reality on the basis of their perceptions, and concepts will be abstracted from immediate sensory experience. Their mental activity and linguistic expressions also are egocentric. They will interpret the meaning of words by assimilating them to their cognitive schemas rather than by accommodating them to conventional meanings. When explaining something to another child, for example, they may use idiosyncratic terms and omit pertinent information. They either fail to understand the other child's point of view or they think that the words they have chosen to describe the object surely convey its properties.

Children's cognitive activity during the preoperational period is dominated by physical experiences. Although they may appear to understand the meaning of relational concepts, they are unable to coordinate them spontaneously. For example, they are less likely to use relational terms like "more" and "less" than absolute terms like "big" and "small." They will probably not simultaneously use such differentiated dimensions as long/short or fat/thin to describe an object. When there is more than one dimension to a problem situation, they may focus on a salient detail and neglect other important but less obvious ones. If preoperational children are presented with two containers of equal size, one tall and thin, and the other short and wide, they are likely to consider height as the critical determinant of size, neglecting the factor of width. When liquid is poured from the short into the tall container, they probably will insist that the tall container now holds more liquid.

Children's symbolic capacity to coordinate simple representations during the preoperational stage is reflected in the gestures and movements that they have *interiorized*. They may use their fingers to represent a quantity of things, and such gestural representations may provide the initial steps toward addition and substraction operations. Their conception of numbers begins with an intuitive feeling of whether more or less is in one configuration or another. Their understanding is based on idiosyncratic experience rather than on a logicomathematical system for representing numbers. In given situations children will focus on the qualitative rather than the quantitative amount of things to be considered. Piaget has demonstrated this in several ingenious experiments. When a candy bar is broken up, for example, children think that the parts are greater than the whole. Children have some idea of equality in physical dimensions, so that when two plasticene balls of equal size are shown to them and they are asked if they are the same size, they will say that they are. But then, even as they watch, if one of the balls is rolled into a sausage shape and they are asked the question again, they are likely to assert that one has more plasticene than the other—either the sausage or the ball, depending on which they happen to view as larger.

Toward the end of the preoperational stage, youngsters acquire the capacity to conceptualize the image of a thing as being independent of their perceptions of its configuration. As the decentering process ascends in cognitive activity, children begin to understand that there are perspectives other than their own. Children might be asked, for example, to imagine how a doll would view the shape of a mountain from several different positions. Borke[72] has shown that when such a task is formulated within the range of children's conceptualization, even three- and four-year-olds are capable of role-taking another person's perspective. But Borke also points out that when the task is confusing, children are likely to resort to their own perspective in an attempt to perform successfully.

3. During the *concrete operations stage,* children acquire the capacity to reason effectively about things, but not yet about verbal propositions.[73] Their reasoning ability is characterized by the development of three important skills— transitivity (relationships and seriation), conservation, and class inclusion. Brainerd[74] suggests that in most concept areas the three skills emerge during the late preschool and middle-childhood years. Moreover, he says, "class inclusion is *never* grasped at a level comparable to transitivity and conservation."

Transitivity is illustrated by children's capacity to arrange elements in a series: If $X = Y$ and $Y = Z$, then $X = Z$, or if $X > Y$ and $Y > Z$, then $X > Z$. Assume, for example, that a child is shown three different balls, A, B, and C, which differ in size. The child can tell by looking at them and without comparing them directly, that if A is bigger than B, and B is larger than C, then A is larger than C. On the other hand, concrete-operational children are less able to reason about verbal propositions than about things. When they are given the problem, "Helen is taller than Mary, and Mary is taller than Jane, who is the tallest of the three," they are unable to solve it despite the fact that it is comparable to the problem with the balls.[75] However, children learn to make limited coordinations as their cognitive operations become more flexible. Elkind[76] has illustrated how the elementary coordinations might occur. Preoperational children who are given a set of size-graded slats and asked to insert them in a set of larger-sized slats, arranged in the form of a staircase, will probably make several mistakes or fail entirely. But children at the stage of concrete operations will experience little difficulty. They see the relation between the two sets: a, b, c, d, e, f and A, B, C, D, E, F, and are able, for example, to compose the relations $A < a < B,$ and so on, recognizing that a must be both larger than A and smaller than B.

Conservation is one of the most significant characteristics of cognitive activity to be acquired during the concrete-operational stage. Children discover the meaning of constancy in the course of any given change or transformation. They discover that there are important features of an object or situation that remain the same within a general context of change; thus, they learn that logical thought permits reversible operations. They recognize that subtraction can cancel addition and division can cancel multiplication. Children recognize that a clay ball can be made into a sausage and then be reconstructed into its original form as a ball, and that water can be heated to become vapor and then condensed back into water. Conservation enables children to compensate for disequilibrium, for example, by assimilating the external transformations of a given object (like a straight line turned into a semicircle), which enables them to hold constant the basic invariant of length.

Children at this stage, for example, develop the capacity to conserve the quantity of various properties even though their arrangement in a spatial configuration has been markedly transformed. First, they learn about the conservation of discrete quantities; if a number of flowers are arranged in vases so that there is one flower per vase, and then they are taken out and grouped together, concrete-operational children will know that the quantity of flowers is the same. At about seven years of age they will understand the conservation of continuous quantities like water. They will recognize that an amount of liquid poured from a tall, thin glass into a short, wide one remains the same. Heretofore, because they had focused primarily on the amount of space the water occupied, they perceived that the amount of liquid changed with its appearance. Conservation of attributes associated with weight is said to be achieved at about nine years of age, and with volume, at about 11 years of age. However, Sheppard[77] has shown that when five- or six-year-old youngsters are trained systematically to observe relations among changes in volume, height, and breadth of water in various cylinders, they are able to develop conservation concepts at this early age. Further, Botvin and Murray[78] have shown conservation of number, amount, mass, and weight can be accelerated in six- to nine-year-old youngsters who either simply observe older children's performance of mass and weight problems or argue about the problems with them in a contrived social-conflict situation.

Children also learn at the concrete operational stage to differentiate the world in terms of logical classification. As they develop a capacity to deal with general classification and subclassification simultaneously, they acquire the ability to conceptualize several pieces of information at once. Further, their growing capacity to combine, order, and reverse elements enables them to categorize and to create hierarchies of classes.

Although children at the concrete level of cognitive operations are beginning to put their thoughts together, the logic of their thinking is dominated by direct personal experience. Children still are unable to differentiate clearly between what they think and what they perceive. Surprisingly, this lack of differentiation stems from their capacity to engage in operational thought.[79] Whereas now they construct hypotheses and strategies, they may, as yet, be unable to distinguish between assumptions and facts. Older persons will test an hypothesis against evidence, but children may reject or reinterpret facts to fit the hypothesis. Elkind[80] thus says that youngsters often operate on the basis of "*assumptive realities,* assumptions about reality that children make on the basis of limited information and which they will not alter in the face of new and contradictory evidence." Elkind points out that assumptive realities resemble delusions, in that both indicate failure to distinguish between thought and reality. Assumptive realities, however, are derived primarily from new cognitive abilities and lack the "systematization and narcissism of true delusions."

4. *The formal operations stage.* Children arrive at the threshold of formal-stage thinking when they have mastered the logic of transitivity of relations, established the conservation of concrete, physical properties, and arrived at the rudimentary concrete operations of classification. Formal-operational thinking is marked, as Peel would say, by capacity to reason in terms of the full range of relevant possibilities. Adolescents can follow the form of an argument whatever its specific content, can consider different hypotheses, and can contemplate what might follow it they were true. Acquisition of formal-operational structures means that "form relative to content" now is more significant to thought processes. Dulit[81] employs three interchangeable terms to describe formal-stage thinking: "formal," "propositional," and "abstract." "Formal" focuses on relations, as in a mathematical equation or a syllogism, for example, where symbols or propositions are used to represent particular variables. "Propositional" emphasizes that mature thinking is cast in terms of principles, statements, and hypotheses. "Abstract" indicates that it deals with attributes derived from external reality—hypotheses, ideas, and concepts—as well as with reality itself.

Adolescents develop cognitive structures with which they can unify the separate thought processes of the concrete operational stage. Hypothetical and deductive-level thought now expresses itself in linguistic formulations. "Formal thinking is both thinking about thought (propositional logic is a second-order operational system which operates on propositions whose truth, in turn, depends on class, relational, and numerical operations) and a reversal of relations between what is real and what is possible. . . ."[82]

The ability to generate all possible combinations within a logical system provides the basis for adolescent intellectual accomplishments. According to

Piaget,[83] two new structures are constructed between 11 and 15 years of age which make propositional manipulation possible. These are the "combinatorial" and "four-group" operations. Combinatorial activity involves classification relative to all possible categories, and is less an entirely new operation than "an operation on other operations." Combinatorial logic may be demonstrated via an experiment in which individuals are presented with five bottles of colorless liquid. Three bottles will produce a brownish color when combined. The fourth contains a color-reducing solution, and the fifth is neutral. The problem is to discover how to produce the colored solution. It is necessary to construct a table to determine all the possible combinations, and to assess the effectiveness or the ineffectiveness of each liquid. Combinatorial analysis thus "refers to the complete and ordered (organized) matrix of all possible combinations of all possible values of all possible variables inherent in a problem."[84]

The second new structure characteristic of formal-stage thinking consists of four interrelated logical operations: Identity, Negation, Reciprocity, and Correlativity. Each of these cognitive operations, which are described collectively as the I N R C group, represents a different way of transforming information. The I N R C group also bears on prior operations. Concrete-operational children readily invoke the I and N operations. They may use various cognitive plans to solve a problem. Identity (I) refers to a cognitive operation that has been performed; Negation (N) is the direct annulment of the operation, that is, a return to its starting point. Acquisition of the concept of conservation of quantity, for example, is facilitated by imagining water being poured from one container into others of different shapes (Identity operations), and by mentally inverting the acts of pouring (Negation operations). Indeed, I is like running a film clip forward for a moment, and N is like running it backward for the same period of time. Since concrete-operational children conceptualize largely in terms of how things go together in classes or orders, they are unable to coordinate relationships easily. They cannot readily invoke the reciprocal (R) operation, for example, which consists of manipulating a related variable such that the situation will be comparable to the state it was in before an I operation was performed. The primary characteristic of an R operation is that when the original operation (I) is combined with the reciprocal, the original equivalence is restored. A correlative operation (C), however, reverses the reciprocal operation so that it is negated. C cancels R in the same way that N annuls I.

The role of the I N R C group of propositional rules can be illustrated by a person's cognitive activity in discovering the significance of proportionality between weight and distance with a balance scale. Let us assume that two equal weights are placed on the balance bar an equal distance from the center of the scale. One might unbalance the scale by adding weight to one side (I); Negation (N) would occur when the new weight is removed. However, let us assume that rather than removing the weight to restore the balance, the weight on either side of the scale is shifted away from or toward the center (R). The latter operation requires an understanding of proportional relationships among weights and distances of weights from the fulcrum. This understanding leads to knowledge of how weights and distances are reciprocal to one another. The individual learns that, beginning with two equal weights at an equal distance from the center, equilibrium is maintained by decreasing one weight but moving it away from the center or by increasing the other weight and moving it closer in. But when the reciprocal change (R) is annulled directly (C), by moving the new weight one way or the other, the scale becomes unbalanced again. The effect is the same as that made by the initial operation (I), and therefore, the operation (C) is "correlated" with the operation (I). The logic of formal-operational thinking thus represents a synthesis into one system of two kinds of reversibility—Negation and Reciprocity. When they become functionally equivalent, adolescents possess the cognitive capacity to structure complex conceptual systems.

Formal Operations and Adolescent Social Expression. Capacity for combinatorial activity and ability to apply the I N R C group to propositional operations enable adolescents to advance to sophisticated stages of equilibrium. Piaget holds that cognitive structural development and adaptation to everyday life are on the same plane of reality. The logic of formal operations is the expression of operational coordination essential to action.[85] Thus the new cognitive structures enable adolescents to assimilate novel events into their frame of reference, to work out a plan of action, and to suspend accommodation until they are convinced that their perceptions of reality are true.

G. Stanley Hall and Sigmund Freud also suggested in different ways that adolescents' acquisition of formal operations is a product of their interaction with the environment. Hall believed that the guiding force of hereditary momentum exhausted itself at adolescence; thus, all subsequent growth of intellect was at the mercy of unpredictable environmental factors. The psychoanalytic approach regards social control of sexual impulses as a major determinant of ability to conceptualize abstract thought. Anna Freud[86] said that adolescents' "mental activity is rather an indication of intense alertness for the instinctual processes and the translation into abstract thought of that which they perceive." At latency, children (at the concrete operational stage) are likely to be primarily interested in actual objects and real things in the environment. But then suddenly, at adolescence, they are unable to deal with the full force of their impulses, and so they try to intellectualize their instinctual lives by representing them abstractly. Their struggle to bring their impulses into accord with reality presumably leads to their adoption of formal operational procedures. Although insights may be nurtured and strengthened, conflict inherent in their lifestyle may thwart their use of abstract logic. All too often, "adolescent intellectualization seems merely to minister to daydreams."[87]

Cognitive learning during adolescence consists of more than piling segments of learning on top of each other; it involves reinforcing perspectives gained from increases in knowledge. Peel and Piaget have demonstrated that before the advent of formal operations children are likely to focus on a single dominant feature in a given situation, whereas adolescents are likely to consider several possibilities, many of which might be only implicit. Children probably will express themselves as if they were stating absolute truths; however, formal-operational thinking leads adolescents to state their conclusions tentatively. The capacity to grasp a metaphor, for example, presupposes the ability to recognize parallels between disparate things and to separate the figure from its literal presentation. The ability to see many possible meanings in a concrete figure, no matter how removed these may be from literal interpretation, is a product of the combinatorial potential of formal operational thought.[88] These higher forms of thought, which were instrumental in eliminating the egocentricity of concrete operational thought, however, now involve adolescents in new forms of egocentricity. Adolescents acquire the ability to conceptualize not only their own thought but also the thought of others, but according to Elkind,[89] the crux of their egocentrism lies in their frequent failure to take account other people's thought and to differentiate between events, the interests of others, and their own interests.

Cognitive growth requires adolescents to continue the decentering process. Elkind believes that changes in physical growth intensify adolescents' thoughts about themselves; because they fail to differentiate between what others are thinking and their own thoughts, they imagine that others are as interested in their appearance and behavior as they are. "It is this belief that others are preoccupied with his appearance and behavior that constitutes the egocentrism of the adolescent."[90] Elkind asserts that adolescent cognitive capacity for introspection fosters a self-consciousness that leads youth to construct and react to an "imaginary audience." He suggests that when adolescents are feeling self-critical, they may be secretive and reluctant to reveal themselves to others, not wishing to encounter criticism. On other occasions they may be self-admiring. Adolescent boorishness, loudness, and faddish clothes are perhaps attributable to their failure to differentiate between what they believe is attractive and what significant others admire. Elkind[91] says that the beliefs adolescents develop about their own feelings represent "personal fables"—untrue stories that they tell themselves. Elkind suggests that the evidence for personal fables is common in adolescent diaries, which are often written seemingly for posterity in the belief that the authors' experiences, crushes, and frustrations are of universal significance.

Adolescent exaggerations end as they are obliged to assume responsibilities. Inhelder and Piaget[92] suggest that one point at which the adaptation or "decentering" may occur is when adolescents contemplate entering the occupational world. The adolescent "is transformed from an idealistic reformer into an achiever." As Elkind[93] puts it, the imaginary audience is modified in the direction of the real audience, and personal fable is overcome by development of real intimacy—the integration of the feelings of others with one's own.

Generality of Formal Operations. Formal-operational thought has its roots in concrete operations, and "all healthy persons in all societies and ranks of life reach the stage of concrete operation."[94] Piaget once presumed that formal thinking was equally universal.[95] His model of cognitive development certainly would lead one to assume that formal-operational reasoning is generalizable to a wide variety of tasks. However, research evidence amassed during the past few years has led Piaget today to acknowledge that social interests and aptitudes may critically affect usage of formal reasoning. For example, Dulit[96] has reported that formal-stage thinking emerges in adolescence as a potentiality "only partially attained by most and fully atttained only by some." Dulit conducted two formal-stage experiments, one involving a proportionality problem and the other a combinatorial problem. Dulit's experimental comparisons were made among four different groups: (a) 14 year olds of average academic performance. (b) 16 to 17 year olds of average academic performance, (c) 16 to 17 year olds of superior academic performance, especially in the sciences, and (d) 20 to 55-year-old adults, randomly selected. Subjects were asked in the proportionality experiment to place rings in sets of two somewhere between a candle and a screen such that when the candle is lit it would cast a single shadow of the rings on the screen. The solution required that subjects recognize that the size of the shadows is directly proportional to the ring diameters and inversely proportional to the distance between the rings and the candle. Subjects were required in the combinatorial problem, via paper and pencil simulation, to derive a yellow-colored liquid from plain-colored fluids placed in five containers of equal size. The yellow solution could be obtained by two different combinations, one somewhat more complex than the other. Dulit found that none of his subjects in the youngest group functioned at the fully formal level on both problems. One-quarter to one-third of the average-adolescent and adult groups, respectively, and 60 percent of the gifted group, however, functioned at the formal level.

Dulit's[97] findings have been confirmed by other investigators. Ashton[98] reports that cross-cultural studies have failed uniformly to demonstrate that development of formal operational thought is universal. Studies conducted in Sardinia, Papua-New Guinea, Australia, and the Belgian Congo have revealed low rates of formal reasoning. In several societies, the data indicated that the majority of adults had failed to progress beyond concrete modes of operation. Barratt[99] administered several combinatorial pretests to 12-, 13-, and 14-year-old youth, who were gifted in high school mathematics. Combinatorial performance was relatively poor overall, but more successful in problems involving only a few elements. The researcher reports, however, that after two training sessions in combinatorial problem-solving, skills of the 14 year olds of both sexes increased.

Such evidence has led Piaget[100] to suggest that formal structures are applied differently by each person in his or her particular activities. According to Piaget, a physical scientist might exhibit logicomathematical reasoning, an attorney might work with legal propositions, and a carpenter might deal frequently in proportions. However, as Elkind[101] indicates, the question of the universality of formal operations remains open. Many areas of specialization, for example, may not require formal operations at all. Dulit[102] has suggested that formal-stage reasoning is a function of "demand" for it. He notes that demand for concrete-operational thought—conservation of number, mass and volume, serial ordering, correspondence, association, and so forth—is an everyday occurrence in a wide range of societies; however, only a few individuals, even in the advanced technological societies, are required to engage in formal thinking. It is probable that many individuals function in their daily lives, in the face of conflicts and crises, by processes of reasoning that are unlike formal-operational thought.[103] Tomlinson-Keasey[104] suggests that there may be a hierarchy of skills that comprise formal thought. Certain operations, for example, may constitute "transition skills," which are basic to abstract formulations, others may relate to isolating variables, and still others, to the integration of operations.

SUMMARY

The study of adolescent cognitive or intellectual functioning consists of two distinct areas. The first encompasses evaluation of developed abilities or previous learning. This includes the achievement test, which measures how much a person has learned in a particular area or school subject; the aptitude test, which predicts how well an individual might learn a new subject, skill, or task; and the intelligence test, which assesses an individual's previous experience relative to future success in a wide variety of situations. The second area is the study of changes in mode of cognitive functioning from infancy through adolescence. Cognitive development usually is described as a series of stages, each of which provides an essential foundation for succeeding stages.

The usefulness of a cognitive test lies in its capacity to discriminate individuals on the basis of socially relevant criteria. Many tests today thus are based on scales that measure attributes of abstract reasoning. The testing movement, however, has recently become the object of social concern on the grounds that minority and economically disadvantaged young people may be misclassified by conventional tests. Consequently, interest is growing in such alternative procedures as: (1) lotteries, evaluation of prior experience, demographic considerations, subjective assessments, and academic grades; (2) tests of temperament, interests, physical skills, and motivation; and (3) new varieties of intelligence tests like those based on diagnosis and mastery learning.

A variety of family socialization factors influence children's intellectual growth. Research has shown that optimal conditions for intellectual growth occur in family environments where parents attempt to accelerate intellectual behavior in a context of moderate structure and discipline. Early pioneers in the field of mental testing assumed that intellectual abilities decline with age and that performance levels reach a peak either in late adolescence or in the early twenties. But these early pioneers overlooked the possibility that education and cultural stimulation after adolescence might affect intelligence. Individuals with a sophisticated educational background who continue to have stimulating experiences in life tend to improve their scores on intelligence tests as they grow older.

Psychological theory holds that cognitive growth advances from elementary to complex thought processes. It appears to take place in an invariant sequence, and for purposes of contrast, the child's cognitive developmental status is usually called *concrete* and the adolescent's, *abstract*. Two European psychologists, E. A. Peel and Jean Piaget, have carefully described and explained how children and adolescents acquire conceptual structures at different ages. Peel holds that each individual strives to maintain cognitive equilibrium between himself or herself and the environment. He believes that intellectual growth between 11 and 20 years of age largely consists of a change from descriptive to explanatory thinking. In the former, the attributes of an event are merely related together; in the latter, they are related to previously explained phenomena and to appropriate generalizations and concepts. In Peel's view, an individual comes to terms with his or her environment by forming concepts—by considering events in terms of hypotheses from previous experience and invoking independent ideas.

Piaget believes that motor activity provides the basis for mental behavior. The cognitive operations that are necessary to cope with life are constructed as the individual interacts with his or her environment. A person begins life with a few unchangeable, innate reflexes and a variety of modifiable reflexes, or *schemas,* which together constitute the primary units of cognitive organization. The notion of schema accounts for changes in perception and the modification of responses during the course of learning. Cognitive growth takes place as the child becomes more and more dependent on an internalized organization of schemas. There are two major dimensions of learning: *assimilation,* whereby the child learns to construe environmental reality in terms of its cognitive structures, and *accommodation,* whereby the child learns to modify its cognitive structures on the basis of reality. The child's cognitive activity is generally within range of either accommodation or assimilation. The process of maintaining internal balance and reaching beyond to more advanced levels of cognitive organization is known as *equilibriation.*

According to Piaget, cognitive growth is divided into several stages: sensorimotor, preoperational, concrete operational, and formal operational. During childhood cognitive activity is largely preoperational. Later, however, the child becomes familiar with the world in terms of logical classifications and learns the meaning of *conservation*— the principle that there are certain features in every context that remain invariant. During the formal operational stage, adolescents may construct two new structures, the "combinatorial" and "four-group" operations, which make propositional manipulation possible. Combinatorial activity involves classification relative to all possible categories, and the four-group operations consist of four interrelated logical operations, Identity, Negation, Reciprocity, and Correlativity, which represent different ways of transforming information. Capacity for combinatorial activity and ability to apply the I N R C group to propositional operations enable adolescents to advance to sophisticated stages of equilibrium; however, research has shown that social interests and aptitudes may critically affect development of formal reasoning.

REVIEW QUESTIONS

1. What are the two distinct traditions in the study of cognitive functioning?
2. Contrast early and contemporary definitions of intelligence.
3. What is the concept of heritability?
4. Distinguish among tests of intelligence, achievement, and aptitude.
5. What are the alternatives to competitive ability testing?
6. What are the effects of parental involvement and standards on the intellectual performance of boys and girls, respectively?
7. What aspects of family background show strong correlation with children's intellectual performance?
8. What kinds of child-rearing practices may lead young people to gain or lose, respectively, in intellectual performance from childhood to adolescence?
9. What is the present status of the "decline assumption"—the belief that intellectual competencies begin to deteriorate after age 20?
10. What attributes distinguish the intellectual processes of children and adolescents?
11. Describe the ways in which adolescents may apply deductive reasoning.

12. Name the basic criteria Peel believes to be useful in analyzing the quality of adolescent judgments.

13. Why should Piaget's theoretical outlook be interpreted in the context of evolutionary theory?

14. What is Piaget's view about how cognitive knowledge is acquired?

15. Describe the roles of schema, assimilation, accommodation, equilibration, and centration in Piaget's system.

16. What factors must equilibration coordinate to foster intellectual growth?

17. What are the characteristics of preoperational thought?

18. Describe transitivity, conservation, and class inclusion as aspects of concrete operational thought.

19. What is the significance of the combinatorial and four-group (I N R C) operations?

20. What does Elkind mean by "imaginary audience" and "personal fable," respectively?

21. Why does development of formal operational thinking vary cross-culturally?

DISCUSSION QUESTIONS

1. Do you accept the assumption that conventional ability testing limits the educational opportunities of minority and economically disadvantaged adolescents? How might the validity of the ability tests be improved? What alternatives to them would you consider?

2. How would you design a family environment to ensure optimal conditions for intellectual growth?

3. What problems, other than that of the balance scale, are applicable to the I N R C group of propositional rules?

4. What sort of experiences in adolescence are especially likely to foster egocentrism?

5. What steps would you take to modify high school instructional programs to facilitate formal operational thinking?

NOTES

1. J. Fiske. *A century of science.* New York: Houghton Mifflin, 1900, p. 107.

2. Fiske, *op. cit.,* p. 108.

3. A. Binet and T. Simon. *The development of intelligence in children,* trans. by E. S. Kite. Baltimore: Williams and Wilkins, 1916, p. 42.

4. L. M. Terman. *The measurement of intelligence.* Boston: Houghton Mifflin, 1916.

5. D. P. Ausubel and P. Ausubel. Cognitive development in adolescence. *Review of Educational Research,* 1966, **36,** 403–413, p. 412.

6. D. Wechsler. *The measurement and appraisal of adult intelligence* (3rd ed.). Baltimore: Williams and Wilkins, 1952, p. 3.

7. D. Wechsler. Intelligence defined and undefined: a relativistic appraisal. *American Psychologist,* 1975, **30,** 135–139, p. 136.

8. Wechsler, Intelligence defined, *op. cit.*

9. T. A. Cleary, L. G. Humphreys, S. A. Kendrick, and A. Wesman. Educational uses of tests with disadvantaged students. *American Psychologist,* 1975, **30,** 15–41.

10. Cleary, et al. *op. cit.*

11. F. L. Goodenough and D. B. Harris. Studies in the psychology of children's drawings: II. 1928–1949. *Psychological Bulletin,* 1950, **47,** 369–433.

12. A. R. Jensen. Heredity, environment, and educability. *Encyclopedia of Education.* New York: Macmillan, 1970, pp. 368–380.

13. Cleary et al., *op. cit.*

14. Ibid.

15. L. J. Cronbach. Five decades of public controversy over mental testing. *American Psychologist,* 1975, **30,** 1–14.

16. Cleary et al., *op. cit.*

17. Ibid.

18. Ibid.

19. Cleary ct al., *op. cit.,* p. 34.

20. Cleary et al., *op. cit.*

21. Ibid.

22. Ibid.

23. Ibid.

24. N. Bayley. Behavioral correlates of mental growth: birth to thirty-six years. *American Psychologist,* 1968, 1–17.

25. M. P. Honzik. Environmental correlates of mental growth: prediction from the family setting at 21 months. *Child Development,* 1967, **38,** 337–364.

26. M. P. Honzik. A sex difference in the age of onset of the parent-child resemblance in intelligence. *Journal of Educational Psychology,* 1963, **54,** 231–237.

27. Honzik, Correlates of mental growth, *op. cit.,* p. 361.

28. H. A. Moss and J. Kagan. Maternal influences on early IQ scores. *Psychological Reports,* 1958, **4,** 655–661.

29. Honzik, Correlates of mental growth, *op. cit.*

30. Honzik, Correlates of mental growth, *op. cit.,* p. 360.

31. Moss and Kagan, *op. cit.,* p. 660.

32. National Center for Health Statistics. *Family background, early development, and intelligence of children 6–11 years, United States,* (DHEW Pub. No. [HRA] 75-1624.) Series 11, No. 142, 1974.

33. R. B. McCall, M. I. Appelbaum, and P. S. Hogarty. Developmental changes in mental

performance. *Monographs of the Society for Research in Child Development,* 1973, **38,** 1–84.

34. Ibid.

35. McCall et al., *op. cit.,* p. 67.

36. McCall et al., *op. cit.,* p. 68.

37. McCall et al., *op. cit.*

38. McCall et al., *op. cit.,* p. 68.

39. R. F. Green. Age-intelligence relationship between ages sixteen and sixty-four: a rising trend. *Developmental Psychology,* 1969, **1,** 618–627.

40. J. McV. Hunt. *Intelligence and experience.* New York: Ronald Press, 1961.

41. B. S. Bloom. *Stability and change in human characteristics.* New York: John Wiley, 1964; Green, *op. cit.*

42. Green, *op. cit.,* p. 626.

43. W. A. Owens. Age and mental abilities: a second adult follow-up. *Journal of Educational Psychology,* 1966, **57,** 311–325.

44. J. D. Nisbet. Contributors to intelligence testing and the theory of intelligence, IV—intelligence and age: retesting with twenty-four years' interval. *British Journal of Educational Psychology,* 1957, **27,** 190–198.

45. Bloom, *op. cit.*

46. J. M. Fitzgerald, J. R. Nesselroade, and P. B. Baltes. Emergence of adult intellectual structure: prior to or during adolescence? *Developmental Psychology,* 1973, **9,** 114–119.

47. K. W. Schaie, G. V. Labouvie, and B. U. Buech. Generational and cohort-specific differences in adult cognitive functioning. *Developmental Psychology,* 1973, **9,** 151–166.

48. Schaie et al., *op. cit.*

49. P. A. Storck and W. R. Looft. Qualitative analysis of vocabulary responses from persons aged six to sixty-six plus. *Journal of Educational Psychology,* 1973, **65,** 192–197.

50. Storck and Looft, *op. cit.*

51. Hall, G. S. *Adolescence.* New York: Appleton, 1904, 2 vols.

52. D. Elkind, R. Barocas, and P. Johnsen. Concept production in children and adolescents. *Human Development,* 1969, **12,** 10–21.

53. E. A. Peel. *The nature of adolescent judgment.* New York: John Wiley, 1971.

54. E. A. Peel. Intellectual growth during adolescence. *Educational Review,* 1965, **17,** 169–180, p. 178.

55. Peel, Adolescent judgment, *op. cit.*

56. Ibid.

57. Peel, Adolescent judgment, *op. cit.,* p. 90–91.

58. Peel, Adolescent judgment, *op. cit.,* pp. 41–42.

59. Peel, Adolescent judgment, *op. cit.,* p. 153.

60. D. Elkind. *Children and adolescents: interpretive essays on Jean Piaget.* New York: Oxford University Press, 1974.

61. H. G. Furth. *Piaget and knowledge.* Englewood Cliffs, New Jersey: Prentice-Hall, 1969.

62. J. Piaget. Piaget's theory. In P. H. Mussen (Ed.). *Carmichael's Manual of Child Psychology.* Vol. 1. New York: Wiley, 1970, p. 704.

63. Piaget, *op. cit.,* p. 707.

64. Elkind, Children and adolescents, *op. cit.,* p. 8.

65. Piaget, *op. cit.*

66. Furth, *op. cit.*

67. Elkind, Children and adolescents, *op. cit.*

68. R. D. Tuddenham. Jean Piaget and the world of the child. *American Psychologist,* 1966, **21,** 207–217.

69. Furth, *op. cit.,* pp. 48–49.

70. Elkind, Children and adolescents, *op. cit.*

71. J. H. Flavell. Piaget's contributions to the study of cognitive development. *Merrill-Palmer Quarterly of Behavior and Development,* 1953, **9,** 245–252.

72. H. Borke. Piaget's mountains revisited: changes in the egocentric landscape. *Developmental Psychology,* 1975, **11,** 240–243.

73. Elkind, Children and adolescents, *op. cit.*

74. C. J. Brainerd. Structures-of-the-whole: is there any glue to hold the concrete-operational "stage" together? Paper presented at the Canadian Psychological Association, 1974, p. 8.

75. Elkind, Children and adolescents, *op. cit.*

76. D. Elkind. Cognitive development in adolescence. In J. F. Adams (Ed.). *Understanding adolescence.* Boston: Allyn & Bacon, 1968, pp. 128–158.

77. J. L. Sheppard. Compensation and combinatorial systems in the acquisition and generalization of conservation. *Child Development,* 1974, **45,** 717–730.

78. G. J. Botvin and F. B. Murray. The efficacy of peer modeling and social conflict in the acquisition of conservation. *Child Development,* 1975, **46,** 796–799.

79. Elkind, Children and adolescents, *op. cit.*

80. Elkind, Children and adolescents, *op. cit.,* p. 79.

81. E. Dulit. Adolescent thinking à la Piaget: the formal stage. *Journal of Youth and Adolescence,* 1972, **1,** 281–301.

82. B. Inhelder and J. Piaget *The growth of logical thinking.* New York: Basic Books, 1958, p. 341.

83. Piaget, *op. cit.* p. 727.

84. Dulit, *op. cit.,* p. 284.

85. Inhelder and Piaget, *op. cit.,* p. 342.

86. A. Freud. *The ego and the mechanisms of defense*. New York: International University Press, 1946, p. 177.

87. Freud, *op. cit.,* p. 176.

88. Elkind, Children and adolescents. *op. cit.*

89. D. Elkind. Egocentrism in adolescence. *Child Development,* 1967, **38,** 1025–1034.

90. Elkind, Egocentrism in adolescence, *op. cit.,* p. 1030.

91. Elkind, Egocentrism in adolescence, *op. cit.*

92. Inhelder and Piaget, *op. cit.,* p. 346.

93. Elkind, Egocentrism in adolescence, *op. cit.*

94. H. G. Furth. Piaget, IQ, and the nature-nurture controversy. *Human Development,* 1973, **16,** 61–73.

95. Inhelder and Piaget, *op. cit.*

96. Dulit, *op. cit.,* p. 281.

97. Dulit, *op. cit.*

98. P. T. Ashton. Cross-cultural Piagetian research: an experimental perspective. *Harvard Educational Review,* 1975, **45,** 475–506.

99. B. B. Barratt. Training and transfer in combinatorial problem-solving: the development of formal reasoning during adolescence. *Developmental Psychology,* 1975, **11,** 700–704.

100. J. Piaget. Intellectual evolution from adolescence to adulthood. *Human Development,* 1972, **15,** 1–12.

101. D. Elkind. Recent research on cognitive development in adolescence. In S. E. Dragastin and G. H. Elder, Jr. (Eds.). *Adolescence in the life cycle.* New York: John Wiley, 1975, pp. 49–61.

102. Dulit, *op. cit.*

103. M. D. Berzonsky, A. S. Weiner, and D. Raphael. Interdependence of formal reasoning. *Developmental Psychology,* 1975, **11,** 258.

104. C. Tomlinson-Keasey. A search for the component operation of formal operations. Paper presented at the American Educational Research Association, Washington, D.C., 1975.

Chapter 7

Identification and Family Antecedents of Identity Formation

CHAPTER HIGHLIGHTS

ISSUES

Identity formation is best understood in the context of motivation and role acquisition.

Adolescents develop an emotional commitment to meet the role expectations of parents, peers, teachers, and employers.

Sex-role learning has meant traditionally that boys learn instrumental roles and that girls learn expressive roles.

Efforts to redefine sex-role expectations are part of life in America today, but sex-role stereotypes still are pervasive.

Lynn suggests that sex-role learning is easier for girls during childhood and easier for boys during adolescence.

Adolescent initiation rites provide perspective on how young people establish sex-role identities in different societies.

The verbal socializing skills parents acquire are associated with social-class membership.

Adolescents generally attribute more family power to their same-sex parents.

Patterns of parental control may be divided into three modes: permissive, authoritarian, and authoritative.

The Berkeley Growth Study data show that child-rearing dimensions of love-hostility are more consistent over time than those of autonomy-control.

Early maternal ratings correlate more highly than do concurrent ratings with older children's behavior.

Moss and Kagan say that behavior will show long-term stability if it is congruent with appropriate sex-role expectations.

Elkind says that parent-adolescent conflict varies as a function of the age of the adolescent and the maturity of the parents.

Intergenerational conflict is heightened when parents fail either to anticipate future events or to cope with youth's growing need for autonomy.

Most parents say that they experienced little or no trouble bringing up adolescents.

Young people tend to be favorably oriented toward the values and attitudes of their parents.

Self-assured young people appear to develop life styles that are relatively immune to pressures from either parents or peers.

Runaway youth often have a history of poor communications with their parents.

Effects of birth order vary as a function of family size.

Working mothers are likely to emphasize responsibility and independence training and to enhance their children's educational aspirations.

Father absence deprives both boys and girls of a source of sex-role sanctions and expectations.

Adolescent girls living in father-absent families may have difficulty interacting appropriately with males.

A significant aspect of the adolescent's socialization takes place in the family. To function effectively in society, one must acquire certain motives, attitudes, and interpersonal skills. Children and adolescents learn in a variety of family settings to fulfill the expectations of others and share role obligations. Erikson's[1] analysis of identity formation is a useful starting point in discussing the influence of the family on the adolescent's socialization. He says that every adolescent makes irrevocable decisions about school, a prospective mate, and an occupation. Each decision may represent a significant turning point in the adolescent's life, as well as contribute something to the realization of selfhood. He also says that it is helpful to the adolescent to have a "moratorium" on the assumption of responsibilities as early-life experiences are integrated and placed in perspective. An adolescent may not wish to assume any obligations until opportunity arises to reflect on the consequences of earlier experiences, experiment with different life styles, formulate work goals, resolve sexual conflicts, establish responsiveness to authority, and ultimately, construct a basic philosophy, ideology, or religion. The goal of identity formation in adolescence is to align "the individual's *basic drives* with his *endowment* and his *opportunities*."[2] Chapter 7 is divided into three sections, each of which is centered on a different aspect of identity formation. The first section considers developmental dynamics, the second describes the impact of parental role functions and explores parent-adolescent relations, and the third reviews how three major dimensions of family structure—birth order, maternal employment, and father absence—affect adolescent socialization.

The dynamics of identity formation are most easily understood when analyzed in respect to two basic processes: motivation and role acquisition. The motivation for identity formation is shown in the first section of Chapter 7 to stem from the process of *identification*. Freud aroused interest in the concept of identification, but he gave it an ambiguous meaning that still persists today. Social scientists generally hold that the core of identification consists of an emotional tie with an object. Since the family provides the basic nurture and safety of the child, its emotional tie is usually to the mother.[3] The identification process begins when the child attempts to imitate its parent's behavior. Kerckhoff[4] says that the distinguishing features of identification include "a very special person in the child's life" and that it "occurs early in the child's life and thus is viewed as having a delimiting or guiding influence on his responses to later events." The motivation to imitate the parent is replaced later by role-playing, which may lead the child to act quite differently from its parents. First the child learns a set of behaviors involving itself and the parent; later it learns to anticipate how the parent will act and to pattern its own behavior so as to elicit desired reactions from the parent. The ability to role-play develops as a result of interaction with significant persons. The emotional dependency of childhood yields in adolescence to an emotional commitment to meet the expectations of others—parents, peers, teachers, and employers. If adolescents fail to meet them, they usually feel pressed to modify their motives, skills, or attitudes. Such learning—involving endless repetitions of the expectation-performance-appraisal cycle—occurs cumulatively in the context of an expanding social environment. Without such role-learning through interaction and mutual expectations, preparation for various role performances in society would be impossible.

Significant changes have occurred in recent decades within the family on matters of division of labor, responsibility, distribution of authority, decision making, patterns of communication, and family emotional support. However, the majority of contemporary adolescents, who were born in the early 1960s, were reared in a traditional "nuclear" family, consisting of husband, wife, and children living relatively independently of other relatives. An adolescent's family helps to fulfill one's personal needs (especially in childhood), teaches one cultural patterns of behavior, and prepares one for adult role performances. The family orients a child to its kin and an adolescent to the wider society. As shown in the second section of Chapter 7, a major characteristic of the nuclear family is its power-structure differentiation. Although both husband and wife may simultaneously attempt to fulfill the dominant roles on occasion, usually there is some degree of patriarchal or matriarchal organization, and different patterns of parental control are likely to lead to different socializing practices and outcomes. The effect of consistency in patterns of parental control and degree of conflict in parent-adolescent relations also is discussed in this section.

The typical American family is an isolated unit, comprised of mother, father, and children, living in households separated from relatives. The degree of isolation may vary from complete aloneness to membership in a nearby clan, but in the context of the traditional nuclear family, research has shown that birth-order position, maternal employment, and father absence may cumulatively influence development of family structure, and hence, affect adolescents' sex-role identification. The implications of each of these factors is discussed in the third section of Chapter 7. Socialization is believed, for example, to be more stressful for first-borns since they must blaze a trail for their younger siblings. Maternal employment may perhaps be associated with escaping from the pressures of family life or a means of personal fulfillment, and the circumstances of maternal employment may greatly affect the mother's outlook. And, as the discussion shows, the father is an important factor in the sex-role learning of both sexes.

IDENTIFICATION AND ROLE ACQUISITION

Oedipal Rivalry and Motivation

The question of motivation in the identification process appears to be distinctly different at various developmental periods.[5] The very young child cannot distinguish between itself and the object of its identification, presumably its mother. As it matures and becomes more aware of the boundaries of reality, it is motivated to try to avoid frustration by imitating her behavior. It will stop trying to be the mother and try to be like her. By emulating the behavior of significant persons and anticipating their expectations, the child prepares itself for sex-role identification.

According to psychoanalytic theory, boys and girls achieve sex-role identification by resolution of the oedipal complex. For a boy the process begins when he becomes sexually attracted to his mother and begins to perceive his father an an unwelcome, aggressive competitor. But the father has substantially more power and can punish the child. The boy fantasies that he will be castrated if he tries to compete for the mother's affection. To cope with this fear, he identifies with or tries to become like his father, the aggressor, and represses his desire for his mother. A girl does not have the fear of castration, but she is afraid of losing her mother's love since her infantile identification is with her mother. However, after discovering that she lacks a penis, she blames her mother for having severed it, thus denying her the pleasures associated with it. She then turns to her father and tries to supplant her mother in his affections, but, torn between the impracticality of her objective and her fear of losing her mother's love, she begins to identify with her mother. The processes of the boy's and girl's identification differ in that the former is through fear and the latter is through love. It is hypothesized that the boy's identification process depends on aggression, threats, and hostility; for girls it depends on a positive, affectionate relationship. Psychoanalytic theorists have described these two processes as "identification with the aggressor" and "anaclitic identification," respectively.[6] The either-or implications of this formulation have troubled many psychologists, and Freud[7] himself was never satisfied with the distinctions, thus leaving the way open for other theories.

Subsequent theorists have reformulated Freud's two types of identification into complementary rather than contradictory processes. After reconceptualizing identification with the aggressor as "defensive identification" and anaclitic as "developmental identification," Mowrer[8] insisted that both forms were necessary to boys and girls in normal personality development. Both sexes reproduce "bits of the beloved parent" in order to avoid feeling that love has been lost when the parent withdraws rewards or is absent. The more the boy loves and respects his father, or the girl her mother, the greater the degree of warmth and affection between them, and thus, the more significant either approval or punishment. Sears, Maccoby, and Levin[9] also view the two mechanisms as interactive and relatively similar for both sexes. They believe that the motive for identification comes from the process of obtaining satisfactions for learned needs, which makes the child dependent on its parents. For example, the infant's more pressing needs—eating, warmth, and sleep—are nearly always gratified by its mother. Thus, it is likely to incorporate some of her habitual actions into its own behavior as its internal needs are being met. If its needs arise during her absence, it may imitate her affectionate gestures and attitudes itself, thus partially satisfying its needs and reinforcing its own behavior as its mother previously had. Once interaction of this kind results in dependency, there is motivation to identify, especially when the mother continues to nurture the child affectionately, places reasonable demands on the child, uses withdrawal of love (rather than physical discipline) when the child fails to conform to expectations, and requires the child to fulfill expectations itself. The first condition serves to keep the child oriented toward her as a model; the second forces the child to adopt more mature behavior; the third fosters doubt and emotional anxiety since the child does not know if it has met its mother's expectations; the fourth requires it to develop appropriate skills by actually doing certain things. Sears et al.[10] noted that a mother who is largely nurturant will seldom give her child reason or opportunity to emulate her behavior. On the other hand, if she is punitive, her child will have little motivation to follow her example. They hold, therefore, that identification should be maximized when parents make rewards contingent on approved behavior while simultaneously threatening punishment for disapproved behavior. Mussen and Distler[11] reported that young boys who had made "substantial father-identifications perceived their fathers as both more nurturant *and* more punitive"; their findings suggest that Freud's two types of identification are indeed complementary.

In a restatement of identification theory, Burton and Whiting[12] hypothesized that children will model their behavior after the parent who controls coveted goals and resources (the rewards of pleasure and freedom from punishments). Their formulation—the "status-envy hypothesis"—holds that motivation for identification depends on the child's perception of a discrepancy between its own access to desirable resources and that of a model and on its envy of the greater privileges and status of the model. Thus the child is led to emulate the behavior of the model, feeling that in this way it, too, will have access to the latter's privileges. Lynn[13] pointed out that the child is expected to envy the status of the person who deprives it of coveted resources more than that of the person who gives them to it. When the child has easy access to the things it wants, it controls them functionally and develops little motivation to identify with the giver. Lynn also pointed out that status envy may lead to identification with a recipient of resources if they are withheld from the child but given to a third person who then acquires the envied status. Lynn makes a distinction, too, between "power envy" and "status envy" as a source of motivation in the process of identification. According to the "power-envy" version, the control of resources is more critical than the status generated by the possession, enjoyment, or consumption of them. The child perceives the discrepancy in control between itself and the model in terms of its relative helplessness as compared with the power of the model. Thus, the child is motivated to want the model's power and to identify with it. The significance of models in the lives of adolescents probably is a function of their interests. One adolescent may covet the skill of a biologist

These youngsters appear to have acquired the rudiments of identification—status envy and motivation.

and attempt to imitate the role of a biology teacher, another may struggle to develop skills in the art of automotive servicing and look to nearby garage mechanics, and someone else may want to be a good tennis player and seek to attain the role characteristics of accomplished tennis players.

Role Acquisition and Sex-Role Learning

Role Acquisition.   Role learning involves knowledge, ability, and motivation. The interactive effects of nurturance and control, which are associated early in life with dependency, foster motivation for identification and affect the eventual course of role learning. The significance of the effects relative to self-concept development is enhanced when explanations increase clarity and level of understanding.[14] A role may be defined "as a set of expectations impinging on an incumbent of a social position."[15] Thornton and Nardi show that a role incumbent's expectations may be derived from several sources—"society at large" (mass media, legal system, entertainment idols, etc.), complementary role relationships (other individuals enacting either the same or reciprocal roles relative to the incumbent), and personal value systems (conscience or superego). The expectations may be centered on ways the incumbent of the role should behave, shared attitudes and values, and knowledge and skills that should be possessed. Thornton and Nardi[16] distinguish four stages—anticipatory, formal, informal, and personal—in the learning of new roles. The process is in fact continuous, but their characterization of it by stages emphasizes the different kinds of expectations that may arise. An adolescent's first attempt at performing a role, for example, is likely to be tentative. Certain features of the role may be recognized whereas others may be ignored. Initial success is partly dependent on whether anticipatory expectations agree with or are modifiable by actual experiences. As role performance ensues, the process of learning and reacting to more formalized expectations begins; these expectations usually relate more to behavior, knowledge, and skills of role enactment than to attitudes. Successful role-learning, however, also is a function of mastering the unofficial or informal expectations associated with role performance. Informal expectations are produced in social interaction with other individuals. They are really uncodified attitudes that lead to differences of opinion, and one may now begin to weigh one's own personal expectations against those of others. Adolescents who have opportunity to impose their own conceptions on a role, to shape it to meet their needs and future objectives, have opportunity to reach the fourth stage of role development; that is, they can personalize the style of their role performance.

Sex-Role Learning. Sex-role learning is made up of the performances and attitudes that coincide with the cultural stereotypes of masculinity and femininity. Adult masculinity, according to the stereotype, is comprised of being very aggressive, independent, unemotional, logical, direct, adventurous, self-confident, and ambitious. The stereotype of adult femininity, on the other hand, is characterized by being very talkative, tactful, gentle, aware of feelings of others, religious, needful of security, and interested in art and literature.[17] These stereotypes are related to Parsons'[18] belief that "instrumental activism" pervades the socialization practices of American parents, leading them in dealing with their children to diverge into distinctly different roles, the father taking the instrumental aspect and the mother, the expressive. Parsons perceived the family as an achievement-oriented subsystem of a larger system—society—and assumed that every successful group within the total system would find ways of differentiating these two functions. One practical approach, for example, is to differentiate them in terms of sex-roles. Thus, Parsons described the father as the prototype of the instrumental masculine role. He makes decisions for the family and sets limits for the children, but since he provides for the family's needs, he must center his attention on the occupational world. The mother fulfills the expressive role. Since she cares for individual family members, she must focus her attention on the emotional relationships among them. By bestowing pleasures and by being solicitous, appealing, and understanding, she may foster emotionally satisfying patterns of behavior among them. The two roles are incompatible in the sense that the first requires a disciplined pursuit of future goals while the second calls for appropriate affective behavior at the moment. The essence of masculinity and femininity presumably resides, respectively, in instrumental and expressive orientations. Early maternal relationships enable children of both sexes to learn expressive behavior and establish interpersonal patterns that may continue throughout life. Role relationships with the father, however, are the key to masculine sex-role identification for boys and feminine sex-role identification for girls. Interactions with the father bring about different behaviors and expectations. The father encourages instrumental-activism with his sons and expressivism with his daughters, thus providing an important, early differentiation in the sex-role learning for boys and girls.

Sex-Role Stereotyping. The instrumental-expressivism perspective suggests that traits of masculinity and femininity are polar opposites. American families, however, appear to distribute their instrumental and expressive tasks, which tends to minimize parental sex-role differences.[19] McIntire, Nass, and Dreyer,[20] for example, asked several hundred high school students whether they perceived their parents as instrumental or expressive. Girls perceived both parents as equally instrumental and expressive. Boys perceived their father as more instrumental, but saw both parents as comparable in expressivism. The researchers concluded that "the instrumental-expressive dimensions have been used much too globally and uncritically."[21] A dissatisfaction with traditional patterns of sex-role assignment underlies the growing inapplicability of the instrumental-expressive role. An exhaustive investigation of the socialization of achievement orientation in young women led Stein and Bailey[22] to conclude, for example, that "reduced achievement efforts occur for many young women as they reach adolescence and adulthood partly because there is pressure to adhere to feminine role definitions and because females internalize the low expectations of the culture for their continued achievement." During a perceptual discrimination task, Deaux and Emswiller[23] found that a male's successful performance was explained by young persons of both sexes to be a function of skill whereas a comparable female's performance was attributed to luck. Thus, it would appear "sex-role stereotypes are with us and are outmoded and burdensome."[24]

The ideal in America today is androgyny—no sex-role differentiation—a role system whereby cultural aspects of gender are not mandated by biological sex differences.[25] The ideal calls for socializing young people to define themselves in terms of "humanness" rather than in terms of "what men do that women should not do."[26] It is expressed in feminist efforts to ensure that persons of both sexes have the freedom to realize individual potential, whether in athletics, home, or career. Ellis and Bentler[27] point out that research indicates that sex stereotypes contradict current conceptions of the "ideal" traits males and females should possess, produce unnecessary internal conflicts, are incompatible with both personal and societal interests, and appear to have negative consequences for personality development, marital harmony, originality, and achievement motivation. Although a concerted effort to redefine societal sex-role expectations is very much a part of life in America today, realization of sex-role equality will in all likelihood be a slow process. Ellis and Bentler[28] suggest that many males are uneasy about changing sex-role styles "because their sex-role identity depends on females being different. Further, people tend to believe that equality of the sexes would mean that men would no longer be 'men,' women no longer 'women.'" Lynn[29] calls attention to the fear that sex-role equality of the sexes would mean retrenchment into a matriarchal society that would stand in the way of "technical, rational, and artistic progress." After several years of study, Broverman[30] and his colleagues found that "despite apparent fluidity of sex-role definition in contemporary society as contrasted with the previous decades, our own findings to date confirm the existence of pervasive and persistent sex-role stereotypes." Clavan and Robak,[31] who made a survey of the sex-role attitudes of husband and sons, concluded that "belief in traditional sex-role differentiation is weakening, is less than dominant, but is still very much present." Nonetheless, eventually the practice of determining role expectations by sex may diminish, and as it does, perhaps individuals will find an expansion of role opportunities in that opposite sex as well as same sex roles will be available to them.

Sex-Role Learning in the American Society. In a series of investigations and reports spanning a decade, Lynn[32] formulated a comprehensive set of hypotheses to account for both the processes and outcomes of traditional sex-role learning. First, he distinguished between "parental" and "sex-role" similarity, the one pertaining to similarity to the same-sex parent and the other to different persons of that sex. Then he used such concepts as "preference," "perceived similarity," "behavior adoption," and "identification" to specify degrees of similarity to both the parent and others of the same sex. Parental or sex-role "preference" appears to be a function of motivation; "perceived similarity" relates to perception of oneself; "behavior adoption" is associated with comparability of behavioral performances; and "identification" means internalization of personality characteristics and "unconscious" reactions. Lynn pointed out that although similarity to one's own parent and other members of the same sex is usually taken for granted, major inconsistencies sometimes occur. A boy, for example, could identify with his father, but his father's traits may not be typically masculine according to ordinary cultural standards. Or the boy might like to identify with his father, but perceive himself as dissimilar, and therefore adopt behavior totally unlike his father. Alternatively, the boy might want to be like other males in general, perceive himself as similar to them, adopt their behavior, and internalize their values.

Lynn[33] makes four major assumptions about traditional sex-role learning: (1) both boys and girls initially identify with their mother; later boys must shift from this early identification to a masculine model; (2) the young girl interacts more with an appropriate sex-role model than the young boy because the mother is more active in child-rearing; (3) the young boy usually learns some stereotype of a masculine sex-role (despite the shortage of male models) from his mother and women teachers. By virtue of a highly developed reward system for typical masculine behavior and the sanctions against feminine behavior, the boy replaces early maternal identification with the masculine stereotype; (4) American society is male-dominated and allocates more privileges and greater prestige to the male than to the female sex-role.

Lynn[34] explored how each of these assumptions affects sex-role learning. He sees the father as a model as comparable "to a map showing the major outline but lacking most details, whereas the mother, as a model for the girl, might be thought of as a detailed map."[35] Given the relatively greater availability of the mother and assuming that there exists status-envy or power-envy, girls can more closely identify with their mother. But the relevance of the father will lead boys to identify with both parents and to relate to a culturally defined masculine role. In the process of learning sex-appropriate roles, Lynn[36] holds that each sex will develop distinct styles of perceiving and learning that are applicable later to tasks. Traditionally, "the little girl acquires a cognitive style that primarily involves (1) a personal relationship, and (2) imitation rather than restructuring the field and abstracting principles. In contrast, the little boy acquires a cognitive style that primarily involves: (1) defining the goal, (2) restructuring the field, and (3) abstracting principles." Lynn believes that a girl maintains her orientation toward her mother as she learns her sex role. She is expected to identify with her mother partly through imitation and partly through the mother's selective reinforcement of behavior similar to her own. On the other hand, the boy must discover what the salient features of masculine role-behavior are, either from his father or from the rewards and punishments administered by his mother or teachers; he must abstract the principles of the masculine role much more than the girl must for the feminine role.

Lynn[37] agrees that the shift of the young boy from mother identification to masculine sex-role identification may be viewed as a period of crisis. As Lynn sees it, masculine sex-role behavior may be defined for the boy through negative admonishments. His teacher may tell him not to be a sissy, but not tell him how he should act. These negative admonishments usually occur early in elementary school where there are few male teachers as models and at a time when his father may seem remote to him. Thus, the boy must restructure the admonishments into their reciprocals in order to understand what the masculine sex-role is, and this cognitive task is likely to be extremely difficult for him at such an early age. Later, the preadolescent boy faces several hazards that may make sex-role learning relatively more difficult for him than for a girl. Consequently, boys are probably more anxious about sex-role identification than girls. Parents probably exert less pressure on girls than on boys to avoid opposite-sex activities, and girls may not be punished too severely for adopting masculine behavior. As boys struggle to develop masculine sex-role identity and reduce possible conflict, they may also develop an overgeneralized hostility toward feminine roles. According to Lynn, men make more derogatory comments about female behavior than women do about male behavior. An aggressive female may be called "a castrating female." Irritable persons are told "don't be bitchy" and fussy persons are admonished not to be "old maids." A woman who attempts to usurp traditional masculine functions may be advised to "stop trying to wear the pants in this family."

The tribulations of young boys and the favorable climate for socializing young girls are reversed at adolescence.[38] The traditionally male-dominated culture accords greater prestige and prerogatives to an adolescent boy and reinforces his learning of masculine sex-role identification more thoroughly than it does a girl's learning of feminine sex-role identity. The early pressure on a boy to shift from mother identification to the masculine sex-role and the powerful rewards offered for adopting it, which caused so much conflict in childhood, greatly strengthen his learning of masculine identification in adolescence. By contrast, a girl is less likely than a boy to be admonished for adopting aspects of the opposite-sex role; she would probably not be censured for being a tomboy whereas a boy could expect criticism for being a sissy. Girls may wear T-shirts and jeans but skirts and dresses are generally taboo for boys. A girl seems to have more freedom to express dissatisfaction with the female sex role and to indicate her preference for the male sex-role. As a girl becomes an adolescent, her earlier pleasures in being a tomboy and the prejudices against the feminine role that she encounters are likely to disillusion her with that role. Consequently, with increasing age, males appear to become relatively more firmly identified with the masculine role than girls with the feminine role, and a growing number of females begin to express a preference for the opposite sex role. Lynn believes that adolescent males develop fewer psychological disturbances associated with inadequate same-sex identification than females. He also believes that as a result of childhood socialization, when a discrepancy exists between sex-role preference and sex-role identification, adolescent males will tend toward same-sex role preference with an underlying opposite-sex identification, whereas girls will tend toward opposite-sex role preference with an underlying same-sex identification. He says that a higher proportion of adolescent girls than boys will adopt aspects of the opposite sex role, since the masculine role has greater prestige and girls are not likely to be particularly ridiculed or punished for overt opposite-sex behavior.

Adolescent Initiation Rites in Preliterate Societies.   These initiation rites often seem foreign and baffling to Westerners. They seem to provide a formal, institutionalized procedure for inducting youth into appropriate sex-role behavior and are an alternative to the prolonged, sex-role learning that is typical in American families. The variety in rites is tremendous. The ceremonies may take place anywhere between 8 and 20 years of age and are usually different for each sex. One rite may require only a few hours while another may require years. In one case the initiates may eagerly anticipate the events; in another, they may fearfully await harsh and painful treatment. Sometimes the rite is public and guests may come from a considerable distance, but often it is cloaked in secrecy.[39]

Van Gennep's[40] classic *Rites of Passage* provided the first theoretical framework to explain initiation rites. Van Gennep recognized that societies organized the life cycle into such periods as infancy, childhood, adolescence, and adulthood, and he assumed that the rites marked transition from one period to another. Subsequently, Freud interpreted the rites to be techniques of enforcing incest taboos, and Bettelheim[41] viewed them as society's means of minimizing cross-sex envy and castration anxiety. Whiting, Kluckhohn, and Anthony,[42] however, were among the first researchers to investigate empirically the probability that different patterns of socialization were related to the occurrence and function of initiation rites. They studied 56 different societies and found that those that fostered strong mother-son relationships, as defined by a period of mother and son sleeping together exclusively after birth and a taboo on sexual relations between the mother and father during this period, tended also to have male initiation rites that included painful hazing, tests of manliness, seclusion from women, genital operations, and a change of residence. A particularly severe rite, that of the Thonga tribe of Africa, is as follows:[43]

When a boy is somewhere between ten and sixteen years of age, he is sent by his parents to a 'circumcision school' which is held every four or five years.

Here in company with his age-mates he undergoes severe hazing by the adult males of the society. The initiation begins when each boy runs the gauntlet between two rows of men who beat him with clubs. At the end of this experience, he is stripped of his clothes and his hair is cut. He is next met by a man covered with lion manes and is seated upon a stone facing this 'lion man.' Someone then strikes him from behind and when he turns his head to see who has struck him, his foreskin is seized and in two movements cut off by the 'lion man.' Afterwards he is secluded for three months in the 'yard of mysteries,' where he can be seen only by the initiated. It is especially taboo for a woman to approach these boys during their seclusion, and if a woman should glance at the leaves with which the circumcized covers his wound, and which form his only clothing, she must be killed.

During the course of his initiation, the boy undergoes six major trials: beating, exposure to cold, thirst, eating unsavory foods, punishment and threat of death. On the slightest pretext he may be severely beaten by one of the newly initiated men who is assigned to the task by the older men of the tribe.

Whiting et al. initially favored an oedipal-rivalry explanation to account for the early exclusive relationship between the mother and son and the severe initiation rites at adolescence. The sleeping arrangements during the first two or three years of the son's life were presumed to engender a strong dependency in the boy; with its abrupt ending at the time of weaning, the boy might have relatively strong feelings of rivalry toward his father. They thought that at adolescence the boy's incestuous feelings toward his mother and hostility toward his father, which could disrupt society, would be defused by the initiation rite. Whiting[44] has since modified his view, suggesting an explanation based on status envy rather than oedipal strivings. His status-envy hypothesis holds that a child would be motivated to identify with the parent who possesses the valued resources that it covets. In societies that have exclusive mother-son sleeping arrangements, the male child's early feminine orientation must subsequently be contradicted, especially if the power and privileges of the society are fundamentally masculine. According to the status-envy hypothesis, the purpose of initiation ceremonies in such societies is to erase the young boy's primary identification with his mother and motivate him toward masculine sex-role learning. Following a similar line of reasoning, Young[45] believes that initiation rites serve mainly to dramatize sex-role recognition. The rite enhances the adolescent boy's status in the society and promotes "symbolic interaction" and "solidarity" among males; it creates shared evaluations of sex-role performances, promotes same-sex solidarity, and strengthens cooperation in activities vital to the welfare of the society. Young also argues that Whiting's explanation focuses too much on resolution of intrapsychic conflict rather than development of sex-role attitudes that help to integrate the social system; however, he may have misconstrued the meaning of Whiting's status-envy formulation.

Initiation rites for girls appear to be substantially different from those for boys.[46] Very rarely is the female initiate subjected to harsh treatment or genital operations. "The usual female initiation rites contain one or more of the following elements: bathing, beautification, such as a new hair arrangement, isolation in a special place, dietary restrictions, an announcement of the initiate's changed status and instruction in such matters as womanly tasks, etiquette, behavior toward in-laws, menstrual observances, contraceptive devices and observances during pregnancy."[47] The initiation ceremony is often related to menarche, betrothal, or marriage; frequently menarche is a prerequisite for initiation, which is itself a prerequisite for betrothal and marriage. Brown[48] reported that female initiation rites may evolve because: (1) the adolescent girl is likely to live in the same household as her mother after marriage. Under such circumstances, the rite emphasizes to the initiate and her family that her status has changed—that she is grown up; (2) the adolescent girl lives in a society that has painful male initiation rites, and thus may have a similar kind for girls. Because such a society is often patrilocal in orientation, there may be sex-role learning conflicts for both sexes; (3) the adolescent girl lives in a society in which women make a sizeable contribution to the economy. The rite in this society will assure the girl of her competence and proficiency. Brown thus suggests that initiation rites for girls may be primarily educational.

PARENTAL ROLE FUNCTIONS AND PARENT-ADOLESCENT RELATIONS

Parental Role Functions

Social Class as a Factor in the Allocation of Parental Role Functions.
Social class membership is known to be related to family decision making, division of labor, and style of parental socializing roles.[49] Kohn maintains that the members of different social classes, as a consequence of variation in levels of educational attainment and experience, see the political and economic worlds differently, develop distinguishable conceptions of social reality, distinct aspirations, and different conceptions of desirable personality characteristics. In particular, he views the principal difference between working- and middle-class parents to be the specific conditions under which children's misbehavior is punished. "Working-class parents are more likely to punish or refrain from

punishing on the basis of the direct and immediate consequences of children's actions, middle class parents on the basis of their interpretation of children's intent in acting as they do."[50] Kohn reasons that middle-class parents typically deal with ideals, symbols, and interpersonal relations, whereas working-class parents generally relate to physical objects and are less concerned about social skills. Moreover, middle-class parents are involved in complex work, requiring flexibility, thought, and judgment but demanding less supervision. Working-class parents, in contrast, are more closely bound to bureaucratic practices, routinization of work, and close supervision. Middle-class parents thus develop values related to self-direction, such as, freedom, initiative, creativity, individualism. Working-class parents, on the other hand, are more likely to stress values associated with conformity to external standards, for example, orderliness, neatness, and obedience. Kohn's research shows that middle-class parents favor "internal" standards as guides to their children's interaction with others, whereas lower-class parents emphasize conformity to *external* constraints, controls, and rules. These value orientations then are reflected in parental styles of discipline. Middle-class parents, stressing self-direction and learned standards of conduct, are likely to discipline on the basis of their interpretation of the children's motives for their actions. Lower-class parents, on the other hand, are likely to demand conformity, base discipline on the consequences of behavior, and react punitively when children are annoying, disturbing, or disobedient.

Kohn's investigation of the influence of social-class factors on socialization practices suggests that middle-class parents view their parental responsibilities as mainly supportive and they seek to train their children to make their own decisions. Working-class parents see their main responsibility as that of imposing constraints, and they want to train their children to act reputably and to obey proper rules. The major antecedent of social class differences in such instances may be the fact that middle-class parents possess greater sophistication in interpersonal relations, which helps them structure their socializing efforts, especially during adolescence. For example, Gecas and Nye,[51] drawing from a large study of sex and class differences in styles of parental discipline, found that the only major difference to appear between the middle- and lower-class parent was the extended range of verbal reprimands available to middle-class parents. The researchers also reported that parents of both social classes were equally sensitive to the circumstances of children's misbehavior and to their intentions and motives. And Erlanger[52] dismisses physical punishment as having no practical significance as an antecedent of social class differences. Hence, the limited evidence available suggests that it is parental verbal skills that produces relationships between social class and socialization.

Patterns of Conjugal Power.   Conjugal power is generally conceptualized as the ability of one marriage partner to influence the other's behavior. The power of the father vis-à-vis the mother in determining family activities was clear-cut during the Victorian era. Gilloran[53] described the father as a "fixed and constant star' around which his wife and children quietly maintained their insignificant orbits." He was the law, addressed with respect, and spoken of in awe. The oft-quoted phrase, "children should be seen and not heard," illustrates the height of his omnipotence. Since then, however, the patriarchal family system has largely evaporated. The weakened control of the family over individual behavior, the emancipation of women, increased education and employment of women, and the trend toward fewer children have led to equalitarian parental relationships. Many roles that were once performed almost exclusively by either the mother or the father are now shared. Burchinal and Bauder[54] point out that today only two or three family tasks are securely monopolized by one sex—child-bearing and sewing by the wife and arduous physical tasks by the husband.

According to the status-envy and power theories of identification, it is believed that young people identify with the model who controls most of the resources that they covet. As adolescents develop different sex roles and accept adult standards and responsibilities, one might expect that girls would interact more frequently with their mothers and be strongly oriented toward their feminine characteristics; one might also expect boys to be oriented toward the masculine characteristics of their fathers. Especially when adolescents see a same-sex (rather than opposite-sex) parent occupying a relatively high status role, they are presumably motivated to want to assimilate that parent's interests, attitudes, and behavior patterns.

Sometimes, however, conjugal power is unbalanced when power accrues to the adolescent. Jacob[55] has investigated the interaction of social class, age, and patterns of family dominance and conflict in fifth, sixth, tenth, and eleventh-grade boys. The younger boys from middle- and lower-class families perceived their fathers as more powerful than their mothers and saw both parents as more influential than themselves. But adolescent sons from the middle-class families saw themselves as gaining family influence at the expense of their mothers but not their fathers. Jacob also reports that whereas the relative influence of fathers in middle-class families remained the same regardless of the boy's age, in lower-class families, the relative power of fathers *and* mothers decreased significantly with the advent of adolescence, resulting in an unstable family structure, in which fathers, mothers, and sons were equal in power. One might expect in such situations that motivation among adolescents to identify with their parents would be greatly diminished.

Sex differences in adolescents' perception of relative parental power, nonetheless, are in general quite stable. A comparative study involving young people in the United States, West Germany, Puerto Rico, Spain, and Mexico reveals that in each of the cultures, adolescent boys attributed more power and final say to their fathers than to their mothers; in contrast, adolescent girls consistently assigned more power to their mothers than to their fathers, and in four of the five cultures, viewed their mothers as having final say.[56] Research corroborates the cross-cultural findings of strong sex differences in perception of conjugal power. Bronfenbrenner's[57] finding that adolescents view their same-sex parent as the principal decision maker in the family was confirmed by Grinder and Spector,[58] who developed a questionnaire in which youth could compare their mothers and fathers in terms of (1) parental authority to grant autonomy and permit various activities, (2) parental capacity to arouse a sense of well-being or despair through nonmaterial rewards and punishments (such as praise or ridicule), and (3) parental control of desirable material incentives (such as use of the telephone, car, or home; and spending money). The subjects were boys and girls in the ninth, tenth, and twelfth grades of a community high school. The questionnaire results showed that girls attributed relatively more power and status to their mothers whereas boys attributed these characteristics to their fathers. In a study of family power structure, King[59] found that ninth-grade black youth in a metropolitan area of Florida reported that their same-sex parent was the major decision maker in their families.

Although adolescents tend to look to the same-sex parent for identity-formation, and appear to be most successful in equalitarian homes, research on conjugal power suggests that parental dominance may influence the manner in which adolescents model themselves after their parents. In families where one parent is perceived as having relatively great power, adolescent girls tend to hold their orientation to the mother even when her power is greatly eroded, but adolescent boys appear to encounter considerable difficulty in achieving father-identification when the power of the father is perceived as subordinate to that of the mother. Bowerman and Bahr,[60] for example, conducted a study of 18,000 adolescents, grades seven through twelve, and found, as expected, that identification was highest toward the same-sex parent. They reported, too, that the proportion of young people who desired to be like their same-sex parent was highest in families where conjugal power was equal. Furthermore, the girls averaged higher identification with their mothers than with their fathers, even when the mothers were perceived as the less dominant parent, but the boys who viewed their mothers as the more dominant parent, appeared to identify much less with the father than those who regarded him as dominant. Van Manen[61] explains that because the father is expected to serve as the prototype of authority in the family, interaction patterns developed with him carry over into other social situations. But in a family where the husband is dominated by the wife, boys may devalue his parental role and avoid opportunities to identify with his masculine traits. In this context, Vogel and Lauterbach[62] reported that adolescent boys with behavior problems tend to view the mother as their chief source of nurturance, acceptance, affection, and control; the sons and the mother frequently allied themselves against the father. Several other investigators reported similar findings. Nikelly,[63] for example, found that 111 19-year-old psychiatric outpatients, as compared with a control group of normal adolescents, rated their mothers as more indulgent and overprotective. After studying 445 children, Hoffman[64] said that "boys from mother-dominant families are aggressive, impulsive, unfriendly, and unsuccessful in their influence attempts." She summarized her investigation as follows: "In this study, we found that when the father is more powerful than the mother, disciplines his children, and has a warm companionship with them, the boys—and to a lesser extent the girls—will have self-confidence and feel accepted by others, show a positive assertiveness in the peer group, have skills, like others, be well liked, and exert influence."[65]

Patterns of Parental Control.   Since successful socialization requires in part the internalization of appropriate sex-role behavior, the presence of clearly differeniated parental models greatly facilitates sex-role identification. But even if parental roles mutually reinforce sex-role identification, parents still use different approaches in disciplining their children. Baumrind[66] contrasted three modes of parental control: *permissive, authoritarian,* and *authoritative.* "The permissive parent attempts to behave in a nonpunitive, acceptant, and affirmative manner toward the child's impulses, desires, and actions."[67] Reason and manipulation rather than overt power prevail. The child is consulted about family decisions, it has few household responsibilities, it is admonished infrequently about disorderly behavior, it is not controlled too much, and it is encouraged to regulate its own activities as much as possible. Parents may serve as a resource for the child to act as it wishes, but are not likely to be models to emulate or active agents to shape its behavior. Permissive parents develop little power and prestige over time, and adolescents are not likely to be motivated to learn either parental instrumental roles or value systems. The door thus is open for nonfamily models—neighbors, peers, entertainment figures—to serve as status resources. The authoritarian mode, however, is more traditional among American families.[68] "The authoritarian parent attempts to shape, control, and evaluate the behavior and attitudes of the child in accordance with a set standard of conduct, usually an absolute standard, theologically motivated and formulated by a higher authority."[69] There is no verbal give-and-take, and the child is expected to accept its parents word as right. The parents value obedience as a virtue and favor punitive, forceful measures to curb the child whenever its behavior conflicts with their conceptions of appropriate conduct. The child is kept in its place, restricted in autonomy, and assigned houschold responsibilities in order to teach it respect for work. Parents oriented toward authoritarian socialization practices are likely to adhere strongly themselves to traditional values. They may be both warm and strict toward children, but their very firm control may be relaxed upon attainment of adolescence. Adolescents living in authoritarian homes generally acquire a belief system strong enough to shield them from the role confusion characteristic of much of adolescence and to keep them oriented toward their familial perspective on social reality.[70] Authoritative parents, on the other hand, are willing to listen to children when directing them and to offer justification for their directives. Authoritative parents direct children firmly, consistently, and rationally. Parents value both obedience to their expectations and independence in the children, and they are likely to set standards and enforce them firmly. However, they are not likely to regard themselves as infallible law-givers. "Autonomous sclf-will" and "disciplined conformity" are valued, and children are encouraged to participate in verbal give-and-take, are told of reasons for certain decisions, and are given opportunity to discuss their objections.

Investigators unanimously agree that different parental control patterns produce different effects on socialization; however, behavioral scientists and philosophers still argue about the merits of freedom versus control in the identification process. As Baumrind[71] observed, "For a person to behave autonomously, he must accept responsibility for his own behavior, which in turn requires that he believe that the world is orderly and susceptible to rational mastery and that he has or can develop the requisite skills to manage his own affairs." Baumrind's discussion of parental disciplinary practices indicates that the authoritative approach may best enable children to conform to social standards with minimum jeopardy to "individual autonomy or self-assertiveness." The researcher notes that it is important in the socialization of adolescents to distinguish between the effects of firm control and restrictive discipline. All sorts of arbitrary limits may be imposed on youth's autonomous efforts to express initiative, try out new skills, and make decisions for themselves. Unrealistic parental demands to supress or avoid conflict may prevent adolescents from attaining the experiences that are prerequisite to successful socialization. Several other investigators support this view. Elder[72] found that young people from the seventh through the twelfth grade were more likely to model themselves after their parents and to associate with parent-approved peers if their parents tended to explain various decisions and restrictions. He compared autocratic, democratic, and permissive parents on the basis of high-, moderate-, and low-parental power, and found that the most attractive parents as models tended to be the democratic ones. The young people with democratic or permissive parents, power level notwithstanding, tended to be confident about their own ideas and opinions and to be independent in their own decision making. On the other hand, those with autocratic parents had little confidence and independence in their decision making. Elder concluded that by legitimatizing parental dominance through explanations, parental power becomes more acceptable and heightens confidence and willingness to depend on parents. Longstreth and Rice[73] compared high school boys—including aggressive, "acting-out" boys; nonaggressive, underachieving boys; and well-adjusted boys—in terms of perceived parental "love" and "control." They found that the boys who described their parents as high in both love and control also tended to identify themselves with their parents. The aggressive boys (as compared with the well-adjusted boys) described their parents as lower in love and indicated that they identified less with their parents than with their peers. In general, loving, controlling parents fostered more parent-identification than less loving, less controlling parents. Similarly, a recent study of junior high boys, in which traits of "internal control" (belief that events, rewards, and punishments are contingent on one's behavior) versus "external control" (belief in fatalistic determination of one's destiny) were compared, suggests that the boys who were oriented more toward internal than external control perceived their parents as more supportive.[74] And Nowicki and Segal,[75] in a study of high school seniors of both sexes, report that parental nurturance is related to "internality," a trait which the researchers say is strongly correlated in high school with higher achievement in boys and more extracurricular participation among girls.

Consistency in Patterns of Family Socialization. Consistency is important in socialization. A stable environment provides an adolescent with assurance that tasks to be mastered and skills to be learned will have meaning over time. Macfarlane[76] observed that adolescents' potential capacities, physical makeup, temperament, and health, as well as their relations with brothers, sisters, parents, and others may affect the consistency of socializing experiences. Growing up in a family is continuous and prolonged; adolescence is the twilight of a long period of intense interaction. The family is the principal socializing agent from which adolescents acquire their unique life style. American families vary substantially in affectional relationships, allocations of authority, and division of labor between the parents and between parents and children. Most responsible parents strive to develop in their children feelings of well-being, belonging, and security, and to reinforce such personality attributes as honesty, punctuality, and reliability. In these areas there is usually considerable consistency. The teaching of self-discipline and self-control, however, appear to depend on the age of the child; since the parents are likely to shift their approach from childhood to adolescence, they may introduce inconsistency in their socializing practices. Unbridled disregard for the rights and property of others, for example, might be tolerated in young children, but few parents would condone such behavior in adolescents. Clausen[77] observed that there is an optimum range of parental control at every age level. Too much control may lead either to submissiveness and timidity or to rebelliousness; too little control may result in immaturity and irresponsibility. The power difference between the parent and young child is so great that the child is seldom able to challenge parental power. Adolescents, however, approach both the physical and intellectual status of their parents, and they can fight back. At adolescence it is psychologically and physiologically impossible for parents to assert the same kind of power they did in early childhood. Clausen holds that when the growing child is given autonomy and when parental restrictions are accompanied by explanations and understanding, the potential for conflict will be lessened. Since parental control can thus be consonant with the adolescent's own long-range goals and self-image, it can provide a consistent frame of reference for socialization.

Baumrind[78] has contrasted the use of power for children and reason for adolescents as mechanisms of parental authority. Parents exercise power over the child by manipulating rewards and punishments. Power per se legitimates authority, and it is unilateral during childhood; by virtue of greater physical size, experience, and control of resources, a parent can exercise control, impose restraints, and restrict autonomy. There is little the child can do to resist. The parent might say "'you must do it because I say so'; and the child will accept such a parental maneuver as legitimate even if he continues to have objections on hedonistic grounds, because he is not yet capable of principled objections."[79] The child learns to express its individuality within the range of behaviors acceptable to its parents, and an orderly series of experiences will enable it to distinguish between conforming and deviant behavior. By early adolescence, it is capable of formal operational thought and can formulate principles by which to judge its own activities and those of others. The child has the conceptual ability to be critical even though it may lack the wisdom to be moderate. Because the adolescent can see alternatives to parental directives, the parent must be ready to defend them on a rational basis. The parent can thus make only limited use of power to settle differences. As Baumrind observed, adolescents develop their own position by having someone with whom to argue. The legitimacy of demands and control may be recognized when both parents and adolescents can vigorously defend their positions until consensus is reached.

The Berkeley Growth Study has provided empirical insights into the nature of parental consistency. Two sets of maternal behaviors, separated by an interval of about 10 years, were compared: love versus hostility and autonomy versus control. The maternal ratings and the children's behavior from infancy to adolescence were also compared.[80] The mothers' behavior was observed in routine testing sessions from the time of birth until about 3 years of age. About 10 years later, when the children were between 9 and 14, a skilled clinical psychologist interviewed the mothers in their homes. The material obtained from the interviews was organized into two sets of scales (love versus hostility and autonomy versus control), each of which included several specific behaviors; from this empirical organization, a conceptual model for maternal behavior was developed. The model, a "circumplex" organization of maternal behaviors, is presented in Figure 1. Part A includes birth to 3 years; part B includes 9 to 14 years.

The organization of the maternal behaviors into theoretical models simplifies the interpretation of the Berkeley Growth Study data. The behaviors, arranged 180° apart, are taken to be polar opposites, for example, accepting versus rejecting. Figure 1 shows that there is considerable consistency in maternal treatment over time, as reflected in the placement of certain behaviors along the scales. For both sexes, behaviors related to love-hostility showed greater consistency than those related to autonomy-control. Also, the boys' mothers showed generally high correlations for love-hostility and generally lower correlations for autonomy-control than did the girls' mothers. Presumably there was consistency in love-hostility behaviors because the mother's capacity to satisfy this need and the child's need for a positive relationship with her may be relatively stable. The lack of consistency over time of autonomy-control behaviors, especially for boys, may be due to the mother's response to the child's increasing need for autonomy. The relatively greater consistency for girls on this dimension suggests that mothers may be reluctant to grant their daughters increasing freedom.

Four sets of personality ratings, based on systematic observation of overt behavior (and not interpretations from tests of motives, attitudes, or underlying drives), were obtained for the children whose mothers participated: 10 to 36

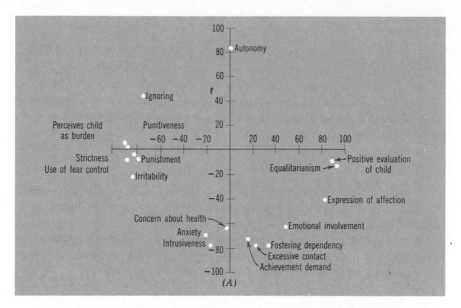

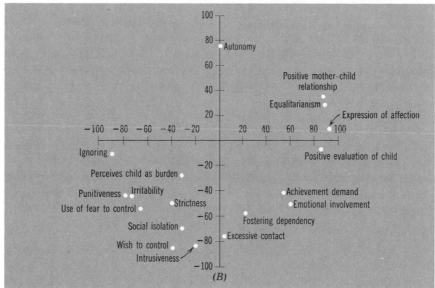

Figure 1
Circumplexes of maternal behavior. (*A*) **Birth to three years.** (*B*) **Nine to fourteen years.**
(Reprinted by permission S. Karger, Basel 1964).

months, 27 to 96 months, 9 to 12 years, and 12½ to 18 years. Comparisons between maternal behavior and children's behavior revealed, first, that there was a high degree of correspondence between maternal love and very young children who were relatively happier, calmer, and positively oriented. Behavior pertaining to autonomy-control—intrusiveness, concern about health, achievement demands, excessive control, and fostering dependency— failed to show a clear correlation with early childhood behavior. Second, early maternal love was also significantly related to preadolescent boys' friendliness, cooperativeness, and positive, task-oriented behavior, but this love was not related to adolescent boys' behavior. On the other hand, early maternal autonomy-control actions were not correlated with the sons' behavior through age 12, but became significantly correlated with it at adolescence. Maternal hostility at adolescence was positively related to maladjustment in adolescent boys. Emotionally close, indulgent, and protective behavior on the part of the mother at an early age was associated at adolescence with either desirable or undesirable extroverted behavior in boys; that is, a boy could be favorably evaluated (considered friendly, social, or independent) or negatively evaluated (considered bold, irritable, or rude). Schaefer and Bayley[81] suggested that the boys who received excessively indulgent, overprotective maternal care during the first three years of life may have been spoiled and pampered; at adolescence this could have led to disobedient, impudent, and hostile behavior. Third, early maternal behavior pertaining to love-hostility and autonomy-control seemed to have no relationship to girls' behavior between 10 months and 12 years; however, maternal hostility and control at adolescence were significantly correlated with girls' maladjusted behavior.

From 1929 to 1939, the Fels Research Institute enrolled at birth 36 males and 35 females from middle-class families in order to make a longitudinal study of personality development.[82] The mothers of the children in this study were also evaluated with respect to the following variables of child-rearing: hostility, protectiveness and nurturance, acceleration of cognitive and motor development, and restrictiveness. Moss and Kagan[83] reported that maternal protectiveness and acceleration were moderately stable variables for boys but not for girls; on the other hand, restrictiveness and hostility were more stable for girls than for boys. Moss and Kagan suggested that the differences indicate that the mother's behavior depends on the sex of the child and that she selectively relates either to the boy's or the girl's behavior.

Moss and Kagan also said that the Fels data suggested that maternal ratings from birth to 3 years of age were more likely to correlate with the child's behavior when it was older than were later concurrent maternal ratings. For example, maternal protectiveness of boys from birth to 3 years was related more to the boys' passivity from 6 to 10 years than were comparable maternal ratings at that age. Further, maternal protectiveness ratings from birth to 3 years were more predictive of achievement and conformity in boys from 6 to 14 than were ratings of these variables made at adolescence. These data led the researchers to point to a "sleeper effect"—an instance in which early maternal behavior was correlated more closely than later behavior with the way the boy or girl acted in adolescence and adulthood. Many of the "sleeper effects," which manifested themselves in adulthood, appeared to corroborate the findings of the Berkeley Growth Study. Protectiveness of a daughter from birth to 3 years of age, for example, was significantly correlated with withdrawal in adult women, but maternal protectiveness from 3 to 10 years was negligibly correlated with this variable. Also hostility toward daughters during the first three years of life, more than during later years, tended to bring about a withdrawal from stress during adulthood. Moss and Kagan explain that a specific maternal treatment during infancy seems to initiate a chain of developmental events, which may lead to a certain orientation later in life. Protectiveness during the early years thus can lead in adolescence to dependency on the affections of others. As the boy or girl matures, he or she is inclined to conform to adult standards in order to maintain the same kind of attention from adults. Such a developmental progression could account for the delayed association between early protectiveness and later conformity. Moss and Kagan have pointed out that maternal hostility and protectiveness during the first three years (rather than later on) have a greater impact on the child because these early attitudes are a more basic and accurate index of the mother's approach to the child. The researchers believe that most mothers have a mental image of what they expect their child to be like, and they are likely to exert pressure on the child to behave in accordance with this image. Since the child's personality is relatively ambiguous during infancy and there is little discrepancy between the mother's standards and what she perceives in the child, she is likely to treat it differently at that time than later on when the child acts more independently.

Longitudinal studies show that while maternal nurturance is relatively stable, there is generally a shift from control toward greater autonomy as children grow older, but the personalities of the children through adolescence do not show a corresponding degree of consistency. Biological impairments, harsh social pressures that may push adolescents beyond tolerance, and perhaps some derision for their coping efforts are among the obstacles listed by Macfarlane,[84] who wondered "how *anyone* achieves even relative coherence." In charting the lives of 166 persons from babyhood to about age 30, Macfarlane[85] and others who participated in the University of California Guidance Study illustrated the enormous difficulty of trying to predict the effects of socializing experiences on personality development across time. In the study only 30 percent of the youth turned out as expected, 20 percent turned out somewhat as expected, but 50 percent surprised the researchers by becoming more "stable and effective" than had been predicted. Those who were severely retarded intellectually were readily detected and were included among the 30 percent whose future maturity level was accurately predicted. Correct predictions were also made for those who at a young age were "overcontrolled, constricted compulsives." This early behavior was so entrenched and rigid that it was obvious they had closed themselves to new learning experiences, and many of them chose mates who reinforced their constraints. The remainder of the 30 percent group was composed of youth whose family treatment had been so variable—alternatively indulgent and harsh—that they had little self-confidence and few stable, integrated behavior patterns by the age of 30. The researchers thus only seemed to be successful at selecting those whose maturity would fall far short of the ideal.

They were notably wrong in predicting that 20 percent of the youth who showed exceptional promise on the basis of high scholastic ability, artistic talent, or athletic ability and enjoyed good family and social relationships would turn out to be the most mature. Among the boys the more successful athletes and among the girls those who were most glamorous turned out totally different than expected. The researchers speculated that the experiences of these boys and girls in young adulthood failed to sustain the excessive approval they had previously received from peers, teachers, and parents. They had achieved extravagant success before they could absorb it gracefully; therefore, too much of their energy had gone into maintaining an image that could not be perpetuated. Apparently too much success at one age can be a millstone, especially if it is not earned or integrated into a total life style.

The researchers anticipated that 50 percent of the youth would have a dismal future, but they were wrong. Many of these youth had been defiant of school regulations and, though capable, received marginal and failing grades; in adulthood they turned out to be responsible citizens and understanding parents. Macfarlane[86] admits that the researchers gave too much attention to failing grades and not enough to the compensating influences of apparently unsatisfactory families; they also overestimated the durability of well-learned behaviors and attitudes. Apparently certain habitual behaviors were dropped or modified as required in later life. Experiences that seemed traumatic and nonmaturing perhaps forced the youth to resolve their conflicts and clarify their goals. Many youth also seemed to be suspended in crises of identity until they married and became parents, when they had new opportunities to acquire a sense of worth by being responsible to others. Finally, the researchers observed that many long-standing patterns of behavior became converted into their opposites with the assumption of responsibilities. Many overdependent children later became nurturant adolescents. Many youth ultimately identified themselves more with the role behavior of their models than with the expectations of these models for them. Although it might have been expected that overdependent boys with energetic, dominant mothers would select wives like their mothers in order to maintain their dependency relationships, nearly all of the dependent boys in the sample chose mates who lacked confidence, thus enabling the boys to play the role of male protector and provider of support. Many participants in the Guidance Study at age 30 believed that their earlier disruptive behaviors had actually provided them with "maturity-inducing benefits." As one former rebel put it:

Granted that my defiance of authority precluded a college education. I desperately needed approval, even if it was from kids as maladjusted as I was. Yet I can see positive results, too. To maintain my rebel status called for a commitment that demanded I discipline all of my intelligence and stamina which, I believe, has contributed to my adult strength and to my self-confidence in tackling later tough problems. I hope my children find less wasteful ways to mature—but who knows?[87]

The Fels[88] analysis dealt with longitudinal observations of each child's behavior in three salient areas: achievement, passivity and dependency, and aggressiveness. As compared with the modest results of the California Guidance Study, the Fels study showed that much adult behavior is established and stabilized during childhood. Children's ratings for aggressiveness, passive-dependency, and achievement were correlated with similar behaviors in adulthood. The ratings in these areas, however, showed a different stability for the two sexes. Childhood aggression beginning about three to six years showed a correlation with adult aggression for boys but not for girls. On the other hand, childhood passive-dependency was associated with adult dependency for girls but not for boys. But the continuity of childhood achievement into adulthood appeared as early as the preschool years for girls and was well established in both sexes by early school years. Moss and Kagan[89] hypothesized that these sex differences in continuity between childhood and adult behaviors can be explained according to the principle: "a behavior will show long-term stability if that behavior is congruent with the cultural definition of the sex-role of the individual." Since aggression is sex-appropriate behavior for boys and passive-dependent behavior is acceptable for girls, aggression would probably show long-term continuity in boys and dependency would do likewise in girls. Since achievement is approved for both sexes, once such a response system is established it tends to be maintained.

Parent-Adolescent Relations

Conflict in Intergenerational Relations. As adolescents begin to adopt more mature life styles, parental expectations of their behavior may or may not change. Long-standing caretaking and supervisory functions should cease—control should yield to autonomy. Adolescents must enjoy increasing independence from parental domination if they are eventually to assume adult responsibilities.

To assess the expectations of adolescents, Wheeler[90] asked 17 to 18 year olds living in Australia to write an essay on the following topic: "By this time you probably know a good deal about how *not* to bring up teenage children. So that you won't some day repeat the errors of your parents, write yourself a cautionary letter for use in, say, 1980." In analyzing the essays of 112 boys and 66 girls, Wheeler found that both sexes were ambivalent about how they would fulfill the parental role. In the area of friendships, the young people felt that parents should scrutinize their friends carefully but not interfere with their choices. Parents should encourage boys and girls to invite their friends, especially of the opposite sex, into their homes but not intrude after they arrive.

Parent-adolescent conflict is mitigated when communication channels are kept open.

They hoped very much that they would be the kind of parents in whom their adolescent children could readily confide their emotional problems. They would refrain from teasing their children about certain of their friends and would avoid exposing them to embarrassment or humiliation in front of their friends. On the subject of late hours, the youth varied in their responses; some felt that parents should rely on the good sense of the adolescent, and others argued for a definite, fixed hour to be home. Young people tended not un understand why their parents became anxious. Many of the adolescents hoped that, as parents, they would encourage their own children to participate in sporting activities; to have hobbies; to learn correct manners and etiquette, good speech, music, and the arts—in general, they wanted their children to develop confidence about new social situations. Several youth felt that sex education was needed in the home, and they recognized the benefits of parental help and advice, including answering questions. Some were afraid that, as parents, they would embarrass and make it difficult for their children to broach the subject of sex rather than promote a natural and healthy attitude toward it. The youth also believed that parents should keep pace with the changing world. Tolerance and understanding were prized attributes, for clearly such traits would mitigate the possibility of conflict between peers and family. The adolescents decidedly did not want to be old-fashioned or inconsistent, arbitrary parents.

Elkind[91] has interpreted parent-adolescent conflict as a stage in the process of self-differentiation. He held that the nature of the conflict varies as a function of the age of the adolescent and the maturity of the parents. The issues arise in real or imagined violations of three kinds of contractual arrangements between the parents and the adolescent: the bargain, the agreement, and the contract. In the *bargain,* the parent initially offers to give a reward or withhold punishment in return for the child's compliance, but at an early age the child learns to make its own bargains. "I'll get undressed and brush my teeth if I can stay up a little longer." Such bargains shift in content but the basic arrangement persists as the child grows up. The *agreement* is usually more complex and lasts longer than the bargain; when one is reached, the parents and child agree to abide by certain rules over a period of time. Elkind points out that with the younger child, agreement may include the threat of punishment: "'If you hit your little brother again you will have to go to your room and miss the cartoons; which can be translated as, "If you agree to leave your little brother alone we agree to let you watch the cartoons'''. But at a later age, agreements are often more positive: "'If you clean up your room every day, I will increase your allowance.'" Agreements appear to predominate over bargains by the time adolescence is reached. The *contract* is the process whereby parents and child interact with one another on the basis of mutual expectations. This arrangement is largely implicit and unspoken; its existence may be acknowledged only after it is breached. "The mother, for example, who says, 'Look how they treat me after I worked and slaved for them' reveals her belief in an implicit contract as does the remark of an adolescent, 'No matter how much I do around the house, it is never enough'".

Elkind hypothesized that each of the contractual arrangements has three complementary "invariant clauses" whose content varies with age level. The contractual differences, plus the variation in the content of the clauses, make the intergenerational conflict distinctive. The first clause is *responsibility-freedom*. During socialization the parents demand that the child fulfill certain responsibilities, while the child contracts for complementary freedoms. The intensity of the arragement increase with age. The period of infancy has few responsibilities and little freedom; the preschool years include responsibilities for feeding, dressing, bowel and bladder control, and some emotional control. The child asks for freedoms made possible by more mobility and motor control. There are additional responsibilities for older children who may be asked to look after their clothing, rooms, and younger siblings; these children, in turn, will seek more freedom in terms of staying away from home for longer periods, staying up later in the evenings, and so forth. The content of this clause changes again in adolescence when parents urge their children to take responsibility for social control, money management, and motor vehicles, and the adolescents insist on new freedoms in the area of later hours, individual dress, and friendship choices. The second clause, *achievement-support*, pertains to developing a sense of competence. Parents begin to insist that the child meet their standards of social etiquette, linguistic usage, and social behavior. In school, parents expect successful academic performance, athletic prowess, and social popularity. At adolescence, parents may intensify these expectations. Throughout socialization, children expect parents to praise them for their accomplishments and to supervise and instruct them. In the third clause, *loyalty-commitment*, parents are likely to expect only affection from the infant, but in the preschool and school periods parents may want the child's affection for them to continue in spite of contact with new adults and peers. Parents may expect children to give their primary allegiance to the family (rather than to teachers and peers), and in adolescence they may expect loyalty to their beliefs and values. The child or adolescent, in turn, wants parents' emotional support as demands are made on parental time and energy. An adolescent may also want his or her parents to commit themselves to the adolescent's beliefs and values.

Elkind's theory of interpersonal relations, based on implicit and temporal contracts, accountability, competence, and commitment clauses, highlights how tensions between responsibility and freedom or control and autonomy are significant sources of intergenerational conflict. If parents exert legitimate pressures on an adolescent to take responsibility and if they refrain from imposing arbitrary authority, conflicts with the adolescent may be infrequent and inconsequential. At every age level there is probably an optimum range of parental demands and expectations, but parents often find it difficult to exercise skillful leadership and to balance control with freedom. First, well-meaning parents may be baffled to find that parental prompting that had been taken in good grace is suddenly resented when adolescents decide that they are old enough to do what is expected of them without being reminded. Second, parents may define standards of responsibility differently for themselves than for the adolescent. Consider, for example, the following:[92]

If your parents make plans and they want to do something and the dishes aren't done, they say, 'Oh, let them wait until tomorrow.' But if the kids make plans, the dishes have to be done right now, no matter what! Because the kids have to grow up to be RESPONSIBLE PEOPLE. . . . So when we get older we do the same thing—we're not responsible. We let the dishes wait, just like our parents do.

Why are well-meaning parents often insensitive to an adolescent's need to grow up? There are numerous answers, of course, and they depend largely on individual differences in family patterns of socialization. However, two distinct groups of reasons will be discussed: (1) parental cultural impoverishments and (2) parental personality constrictions.

1. Parental cultural impoverishments reflect parental inability to anticipate future events or tendency to enter into ill-advised or unduly restrictive contracts or covenants with the adolescent. Kandel and Lesser[93] investigated the extent to which parents in the United States and Denmark grant independence to adolescents and how adolescents feel about having independence. The survey of 2,327 American and 1,552 Danish adolescents showed that an authoritarian pattern of decision making predominates in the United States whereas a democratic pattern prevails in Denmark. American parents impose may more specific rules on adolescents and apparently need to enforce specific rules in order to make sure that the youth do what is expected to them. American parents apparently do not limit the behavior of their young children enough to help them acquire self-discipline at an early age. By contrast, Danish parents (like German parents as described by Karr and Wesley[94]) appear to be less permissive during childhood and to provide more explanations for rules. The Danish parents imposed rules during adolescence only when their children could not know what was expected of them. Because Danish parents exercise greater control during childhood, their children develop self-discipline; thus Danish adolescents are more likely to behave in an approved fashion without external constraints. Kandel and Lesser suggest that, in the face of temptation, American youth are more likely to rely on external constraints whereas Danish youth rely on internalized norms. As the adolescents become older in both countries, the number of rules decreases and the proportion who experience adequate freedom increases. However, Americans at the age of 18 are still subject to more rules than the Danes are at 14. American parents apparently treat their adolescents as youngsters for a longer period of time than the Danes; thus, Danish youth experience increasing independence through their adolescent years while American youth seem to remain at a relatively stationary level. The proportion of young people in the United States who want more adult prerogatives remains at a constant level from age 13 through 18 whereas in Denmark the proportion decreases consistently with age. The percentage of adolescents satisfied with the amount of freedom granted them by both parents is at the same level for the 14-year-old Danes and 17-year-old Americans; at 18 years of age, 59 percent of the Americans said that their parents should treat them more like adults while only 18 percent of the Danes felt this way. Danish adolescents were not only treated more like adults by their parents but also felt subjectively more independent of their parents than the American youth; in instances of conflict with parents, Danish youth were more likely to act according to their own rather than their parents' wishes. Kandel and Lesser suggested that the American adolescents' greater dissatisfaction with the amount of freedom granted them by their parents might lead them to make more absolute demands on their parents than would the Danish youth.

The extent to which parents are disenchanted with social institutions—schools, churches, and government—may make it difficult for them to uphold the traditional standards of conformity and social conduct. Baumrind[95] has pointed out that before the 1960s most parents could readily believe that by maintaining order within their family they were also upholding a higher order defined by religious teachings, cultural traditions, and national patterns. But in the late 1960s and during the early 1970s some parents developed irreverence and cynicism toward many political and economic institutions in America, and they do not care whether their adolescents are raised to act responsibly toward those that uphold the values that they question. Parental problems in establishing covenants with adolescents are especially aggravated when their experiences also impose limits on their ability to comprehend contemporary reality.

Ausubel's[96] description of the plight of Maori youth in New Zealand is illustrative. Maori parents are less sophisticated than their European counterparts about vocational matters and therefore are less capable of providing their children with appropriate information, advice, and guidance. Maori parents have smaller incomes and larger families, are reluctant to apply coercive pressure or support long-term vocational preparation, and have relatively permissive and laissez-faire attitudes about their children's careers. Some parents are confused about the standards of behavior they should expect and demand from their adolescents and others are ambivalent about letting them leave home in search of better vocational opportunities. Maori parents encourage the short-term view: they are unlikely to defer immediate hedonistic satisfactions in favor of the effort necessary to attain long-range academic and occupational goals; Maori adolescents, consequently, can seldom resist the lure of immediate "big" money from unskilled laboring jobs.

Strong parallels exist between the Maori situation and that of many ethnic minority, rural, and lower-class working families in America. Parents who are swept on by uncomprehensible forces or who cling to traditional standards, may find it difficult to accept the fact that adolescents may be turning their backs on the achievement ethic that has given meaning to parental work and life styles. Gallagher,[97] for example, compared differences in social attitudes across three generations: contemporary adolescents, parents, and grandparents; the researcher found the two older generations to be relatively conservative and to hold similar attitudes. The adolescents, however, differed from their elders in their emphasis on individual autonomy, rejection of physical punishment in child rearing, liberal political attitudes, political activism, irreverence toward traditional interpretations of religion, sex-role egalitarianism, and freer expression of sexuality. Gallagher's data reveal that many parents fail to maintain a flexible outlook and, therefore, may fail to recognize adolescents' needs to adapt to a social reality that is unlike that which they encountered when they were adolescents themselves.

2. Parental personality constrictions reflect the parents' inability to cope with the adolescent's growing need for freedom because of their own personality needs. One of the principal tasks of socialization is to help the adolescent develop independence, yet parents are often ill-prepared to help with this essential task. Keith and Barranda[98] and Kandel and Lesser[99] observed that American parents provide their children with more money and possessions than parents elsewhere. With automobiles, motorbikes, cameras, and opportunities for travel, adolescents can do more things independently. But parents may continue to conceptualize an adolescent's role-behavior as they had defined it in childhood and thus attach the same importance to their own functions as they did earlier. Lerner and Knapp[100] note that both mothers and fathers underestimate major attitudinal differences between themselves and adolescents. American society expects adolescents increasingly to make their own decisions; although most parents want adolescents to be independent, what they really mean is that they want them to be able to wash their own hands, turn on the light, or take the bus by themselves.[101] Kemp[102] for example, asked 45 parents to assess the self-reliance of their children, all of whom were in early adolescence. The youth were also asked to evaluate their own personal adjustment. The data indicated that the parents perceived their children as having less self-reliance than the youth believed they had. According to Hsu et al., who compared the practices of Chinese and American parents, once the American child becomes independent, parents have few honored places in the scheme of things; consequently, they try to maintain their control as long as they can. Because American parents have a psychological need to hold on to the adolescent, their control tends to be heavy. Other researchers have said that parents tend to be overcontrolling because of unresolved conflicts in their own development. If a son or daughter shows psychological maturity, the parents may experience a conflict that had only been latent before but now prevents them from letting the adolescent separate himself or herself from the family.[103]

As Scherz[104] observed, the middle years of adolescence frequently coincide with the middle years of the parents. While the adolescent is struggling to establish sex-role identity, master vocational skills, develop long-range goals, succeed in heterosexual relations, experiment with a life style different from that of parents, and generally learn new roles both inside and outside the family, the parents are struggling with changes in their sex life, career status, and family relations resulting from the adolescent's impending physical separation. The parents' conflict over their own responsibilities often engenders self-doubt and loss of self-esteem, which makes them less able to respond to the adolescent's need for independence. The necessity of adjusting to menopause and fears about or changes in sexual vigor and activity may come at a time when the adolescent is showing sexual interests and propensities. Parental anxiety may increase with sudden changes in adolescents' behavior, and their sexuality may arouse parents' dormant sexual conflicts. The son may be criticized as "loose" for keeping late hours, although he had generally been encouraged to be independent and self-sufficient. The daughter may use cosmetics and wear provocative dresses as she approaches womanhood, but her parents may fear she is promiscuous. The career problems of parents in their middle years may also raise havoc in their relations with adolescents. Many men, for example, may find themselves situated in a job that will not alter appreciably in the future. The thought of the father reaching a plateau may make both parents uneasy, but it is difficult to change jobs when a person is in his 40s or 50s. The parents may be dissatisfied with their achievement and status just as the adolescent is struggling to find vocational goals. Parents may believe that life was harder for them and thus resent their adolescent son or daughter because each has more opportunities for success. There may also be intense anxiety over the thought of separation. Scherz noted that much of American life is organized around child-rearing, and when the adolescent leaves home the parents must face each other with a closeness that may be disturbing. Parents may try to cling to the adolescent, pay too much attention to their younger children, or find new interests outside the home in an effort to maintain marital equilibrium. The situation may resolve itself as the parents recognize that a different type of family is emerging.

Vincent[105] anticipates that American parents will move increasingly toward greater restrictiveness in child-rearing practices. He suggests that many parents are members of the "caught" generation. These are the parents who were born and socialized during a restrictive child-rearing era (1915–1935) and have been strongly influenced by the economic depression and the work and save ethic of the 1930s. They became parents themselves during the permissive "children-youth" era of 1945–1965, and they have sought to provide their children with the material advantages that they had been denied during the depression. Vincent also believes that tomorrow's parents, the 15 to 25 year olds of today, will be accustomed to having their "wants" regarded as "needs" to be satisfied "here and *now*." He speculates that the abuses of the children-youth era, of which youth's heightened drug consumption, alcoholism, and social anomie are symptoms, will lead the parents of the 1970s and 1980s to usher in another restrictive child-rearing era. Although Vincent may overestimate the extent to which parental child-rearing practices oscillate between "permissive" and "restrictive" eras, he makes the important observation that conventional parental child-rearing practices usually are a decade or two out of step. Well-meaning parents may try to provide youth with the formative influences that will serve them well during adolescence and young adulthood, but unfortunately, their own personality constrictions may impair their vision.

Congruence in Intergenerational Relations. According to sex-role identification theory, children model themselves after their parents. Family structure, the personality characteristics of family members, and the intensity of interpersonal relations affect the identification process, but in general it is assumed that adolescent sons and daughters would prefer the values and life styles of their parents. The notion that parents and adolescents would share a great deal in common runs contrary to the belief that conflict is virtually inevitable because of the gap between the generations in terms of their experiences and outlooks on life; however, evidence shows that parents and adolescents agree rather extensively on basic values and that the differences between them often pertain to specific situations and are transitory. Wright,[106] for example, showed that boys and girls in secondary school rated their parents as closer to their ideals than they themselves. He concluded that "the opinion sometimes expressed that adolescents are, in general, rejecting parental influence, receives no confirmation here." Houdek[107] administered brief questionnaires to 3,382 adolescent boys and girls and found that about 40 percent denied having experienced any frustration in communicating with their parents. Most felt that they could discuss anything freely with them; some reported that they had no hesitation about talking things over with their parents even though they might not get the answers they wanted. Chand, Crider, and Willits[108] examined the comparability of parent-youth attitudes in a longitudinal study involving about 10,000 adolescents from three different periods—1947, 1960, and 1970. At each period, high school students of both sexes were asked whether they viewed the attitudes of their parents as highly critical, sensible, or uncritical in respect to loafing uptown, staying out late, failure in school, ways young people spend their money, use of makeup, irregular church attendance, divorce, drinking, use of tobacco, card playing, Sunday movies, and Sabbath labor. When adolescents indicated a "sensible" response, the researchers interpreted it to mean that in this respect the attitudes of the adolescents and their parents were approximately the same. The results revealed a homogeneity of attitudes across the three time periods and projected an image of young people accepting their parents' norms of conduct. The findings are striking, given the constraining nature of the criteria by which the attitudes were assessed.

To ascertain parental attitudes toward adolescents, the National Center for Health Statistics conducted a survey of American parents of youth, 12 to 17 years of age.[109] The survey was carefully designed to be closely representative of young people with respect to age, sex, race, region, and socioeconomic factors. Questions were asked of the parents concerning the amount of trouble adolescents were "to bring up," adolescents' ease in making friends, frequency of overnight visits to friends, parental acquaintance with adolescents' friends, and frequency of meals eaten with the family. As Table 1 reveals, more than 85 percent of parents stated that they experienced little or no trouble bringing up adolescents; it is noteworthy that boys are reported as only slightly more difficult to bring up than are girls. Eighty-two percent of the adolescents were

Table 1
Selected Characteristics of Social Behavior of Youth aged 12–17, as Reported by Parents, United States, 1966–1970

Characteristic	Both Sexes	Boys	Girls
	Percent reported to be little or no difficulty to bring up		
All youth 12–17 years of age	87.1	85.3	88.8
Ease in making friends	82.0	82.3	81.7
Frequent overnight visits to friends	54.7	46.6	62.9
Parents acquainted with most of friends	77.0	75.1	78.9
Two or more meals per day eaten with family	61.0	63.5	58.3

Source: National Center for Health Statistics. Parent Ratings of Behavioral Patterns of Youths 12–17 Years, United States. (DHEW Pub. No. (HRA) 74-1619.) Series 11, No. 137, 1974. Reprinted by permission.

reported to make friends easily and 55 percent to have visited overnight with their friends fairly frequently. As one might expect, frequency of overnight visits increased steadily for the adolescents as age increased, and as Table 1 indicates, a higher proportion of girls than boys were reported to make frequent overnight visits. Further, three-fourths of the parents reported that they were well acquainted with most of their adolescents' friends, and three out of five adolescents were said by their parents to eat at least two meals a day with other members of the family. On the whole, then, as the findings presented in Table 1 collectively show, parents in the United States are very favorably oriented toward adolescent conduct in their own families.

Young people and their parents also appear to be relatively congruent in respect to their social and political values, and where differences of opinion exist, they do not appear to signify areas of basic conflict. In a study of 250 junior high school students, Eckhardt and Schriner[110] report, for example, that adolescent boys (but not girls) tended to diverge from their parents' political views, but these views were not related to conflict with parents. Further, Troll, Neugarten, and Kraines[111] found that parents and adolescents share more values with each other than with unrelated persons. They interviewed Chicago-area parents and approximately 90 sons and daughters home on vacation from 26 colleges across the country. The interview schedules were quite similar for both adolescents and parents; they included values, interests, and aspirations; literary, artistic, and recreational pursuits; family relations; views of each other;

and attitudes toward social issues. The results showed a greater congruence between the mother and father than between parents and children; however, the results also showed that the primary values of the adolescents tended to be those of the parents. If one member of the family was a liberal or a conservative, it was found that other members shared similar dispositions, even though the causes that they espoused might differ. And Epperson[112] found that 80 percent of a sample of 619 preadolescents and 159 adolescents reported that it would make them "most unhappy if their parents did not like what they did." Given the close relationship of younger children to their families, the researcher hypothesized that the adolescents would be less concerned than the younger ones about their parents' reactions; the data, however, revealed that the adolescents were even more concerned. In a comparative study of adolescents in the United States and Denmark, Kandel and Lesser[113] noted that in both countries adolescents who felt that they had adequate independence from their parents also had a close, positive relationship with them. Enhanced feelings of independence augmented respect for parental values, not estrangement from them.

The primary sources of conflict between parents and adolescents tend to be similar in most families. Parents insist on relative quiet and tidiness, good relations with siblings, responsible behavior, and fulfillment of home duties. Adolescents want greater independence in going out at night, use of family resources, and freedom in choosing friends. As youth grow older, their interest in freedom outside the home begins to take precedence over interest in complying with their parents' wishes at home.[114] But such conflicts may not persist for long. Bath and Lewis[115] investigated the extent to which parents and adolescents agreed about these potential areas of conflict. The researchers administered two questionnaires (two days apart) to 103 girls, most of whom were about 20 years of age. On the first questionnaire, the girls were asked to indicate how much they agreed or disagreed with several statements about the way in which a 16-year-old girl should be treated by her parents. Three general areas were covered: (a) family rules and regulations—the hour to be in after a date, number of dates per week, use of the family car, and home duties; (b) behavior with respect to the family—conflict with siblings or relatives, extent of discipline used, and weekly allowance; (c) freedom in making personal choices—the girl's own clothes, hair style, make-up, college, occupation, boy and girl friends, and movie and TV programs. On the second questionnaire, each girl was asked to indicate how several statements on parental practices related to her own family. As expected, the results showed that families were more restrictive where there was conflict or where parental practices were inconsistent; also whatever conflicts arose had to do with emotional relationships involving acceptance, rejection, and overprotection. It was found, however, that the adolescents' attitudes about issues and practices were similar to those of their own families. Most of the girls would treat their own 16-year-old daughters pretty much as they themselves had been treated at that age. Those who believed that parents should set an hour for a girl to be home after a date had parents who did just that. Bath and Lewis also reported that some of the girls would be stricter with their own 16-year-old daughters than their parents had been with them. Those who had been allowed free use of the family car at 16 believed that there should be stricter limits, and those who had been permitted to have several dates on the weekend felt that a 16-year-old girl should be limited to only one. The researchers speculate that because these girls were so close to the tribulations of adolescence, they were especially reluctant to grant younger girls too much freedom.

Parents Versus Peers. Parents *and* peers constitute the most important reference groups in the lives of most adolescents. Day-to-day activities confront adolescents with different sets of behavioral norms. Namely, on one occasion an adolescent may be inclined to meet the role expectations of parents, and on another, to conform to peer pressures. Larson[116] points out that adolescents may opt for peers "because of what they obtain by doing so or because of what they would lose by not doing so. Similarly, parent-oriented adolescents may be expected to be 'getting' something from their relationship with their parents."

Havighurst, Robinson, and Dorr[117] identified a developmental sequence of the kinds of persons adolescents model themselves after. In early childhood there are the parents, in preadolescence there is a transitional stage of "romanticism and glamour," and finally in adolescence there is an attractive, known young adult or a composite, imaginary figure. When young people are asked to write a brief essay on the topic, "The person I would like to be like," the resulting models can be classified as follows: (1) parents; (2) parent surrogates such as grandparents and teachers; (3) glamorous adults with romantic or ephemeral fame resulting from superficial qualities of behavior and acceptance (for example, athletes, military figures, movie and television stars); (4) heroes; (5) saints or religious figures; (6) attractive adults who are well known to the adolescent (for example, younger neighbors, siblings or relatives, youth leaders); (7) composite or imaginary characters who may be abstractions of several persons; (8) friends of the same age; (9) miscellaneous.

Peer-orientation in general increases during adolescence. Musgrove,[118] reported, for example, that with increasing age young people prefer their peers to their parents as leisure-time companions. Peak hostility toward parents emerged in the study at about 15 for boys and 14 for girls. Similarly, Floyd and South[119] found that peer orientation increases for both boys and girls until about tenth grade after which it tends to decrease. An explanation for the developmental trend may lie in Goodman's[120] analysis of adolescent models into two broad groups. The first group is made up of "reference-set members"—those persons whom adolescents take into account when they act; the second group is composed of an "extra-local social system"—those reference-set members who are not physically present and/or not necessarily relevant models in a specific situation. The second group enables adolescents to resist immediate demands and to preserve their autonomy and integrity in devisive confrontations. This group seems to be comparable to a conscience because it suggests that internalized norms derived from reference-group members will be utilized in a given situation even though the members themselves may be absent. To test his assumptions, Goodman asked 1,303 sophomores, juniors, and seniors in several different high schools what each expected of themselves and what they believed their fathers, mothers, friends, and best-liked teachers expected of them in three basic roles—family member, peer-group member, and student. The adolescents were asked how they felt and how the groups of significant persons (parents, friends, and teachers) felt about the roles. The study revealed that adolescents see themselves as being confronted with different sets of norms for their behavior, depending on the reference-set members. Adolescents apparently believe that they do not have much autonomy. They perceive the internalized norms for their behavior to be more like the demands made by their parents than those made by their friends, and in spite of peer pressure to conform to peer norms, they actually conform more to those of parents than to those of friends. Goodman believes that their pattern of choices is part of a developmental sequence leading to increased autonomy and responsibility. On the one hand, for example, adolescents have "economic, legal, and emotional ties," that still bind them to their parents, and on the other, they have "personal and social ties" that keep them sensitive to the demands of their peers.[121] They may take a step toward autonomy by deviating from the demands of parents, but since they are not ready to break their ties completely, they conform in part to parental demands. In this way adolescents reduce the number of persons who can control their behavior in social situations, they assume some of the control themselves, and they achieve a measure of integrity and self-esteem by resisting the immediate demands that are thrust on them.[122]

Adolescents obviously develop an orientation toward their peers, but one must be cautious in estimating its significance. Musgrove[123] has reported, for example, that both boys and girls from 9 to 15 years of age prefer their parents to their peers when the situation requires coping with difficult tasks. Won,

Social ties keep young people sensitive to the expectations of peers.

Yamamura, and Ikeda[124] assessed the relative influence of parents and peers on the independence behavior of adolescents. Boys and girls who were randomly selected from two high schools in Hawaii were asked to indicate, first, the extent to which they thought about such things as future educational and occupational plans, financial matters, and academic and social problems encountered in school, and second, to indicate the person whose advice they might seek about these issues. It was found that, in general, young people relied more on their parents than their peers. Schwartz and Baden[125] sought to determine the relative influence of parents versus peers on adolescent self-concept development, and found "that there is virtually no support for a view of adolescents as social-psychologically cut off from adults." And after a comprehensive review of earlier studies bearing on the relative influence of parents and peers and a thorough investigation of the attributes of family structure that appear to affect adolescents' interaction with peers, Larson[126] "calls into serious question much of the parental rejection literature of the sixties."

Whether young people are, in general, more likely to view either parents or peers as having the more important influence on their actions is perhaps less significant to an understanding of their behavior than knowing the conditions under which the relative influence develops. An early investigator of parent-peer orientation, for example, Brittain[127] demonstrated that adolescents tend to be influenced by parents or peers according to whichever appear to be competent guides in different areas of judgment. A cross-pressures test comprised of 12 situations that have to do with an adolescent girl who is trying to choose between two alternatives, one of which is favored by her parents and the other by her friends, was presented to 280 girls in Grades 9 through 11. Brittain showed that peer-conformity in adolescence varies according to the situation. The decisions of adolescent girls in matters of moral judgment, part-time work, and long-range adult status were more likely to be influenced by their parents than by their peers. Brittain also pointed out that decisions may comply more with the parents' wishes when the girls believe they are important to both their parents and peers, but comply with their peers' wishes when the decisions are seen as relatively unimportant to both groups. The girls generally conformed to their peers in buying clothes, dressing for a football game or party, and friendship choices. Brittain[128] concluded that adolescents are more strongly oriented toward peer-conformity in areas where social values are changing rapidly and where the choices hold immediate consequences.

Larson,[129] however, has raised two critical questions about the "situational" explanation. First, he has pointed out that situational dilemmas may indicate adolescents' choice of action rather than the nature of parent-peer relationships. Parent-peer orientations must be assessed independently of situations, he contends, because situational compliance may also reflect fear, respect, appreciation, assessments of special competence, reactions to recent events, and so on. Second, he questions the consistency of either parent or peer importance across situations. Do adolescents who choose their parents' position in a party situation also choose to be parent compliant in a moral dilemma, in an educational dilemma, and so on? Larson[130] says that, in fact, whether an adolescent is influenced by either parents or peers depends on whether the influence each exerts fits with his or her self-concept. Larson conducted an empirical investigation of the conditions under which parents versus peer compliance occurs, and the researcher found strong support for his assumption. Larson's data suggest that neither parents nor peers influence youth who are (1) self-assured, for example, familiar with characteristics of future roles and statuses and sufficiently independent to make decisions about them; (2) able to sort alternatives into levels of priority, assigning moral dilemmas highest priority and attaching lesser significance to issues of temporal importance; and (3) realistic about counsel of either parents or peers. Thus, Larson's data suggest that young people who have developed a relatively strong value structure are relatively immune from the pressure of either parents or peers.[131]

Runaways. Running away from home has been an attractive option to a small proportion of adolescents since time immemorial. Literary figures like Tom Sawyer and Holden Caulfield have even made running away seem romantic. But running away from home today usually represents an often unproductive solution to long-standing conflict in parent-adolescent relations.[132]

Many parents permit their own imagination free reign when an adolescent runs away from home, fearing that the missing son or daughter was kidnapped, a victim of drugs, or (in the case of girls) raped. Probation workers, judges, counselors, police officers, and others engaged in law enforcement programs often are exasperated by the problems runaways cause them. However, Gold and Reimer,[133] drawing from findings and conclusions based on a recent nation-wide survey of youth (conducted by the Institute for Social Research, University of Michigan), report that the size of the runaway youth problem is often exaggerated and that the nature of the problem is generally misunderstood. Their findings contradict the popular image of runaways as a growing legion of adolescents who depart home for distant parts of the country. The researchers report that about 1.5 to 2.4 million adolescents, ages 11 to 18, ran away from home between mid-1969 and 1972. However, 70 percent of the young people merely ran away to the house of a friend or relative. Only 13 percent actually "hit the road," leaving their city or community. The researchers point out that over two-thirds of the runaways who came to the attention of the police were from out of town. Adolescents in the age range 15 to 16 years were most likely to run away from home, and the runaways emerged equally from all social classes. Further, the act of running away seldom was accompanied by other acts associated with breaking the law, but a higher proportion of the runaways, relative to the general population of adolescents in the country, had on other occasions engaged in delinquent activities.[134]

Shellow et al.[135] conducted a study of several hundred 10- to 17-year-old boys and girls in a rapidly growing suburb of Washington, D.C. They found that 50 percent of the runaways came from families with incomes between $6,000 and $12,000; 15 percent from families with incomes over $12,000; and about 25 percent from families with incomes of less than $6,000. Educational and socioeconomic factors appeared to be only indirectly related to an adolescent's decision to run away; most of the runaways came from broken or reconstituted homes. The researchers also found that the majority of the runaways were the oldest children in their families. Girls tended to run away between 6 p.m. and midnight on Friday or Saturday, whereas boys tended to run away during the daytime and on weekends, suggesting that dating for girls and school for boys may be precipitating factors. Girls often ran away with a boyfriend "who provided transportation, financial resources, and a reason." On the whole, the runaway episodes seemed to be impulsive and poorly planned. About one-third of the youth started from home with less than $1.00, and many left without food or enough clothing. Girls frequently took only a set of curlers and a can of hairspray. Runaways often sought makeshift sleeping arrangements in hallways, laundromats, and parked cars. Shellow et al. suggested that the apparent lack of planning indicates "a timidity and tentativeness" that is typical of many runaways. An analysis of hundreds of episodes indicates that the youth usually travel only a short distance. Within about 48 hours half return on their own volition and the other half are returned with the help of the police. Shellow et al. noted that about 50 percent of the episodes are reported to police within four hours and 60 percent within six hours. It was found that first-time episodes were reported quite promptly. However, an increasing amount of time elapsed in reporting the second, third, and fourth episodes, perhaps reflecting "the parents' confidence—born of past experience—that the child would return soon on his own."[136]

An investigation of the problems of runaways in two New York City neighborhoods—a low-income, high-crime area and a middle-income area—provides further insight into the characteristics of runaway adolescents.[137] Hildebrand found that the number of runaways in the high-crime area was six times that of the middle-income area, and that children in the former area began running away from home at an earlier age than did those in the latter area. He also found that among runaways there was extensive deterioration of family life and general apathy toward education, especially in the low-income section. Low-income girls tended to run away from home around age 14; low-income boys around age 13. These figures are lower than those cited by Gold and Reimer above, but they must be considered from the perspective of low-income parents, who may think of their 15 or 16 year olds as mature enough to be away from home on their own. Thus, a low-income youth about this age who ran away might not ever be reported to the authorities. Hildebrand also pointed out that low-income parents often did not know the name or the location of the school that their runaway child was supposed to be attending. These parents usually adopted a nonchalant attitude toward their child's absence, feeling that their responsibilities ended when they reported the incident to the police. Some may even have known the whereabouts of the runaway but did nothing, preferring to depend wholly on the police.

Posting a reward for information is one way in which parents attempt to restore communications with a runaway.

Hildebrand's observation that parents may not even know the name or location of their runaway adolescent's school points symbolically to a striking absence of communication among members of the family. Blood and D'Angelo[138] suggest, moreover, that the issue of communication, as reflected in absence of demonstrable love and affection, heightened manifestations of parental rejection, and higher rate of physical abuse on the part of parents, may be at the core of the runaway's problems. Further, Goldmeier and Dean[139] report that runaways, in comparison with adolescents who do not run away, feel ill at ease and unhappy at home, experience less "warmth" and affection with parents, and believe that they are excessively and undeservedly punished. Goldmeier and Dean also reveal that runaways tend to avoid contact with adults in general, perhaps because the absence of parental models impedes their development of the skills necessary for interaction with adults. But the researchers found that runaways are willing to relate to peers, and they suggest that professional intervention programs for runaways might be well advised to support more halfway houses and such self-help sources as "walk-in," "hot line," and other kinds of crisis centers.

FAMILY ANTECEDENTS OF IDENTITY FORMATION

The structural outline of the conventional American family has long been influenced by the forces of industrialism. The traditional family has learned to orient itself to society by an instrumental, achievement ethic, which has tended to cause it to develop into a relatively isolated unit. The family has been held together largely by ties of affection, and the sex-role learning of daughters has emphasized effective interpersonal relations and that of the boys has emphasized achievement, efficiency, and rational mastery of the environment. Industry has employed workers on the basis of their skills for particular jobs, kinship ties and nepotism seldom have interfered with the efficient organization of an enterprise. Workers and their families have been almost entirely dependent on their occupational earnings. As a result of geographic mobility, the nuclear family (headed usually by a male worker) has become separated from relatives by enormous distances. As large industries have taken over economic production, schools, peer groups, hospitals, and community organizations have assumed responsibilities for education, health, and other functions formerly performed by the family.[140]

The ideal family structure from the perspective of industrialism—an independent, isolated, mobile unit—emerged only in relatively few instances. Kinships have survived, occupational and geographical mobility notwithstanding, especially in large urban areas.[141] It is easy, for example, to overlook the aid and service activities that link American families into functioning systems. According to Sussman and Burchinal,[142] the aid, services, and support provided by related families supplement the resources of the nuclear family unit. Decisions are still made by the nuclear family; relatives seldom direct its course of action in given situations. But a flow of financial aid runs along generational lines, either from parents to young married children or from a middle-aged couple to aged parents. Although financial aid for emergencies is important, money may also be given for education, starting a family, beginning a marriage, or launching a career. Such support may be given in the form of gifts for weddings, children's births, Christmas, anniversaries, or birthdays. Substantial parental support may often be given to adolescents who marry while still in high school or college. Among middle- and working-class families, relatives may be especially helpful during times of disaster or on ceremonial occasions. Sussman and Burchinal have also observed that everyday or weekly activities often bring together members of related families. Reduction in the work week, automobiles and superhighways, and telephones as household necessities have facilitated social interaction and communication among relatives. Among urban working-class families, leisure-time activities consist of joint get-togethers and recreational pursuits. Suburban middle-class families may want to get together but be unable to do so because of the distance separating nuclear units.

The image of the contemporary American family is that of a relatively flexible and adaptive socializing agent. Aldous[143] has pointed out that the contacts a nuclear family may have with other related nuclear families is likely to vary according to its phase in the family life cycle. A newly married couple would probably focus on developing a common bond and a division of labor to supplement their romantic love. Since relatives may represent a threat to the fragile unity of a newly married couple, they may try to keep their contacts with kin to a minimum. But during the child-bearing phase and the aging period, the nuclear family may need contacts with relatives, for during these periods the problems of physical maintenance can demand substantial energy and financial support.

Three major modifications in the structural elements of the nuclear family—family size and birth order, maternal employment, and father absence—have affected family socialization patterns in significant ways. Rapidly depleting ecological resources and changes in the industrial society call for a smaller world population; hence, changes in family size and sibling birth order now exert a different kind of impact on parental socializing practices. Women today have more freedom and authority and their changed status has influenced the family structure. The need for women workers, especially during World War II, helped to equalize their opportunities. Women's personal and economic independence derived from earning a living led many to develop a more achievement-oriented outlook on life; to some extent, this has undermined the traditional role of the father as the primary wage-earner, head of household, and carrier of instrumental values. A mother, for example, may use her intelligence and skills to acquire even greater earning power than a father; since housework must be done in the evenings, husbands must share in performing an increasing amount of domestic work and child care, all of which affect parental expectations toward socialization. Further, all theories of identification emphasize the impact a father may have on the sex-role learning of both sexes. When a father is absent for a prolonged period because of the requirements of his job, he deprives his children of a model for sex-role learning. But if he deserts the family or dies, there are additional problems. Under these circumstances, a mother may have to assume all parental tasks on a long-term basis, and this, too, may exert important variations in the role learning of young people. What actually occurs in a family in the context of birth control, maternal employment, and father absence, respectively, depends on many circumstances, the more significant of which are discussed in the following portions of this chapter.

Birth Order and Family Size

When Francis Galton published *English Men of Science* in 1874, he found from the biographical data of the scientists that the proportion of only sons and first-born sons was greater than would have been expected by chance alone. Galton invoked the ancient laws of primogeniture to explain his findings: the eldest son usually inherited the wealth of his parents and thus was free to pursue such matters of interest as science.[144] Galton's pioneering research has inspired further study of the relationship between birth order and socialization. Rosenberg and Sutton-Smith[145] reason that birth order today is an ecological variable that "operates chiefly as a determinant of the availability of the major rewards in the child's family of origin." The differential effects of birth order would appear to be more significant in childhood than in adolescence when boys and girls have access to other models and rewards than those of their parents. Thus many early internalizations of role behaviors that persist in adolescent identity-formation and the adult personality have been shown to be related to birth order. Galton suspected that parents favored either the only child or the first-born (who was actually an only child for a time) as a companion and assigned that child more responsibilities than other children in the family.[146] Warren's[147] studies show that Galton's early assumption was correct: it has been consistently shown that the socializing experiences of first-born and later-born children are qualitatively different. Socialization is believed to be more stressful for the first-born; it must blaze a trail for its younger brothers and sisters in attaining privileges from its parents, and both the first-born and its mother are likely to have a number of anxiety-provoking conflicts. The first-born's parents are likely to be relatively young and immature and to be over-eager for their first-born to accomplish things. The social-learning experiences among first-borns may include parent-surrogate training, and its concomitant intensive identification may lead to such traits as conformity, affiliation, and dependency; these, in turn, may contribute to academic success and a readiness to take on such parent-surrogate roles as teaching.[148] Social learning in the male dyad (two-boy family) presumably leads to strong sex-role masculinity. The socialization experiences of the two may lead the first-born, as a consequence of intense parental attention, to differ from the second-born by developing a strategic or conniving style of social interaction. Social learning in the female dyad may result in strong femininity. Since the first-born daughter is less likely than the first-born son to experience strong achievement pressures, it is the second-born daughter, perhaps in an effort to keep up with the first-born, who tends to develop the strategic or conniving style. When there are two opposite-sex siblings, there seems to be more innovative sex-role learning.[149]

In general later-borns are expected to learn vicariously from the tribulations of the first-born, and when it is their turn, to face the same situations with aplomb. The family is likely to be less demanding and more protective of younger children. Although first-borns enjoy the undivided attention of their parents, their wants may be satisfied to the point of indulgence; thus, the birth of a second child may engender feelings of jealousy and hostility which may lead the first-born to adopt immature modes of adjustment. Although later-borns must compete more for parental attention, they also enjoy the advantage of having first-borns as models. In adolescence, the first-born may be expected to stay on the farm or run the family business while each later-born is free to enter an occupation of his or her choice. The socializing experiences of only children tend to parallel those of the first-born.[150] Although they may receive undivided parental attention and stimulation throughout childhood, they are frequently coddled and may lack the experiences necessary to prepare them to face competition and adversity. Without siblings only children may not develop sensitivity and consideration for the feelings of others; their incomplete socialization may handicap them in peer relations at adolescence.

Rosenblatt and Skoogberg[151] confirmed these general interpretations in a cross-cultural comparison of regularities in sibling relationships with the adult roles of persons. The researchers examined ethnographic materials from 39 unrelated, preindustrial cultures scattered throughout the world. Their findings revealed that first-born children of both sexes were likely to have more authority over siblings in childhood and receive more respect from them. In adulthood, first-born daughters were more likely than later-born daughters to be respected by siblings, and first-born sons relative to the later-born were more likely to head a kingroup, acquire authority over and gain respect of siblings, control property, and attain power and influence over others. Another confirmation of the belief that first-borns generally tend to acquire skills associated with status and power while later-borns learn more adaptive skills may be derived indirectly from Weller, Natan, and Hazi's[152] study of marital happiness. One might anticipate that marital happiness would be highest among partners of complementary rather than of similar birth-order ranks. The researchers found, as expected, in a study of the marriages of 258 Israeli women, that marital happiness was highest among first-born males married to later-born females and nearly as high among first-born females married to later-born males. Adjustment of first-borns married to first-borns was relatively low; least satisfaction was reported by only-born women who were married to only-born men.

The impact of birth order on socialization in the United States tends to be masked relative to its influence in non-Western societies. In the United States, for example, kinship groups in which children care for other children are limited in number, long periods of formal schooling keep siblings isolated from one another, and parental control of socialization continues nearly to attainment of adulthood. As a consequence, family size appears to be a key variable in determining whether ordinal position affects socialization in American families.

Rosenberg and Sutton-Smith[153] discuss how the size of a family affects the distribution of parental reinforcements. One child to one parent may provide a match up in a two-child family, but one of the children may be excluded in a three-child family. This child may try to compete by acting either like a child to obtain a share of the resources or an adult (by looking after the other children) to receive special recognition from its parents. The oldest child usually receives explicit recognition from both its parents and younger siblings for assuming the role of parent-surrogate, especially in large families. Rosenberg and Sutton-Smith also point out that more rivalry should be expected in same-sex, two-child families than in opposite-sex families since same-sex siblings compete for the same rewards. The rivalry should have the greatest impact on a first-born, who has undisputed claim to the family rewards until a second-born challenges its supremacy. When the second child arrives, a pattern for distributing the rewards must be developed, but it is helped in its struggle by the older sibling, who, though a rival, is also a model. But an older opposite-sex sibling may not facilitate sex-role learning. Assuming the stereotype that girls are supposed to be more obedient, responsible, and nurturant, and boys more achieving, self-reliant, and independent, modeling one's behavior after that of an opposite-sex sibling might make it difficult to identify with either feminine or masculine roles. In a study of 900 children in the fourth through the sixth grades in 14 Ohio schools, Rosenberg and Sutton-Smith[154] found support for most of these notions; for example, as family size increased, sex-role anxiety in both first- and later-borns decreased. But in two-child families, there seemed to be a complementary imbalance—what was good for one sibling was not for the other; a first-born with a younger sibling of the same sex was more anxious, compulsive, and assertive of its masculinity or femininity, but a first-born with a younger sibling of the opposite sex had few of these characteristics. In two-child families boys with a boy sibling were more masculine than boys with a girl sibling, and girls with a girl sibling were more feminine than girls with a boy sibling. In three-child families, however, the first-born with younger siblings of the same sex demonstrated less sex-role anxiety than those with opposite-sex siblings. For the second-born in two- and three-child families, the presence of an older same-sex sibling facilitated sex-role learning with minimal anxiety; the presence of an older opposite-sex sibling led to sex-role conflict and heightened anxiety. On the basis of conclusions drawn from a large-scale study of seventh through twelfth grade young people, Bowerman and Dobash[155] also report that intersibling affect varies as a function of family size. The researchers point out that large families lead to complex relationships, with potential for conflicts, coalitions, and diffusion of sentiments. They found that adolescents in two-child families were more likely to report close feelings toward siblings than were the young people from larger families. Intersibling affect also was influenced by direction of age difference, age of the adolescent, and sex combination. On the average, the adolescents felt closer to an older than to a younger sibling. Further, both sexes felt close to a sibling of the same sex, but girls were more likely than boys to have favorable feelings toward the same-sex sibling. Indeed, the adolescent girls more than the boys were likely to feel close to siblings of either sex.

Maternal Employment

During the past two or three decades, the proportion of women in the work force has increased markedly. Only one women in five was working in 1920, one in four working in 1940, one in three in 1960, and today, almost one mother out of two is employed either part- or full-time. Single-parent families contribute disproportionately to the population of working mothers. Further, the probability of maternal employment is greater among families with adolescents rather than children, since caretaking functions deter many women from seeking gainful employment. Maternal employment occurs for a variety of reasons—to realize a career, to escape from boredom or monotony, to avoid irksome housework, and to augment family income for household possessions, status items, and children's education. Since convention expects the father to provide economic support for the family and the mother to maintain the home, the latter's assumption of a share of family economic obligations entails a change in family structure, and in turn, a change in the pattern of children's sex-role learning.

Maternal employment may affect adolescents in a number of ways. They may be required to shoulder work left behind by the mother, and they may have less time for leisure activities and for taking part-time summer jobs. Parents may be too busy for social interaction, thus depriving the adolescents of modeling behavior.[156] Father-adolescent relations may deteriorate should the balance of conjugal power shift to the mother, leading adolescents to view the father as an ineffectual model.[157] On the other hand, maternal employment may enhance adolescents' acquisition of independence and responsibility. Adolescents of both sexes may prosper when working parents have opportunity to fulfill an active, sharing role in child-rearing, and daughters may be especially fortunate when maternal employment helps sharpen their career perspectives.[158] Such assumptions as these have led Hoffman[159] to set forth the following five hypotheses, which specify the probable effects of maternal employment, and then, to thoroughly examine the research literature in order to assess whether the hypotheses were supported by the results of investigations:

1. Maternal employment leads the mother, and possibly the father, to provide different models of behavior for the children. The self-concept of girls relative to the female role is particularly likely to be affected.
2. Maternal employment influences the mother's emotional state, providing on different occasions, satisfaction, role strain, and guilt, which affect her interaction with her children.
3. The working mother's socialization practices are affected relative to those of nonemployed mothers by different situational demands.
4. The working-mother provides less personal supervision of her children than does the nonworking mother.
5. The working mother's regular absences deprives her children both emotionally and cognitively, and they may perceive her absences symbolically as rejection.

Let us review briefly Hoffman's[160] findings. First (hypothesis 1), maternal employment indeed appears to affect the adolescents' concept of themselves and the way in which they model their parents. Family members associate maternal employment with less traditional sex-role concepts, approve of maternal employment, and develop a higher evaluation of female competence. And Etaugh[161] notes that educational aspirations generally are higher among sons and daughters of working mothers and that the daughters often choose male-dominated careers. The modeling effect of maternal employment leads daughters to become more independent and to develop higher achievement aspirations, which implies that they will also develop positive self-concepts and effective social skills.[162] Second (hypothesis 2), a working mother's morale may be very high. One who obtains satisfaction from her work and whose familial arrangements support her dual role is likely neither to feel guilty about working nor to develop counterproductive attitudes toward her family. Third (hypothesis 3), employed and nonemployed mothers are likely to differ in their child-rearing practices, especially in respect to responsibility and independence training. Hoffman indicates that working mothers of older children and adolescents are more likely than nonworking mothers to expect them to participate effectively in fulfilling household responsibilities. When the young person is not overburdened, the obligations seem conducive to the development of social adjustment and responsibility. Hoffman also points out that, whereas a nonworking mother may have difficulty making the transition from "protector and nurturer" to "independence trainer," because the latter role is not open to her; the working mother may find the psychological threat in the transition of her socializing role lessened because alternative roles and sources of self-worth are in fact open to her. Fourth (hypothesis 4), Hoffman found that working mothers in both lower- and middle-class families do indeed fall short of nonworking mothers in the adequacy of their supervision of young people. Fifth (hypothesis 5), Hoffman reports that investigators have been unable to demonstrate either a positive or a negative relationship between maternal employment and children's emotional and cognitive growth. (Propper,[163] for example, in a study involving "perception of parental interests, parental help with school and personal problems, and closeness to parents" found that adolescents' perceptions of parental support were about the same whether their mother worked.) Hoffman suggests that the absence of negative effects may mean, not that mother's employment is an irrelevant variable in this respect, but that mothers have been sufficiently concerned to counterbalance potential deprivation effects with various forms of support.

Father Absence

The roles and behaviors that family members perform constitute a basic source of sex-role information for children. Adolescents internalize appropriate sex-role expectations as they fulfill adult-sanctioned tasks and obligations. Sex has become a convenient criterion for developing a pathway to adult roles, and the family plays an important function in making young people officially aware of the sex category to which they belong, in stimulating acquisition of appropriate sex behavior, and in ensuring that self-concept development and sex-role identification are congruent. From the perspective of sex-role acquisition, then, father absence is an important variable in socialization. According to Lynn,[164] father absence traditionally means that the primary instrumental leader, the parent who usually stresses delay of gratification in the interest of greater future reward and who epitomizes the roles and privileges of society, is lost to the family. Moreover, Lynn notes that father absence reduces the number of adults in the family to one, which restricts the supervision of young people, limits their recreational opportunities, and deprives them of a model to demonstrate the characteristics of maleness. Aldous[165] contends that "mothers, because of lack of knowledge, cannot transmit in their role expectations of boys, the subtle nuances of masculine behavior." Father absence thus may lead boys to encounter either "learning lags or learning deficits" until they have opportunity to interact at length with a male model. Furthermore, mothers who are forced by circumstances to play paternal roles may present distorted pictures of adult role behaviors to daughters, and thus, father absence may affect girls, too, since it results in loss of a critical cross-sex source of sex-role sanctions and expectations.

The presence of a father as a masculine model appears to be a very important factor in the masculine development of younger boys. Hetherington[166] has shown that boys whose fathers were absent were less masculine, more dependent, and less aggressive than boys whose fathers were present if the absence had begun during the boy's first four years of life, but if the absence occurred after age five, there was little difference on measures of these attributes. Sutton-Smith, Rosenberg, and Landy[167] have reported that the effects of a father's absence are greatest during the early and middle years of childhood. Although the absence of a father appears to affect the younger boy's socialization considerably, the cumulative effects of role-model deprivation may also influence the adolescent's sex-role identification. For example, Barclay and Cusumano[168] reported that male adolescents without a father tended to be less perceptive in their general life style, more passive about their environment, and less self-reliant. Suedfeld[169] reported that a study of Peace Corps volunteers showed that about 45 percent of those who returned to the United States before the completion of their overseas tour because of adjustment and conduct problems had fathers who had been absent from their families for at least five years before their fifteenth birthday. And in a study of 27 emotionally disturbed 11- to 15-year-old male military dependents and 30 comparable normal military dependents, Pedersen[170] found that the extent of the father's absence was predictive of emotional disturbance. His study also showed that the mothers of the disturbed boys were themselves more disturbed than the mothers of the normal youth. No differences in psychological adjustment were found among the fathers of the two groups.

Significantly, boys without brothers seem to be more affected by a father's absence than those with brothers. Biller and Borstelmann[171] pointed out that with increasing age, male siblings and peers may become important masculine models for boys who were without fathers during their preschool years. For preadolescents, however, such interactions may bring about considerable sex-role conflict in the boys whose fathers are absent. The researchers reviewed several investigations showing that preadolescent boys may manifest competing masculine and feminine response tendencies. Feminine behavior may persist as a result of earlier maternal reinforcements, and exaggerated masculinity may emerge as the boy acts out his conception of the masculine role. Wohlford,

Santrock, Berger, and Liberman[172] investigated the role of the older male sibling as a potential surrogate father model for economically disadvantaged, black, preschool boys and girls. They assessed masculinity-femininity, aggression, and dependency. They found that boys were more aggressive but not more independent than girls and that both boys and girls who had one or more older male siblings were more aggressive, less intensely dependent, and less frequently dependent than those without such siblings. Wohlford et al. concluded that the presence of an older male sibling in a family without a father helped make the child more like one from a family with a father; however, since the older siblings may also have been deprived of a father as an adult male model, they may have encountered their first male model in a street corner gang and thus acquired exaggerated male sex-typed, aggressive, and independent behavior, which they then passed on to their younger brothers and sisters.

Research dealing with the effects of father absence on the personality development of adolescent girls is virtually nonexistent, except fortunately, for one very thorough investigation. Hetherington[173] conducted a detailed exploration of the effects of time of and reason for paternal separation on the behavior of father-absent adolescent girls. The girls, ranging in age from 13 to 17, were first-borns without brothers, whose families were white, lower-middle-class. They were divided into three groups: (1) girls from intact families with both parents living in the home, (2) girls from families in which the father was absent as a result of divorce and in which the girls had minimal contact with the father following the divorce, and (3) girls from families in which the father was absent due to death. None of the father-absent families had any males living in the home after separation from the father occurred. Measures of the girls' personality development included (1) observation of each girl's behavior in a recreation center (2) each girl's nonverbal behavior while interacting with a male or female interviewer, (3) ratings based on interviews with each daughter, (4) ratings based on interviews with the mothers, and (5) scores on a variety of personality tests.

Hetherington's study in general revealed that adolescent daughters living in father-absent families, while maintaining traditional sex-type feminine behavior and role preferences, develop an inability to interact appropriately with males. On the whole, the effects of father separation during the preschool years were more pronounced than when the separation occurred later. (This finding corresponds with those of other studies that show that father absence also exerts a long-term effect on the socialization of younger boys.) The investigation also indicated that daughters, widows, divorcees, and mothers from intact families were comparable in their affect toward their daughters and in their control and discipline of them. The groups of mothers were equal in their femininity and the extend to which they reinforced the sex-appropriate behavior of their daughters. The divorcees, however, were more critical of themselves, anxious and unhappy, and relative to the other two groups of mothers, when their daughters began to engage in heterosexual activities, they became more inconsistent, conflictful, and punitive toward the daughters' sexual behavior.

The effect of father absence on the adolescent girls' relationships with males was particularly evident in the nonverbal measures recorded during their interviews. The girls were permitted to sit in one of three chairs relative to the interviewer; one was beside the interviewer, one was directly across a table, and one across the table and somewhat removed. When the interviewer was a woman, the girls in the three groups chose the chairs indiscriminately; however, when the interviewer was a man, the daughters of divorcees chose the closest chair, the girls from intact families selected the chair across the table, and the daughters of widows picked the remote chair. The daughters of divorcees were particularly open and uninhibited whereas the daughters of widows were especially reserved. When talking with the male interviewers, the former tended to lean back in an open arm-and-leg position, show proximity seeking in a smiling, open, receptive manner; in contrast, the latter demonstrated relatively infrequent speech and eye contact, avoidance of proximity, and rigid postural characteristics. Further, the daughters whose mothers were widowed early in their childhood talked, smiled, and made eye contact even less frequently than the girls whose fathers had died when they were older.

Hetherington found that the three groups of girls reported themselves as secure around female adults and peers. The daughters living in intact and widowed families indicated that they were equally close to their mothers and that their mothers were equally warm and permissive toward them. The daughters of divorced parents, however, reported considerable conflict with their mothers. In different ways the daughters of widows and divorcees expressed uncertainty around male peers and adults. The daughters of divorcees were more and the daughters of widows were less heterosexually active than the daughters from intact families. Girls from intact families also were attached to their parents' male friends whereas both groups of father-absent daughters indicated infrequent contact with adult males. Finally, daughters of divorcees in respect to daughters in the other two groups, reported more negative attitudes and conflict with their fathers and saw them as less competent. Hetherington's investigation thus suggests that the impact of father absence on adolescents may depend partly on its effect on the mother's self-image, its length and timing, and on the availability of paternal surrogates. Such factors may influence the course of socialization and the sex-role learning of young people whose family structure departs from the modal, nuclear family unit.

SUMMARY

Identification begins when the child first attempts to imitate its parents' behavior. Several explanations have been advanced to account for motivation in the process of identity formation. Psychoanalytic theory suggests that it stems from resolution of the oedipal complex. Mowrer holds that the more a boy loves and respects his father (and a girl, her mother), the greater will be the degree of warmth and affection between them, and thus, the more significant parental approval or punishment. Presumably, then, children acquire strong motivation to identify with their parents when the parents reward them for appropriate behavior and also threaten to punish them for disapproved behavior. Role taking later replaces the imitation, and children may act quite differently from their parents. The emotional dependency of childhood changes in adolescence to an emotional commitment to meet the role expectations of parents, peers, teachers, and employers. Adolescents who have opportunity to impose their own conceptions on a role, to shape it to meet their needs and future objectives, may personalize the style of their role performance.

Sex-role learning comprises the performances and attitudes that coincide with cultural stereotypes of masculinity and femininity. Traditional patterns of sex-role differentiation anticipate that parents will diverge into distinctly different roles, the father taking the instrumental image (a disciplined pursuit of future goals), and the mother, the expressive image (a focus on affective behavior at the moment). Today, however, the growing inapplicability of the instrumental-expressive role distinction is leading to dissatisfaction with traditional patterns of sex-role assignments. The ideal now is androgyny—no sex role differentiation—a role system whereby cultural aspects of gender are not mandated by biological sex differences. Evidence points, however, to the existence of pervasive and persistent sex-role stereotypes in our society, and according to Lynn, four major assumptions regarding traditional sex-role learning should be noted: (1) both boys and girls initially identify with their mothers, but the boy must shift later to a masculine model; (2) the young girl interacts more frequently with an appropriate sex-role model than does the young boy; (3) despite the shortage of male models, the young boy usually learns some stereotype of a masculine sex-role; (4) American society still is male-dominated and allocates more privileges to the male than to the female, especially during adolescence and adulthood.

Adolescent initiation rites in preliterate societies contrast markedly with the prolonged, incremental sex-role socialization of American young people. The variety of rites is tremendous. One rite may require only a few hours while another may require years. In one instance the initiate eagerly anticipates events; in another, he or she fearfully awaits harsh and painful treatment. Although interpretations of the rites vary, anthropologists generally agree that they provide perspective on the myriad ways in which young people's sex-role identities are established.

Parental role functions affect the socialization of adolescents in several important ways. First, social-class membership appears to be differentially associated with parental verbal skills—middle-class parents appear more effective than lower- or working-class parents in helping young people learn standards of conduct and self-direction. Second, adolescent boys and girls generally attribute more power in the family to their same-sex parent and seek to be like that parent. On the other hand, in families where one parent dominates the other, adolescent girls tend to hold their orientation to the mother even when her power is greatly eroded, but adolescent boys appear to encounter considerable difficulty in achieving father-identification when his power is perceived as subordinate to that of the mother. Third, an adolescent's identification with his or her parents depends also on the pattern and consistency of parental control. The relative merits of permissive, authoritarian, and authoritative patterns of parental control are discussed; in general, young people with authoritative parents tend to possess greater self-confidence than those with either permissive or authoritarian parents. Consistency is an important factor because a stable environment gives an adolescent assurance that tasks to be mastered and skills to be learned will have meaning over time. Longitudinal studies generally show that while maternal nurturance is relatively stable, there is generally a shift from control toward greater autonomy as young people grow older.

Identification also is influenced by the extent to which conflicts ensue. Intergenerational conflict emerges for two general reasons: parental cultural impoverishment and parental personality constrictions. Cultural impoverishment refers to the parents' inability to anticipate future events, which increases the likelihood that they will make ill-advised or unduly restrictive agreements with adolescents. These parents may become authoritarian and insist that the adolescent hew the line. Personality constrictions refer to the parents' inability to cope with the youth's growing need for freedom because of their own emotional needs. When severe friction is engendered between adolescents and their parents, the young people may run away from home, perhaps to express their defiance of parental expectations. On the whole, however, about 85 percent of the parents in a recent nationwide survey said that they experienced little or no trouble bringing up adolescents, and most were favorably oriented toward the way adolescents in their families conducted themselves. Peer orientation usually increases during adolescence, and situations where young people must choose between the views of either parents or peers sometimes arise. Young people who are self-assured, able to sort alternatives into priorities, and are realistic, however, appear to develop life styles that are relatively immune to pressure from either parents or peers.

Three major dimensions of family antecedents of identity formation are set forth in this chapter: birth order and family size, maternal employment, and father absence. Research has consistently shown that the socialization experiences of first-born and later-born children are qualitatively different. Socialization is believed to be more stressful for the first-borns since they must blaze a trail for their younger siblings. The first-borns' socialization (in relation to that of the later-borns) leads them to assume greater responsibilities and to exert stronger effort to achieve authority and status. Effects of birth order vary as a function of family size, since family size affects the distribution of parental reinforcements. In large families, for example, there may be fewer parental pressures on all children to do well and conform to middle-class standards; thus, the children may experience lower levels of achievement anxiety. Also adolescents from large families are less likely than those from small families to feel close to their brothers and sisters.

Maternal employment may affect adolescent self-concept development in different ways. On the other hand, parents may be too busy for social interaction, thus depriving adolescents of modeling behavior, and on the other, adolescents of both sexes may prosper when working parents have opportunity to fulfill active, sharing roles as socializing agents. Maternal employment appears to exert a positive overall effect on the socialization of adolescents when maternal sex-role satisfaction is high.

Father absence appears to affect the sex-role acquisition of boys primarily by depriving them of a role model; the deprivation effects appear to be relatively more serious in respect to the socialization of young boys, but the cumulative effects may also influence adolescents' sex-role identification. Adolescent girls living in father-absent families, while likely to acquire traditional sex-type feminine behavior and role preferences, may develop an inability to interact appropriately with males. On the whole, the effects of father separation on adolescent girls is more pronounced when the separation occurs during their preschool years than when it happens later in their childhood.

REVIEW QUESTIONS

1. How does psychoanalytic theory account for motivation in the identification process?
2. How do dependency, nurturance, and control affect identification?
3. Define the status-envy hypothesis.
4. What are the stages through which young people pass in learning new roles?
5. What is the essence of, respectively, the instrumental and expressive sex-role?
6. Why is androgyny an ideal in contemporary society?
7. What assumptions does Lynn make about the sex-role learning of boys and girls?
8. How do initiation rites motivate young people to adopt appropriate sex-roles?
9. How do parental verbal skills produce relationships between social class and socialization?
10. What conjugal power relationship is most effective in facilitating socialization?
11. Define, respectively, the permissive, authoritarian, and authoritative modes of parental control.
12. What is the significance of consistency in patterns of family socialization?
13. How do love-hostility and autonomy-control variables, respectively, affect the socialization of both boys and girls?
14. What is the "sleeper" effect?
15. Why is it difficult to predict the effects of socializing experiences on personality development across time?
16. Define the parent-adolescent arrangements Elkind describes as the bargain, agreement, and contract.
17. What may happen when parents fail to anticipate future events?

18. How might parental personality needs affect youth's growing need for autonomy?
19. What are the aspects of family socialization upon which parents and adolescents generally agree?
20. What kinds of persons are attractive to young people as models?
21. At what age does adolescent hostility toward parents tend to peak?
22. What are the circumstances that lead young people to respond to parents or peers, respectively, in a parent versus peers conflict?
23. What are the characteristics of the families of runaway youth?
24. Why are first-borns expected to assume greater responsibility than later-borns?
25. How does family size relate to the way ordinal position affects socialization?
26. How is maternal employment likely to affect family socialization patterns?
27. How might father absence affect the socialization of both boys and girls?
28. How does father absence appear to affect the heterosexual relationships of adolescent girls?

DISCUSSION QUESTIONS

1. What are the circumstances in a typical family that would lead adolescents, according to the status-envy hypothesis, to identify with their parents?
2. To what extent do you believe that instrumental and expressive roles are indeed sex-stereotyped in our society?
3. How are the status-envy hypothesis and the authoritative mode of parental control congruent with one another? Describe from a developmental perspective an ideal model of parental socializing practices.
4. If you were asked to predict relative personality integration across a group of high school students when they reach age 35, what variables would you use in making your predictions?
5. What steps would you take to socialize young persons to be relatively independent of pressures emanating from both parents and peers?
6. Why is an ideal family in an industrial society an independent, isolated, mobile unit? What special problems does this kind of family present in the socialization of adolescents?
7. How is maternal employment likely to affect family patterns of socializing adolescents? What might be the effects of maternal employment on the mother's role as a model and on conjugal power relationships? What circumstances would foster socialization in the context of maternal employment?
8. How would you expect adolescent daughters of widows and divorcees, relative to daughters from intact families, to relate to adolescent boys and men? Does your judgment correspond with Hetherington's findings?

NOTES

1. E. H. Erikson. Identity and the life cycle. Part I. In G. S. Klein (Ed.). *Psychological Issues*. New York: International Universities Press, 1959.

2. Erikson, Identity and life cycle, *op. cit.*, p. 89.

3. A. C. Kerckhoff. Early antecedents of role-taking and role-playing ability. *Merrill-Palmer Quarterly of Behavior and Development,* 1969, **15,** 229–247; D. B. Lynn. *Parental and sex-role identification: a theoretical formulation.* Berkeley: McCutchan, 1969.

4. Kerckhoff, *op. cit.*, p. 233.

5. U. Bronfenbrenner. Freudian theories of identification and their derivatives. *Child Development,* 1960, **31,** 17–19; W. C. Bronson. Dimensions of ego and infantile identification. *Journal of Personality,* 1959, **27,** 532–545.

6. Bronfenbrenner, Freudian theories, *op. cit.*; A. Freud. *The ego and the mechanisms of defence,* trans. by C. Baines. New York: International Universities Press, 1946.

7. S. Freud. *New introductory lectures in psychoanalysis.* London: Hogarth, 1949.

8. O. H. Mowrer. *Learning theory and personality dynamics.* New York: Ronald Press, 1950.

9. R. R. Sears, E. E. Maccoby, and H. Levin. *Patterns of child rearing.* New York: Harper and Row, 1957.

10. Sears et al., *op. cit.*

11. P. H. Mussen and L. Distler. Masculinity, identification, and father-son relationships. *Journal of Abnormal and Social Psychology,* 1959, 350–356, p. 354.

12. R. V. Burton and J. W. M. Whiting. The absent father and cross-sex identity. *Merrill-Palmer Quarterly of Behavior and Development.* 1961, **7,** 85–95.

13. Lynn, *op. cit.*

14. Kerckhoff, *op. cit.*

15. R. Thornton and P. M. Nardi. The dynamics of role acquisition. *American Journal of Sociology,* 1975, **80,** 870–885, p. 872.

16. Thornton and Nardi, *op. cit.*

17. C. C. Naffziger and K. Naffziger. Development of sex role stereotypes. *The Family Coordinator,* 1974, **23,** 251–259.

18. T. Parsons and R. F. Bales. *Family, socialization and interaction process.* New York: Free Press, 1955.

19. D. B. Lynn. *The father: his role in child development.* Monterey, Calif.: Brooks/Cole, 1974.

20. W. G. McIntire, G. D. Nass, and A. S. Dreyer. Parental role perceptions of Ghanian and American adolescents. *Journal of Marriage and the Family,* 1974, **36,** 185–189.

21. McIntire et al., *op. cit.*, p. 189.

22. A. H. Stein and M. M. Bailey. The socialization of achievement orientation in females. *Psychological Bulletin,* 1973, **80,** 345–366, pp. 362–363.

23. K. Deaux and T. Emswiller. Explanations of successful performance on sex-linked tasks. *Journal of personality and Social Psychology,* 1974, **29,** 80–85.

24. Naffziger and Naffziger, *op. cit.*, p. 257.

25. S. Clavan and N. Robak. Masculinity: fathers and sons. *Youth and Society,* 1974, **6,** 32–48.

26. Naffziger and Naffziger, *op. cit.*

27. L. J. Ellis and P. M. Bentler. Traditional sex-determined role standards and sex stereotypes. *Journal of Personality and Social Psychology,* 1973, **25,** 28–34.

28. Ellis and Bentler, *op. cit.,* p. 33.

29. Lynn, The father, *op. cit.*

30. I. K. Broverman, S. R. Vogel, D. M. Broverman, F. E. Clarkson, and P. S. Rosencrantz. Sex-role stereotypes: A current appraisal. *Journal of Social Issues,* 1972, **28,** 59–78.

31. Clavan and Robak, *op. cit.*

32. D. B. Lynn. A note on sex differences in the development of masculine and feminine identification. *Psychological Review,* 1959, **66,** 126–135; D. B. Lynn. Sex differences in identification development. *Sociometry,* 1961, **24,** 372–383; D. B. Lynn. Learning masculine and feminine roles. *Marriage and Family Living,* 1963, **25,** 103–105; D. B. Lynn. Divergent feedback and sex-role identification in boys and men. *Merrill-Palmer Quarterly of Behavior and Development,* 1964, **10,** 17–23; D. B. Lynn. The process of learning parental and sex-role identification. *Journal of Marriage and the Family,* 1966, **28,** 466–470; Lynn, Parental and sex-role identification: a theoretical formulation, *op. cit.*

33. Lynn, Learning masculine and feminine roles, *op. cit.*; Lynn, Parental and sex-role identification, *op. cit.*; Lynn, Parental and sex-role identification: a theoretical formulation, *op. cit.*

34. Lynn, Parental and sex-role identification, *op. cit.*; Lynn, Parental and sex-role identification: a theoretical formulation, *op. cit.*

35. Lynn, Parental and sex-role identification, *op. cit.,* p. 466.

36. Lynn, Parental and sex-role identification: a theoretical formulation, *op. cit.,* p. 36.

37. Lynn, Parental and sex-role identification, *op. cit.*

38. Lynn, Parental and sex-role identification, *op. cit.*; Lynn, Parental and sex-role identification: a theoretical formulation, *op. cit.*

39. J. K. Brown. Adolescent initiation rites among preliterate peoples. In R. E. Grinder (Ed.). *Studies in adolescence.* New York: Macmillan, 1963, pp. 75–85.

40. A. Van Gennep. *The rites of passage.* Chicago: University of Chicago Press, 1960. (Originally published in 1909.)

41. B. Bettelheim. *Symbolic wounds.* New York: Free Press, 1954.

42. J. W. M. Whiting, R. Kluckhohn, and A. Anthony. The function of male initiation ceremonies at puberty. In E. E. Maccoby, T. M. Newcomb, and E. L. Hartley (Eds.). *Readings in social psychology.* New York: Henry Holt, 1958, 359–370.

43. Whiting et al., *op. cit.,* p. 360.

44. Burton and Whiting, *op. cit.*

45. F. W. Young. The function of male initiation ceremonies: a cross-cultural test of an alternative hypothesis. *American Journal of Sociology,* 1962, **67,** 379–391.

46. Brown, *op. cit.*; J. K. Brown. Female initiation rites: a review of the current literature. In D. Rogers (Ed.). *Issues in adolescent psychology.* New York: Meredith, 1969, 74–87.

47. Brown, Adolescent initiation rites, *op. cit.,* p. 81.

48. Brown, Adolescent initiation rites, *op. cit.*; Brown, Female initiation rites, *op. cit.*

49. M. L. Kohn. *Class and conformity, A study in values.* Homewood, Ill.: Dorsey Press, 1969.

50. Kohn, *op. cit.,* p. 104.

51. V. Gecas and F. I. Nye. Sex and class differences in parent-child interaction. A test of Kohn's hypothesis. *Journal of Marriage and the Family,* 1974, **36,** 742–749.

52. H. S. Erlanger. Social class and corporal punishment in childrearing: A reassessment. *American Sociological Review,* 1974, **39,** 68–85.

53. J. L. Gilloran. Family happiness. (a) The father's angle. *Royal Society of Health Journal,* 1965, **85,** 211–214, p. 211.

54. L. G. Burchinal and W. W. Bauder. Family decision-making and role patterns among Iowa farm and nonfarm families. *Research Bulletin, No. 528.* Agricultural and Home Economics Experiment Station, Iowa State University, 1964.

55. T. Jacob. Patterns of family conflict and dominance as a function of child age and social class. *Developmental Psychology,* 1974, **10,** 1–12.

56. M. H. Buehler, A. J. Weigert, and D. L. Thomas. Correlates of conjugal power: A five culture analysis of adolescent perceptions. *Journal of Comparative Family Studies,* 1974, **5,** 5–16.

57. Bronfenbrenner, Freudian theories, *op. cit.*

58. R. E. Grinder and J. C. Spector. Sex differences in adolescents' perceptions of parental resource control. *Journal of Genetic Psychology,* 1965, **106,** 337–344.

59. K. King. Adolescent perception of power structure in the Negro family. *Journal of Marriage and the Family,* 1969, **31,** 751–755.

60. C. E. Bowerman and S. J. Bahr. Conjugal power and adolescent identification with parents. *Sociometry,* 1973, **36,** 366–377.

61. G. C. Van Manen. Father roles and adolescent socialization. *Adolescence,* 1968, **3,** 139–152.

62. W. Vogel and C. G. Lauterbach. Relationships between normal and disturbed sons' percepts of their parents' behavior, and personality attributes of the parents and sons. *Journal of Clinical Psychology,* 1963, **19,** 52–56.

63. A. G. Nikelly. Maternal indulgence and neglect and maladjustment in adolescents. *Journal of Clinical Psychology,* 1967, **23,** 148–150.

64. L. W. Hoffman. The father's role in the family and the child's peer-group adjustment. *Merrill-Palmer Quarterly of Behavior and Development,* 1961, **7,** 97–105, p. 98–99.

65. Hoffman, *op. cit.,* pp. 104–105.

66. D. Baumrind. Effects of authoritative parental control on child behavior. *Child Development,* 1966, **37,** 887–907; D. Baumrind. Authoritarian vs. authoritative parental control. *Adolescence,* 1968, **3,** 255–272; D. Baumrind. Symposium on adolescents and their parents. Unpublished manuscript. Presented at the American Psychological Association 76th Convention, San Francisco, 1968.

67. Baumrind, Effects of authoritative parental control, *op. cit.,* p. 889.

68. D. Baumrind. Early socialization and adolescent competence. In S. E. Dragastin and G. H. Elder, Jr. (Eds.). *Adolescence in the Life Cycle,* Washington D.C.; Hemisphere Pub. Corp. 1975, pp. 117–143.

69. Baumrind, Authoritative parental control, *op. cit.,* p. 890.

70. Baumrind, Early socialization and competence, *op. cit.*

71. Baumrind, Effects of authoritative parental control, *op. cit.,* p. 903.

72. G. H. Elder, Jr. Parental power legitimation and its effect on the adolescent. *Sociometry,* 1963, **26,** 50–65.

73. L. E. Longstreth and R. E. Rice. Perceptions of parental behavior and identification with parents by three groups of boys differing in school adjustment. *Journal of Educational Psychology,* 1964, **55,** 144–151.

74. D. C. Scheck, R. Emerick, and M. M. El-Assal. Adolescents' perceptions of parent-child relations and the development of internal-external control orientation. *Journal of Marriage and the Family,* 1973, **35,** 643–654.

75. S. Nowicki, Jr., and W. Segal. Perceived parental characteristics, locus of control orientation, and behavioral correlates locus of control. *Developmental psychology,* 1974, **10,** 33–37.

76. J. W. Macfarlane. From infancy to adulthood. *Childhood Education,* 1963, **39,** 336–342.

77. J. A. Clausen. Family structure, socialization, and personality, In L. W. Hoffman and M. L. Hoffman (Eds.). *Review of Child development research.* New York: Russell Sage Foundation, 1966, pp. 1–54.

78. Baumrind, Authoritarian vs. authoritative control, *op. cit.*

79. Baumrind, Authoritarian vs. authoritative control, *op. cit.,* p. 265.

80. E. S. Schaefer and N. Bayley. Consistency of maternal behavior from infancy to pre-adolescence. *Journal of Abnormal and Social Psychology,* 1960, **61,** 1–6; E. S. Schaefer and N. Bayley. Maternal behavior, child behavior, and their intercorrelations from infancy through adolescence. *Monographs of the Society for Research in Child Development,* 1963, **28,** 1–127; N. Bayley. Consistency of maternal and child behaviors in the Berkeley growth study. *Vita Humana,* 1964, **7,** 73–95; E. S. Schaefer and N. Bayley. Validity and consistency of mother-infant observations, adolescent maternal interviews, and adult retrospective reports of maternal behavior. *Proceedings,* 75th Annual Convention, American Psychological Association, 1967, 147–148.

81. Schaefer and Bayley, Maternal and child behavior intercorrelations, *op. cit.*

82. J. Kagan and H. A. Moss. *Birth to maturity: a study in psychological development.* New York: John Wiley, 1962; H. A. Moss and J. Kagan. Report on personality consistency and change from the Fels Longitudinal Study. *Vita Humana,* 1964, **7,** 127–138.

83. Moss and Kagan, *op. cit.*

84. J. W. Macfarlane. Perspectives on personality consistency and change from the Guidance Study. *Vita Humana,* 1964, **7,** 115–126, p. 120.

85. MacFarlane, Infancy to adulthood, *op. cit.*; MacFarlane, Personality consistency, *op. cit.*

86. MacFarlane, Infancy to adulthood, *op. cit.*

87. MacFarlane, Personality consistency, *op. cit.*, p. 121.

88. Moss and Kagan, *op. cit.*

89. Moss and Kagan, *op. cit.*, p. 129.

90. D. K. Wheeler. Adolescent views of adolescence in Western Australia. *International Review of Education,* 1960, **6,** 248–255, p. 248.

91. D. Elkind. Exploitation and the generational conflict. Unpublished manuscript. Paper presented at the meeting of the American Psychological Association, San Francisco, 1968, p. 3.

92. M. Bates. Themes in group counseling with adolescents. *Personnel and Guidance Journal,* 1966, **44,** 568–575, p. 571.

93. D. Kandel and G. S. Lesser. Parent-adolescent relationships and adolescent independence in the United States and Denmark. *Journal of Marriage and the Family,* 1969, **31,** 348–358.

94. C. Karr and F. Wesley. Comparison of German and U.S. childrearing practices. *Child Development,* 1966, **37,** 715–723.

95. Baumrind, Authoritarian vs. authoritative parental control, *op. cit.*

96. D. P. Ausubel. Acculturative stress in modern maori adolescence. *Child Development,* 1960, **31,** 617–631.

97. B. J. Gallagher. An empirical analysis of attitude differences between three kin related generations. *Youth and Society,* 1974, **5,** 327–349.

98. R. A. Keith and E. G. Barranda. Age independence norms in American and Filipino adolescents. *The Journal of Social Psychology,* 1969, **78,** 285–286.

99. Kandel and Lesser, *op. cit.*

100. R. M. Lerner and J. R. Knapp. Actual and perceived intrafamilial attitudes of late adolescents and their parents. *Journal of Youth and Adolescence,* 1975, **4,** 17–36.

101. F. L. K. Hsu, B. G. Watrous, and E. M. Lord. Culture pattern and adolescent behavior. *The International Journal of Social psychiatry,* 1961, **7,** 33–53, p. 47.

102. C. G. Kemp. Parents' and adolescents' perceptions of each other and the adolescents' self-perception. *Personnel and Guidance Journal,* 1965, **43,** 58–62.

103. D. G. Langsley, R. M. Fairbairn, and C. D. De Young. Adolescence and family crises. Unpublished manuscript. Family Treatment Unit, Colorado Psychopathic Hospital, Denver, 1968; O. Pollak. Disturbed families and conjoint family counseling. *Child Welfare,* 1967, **46,** 143–149; F. Scherz. The crisis of adolescence in family life. *Social Casework,* 1967, **48,** 209–215.

104. Scherz, *op. cit.*

105. C. E. Vincent. An open letter to the "caught generation." *The Family Coordinator,* 1972, **21,** 143–150.

106. D. S. Wright. A comparative study of the adolescent's concepts of his parents and teachers. *Educational Review,* 1962, **14,** 226–232, p. 232.

107. P. K. Houdek. Youth's unasked questions. *Family Life,* 1966, **26,** 1–3.

108. I. P. Chand, D. M. Crider, and F. K. Willits. Parent-youth disagreement as perceived by youth. *Youth and Society,* 1975, **6,** 365–375.

109. National Center for Health Statistics. *Parent Ratings of Behavioral Patterns of Youths 12–17 Years, United States.* (DHEW Pub. No. [HRA] 74-1619.) Series 11, No. 137, 1974.

110. K. W. Eckhardt and E. C. Schriner. Familial conflict, adolescent rebellion, and political expression. *Journal of Marriage and the Family,* 1969, **31,** 494–499.

111. L. E. Troll, B. L. Neugarten, and R. J. Kraines. Similarities in values and other personality characteristics in college students and their parents. *Merrill-Palmer Quarterly of Behavior and Development,* 1969, **15,** 323–336.

112. D. C. Epperson. A re-assessment of indices of parental influence in The Adolescent Society. *American Sociological Review,* 1964, **29,** 93–96.

113. Kandel and Lesser, *op. cit.*

114. M. E. Hebron and W. London. A study of stereotypes in the caretaking of English children. *British Journal of Educational psychology,* 1964, **34,** 125–131.

115. J. A. Bath and E. C. Lewis. Attitudes of young female adults toward some areas of parent-adolescent conflict. *Journal of Genetic Psychology,* 1962, **100,** 241–253.

116. L. E. Larson. An examination of the salience hierarchy during adolescence: The influence of the family. *Adolescence,* 1974, **9,** 317–332, p. 328.

117. R. J. Havighurst, M. Z. Robinson, and M. Dorr. The development of the ideal self in childhood and adolescence. *Journal of Educational Research,* 1946, **40,** 241–257.

118. F. Musgrove. Inter-generation attitudes. *British Journal of Social and Clinical Psychology,* 1963, **2,** 209–223.

119. H. H. Floyd, Jr. and D. R. South. Dilemma of youth: The choice of parents or peers as a frame of reference for behavior. *Journal of Marriage and the Family,* 1972, **34,** 627–634.

120. N. Goodman. Adolescent norms and behavior: organization and conformity. *Merrill-Palmer Quarterly of Behavior and Development,* 1969, **15,** 199–211.

121. Goodman, *op. cit.,* p. 209.

122. Goodman, *op. cit.,*

123. Musgrove, *op. cit.*

124. G. Y. M. Won, D. S. Yamamura, and K. Ikeda. The relation of communication with parents and peers to deviant behavior of youth. *Journal of Marriage and the Family,* 1969, **31,** 43–47.

125. M. Schwartz and M. A. Baden. Female adolescent self-concept. *Youth and Society,* 1973, **5,** 115–128, p. 127.

126. Larson, Salience hierarchy, *op. cit.,* p. 328.

127. C. V. Brittain. Adolescent choices and parent-peer cross-pressures. *American Sociological Review,* 1963, **28,** 385–391; C. V. Brittain. An exploration of the bases of peer-compliance and parent-compliance in adolescence. *Adolescence,* 1968, **2,** 445–458; C. V. Brittain. A comparison of rural and urban adolescents with respect to peer vs. parent compliance. *Adolescence,* 1969, **4,** 59–68.

128. Brittain, Adolescent choices and parent-peer cross-pressures, *op. cit.*

129. L. E. Larson. The influence of parents and peers during adolescence: the situation hypothesis revisited. *Journal of Marriage and the Family,* 1972, **34,** 67–74.

130. L. E. Larson. The relative influence of parent-adolescent affect in predicting the salience hierarchy among youth. *Pacific Sociological Review,* 1972, **15,** 83–102.

131. Larson, Situation hypothesis, *op. cit.*

132. M. Gold and D. J. Reimer. Size of runaway problem exaggerated, new figures from youth survey show. *ISR Newsletter,* 1974, **2,** 1–8.

133. Gold and Reimer, *op. cit.*

134. Gold and Reimer, *op. cit.*

135. R. Shellow, J. R. Schamp, E. Liebow, and E. Unger. Suburban runaways of the 1960's. *Monographs of the Society for Research in Child Development,* 1967, **32,** 1–51.

136. Shellow et al., *op. cit.,* p. 15.

137. J. A. Hildebrand. Reason for runaways. *Crime and Delinquency,* 1968, **5,** 42–48.

138. L. Blood and R. D'Angelo. A progress research report on value issues in conflict and their parents. *Journal of Marriage and the Family,* 1974, **36,** 486–497.

139. J. Goldmeier and R. D. Dean. The runaway: person, problem, or situation? *Crime and Delinquency,* 1973, **19,** 539–544.

140. N. B. Ryder. The character of modern fertility. *Annals of the American Academy of Political and Social Science,* 1967, **369,** 26–36.

141. H. Rodman. Talcott Parsons' view of the changing American family, *Merrill-Palmer Quarterly of Behavior and Development,* 1965, **11,** 209–227.

142. M. B. Sussman and L. Burchinal. Kin family network: unheralded structure in current conceptualizations of family functioning. *Marriage and Family Living,* 1962, **24,** 231–240.

143. J. Aldous. Children's perceptions of adult role assignment: father-absence, class, race and sex influences. *Journal of Marriage and the Family,* 1972, **34,** 55–65.

144. W. D. Altus. Birth order and its sequelae. *Science,* 1966, **151,** 44–49.

145. B. G. Rosenberg and B. Sutton-Smith. Ordinal position and sex-role identification. *Genetic Psychology Monographs,* 1964, **70,** 297–328.

146. Altus, *op. cit.*

147. J. R. Warren. Birth order and social behavior. *Psychological Bulletin,* 1966, **65,** 38–49.

148. B. Sutton-Smith, J. M. Roberts, and B. G. Rosenberg. Sibling associations and role involvement. *Merrill-Palmer Quarterly of Behavior and Development,* 1964, **10,** 25–38.

149. Ibid.

150. R. E. Gordon and K. K. Gordon. The relationship between birth order and psychiatric problems. *College Health,* 1967, **16,** 185–193.

151. P. C. Rosenblatt and E. L. Skoogberg. Birth order in cross-cultural perspective. *Developmental psychology,* 1974, **10,** 48–54.

152. L. Weller, O. Natan, and O. Hazi. Birth order and marital bliss in Israel. *Journal of Marriage and the Family,* 1974, **36,** 794–797.

153. Rosenberg and Sutton-smith, *op. cit.*

154. Ibid.

155. C. E. Bowerman and R. M. Dobash. Structural variations in intersibling affect. *Journal of Marriage and the Family,* 1974, **36,** 48–54.

156. A. M. Propper. The relationship of maternal employment to adolescent roles, activities, and parental relationships. *Journal of Marriage and the Family,* 1972, **34,** 417–421.

157. C. Etaugh. Effects of maternal employment on children: A review of recent research. *Merrill-Palmer Quarterly of Behavior and Development,* 1974, **20,** 71–98.

158. Etaugh, *op. cit.*; L. W. Hoffman. Effects of maternal employment on the child—A review of the research. *Developmental Psychology,* 1974, **10,** 204–228; Propper, *op. cit.*

159. Hoffman, Maternal employment, *op. cit.*

160. Ibid.

161. Etaugh, *op. cit.*

162. Hoffman, Maternal employment, *op. cit.*

163. Propper, *op. cit.*

164. Lynn, The father, *op. cit.*

165. Aldous, *op. cit.,* p. 55.

166. E. M. Hetherington. Effects of paternal absence on sex-typed behaviors in negro and white preadolescent males. *Journal of Personality and Social Psychology,* 1966, **4,** 87–91.

167. B. Sutton-Smith, B. G. Rosenberg, and F. Landy. Father-absence effects in families of different sibling compositions. *Child Development,* 1968, **39,** 1213–1221.

168. A. Barclay and D. R. Cusumano. Father absence, cross-sex identity, and field-dependent behavior in male adolescents. *Child Development,* 1967, **38,** 243–250.

169. P. Suedfeld. Paternal absence and overseas success of Peace Corps volunteers. *Journal of Consulting Psychology,* 1967, **31,** 424–425.

170. F. A. Pedersen. Relationships between father-absence and emotional disturbance in male military dependents. *Merrill-Palmer Quarterly of Behavior and Development,* 1966, **12,** 321–331.

171. H. B. Biller and L. J. Borstelmann. Masculine development: an integrative review. *The Merrill-Palmer Quarterly of Behavior and Development,* 1967, **13,** 253–294.

172. P. Wohlford, J. W. Santrock, S. E. Berger, and D. Liberman. Older brother's influence on sex-typed, aggressive, and dependent behavior in father-absent children. *Developmental psychology,* 1971, **4,** 124–134.

173. E. M. Hetherington. Effects of father absence on personality development in adolescent daughters. *Developmental Psychology,* 1972, **7,** 313–326.

Chapter 8

Adolescent Character and Moral Development

CHAPTER HIGHLIGHTS

ISSUES

Moral growth is predicated upon making decisions about moral issues and learning moral dispositions to facilitate self-control.

Piaget presumes that development of morality parallels the advance of reasoning—a morality of constraint evolves into a morality of cooperation.

John Dewey defined morality in the context of ideal ethical values.

Kohlberg, who has synthesized the theories of Piaget and Dewey, describes moral development in cognitive-developmental terms, says moral judgments progress in an invariant sequence, and views advanced stages of moral reasoning as culturally universal.

Kohlberg describes attainment of a metaphysical perspective as the ultimate stage of moral development.

Cognitive-developmental theorists have been relatively successful in showing that moral development proceeds in a sequence of stages but have been less convincing in demonstrating that the sequence is innate and universal.

Freud's theory of superego development provides a historical basis for the social-learning interpretation of moral development.

Social-learning theorists conceptualize moral conduct in terms of either pre- or posttransgression activity.

282

Temptation generates a pretransgression conflict in which both alternatives, either yield or resist, are highly desirable responses.

Posttransgression behavioral responses—self-criticism, reparation, confession, and reactions oriented toward external punishment—facilitate restoration of disrupted social relationships.

Shoplifting and cheating on examinations are examples of failure to resist temptation.

The anticipation of painful self-criticism may impede subsequent transgression.

Reparation often occurs in response to transgressions involving aggression, dishonesty, property damage, or harm to others.

Confession may produce punishment followed by restoration of affection.

Punishment-seeking behavior may reduce anxiety following transgression.

Techniques of parental discipline categorized as induction emphasize explanatory reasoning in moral dilemmas.

Consistency in moral conduct is likely to be highest in families which emphasize inductive disciplinary practices and where principles of justice and respect for the dignity of human beings prevail.

Moral education from the social-learning perspective is essentially a matter of role clarification.

Moral education from the cognitive-developmental perspective involves development of capabilities in decision making and problem solving.

John Dewey[1] once said that the primary constituents of mature character are strong willpower, good judgment, and social sensitivity. An "individual," he said, "must have the power to stand up and count for something in the actual conflicts of life . . . any other character is wishy-washy; it is goody, not good." Since raw willpower often overrides respect for others, Dewey recognized the role of good sense in moral conduct. "Good judgment is a sense of respective or proportionate values. The one who has judgment is the one who has ability to size up a situation." And he added: "Good judgment is impossible without . . . prompt and almost instinctive sensitiveness to conditions, to the ends and interests of others. . . ." Dewey reasoned that moral conduct not only stands in opposition to behavior governed by hedonistic, self-serving, or instinctual impulses, but also transcends it. Moral character arises as self-interest is subordinated to values that reflect the best interests of all people.

At first, the process of moral development is essentially that of accommodation. Long ago, when men and women first began to live together in groups, they established rules, customs, and laws to ensure harmony and to govern conduct; similarly, children's actions broach the moral realm as they start to obey the culturally defined rules of conduct that the social world imposes upon them. Children learn to behave "morally" as they are rewarded for conforming to the routines of family and neighborhood. Concepts of rules and principles are initially viewed as part of "external reality" and as something to be taken literally. Transgression of social strictures may bring forth swift disapproval, and the ensuing emotional discomfort may provide an affective basis for cueing subsequent self-control; that is, anticipation of disquieting emotion associated with the disruption of ongoing social relationships may foster resistance to deviation. Children may also adopt techniques—self-criticism, reparation, confession, and so on—for dealing with transgressions that they failed to check. Cognitive growth during adolescence, however, transforms the literal rules of childhood into general conduct guides. Previously established generalizations may become moral dilemmas when it is necessary to question conventional practices, to face competing expectations, and to anticipate the probable consequences of different persons and courses of action. As control of moral conduct is displaced from socializing agents to personal, internalized standards, a disposition to obey rules is transformed into a disposition to question rules. Moral autonomy becomes distinctly possible when young people rise above self-serving interests and act in the context of compassion, empathy, and respect for justice and human rights. As McDougall[2] put in in his classic volume in social psychology: "For the generation of moral character in the fullest sense, the strong self-regarding sentiment must be combined with one for some ideal of conduct, and it must have risen above dependence on the regards of the mass of men."

Moral decisions are based ideally on principles that transcend self-interest, that are autonomous of conflicting social pressures, and that promote human dignity. Indeed, common sense perspective on social evolution leads us to hold up morality as one of the more prominent distinctions that separate humankind from the beasts of the jungle. How then is the transition made from the externally constrained child to the more mature, principled individual who stands up to moral dilemmas with strong willpower, good judgment, and social sensitivity? How does an individual acquire the capacity to resist corrupt or misguided authority and avariciousness? Moral philosophers and religious prophets have written countless treatises, tomes, and books to answer these questions, and many, many more will be inspired, for no subject is more profound and inscrutable. Several provocative theorists of the twentieth century have offered, nonetheless, noteworthy insights into the nature of adolescent morality, and these tend to polarize into two distinct viewpoints. Proponents of one stress a *cognitive-developmental* outlook. Moral growth is predicated on children making decisions about moral issues. Moral development is viewed as a process of evolving thought structures that unfold in the same sequence for all individuals. Those endorsing the other viewpoint obtain their inspiration from *social-learning* theory. Moral development is viewed as the learning of moral dispositions to facilitate self-control, that is, internalization of socially sanctioned moral standards. The significant characteristics of each position, as they apply to the moral development of adolescents, are described in the following two sections. The chapter concludes with a third section dealing briefly with the question of moral education in adolescence.

KOHLBERG'S DEVELOPMENTAL-PHILOSOPHIC THEORY

Lawrence Kohlberg, a distinguished developmental psychologist, is today the major spokesperson for the cognitive-developmental interpretation of moral development. He draws inspiration primarily from two eminent authorities— Jean Piaget and John Dewey. Accordingly, Kohlberg[3] labels his theory, *developmental-philosophic,* by which he means "to connote the union of the study of universal stages of development with philosophic definition of development in terms of universal ethical and epistemological principles." Piaget[4] presumed that development of moral judgment parallels the successive transformations of cognitive structures that result in the advance of reasoning from simple to complex logical operations. Piaget described a morality of cooperation following a morality of constraint. The latter is founded upon adult authority and unilateral respect. Children's thought processes are relatively concrete and they are led to develop *moral realism,* that is, to equate "good" with obedience and duty, to focus on literal rather than abstract aspects of rules, and to evaluate actions by their conformity to rules rather than by the motives that prompted the actions. Furthermore, moral realism promotes the belief that transgressions should be atoned for or redressed by powerful physical punishment, and this leads children to affirm the principle of *immanent justice,* that is, the belief that punishments routinely follow transgressions. About middle childhood, however, the passive morality nurtured by constraint is supplanted by the "autonomous rationality" of cooperation. Moral autonomy becomes possible when children comprehend beliefs as hypotheses requiring verification, manipulate logical relations rationally and consciously, structure "laws" for themselves rather than accept them obediently, and conceive rules as subject to modification and adaptation in terms of the intent and purpose of other individuals. Kohlberg sees in Dewey's description of universal principles of moral conduct an extension of the Piagetian system. Dewey saw the development of a free and powerful moral character as the most significant aspect of human behavior. Dewey's philosophical position led him to define and describe mature morality in the context of ideal ethical values. Kohlberg thus maintains that moral development progresses in an invariant sequence; each advance represents a new, hierarchical integration, until ultimately, moral judgments are principled, that is, made on the basis of universal principles.

Kohlberg's reliance on moral philosophy enables him to transcend the perennial dilemma of cultural relativity in moral values and to assert that "the validity of respect for human life as a universal ideal can be logically or philosophically supported.[5] He points out, for example, that the fact all persons do not always act in terms of a given value does not contradict the claim that all persons ought to act in accordance with the value. An exchange between Kohlberg and a young woman is illustrative. In response to a moral dilemma in which a man had to choose between stealing a life-saving drug or permitting his wife to perish, the young woman responded: "I think he should steal it, because if there is any such thing as a universal human value, it is the value of life and that would justify it." Kohlberg then asked her, "Is there any such thing as a universal human value?" She replied, "No, all values are relative to your culture." Kohlberg observed that she started out by asserting that one ought to act in terms of the universal value of human life, thus implying that it is logical and desirable for all persons to respect human life, but that in holding the value to be culturally relative, failed to see it as being part of a larger body of universal moral ideals.[6]

Kohlberg initiated a longitudinal study in 1955 to validate empirically his developmental-philosophic approach to moral behavior. First, he began a study of the development of moral reasoning with adolescent boys. The boys were aged 10 to 16 at the start of the study and were investigated at three-year intervals from early adolescence through young manhood. They were presented a variety of stories about moral dilemmas, and on the basis of their responses to them, Kohlberg identified six qualitatively distinct, sequentually related value orientations: (1) punishment and obedience, (2) instrumental relativist, (3) good boy—nice girl, (4) law and order, (5) contractual-legalistic, (6) conscience or principled. Kohlberg has cast the six value orientations into a typology of moral structures. Table 1 shows how it is conceptualized with three levels of moral reasoning—preconventional, conventional, and postconventional-each level encompasses two of the six value orientations.

Kohlberg additionally has explored changes in the moral development of boys in five cultures other than the United States—Great Britain, Canada, Taiwan, Mexico, and Turkey. He has documented in each of the cultures appeal to such values as Life, Law, Roles of Affection, Property, Contract, Trust, Liberty, Social Order and Authority, and Equity. Although the boys in the course of their development reflected different cultural content in conceiving the values, each value was restructured sequentially in the form of the six stages presented in Table 1. These data have convinced Kohlberg that changes in moral thinking progress through an invariant order that reflects universal moral structures. The six stages, he asserts, are logically or hierarchically ordered so that the higher

Table 1
Definition of Moral Stages

I. Preconventional Level

At this level the child is responsive to cultural rules and labels of good and bad, right or wrong, but interprets these labels in terms of either the physical or the hedonistic consequences of action (punishment, reward, exchange of favors) or in terms of the physical power of those who enunciate the rules and labels. The level is divided into the following two stages:

Stage 1: *The punishment and obedience orientation.* The physical consequences of action determine its goodness or badness regardless of the human meaning or value of these consequences. Avoidance of punishment and unquestioning deference to power are valued in their own right, not in terms of respect for an underlying moral order supported by punishment and authority (the latter being Stage 4).

Stage 2: *The instrumental relativist orientation.* Right action consists of that which instrumentally satisfies one's own needs and occasionally the needs of others. Human relations are viewed in terms like those of the marketplace. Elements of fairness, of reciprocity and equal sharing are present, but they are always interpreted in a physical, pragmatic way. Reciprocity is a matter of "you scratch my back and I'll scratch yours," not of loyalty, gratitude, or justice.

II. Conventional Level

At this level, maintaining the expectations of the individual's family, group, or nation is perceived as valuable in its own right, regardless of immediate and obvious consequences. The attitude is not only one of *conformity* to personal expectations and social order, but of loyalty to it, of actively *maintaining,* supporting, and justifying the order and of identifying with the persons or group involved in it. At this level, there are the following two stages:

Stage 3: *The interpersonal concordance or "good boy—nice girl" orientation.* Good behavior is that which pleases or helps others and is approved by them. There is much conformity to stereotypical images of what is majority or "natural" behavior. Behavior is frequently judged by intention—"he means well" becomes important for the first time. One earns approval by being "nice."

Stage 4: *The "law and order" orientation.* There is orientation toward authority, fixed rules, and the maintenance of the social order. Right behavior consists of doing one's duty, showing respect for authority, and maintaining the given social order for its own sake.

III. Post-Conventional, Autonomous, or Principled Level

At this level, there is a clear effort to define moral values and principles which have validity and application apart from the authority of the groups or persons holding these

Table 1 (Continued)

principles and apart from the individual's own identification with these groups. This level again has two stages:

Stage 5: *The social-contract, legalistic orientation.* Generally with utilitarian overtones. Right action tends to be defined in terms of general individual rights and in terms of standards which have been critically examined and agreed upon by the whole society. There is a clear awareness of the relativism of personal values and opinions and a corresponding emphasis upon procedural rules for reaching consensus. Aside from what is constitutionally and democratically agreed upon, the right is a matter of personal "values" and "opinion." The result is an emphasis upon the "legal point of view," but with an emphasis upon the possibility of changing law in terms of rational considerations of social utility (rather than freezing it in terms of Stage 4 "law and order"). Outside the legal realm, free agreement and contract are the binding elements of obligation. This is the "official" morality of the American government and Constitution.

Stage 6: *The universal ethical principle orientation.* Right is defined by the decision of conscience in accord with self-chosen *ethical principles* appealing to logical comprehensiveness, universality, and consistency. These principles are abstract and ethical (the Golden Rule, the categorical imperative); they are not concrete moral rules like the Ten Commandments. At heart, these are universal principles of *justice,* of the *reciprocity* and *equality* of human *rights,* and of respect for the dignity of human beings as *individual persons.*

ones are conceptually more advanced that the lower ones. A new stage supplants a previous stage, not simply by adding to it, but by transforming elements of the old into the new to create an emergent stage. Further, forward movement in the sequence occurs without skipping stages. Moral reasoning of the conventional (Stages 3–4) type, for example, "never" occurs before preconventional (Stages 1–2) thought has taken place. No adult in Stage 4 has gone through Stage 5, but all Stage 5 adults have gone through Stage 4. Young people may move through the stages at varying speed, depending on stimulation from the social environment, and may be found occasionally half in and half out of a particular stage. Young people may also cease moral growth at any given stage and any age. Kohlberg believes, in keeping with Piaget's assumptions about cognitive stages, that moral stages represent a series of increasingly adequate cognitions of a relatively constant physical and social world. A person at Stage 6 is fully aware of what laws, roles, and previous commitments (Stages 3, 4, and 5) require be done. Further, in every moral dilemma, reasoning at the highest stage comprehended is preferred.

The developmental-philosophic interpretation of moral development assumes that children and adolescents will become moral philosophers. Younger children's first predispositions to acts of conduct, nonetheless, are initiated on the basis of affective feedback. Children's initial orientations toward cultural concepts of conduct are derived from the physical or hedonistic consequences of behavior, that is, threat of punishment or hope of reward (Stage 1). Children eventually recognize, however, that these consequences give direction to their behavior and they begin to equate "right" with what avoids punishment and with what satisfies (Stage 2). Children next observe that unpunished activities are more pleasurable, in that good behavior is pleasing to others, and they begin to differentiate role expectations at home and school (Stage 3). Conformity to the role expectations over time helps children understand the roles that they are expected to play in a larger constellation of roles organized by legal authorities (Stage 4). Young people now use their awareness of lawfulness as the basis for contracts and interpersonal commitments (Stage 5). After much experience in forming and dissolving voluntary commitments, individuals acquire the capacity to abstract and apply moral principles (Stage 6) that render mutual relationships valuable and satisfying. As moral development ensues, the moral expectations adolescents hold regarding their family, peer group, community, and so forth attain significant value in their own right. The youth acquire a sense of duty and respect for authority and an ability to justify and support values of social sharing and love. They attain the capacity to judge behavior by intention—"he means well"—rather than by consequences. Mature morality arrives when young people learn to make "right decisions" using ethical principles based on logical comprehensiveness, consistency, and universality.

Let us now review the changes in respect to the value, "the basis of moral worth of human life," that occurred in the moral judgments of two boys.[7] The responses of Tommy, at ages 10, 13, and 16, illustrate how young people reason at each of Kohlberg's first three stages; those of Jim, at ages 16, 20, and 24, depict reasoning at each of the three advanced stages. Tommy was asked "Is it better to save the life of one important person or a lot of unimportant people?" At age 10, he answered, "All the people that aren't important, because one man just has one house, maybe a lot of furniture, but a whole bunch of people have an awful lot of furniture and some of these poor people might have a lot of money and it doesn't look it." Tommy now is at Stage 1—he makes no differentiation between the values of human life and material possessions. Three years later (age 13), Tommy's conceptions of the value of life were elicited by the question, "Should the doctor 'mercy kill' a fatally ill woman requesting death because of her pain?" He answered, "Maybe it would be good to put her out of her pain; she'd be better off that way. But the husband wouldn't want it; it's not like an animal. If a pet dies you can get along without it—it isn't something you really need. Well, you can get a new wife, but it's not really the same." Tommy's answer is at Stage 2—the value of the woman's life is viewed as contingent on its instrumental value to her husband, who cannot replace her as easily as he can a pet. Three years later (age 16), Tommy's moral outlook on life was elicited by the same question, to which he replied: "It might be best for her, but her husband—it's a human life—not like an animal; it just doesn't have the same relationship that a human being does to a family. You can become attached to a dog, but nothing like a human you know." Now Tommy has moved from a Stage 2 instrumental view of the woman's value to a Stage 3 view based on the husband's empathy and love for someone in his family. Yet it lacks any basis for a universal value of the woman's life, which would hold even if she had no husband or if her husband failed to love her. Tommy, thus, has moved step by step through three stages between the ages of 10 and 16. Sequential movement through the next three stages is shown in Jim's moral judgments. At age 16, he said regarding the mercy killing: "I don't know. In one way, it's murder; it's not a right or privilege of man to decide who shall live and who shall die. God put life into everybody on earth and you're taking away something from that person that came directly from God, and you're destroying something that is very sacred; it's in a way part of God and it's almost destroying a part of God when you kill a person. There's something of God in everyone." Here Jim displays a Stage 4 concept of life. It is viewed as sacred in terms of its place in a categorical moral or religious order of rights and duties. The value of human life is seen as universal and true for all human beings, but it is still dependent on serving the end of a higher authority. It is not yet an autonomous human value. At age 20, however, Jim responded to the same question: "There are more and more people in the medical profession who are thinking it is a hardship on everyone—the person, the family—when you know they are going to die. When a person is kept alive by an artificial lung or kidney it's more like being a vegetable than being a human who is alive. If it's her own choice I think there are certain rights and privileges that go along with being a human being. I am a human being, and have certain desires for life and I think everybody else does, too. You have a world of which you are the center, and everybody else does, too, and in that sense we're all equal." Jim is now reasoning at Stage 5. The value of human life is defined in terms of equal and universal human rights—obligation to respect the basic right to life is differentiated from generalized respect for the socio-moral order. Finally, at age 24, Jim said, "A human life takes precedent over any other moral or legal value, whoever it is. A human life has inherent value whether or not it is valued by a particular individual. The inherent worth of the individual human being is the central value in a set of values where the principles of justice and love are normative for all human relationships." Jim has arrived at Stage 6, for he sees the value of human life as absolute in representing a universal respect for the human as an individual. He has moved step by step through a sequence culminating in a definition of human life as centrally valuable. Jim, at Stage 6, has acquired a means of moral reasoning that is universal and impersonal. He is capable of principled moral judgments.

Erikson's and Kohlberg's Developmental Stages Compared

Erikson and Kohlberg share the belief that emergence of a morality based on principles becomes a potentiality during adolescence. Each derives his position from somewhat different assumptions, and Kohlberg has appended a seventh stage to his outlook to bring the two developmental systems into congruence.[8] Erikson emphasizes the role of the self in his developmental theory. The self faces a major challenge at each of eight stages in an invariant sequence; success-ful resolution stage by stage means progress is fortified with "ego-strength" or "ego-integration," but unsatisfactory resolution jeopardizes capacity to cope effectively with demands faced during subsequent stages. An ideology of morality evolves during adolescence, but moral character is only approximated as the ego gains experience in moral decision making. According to Erikson,[9] adolescence intervenes between the moral tendencies of childhood and the ethical powers of adulthood. He notes that adolescents learn to grasp the flux of time, anticipate the future, perceive abstract ideas, assent to ideals and take ideological positions for which children are unprepared. The capacity to make genuine ethical commitments emerges in adulthood, however, only after extended "testing" and ego development.

Kohlberg's[10] position differs from Erikson's in several noteworthy respects. First, he views the advanced stages of moral reasoning as culturally universal, whereas Erikson sees them as affected by ideological and cultural factors. Second, Kohlberg draws heavily on philosophical distinctions of moral behavior, extend-ing himself to show how each successive stage is philosophically more adequate than the preceding stage. Erikson, in contrast, draws upon psychological considerations to account for growth in ego-strength. Third, in keeping with his strong emphasis on philosophical factors, Kohlberg stresses a "world-pole" view, in which morality is related to universal human values, but Erikson's view, he says, focuses on a "self-pole" outlook, in which competence and satisfaction in the context of society are the primary concerns. Fourth, Kohlberg has long held that Stage 6 placed a ceiling on postadolescent reasoning; Erikson, on the other hand, has viewed adolescence as the period during which the transition from an ideological to an ethical orientation begins. Kohlberg today agrees with Erikson, however; he says that the consistency which develops in adolescent reasoning indicates the continued development of cognitive structures. He now acknowledges the probability of additional structural reorganization and the possibility of a seventh stage. The changes in cognitive growth, he says, are derived from cosmic rather than psychological or philosophical perspective. Kohlberg avows that after attainment of a clear awareness of universal ethical principles, "the loudest of all skeptical doubts" remains: "Why be moral?" "Why be just, in a universe which is largely unjust?" The answers rest in responses to such questions as "Why live?" and "How to face death?" Hence, Kohlberg declares that "ultimate moral maturity" involves the question of the meaning of life itself. Each individual, therefore, to reach the highest stage of moral maturity—Stage 7—must ultimately develop a metaphysical perspective.

Corroborative Evidence

Moral Development as an Invariant Sequence. Kohlberg's developmental view of moralization is predicated on a universal, invariant sequentiality of stage development. At each stage the same basic moral issue is defined; greater differentiation and integration characterize reasoning at the higher stages. At every upward step, lower stages are presumably taken into consideration, but the higher level is preferred. Kohlberg and his colleagues have mustered considerable evidence to demonstrate that the sequential order, the reorganization of stages, and the preference for higher stages do indeed occur. Turiel,[11] for example, devised a role-playing situation for children 12 to 13.5 years of age who were exposed to moral reasoning at levels one stage below and two stages above their own. The children's levels of moral reasoning ranged from Stages 2 to 4. Turiel's results showed that the young people were influenced most by reasoning one stage above and least by one stage below their own. And Rest, Turiel, and Kohlberg[12] asked children 11 to 14 years of age about the resolution of moral dilemmas two stages above and one stage below their own. Their results also revealed that young people preferred moral reasoning at the advanced levels; furthermore, their data indicated that difficulty of comprehension increased for the children from one to two stages above their own whereas comprehension was relatively easy at the stage below. Additionally, Rest[13] asked high school seniors to paraphrase statements characteristic of each of the six stages, compare them with their own ideas, and evaluate and rank them relative to their persuasiveness. Rest examined comprehension at all stages lower than each individual's own stage, thus extending the Rest et al.[14] investigation, and found that individuals readily comprehend all the stages below their own. He reports, moreover, that many persons thoroughly comprehend moral reasoning one level above their predominantly spontaneous level and that about 20 percent of the time they function at that level. Rest[15] holds that "there is an order preference for the highest stage one can comprehend, regardless of one's own spontaneous stage."

Given the preference of adolescents for reasoning at more conceptually adequate stages, what is the likelihood of regression to lower levels of moral reasoning? Kohlberg and Kramer[16] have reported longitudinal data that indicate some high school seniors, who had been assessed predominantly at Stage 4, showed extensive Stage 2 thinking during their college years. By their early twenties, however, the young people had achieved Stage 5 level moral reasoning. Kohlberg and Kramer suggested that social unrest and pressure of college life had induced temporary regression to the lower level. The assumption that an earlier stage may be retrievable also implies that the structure of the stage must persist in memory unchanged. Turiel,[17] on the other hand, rejects the notion of temporary regression and holds that earlier forms of moral reasoning are not recoverable. Each succeeding stage indicates, he contends, more internal consistency and adequacy for understanding moral problems and resolving conflicts. Turiel holds that disorganized expressions of moral functioning only represent situations in which adolescents become incapable temporarily of making the differentiations characteristic of the more advanced stages. The researcher's data reveal that "progressive equilibriation" occurs; that is, as a consequence of awareness of contradictions and inadequacies at one level, the logic at that level is rejected, and a new stage is created. Turiel thus argues that what appears to be regression in moral reasoning is in fact an illusion created by the process of structural reorganization.

Moral Structures as Developmental and Universal. Kohlberg and his colleagues have been relatively successful in showing that the developmental sequence of the moral-judgment stages corresponds with the general pattern of cognitive development. Tomlinson-Keasey and Keasey,[18] for example, found among young people of comparable ages that the level of moral reasoning varied with progress in formal operational thought. Moreover, principled moral reasoning lagged behind functioning in the cognitive realm. Keasey[19] asked two groups of girls, one about 12 years of age and the other about 20 years of age, to evaluate moral judgments that, respectively, agreed and disagreed with their own. The preadolescent girls focused attention on the relatively concrete issue of whether they agreed or disagreed with the opinion of others. The older girls were less influenced by the positions advocated by others, and thus by implication, were more consistent and autonomous in their moral judgments. Anchor and Cross,[20] in a study involving males in their early twenties, also found a degree of correspondence between moral development and social development. The young men who functioned at preconventional levels (Stages 1 and 2) were more intolerant of frustration than those at postconventional levels and were more likely to aggress against other persons. The researchers suggested that preconventional reasoning and maladaptive aggression is a consequence of impoverished social and cognitive development.

Kohlberg has been less successful in showing that the sequence of moral reasoning development is innate and universal. Kohlberg believes that individuals in all cultures go through the same sequence of development, though varying in rate and extent of progress. As Graham[21] says, the assumption of universality would be strongly supported if it could be shown that individuals progress similarly in their moral development across a range of societies with very different value systems and presuppositions. Kohlberg has attempted to assemble empirical support for the assumption with his study of moral reasoning in six cultures. He argues that the data show the stage sequence of moral reasoning to be unaffected by varying social, cultural, or religious conditions. But critics argue that Kohlberg's data fail to provide sufficient evidence for the stage process itself to justify comparing stage sequence across cultures. At age 16, for example, Stage 5 thinking was more prominent among boys in the United States than among those in Mexico or Taiwan; age trends in moral reasoning at Stages 5 and 6 were apparent only in the sample of boys from the United States—the same boys whom Kohlberg had used to derive the six stages in the first place. Moreover, none of the youth in Turkey or Yucatan were able to reach Stage 5, and at age 16 still had not achieved a clear ascendency over preconventional thought. Kurtines and Greif,[22] therefore, argue that Kohlberg's data "provide no support for the claim that the stages are universal." Furthermore, Gorsuch and Barnes,[23] in an investigation of rural and urban Caribbean adolescents, found that they could not ascertain levels of moral reasoning because "these [Kohlberg's] moral dilemmas were insufficient to catch the nuances of this culture's thinking, and might also imply that a different set of 'stages' or typologies of moral reasoning might be developed . . ." in the Caribbean cultures.

Assuming, nonetheless, the universality of stage sequence, how does one explain the finding that young people in isolated, preliterate societies progress through the lower stages of moral development more slowly than Western urban youth and largely fail to achieve principled, postconventional levels of moral judgment? Kohlberg contends that living in a noncomplex, nondifferentiated society may impede persons from reaching the highest stages of ethical reasoning and moral maturity.[24] Does the fact that members of society fail to reach Kohlberg's fifth and sixth stages mean that the society is morally inferior?[25] Kohlberg's position is akin to that of G. Stanley Hall,[26] who concluded his magnum opus with a chapter entitled, "Adolescent Races." Hall assumed that societies whose members were unable to manifest traits of responsibility, punctuality, and delay of gratification were morally and socially inferior on the scale of evolution. Kohlberg appears to skirt the edges of Hall's antiquated ethnocentric hypothesis of social evolution in attempting to cling to his belief that moral structures are culture-free. The answer to the problem may lie in defining stages of moral development in terms of sociological rather than philosophical criteria. It may be necessary to accept the proposition that individuals' comprehension and preference for all stages of judgment are indeed dependent on their learned beliefs and values.[27]

SOCIAL LEARNING THEORY

Sigmund Freud's theory of superego development is the major precursor of social learning approaches to moral behavior. Freud began with the assumption that oedipal rivalry provided children their first impetus to acquire moral behavior. Freud knew that control of children's self-interest, as reflected in instinctual, aggressive, hedonistic tendencies, preceded responsible participation in society. He reasoned that children grew jealous of their same-sex parents as they competed with them for the sexual favors of opposite-sex parents. Fearing harsh retaliation, however, children eventually renounced their incestual claims on their opposite-sex parents. And at the same time they identified with the characteristics of same-sex parents in order to attain parental status. The birth of the process of identification thus also gave rise to the superego or conscience. In his subsequent writings, Freud adopted a more figurative interpretation of oedipal events. He modified his view that oedipal conflicts provide the primary motivation for superego development, and he turned his attention to the cumulative effects of parental rewards and punishments:

The role, which the superego undertakes later in life, is at first played by an external power, by parental authority. The influence of the parents dominates the child by granting proofs of affection and by threats of punishment, which, to the child, mean loss of love, and which must also be feared on their account. This objective anxiety is the forerunner of the later moral anxiety; so long as the former is dominant, one need not speak of superego or of conscience. It is only later that the secondary situation arises, which we are far too ready to regard as the normal state of affairs; the external restrictions are introjected, so that the superego takes the place of the parental function, and thenceforward observes, guides and threatens the ego in just the same way as the parents acted to the child before.[28]

Freud recognized that the need for external coercion receded as parental strictures were adopted or internalized. He speaks above of "objective anxiety," which is derived from children's concerns about parental expectations and mandates, and "moral anxiety," which is independent of parental dominance and which underlies the development of self-control. These two important aspects of social behavior have since been extended and refined in social-learning concepts of moral conduct. The mastery of moral conduct according to social-learning theory is a highly dynamic process. Objective anxiety is life-long. It results from external pressures and demands to meet the expectations of significant socializing agents—parents in childhood and peers and other adults in adolescence and later life. Its arousal serves to impede attainment of forbidden objectives and participation in forbidden activities. Moral anxiety also is life-long. It emerges when children begin to control their impulses and behavior in accord with self-imposed dictates. A necessary precondition is learning to conduct oneself on the basis of patterns of expectations differentially rewarded and punished by important models. Freud noted, for example, the significance of parental "proofs of affection" and "threats of punishment." As children and adolescents accelerate role-seeking experience, and, of course, acquire cognitive skills, they learn to generalize beyond immediate social contexts, to anticipate expectations of society at large, and thus, to abstract general rules that hold in a wide variety of situations. All persons learn in some degree to keep moral anxiety in check by functioning in a social context of rules associated with honesty, punctuality, loyalty, courage, responsibility, and so on. The abstracted moral standards may be expected to foster self-control and minimize moral anxiety to the extent that cultural conditions enable adolescents to develop long-term, stable patterns of moral conduct.

Social-learning theorists, following Freud, generally conceptualize moral development along several personality dimensions, each of which may vary in strength from others, depending on the course of socialization. Moral development is viewed as a continuous process and behavioral expressions of moral character are believed to be products of both cognitive and affective personality processes. The following discussion is divided into four parts in order to discuss the process in greater detail. The first describes the nature of temptation and reviews the pretransgression circumstances under which standards underlying self-control may be compromised. The second considers four relatively common behavioral reactions to transgression; each of the four styles arouses aversive feelings (moral anxiety), the anticipation of which on subsequent occasions may strengthen self-control. The third examines and emphasizes the significance of explanatory reasoning in the resolution of moral dilemmas. The fourth clarifies the question of consistency in moral conduct and raises the question of moral autonomy in character structure.

The Nature of Temptation

Temptation occurs when moral standards and desire for incentives conflict. Temptation is basically a precommitment moral conflict in which individuals, free from danger of detection or external pressures to deviate, must choose between either adherence to moral standards or transgression in order to attain the incentives. A state of temptation occurs when an opportunity arises to increase the probability of behavior that is forbidden because of its incompatability (conflict) with socially expected (moral) behavior. Incentives leading to temptation may be intangibles, such as anticipation of praise or the circumvention of anticipated reproof, or tangibles, such as money, food, and avoidance of corporal punishment. The moral standards may be described from the point of view of virtues, for example, honesty, truthfulness, punctuality, and responsibility, or from that of tabus, such as cheating, lying, procrastination, and carelessness. Temptation generates the kind of conflict in which both alternatives, either yield or resist, are highly desirable responses. The magnitude of the conflict derives from the power or weakness of the attraction to enhance self-interest and the extent "moral anxiety" is aroused and/or one's pride and self-image are in danger of compromise. The conflicting indices of temptation are not independent, since one or the other must be relinquished to resolve the conflict. Weak incentive appeal and strong adherence to moral standards will lead to resistance to temptation whereas strong appeal and weak moral standards will result in transgression; however, both strong incentive appeal versus strong moral standards and weak appeal versus weak moral standards may generate intense precommitment moral dilemmas.

Consider the following justifications adolescents advance for shoplifting and cheating on examinations. Both forms of transgression are readily condoned, and yielding to temptation is currently widespread. The justifications illustrate how easily ethical dictates may be compromised by objectives that supersede them in desirability. El-Dirghami,[29] for example, conducted a study of shoplifting among 112 high school students, randomly selected from a population of several thousand. More than 50 percent of the youth had shoplifted at least once

Moral standards are often foresaken in the face of temptation.

and nearly 30 percent, at least twice. The investigation showed that young
people view shoplifting as exciting. It was all right to shoplift if one needed the
product but could not afford it, if one had use for the stolen item, and if one
needed the item to have what one's best friend had. Cheating on high school
examinations is equally widespread and readily justified, too. LeVeque and
Walker[30] conducted an experiment in which several hundred adolescent boys
and girls were asked to correct and score their own answer sheets on a plane
geometry test; over 50 percent of the youth illegitimately raised their scores.
Schab[31] suggests that the prevalence of cheating in high school derives from
youth's strong desire for success and willingness to use whatever means is
necessary to attain goals. His study, which involved 1500 youth from 22 different high schools, revealed that young people estimated that from 50 to 75
percent of their peers cheated on exams. Schab[32] concluded that "cheating is so
common it is almost a way of scholastic life." A query of undergraduates in two
large urban colleges also showed that approximately 70 percent of the males and
63 percent of the females had cheated at least once on an examination during
the current or preceding semester.[33] When asked whether cheating was a
normal part of life, 93 percent of the young people answered "yes." Most said
that they had grown up believing that cheating was an acceptable way of getting
ahead. Both sexes cheated mainly to relieve the competition among peers for

grades. Girls cheated as a consequence of insufficient time for study and pressure of peer expectations; boys cheated because of insufficient time for study, to meet graduate school requirements, to satisfy expectations of parents, and to please instructors.

Behavioral Reactions to Transgression

The discussion below describes four posttransgression behavioral responses—self-criticism, reparation, confession, and reactions oriented toward external punishment—that individuals adapt to help themselves restore disrupted social relationships.[34] Aronfreed points out that very specific socializing experiences determine the relative preference of the four styles to young people. Aronfreed also observes that the responses acquire their effectiveness through the control that they exercise over the consequences of transgression. They do not introduce alterations in the cognition of the transgression; such distortion is largely a pathological device for coping with anxiety following transgression, and an analysis of it is beyond the scope of the discussion here. Let us note in passing that young people occasionally attempt to justify a transgression by attributing characteristics to the victim that appear to legitimatize the harmful effects of the transgression, for example, "he's rich and can afford it;" by minimizing the magnitude of the transgression, for example, "well, it really was a little thing" or "it's no big deal;" or by denying responsibility for control over events associated with it, for example, "I was spaced out."

1. Self-Criticism.[35]   A form of self-evaluation that young people learn by reproducing criticisms and aspects of punishment which they incur following a transgression: "I feel badly about . . . ." "I am worthless." "This is making me terribly upset." "I can't face anyone." "I ought to be punished." Young people who have been reprimanded successively for particular transgressions will begin to experience anxiety in anticipation of reproof after committing these acts on later occasions. Since "punishment" generally terminates the anxiety (it signifies that transgression has been avenged), verbal criticism accompanying the punishment also acquires anxiety-reducing value. Eventually young people will produce the rebukes in response to transgression, even when the probability of external punishment is remote, as a way of exerting control over their anxiety and redressing the situation. Self-critical behavior may become dominant in their hierarchy of responses to transgression because their parents had reinforced it by forgiving them and reinstating them to favor. On the other hand, parental socializing practices may entirely suppress self-critical responses. The behavior of socializing agents who inflict severe punishment may lead young people to acquire avoidance or withdrawal reactions to transgressions, rather than to acquire responses that reproduce verbal aspects of the socializing agents' punishment. It is noteworthy that anxiety anticipatory of self-criticism may affect intentions in a temptation dilemma. Young people who find their resolve being sorely tested may gain support for resisting temptation by recognizing that yielding to temptation also would bring on harsh self-evaluation. The moral standards in question thus attain an ally in the anticipatory anxiety, and once resolve is strengthened, the appeal of the forbidden objective is lessened.

2. *Reparation.*[36]   A form of response to transgression in which young people attempt to reverse the socially disruptive effects of their actions. All forms of reparative or restitutive action possess a corrective orientation, and require that young people exercise a relatively high degree of control over the resolution of their transgressions. Reparative reactions to correct the consequences of transgression will vary in respect to directness and relevance. Most reactions are aimed at benefiting directly those who have sustained the effects of transgression, The more clearly discernable forms literally repair the damage— as when a stolen bicycle is fixed and returned to its owner or money is handed over to a clerk to pay for shoplifted merchandise. When transgression cannot be redressed in terms of concrete material consequences, restitutive acts may be indirect and symbolic. Young people, for example, may attempt to reaffirm their love for the victim of their transgression. Others may voluntarily engage in acts of atonement, for example, after disobeying their parents, adolescents may weed the garden, mow the lawn, or paint the fence. Reparative behavior tends to dominate young people's hierarchy of responses to transgression when the acts involve aggression, dishonesty, and property damage or cause harm to others. In general, young people acquire the capacity to make reparative responses to their transgressions as they learn to assume responsibility for the consequences of their actions. Young people who learn to carry out reparative acts presumably strengthen their moral disposition to conduct themselves honestly, responsibly, and compassionately. Parental and peer models encourage them to return what they have appropriated, clean up and repair what they have broken, and to be solicitous toward the victims of their aggression. Such expressions of redress reduce anxiety associated with transgression, but more significantly, the social degradation they entail leads to anticipatory anxiety, and thus strengthens resistance to temptation.

3. *Confession.*[37]   This is a form of response to transgression in which young people inform other persons of their wrongdoing. Confession is more externally oriented than either self-criticism or reparation since it requires the intervention of someone to whom it can be addressed. Confession develops as a characteristic response to transgression when it is followed by restoration of affection. Parents

may assure children repeatedly that confession following a transgression will result in less severe consequences for them than will failure to confess. Sometimes socializing agents exert strong pressures on young people to confess because they want an opportunity to reinforce honesty and because they want more information in order to respond appropriately in the situation. Confession paradoxically also develops as a response to transgression when socializing agents follow the wrongdoing with some form of punishment. Every transgression arouses some anxiety about potential aversive consequences, and young people can at least reduce the anxiety by confessing their misdeeds and accepting the punishment. Confession and self-criticism thus share a "kinship," in that "confession can *produce* punishment, while self-criticism can *reproduce* punishment."[38] Whether followed by either nurture or punishment, the emotional stress inherent in the act of confession generates anticipatory anxiety that also contributes to resistance to temptation. However, when confession is too often followed by excessively adverse consequences, a young person may turn instead to various forms of escape or withdrawal from agents of socialization, which in turn, may impede the growth of moral character.

4. Reactions Oriented Toward External Punishment.[39] This style represents responses to transgression that are oriented toward either punishment or punishment-avoidance. Young people may disperse clues and incriminating evidence after a transgression in such a way that they ensure others will recognize and punish them for it. Sometimes they will engage in forms of self-punishment, for example, by "accidentally" hurting themselves, by deliberately asking for trouble, or even by attempting suicide. Punishment-seeking behavior acquires its reinforcement value from reducing anxiety following transgression. It is somewhat like self-criticism, but each is an outcome of a different pattern of socialization. Self-criticism evolves from learning to use one's own resources in the control and resolution of transgression, but punishment-seeking is an outgrowth of dependence on external direction for control of behavior. When parental discipline has been inconsistent and verbal explanations have been lacking in disciplinary matters, young people are unlikely to acquire the cues necessary for satisfactorily reducing moral anxiety following transgressions. Consequently, they are likely to look to others rather than to themselves for solutions to their moral dilemmas. Punishment avoidance, however, may eventually emerge as an alternative to punishment-seeking, especially among young people who have been severely punished following transgression. Young people may follow wrongdoing by withdrawing from the vicinity of socializing agents, hiding the consequences of transgression, or becoming wary of cues that signal impending punishment. Such reactions are reinforced when they are successful. Punishment-avoidance behavior, however, holds anxiety at a relatively high level since considerable time must pass before the danger of detection expires. Under such circumstances, externally oriented reactions to transgression can be instrumental in fostering anticipatory anxiety, and thus, in strengthening resistance to temptation. On the other hand, they are less likely than such corrective responses as reparation and confession to become stable personality response styles, since the latter are more likely to lead to immediate reduction in anxiety, restoration of social relationships, and thus more consistent social reinforcement.

Parental Discipline and Moral Conduct

The parental disciplinary practices that foster moral conduct have been divided into three groups—power assertion, love withdrawal, and induction.[40] Power assertive techniques are comparable to authoritarian techniques of control.[41] Parents value obedience as a virtue and favor forceful measures of discipline, for example, physical punishment, deprivation of privileges and resources, and verbal reprimands such as scolding, ridicule, and bawling out.

Scolding exerts pressure on the child to conform to parental standards, but it may lead in the long run to inhibition of behavior instead of moral autonomy.

Such practices socialize young people to avoid both punishment and the development of self-initiated, corrective reactions like self-criticism, reparation, or confession.[42] Love-withdrawal techniques, on the other hand, are those in which parents express anger or disapproval of wrongdoing in nonphysical ways.[43] Love-withdrawal, like power-assertion, stimulates emotional arousal that is specifically relevant to general parental objectives regarding obedience, but neither promotes emotional control nor understanding in resolving moral conflicts. Parents may literally ignore young people, turn their back of them, refuse to speak or listen to them, express dislike of them, or isolate and threaten to abandon them. Such expressions of hurt and disappointment arouse unpleasant feelings that persist during parental absence. Love-withdrawal techniques vary in duration, heighten uncertainty, and may exert severe emotional impact upon young people. The consequences of love-withdrawal are so anxiety-arousing that parents who emphasize this disciplinary technique may instill in young people so much responsibility for evaluating and modifying their behavior that they acquire "too much" resistance to temptation. The apparent self-control may be less reflective of a strong moral character than it is of inhibition of willingness to explore, investigate, and take risks in novel situations.

Techniques of parental discipline categorized as induction emphasize explanatory reasoning in moral dilemmas. They exemplify the efforts of authoritative parents to induce cognitive skills in the course of socialization.[44] Such techniques may appeal to young people's pride, concern for others, striving for mastery, and desire to be "grown up."[45] Parents who encourage young people to question why they acted as they did, insist that they correct the consequences of their action, or refrain from punishing them when they initiate corrective actions, foster self-examination, responsibility, and acquisition of self-control.[46] Induction techniques rely on persuasiveness to convince young people that they should modify their behavior. Their effectiveness lies both in helping young people comprehend the consequences of their moral behavior and in directing them to initiate appropriate corrective responses.

Hoffman[47] views inductive disciplinary encounters as more significant in the development of morality than cognitive structural changes. Hoffman reasons from the following series of assumptions. Children's initial motivation to subordinate hedonistic impulses to social expectations is a product of social learning. The "most" important socializing experiences in the development of self-control are those disciplinary encounters in which children must choose, starting early in life, between their own self-interests and parental "moral demands." These conflicts provide children with their first opportunity to face and resolve conflict; moreover, they continue "throughout childhood and possibly well into adolescence" as young people's major confrontation with the "moral standards of society." The effects of the disciplinary encounters accrue slowly. Whereas both power-oriented and inductive encounters exert pressures to conform, the inductive direct young people's attention to the consequences of their behavior for others, encourage them to make realistic assessment of the significance of their actions, and offer sufficient autonomy to process the information for future reference in the resolution of subsequent moral dilemmas.[48] Hoffman[49] contends that the cognitive-structural changes occur in moral reasoning primarily when parents stress inductive techniques. He argues then that cognitive-developmental structural changes are secondarily important to inductive experiences in producing moral conduct. Also he points out that there is "no evidence that children are ordinarily exposed to the necessary progressively increasing levels of moral reasoning." Holstein,[50] for example, found with eighth grade boys and girls that upward movement in the sequence of Kohlberg's moral stages was facilitated in families where principled parents reasoned about moral dilemmas with the young people. Moir[51] also found that, among young girls, correlation was strong between level of moral reasoning and possession of a wide range of social skills involving situations in which the girls were required to perceive the feelings and motives of others. Thus, a growing body of evidence supports Hoffman's contention that inductive disciplinary techniques are a necessary prerequisite to the development of moral-judgment capacity.

Consistency in Moral Conduct and Autonomy in Moral Character

In nineteenth-century genetic psychology, moral conduct was said to issue from a unitary moral faculty. It was assumed that a person's moral conduct would be relatively consistent across situations unless arrested in its growth toward maturity by childhood reversions. The belief appears to have flourished until shortly after the turn of the century. Social scientists were then beginning to recognize the effects that social factors might exert on personality development, and none was more damning in his criticism than McDougall:[52]

Because they treated the individual in artificial abstraction from the social relations through which his moral sentiments are formed, they [older moralists] were led to maintain the hypothesis of some special faculty, the conscience, . . . in seeking to account for moral conduct.

In the early 1920s, Hartshorne and May[53] set out "to test scientifically the truth or falsity of this theory . . . that honesty is a unified character trait."[54] Over a period of five years, the researchers studied the behavior of several thousand children in 29 temptation situations. On the basis of low correlations among the temptation measures, Hartshorne and May[55] concluded that moral behavior could not be conceptualized as emanating from "an inner entity operating independently of the situation in which individuals are placed." The Hartshorne and May[56] exclusive emphasis on situational factors, however, has been challenged recently by Burton,[57] and Nelsen, Grinder, and Mutterer,[58] whose evidence suggests that the problem cannot be conceptualized in polarized terms. After reanalyzing the original Hartshorne and May data with sophisticated procedures, for example, Burton[59] concluded:

The strong emphasis on lack of relationship between the tests is removed. Our analyses indicate that one may conclude there is an underlying trait of honesty which a person brings with him to a resistance to temptation situation. However, the results strongly agree with Hartshorne and May's rejection of an "all or none" formulation regarding a person's character.

The social-learning interpretation of moral development also suggests the probability of underlying consistency in moral behavior. Whether a moral disposition is learned depends in part on the structure of socializing experiences. The repetition of response patterns following a series of wrongdoings that successfully reduce anticipatory anxiety should contribute to the development of a generalized disposition to resist temptations. Following wrongdoing, for example, certain young people will verbally reproduce responses of self-criticism, others will attempt to reverse their actions by making reparation or restitution, others may inform persons of the transgression, and still others may actively seek some form of punishment. Stable socializing experiences will lead them to acquire consistent response styles, even though each person may develop a personally unique one. Consistency in moral conduct also depends in part on the nature of parental discipline. It should be highest in families that emphasize inductive disciplinary practices. Power-assertive and love-withdrawal techniques, (the "do as I say" or "I won't love you if . . ." admonitions) frequently lead to conceptually void, blindly imitative behavior, which may attain situational relevance but will lack generality in novel contexts. Induction, on the other hand, should promote the understanding of moral principles, such as, honesty, courage, responsibility, and punctuality. It should enable young people to develop a coherent moral ideology, to generalize in a wide variety of situations, and hence, to exhibit consistency in their moral conduct.[60]

Dienstbier et al.[61] suggest that behavioral outcomes of moral dilemmas are consequences of complex interaction between affect and cognition, and they predict implicitly that inconsistency will be a function of the extent to which emotion confounds cognition in a moral situation. The investigators advance an "emotion-attribution" hypothesis to account for the role of emotion in moral conflicts. Affect will play a role when emotion aroused in a conflict is perceived as relevant to it. The investigators begin with the assumption that self-control in the face of temptation is strongly influenced by states of emotional discomfort. Every moral issue faced by adolescents and adults—stealing, dishonesty, disloyalty, hurting others, and destroying property and life—arouses emotions in the face of temptation. As socialization ensues and as advanced moral structures are attained, the pertinence of emotional discomfort takes on new meaning and affects moral conduct differently. A person's cognitive understanding in any given situation will determine how the emotional state is interpreted. The thought of a dishonest act might lead one person to worry anxiously about acting irresponsibly toward societal rules and another to be deeply concerned about violating self-chosen internal principles. Dienstbier et al. assume that many moral dilemmas will evoke a "phobic-like" response, which will cause considerable emotional discomfort as the individual seriously considers the option of transgression. When affective dimensions confound an individual's reasoning about a course of action, little consistency in moral behavior is probable. However, "in the normal middle ground of life," cognitive reasoning acquires dominance over emotional factors. When this happens, the likelihood of consistency is enhanced, but whether this happens "seems to depend heavily on our ability to experience emotion as inoperative by attributing it to causes not relevant to the present situation."[62]

Kohlberg's developmental-philosophic theory of morality presumes consistency at the principled level of moral conduct, where universal principles of justice and respect for the dignity of human beings prevail. To the extent that individuals rise to advanced stages of moral conduct, Kohlberg believes that they may transcend their cultural conditioning, lifting themselves above the "mass of men," and respond to moral dilemmas with "logical comprehensiveness, universality, and consistency." Persons whose moral judgments are conceptually inadequate will be less objective, and they will address moral dilemmas in terms of self-interest and personal bias. Their behavior will be relatively situation-specific. The cognitive-developmental view thus suggests that moral reasoning at the lower stages will be culturally conditioned and at the higher stages will be truly abstract and autonomous of social relations. Kohlberg,[63] therefore, perceives the learning of moral standards such as honesty, loyalty, and courage as insignificant relative to the structural development of moral reasoning. Although the standards point approvingly to certain behaviors, they may be so loosely defined and bound to low levels of moral reasoning that individuals will apply them indiscriminately. In the absence of their integration into the process of cognitive structural reorganization, moral standards constitute no more than a "bag of virtues." Kohlberg asks: "Who's to decide what goes on the list?" By adding enough moral principles to the list, it would be long enough eventually to suit everyone. In respect to honesty, for example, Kohlberg observes that almost everyone cheats sometime, however, whether a person cheats in one situation is of little value in predicting whether he or she will or will not cheat in another situation. Kohlberg[64] also points out how difficult it is to agree on the definition of virtue. "What is one man's '*integrity*'" he says, "is another man's 'stubbornness,'" "what is one man's honesty in 'expressing your true feeling' is another man's insensitivity to the feelings of others." The solution to the question of consistency, from Kohlberg's viewpoint, is to attach meaning to virtuous behavior as moral structures evolve. As individuals acquire the capacity to abstract and apply moral principles, they will adopt self-chosen ethical principles.

Kohlberg's criterion for consistency in moral conduct, however, is rooted in philosophy rather than psychology. What is predictable about the moral behavior of "autonomous," internally oriented individuals who reason at Stage 6? After making an exhaustive analysis of Stage 6 moral reasoning, Simpson[65] states: "As a description of a structural element of the principle actor's conduct, this is an eloquent statement, but we are no closer to knowing how he would actually behave, what decisions he would make, and how he learned that such choices were available to him." Hogan and Dickstein,[66] however, have attempted to describe how persons differ in moral conduct at the highest levels of principled reasoning. The investigators show how individuals differ, as a function of socializing experiences, in their regard for legal procedures in regulating society and in protecting the welfare of citizens. Persons may be persuaded over time to favor law as the best guide to social action and to believe that civil-rights guarantees should be built into the structure of society. These individuals develop a disposition that Hogan and Dickstein label "the ethics of responsibility," and they may hold suspicious attitudes toward other people who fail to share their respect for law and order. In contrast, other persons deemphasize the utility of legal procedures and distrust institutional sources of law, preferring to rely on intuition as a moral guide. These individuals develop a disposition the researchers label "the ethics of personal conscience;" they tend to believe that everyone can be taught to respect the rights of others and they look to educational programs as vehicles for perfecting human nature. Given the probability that the moral conduct of persons in general is affected by their position relative to these two distinct dispositions, Hogan and Dickstein[67] argue that moral reasoning can be properly understood only in the context of "total character structure." Baumrind,[68] for example, has distinguished how a devout Buddhist and a devout Christian might exemplify contrasting outlooks in respect to Kohlberg's dilemma about whether a man should steal drugs to save his wife. The former appears to illustrate "the ethics of responsibility" whereas the latter appears to reveal "the ethics of personal conscience."

The Buddhist: "I personally feel that death under certain circumstances and in spite of the fear it produces is not worth violating one's moral essence to avoid. The proscription against stealing is a universal truth, as is accepting one's death. If in any particular case one violates a value judgment, then the truth has no essence. I definitely would not steal for it. I would try to convince my wife to accept her death."

The Christian: "Yes, the man should steal for his wife. A life is worth that. I would penalize the druggist. Wherever there is life there is hope. Even if it only prolonged her life, that would be something. The druggist is trespassing against a higher law than Thou Shalt Not Steal."

Simpson,[69] moreover, indicates how moral reasoning that appears on the surface to be philosophically independent, may in fact be derived from past experiences as a function of social-group membership. The investigator suggests that the postconventional levels (Stages 5 and 6) of principled morality may be a product of adopting intellectualized, moral styles of small, relatively sophisticated reference groups. The acquisitions may be so completely internalized that members of a reference group delude themselves into believing that they are functioning autonomously. Simpson wonders whether some individuals learn moral autonomy as a norm, and to meet continued expectations of reference groups, "learn to reason abstractly about morality and to emphasize the kind of morality which admits them to elevated ethical status."

Moral Education: Social Learning and Cognitive-Developmental Perspectives

Moral maturity arises with acquisition of skills of moral analysis and motivation to act consistently. Social-learning theorists and cognitive-developmentalists recognize that adolescents must learn emotional self-control, acquire the capacity to abstract moral principles, and transcend self-interest in moral decision making in order to develop stable, relatively autonomous patterns of moral conduct. The former stress self-examination of moral action, role development and identity formation, and culturally derived values; the latter emphasize the developmental significance of advanced logical reasoning, structured competencies, and adherence to universal values. Proponents of each position reject doctrinaire efforts to induce unreflective conformity to parental, teacher, school, or community values. Kohlberg[70] attacks "indoctrinative moral education" as if it were a reasonable alternative, but no social scientist today seriously believes that either preaching or exhortation provides a basis for character development. As a matter of fact, responsible developmental theorists have unequivocally repudiated doctrinaire efforts for decades, for example, "it is cruel to teach [moral and] religious doctrines that cannot be understood, and that may have to be unlearned or rejected later."[71] An effective moral education curriculum, all agree, will lead young people to relinquish childhood forms of imitative conformity as they reach for carefully reasoned, ethical principles.

Moral education from the perspective of social learning is essentially a matter of role clarification. During socialization it is a question of forestalling moral anxiety and strengthening resistance to temptation (self-control) by emphasizing inductive disciplinary encounters. Young people's attention is directed to the consequences of their behavior; they are encouraged to assess how their moral choices affect the rights and intentions of others, and they are provided with sufficient autonomy to process information into an objective, comprehensive system of values. Unfortunately, parents often fail at the task. Their efforts to foster moral character development often are poorly conceptualized, and their successes are frequently a product of luck. The social-learning approach to moral development is a long-term process, and it is difficult to abbrieviate it. A recently developed educational strategy, however, known as "values clarification," may represent a useful, short-term approximation. The values clarification approach to moral education centers on open or Socratic peer discussion of moral dilemmas. It aims to help young people become more purposive, creative, productive, analytical, and respected.[72] Specifically, in encouraging young people to explore their own judgments about issues in which values conflict, the strategy leads them to clarify interpersonal role relationships. "What is expected of me by my parents, peers, teachers, and myself? How will I feel if I transgress either my own standards or those of persons whom I greatly respect?" On the matter of whether to use drugs, a values clarification session might help young people put their lives into broad perspective, for example, review the qualities inherent in persons with whom they interact closely and think about the consequences of their actions upon them. Another session, organized around introspective issues, might ask young people to rank the following ten items from highest to lowest on a "priority ladder:"[73]

I want to have a clarified set of values to live by.
I want more intimacy with more people different from me.
I want to learn how to change.

I want to live more fully.

I want to help make the world a better place in which to live.

I want more ritual and celebration in my daily living.

I want feedback from people so I know how to act.

I want to be more authentic, open, and trusting.

I want to handle my anger more constructively.

I want to live more justly.

Afterward the young people might be grouped according to the order of their rankings to discuss with one another the bases they used for establishing their "priority ladders." The values clarification approach thus leads the participants to examine the different choices available to them and to make decisions in the context of what is most meaningful. Many critical issues, however, may fail to surface during values clarification sessions, and young people may attain resolution inadvertently on the basis of superficial and trivial choices. The values clarification strategy with its emphasis on public affirmation also may cause participants to avoid extreme positions and to seek a safe middle ground. Its social aspects, too, may exert pressure to conform to the values of others rather than to clarify one's own moral standards.[74]

Kohlberg[75] views the values clarification strategy as a useful "first step" because it implies a "rational" approach. He criticizes it, nonetheless, on the grounds that it presupposes ethical relativity, particularizes values, assumes raising issues to transitory awareness can lead to lasting value orientations, and fails to recognize differences in moral judgment strategies. Kohlberg's[76] version of cognitive-developmental moral education, in contrast, aims to stimulate moral structural organization through development of capabilities in decision making and problem solving. "The focus is upon the acquisition of structured competencies that transfer to later life and have a *cumulative* effect in enhancing and enriching life."[77] As young people find established cognitive structures inadequate, they are encouraged to revise their ways of thinking. According to Rest,[78] "the essential condition for the cumulative elaboration of cognitive structure is the presentation of experiences which 'stretch' one's existing thinking and set into motion this search-and-discovery process for more adequate ways to organize experience and action." It is the teacher's function to stimulate the "stretching and searching." Kohlberg[79] recommends that teachers expose young people (1) to their next higher stages of moral reasoning, (2) to situations posing problems and contradictions for their current moral structures, leading to dissatisfaction with these levels, and (3) to an open atmosphere of interchange and dialogue in which conflicting moral values are compared. Furthermore,

Kohlberg[80] emphasizes the following four distinctive features of the cognitive developmental approach in stimulating movement to more advanced stages:

1. Change is in the way of reasoning rather than in the particular beliefs involved.
2. Students in a class are at different stages; the aim is to aid movement of each to the next stage, not converge on a common pattern.
3. The teacher's own opinion is neither stressed nor invoked as authoritative. It enters in only as one of many opinions, hopefully as one of those at the next higher stage.
4. The notion that some judgments are more adequate than others is communicated. Fundamentally, however, this means that the student is encouraged to articulate a position which seems most adequate to him and to judge the adequacy of the reasoning of others.

Kohlberg has criticized moral education programs in general for failing to match curricula with students' developmental levels. An underestimation of their sophistication may result in trying to teach a simplistic "virtue-always-pays" morality and an overestimation may mean overshooting their comprehension "with abstract and abtruse doctrines." However, Rest questions whether any teacher possesses the skills to facilitate moral education in terms of structural growth. Certainly it is essential for the teacher to be familiar with stage characteristics and recurrent themes in order to "reflect, summarize, and amplify" young people's moral judgments. But Rest[81] asks:

Is it really possible for a teacher to code a child's statement, to decide what stage is above it, and to compute a response all in the time frame of conversational exchanges? Judging from the amount of time it takes to stage score a regular interview and the amount of time it takes to compose unambiguous stage-prototypic statements, it is unrealistic to expect a teacher to be computing + 1 retorts to students in a group discussion. Perhaps with special training, such responses to recurrent statements would be possible—but in any case, Kohlberg's advice to teachers is enormously difficult to carry out.

Kohlberg's approach to moral development has been more actively discussed and researched during the past decade than that of the social-learning theorists. Scores of researchers have published papers investigating, supporting, and criticizing his position. Some are intrigued by its coherence and comprehensiveness, others are drawn to it by his belief that moral education can be advanced by stimulating persons to higher levels of moral judgment, and still others, by his metaphysical insistence that principled morality (respect for the dignity of human beings as individuals) is the core of the mature moral character. These features enhance its appeal relative to the empirically based, metaphysically void, social-learning explanation of character development. The verification of either perspective, however, is far from complete, and perhaps the general conclusion to be drawn from the foregoing review is that application of theoretical principles to moral education still has a very long way to go. Whatever the theoretical orientation that we choose to adopt, the socializing experiences that structure disciplinary encounters in an inductive vein lead to both role-clarification and enlarged capacity for moral judgment. The differences between the two positions are relatively inconsequential during the course of early socialization; it is only when principled morality emerges that the two part on the question of relative versus absolute moral values. The issue is so complex that Kohlberg[82] restricts his moral education program "to that which is moral or, more specifically, to justice," in order to ensure himself a rational basis for inferring moral autonomy. He observes, for example, that "it is not clear that the whole realm of personal, political, and religious values is a realm which is nonrelative, i.e., in which there are universals and a direction of development." Is there, then, a point in moral development at which "right comprehension" ensures "right" conduct, that is, the capacity to resist compromise in the face of tempting pressures involving personal, political, and religious values? John Dewey[83] put the age-old problem in these terms: "We need to translate the moral into the conditions and forces of our community life, and into the impulses and habits of the individual. All the rest is mint, anise, and cummin."

SUMMARY

Moral character arises as self-interest is subordinated to rules that reflect the best interests of all people. Children's actions broach the moral realm as they start to obey the culturally defined rules of conduct that the social world imposes upon them. Concepts of rules and principles are initially viewed as part of external reality, and children learn to behave "morally" as they are rewarded for conforming to the routines of family and neighborhood. Cognitive growth during adolescence, however, transforms the literal rules of childhood into general conduct guides. As control of moral conduct is displaced from socializing agents to personal, internalized standards, a disposition to obey rules is transformed into a disposition to question rules. Moral autonomy thus becomes possible when young people rise above self-serving interests and act in the context of compassion, empathy, and respect for justice.

This chapter describes young people's moral development from two viewpoints: (1) the cognitive-developmental, which predicates moral growth on children's making decisions about moral issues, and (2) the social learning, which presumes moral growth to be a product of the internalization of socially sanctioned standards. The cognitive-developmental outlook was inspired by the early work of Piaget, who believed that moral development paralleled the successive transformations of cognitive structures. The social-learning approach starts from Freud's distinction between "objective anxiety," which is a product of concern about external expectations and mandates, and "moral anxiety," which, being independent of external dominance, provides the basis for self-control.

Lawrence Kohlberg is today the major spokesperson for the cognitive-developmental interpretation of moral development. He maintains that moral development progresses in an invariant sequence; each advance represents a higher level of integration until, ultimately, moral judgments are based on universal principles like respect for human life, liberty, and equity. Kohlberg has identified six qualitatively distinct, sequentially related value orientations: (1) punishment and obedience, (2) instrumental relativist, (3) good boy—nice girl, (4) law and order, (5) contractual-legalistic, (6) conscience or principled. He has cast the six value orientations into a typology of moral structures. They comprise six stages that are presumed to be logically ordered so that the higher ones are conceptually more advanced than the lower ones. In every moral dilemma, young people are expected to prefer reasoning at the highest stage comprehended. Mature morality arrives when young people learn to make "right decisions" on the basis of ethical principles that have logical comprehensiveness, consistency, and universality.

Kohlberg and his colleagues have mustered considerable research evidence to show that the sequential order of the stages, conceptual reorganization of moral reasoning, and preference for higher stages occur. Their research effort has been less successful, however, in demonstrating that the process of moral development is innate and universal to all persons. Attempts have been made to show that individuals in a wide range of societies proceed similarly in their moral development, but the data are inconclusive.

Social-learning theorists have (1) operationalized moral behavior and (2) have integrated cognitive and affective components in describing moral development. Moral conduct is distinguished from other forms of behavior in that it usually involves either pre- or posttransgression activity. Conduct that precedes a moral decision is conceptualized as temptation behavior. Temptation occurs when a situation arises to engage in behavior that becomes forbidden because it conflicts, in this particular context, with socially expected (moral) behavior. (A hungry adolescent at home may take and eat an apple from a bowl on the kitchen table, but a hungry adolescent on a hike may not climb a fence and take and eat an apple from a private orchard.) Temptation generates a conflict in which both alternatives, either yield or resist, are highly desirable. When transgression is the outcome of a moral decision, persons are likely to engage in one or more of the following four response patterns to help themselves restore disrupted social relations: *self-criticism,* a form of self-evaluation based on experiences that followed earlier transgressions; *reparation,* a form of corrective or restitutive activities, *confession,* a way of informing other persons of the transgression; and *reactions oriented toward external punishment,* a style of response to transgression that leads explicitly to punishment or punishment-avoidance.

Hoffman describes the effects of three parental disciplinary practices, power assertion, love withdrawal, and induction, upon moral development. Power assertion and love withdrawal promote neither emotional control nor understanding in resolving moral conflicts. Techniques of induction, however, foster development of these attributes. They are based on explanatory analyses, and they exemplify efforts of parents to induce cognitive skills in moral reasoning. Hoffman contends that inductive disciplinary encounters are more significant than cognitive structural changes to the development of morality.

The question of consistency in moral conduct has long been of concern to social scientists. Kohlberg's developmental-philosophic theory of morality presumes consistency at the higher levels of moral conduct, where universal principles of justice and respect for the dignity of human beings predominate. Social learning theorists assume that inductive disciplinary encounters, which promote understanding of moral principles such as honesty, courage, and responsibility, should enable young people to develop a coherent moral ideology, to generalize in a wide variety of situations, and hence, to be consistent in their moral conduct.

Moral education in the schools from the cognitive-developmental viewpoint aims to stimulate moral structural reorganization through development of skills in decision making and problem solving. Moral education from the perspective of social learning theory focuses upon these skills in the context of role clarification. A recently developed educational strategy known as "values clarification" may prove highly useful in the refinement of educational strategies.

REVIEW QUESTIONS

1. In what respect is moral development a matter of accommodation?
2. What do decision making and self-control have to do with morality?
3. Why does Kohlberg use the label developmental-philosophic theory to describe his interpretation of moral development?
4. What is moral realism, immanent justice, and moral autonomy, respectively?
5. Why does Kohlberg assert that respect for human life is a universal ideal?
6. Describe the six value orientations that Kohlberg has cast into a typology or moral structures?
7. Describe the course of moral development in Kohlberg's system.
8. What evidence suggests moral development is sequential?
9. Why do critics argue that Kohlberg has failed to show that the stage sequence of moral reasoning is universal?
10. What is the Freudian perspective on the role of superego in moral development?
11. What are the characteristics of a temptation conflict?
12. Why is self-criticism described as a form of self-evaluation?
13. Why are reparative responses to transgression closely related to responsibility?
14. How do parents foster confession in young people as a response to transgression?

15. Why does punishment-seeking following transgression seem an outgrowth of dependence on others for direction?
16. How do parental emphases on moral reasoning foster acquisition of self-control?
17. What circumstances lead to consistency in moral behavior from, respectively, the social-learning and the cognitive-developmental viewpoint?
18. What is moral education from the perspective of social-learning theory?
19. Why does Kohlberg criticize the values clarification strategy?
20. What are the four distinctive features of the cognitive-developmental approach to moral education?

DISCUSSION QUESTIONS

1. What is morality from your viewpoint? What are its major components?
2. Why does Kohlberg make a strong effort to connect moral development and moral philosophy?
3. Why do both Erikson and Kohlberg believe that moral development continues beyond adolescence?
4. How would you account for Freud's concepts of "objective anxiety" and "moral anxiety" in Kohlberg's typology of moral structures?
5. What steps would you take as a social learning theorist and as a cognitive-developmental theorist, respectively, to increase the capacity of adolescents to resist temptation in the context of shoplifting?
6. What are the points of congruity and incongruity between the social-learning and cognitive-developmental theories of moral development?

NOTES

1. J. Dewey. *Moral principles in education.* Boston: Houghton Mifflin, 1909, pp. 50–52.
2. W. McDougall. *An introduction to social psychology.* Boston: John W. Luce, 1910, p. 261.
3. L. Kohlberg. The contribution of developmental psychology to education—examples from moral education. *Educational Psychologist,* 1973, **10,** 2–14.
4. J. Piaget. *The moral judgment of the child.* New York: Free Press, 1948.
5. Kohlberg, *op. cit.,* p. 6.
6. Kohlberg, *op. cit.*
7. L. Kohlberg. The child as a moral philosopher. *Psychology Today,* 1968, **2,** 25–30.
8. L. Kohlberg and E. Turiel (Eds.). *Moralization, the cognitive developmental approach.* New York: Holt, Rinehart and Winston, in press.
9. Ibid.
10. Ibid.

11. E. Turiel. Developmental process in the child's moral thinking. In P. H. Mussen, J. Langer, and M. Covington (Eds.). *Trends and issues in developmental psychology.* New York: Holt, Rinehart and Winston, 1969.

12. J. R. Rest, E. Turiel, and L. Kohlberg. Level of moral development as a determinant of preference and comprehension of moral judgments made by others. *Journal of Personality,* 1969, **37,** 225–252.

13. J. R. Rest. The hierarchical nature of moral judgment: a study of patterns of comprehension and preference of moral stages. *Journal of Personality,* 1973, **41,** 86–109.

14. Rest et al., *op. cit.*

15. Rest, *op. cit.,* p. 106.

16. L. Kohlberg and R. B. Kramer. Continuities and discontinuities in childhood and adult moral development. *Human Development,* 1969, **12,** 93–120.

17. E. Turiel. Conflict and transition in adolescent moral development. *Child Development,* 1974, **45,** 14–29.

18. C. Tomlinson-Keasey and C. B. Keasey. The mediating role of cognitive development in moral judgment. *Child Development,* 1974, **45,** 291–298.

19. C. B. Keasey. The influence of opinion agreement and quality of supportive reasoning in the evaluation of moral judgments. *Journal of Personality and Social Psychology,* 1974, **30,** 477–482.

20. K. N. Anchor and H. J. Cross. Maladaptive aggression, moral perspective, and the socialization process. *Journal of Personality and Social Psychology,* 1974, **30,** 163–168.

21. D. Graham. *Moral learning and development.* New York: John Wiley, 1972.

22. W. Kurtines and E. B. Greif. The development of moral thought: review and evaluation of Kohlberg's approach. *Psychological Bulletin,* 1974, **81,** 453–470.

23. R. L. Gorsuch and M. L. Barnes. Stages of ethical reasoning and moral norms of Carib youths. *Journal of Cross-Cultural Psychology,* 1973, **4,** 283–301.

24. E. L. Simpson. Moral development research. *Human Development,* 1974, **17,** 81–106, p. 91.

25. Simpson, *op. cit.*

26. G. S. Hall. *Adolescence.* New York: Appleton, 1904.

27. M. L. Hoffman. Moral internalization, parental power, and the nature of parent-child interaction. *Developmental Psychology,* 1975, **11,** 228–239; Rest, *op. cit.*

28. S. Freud. *New introductory lectures on psychoanalysis.* New York: Norton, 1933, p. 89.

29. A. El-Dirghami. Shoplifting among students. *Journal of Retailing.* 1974, **50,** 33–42.

30. K. L. LeVeque and R. E. Walker. Correlates of high school cheating behavior. *Psychology in the Schools,* 1970, **7,** 159–163.

31. F. Schab. Cheating in high school: A comparison of behavior of students in the college prep and general curriculum. *Journal of Youth and Adolescence,* 1972, **1,** 251–256.

32. Ibid.

33. C. P. Smith, E. R. Ryan, and D. R. Diggins. Moral decision-making: cheating on examinations. *Journal of Personality,* 1972, **40,** 640–660.

34. J. Aronfreed. *Conduct and conscience.* New York: Academic Press, 1968.

35. Aronfreed, *op. cit.,* pp. 217–226.

36. Aronfreed, *op. cit.,* pp. 227–234.

37. Aronfreed, *op. cit.,* pp. 235–237.

38. Aronfreed, *op. cit.,* p. 237.

39. Aronfreed, *op. cit.,* pp. 238–240.

40. Aronfreed, *op. cit.;* M. L. Hoffman. Moral development. In P. H. Mussen (Ed.). *Carmichael's manual of child phychology.* Vol. 2. New York: Wiley, 1970.

41. See p. 230.

42. Aronfreed, *op. cit.*

43. Hoffman, Moral development, *op. cit.*

44. See p. 231.

45. Hoffman, Moral development, *op. cit.*

46. Aronfreed, *op. cit.*

47. Hoffman, Moral internalization and parent-child interaction, *op. cit.*

48. Aronfreed, *op. cit.*

49. Hoffman, Moral internalization and parent-child interaction, *op. cit.*

50. C. E. Holstein. The relation of childrens' moral judgment level to that of their parents and to communication patterns in the family. In R. C. Smart, and M. S. Smart (Eds.). *Readings in child development and relationships.* New York: Macmillan, 1972.

51. D. J. Moir. Egocentrism and the emergence of conventional morality in preadolescent girls. *Child Development,* 1974, **45,** 299–304.

52. McDougall, *op. cit.,* p. 229.

53. H. Hartshorne and M. A. May. *Studies in the nature of character.* Vol. 1. *Studies in deceit.* New York: Macmillan, 1928.

54. H. Hartshorne. *Character in human relations.* New York: Scribners, 1932, p. 209.

55. Hartshorne and May, *op. cit.,* p. 385.

56. Hartshorne and May, *op. cit.*

57. R. V. Burton. Generality of honesty reconsidered. *Psychological Review,* 1963, **70,** 481–499.

58. E. A. Nelsen, R. E. Grinder, and M. L. Mutterer. Sources of variance in behavioral measures of honesty in temptation situations. *Developmental Psychology,* 1969, **1,** 265–279.

59. Burton, *op. cit.,* p. 492.

60. Hoffman, Moral internalization and parent-child interaction, *op. cit.*

61. R. A. Dienstbier, D. Hillman, J. Lehnhoff, J. Hillman, and M. C. Valkenaar. An emotion-attribution approach to moral behavior: interfacing cognitive and avoidance theories of moral development. *Psychological Review,* 1975, **82,** 299–315.

62. Dienstbier et al., *op. cit.,* pp. 313–314.

63.   Kohlberg, Developmental psychology and moral education, *op. cit.*

64.   Kohlberg, *op. cit.*, p. 5.

65.   Simpson, *op. cit.*, p. 94.

66.   R. Hogan and E. Dickstein. Moral judgment and perceptions of injustice. *Journal of Personality and Social Psychology*, 1972, **23,** 409–413.

67.   Hogan and Dickstein, *op. cit.*, p. 412.

68.   D. Baumrind. Metaethical and normative considerations covering the treatment of human subjects in the behavioral sciences. In E. Kennedy (Ed.). *Human rights and psychological research: A debate on psychology and ethics.* New York: Crowell, 1975, pp. 37–68.

69.   Simpson, *op. cit.*, p. 94.

70.   L. Kohlberg. The cognitive-developmental approach to moral education. *Phi Delta Kappan,* 1975, **51,** 670–677.

71.   N. Norsworthy and M. T. Whitley. *The psychology of childhood.* New York: Macmillan, 1918, p. 250.

72.   S. B. Simon and P. deSherbinin. Values clarification: It can start gently and grow deep. *Phi Delta Kappan,* 1975, **51,** 679–683.

73.   Simon and deSherbinin, *op. cit.*, p. 680.

74.   J. S. Stewart. Clarifying values clarification: A critique. *Phi Delta Kappan,* 1975, **51,** 684–688.

75.   Kohlberg, Cognitive-developmental approach to moral education, *op. cit.*

76.   Ibid.

77.   J. Rest. Developmental psychology as a guide to value education: A review of "Kohlbergian" programs. *Review of Educational Research,* 1974, **44,** 241–259, p. 242.

78.   Rest, *op cit.*, p. 245.

79.   Kohlberg, Cognitive-developmental approach to moral education, *op. cit.*

80.   Ibid.

81.   Rest, *op. cit.*, pp. 248–249.

82.   Kohlberg, Cognitive-developmental approach to moral education, *op. cit.*, p. 674.

83.   Dewey, *op. cit.*, p. 58.

Chapter 9

Youth Culture and Peer Group Relations

CHAPTER HIGHLIGHTS

ISSUES

Freedom from parental control fosters peer interaction.

Purchasing power, advertising, and shopping tastes affect youth-culture distinctiveness.

Status terms and peer-group standards provide bases for youth cultures.

Youth-culture styles are distinguishable on the basis of value differences between youth and the established society.

The emergence of "freak culture" represents an extreme expression of values in the counterculture.

Countercultural religious groups are unlike conventional churches and ignore the complexities of modern society.

Social disequilibrium gives rise to generation gaps because of either youth's alienation from established societal roles or youth's participation in evolving new social systems.

The lyric themes of popular music acquaint youth with ways of experiencing basic emotions.

Forms of social organization like cliques, crowds, and sororities serve mainly to enhance heterosexual prowess.

THE QUESTION OF YOUTH-CULTURE DISTINCTIVENESS

The transition of adolescents from their families through the peer world and into adulthood encompasses a major aspect of their socialization. They spend a long time in a relatively segregated peer world. Although the American culture lacks rites of passage and ceremonies that formally specify the passing of childhood dependency and the assumption of adult responsibilities, a series of largely irrevocable decisions—pertaining to mate selection, educational attainment, career choice, place of residence, and so forth—take adolescents away from their families and childhood into peer activities, and toward participation in adult life. Almost all adolescents in America eventually leave their family circles for a life in which they are appreciated for *what* they are rather than *who* they are.[1] The contemporary prominence of peers in the socialization of youth stems from a cultural context that fosters, on the one hand, youth's freedom from parental control and on the other, a wide discrepancy between youth's power to consume goods and their capacity to earn them. First, few adolescents live on farms where they care for crops and animals or work in family businesses; their family obligations are minimal; they have little responsibilities around home, and neither opportunity nor occasion for part-time gainful employment is readily available. Second, youth have grown up for several generations in an expanding economy, have experienced successive rises in the purchasing power of their families, and have been provided with ample rationale for taking affluence for granted. Young people today have more time and money than ever before to purchase and consume goods and services, and they possess a large share of the discretionary income of society. Further, the age at which they become consumers (i.e., possess the resources to purchase goods and services freely in the marketplace) has become progressively younger.[2] At the same time, the age at which youth assume full-time productive roles in society and acquire independence in terms of residence has become older.

Adolescents, thus, with time on their hands, turn to their peers for social activities and companionship. About the time children start riding their bicycles around the block and out into the neighborhood, they begin to decide for themselves who their friends will be. Peers give young people their first social independence from adults, and the relationships they engender facilitate their transition from reliance on their families to relative freedom in adolescence and adulthood. Peers offer adolescents new patterns of reciprocity: they reverberate thoughts, feelings, expectations, and demands. Peer interaction permits adolescents to see how their friends respond to their parents; it encourages them to examine new values and relationships.

As young people interact, sharing hopes and aspirations, meeting each other's demands and expectations, and coming to terms with rights and obligations, the common repertoire of language, slang, grooming, clothing, music, and so forth that they adopt leads them to express collectively, in varying degrees of cohesiveness, a cultural distinctiveness; that is, a *youth culture*. Their sensibilities, however, will be affected by differences in age, social-class, geographical, ethnic, and family background. Youth cultures thus arise pluralistically to serve young people differently depending on their social and psychological needs. Some adolescents will rely on a youth culture for a reward system alternative to that of the adult society, some will use a youth culture to support and facilitate their transition to adulthood, and others, denied access to youth-culture pleasures by their peers, may withdraw from both peer and adult value systems.

A few researchers deny the fact of *any*-youth culture distinctiveness. It is said adults and adolescents are more alike than dissimilar. Jahoda and Warren[3] have said the question of youth-cultural distinctiveness is a "pseudo-issue" unworthy of debate. They say that all social groups can be studied usefully from two viewpoints: what they share and what they do not share with the larger culture. So, they ask, why should youth's activities be singled out for special attention? Smith and Kleine[4] believe that the debate about the uniqueness of youth-culture will suffer a fate similar to that of the old controversy about heredity and environment (for a time it was believed that the influence of each of these forces on development could be studied separately). Smith[5] holds also that the use of the concept of youth-culture is unproductive. He says that it exaggerates the significance of age as a variable in explaining cultural differences. Attitudes toward glamour and athletics, for example, may vary more among older persons than between adults and young people. These reservations gain credence from evidence in at least one area—shopping tastes—in which adults and youth share strikingly similar views. Young people are almost always consulted about family vacations and about the purchase of a family car, TV set, and home. They seek parental advice in shopping for personal clothing, toiletry articles, sports equipment, small appliances, and forms of transportation.[6] Adolescent boys buy more than 40 percent of the male sportswear; adolescent girls buy about 20 percent of the women's apparel and account for 30 percent of all cosmetic purchases, 25 percent of all greeting card sales, and 50 percent of all record album sales. A survey made by the Los Angeles Chamber of Commerce,[7] primarily for business executives, recommended using appeal created by advertising to diminish the distinctiveness of youth-culture tastes. The report stated: "As a child progresses through the teens it becomes much more important to sell the child than to sell the parent. And a child, once sold, exerting peer influence, will tend to steer others in his group toward your product, your brand, your service, or your store. . . . Childhood items tend to be low priced/convenience; while the teenager not only buys low priced items, but also more costly items, and should be advertised to with an eye for long-range impression. . . . 'Instead of parents influencing children it's vice-versa—mothers dress like daughters and fathers like sons.'"

Similarity in shopping tastes notwithstanding, young people occupy a common position in society, and peer-group standards dominate adolescent social situations in ways that appear to lead youth to develop unique expectations of themselves. By virtue of their age segregation youth respond with an intensity toward each other that is largely lacking after decisions about marriage and career prospects are settled. Schwartz[8] argues that peer standards associated with "personal excellence and interpersonal competence" cause youth to disassociate from the adult world and to develop independent status systems and styles of life. Schwartz holds that whether young people attain prestige in their particular status system depends on how highly peers regard their masculinity or femininity. He also believes that the youth-culture distinctiveness young people engender via their efforts to differentiate themselves in terms of masculine or feminine status is so basic to youth interaction that it holds across variations in both social class and social values. Youth employ special terms and categories that pertain to social virtues and defects to segregate themselves. They also estimate their own competence and rank in the prestige hierarchy by whether peers identify them by terms that have positive or negative connotations. These terms signify both attributes and dispositions; the former describe persons as admirable or reprehensible and the latter indicate what kinds of things persons say and do. They suggest images by which adolescents can measure their own worth. The more desirable terms indicate that they are viewed as being able to present "cool" self-images under highly competitive social conditions.

According to Kluckhohn and Kelly,[9] culture is "a historically derived system of explicit and implicit designs for living, which tend to be shared by all or specifically designated members of a group." A culture thus may be regarded as an abstraction, including both acts and artifacts, that is made up primarily of historically developed, shared, and learned behavior patterns. Applying the Kluckhohn and Kelly[10] definition, the major criterion by which to decide if there is a basis for youth-culture distinctiveness is whether there are systems of communication and patterns of behavior among adolescents that distinguish them from children and adults. Schwartz[11] contends that the manner in which youth regard each other in the peer status hierarchy constitutes a culturally distinct communications system.

In a study of middle- and lower-class youth attending a high school which drew its students from stable, working-, lower-, middle-, and upper-middle class areas of a community, Schwartz and Merten[12] provided empirical support for

Schwartz' view. The researchers discovered that the students had indeed structured a status system and had adopted certain key terms to describe the positions peers occupied in it. Schwartz and Merten found the youth in their particular study had adopted the terms "socie" and "hoody" to differentiate their statuses. (Youth in other parts of the country will employ regionally appropriate terms to differentiate their life styles, dress, speech, and interpersonal relationships—see Figure 1.) An adolescent was labeled a "socie" or "hoody" according to his or her overt commitment to a particular style of life. Most of the youth in the high school perceived the socies to be in the top stratum of the prestige system, and the socies with the most status of all were known as "elites." The youth who adopted conventional patterns of life (neither socie nor hoody) gained social recognition only to the extent that they imitated the socies. But as viewed by the socies, these youth failed to qualify as even "out of it," and were often regarded as "others," which signified that they had no definite identity in the social system. The socies saw them as faceless because they were not demonstrably attached to any discernable adolescent style.

A socie participated in formal high school activities and belonged to adult-sanctioned cliques, clubs, fraternities, and sororities. The socies tended to divide themselves on the basis of their commitments to the achievement orientation of the high school. The group that held steadfastly to adult standards of accomplishment were known as "clean-cut" and "all-around." They would do well in team sports, get fairly good (but not necessarily high) grades, and, importantly, know how to get along with their teachers and classmates. They were very "sociable" and mastered the "cool" patterns of adolescent social life. The social circle from which the clean-cut socies selected their dating partners partially established their standing in the social system, and thus it was essential that the socie succeed in the intense competition for dates with other high-status persons. The socie boys were supposed to "make out" and be able to provide concrete evidence of their sexual prowess. Girls were also required to prove their worth in the sexual arena. They were expected to attract high-status boys as dates, but this meant that they had to engage in intense petting occasionally without endangering their "reputations." Their prestige rested partly on the status that their presence could bring to the boys who dated them, and it could be compromised if they gave sexual favors too freely. The socies who moved away from the school's achievement orientation, but not so far as to openly reject it, were known as "hoody-socies." They evinced little interest in academic pursuits, but they participated enthusiastically in high school social life and they spent a good deal of time and energy systematically refining their dating and drinking techniques. The hoody-socies were the pacesetters in musical taste, grooming styles, and so forth. They rarely defied adult authority openly, committed acts of serious delinquency, or dropped out of high school before graduation. The two socie divisions regarded the hoodies as being "out-of-it." Indeed, they tended to see anyone who deviated from their prestige criteria as being "out-of-it." To diminish the image of masculinity or femininity that the hoody or "out-of-it" young people might project, the socies stereotyped these youth, in many respects erroneously, as caring little about their personal appearance, morals, grades, or school activities.

An adolescent's estimation of his or her own status depended on the particular reference group to which he or she belonged. The hoody youth, for example, viewed the socies as hypocrites. The hoodies recognized that their mode of life was not consistent with the esteemed features of the socie system, and they saw their life style as partly antagonistic to socie values. They seemed to have evolved an independent life style, representing in the school an exceedingly heterogeneous category of persons—the rebels, slow learners, and intellectuals. A hoody might or might not be oriented toward the academic achievement values of the high school, but he or she was definitely deviant in terms of the prestige criteria of the social system. As one socie described hoody girls: "They're misfits; they're insecure. They don't think they're cute enough, or they're awkward, or they have a lisp or something."[13]

The distinctions Schwartz and Merten drew among the terms young people employ to differentiate peer statuses have been corroborated by Gordon[14] who conducted a somewhat comparable study. Gordon collected a sizeable list of common high school status terms prevalent in the 1950s and 1960s. He developed the list from personal observations, interviews, and student newspapers, and it is presented in Figure 1. A few terms common in the 1970s (those that are italic) have been added. The data in Figure 1 are ordered in terms of achievement orientation toward high schools and of social acceptance by the school's "leading crowd." The status terms are placed in Figure 1 to show both degree of orientation toward each dimension and degree of integration between the two dimensions. Further, the social acceptance dimension is divided into two areas to indicate whether the status terms signify orientation toward either "outside," that is, peer-dominated values, or institutionalized school values. A "jock," for example, is typically a youth who enjoys both high peer orientation and high school integration. A "cowboy," in contrast, signifies a young person whose orientation is low relative to each dimension. The cowboy's rankings in the two areas are correlated, however, in the sense that the individual is neither achievement nor school oriented. A "brain," on the other hand, is high in achievement orientation and low in social acceptance, which suggests that "brains" are poorly integrated on the two dimensions. It is noteworthy that Figure 1 shows no status term to indicate that there are youth in high school who are highly

	Orientation toward acceptance by the "leading crowd"					
	Low		Medium		High	
Achievement orientation	Outside Values	"Official" Values	Outside Values	"Official" Values	Outside Values	"Official" Values
High	Prudes Pilgrims	Brains Grinds Wonks Brown-nosers Weanies Curve-breakers Super jocks			Lovers Hot dogs In-group Popular kids Soshes	Gentlemen jocks Big wheels Politicos Student council types
Medium	Fags Queers Pansies Fairies			Invisibles Losers Nebbishes Frumps Nerds Rednecks		Cheer leaders Colleeges
Low	Shop-boys Animals Surfers Goof-offs Heads Hoods Grubbies Goers Pigs Thugs *Turkey Honky Creep Cowboy*		Heads Hippies Freaks Hodads Longhairs Swingers *Juicer Doper*			Bible clubbers Service clubbers

Figure 1

High school social types of the 1950s, 1960s, and 1970s, based on student papers, interviews, and personal observations. (From Gordon, see text. Reprinted by permission.)

accepted by the "leading crowd" in terms of "outside," peer-dominated values and also low in achievement orientation. These data, as well as those of Schwartz and Merten, suggest that a positive orientation toward high school achievement standards may be a necessary antecedent to peer acceptance at the higher prestige levels.

THE QUESTION OF YOUTH-CULTURE STYLES

Although the way young people use status terms contributes to youth-culture distinctiveness, the differentiations that they make are common to all youth-culture styles. The clean-cut socies, emphasizing handsomeness, glamour, and cool demeanor, approximate the image adults uphold to adolescents as ideal. And the hoodies appear out-of-step with the adult world more in respect to standards of heterosexual prowess and achievement orientation than in any ideological fashion. The question of youth-culture styles emerges most clearly when one considers the differences among the value structures of youth and those of the established society. According to Coleman,[15] the values youth develop today are conditioned by circumstances particular to our times; for example, youth are segregated by economic and educational institutions, are outsiders relative to the dominant social institutions, are subordinate and powerless in relation to adults, obtain psychic support from peers that once came from families, and have plenty of spending money and access to a wide range of communication media. Since not all youth develop the same relationship to society, youth-culture styles may vary all the way from the conventional, where youth's values are closely aligned to those of the adult society, to the countercultural, where youth's values may be diametrically opposite to those of adults. Coleman and his colleagues have identified five ways in which youth characteristically respond to the circumstances prevailing in the American society. These responses run through youth cultures in varying degrees of intensity, and it is the pattern by which they come together that culminates in different youth-culture styles. Therefore, let us first consider the five characteristic ways of responding, and second, three probable youth-culture styles—conventional, hedonistic, and countercultural—to which variations in the responses may give rise.

1. *Inward-Lookingness.* Youth today look largely to one another. Their togetherness is enhanced by the prolongation of their education, and they are apart more and more from adults as the latter's work in large organizations increases proportionately. Their friends are other young people and their communications about music, entertainment, clothes, and movies are peer oriented. Many of their families have sufficient money to provide some of it to them to spend on things that they want, and they can purchase records, patronize the pop food chains, buy the clothing and cosmetics that they prefer, and so on. A marketplace of goods and services, provided by young designers, has evolved to serve the young. Their inward-lookingness thus is fostered both by their isolation and the extent to which exercise of purchasing power offers a reinforcing social environment.

2. *Psychic Attachment.* Contemporary society makes attainment of close interpersonal relationships a difficult process. Young people turn to each other much more than they once did. Kinship structure is weakening, and contemporary American families find it hard to provide sufficient psychic

strength for adolescents. Thus psychic need for closeness, intimacy, and attachment must be met from outside. Coleman suggests that as the power of the family to service psychic-attachment needs has diminished, youth have turned to the dating system, communal groups, drugs, and religious movements for solace.

3. *Press for Autonomy.*   This response manifests itself among youth as a high regard for those who successfully challenge adult sanctions or who act autonomously of them. Coleman describes youth as "a subordinate nation," and he says that the young regard peers who stand up ideologically to adults with "a certain amount of respect, awe, and admiration." He also indicates that the proliferation of communication outlets that cater to youth—movies, radio stations, and newspapers—have fueled the rise of youth cultures, because they can widely disseminate ideas that once might have been confined to a small, isolated minority. When television drew the mass audience away from movies in the 1950s, movie makers concentrated on appealing to young people, and films associated with unconventional social causes and mores attracted a great deal of attention. Radio stations also lost their mass audience to television, and station managers began to search for ways to build listeners among adolescents. Many radio stations today are "youth" stations, for example, and play forms of music largely of interest to adolescents. Further, many radio "talk" shows today are youth-oriented, and they deal with issues of interest to youth: drugs, ecology, sexual expression, questions of dress, and problems with police, school, and parents. To a lesser extent youth have also found an outlet for their communications in newsprint. An "underground" press has risen on college campuses and some high schools. High school underground papers usually follow the adult underground press in discussing such concerns as political issues, mood-modifying substances, participation in rock concerts, experimental sexual behavior, meditation, venereal diseases, contraception, and abortion.

4. *Concern for the Underdog.*   Since youth are kept from positions of responsibility and authority, denied admission to the organizations in which adult men and women work, and "brushed aside" into schools "to prepare themselves," Coleman says youth of all social classes are outsiders in society, and a large proportion of them fail to develop sympathy and loyalty for ongoing societal institutions. Many young people acquire instead an intense appreciation for the outside pressures that impinge upon the institutions, that is, for underdog positions and causes, for instance, economic equality for third world countries, social justice for ethnic minorities and women, and opportunity for all to find meaningful work in the corporate structure of society.

5. *Interest in Change.* Youth appear to show a greater interest in social change than do adults. Their posture toward change is closely related to their concern for underdog causes. Being outsiders, they have limited stake in existing social institutions, and thus their support for the status quo is usually at a relatively low ebb. As a consequence, they readily embrace systems that promise to change societal structures in directions that they endorse. Coleman suggests that young people today may be upholding the left dimension of politics more than did the young of some years ago, and adults, to preserve the status quo, may be leaning more to the right.

One may study the question of youth-culture styles in terms of the patterns by which young people adapt as part of their life styles the five elements Coleman has identified.[16] As Table 1 suggests, at least three basic classifications may be differentiated. The young people categorized as "conventional" maintain their ties to the adult world. They may question an issue here and there, but seldom do they renounce their plans for an ordinary adult career. Perhaps these youth participate in the youth culture no more than at the level of assigning their peers to prestige categories. The young people shown in Table 1 as "hedonistic" are those who have come to believe that the structure of the American society will not help them realize their ideals and who reject it as incompatible with their interests. They seek primarily to indulge in the pleasures of society. These youth may indeed turn inward, develop psychic attachments toward peers, and press for autonomy, but they are unlikely to show much concern for either underdog causes or social change. They create a distinct youth-culture style because, in their search for immediate gratification, they deviate from the instrumental work ethic that adults generally expect them to hold. The third group identified in Table 1 as "countercultural" comprises those youth who are not only estranged from society, but who are also working actively to establish a cultural context for themselves that is congruent with their interests and values. Some may seek a more detached and meditative life, others may attempt to create new societies, and others may try to change the aspects of the American society that they find undesirable. They are likely to develop an inward-lookingness, participate in a variety of novel experiments in a search for meaningful psychic attachments, and seek autonomy from the social institutions that they view as oppressing them. They are likely to view themselves as underdogs, support others whom they see in an underdog position, and seek social change rather emphatically.

Table 1 suggests analytically how variations in the five ways youth respond to the circumstances of life may seem to yield three youth-culture styles—conventional, hedonistic, and countercultural. The typology is admittedly crude,

Table 1
Response Patterns in Youth-Culture Styles

Response pattern	Youth-Culture Style		
	Conventional	Hedonistic	Countercultural
1. Inward-lookingness	no	yes	yes
2. Psychic attachment	no	yes	yes
3. Press for autonomy	no	yes	yes
4. Concern for the underdog	no	no	yes
5. Interest in change change	no	no	yes

for actually there are dozens of different ways in which youth-culture styles emerge. The three categories, nonetheless, provide us with a useful framework for looking at youth's activities from three distinct perspectives.

The Conventional Style

A large proportion of adolescents in America are satisfied with their lives. They have found satisfying pathways to adulthood and are happy with the prospects ahead of them. They are reasonably popular with their friends, have few significant conflicts with their parents, and have few serious quarrels with the value system in which they are being socialized. They generally accept work as a principal source of self-esteem and take pride in educational achievement. They accept the instrumental-activism and upward-mobility that dominates so much of American life. An investigation of middle-class youth conducted by Elkin and Westley[17] was one of the first to demonstrate youth's conventionality. The researchers found that adolescents had learned to accept adult guidance and to view immediate activities as instrumental to more remote goals. Elkin and Westley also found that adolescents were neither compulsively rejecting of parental values nor excessively independent of them. Those youth-culture activities that had appeared carefree, irresponsible, and hedonistic revealed (upon close scrutiny) a high degree of sophistication. The young people themselves recognized that "kidding around" represented a temporary, passing phase in their lives.

A decade ago, *Newsweek*[18] reported, after an extensive survey, "What they're really like." It said of adolescents that "a solid majority are builders, not breakers—not hot-headed hoodlums and hoodlettes churning up the drag strips with their hot rods, rolling in the hay, thumbing their noses at organized society and getting blind drunk today in the belief that their tomorrows will run dry. They like it here. They want what the adults want them to want. They are essentially content with their lot. They feel at one with the world today and have little doubt their tomorrows will be even better." Adelson,[19] in an investigation of 3,000 representative young people from 12 to 18, came to virtually the same conclusion. He acknowledged that at the outset he expected to find that adolescence was a period of crisis, upheaval, and radical personality change. He assumed that adolescents' need to disengage themselves from their families and establish autonomy would result in conflict with their parents and perhaps with authority in general. His research was carefully designed to probe the tensions and troubles he expected to find. The data, however, did not confirm these expectations. Questions asked directly, indirectly, and projectively uniformly revealed little serious discord between adolescents and their parents. Although young people's pursuit of autonomy led them to test parental limits and contentions did arise, the conflicts themselves were short-lived. The conflicts generally dealt with rules and restrictions, cars and curfews, or matters of personal style, clothes, and cosmetics; seldom was the legitimacy of parental authority or the values of the larger society challenged. Adelson[20] found that the prevailing ethos in the American family was equalitarian; give-and-take negotiation and compromise prevailed. No one pushed an advantage too hard—concessions were made now in the expectation that reciprocal concessions would be won later. Adelson concluded that for a substantial majority of adolescents there is a continuity in the generations. Their transition is a psychologically conservative one, involving retention of traditional and familiar values and producing no fundamental restructuring of their commitments.

Friedenberg[21] has long believed that so many adolescents are conventional that he has scathingly criticized society for permitting it to happen. He believes that personality development requires a high degree of differentiation; therefore, he feels that it is good for young people to have conflict with the social institutions that hold the keys to adult statuses in order for them to meet the challenges of struggle, to place themselves in perspective, and thus, to develop their full individual identities. Friedenberg deplores the extent to which critical opportunities for self-clarification are manipulated by a bureaucracy insistent on conformity. An elaborate structure of pseudo- and quasi-adult organizations and activities in the school, he says, such as student councils, courts, governments, and world-affairs clubs imposes on adolescents the trappings of an adult milieu, absorbs them in bureaucratic activities, and leads them into modes of adaptation before they have developed a clear self-identity. Friedenberg contends that adolescence should be a period relatively free of adult pressures and responsibilities, a period in which boys and girls can engage in "identity play" and other forms of interpersonal experiments to find out who and what they are.

The Hedonistic Style

Parsons[22] was among the first social scientists to describe hedonism in the youth culture. He contrasted the behavior of young people with that of adult males who had exhibited responsible, professional, and executive achievement (conventional style). He observed that "the youth culture has a strong tendency to develop in directions which are either on the borderline of parental approval or beyond the pale, in such matters as sex behavior, drinking, and various forms of frivolous and irresponsible behavior."[23] Adolescent boys appeared to bask in a "having-a-good-time" kind of irresponsibility and to strive unduly for success in athletics; analogously, girls appeared to exploit the advantages of "glamour-girl" sexual attractiveness. Youth compulsively conformed to peer standards, resisted adult expectations, repudiated adult standards, and failed to develop concern for political affairs. Both the older and the younger generation (but especially the latter) relieved themselves of social pressures and the strain of becoming adults by idealizing "the isolated couple in romantic love," which Parsons[24] defined as "the devotion to expectations unrealistically simplified and idealized with respect to actual situations." Parsons[25] couched his early interpretation of the youth culture in psychoanalytic terms, reasoning that children become highly dependent emotionally on their parents, particularly their mother. The intensity of these attachments is enhanced by the fact of small families, which provide few "objects of cathexis," and by the children's early exposure to competitive pressures outside the family. Then, in adolescence, there is a reaction-formation against these dependency needs, leading young people to compulsively assert their independence and defy adult standards. The focus of dependency needs shifts from parental figures to the peer group so that young people compulsively conform to peer standards. These tensions, coupled with a general tendency to romanticize adult society, lead to the adolescent emphasis on romantic escapades and sexual indulgences. Subsequently, Parsons[26] modified his psychoanalytic interpretation of youth culture. Dependency, he said, develops because parents motivate their children to please them by manipulating their behavior through rewards and withdrawal of love. To this developmental sequence, Parsons added that, concurrently, separate needs for autonomy and independence are being promoted through the demands of society. Not only do school functions maintain their own discipline and reward system, but increasingly, parents are relaxing their restrictions upon children's activities outside the home. During adolescence, then, inasmuch as the socialization practices of adult agencies and parents themselves now strongly encourage the development of individuality, youth may grow rebellious and disdainful of adult customs and lean toward the more hedonistic youth culture.

Parsons' general view received strong support from Coleman[27] who concluded, after analyzing youth-culture activities in ten Illinois high schools, that the values and interests of this culture systematically diverted the students' energies away from academic goals. Coleman found that adolescents cared more about high school status and popularity than academic achievement. Boys were primarily interested in automobiles, sports, and athletic prowess; girls, in beauty, glamour, and attractiveness. Both sexes regarded dating and extracurricular activities as important, but the high school "elites" considered them very, very important. Brains and good grades brought forth few tangible rewards from the peer group. Coleman also found that good grades and concentration on academic work were seen by adolescents as an expression of acquiescence and conformity to adult pressures, but social affairs, extracurricular activities, and athletics reflected frivolous, leisure-oriented values, which the youth felt were their own.

Parsons' analysis of youth-culture hedonism suggests that in this youth-culture style three of the response patterns identified by Coleman are present—inward-lookingness, psychic attachment toward peers, and press for autonomy. The hedonistic youth-culture style is an outgrowth of youth's inability to cope with the strain of moving into adulthood. Although youth may feel thwarted in realizing their ideals, they are not likely to repudiate the social institutions that foster moral values and control access to the world of work. And hedonistic youth probably are too self-serving in outlook to worry much about underdog causes or social change. Indeed, much of the fun-loving, glamorous image youth express may actually be endorsed and supported by the wider adult community. For example, Berger[28] observed that almost all of the values and interests of adolescents, as revealed by Coleman,[29] were derived from and shared by the majority of their parents. The parents were also concerned about prestige and popularity and cared as much as adolescents about masculine prowess, feminine glamour, social activities, sex, wearing the right clothes, and belonging to the right family. Parents had taken over certain adolescent dances, long-hair styles, tight pants, and a dozen other fashions. Avant-garde tastes have reached the adult world both by adolescents who have grown up and by adults who adopted these tastes themselves (and sometimes even originated them); in any event, there is a great deal of continuity between the generations on the status symbols of glamour. Berger[30] points out that social affairs, extracurricular activities, and athletics are initiated and supported by schools, sponsored and run by faculty advisers, coaches, and local advisory groups, and considered by adults to be organized training grounds for the assumption of adult responsibilities. Berger wondered whether the anti-intellectual and hedonistic character of adolescent life should be attributed to autonomous social processes within the young people themselves or to values in the wider culture that they merely reflect.

The Countercultural Style

Modern societies are structured bureaucratically. Most work settings, government agencies, high schools, traditional religious institutions, and forms of entertainment and leisure activities are functions of large organizations. Bureaucratic institutions are forms of organization that attempt to fulfill their aims efficiently. They function as rationally as possible, accommodate a hierarchical status system, operate with formal rules governing relationships and responsibilities, which foster strict affective neutrality among participants, and frequently subordinate individual rights for the greater good of the organization. The growth in bureaucratic control of society has been accompanied by a rise in an "alienating sense of powerlessness experienced by youth."[31] Social scientists at the turn of the century recognized signs of stress among adolescents, but rather than seeing them as an outgrowth of cultural alienation, proclaimed them to be biologically foreordained—an inevitability of growing up. According to the dictates of recapitulation theory, for example, G. Stanley Hall[32] insisted: "at dawning adolescence, this old unity and harmony with nature is broken up; the child is driven from his paradise and must enter upon a long viaticum of ascent, must conquer a higher kingdom of man for himself, break out of a new sphere, and evolve a more modern story to his psychophysical nature." Contemporary researchers, in contrast, are inclined to explain youth's disquiet in terms of their effort to find self-fulfillment and personal expression in the face of the imposition of technology on their personal lives.[33]

At the core of the counterculture value structure is a strong belief in equality and justice. Individuals committed to the counterculture may create identity crises for themselves in coming to terms with the bureaucratic practices that weaken or threaten these values.[34] Countercultural values are, above all, liberating. They stress raising personal states of consciousness—feelings, beliefs, interests, talents—whatever is most meaningful for the individual. According to Light and Laufer, "a fulfillment ethic is replacing the puritan work ethic, which makes a virtue out of any kind of work. The counterculture value structure insists that work and marriage, for example, become means of self-exploration. Thus, the new culture has created lifestyles that lend support to those who do not wish to work at a desk, get married, buy a house in a community mostly of strangers, and settle down."[35]

Distler[36] has provided a useful nomenclature for distinguishing between traditional American values and those of the counterculture. He points to a shift from a "patristic" to a "matristic" value system. The former refers to socialization for instrumental roles, including achievement, goal directedness, delay of gratification, rationality, autonomy, and individual responsibility as the cultural ideal for both sexes, but especially males. It includes a prestigious vocational choice and excellent school performance as important sources of self-worth. Morality is based on either social or religious authority, and self-control of impulses is rewarded. Artistic expression in music, literature, and fine arts is valued more for the quality of the product than the creativity. Participation in social and religious activities is valued more as an opportunity to acquire status and fulfill social responsibilities than to satisfy affiliative needs. Youth's answer to these bureaucratic, instrumental roles is an emerging matristic culture, which values expressive roles, including feelings, intimacy, sensory experiences, and self-exploration. It represents a diminished emphasis on instrumental goals. Meaningfulness has more to do with being than with doing or becoming; the here-and-now is more important than the future. Spontaneity is esteemed and artistic activity is viewed as a process of sharing and participation, which is more valued than the final product. Morality is personal and relativistic; authority largely comes from personal conviction and not from institutions. There is an affinity for the mystical, transcendental, and existential. "Such traditionally maternal attributes as nurturance, succorance, affiliation, and the desire for close personal relationships are valued over such attributes as endurance, order, autonomy, and independence."[37]

Wieder and Zimmerman[38] studied recently the emergence of "freak culture" within the present generation of middle-class youth, and their data provide empirical support for the main points of Distler's distinction between "patristic" and "matristic" value structures. The researchers studied the life styles of a settlement of former college students who were living on the California coast. The youth were in the process of forging identities for themselves apart from their families and familiar societal props, and were formulating and living out new conceptions of work, consumption, and achievement. Wieder and Zimmerman suggest that they were trying to evolve a social structure that would enable them to ignore in their life styles the biological fact that they were aging. Although not necessarily youthful in age, through participation in their culture, they retained a youthful social position from both their perspective and that of the established society. Wieder and Zimmerman view the life styles of these young people, who called themselves "freaks," as constituting a sharply differentiated reaction (matristic) within the counterculture to the conditions imposed on them by a bureaucratic (patristic) society.

Freak culture rejects conventional attitudes toward financial and occupational success. The freak culture point of view holds that the future should be free and unconstricting—unplanned—and thereby open to whatever each successive "present moment" offers. Freaks place high ideological valuation on spontaneity and open-endedness and try consciously to "turn middle-class standards on their heads, e.g., in 'freaky' dress and hair, highly expressive speech, and unconventional living arrangements."[39] In general, freaks reject the use of cosmetics, perfumes, and deodorants as "corrupt artifices." They value naturalness, including body odors. They view the use of underwear as a useless custom, and they seek to break down inhibitions concerning nudity, and practice nudity in both private and public places. A good life in the freak culture thus is one in which a pleasurable relationship between self and environment emerges. Freaks insist that it is virtuous to seek continuous satisfaction, and no one should suffer in order to enjoy. They observe that "the important satisfactions are basic, direct, readily at hand, and inexpensive, e.g., food, sex, affection, and the somewhat less basic but still direct, readily at hand, and inexpensive pleasures of dope, watching a sunset, making music, or engaging in a craft."[40] It is noteworthy, however, that the use of psychoactive drugs was not critical to participating in the freak culture—many freaks are involved in "meditation" or other activities that prohibit the use of drugs.

Freaks are especially contemptuous of concern for property. They disdain the notion that ownership and career achievement are measures of moral worth, and they avoid the acquisition of property. They devalue property on practical grounds as well, for they say that to accumulate it requires commitment to the system and to possess it restricts one's mobility and undermines control of one's time. Freaks "get by" through marginal jobs. Some of these are low-status, undemanding, part-time jobs, others are part- and full-time jobs in making crafts. Sometimes freaks "get by" through illegal or unrespectable pursuits like selling drugs. A few rely on the good graces of other freaks in order to "get by," which "means augmenting their resources through panhandling, hitchhiking, welfare programs, parental largesse, generous and more economically secure friends, and the like."[41] Freaks have no moral qualms about these matters and feel that it is as proper to receive as to give. Freaks "get by" on very little, but they do not experience their deprivation as failure to succeed. They reject middle-class standards of consumption, and they do not experience disinterest in living up to these standards as degrading.

Countercultural Religiosity among Youth.   Religiosity functions in several ways to reinforce one's moral convictions. Rohrbaugh and Jessor[42] point out that participation in religious rituals and observances encompasses one in an organized network of supportive sanctions, religious teachings socialize concern and awareness of moral issues and standards of appropriate conduct, religious ideology such as anticipation of God's wrath serves as a deterrent to transgression and affects one's commitment to given courses of action, and a devoutness or reverence generated by religious experience engenders an obedience orientation to established authority. Traditionally, young people who have been high in religiosity, whatever their denominational affiliation, whether fundamental or liberal, have tended to be relatively conservative—they embrace social contexts that minimize opportunity for departure from conventional norms, adapt values that sustain conformity, avoid self-assertion and autonomy, and seek to conserve existing social institutions.[43]

A very different kind of religious sensibility has emerged in the lives of many American young people during the past decade. The "new" religiosity has been described variously as a "New Reformation," a "New Spiritualism," or a "New Mysticism." It has a number of different manifestations—meditation, mystical experience, and participation in countercultural spiritual groups like the Children of God Sect, the Unification Church, the Divine Light Mission, and the Hare Krishna movement. These countercultural spiritual groups share in common with the wider counterculture a "vision of a highly personalistic, experiential, communally oriented society replacing a bureaucratic or technocratic one."[44] They are basically "attempts at establishing religious communities as alternatives to the established churches and synagogues, which are seen as 'dead, hypocritical things.'"[45] Many feel that the traditional churches have sold out their simple faith for the pleasures of an industrial society. According to Graham,[46] countercultural religious youth see their perceptions systematically ignored, view the universe as cold and meaningless, and regard "dropping out" as being their only alternative. The countercultural spiritual groups have become answers to this emptiness. Consider, for example, the following four contemporary spiritual movements. These contemporary manifestations of religiosity have provided youth a unifying experience, a focus for their lives, and an opportunity to acquire new values. The ritual procedures of each produce and reinforce a sense of social "belongingness" to a group not part of the mainstream culture.

1. *The Children of God* is a highly secretive sect that demands total devotion from its members who are militantly antagonistic toward established society and who regard themselves as the enlightened "children of God." The sect was founded in 1968; it sponsors self-sufficient communes in which the lives of the converts are wholly regimented. They are segregated rigidly from

society, renounce their families and material possessions, take on biblical names, and follow monastic schedules.

2. *The Unification Church* is a highly ascetical sect whose members are opposed to free love, alcohol, and drugs. The hard-core devotees live in communes, proselytize on street corners, sell flowers to raise money, relinquish their savings and personal property, and even permit the founder of the sect, Rev. Sun Myung Moon, a Korean evangelist, to select their marriage partners. Rev. Moon teaches that Christ will come again, take a bride, and father a blessed race. Rev. Moon is believed to have come as a spiritual father and to be an individual through whom God speaks.

3. *The Divine Light Mission* is an Indian sect led by Guru Maharaji Ji, who is compared by his followers with Jesus, Buddha, and Krishna. He is called the Perfect Master of the mission, which was founded by his father in India. He has promised to reveal God and establish world peace. The mission claims about a half-million followers in America, and eight million in India. Many of the devotees live in ashrams—communes for celebate living and meditation. The disciples must meditate in order to receive knowledge and practice tongue contortion and eyeball pressure to taste "Divine Nectar" and see "Divine Light."

4. *Hare Krishna* is a sect that is part of the international society for Krishna Consciousness. "Krishna" means Supreme Being in Sanskrit and followers believe that they can achieve ecstasy by leading an ascetic life, swaying and chanting "Hare Krishna." The members believe that salvation or Krishna consciousness comes not through thinking, but through the senses, and devotees frequently dance and chant themselves into trances. It is a strictly disciplined monastic order, and many of the members are segregated in temples which totally organize their lives, although there are "householders" who live outside the temple and hold conventional jobs. The followers with their shaven heads and pigtails are a familiar sight on many street corners, airports, and subways, where they sell flowers and seek donations for their cause.

The involvement of young people in countercultural religious movements is generally viewed as substantially more socially legitimate than being into either "drug abuse" or political radicalism. As Graham[47] observes, ascetical renunciation of sex, glamour, and drugs purchase credibility for the basic countercultural values. Furthermore, to the extent youth's sensibilities become wholly consumed in spiritual activities, interest diminishes in political protest and social reform.[48] Nonetheless, countercultural religious movements in general fail to address themselves significantly to problems concerning modern society. The commit-

These young people cope with modern complexities through spiritual asceticism.

ments of countercultural religious youth "seem to be made in tentative, explora-
tory, experimental ways, and to lack the sense of dedicated permanence of the
early Christian apostles."[49] The members seem unconcerned about working out
the complex cosmological, theological, and ethical issues that would result in
improving the social conditions that have alienated them, and the elements of
the movement do not appear sufficiently viable to penetrate the dogma of
established religions. Carroll[50] also suggests that countercultural religiosity may
be both unrealistic and irresponsible. He says that glossing over societal problems while longing to relive some form of paradise ignores the complexity of life
in the modern world. Carroll[51] characterizes countercultural religious youth as
being vulnerable to a particular form of escapism, which leads them to avoid
critical analysis and socially responsible action—it leads them instead to be
concerned primarily with individual transcendence—the naive belief that if individuals change, social problems will somehow go away.

Why Countercultural Generation Gaps?   Two major models or explanations have been advanced by sociologists to account for the rise of countercultural
orientations. Each starts from the basic assumption that young people engender
some degree of social stress in their transition to adulthood. The first model
views the social disequilibrium as occurring in a relatively stabilized,
well-organized, industrialized society. It has been labeled the "structural-

functionalist" model, and it presumes that youth give rise to generation gaps because they perceive that they have only limited opportunity to attain the perquisites of the adult world and they are reacting against the social forces that impede them. This perspective suggests that youth find no major contradictions in the adult society; rather, they want to redress social inequities, promote egalitarian ideals, and distribute the resources of society fairly. Although young people often indulge in threatening rhetoric and sometimes appear to hold values sharply deviant from those of the established society, from the perspective of the structural-functionalist model, their primary goals are maintaining and distributing the resources of society.[52] Consequently, from this viewpoint, generation gaps should be regarded as pseudo-countercultures, in the sense that youth are not represented as advocating new value structures. The functionalist model implies, for example, that the effort of black, chicano, native-American, and other ethnic minority young people to realize their aspirations is primarily an effort to participate in "the dominant social order and share in the technology and affluence of the privileged classes or elites."[53] The conflict experienced by these young people may be characterized, not by their search for a new, synthesized responsiveness in society, but by their "feeling of inadequacy, alienation, and search for structural or institutional order and closure."[54]

The second model views young people less as rebelling against society than as creating new forms of consciousness. This model, usually identified as Mannheim's generational unit model, suggests that as a consequence of biological, social, and cultural forces operating at a particular moment in history, youth may coalesce as a unique generational unit and exert pressure for change on the relatively stable structures of society. The model presumes that a society, like an organic being, (1) will grow over time and in the process will experience continuous tension between the forces of stability and change and (2) will progress toward higher and more sophisticated forms of social organization and integration. Countercultural movements are thus very real from the perspective of the generational unit model. They represent "destabilizing forces within society" and "the newer units represent the vanguard or 'cutting edge'" of different expectations of the future.[55]

Let us now consider how each model describes the development of youth's estrangement:

1. *The Structural-Functionalist Model.* The structural-functionalist model suggests that youth cultures reflect generational alienation as a consequence of efforts of youth to integrate themselves into the mainstream of society and to achieve parity with adults.[56] Youth are expected to hold "rightful expectations to succeed the parental generation."[57] They "wish to enter and

celebrate society rather than destroy it."[58] The problem is that complex, impersonal forces may pull youth apart from the wider society and its structure may become nonfunctional for them. According to Eisenstadt,[59] the principal architect of the structural-functionalist model, the rise of youth-culture consciousness occurs in societies where the division of labor isolates youth from participating in meaningful roles, and, eventually, when they are admitted as young adults to responsible roles, increasing age is unrelated to attainment of progressively greater responsibilities. When the division of labor is simple, as in preindustrial societies, where physical vigor and seniority largely determine social, economic, and political role assignments, a great deal of symmetry exists between age and the functions of the total society. The degree to which all age groups participate in ceremonial and communal activities is well delineated and the prevailing role clarity facilitates the transition of individuals both into responsible work roles and from one age group to another. In contemporary, technological societies, however, adolescents are unable to participate in the work force as readily as they might wish. Wealth, acquired skills, specialization, and knowledge determine role allocations, and smooth transition to responsible, fulfilling roles becomes problematical.

The problem is made worse when parents push their children to learn professional skills requiring commitment to long-range goals but are unable to prepare them adequately to achieve the goals.[60] Few adolescents are able to learn exclusively from their families the competitive prowess, poise, and self-assurance that they need for acquiring desirable adult perquisites and privileges. Educational, religious, economic, and political functions have been increasingly assumed by outside institutions, and the relative decline of the family's influence (especially since it no longer includes grandparents, uncles, and aunts) has constricted its significance in assisting youth make the transition to adulthood.[61] These circumstances may lead adolescents to turn to peers who can help them develop and crystallize their identity, attain personal autonomy, and facilitate their transition to adulthood. In the struggle to achieve and preserve peer-status, however, adolescents easily slip under the tyranny of peer pressures.[62] The youth-culture orientation suggested by the structural-functionalist perspective thus appears more hedonistic than countercultural, since the young people are seen more as rebelling than as creating new values.

2. *Mannheim's Generational Unit Model.* The generational unit model looks more to youth's "emerging consciousness" than to "lack of social integration" to explain the rise of generation gaps. Mannheim presents a dynamic, evolutionary image of culture, for he assumes that emerging forces give birth

over time to new forms of social organization. As Buss[63] interprets Mannheim, "each successive biological generation (continuously emerging and therefore aging) comes into contact anew with the existent cultural heritage. Each new generation interprets reality without the years of commitment to a previous ideology and thereby transforms that reality." The generational unit model attributes youth-culture generation gaps

"to youth's reaction to the major issues and contradictions that exist in modern society. Youth groups take sides and mobilize over issues like their parents before them, but unlike their parents and because of their fresh contact, they are more attuned to the current issues that confront their generation. When the contradictions are historically new (women's rights, minority rights, ecology), when they appear to be anchored in the future rather than the present, when adults are more committed to the past and when future interests cross-cut the old conflict of interests, there is a greater probability that society will experience youth dissent."[64]

Mannheim refers to a generational unit as a group of contemporaries that attempts to integrate economic, political, and moral values into an outlook that will help it realize a common destiny. A generational unit, then, is somewhat comparable to a social class in that its members are similarly located in respect to the social, political, and economic power structure.

Mannheim also distinguishes between "actual" and "potential" generational units. Braungart[65] points out that membership in a particular social-historical community is a crucial ingredient for generational location and solidarity. A generational unit thus emerges only when a psychosocial bond is created among its members as a consequence of exposure to similar social forces. Mannheim suggests that whereas isolated, rural youth may have the potential for experiencing youth-culture solidarity, they rarely become involved in youth-culture movements because they are seldom able to coalesce as a unit and thereby influence the "dynamic destabilization" of society. The structure and content of each generational unit depends on the collective values and goals to which its members subscribe. It is possible, therefore, that youth who encounter the same historical problems, and who may be said to be part of the same generation, will, nonetheless, constitute separate generational units, and thus, evolve different outlooks, life styles, and countercultural values.[66] According to Braungart,[67] relative "stabilization of experience" is the critical factor that determines whether competing generational units arise within a given biological generation.

Popular Music and Youth-Culture Styles

During the past quarter of a century, a significant rise has occurred in the relevance of popular music to young people, whatever their youth-culture orientation—conventional, hedonistic, or countercultural. From the birth of the phonograph around the turn of the century until the explosion in electronic technology following World War II, popular music was geared to the tastes of urban, upper-middle-class adults. Manhattan and Hollywood professionals controlled the recording radio-musical market. Only a few recording firms possessed the technical sophistication necessary to produce the 78 rpm records, which constituted the only means of production for decades. Each firm employed "house stars" who recorded a steady stream of "smoothly-crafted" bland, "moon-June-spoon" songs.[68] Jerome Kern, George Gershwin, and Cole Porter dominated the popular music world and monopolistic practices coupled with cumbersome, expensive production procedures effectively stifled any thoughts of expansion. Television drew away from radio much of the adult audience in the early 1950s, and radio programmers began to seek new markets in the youth population, which was beginning to accelerate swiftly as a consequence of the postwar baby boom. The major radio networks were dismantled; many of the high-powered stations became "independent," and these stations, to modify their programming to accommodate the emerging youth audience, created the "top-40" format.[69]

The market appeal to youth was augmented also by technical advances in the electronic industry. The youth market burgeoned in the late 1950s with the introduction of the cheap, highly portable transistor radio and the stereo tape deck, which became especially popular as an automobile accessory. Perhaps the most significant of the technical advances was the early development of the tape recorder, which was followed a decade later by cartridge and cassette tape equipment. The tape recording devices made the initial task of recording a performer readily accessible to small producers.[70] They also signaled the death knell for the big bands of the 1930s and 1940s, since the big band effect could be achieved by fusing parallel tapings into one big production.[71] The slower-speed, microgroove vinyl records were introduced about the same time as the tape recorder. The new records were a vast improvement in audiofidelity, durability, and convenience over the 78 rpm records, and a speed battle endured for several years over the relative merits of 33 rpm and 45 rpm discs. The former eventually was established as a multiple-record LP, while the 45 rpm became popular as a "single" disc.[72] Suddenly, it was possible for small recording companies, with very little investment, to record performances, and even press their own discs.[73] Recording companies thus proliferated, and by the early 1960s there were hundreds of them vying for a share of the market. Styles and subject matter expanded immensely. Instrumentation became more varied, and overdubbing, multitrack recording, and mixing became routine. All in all, the advanced techniques made possible a variety of new effects, which resulted in increasingly sophisticated and intricate forms of music.

The trend of popular music toward youth's tastes and the technological advances in electronics led particularly to a new form of musical expression called rock, or rock and roll. Harmon[74] likens rock music, with its powerful beat, to good poetry, which because of its nonspecific nature, is open to a multitude of interpretations. One person will not necessarily hear what another hears in a piece of rock music. The "meaning" or "message" may be triggered by a word, phrase, chord, or even a combination of sounds. Moreover, such triggering may be idiosyncratic to the listener and the "meaning" may not lend itself to verbal description. Harmon also points out that a particular song may induce responses in individuals that range from negligible ("yeah, I heard it but it doesn't do anything for me") to intense ("oh, wow, dig that"). He suggests that the more intense emotional responses may serve to weaken or reinforce attitudes, depending on the inclinations of the listeners. Finally, Harmon says that the lyrics of rock need not necessarily be heard in their entirety, for the image stimulates "full meaning" in the listeners. Indeed, for some young people, the music alone constitutes the message. In such instances, it makes little difference whether lyrics are absent or present to "anticipate" an image.

The beat and rhythm of rock music requires of listeners an intense level of concentration.[75] The rise in the significance of popular music to youth, however, has also resulted in emphasis on lyric themes. The meaning of these themes is much more explicit. Much of the popular music before 1955 was dubbed "easy listening" and was recorded for adults, but it has been replaced today by a new kind of formula music, sometimes called "bubble-gum" or "aural wallpaper," which is primarily for adolescents.[76] This particular variety of popular music produces an interesting and "meaningful" lyric that can be listened to, thought about, experienced, and perhaps discussed with friends. It is in considerable demand as a pleasant background to such activities as working around the house or studying; however, whether it is helpful in such circumstances is questionable, for one recent investigation has shown that listening to the "top-40" seemingly interferes with youth's study of school subjects.[77]

Kantor[78] analyzed the lyric themes of 772 popular songs between 1955 and 1972, and he found that drug usage and protest songs, which first appeared about 1964, rose in the 1970s to account for 7 percent of the lyrics. (The airplay of drug-related songs has been drastically reduced since the Federal Communications Commission in 1971 questioned their acceptability.) Religious songs pertaining to the new spiritual movements encompassed 1 percent of the popular music in the 1960s and 17 percent in the 1970s. Approximately 15 percent of the songs Kantor compared contained slurred or undecipherable lyrics. Most of the popular songs that he studied, however, nearly three-fourths of them between 1955 and 1969 and two-thirds between 1970 and 1972, dealt with romantic love and courtship. Further, the message content of these popular love songs today depicts courtship more dynamically than it did during the 1950s.[79] Lyrics during the 1950s described love as being in the hands of fate. Romance was a matter of waiting for a lasting, ideal love relationship to "happen."[80] Love often was depicted as an externally controlled commodity over which the lovers had little influence—whether partners fell in love was attributed to good luck and whether their love was stolen away from them was a matter of inescapable misfortune. But by the mid-1960s, romantic love songs were reflecting the reality of current patterns of heterosexual relations—the new music emphasized that the affair was actively sought by both partners. And the basis for the romantic liaison had changed, too. Both partners prized their freedom; neither expected the affair to be permanent, and neither regarded a deep sense of romantic love as being a strong requirement for engaging in an active sexual relationship.[81] The message of romantic popular songs thus had become more "sensual, direct, sexual, and 'gutsy.'"[82]

Although youth-oriented popular songs are more realistic today in portraying boy-girl relations, their lyric themes are derived from an underlying range of basic emotions that are fairly timeless relative to romantic settings. These emotions are associated with loneliness, adoration, separation, loss of love, and so forth. A content analysis of 660 songs selected randomly from the "popular" file of an independent, Midwestern radio station identified the following nine emotions that appear frequently in the lyrics of youth-oriented music.[83] Lyrics in popular songs express these emotional themes over and over again in a countless variety of romantic settings, and thereby, youth who listen to them learn how other persons do in fact feel when they are alone, saddened, or exhilarated. The themes have long served to help youth learn of the emotions that they should expect in others and of how others might be expected to respond to them when they are experiencing a particularly deep emotional reaction. Young people thus learn to interpret emotional arousal and to ascribe meaning to the experience.[84]

1. *Loneliness*—the feelings of a boy or girl who is unsuccessful in finding a boyfriend or girlfriend. The inability to participate emotionally in heterosexual relationships is sometimes explained by shyness, lack of sophistication, or bad luck.
2. *Adoration*—love or adulation for a specific member of the opposite sex pre-

dominates. Adoration songs usually include exaggerated descriptions of desirability, beauty, or handsomeness; the love expressed is happy, and it is often seen as reciprocated.

3. *Disruption*—emotions that arise from the permanent dissolution of relations with a specific member of the opposite sex. Songs encompassing the disruption theme usually express extreme unhappiness, abject loneliness, fantasy, revery of past happiness, and jealousy.

4. *Pleading*—a member of the opposite sex is implored to be faithful or to reciprocate love. Feelings such as adoration, surrender, impotence, and masochism often accompany the pleading.

5. *Lovelife*—a general expression, usually in personal terms, of the pleasure and pains of love. Lovelife songs may present the facts of social life or give advice to the socially unskilled.

6. *Independence*—the individual's ability to achieve status by his or her own initiative and fortitude is stressed. This includes:

   (a) Songs about a hero who displays courage, physical strength, or, occasionally, wisdom;

   (b) Songs that describe a teenager who has become successful among his or her peers;

   (c) Songs that stress a teenager's resolution to be strong in the face of frustration, such as the impending loss of a boyfriend or girlfriend.

7. *Misunderstanding*—feelings of a boy or girl who finds little sympathy in an adult world but gains solace when peer relations are described. Exclusion from the adult world results from having lower social-class standing, breaking adult rules, simply being a teenager, and so forth.

8. *Death or mutilation*—either the death or the mutilation of a loved one is romanticized. Remorse, grief, and guilt are the chief emotions expressed.

9. *Aphrodisiac*—a hard-driving, frenzied sound or seductive background is featured, accompanied by shouting or other meaningless vocalizations which tend to be sexually stimulating.

The formula music prepared for young people clearly is geared to their interests, and economics determine its content.[85] Nothing is produced unless it is marketable. Creators and producers thus, in an effort to maximize sales, attempt to mirror the concerns and preferences of their listeners and try to find "meaningful" lyric themes which evoke experiences of significance to them. They are unable, however, to control the destiny of their creations. The "cultural gatekeepers" in the recording industry are highly problematic individuals.[86] On the one hand, radio program directors determine which records will be aired, and given the "top-40" format, their choices generally involve 30 to 40 songs per week. Depending on the fluctuations in the charts, new records selected for play each week range from two to four. The choice of these is made from approximately 150 to 200 recordings released each week. Obviously, very few reach the public, and the judgment of the program director determines those that do. On the other hand, record reviewers, who write critiques of newly released recordings for music publications, perform a role similar to that of radio program directors. The reviewer tends to stick to established performers and groups since coverage about known acts is more likely to be published.

PATTERNS OF PEER INTERACTION

Youth's learning experiences among their peers furnish them with their first measure of independence from adults. Peers facilitate young people's transition from reliance on their families to relative freedom in adolescence and new patterns of responsibility in adulthood. Their families can provide only a small range of role-participation opportunities, but peer interaction offers them trial runs in preparing themselves for places in the social structure. In the first place, adolescents can see how their friends are responding to their own parents' demands. They can also examine the status and reward system of youth cultures and decide how much they wish to uphold their values and relationships. The peer group allows each adolescent opportunity to assume a variety of roles—to be temporarily a leader or follower, a deviant or conformist. The values and behavioral norms of the peer group permit adolescents to acquire some perspective on their own values and attitudes. Untested social skills can be tried and modified, and impractical aspirations can be changed. Once adolescents identify with the values of a given peer group, it becomes a reference point for their behavior. It enforces conformity to its definition of appropriate activities and norms. Over the course of time, satisfying experiences with peers contribute to the development of a firm self-identity, whereas unsatisfactory experiences may precipitate identity crises.

Cliques and Crowds

The specific values and norms of the majority of peer groups are usually remote from school objectives. They are, however, avowedly central to the improvement of heterosexual prowess. During adolescence, as at no other time in life, there is a tremendous increase in the volume of heterosexual social relationships. Whether or not adolescents belong to a peer group, their lives are affected by one, either by the advantages inclusion provides or by the disadvantages that exclusion fosters. As Schwartz and Merten[87] underscore, achieving the personal qualities that make a male admirable and a female desirable are

Cliques and crowds are fun and rewarding except for the young people who are left out.

the prime objectives of participating in the youth culture. The development for this explicit purpose of two closely related peer groups, the *clique* and the *crowd,* has been carefully analyzed by Dunphy.[88] Since his masterful investigation has contributed a great deal to understanding adolescent peer groups, it is reviewed in detail here.

Dunphy made his initial contacts with adolescents in Sydney, Australia, through institutions; then, after establishing rapport, he began to work with them informally. He spent hours on street corners and beaches, at homes, and at parties. The youth were informed that he was investigating their grouping patterns and agreed to cooperate. Questionnaires were administered to all the participants; the majority were also interviewed at length, and diaries were kept concurrently by members of each group. Dunphy distinguished two kinds of peer groups—the clique and the crowd—which differed by size rather than by internal structure or function. The clique is the smaller, more cohesive unit. The crowd is the largest adolescent peer group and is usually made up of a cluster of cliques. His investigation included 44 cliques, ranging in size from 3 to 9 members, with an average membership of 6.2. Twelve crowds were studied, ranging from 15 to 30 members, with an average size of 20.2. The crowds were about three times the size of cliques, and were made up of between two and four of them. None of the groups had memberships ranging from 10 to 14 persons, which suggests that groups of this size are conducive to development of neither cliques nor crowds.

The intimacy and cohesiveness necessary for a clique appeared to be reached with an upper limit of about 9 members. The cliques of younger adolescents were made up of either boys or girls of similar age and social maturity. The cliques of older adolescents, however, were heterosexual, and the boys tended to be between 3 months and 22 months older than the girls; the average was about 10 months older. Residential proximity was a major criterion of membership. In certain suburbs, there were two or three crowds whose members were of similar peer status and age. The age differences between adjacent crowds varied from seven months to three years, with the average being about two years. The extent to which crowds shared the same social activities varied according to the difference between the mean age of their members. All of the crowds were heterosexual, and in all of them (as in cliques) the boys averaged about 10 months older than the girls. The upper peer-status members of a younger crowd tended to hold lower status positions in the adjacent older crowd. Within a crowd, the "real buddies" were those who retained their clique identity. Many of the youth who belonged to a clique were not in a crowd, but no one belonged to a crowd who lacked clique membership.

The two groups served different purposes for their members. Clique activities largely focused on talking, which provided an important instrumental function in preparing clique members for crowd activities and disseminating information about crowds, enabling clique members to evaluate crowd events. The crowd was the center of larger, more organized heterosexual social activities, such as parties and dances. Most important, it offered a pool of acceptable young people who could be drawn on for various social activities. There was a tendency for clique and crowd activities to be distributed differently throughout the week. For example, Dunphy's[89] analyses showed that there were 25 crowd activities during the weekend; on the other hand, there were 47 clique events during the week and only 22 on the weekend. Weekends appeared to be for crowds; weekdays for cliques.

Dunphy said that the boundaries of the peer groups were clearly defined and adherence to them served as a form of social control; however, establishing these boundaries was a ceaseless process. Decisions always had to be made as to who would be invited to parties. The crowd boundaries were more sharply defined than those of cliques. When young people were asked to choose others to join them in various activities, fewer than 10 percent of the choices were outside the crowd. The majority of choices were made within the respondent's own clique; but about half were outside the clique yet were within the same crowd. Thus, cliques in the same crowd tended to stay together for various activities, but the boundaries between cliques were not strictly enforced. Adolescents who did not belong to a component clique were not accepted by a crowd, even if they attempted to relate themselves to it.

Individuals passed from the outside through a clique boundary by means of achievement and conformity. They had to push themselves forward and "fit in." "'Someone who gets in and pushes, gets into a group easiest. You just have to get in and push. People who stand back just don't make the grade'. . . . 'All groups have a certain temperament of their own. Anyone new has to fit in; he must have similar aspects and outlooks and like similar things.'"[90] As Dunphy pointed out: "The basic consensus of values which results is a major factor in the strong *esprit de corps* of most adolescent peer groups." Just as entrance to a peer group depends on achievement and conformity, failure in these respects may mean exclusion from the group. Adolescents could lose their status and eventually their membership by failing to maintain heterosexual achievements at the level of their peers. They could also be ostracized if they rejected the authority of the group, regarded themselves as superior to others, or viewed their judgment as better than that of others.

Although many of the respondents claimed that their peer groups were leaderless, Dunphy found that one individual in each group, usually a male, appeared to play an important and distinctive role in relating it to the larger society. Indeed, cliques were referred to by the name of one person, for example, "John Palmer's group." The clique leaders were "group representatives," had more frequent contact with others outside the clique, and thus were more socially mobile than their followers. The strategic role of the clique leader made him the best informed person in the smaller group about events transpiring in the crowd. He had "to play an advanced heterosexual role since the crowd is essentially a heterosexual association."[91] He was expected to date more often, to go steady, and to form a steady relationship earlier than the other members of his clique. The leaders constituted an elite corps who served as confidants, models, and sources of pressure on other clique members to advance to more sophisticated levels of heterosexual development. Clique leaders were better informed than their followers about what was going on in the crowd because they participated in crowd decision making. Among the clique leaders a crowd leader emerged as the coordinator of its social structure. His presence assured the success of a crowd activity. This leader was always a male, and he was usually the leader of the largest and most heterosexually advanced clique in the crowd. Dunphy also noted that, whereas the crowd leader performed a functional (or instrumental) role, another adolescent, a specialist in humor, performed an expressive role. This position existed in every crowd, and the incumbent was always popular, well-liked, and the most extroverted member of the crowd. He dominated crowd gatherings with his witticisms and jokes. The attention he received frequently caused adults to mistake him for the leader and thus see the group as frivolous in character.

In Figure 2, Dunphy[92] has abstracted an "ideal-type," illustrating the structural development of cliques and crowds. Each of the five stages from early to late adolescence is marked by age variations; however, the pattern of social development is relatively uniform. Stage 1 shows that the younger peer groups are comprised of either boys or girls and that their activities do not include heterosexual social relationships. During Stage 2 cliques of boys and girls begin to participate in activities together. At this stage such interaction is regarded as daring and takes place only in settings where adolescents can be supported by the presence of members of their own clique. This initial interaction is often "superficially antagonistic." At Stage 3 the heterosexual clique emerges. The upper status members of the unisexual cliques initiate heterosexual relationships on a person-to-person basis. Young people begin to date; if the clique leaders demonstrate an aggressive attitude toward the opposite sex, they may lose their leadership at Stage 3 (although such behavior might have been admired at Stage 2). Adolescents who belong to the emergent heterosexual groups continue as members of their unisexual clique. Heterosexual activities lead to an extensive transformation of the peer groups; at Stage 4 heterosexual cliques exist as small intimate groups and are closely associated with other cliques as a crowd. At Stage 5, when most members are engaged or going steady, the crowd slowly disintegrates. Figure 2 shows that the crowd offers the adolescent opportunity to develop appropriate heterosexual role behavior. According to Dunphy, the crowd consolidates the heterosexual learning appropriate to each stage of development.

The High School Sorority: A "Formal" Peer Group. Marriage has traditionally been a more important determinant of social status for a girl than for a boy; hence, adults have actively formalized certain social practices and peer groups to ensure that girls' heterosexual experiences will prepare them for the "best" possible marriage. The modern social event known as the debut represents a significant ritual for a girl who is conscious of her social status. It is the culmination of her socialization to elitism.[93] Her "coming out" is the result of long years of preparation. Indeed, Knudsen holds that the most significant factor in producing a debutante is the persistent effort of her parents. The "debutante-producing environment" includes upper-status nursery schools, dancing classes, elite boarding schools, and exclusive junior colleges. In such settings the daughters of upper-class and nouveau riche families become familiar

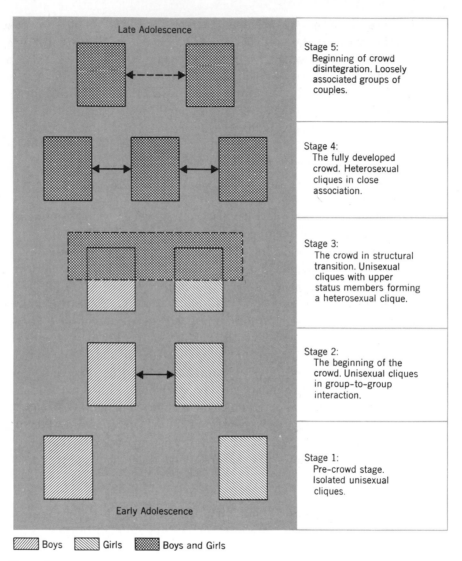

Figure 2
Stages of group development in adolescence. (From Dunphy, see text. Reprinted by permission.)

with the customs and attitudes of persons with high status. The debut is a *rite de passage* into adulthood, providing a context for introducing the young lady to eligible young men. More important than this, according to Knudsen, is that the debut acknowledges that the girl is a "marriageable young woman of high status." In Knudsen's view, the debut is part of a strategy to help solve the marriage problem for women whose pool of upper-class potential husbands is being decreased by the tendency of these males to marry girls of lower social class.

The fervor with which parents promote their daughters' debut is matched by parents who support their daughters' participation in sororities. Many debutantes join sororities, but only a minority of sorority members are debutantes. According to Scott[94] the sorority exerts control over the heterosexual interests, and ultimately marital arrangements, of the young girl out of reach of direct family control. The sorority wards off boys of dubious wealth and ethnic background, facilitates upward movement for middle-status girls, and promotes interaction between boys and girls of comparable status.

Organizations that resemble college sororities began to appear at the high school level about 1890.[95] The high school sorority is usually structured to enhance the adolescent girl's status and heterosexual prowess. Whereas college administrators have joined with parents in fostering a strong sorority system at the college level (perhaps because of its value in the mate-selection process), high school administrators have generally opposed sororities for their students. They feel that the high school should uphold egalitarian ideals and teach democratic principles, and they view sororities as elitist. Moreover, high school students have less experience in social competition and cannot easily cope with the pressures associated with either membership or nonmembership in a sorority or fraternity. Consequently, about half the states have outlawed membership in any secret society in the public schools.[96] The principle of egalitarianism, however, has been subverted readily by the elevation of officially sanctioned, "service" clubs to more significant standing in the prestige hierarchy. Figure 1 shows the service clubs to be "low" relative to achievement criteria; however, such organizations have risen in standing over the past quarter-century as a consequence of the official extinction of high school sororities. The service club-bers are selected ostensibly for the significance of their contributions to the high school, for example, but often are selected in terms of whether they exemplify complete adolescent virtue, that is, are both cool and popular. The high school sororities that have maintained their basic identity have largely removed themselves from the auspices of the school. Most of them exist today as extracurricular activities. Few school administrators take much notice of the elitest structure of many service clubs or of the activities of the off-campus sororities, perhaps in deference to status-minded parents, who want their children to associate with peers of a certain social, ethnic, or religious background.

Schwartz and Merten[97] examined the initiation rites of several urban high school sororities. The sorority members attended a public high school whose students were from all social classes. The researchers found the rites to be "elaborate and exotic." Although the parents clearly supported their daughters' participation by providing their homes for meetings and sufficient money for activities, both the parents and the girls were naive about the meaning of the ceremonial rituals. Schwartz and Merten reported that none of the participants could offer even a minimal rationale for the ritual complex or explain the significance of particular acts or symbols. Although oblivious to the symbolism itself, the girls were very much emotionally involved in the ritual process; this discrepancy may have arisen because the ritual symbols evoked a sense of superiority over other girls from different social strata. It is noteworthy that the members of the high school sororities manifested an egalitarian ideology, believing that anyone with proper motivation could move to the apex of the adolescent social hierarchy; however, in actuality, mobility in the status system was virtually impossible for girls outside it. Schwartz and Merten's[98] analysis of high school sororities suggests that the purpose of the initiation rites is to affirm the moral solidarity of persons who claim similar virtues and who deny the same virtues to others. The function of the sorority is to "support the ideology of groups that try to maintain their hegemony over the adolescent status system."

SUMMARY

Peer groups help children establish their independence and make the transition from reliance on their families to relative freedom in adolescence and adulthood. Peers offer new patterns of reciprocity: they reverberate thoughts, feelings, expectations, and demands. When adolescents can see how their friends respond to their parents, they are encouraged to examine new values and relationships. The common repertoire of language, slang, grooming, clothing, music, and so forth that young people adapt in their interactions with one another leads them to express collectively, in varying degrees of cohesiveness, a cultural distinctiveness, that is, a *youth culture*.

Youth-culture distinctiveness tends to be blurred by the continuity in tastes that extends from adolescence into adulthood. It is brought about in part by advertising that encourages adolescents to develop long-term purchasing practices. On the other hand, peer group communications seem to contribute to youth-culture distinctiveness. The language, values, beliefs, and standards of adolescents tend to create patterns of interaction that set them apart from adults.

Youth-culture styles vary from being closely aligned to the established adult society to being wholly alienated from it. This chapter identifies, first, five characteristic response patterns that run through youth-culture styles in varying degrees of intensity, and second, three probable youth-culture styles to which these variations may give rise. The five characteristic response patterns have been described by Coleman and his colleagues as *inward-lookingness,* which is fostered by youth's isolation from adults and the extent to which purchasing power creates a mutually reinforcing social environment; *psychic attachment,* which results from the need to satisfy desire for closeness and intimacy outside the family; *press for autonomy,* which is stimulated in part by the respect youth earn from one another as they challenge adult sanctions; *concern for the underdog,* which arises from the fact that youth, being "outsiders" in society, may fail to develop sympathy and loyalty for ongoing societal institutions; and *interest in change,* which occurs because youth, as outsiders, may fail to support the status quo and, instead, embrace systems that promise to change society. The ways in which young people adapt to these five response patterns lead roughly to three basic classifications of youth-culture style: *conventional,* which includes youth who maintain their ties to the adult world; *hedonistic,* which encompasses youth who seek, perhaps because they are impeded from realizing their ideals, to indulge in the pleasure of society; *countercultural,* which describes youth who are estranged from established society and who are working actively to establish a cultural context for themselves that is congruent with their interests and values. Countercultural values tend generally to be associated with feelings, beliefs, interests, and talents that raise personal states of consciousness. These values diminish emphasis on instrumental goals. Morality is relativistic; authority stems more from personal conviction than from institutions. Countercultural values find explicit expression in the life styles of young people who call themselves "freaks." Young people who espouse countercultural values also have found an outlet in the new spiritual movements, such as the Children of God, the Unification Church, the Divine Light Mission, and the Hare Krishna, which share with the wider counterculture a vision of a highly personalistic communally oriented society.

During the past quarter of a century, popular music has become more relevant to young people, whatever their youth-culture orientation. For some young people, the music alone conveys meaning, and it makes little difference to them whether lyrics are absent or present. Other young people find that the lyric themes of popular music communicate a great deal of significance to them. The lyrics of most popular songs deal with romantic love and courtship, and the themes are derived from an underlying range of basic emotions associated with loneliness, adoration, separation, loss of love, and so forth. Such themes have long served to help youth learn about how they should react to the romantic emotions of others and how they might expect others to respond to their own emotional experiences.

A peer group may become a reference source for the behavior of adolescents. The peer group allows youth to assume a variety of roles—to be temporarily leaders or followers, deviants or conformists. The values and norms of the group permit adolescents to acquire perspective on their own values and attitudes. Most peer groups are largely interested in the improvement of heterosexual prowess. Two closely related peer groups—the clique and the crowd—serve this objective admirably. According to Dunphy, the crowd is the largest adolescent group and is usually made up of a cluster of cliques. Adolescents tend to move developmentally from neighborhood play activities through "superficially antagonistic" heterosexual interaction into compatible heterosexual cliques; with increased prowess in boy-girl relations, they form a relatively intimate clique that is associated with similar cliques in a crowd.

Although about half the states have outlawed secret societies in public schools, the high school sorority thrives off campus in many communities (largely urban). Its primary goal is to enhance the adolescent girl's status and heterosexual sophistication. Membership is restricted; pledging and initiation usually involve an elaborate ritual.

REVIEW QUESTIONS

1. What are the factors in socialization that lead to the prominence of peers?
2. Why do youth cultures arise pluralistically?
3. What is the basis for denying youth-culture distinctiveness?
4. How do life style commitment and academic orientation affect an adolescent's peer status?
5. Name five characteristic ways youth respond to circumstances prevailing in the American society.
6. What is the basis for suggesting that some youth represent a (a) conventional youth-culture style, (b) hedonistic style, and (c) countercultural style?
7. Distinguish between "instrumental" and "expressive" values.
8. What are the characteristics of the "freak culture"?
9. What do countercultural religious groups share in common?
10. What do countercultural movements represent in, respectively, the structural-functionalist model and the generational-unit model?
11. What are the emotional themes in the lyrics of popular songs that appeal to young people? Why?
12. Distinguish between the characteristics of cliques and crowds.
13. Why are high school restrictive organizations no longer sanctioned?

DISCUSSION QUESTIONS

1. What are the systems of communication and patterns of behavior among adolescents in your community that distinguish them from children and adults?
2. What are the bases for the status hierarchies in the high schools with which you are familiar? What status terms do the youth employ?
3. Do you agree that dividing values into instrumental and expressive categories provides a basis for distinguishing the values of youth cultures from those of the established adult society?
4. Which of the youth-culture styles predominates among the young people with whom you are familiar?
5. Describe experiences relative to identity formation and moral development that might lead youth to join one of the new spiritual movements.
6. Why is the rise of countercultural values more readily deduced from the generational-unit than the structural-functionalist model?

7. Which of the emotional themes in the lyrics of popular songs might show developmental change through adolescence? Why?

8. What are the characteristics of the cliques and crowds in the high schools of your community? How are these characteristics related to youth-culture status terms and styles?

NOTES

1. G. Schwartz and D. Merten. The language of adolescence: an anthropological approach to the youth culture. *American Journal of Sociology,* 1967, **72,** 453–468.

2. D. Gottlieb and A. L. Heinsohn. Sociology and youth. *Sociological Quarterly,* 1973, **14,** 249–270.

3. M. Jahoda and N. Warren. The myths of youth. *Sociology of Education,* 1965, **38,** 138–149.

4. L. M. Smith and P. F. Kleine. The adolescent and his society. *Review of Educational Research,* 1966, **36,** 424–436.

5. D. M. Smith. The concept of youth culture: a reevaluation. *Youth and Society,* 1976, **7,** 347–364.

6. P. Gilkison. Teen-ager's perceptions of buying frames of reference: a decade in retrospect. *Journal of Retailing,* 1973, **49,** 25–37.

7. Los Angeles Chamber of Commerce. *The dynamics of the youth explosion—a look ahead.* Los Angeles: Chamber of Commerce, 1967, pp. 16–17.

8. G. Schwartz. *Youth culture: an anthropological approach.* Reading, Mass.: Addison-Wesley, 1972, pp. 1 47.

9. C. Kluckhohn and W. Kelly. The concept of culture. In R. Linton (Ed.). *The science of man in the world crisis.* New York: Columbia University Press, 1945, 76–106.

10. Kluckhohn and Kelly, *op. cit.*

11. Schwartz, *op. cit.*

12. Schwartz and Merten, *op. cit.*

13. Schwartz and Merten, *op. cit.*

14. C. Gordon. Social characteristics of early adolescence. *Daedalus,* 1971, **100,** 931–960.

15. J. S. Coleman. *Youth: transition to adulthood.* Chicago: University of Chicago Press, 1974.

16. Coleman, *op. cit.*

17. E. Elkin and W. A. Westley. The myth of adolescent culture. *American Sociological Review,* 1955, **20,** 680–684.

18. *Newsweek.* The teen-agers. March 21, 1966.

19. J. Adelson. The myths of adolescence: a polemic. Paper read at the meeting of the American Psychological Association, San Francisco, 1968.

20. Adelson, *op. cit.*

21. E. Z. Friedenberg. *The vanishing adolescent.* New York: Dell Publishing Company, 1959.

22.   T. Parsons. Age and sex in the social structure of the United States. In W. E. Martin and C. B. Stendler (Eds.). *Readings in child development.* New York: Harcourt, Brace, and Co., 1954, pp. 301–309.

23.   Parsons, *op. cit.*, p. 303.

24.   T. Parsons. Youth in the context of American society. *Daedalus,* 1962, **91,** 97–123.

25.   T. Parsons. Psychoanalysis and the social structure. *Psychoanalytic Quarterly,* 1950, **19,** 371–384.

26.   T. Parsons. The school class as a social system: some of its functions in American society. *Harvard Educational Review,* 1959, **29,** 299–318; Parsons, Youth in the context of American society, *op. cit.*

27.   J. S. Coleman. *The adolescent society.* New York: The Free Press of Glencoe, 1961.

28.   B. M. Berger. Adolescence and beyond. *Social Problems,* 1963, **10,** 394–408.

29.   Coleman, Adolescent society, *op. cit.*

30.   Berger, *op. cit.*

31.   J. W. Carroll. Transcendence and mystery in the counter-culture. *Religion in Life,* 1973, **42,** 361–375, p. 367.

32.   G. S. Hall. *Adolescence.* New York: Appleton, 1904, 2 vols.

33.   D. Light, Jr. and R. S. Laufer. College youth: psychohistory and prospects. In R. J. Havighurst and P. H. Dreyer (Eds.). *Youth—seventy-fourth yearbook of the National Society for the Study of Education.* Chicago: University of Chicago Press, 1975, pp. 93–114.

34.   Light and Laufer, *op. cit.*

35.   Light and Laufer, *op. cit.*, p. 105.

36.   L. S. Distler. The adolescent "hippy" and the emergence of a matristic culture. Unpublished manuscript. Paper presented at the American Psychological Association, 1968.

37.   Distler, *op. cit.*, p. 7.

38.   D. L. Wieder and D. H. Zimmerman. Generational experience and the development of freak culture. *Journal of Social Issues,* 1974, **30,** 137–161.

39.   Wieder and Zimmerman, *op. cit.*, p. 142.

40.   Ibid.

41.   Wieder and Zimmerman, *op. cit.*, p. 144.

42.   J. Rohrbaugh and R. Jessor. Religiosity in youth: a personal control against deviant behavior. *Journal of Personality,* 1975, **43,** 136–155.

43.   Rohrbaugh and Jessor, *op. cit.*

44.   Carroll, *op. cit.*, p. 372.

45.   Carroll, *op. cit.*, p. 365.

46.   W. F. Graham. Technology, technique, and the Jesus movement. *Christian Century,* 1973, **90,** 507–510.

47.   Graham, *op. cit.*

48. T. Robbins, D. Anthony, and T. Curtis. Youth culture religious movements: evaluating the integrative hypothesis. *Sociological Quarterly,* 1975, **16,** 48–64.

49. B. Lidz. Comments on the religiosity of contemporary cultural movements. *Sociological Inquiry,* 1972, **42,** 161–168, p. 165.

50. Carroll, *op. cit.*

51. Carroll, *op. cit.*

52. R. G. Braungart. The sociology of generations and student politics: a comparison of the functionalist and generational unit models. *Journal of Social Issues,* 1974, **30,** 31–54.

53. Braungart, *op. cit.,* p. 49.

54. Ibid.

55. Ibid.

56. Braungart, *op. cit.*

57. V. L. Bengtson, M. J. Furlong, and R. S. Laufer. Time, aging, and the continuity of social structure: themes and issues in generational analysis. *Journal of Social Issues,* 1974, **30,** 1–30.

58. Braungart, *op. cit.,* p. 38.

59. S. N. Eisenstadt. Archetypical patterns of youth. *Daedalus,* 1962, **91,** 28–46.

60. Parsons, Youth in the context of American society, *op. cit.*

61. S. N. Eisenstadt. *From generation to generation.* New York: Free Press, 1956; Eisenstadt, Archetypical patterns, *op. cit.*

62. F. L. K. Hsu, B. G. Watrous, and E. M. Lord. Culture pattern and adolescent behavior. *The International Journal of Social Psychiatry,* 1961, **7,** 33–53.

63. A. R. Buss. Generational analysis: description, explanation, and theory. *Journal of Social Issues,* 1974, **30,** 55–71, p. 67.

64. Braungart, *op. cit.,* p. 47.

65. Braungart, *op. cit.,* p. 44.

66. Mannheim, as cited in Braungart, *op. cit.,* p. 41.

67. Braungart, *op. cit.*

68. H. Mooney. Just before rock: pop music 1950–1953 reconsidered. *Popular Music and Society,* 1974, **3,** 65–108; J. H. Rieger. The coming crisis in the youth music market. *Popular Music and Society,* 1975, **4,** 19–35.

69. P. Hirsch, J. Robinson, E. K. Taylor, and S. B. Withey. The changing popular songs: an historical overview. *Popular Music and Society,* 1972, **1,** 83–93.

70. Rieger, *op. cit.*

71. Mooney, *op. cit.*

72. Rieger, *op. cit.*

73. Mooney, *op. cit.,* p. 92.

74. J. E. Harmon. Meaning in rock music: notes toward a theory of communication. *Popular Music and Society,* 1972, **2,** 18–32.

75. G. Murdock and G. Phelps. Responding to popular music: criteria of classification and choice among English teenagers. *Popular Music and Society,* 1972, **1,** 144–151; Harmon, op. cit.

76. J. E. Harmon. The new music and counter-culture values. *Youth and Society,* 1972, **4,** 61–83.

77. J. C. LaVoie. and B. R. Collins. Effect of youth culture music on high school students' academic performance. *Journal of Youth and Adolescence,* 1975, **4,** 57–65.

78. I. Kantor. This thing called rock: an interpretation. *Popular Music and Society,* 1974, **3,** 201–214.

79. Hirsch et al., *op. cit.*

80. Ibid.

81. Hirsch et al., *op. cit.*

82. J. Carey. As cited in Hirsch et al., *op. cit.*

83. R. S. Burke and R. E. Grinder. Personality-oriented themes and listening patterns in teen-age music and their relation to certain academic and peer variables. *School Review,* 1966, **74,** 196–211.

84. Burke and Grinder, *op. cit.;* Kantor, *op. cit.*

85. R. S. Denisoff and M. H. Levine. Youth and popular music: a test of the taste culture hypothesis. *Youth and Society,* 1972, **4,** 237–255.

86. Denisoff and Levine, *op. cit.*

87. Schwartz and Merten, *op. cit.*

88. D. C. Dunphy. The social structure of urban adolescent peer groups. *Sociometry,* 1963, **26,** 230–246; D. C. Dunphy. Peer group socialisation. In F. J. Hunt (Ed.). *Socialisation in Australia.* Sydney: Angus and Robertson, 1972, pp. 200–217.

89. Dunphy, Social structure of peer groups, *op. cit.*

90. Dunphy, Social structure of peer groups, *op. cit.,* pp. 238–239.

91. Dunphy, Social structure of peer groups, *op. cit.,* p. 240.

92. Dunphy, Social structure of peer groups, *op. cit.*

93. D. D. Knudsen. Socialization to elitism: a study of debutantes. *Sociological Quarterly,* 1968, **9,** 300–308.

94. J. F. Scott. Sororities and the husband game. *Trans-Action,* 1965, **2,** 10–14.

95. M. L. Papista. Secret societies and Michigan schools. *Michigan Educational Journal,* 1963, **40,** 366–368.

96. Papista, *op. cit.*

97. G. Schwartz and D. Merten. Social identity and expressive symbols: the meaning of an initiation ritual. *American Anthropologist,* 1968, **70,** 1117–1131.

98. Schwartz and Merten, Meaning of an initiation ritual, *op. cit.*

Chapter 10

Friendships and Heterosexual Relations

CHAPTER HIGHLIGHTS

ISSUES

Friendships develop between persons as a function of the rewards a liking relationship produces.

Trust, intimacy, admiration, and similarity are among the important ingredients of friendships.

Personal and social adjustment, intelligence, physical attractiveness, and peer status are key dimensions of popularity.

Cognitively unsophisticated youth perpetuate stereotypes of others and accept simple-minded views of themselves.

Segregation of friendship choices by sex diminishes markedly between 10 to 11 and 14 to 15 years of age.

Dating facilitates development of social skills, ranges from casual meetings to engagement, and offers such incentives as companionship, sexual gratification, and status.

Mate selection is characterized by self-selection in America, but cultural factors may limit options and romantic love may lead to unwise choices.

Traditional attitudes toward marriage still predominate in America, but a sizeable minority of young people today see marriage less as an institutional requirement for living together than as a crucial step in their identity formation.

Prospects for the success of an early marriage are generally poor, for young people usually cannot reconcile high expectations with low financial resources.

High schools are becoming more responsive to the needs of married students and supportive learning activities are beginning to emerge.

FRIENDSHIPS

Interpersonal Attraction and Friendship Formation

Friendships provide emotional and instrumental support for day-to-day activities. Being relatively free of work and family responsibilities, adolescents have enough leisure time to explore a variety of friendships. The continuous feedback they receive from friends helps them develop a sense of personal autonomy and achieve a consistent and stable role identity. Douvan and Adelson[1] observe that friendships prepare adolescents for adult love. They learn something of the vicissitudes of affection, loving, and being loved. Friendships enable adolescents to engage, cultivate, and resolve passions and problems of socialization. They carry so much of the burden of adolescent growth that they acquire at this time "a pertinence and intensity" that they never had before nor may ever have again.[2] Friendships also offer adolescents opportunity for exploring and enlarging their sphere of interaction.

Interpersonal attraction, a prerequisite to the developed relationships we think of as friendships, is fundamentally a function of attitudes comprised of cognitive, affective, and dispositional components. According to Tedeschi[3] the cognitive component involves an expectancy of the benefits that another person will provide across situations and time; the affective component relates to the intensity of emotions that are aroused and acknowledged in response to the other person; the dispositional component refers to a general readiness to act in certain characteristic ways with respect to the other person. Considerable interaction occurs among the three components. The cognitive component, for example, functions to organize different emotions with respect to the other person (feelings of confidence, well-being, and the like may be engendered because the other person can be trusted to carry out responsibilities). These expectations may give rise to affective labels—the other is "trustworthy," "honorable," and "just," and these may in turn enhance dispositional readiness to participate in activities with the other.

Psychoanalytic theory holds the affective component to be the preeminent factor in shaping the characteristics of adolescent friendships. The theory holds that an adolescent ego's first task is to revoke postoedipal fantasies at all costs; thus, young persons may isolate themselves and behave like strangers with members of their own families because of the residue left by these incestuous impulses.[4] Postoedipal young persons will turn from their parents to peers for emotional satisfaction: "All in all, it would seem that the adolescent does not choose friendship, but is driven into it."[5] Egocentrism dominates the search for self-definition. Adolescents enter into friendships with remarkable eagerness and flexibility. The friendships are likely to be short, but of passionate intensity. Psychoanalytic theory suggests that adolescents view their friends as

Friendships provide emotional support and social reinforcement for day-to-day activities.

objects; they choose and abandon them with little regard for their feelings. As viewed by psychoanalytic theorists, the adolescent's groping results in a loss of personality, a regression in libidinal life to "narcissism." The theorists believe that the adolescent's capacity for narcissism expresses itself in self-consciousness—concern about clothing, posture, appearance, and exaggerated withdrawal or extroverted behavior. The narcissism, however, interacts with cognitive needs. A friendship, for example, may represent a need for a forum where, by mutual consent, each participant is allowed equal time to talk about the problems of growing up.[6] Narcissism also leads adolescents to place themselves at the center of their peer universe, and they may misinterpret the behavior of others. A friend's casual gesture of boredom or the passing mention of another adolescent may become magnified into something of great significance. If adolescents are touchy and hypersensitive about rejection, they may become convinced that their friends are talking about them or are out to exclude, wound, or humiliate them. Indeed, their sensitivity to rejection may be so great that they cannot abide any friendships.

The psychoanalytic interpretation of friendship development appears to exaggerate its self-serving aspects and to minimize the influence of cognitive and dispositional factors on the development of trust and confidence, and ultimately, on the permanence or nonpermanence of friendship patterns in adolescence. An alternative interpretation of friendship development, based on social-developmental factors, holds that friendships emerge from interpersonal attraction when persons share expectations of a rewarding relationship and are disposed to act cooperatively and kindly toward each other.[7] Douvan and Adelson[8] regard mutual trust as a major dimension of friendship. They say that a deep friendship permits free expression of emotion, shedding of privacy, absorption of minor conflicts, discussion of personally crucial matters, and opportunities for enriching and enlarging one's self-concept. "A friend is expected to be reliable, to invest himself and give of himself in the relationship, to be both tolerant and loyal, to respond to his partner as a whole person, and to respect his friend and his friend's vulnerabilities."[9] Tedeschi[10] believes that persons are attracted to one another in friendship patterns as a function of the rewards that a positive liking relationship brings to each of them. He notes that one of the reasons persons like to be liked is that they expect that friends will provide them with "benefits;" they can count on others when help is needed. And "the stronger the attraction between persons, the more willing each should be to provide favors, help, or benefits whenever the other requests or needs them."[11] Tedeschi likens a friendship to a social insurance policy—one that accrues cash value and can be borrowed against any time without collateral, for an unstated interest rate and premium payment. The timing and nature of repayment is up to the borrower, but the friendship may be destroyed and future credit forfeited if the borrower waits too long or repays too little.

The various functions of attraction as resources in the development of friendships have been described in an unpublished investigation cited by Tedeschi.[12] The researchers reduced 1,800 friendship statements, which had been obtained via open-ended interviews from college students, to 152 relatively distinct items, and asked 30 judges to rate them as "most essential" or "least essential" relative to five levels of friendship: best friends, close friends, good friends, social acquaintances, and casual acquaintances. From these data, a rating scale was developed which was administered to over 1,000 high school and college students, who were asked to determine which items were most important for each level of friendship. These data revealed the following eight major factors, which were judged to be essential to friendship, whether the level was "best friend" or casual acquaintance.

1. *Genuineness*—the expectation that a friend will be open, honest, and straightforward—liking induces trust.
2. *Intimacy Potential*—the emotional accessibility of a friend—friends can ascribe qualities to one another and accept them in each other—"friends let down 'face.'"

A friendship is a product of shared expectations based on trust, emotional accessibility, and mutual esteem.

3. *Acceptance*—the unconditional positive regard of a friend.
4. *Utility Potential*—the willingness to endure high costs as the intensity of the relationship increases—self-assurance that one's favors, help, or benefits are given in a spirit of altruism.
5. *Ego-reinforcement*—the expectation that a friend will provide social reinforcement in the form of sympathy or empathy.
6. *Admiration or Esteem*—the expectation that a friend will possess qualities that engender respect and status.
7. *Similarity*—the expectation that a friend will possess similar attitudes and needs.
8. *Ritualistic Social Exchange*—the assumption that friends will exchange gifts, for example, on birthdays and Christmas.

Popularity and Peer Status. Popularity is an index of a person's desirability as a friend. Popularity forecasts the extent to which others believe that the attributes of a potential friend are possessed by an individual—similarity of attitudes, needs, genuineness, trust, mutual acceptance, and so forth. Wheeler has reported, for example, that the components of adolescent popularity include an attractive appearance; kindness and sympathy, a cheerful, jolly, and carefree outlook; an active participation in sports; and some degree of intelligence in school and out-of-school activities. The youth's expectations for themselves were consistent with adult expectations. Popularity with the opposite sex required about the same attributes and behavior as popularity with one's own sex.[13]

Good personal and social adjustment appear to be the sine qua non of popularity. In her now-classic investigation, Tryon[14] found that for youth between 12 and 15 years of age, girls had to be more flexible than boys in modifying their behavior, adjusting to ideals, and reorienting themselves in order to stay popular. The 12-year-old girl was expected to be quiet, sedate, nonaggressive, friendly, likeable, good-humored, and attractive. By 15 years of age, there was no longer any admiration for the demure, docile, prim and ladylike girl; now she had to be an extrovert and good sport—like the idealized boy. The ability to organize games for heterosexual parties and to keep social activities lively and entertaining was especially admired; the possession of social skills, personal charm, and ability to fascinate boys had also become important. For boys it was less important to be flexible; at both 12 and 15 years of age, the idealized boy was expected to be a leader in games, physically skilled, moderately aggressive, and fearless. Other researchers have also shown that responsiveness to the age-graded expectations of peers and adults is very important in maintenance of relative popularity. Livson and Bronson[15] found that in the matter of impulse control, boys have to change more than girls in order to hold their popularity. In the fifth grade, boys who took chances and were daring tended to be relatively popular. In early adolescence excessive control over aggressive impulses thus was a social handicap among boys, but in later adolescence such control was necessary for popularity. Girls were not rewarded for such traits as impulsivity and daring at any time; to be popular, girls at all age levels were expected to control their assertive and aggressive impulses. Further, Emmerich[16] asked more than 600 children and adolescents in the fourth through eleventh grades to assess the value in other persons of such traits as kindness, cooperation, sociableness, leadership, independence, forcefulness, conformity, and self-centeredness. Emmerich assumed that age changes in conceptions of popularity could be assessed by determining the degree to which persons at different ages liked or disliked the traits in other persons. Emmerich found that the measures revealed virtually no developmental changes in traits of popularity. Nearly everyone, whatever their age, valued kindness, cooperation, sociableness, and leadership and consistently devalued conformity and self-centeredness. Although the "social desirability" of the traits remained constant, the researcher reports, nonetheless, that as a function of cognitive growth, the capacity of individuals to process information about kindness, cooperation, and so on increased with age, and thus they became more sophisticated in associating personality qualities with each of the traits. For example, the observation of a benevolent act might lead young people to view the other as "kindly," but older persons might raise questions about the relationship between motives and performance before developing a disposition to view the other as "kindly."

As Wheeler noted above, possession of a higher than average level of intelligence is generally regarded as an important determinant of popularity among adolescents. Although the youth-culture stereotype of the hedonistic, antischolastic adolescent has led many to believe that intelligence does not promote popularity, the image of an introverted "egg head," whose sole extracurricular activity is playing chess, has also contributed to this misconception. But Elkins[17] reported that very popular youth have relatively high intelligence, whereas unpopular youth have relatively low intelligence. Peck and Galliani[18] insist that intelligence "is positively and significantly" related to age-mate acceptance. They found that adolescents picked the brighter boys and girls to be leaders and innovators and appropriately assigned a "brain" role to brighter youth. Marshall[19] also found that sociometric popularity was related to the knowledge and skills necessary to achieve group goals. In a study of the sociometric choices of 3,000 high school students, Horowitz[20] confirmed Coleman's[21] finding that "the most popular of all" youth were the "athlete-scholars." Horowitz reported that the following variables were the best predictors of popularity in both sexes: the English test total, interest in sports, and the self-rating personality scales of sociability and leadership.

Physical attractiveness also appears to be an important correlate of popularity. Physically attractive persons are assumed to possess more socially desirable personality traits than persons of lesser attractiveness and to lead happier and more successful lives.[22] Whether initial social contacts among opposite-sex adolescents are viewed positively or negatively appears to be affected by physical attractiveness.[23] Further, because handsome young people are expected to possess favorable personality qualities, adolescents tend to believe that associations with attractive partners will lead others to view them favorably, too.[2] What, then, is so significant about good looks to interpersonal attraction and popularity? Sigall and Landy[25] note that kindness, intelligence, and so forth may be more desirable than physical attractiveness to the endurance of a friendship, but considerable interaction must ensue before insight into these traits is acquired. Physical appearance, on the other hand, is a person's most easily observable characteristic. Hence, they say, it is the immediate availability of information about beauty that contributes to its importance as a factor in friendship formation. Indeed, there is some evidence that perceptions of physical attractiveness partially determine popularity. Cavior and Dokecki[26] state that it is difficult to imagine that many people will like a partner, especially for sustained interaction as in dating, whom they perceive as physically unattractive, no matter how positively they evaluate his or her other personality qualities. The researchers suggest that perceptions of popularity and physical attractiveness may exert a reciprocal effect on one another. They found, for example, that persons average in attractiveness may become popular largely because of their physical attractiveness, and once they are perceived as popular, they are also perceived as being relatively more attractive than before. It appears that physical attractiveness initiates a sequence of circular reactions, which reinforces its significance as an attribute of popularity.[27] Physical attractiveness may also affect social relationships early in life; those who are attractive are admired and pursued; their attractiveness enables them to develop a high level of self-esteem and to acquire the traits that would lead others to view them as potential friends. On the other hand, physical unattractiveness may evoke unfavorable trait attributions; the physically unattractive may be ignored, which forces them to withdraw from social relationships and perpetuates their isolation since they are deprived of the feedback necessary to develop socially effective personalities.[28]

Peer status is another facet of interpersonal attraction and friendship formation. It is a function of either *achieved* or *ascribed* popularity. On the one hand, adolescents may win admirers and friends because of their superior insight into how to select alternatives to maximize goal attainment, their ability to organize available resources well, and their capacity to act effectively in socially approved ways. On the other hand, they may be ascribed popularity because they possess the perquisites that facilitate its development—homes for parties, cars, clothes, and so forth. Snyder[29] asked several hundred members of a high school class the following question: "What does it take to be a 'big wheel' in the high school?" The responses fell logically into five categories, four of which reveal achieved status qualities and one of which suggests ascribed or unearned qualities. The first four qualities prescribe the basic attributes of popularity: (1) personal qualities, good looks, and neatness; (2) social activities and athletics—joining the "right" clubs and having athletic status; (3) academic achievement—obtaining good grades; (4) associating with "right" friends—having a "cool" girlfriend and "connections." The fifth of the categories pertained to material possessions—money, car, clothes, and parents having an impressive house. The latter possessions are extras in the lives of many adolescents; popularity is ascribed rather than achieved to the extent that it is determined by them. Snyder's finding that material possessions affect popularity is corroborated by the data presented in Table 1, which reveals empirically just how much popularity is a function of socioeconomic variables like family income and parental level of education. The data are drawn from the nationwide Health Examination Survey conducted by the National Center for Health Statistics.[30] They are

Table 1

Percent Distribution of Youth Aged 12–17 Years by Popularity According to Selected Socioeconomic Variables: United States, 1966–70

	Popularity			
Selected Variables	Above Average	Average	Below Average	Don't Know
Income				
Less than $3,000	8.6	64.4	15.7	11.3
$3,000–$5,000	7.5	66.9	14.2	11.4
$5,000–$7,000	9.5	64.5	12.7	13.3
$7,000–$10,000	13.8	62.0	9.8	14.3
$10,000–$15,000	15.0	63.6	6.5	14.9
$15,000 or more	19.2	63.4	5.8	11.5
Parents' Education				
Elementary	9.7	64.5	14.4	11.5
High School	10.8	64.4	9.9	14.9
Beyond High School	19.5	62.1	6.4	12.0

Source: National Center for Health Statistics. *Health attitudes and behavior of youths 12–17 years: demographic and socioeconomic factors.* (DHEW, pub. no. [HRA] 76–1635.) Series 11, No. 153, 1975, p. 29. Reprinted by permission.

based on teacher ratings of youth's popularity, 12 to 17 years of age. Table 1 indicates that popularity increases markedly with increase in socioeconomic status and that it drops sharply with decrease in status.

On the whole, young people are likely to gravitate toward the viewpoint of the high-status adolescent, and adolescents who attain high status among their peers usually acquire a large advantage in controlling their own destiny and that of others. Feshbach[31] reported, for example, that high peer-status youth were freer than those of low status to deviate from group norms. In a study of the influence patterns in small informal groups, Harvey and Rutherford[32] questioned 405 youth from the third, sixth, ninth, and eleventh grades. The study involved two sessions conducted in conventional classrooms; the subjects were first asked in small groups to indicate their preference for one out of two pictures taken from an art judgment test. During the first session, sociometric measures of peer status were also obtained. A week later, the subjects were again asked to make a choice between the two pictures as well as between four other pairs of noncritical pictures. Before making their second choice, they were informed of the choices made by the highest- and lowest-status members of the informal group to which they belonged. In one experiment, the highest-status member of the group was presented as having disagreed with the subjects' earlier choices while the lowest-status member was depicted as having agreed. In another experiment, the highest-status member was represented as having agreed and the lowest status member as having disagreed. The researchers reported that the overall effect of simultaneous disagreement with the high-status member and agreement with the low-status member resulted in a shift toward the judgment of the higher-status individual. Conversely, agreement with the higher status person coincident with disagreement with the lowest-status member tended to reinforce the youth's initial preferences.

Ethnicity and Prejudice.   Rokeach, Smith, and Evans[33] suggest that prejudice serves in essence to repulse interpersonal attraction. The researchers assume that one major component of prejudice is perceived dissimilarity of beliefs, between either individuals or groups. Prejudice and aversion are likely outcomes when stereotypical judgments are permitted to distort interpersonal involvement. Although a complex array of factors affects prejudice, ethnicity certainly is one of the major correlates. The findings of investigations in general reveal fairly conclusively that adolescents, whether attending either segregated or desegregated schools, choose to group themselves along ethnic lines—chicano with chicano, black with black, white with white.[34] The magnitude of the isola-

Social segregation is a functional reality in many high schools.

tion that may arise is illustrated by the following description of social segregation in a desegregated high school. It is drawn from extended observations made of youth attending a moderately large, urban high school in a northern industrial city:[35]

The "freaks" who gather by the entrance to the gym are all white, the boys in the corner are all black, white girls are with white girls, white boys are with white boys. The couples are either both white or both black. Although there were rumors of interracial dating, only twice did we see a white girl openly conversing with a black boy in the school, and never did we see a white boy with a black girl.
Between classes, although there are three times as many whites as blacks, the blacks seem to hold their own. That is, they are not a reticent minority, but constitute a vocal and vigorous group. It almost seems that the whites are the most quiet, reserved, and private in their interactions, the blacks more likely to greet each other and interact in loud voices and with vigorous gestures. But they carry on their interactions only with other blacks. There is no interracial interaction in the halls.
The cafeteria is the same way. The blacks always occupy the southeast quarter and never in six months did we see a white student with blacks. Nor did we ever see blacks interspersed in the other part of the cafeteria. It just did not happen.

The above scenario represents the instance of a single northern high school, but Nelsen and Uhl,[36] drawing upon a study involving nearly 100 southern high schools, also report findings of friendship segregation among black and white high school students; however, the degree of social segregation they describe appears to be less severe. Their data are based on comparisons of high school social climates which were obtained from black males from 45 high schools and black females from 85 high schools who had matriculated as first-year college students to a predominantly black university. The investigators' analyses concentrated primarily on black adolescents of both sexes who had attended predominantly white schools. These youth indicated that they tended to be excluded from the extracurricular activities and programs of their high schools. They believed that their participation would have been unwelcome; they made little effort to participate, but when they did try, they often found themselves outnumbered and outvoted on matters of concern to them. Moreover, the black females felt not only that their own social life was poor, but also that the social life of black males was equally poor. But the black males contradicted the females' perceptions, for they saw their social life as adequate. Nelson and Uhl speculate that black males may have developed more aggressive means for coping with interpersonal problems associated with prejudice, and that black females, because they possess less effective coping mechanisms, experience prejudice more intensely when they are substantially in the minority.

What accounts for the development of prejudice among adolescents? Glock, Wuthnow, Piliavin, and Spencer[37] conducted a detailed analysis of the antisemitic attitudes of several thousand black and white adolescents living in three different communities near New York City to find out. The researchers found prejudice to be especially prominent among the academically deprived; youth whose school performance was weak manifested greater prejudice than those who made good grades, completed their homework, and planned to attend college. Academic deprivation was an important correlate of prejudice in two ways: cognitively unsophisticated modes of thought led not only to discriminatory behavior toward minority groups by the unsophisticated members of majority groups, but also led the unsophisticated minority group members to think of themselves in terms of stereotypes. As the researchers say: "the cognitively unsophisticated teenager is more likely both to perpetuate stereotypes of others and to accept the simple-minded notions when they are applied to himself."[38] From this perspective, prejudice arises not so much from the perceptions young people may have of a given ethnic group but by a "'racist' mode of explaining" what is perceived. Young people who view black teenagers, for example, to be more in trouble with school authorities than white youth because of racially innate differences have acquired higher levels of prejudice than those who view the variance in troubles as a consequence of institutional, economic, and historical processes. The researchers account for their findings in terms of a "cognitive theory of prejudice." They hold that "prejudice is rooted in a failure cognitively to recognize and understand it, and therefore to be armed to combat it."[39] Glock et al. suggest, therefore, that by increasing cognitive sophistication, prejudice may be lessened, that is, by creating an aversion to the simplistic generalities inherent in stereotyping and by creating a better understanding of why ethnic differences exist. These assumptions have led them to propose that the following three kinds of educational input are needed to teach young people to avoid falling victim to simplistic and stereotypical thinking:[40]

1. Instruction in the logic of inference is called for so that youngsters can come to recognize when group differences are being falsely accounted for. . . . Learning the logic of inference requires instruction in the notion of causality; that is to say, the necessity of looking beyond surface characteristics, beyond easy explanations, to discover more subtle reasons for human behavior. It also requires instruction in the rules of evidence. Just as a teenager learns to inspect a chemical solution to judge its properties, he

needs to be able to examine human situations and decide what conclusions he reasonably can and cannot infer.

2. Specific instruction is needed about how group differences come about. This means going into the historical background of group differences to reveal their cultural and social sources. Why black teenagers are less successful and why Jewish teenagers and their parents are prone to clannishness, for example, have to be explained so that their historical roots are understood and the social forces making for their persistence in contemporary society comprehended. Especially necessary, it seems, is instruction showing that group differences are not exclusively the result simply of genetic traits or attributable simply to the acts of individuals without respect to social, cultural, and historical pressures.

3. Instruction is required to make clear the size of group differences so as to guard against the common tendency for relative differences, which virtually all groups are, to be generalized. For example, it needs to be made clear that all Jewish teenagers are not successful in school, nor are all non-Jewish teenagers unsuccessful. The differences are, as most human differences, matters of degree. Instruction is required which makes it evident that this is the case even though stereotypes and generalizations are often used as shorthand ways of describing differences.

The Developmental Pattern of Heterosexual Friendships

Figure 1 depicts a U-shaped curve showing the proportion of children from grades 2 through 8 who are likely to make friends of the opposite sex.[41] The figure is based on an early sociometric study[42] showing that boys and girls from kindergarten through grade 8 made more opposite-sex choices in the lower three and upper three grades than in the middle grades. Thus more heterosexual choices appear at either end of Figure 1 than at its center. The shape of the curve could be predicted from psychoanalytic theory. The "trough" that appears around grade 5 is comparable to the latency period, presumably a biologically determined period of low heterosexual interest. According to this viewpoint, the sequence of events leading to mature heterosexuality can be divided into three periods:[43] (1) initial heterosexual orientation, when sex identification and social and emotional skills are learned in the family; (2) sexual latency and segregation, when interaction with children of the opposite sex is relatively insignificant; and (3) adolescence, when sexual propensities and members of the opposite sex become important. The curve and its theoretical aspects, however, have been modified by Kanous, Daugherty, and Cohn,[44] who repeated Moreno's study, but found that it held more for upper-class than lower-class youth. The researchers viewed the classic U-shaped curve as an artifact of the socialization experiences of upper-class families, for the children from lower-class families appeared to develop heterosexual interests during elementary school, thus distorting or flattening the curve.

The shape of the curve for any given group of boys and girls probably depends on the nature of their socialization experiences. From the viewpoint of friendship theory, one might expect that both sexes would have proportionately greater same-sex rather than opposite-sex choices well into adolescence. The early, positive expectations acquired during the preschool years concerning the behavior of same-sex children should be reinforced and maintained throughout the school years. An antagonism toward the opposite sex also may develop as children identify very closely with their own sex.[45] Mutual withdrawal provides support for the unique values of one's own sex and is reinforced by rejection of the values of the opposite sex.[46] Meyer,[47] for example, administered a test of social relations that tapped the capacity "to make people have a good time" and "to be kind and sympathetic" to 370 boys and girls from grades 5 through 12. His results showed that same-sex social activities were perceived as more reinforcing than those with the opposite sex at all ages. In looking for "kind and sympathetic" persons, the proportion of youth at each grade level who looked to their own sex remained constant. In looking for those who could help one "have a good time," the proportion of boys who preferred their own sex also remained

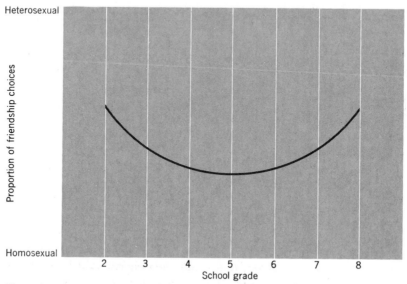

Figure 1
Hypothetical curve depicting the latency concept. (From Kanous, Daugherty, and Cohn, see text. Reprinted by permission.)

the same, but after grade 7, girls began to view boys more favorably, although the proportion of girls at each grade level who preferred female companions still was larger.

Broderick[48] describes a typical developmental pattern of heterosexual choice among contemporary boys and girls. He studied about 1,000 youth in four age groups—10 to 11, 12 to 13, 14 to 15, and 16 to 17—who lived in an upper-middle-class suburb of a medium-sized town. More than one-half of their fathers had professional or managerial jobs, nearly one-third of their mothers worked, and more than three-fourths of the youth were expected to go on to college. Broderick found that serious heterosexual interest may begin as early as 12 years of age. Although Douvan and Adelson[49] believe that the average age to begin dating is 14 years for girls and 15 for boys, they agree with Broderick that by age 17 nearly all American young people have begun to date.

1. The 10 to 11 year olds. A reciprocal, same-sex friendship of two or three children prevailed among this age group. On the fringe of these units was a web of less intimate, nonreciprocal, heterosexual relationships. The network was held together uneasily. Different situations elicited certain negative sanctions for socializing with a member of the opposite sex. Broderick,[50] for example, compared the negative feeling of being with a member of the opposite sex while eating in the school cafeteria, taking a walk, and going to the movies. The feeling was greatest in the cafeteria and least in going to the movies. He hypothesized that eating together is a symbol of "fraternal acceptance and social solidarity," and because of the visibility of the cafeteria, few youth would want to break rank in order to sit next to a member of the out group, no matter what the personal attraction. But group solidarity was less threatened by heterosexual pairing in private. Attending the movies and, to some extent, taking a walk with a member of the opposite sex was associated with dating and romanticism. Over 90 percent of the 10-to-11-year-old boys, nonetheless, viewed walking with a girl to be as unacceptable as eating with one, but about one-fourth of them expressed an interest in going to a movie with a girl. Twice the number of girls as boys was ready to cross the sex barrier in the lunchroom, four times as many were ready to walk with a boy, and more than one-third of them were willing to go to a movie with a boy.

A majority of the 10 to 11 year olds of both sexes, but a much larger proportion of girls, reported that they had had a "sweetheart." The relationships were largely unilateral since seldom did anyone else—especially the object of affection—know about them. Although nearly all of the youth were unsure about how the "sweetheart" felt, about half believed that their feelings were reciprocated. The girls were more likely than the boys to confide their romantic inclinations to their friends and parents; for both sexes, friends were more often confidants than parents. A small minority of the youth (more boys than girls) described the relationship with their sweetheart as "going steady;" the discrepancy suggested a lack of consensus between the sexes as to whether a relationship should be called "going steady." One-fifth of the boys and girls claimed that they had gone steady, although several of them had never had a date. Apparently going steady at 10 or 11 could be accomplished without meeting outside of school.

Broderick[51] also reported that at 10 or 11 years, as well as later on, a large proportion of both boys and girls said that they had "fallen in love" for the first time within the preceding year. He suggested that "love" might be redefined following each increment in heterosexual maturity. The earlier loves may have been explained away as something less than love as new attachments and dimensions were added to relationships.

"Crushes" (or what Broderick called "practice emotions") appeared at the 10-to-11 age level. He suggested that crushes on movie, TV, and recording "stars" and familiar adults (like teachers and attractive married neighbors) represented a safe expression of love; in this way young people may wish, yearn, and dream without risk of being rejected. The "crush" phenomenon included about one-fourth of the boys from 11 to 12 but seemed to disappear in older boys. By contrast, at least half the girls from 11 to 12 indulged in this form of romantic fantasy, and large numbers continued until much later in adolescence.

2. *The 12 to 13 year olds.* Both social segregation and romantic interests increased among the 12 to 13 year olds. The widest cleavage between the sexes occurred at age 12, where there were the fewest cross-sex friendship choices among both boys and girls. It was still unpopular to eat in the cafeteria with the opposite sex, but in situations with more romantic potential—such as taking a walk or going to the movies—the preference for opposite-sex companions had increased from its 10-to-11-year-old level. By age 12, one-half of the boys and three-fifths of the girls had dated; the proportion rose to seven-tenths for both sexes by age 13. The youth expected more reciprocity and they got it, a fact that Broderick felt reflected an important step away from the largely imaginary characters of earlier relationships and toward real romantic interaction. The youth were also more willing to reveal their romantic attachments. Boys confided much more in their friends and parents, but not as much as girls. Girls were more likely to talk to their parents and friends, but especially the latter. Girls were also more likely to tell their girlfriends how they felt about a boyfriend than to let the boy himself know.

At the 12-to-13 age level there was a marked tendency for girls to choose older boyfriends and for boys to choose younger girlfriends. The percentage of boys and girls who claimed that they had ever gone steady was the same as for the 10 to 11 year olds. Approximately half the youth reported that they had been in love, perhaps once or twice, usually within the past two years. Crushes on famous entertainers and familiar adults had passed for 12-to-13-year-old boys; from this point onward fewer than 15 percent of the boys admitted that they had had such feelings. Whether the older boys had actually had fewer crushes is not clear; since the older boys publicly considered crushes as ridiculous and juvenile, they may have denied having them. By contrast, a large proportion of the 12-to-13-year-old girls reported that they had had crushes.

3. *The 14 to 15 year olds.* Segregation of friendship choices by sex diminished markedly among the 14 to 15 year olds. Girls began to report as many as two boys among their friends. Boys and girls continued to be reluctant to choose one another as companions in the school cafeteria, but now about two-fifths of the boys preferred a girl companion to walk with and about two-thirds preferred a girl at the movies; for the girls, the proportions were now about one-half and three-fourths, respectively. At this age level, more than eight-tenths of the boys and girls were dating. Approximately one-fourth of them dated once a week, but the majority still dated less than once per month. Girls were more likely than boys to have dated different persons.

The 14 to 15 year olds sharply revised their definition of "sweetheart," and fewer now claimed to have one. At this age two out of three young people expected reciprocity, and reciprocity continued to rise. At this age boys were as likely as girls to list a sweetheart as a friend (however, this was not done significantly until 16 or 17), and there was increased openness of communication. Nearly all the boys and three-fourths of the girls were sure that the sweetheart knew how they felt. Furthermore, most of their friends knew about it and about two-thirds of their parents of both sexes also knew. The age spread between the partners continued to prevail, and girls were more likely to choose upward than boys were to choose downward on the age scale. More than twice as many at this age (as compared with earlier ages) reported that they had gone steady at least once. At 14 or 15, a very large number of boys and a relatively small number of girls reported that they had ever been in love. As at all ages, they reported that they had been in love for the first time within the past year; however, since the girls appeared to be more systematic than the boys in repudiating past loves, fewer girls felt that they had ever been in love. By contrast, boys appeared to be more willing to accept earlier attachments as "real love"— an interpretation that is supported by the finding that more boys than girls claimed that they had been in love two or more times.

At this age Douvan and Adelson[52] found that boy-girl relations were characterized by a "combative image." A girl is not likely to modify her positions or compromise what she wants to do at the request of a boy; when a problem arises, the girl is likely to suggest that her girlfriend help them solve it.

The girl's approach is to manipulate the boy in collaboration with a loyal girlfriend.

4. The 16 to 17 year olds.   Reaching 16 or 17 years of age marks the passing of serious negative feelings about the opposite sex; the basic friendship unit has been restructured. At least half the boys and three-fourths of the girls name one or more members of the opposite sex among their best friends. At 16 or 17 nearly everyone had begun to date. Broderick reported that only 4 percent of the boys and 3 percent of the girls in his sample indicated that they had never dated; however, he acknowledged that other studies found that one-fourth of the boys and less than two-tenths of the girls still were not dating at ages 16 or 17. In Broderick's study four out of five of those who dated had gone out with at least four different persons. The frequency of dating was also higher among this age group; most of the girls and half the boys dated at least once a week (on the weekend). The single date continued to be most popular among boys, but more girls still preferred the double date.

Sweetheart choices became more significant at 16 or 17. The proportion of youth making sweetheart choices was comparable to that at earlier ages, but now nine-tenths were certain of reciprocation; there was almost no gap between expected and received reciprocity. Girls generally communicated more about their boyfriends than at younger ages. A few girls were still uncertain of their boyfriend's feelings (a very few did not even know if he knew of their interest) and were uncommunicative about their own feelings, but most participated in open, reciprocal relationships. These relationships were known to their friends and parents and usually approved by their parents. Boys communicated less about these relationships to their friends and parents. Both boys and girls of this age were likely to have listed their sweethearts among their close friends, increasing the overlap between sweetheart and bestfriend. The girls' preference for older boyfriends leveled off somewhat; however, the majority of girls continued to date older boys, which meant outside the high school. At this age there was a high rate of going steady, and the majority of the youth reported that they had gone steady at one time. Most of the young people apparently felt that going steady was a desirable social arrangement, but that it did not necessarily involve deep emotional attachment. Love was not generally considered a prerequisite for going steady, but about two-thirds of the boys and girls reported that they had been in love and had experienced it for the first time within the past year.

DATING

This is one of the major social activities of adolescents, who usually begin dating many years before they seriously contemplate marriage. Parents may encourage their children to start dating as early as elementary school and may become distressed if their daughters have no boyfriends by senior high school and their sons show little interest in girls by late adolescence. Dating performs an important function in America since parents do not arrange marriages and there are no longer any marriage brokers. Dating is an integral part of the courtship to marriage sequence; it is the closest phenomenon in America to a *rite de passage*.[53] Our society stresses love as the main motive for marriage and upholds free choice among partners as an ideal. Dating facilitates mate selection because it enables adolescents to acquire a wide range of social skills, especially in respect to interpreting their own moods and refining their perceptions of the opposite sex. At any given age after 12 years, more girls than boys are dating; older youth will tend to date the younger; those who begin dating at an early age will date more frequently during adolescence. Among boys, possession of an automobile and a job accelerates likelihood of dating. On the other hand, high academic aptitude and school achievement tend to lessen dating frequency. In general, boys and girls who date frequently are inclined to marry at an early age.[54]

The Structural Dimensions of Dating

The dating system may serve one end, courtship, or a variety of subsidiary ends associated with socially satisfying experiences. It appears to increase in structure with involvement and commitment. Delora[55] has analyzed the characteristics of dating by considering a dating couple as a social system with structural elements consisting of ends, norms, and status roles. Table 2 shows how types of dating may be distinguished in accordance with different structural elements. Delora identified the purpose of casual dating as "getting acquainted." Both the boy and the girl try to make the best possible impression and are "formal" with each other. Conversation is general and uninvolved. Group and double dating may take place as often as single dating, especially at movies and athletic events. Entertainment is the main purpose of dating "steadily." The boy is likely to initiate most of the action and to be the aggressive, dominant partner. The partners are free to date other persons but are attracted to each other at the moment. Dating "steadily" represents an individualistic social system in which the goals of each partner tend to transcend the mutual roles of the relationship, that is, enjoyment supersedes companionship. Companionship usually is the objective of young people who are "going steady," although in high school it may be convenience.[56] The arrangement calls for monogamous interaction, and daily contact is often maintained between the partners. Since the relationship is more democratic, both partners may initiate

Table 2
Types of Dating Compared on Basis of Social Structure (Type of Dating)

Structural Element	Casual	Steadily	Going Steady	Engaged to Be Engaged	Engaged
Ends*	Getting acquainted	Entertainment Enjoyment	Companionship	Trial engagement	Getting ready for marriage
Norms	Impersonal Uninvolved Rational	Individualistic Free No Commitment	Personalized Monogamous Intimate Emotional	Personalized Monogamous Intimate Emotional Oriented to future	Personalized Monogamous Intimate Emotional Oriented to future Rational plans
Status-role	Initiation of action by male Dominance of male authority	Initiation of action by male Dominance of male authority	Two-way initiation of action Equal authority	Two-way initiation of action Equal authority	Two-way initiation of action Equal authority Male-female assumption of specific responsibilities

Source: J. Delora. Social systems of dating on a college campus. *Marriage and Family Living*, 1963, **25**, 81–84. Reprinted by permission.

* The *ends* of dating tended to be compounded as a couple moved from one type to the next.

381

action and reciprocation. The types of dating identified by Delora as "engaged to be engaged" and "engaged" represent the courtship phases. The partners spend considerable time together, there is a state of "mutual trust" between them, and an increasing degree of physical intimacy develops. Initiation of action is reciprocal, and in contrast to the less involved types of dating (where dating may be a means to some other end), interaction is the end, and thus, there is a general fusion of means and ends.

The Incentives of Dating

The most salient incentives of dating are companionship and mate selection, and some researchers have viewed each of these as *the* attraction of dating. For example, Burgess and Locke[57] said that dating is "a social engagement between two young people with no commitment beyond the expectation that it will be pleasurable to both." But Lowrie[58] held that dating is "a gradual, almost unconscious development from the customs of courtship whereby people obtain the training and experience needed for sensible selection of mates." At a more down-to-earth level, of course, there are other incentives that may or may not facilitate companionship and mate selection.

In a classic analysis of dating, Waller[59] emphasized the prestige factor. Observing the dating behavior of college students during the academic year 1929–1930, he found that competition for dates among both sexes was extremely keen. Success in dating, he said, was achieved by the men who valued money and the things that money can buy—car, good clothes, and fraternity membership. Men who dated extensively also had a "good line," "smooth manners and appearance," and the ability to dance well. The good line, fashionable clothes, and dancing skills also enhanced the value of girls; but they had the extra task of maintaining propriety with respect to social drinking and other forms of unconventional behavior. They key factor for girls was "nothing succeeds like success." Girls achieved top status by managing to be seen in the right places with the right ("Class A") men, but not too often with the same one. Waller's analysis has long been used in discussing the basic incentives of dating. It is consistent with Schwartz and Merten's[60] description of the status values of socie girls. Coombs and Kenkel[61] demonstrated the incentive value of dating a member of the opposite sex who is physically attractive. They also showed how such attributes as being a good student, popular, an excellent dancer, a fraternity member, and stylishly dressed enhance one's dating status. Similarly, Walster, Aronson, Abrahams, and Rottmann[62] reported that for both sexes physical attractiveness was more important than personality and intellectual measures in predicting partner desirability. Indeed, relative to the judgments of impartial observers, both boys and girls tended to view their partner (someone each had been dating regularly) as being more attractive than they really were.[63]

Several types of incentives make dating attractive. Grinder[64] compiled a comprehensive list of dating attractions from the interpretations of sociologists, the replies of several adolescents who were queried about dating, and the columns of various newspapers and teenage magazines. Consideration was only given to situations in which the dating partners constituted a heterosexual pair, were unmarried, and were unchaperoned. The following four categories represent the major incentives of dating:[65]

1. *Sexual gratification.* Dating offers sanctioned opportunities for physical contact with members of the opposite sex; for example, to dance cheek to cheek, to hold hands at the theater, to stroll with an arm around the consort's waist, to caress, to neck in some secluded place, and so forth.

2. *Independence assertion.* Dating provides a means to achieve independence from adults and the accepted standards of society; for example, drag-racing on lonely streets, fudging one's age in order to gain admittance to an "adults-only" movie, and dating members of the opposite sex whose reputations are tarnished. Dating may also serve as a means for deviating from one's family religious practices, disdaining one's family political beliefs, ignoring parental strictures on curfew hours and sex-conduct rules, and being heedless of family propriety in crossing of social-class lines, in smoking, and in drinking.

3. *Status seeking.* Dating offers opportunities for associating with prestigious members of the opposite sex. One may prefer consorts who are champions or leaders in debating, athletics, or dramatics. Dating may be a vehicle for entering an "in group," or partners may be sought who are excellent models for developing social etiquette, grace, and sophistication.

4. *Participative eagerness.* Dating sometimes appeals to adolescents so that they can avoid loneliness, boredom, anxiety, work responsibilities, or activities with parents or same-sex peers.

Skipper and Nass[66] have also listed four categories of incentives. Although they focus on the social functions of dating, they acknowledge that the social functions are indicative of the incentives of dating.

1. *Recreation.* "Dating may be a form of recreation. It provides entertainment for the individuals involved and is a source of immediate enjoyment."

2. *Socialization.* "Dating may be a form of socialization. It provides an opportunity for individuals of the opposite sex to get to know each other, to

learn to adjust to each other, and to develop appropriate techniques of interaction."

3. *Status achievement.*   "Dating may be a means of status grading and status achievement. By dating and being seen with persons who are rated 'highly desirable' by one's peer group, an individual may raise his status and prestige within his group."

4. *Courtship.*   "Dating may be a form of courtship. It provides an opportunity for unmarried individuals to associate with each other for the purpose of selecting a mate whom they may eventually marry."

Skipper and Nass have also suggested that every dating partner's "primary motivations" may be identified at points on two independent continua, which are bipolarized respectively as expressive-instrumental and low-high emotional involvement. For example, dating may be an end in itself (expressive) or a means to a larger goal (instrumental). Emotional involvement may range from zero-level to total consummation. Although a partner's motivation could conceivably fall anywhere along both continua, the researchers speculate that certain configurations are more probable. For instance, when recreation is the main incentive, a youth's motivations may be relatively expressive and uninvolved emotionally. If the interest is primarily socialization or status seeking, there would be a high instrumental orientation and a low emotional involvement. When the principal incentive is mate selection, there will probably be both a strong instrumental orientation and a strong emotional involvement. Skipper and Nass pointed out how the above framework can be used to judge how much conflict may emerge in a relationship, which partner is likely to control it, and which partner is likely to experience the most distress. When either emotional involvement or instrumental orientation is shared, there will be a desire to continue the relationship; when there is disparity between either the instrumental or the emotional dimension; conflict and distress are likely. The partner who has the greater involvement of either sort is likely to suffer the greatest distress and to have the least control over the relationship. The partner who has the least to gain from continuing the relationship is in the best position to control it and to maintain better bargaining positions. He or she can win concessions from the other by threatening to discontinue it.

Although dating is expected to facilitate personal growth and mate selection, it can be a despairing experience for many young people. Dating encompasses complex motives and different kinds of role relationships that in several respects imperfectly facilitate socialization. The intense competition of social dating may lead an adolescent to role-play and thereby conceal his or her individuality. "The dating code, the implicit prescriptions for behavior and affect, are designed to keep the relationships casual, superficial, emotionally noninvolving. There develops a kind of characterological fiction—the 'good date.'"[67] The good date is expected to be cheerful, verbally facile, skilled in controlling impulses and moods, and well-mannered. "The boy can exercise some inventiveness in arranging the evening's activities, but not to the point of deviation. The girl's behavior is probably more strictly regulated than the boy's; . . . she must be at the least polite and if possible enthusiastic about it, whatever her secret inclinations may be."[68]

Douvan and Adelson are pessimistic about the dating situation in America, pointing out that it may drive "the American youngster to displays of emptiness, silliness, artificiality, vanity, vulgarity and among girls, outright 'tigerish bitchiness.'"[69] Thus, dating may teach one only certain superficialities, and two aspects of personality growth—sexual development and self-esteem—may receive little attention at all. Douvan and Adelson emphasize that in dating there are no external controls (such as chaperones) and that the burden of constraint is on the young people themselves. In an unstable situation, young people may find it difficult to control their impulses. Also, adolescents may retreat to the safety of role-playing to protect themselves from the danger of humiliation. The salient status-seeking rewards come from the appraisal of others, and a great deal of prestige is at stake. Since adolescents know that they can easily be embarassed, they may turn to external grace, poise, and nonchalance to avoid unnecessary exposure of their feelings. Unfortunately, the diverse subterfuges of social dating may ill-prepare the adolescent for the affective demands of more intense relationships.[70]

Mate Selection

Romanticists are inclined to believe that dating and courtship choices are made freely in a worldwide pool. The fiction exists that once commitment to the desirability of a heterosexual relationship is made, adolescents may differentiate progressively among attractive prospects and pick mates according to their inclinations. But, however approvingly societies may condone companionship and love, few leave love and mate choice wholly to adolescents themselves. Goode[71] believes that in most societies parents attempt to control and channel the direction of adolescent affection in order to preserve social stratification and lineage patterns. Random mating across ethnic and social-class lines is a threat to traditional social structures. Goode[72] identified five patterns that societies have used worldwide to control mate selection. These are briefly described below:

1. *Child marriage.* A child may be betrothed, married, or both before it has any opportunity to interact intimately with its peers. Since the child is socially dependent on and dominated by its elders, it has no resources with which to oppose the union. Goode described an instance of child marriage that took place in India where the young bride went to live with her husband; the marriage was consummated physically at a much later time, while the young couple was still living in the husband's household.

2. *Kinship rules* prescribe rigid rules to control the eligibility of spouses. Whom the individual can marry may be determined within narrow limits by birth. The kinship rules may go so far as to specify, for example, that a man's sister's child marry his wife's brother's child.

3. *Social isolation* is a practice whereby adolescents who might fall in love are kept socially isolated. Elders may thus arrange marriages for their offspring, knowing that their plans cannot be disrupted by inappropriate love attachments. This system can work where youth seldom, if ever, see one another. It is also found among the upper social strata of certain societies, where both social and physical segregation are economically possible. Goode reported that in China marriages have taken place between young persons who had not previously met because they lived in different villages.

4. *Chaperonage* is a practice whereby close supervision displaces social isolation. It is less expensive and more practical. Marriage is seen as a duty, and family elders choose the mate. In societies practicing chaperonage, there is usually a high value placed on female chastity. Goode said that because of "a complex tension Christianity has fostered between "asceticism and love," the use of chaperones to control mate selection has prevailed throughout the industrial societies.

5. *Self-selection* is a practice whereby individuals are free to choose one another as mates, and ideally, it is unencumbered by cultural customs and restrictions. Self-selection has increasingly characterized the process of mate selection in America. During the seventeenth and eighteenth centuries, a "stable parental-run marriage system" prevailed in America.[73] Families of birth ("the family of origin") dominated those newly created by marriage ("the family of procreation"). Households were likely to be extended in structure, and marriages often took place at an early age and were arranged. But during the nineteenth century, a "stable, participant run system" emerged. With the rise of industrialism, and the shift of economic control and of access to social status to the marketplace, the significance of the family in the mate-

selection process diminished. And the recent successes of women in achieving satisfaction in the workforce are leading many young girls to view employment and career as legitimate alternatives to courtship.[74] Consequently, freedom of choice in mate-selection characterizes contemporary America.

The success of freedom of choice in the mate-selection process is predicted on opportunity to meet persons who are eligible as mates. When an individual is seeking a mate, the task of making contacts at work, school, social events, and parties becomes very important.[75] Dances are a particularly significant source of male-female contact. They provide a gathering place for eligible persons who might not otherwise meet in daily activities. Dances offer opportunity, without much risk of self-esteem, for testing whether acquaintances might lead to worthwhile relationships. They may heighten "interpersonal attraction through the combination of rhythm, expectation of romance, special adornment and the like." And the emotions aroused may stimulate the dancers to believe that they are experiencing strong feelings of attraction.[76]

The extent to which mate selection is affected by cultural factors, however, makes freedom of choice more an illusion than a reality. Researchers overwhelmingly agree that the practice of homogamy—the tendency of similar persons to seek out one another—serves to restrain free choice in mate selection.[77] Homogamous tendencies result from youth's acquired motives to associate with others who share their life styles (or perhaps, complementary life styles). They experience discomfort when their system of values is challenged; therefore, they are likely to want the emotional security of companionship with others who share similar values. Such consensus enhances interpersonal attraction through reciprocal rewards, ease of communication, and self-validation of beliefs.[78] But consensus also rules out pursuit of many eligibles whom one meets at dances and the like because dissimilarities in physical and social characteristics preclude interaction. Eshleman and Hunt,[79] for example, reported that an adolescent from a high-status home whose father is in a professional or managerial occupation is more likely to marry someone whose father has the same occupational status. The same holds true for adolescents whose fathers are in business, secretarial, and minor governmental jobs or in skilled, unskilled, and farming occupations.

Murstein[80] says that good courtship progress is dependent on the ability of each partner to predict features of the self-concept of the other and to confirm them on the basis of the capacity of the other to live up to expectations. The confirming process, however, is affected externally in countless ways by persons outside the couple relationship. One major source of social influence is friends who may contribute their evaluations of a potential mate's qualities. Friends may accept a couple as a pair, for example, acting approvingly toward the two. On the other hand, friends may assert "he is not good enough for you"; or "you can't make it with her; she is out of your class." Parental control over youth's informal relationships also helps focus their affections. Parents may "threaten, cajole, wheedle, bribe, and persuade their children to 'go with the right people,' during both the early love play and later courtship phases."[81] Parents may even control mate selection by influencing youth's informal social contacts. They might move to more appropriate neighborhoods with better schools, give parties, prepare invitation lists, and in innumerable ways make the adolescents aware that certain individuals are more eligible as mates by virtue of manners, tastes, clothing styles, and so forth. Lewis[82] argues that friends and relatives initiate, perpetuate, and crystalize mate selection by evaluating the pair as "viable or nonviable," by attaching labels to the two on the basis of the way in which they have evaluated them, and then, by responding to the couple relative to their preconceptions. Thus, as Goode[83] points out, it is no accident that most marriages are between couples of the same social class, religious, ethnic, and educational levels.

The mate-selection process also is strongly influenced by the phenomenon of romantic love. Rubin[84] says its "distinguishing features include the beliefs that love is fated and uncontrollable, that it strikes at first sight, consumes the lovers with single-minded passion, transcends all social boundaries, and lasts throughout life." He points out that the socialization of young people to believe in romantic love begins in the nursery schools with the recounting of fairy tales even before they are old enough to attend movies and read comic books. The Cinderella story, for example, tells how a handsome prince overcomes obstacles to win the hand of a poor maiden with whom he has fallen in love. The last line of the typical fairy tale relates that the couple lived happily ever after, but the unsaid last line in each story is "'some day this may happen to you.'"[85] There is some evidence, too, that young people are often seduced by romantic love to ignore practical considerations—dissimilarities associated with social class, education, religion, aspirations, and personal traits. Rosenblatt and Cozby[86] observe that so much freedom of choice in mate selection sometimes leads to impractical decisions and unwarranted emotional involvement in courtship. Perhaps, they say, the need to justify a mate choice, when one has not used clear, objective grounds for making it in the first place, especially when external pressures have been fairly light, results in emphasis on affection, exaggeration of qualities, and so on. Finally, romantic love may distort mate selection by reflecting efforts to avoid loneliness or to cope with feelings of depression or dependency. Young people may observe their friends becoming engaged or marrying, and then, make unwise choices more for the sake of obtaining a mate per se than the right mate.

MARRIAGE AS A SOCIAL INSTITUTION

The marriage-family unit in the United States represents a bridge between "the needs of society to maintain itself and the needs of individuals to fulfill themselves."[87] Marriage is an institutionalized structure for satisfying both societal and personal expectations. It is one of the more significant rites of passage from childhood dependence and freedom to adult responsibility and commitment. Dreyer[88] describes marriage in the traditional sense as a means to achieve personal and social ends. It is entered into as a legal contract by means of a ritualized ceremony. It satisfies a general expectation in society about the manner in which persons become husbands and wives; it establishes formally the right of young people to residential separation from their families of origin; it offers a legitimate, relatively secure context in which to satisfy sexual needs; it provides a stable environment for child bearing and child rearing; and it serves to meet psychological expectations for intimacy, understanding, communication, and love.[89] Within the traditional marriage unit, as Dreyer points out, instrumental or task accomplishment roles are usually performed by husbands and expressive or group maintenance roles are usually fulfilled by wives. He notes that these expectations are fairly rigid, allowing for little variation throughout the life span.

Perhaps one-third of today's young people are actively seeking new forms and meanings in marriage, while two-thirds continue to hold fairly conventional views about marriage.[90] A variety of trends are converging to alter youth's outlook toward marriage. During the past decade (1) advances in contraceptives (symbolized by the "Pill") and the liberalization of attitudes toward abortion have allowed for greater sexual freedom and have reduced fear of unwanted pregnancies; (2) a growing commitment to a zero population growth policy has eliminated guilt over turning away from child-bearing; and (3) the ideology of the women's movement is making cooking, washing, and diapering as secondary to women as to men in the development of career aspirations. The profile of attitudes of youth toward marriage and family issues, which is shown in Table 3, is indicative of the sizeable and growing minority of young people who are actively interested in exploring life styles alternative to those implied by traditional marriage roles. Table 3 shows that the attitudes toward family structure of the respondents, who were college students, could be categorized as radical

Table 3
Percentage Distribution of Students' Attitudes Toward Family Issues (N = 216)

Family Issue	Attitudes and Percent				
1. Communal Living*	Very attractive 7.4	Attractive 34.2	Somewhat attractive 58.3		
2. Group Marriage*	Extremely attractive 6.5	Very attractive 16.7	Attractive 57.9	Not attractive 19.0	
3. R's Marriage Intention	W/o legal ties 8.3		W/legal ties 91.7		
4. Marital Roles (Work-Home)	Reverse Roles 0.0		Equalitarian 54.6	Intermediate 30.1	Patriarchal 15.3
5. Involvement Justifying Intercourse	Physical attraction 7.9	Some emotion 35.2	Deep emotion 43.0	Marriage Intention 10.2	Marriage Only 3.7
6. Legalized Abortion			Approve 78.7	Disapprove 21.3	
7. Homosexuality	Desirable alternative 6.9	Possible alternative 35.2	Illness 53.7	Family Problem 2.3	Immoral 1.8
Conventionality Index		Radical 16.2	Conventional 67.6		Conservative 16.2

Source: E. D. Yost and R. J. Adamek. Parent-child interaction and changing family values: a multivariate analysis. *Journal of Marriage and the Family*, 1974, **36**, 115–121. Reprinted by permission.

* Attitudes toward these issues were measured by more than one item, and the percentage distributions reflect the respondents' distributions on the indexes formed by these items. The other issues were measured by one item each.

(16.2 percent), conventional (67.6 percent), and conservative (16.2 percent).[91] The radical youth saw attractiveness in communal living, favored group marriage for society in general, preferred marriage and parenthood without legal ties, viewed physical attractiveness as the minimum level of involvement that should precede sexual relations, characterized homosexuality as a desirable alternative to the cultural norm of heterosexuality, and favored equalitarian marital roles and legalized abortions. On the other hand, the traditional or conservative youth disapproved of communal living, group marriage, premarital sex, abortion, and homosexuality. They saw marriage as a relationship with a spouse where the male had an outside career and the female was primarily responsible for the home. The conventional youth, who represented the majority, saw communal living as having some attractive aspects, held permissive attitudes toward experimenting with group marriages, preferred marriage with legal ties, including a commitment to have children, and wanted a relationship where they and their spouses shared equally in career and family responsibilities. They also felt that a deep emotional involvement was the minimal level which should precede sexual relations. They expressed approval, too, of legal abortion and regarded homosexuality as an illness.[92] The data presented in Table 3 bear out Dreyer's[93] contention that marriage has lost its significance to some youth as a social necessity. He observes that persons of the opposite sex can live together today, can participate in sexual intercourse, can have children, either naturally or by adoption, and will be accepted by many groups as a fully functioning family unit—without being married in the legal or official sense. Table 3 also shows, however, that more than 90 percent of young people prefer marriage. On the one hand, marriage is universally sanctioned in Western societies and it is the long-term living arrangement most socially approved by the adult generation. On the other hand, marriage conveys joint ownership of property, protection from liability, tax benefits in the lower income brackets, increased credit, inheritance guarantees, and dependency protection for wives and children.[94]

Marriage, nonetheless, is acquiring new meanings among contemporary youth. Many young people no longer look upon marriage as an institutional prerequisite to living together, but they do see marriage as "a goal representing affirmation of personal identity, psychological intimacy, mutual pleasure giving, the promise of continued personal growth, and a transcendent relationship between two human beings."[95] Marriage in this sense becomes a means to interpersonal growth. Dreyer says that young people today are taking marriage seriously not because the legal contract is inviolate or because divorce is impossible but because young people see marriage as a crucial step in their identity

Love and commitment are being celebrated today in uniquely expressive ways.

formation. Their changing views about marriage are finding expression in new rituals regarding the marriage ceremony. Seligson[96] describes the rise in the 1970s of a "new kind of wedding that aims to celebrate the love and commitment of the couple in uniquely expressive ways. Whereas the traditional wedding ceremony is largely conducted by parents as their day, since it symbolizes the final chapter of their parenthood, the 'new' wedding is focused primarily around the values of the couple about to be married. It is likely to take place on a beach, hilltop, or meadow." Seligson[97] says that key word in the "new" wedding is "meaningful." One girl who was married on a beach in Virginia said: "When Tom and I planned our wedding, we talked about all the formal church and hotel affairs we'd been to—those of friends and relatives—and realized how empty they were. Phony, with all that etiquette junk and everything done for the parents who just wanted to show off for their friends. You never knew what the couple was like, and you never cared. And there was no real joy at all. We knew we wanted to have something that would be more than just another drunken party—something uniquely ours.'' Marriage contracts constitute another aspect of the change in outlook. Many young couples are writing contracts to ensure that they have a clearly defined relationship. The idea of a definitive contract has received impetus from young women who want to combine career and a family but are fearful that they might be trapped in a traditional marriage. The contract also is appealing to young people who want to spare themselves the emotion and trauma often associated with divorce. A contract, for example, might cover such areas as household duties, child care, and property ownership. It might also go so far as to include a proclamation that sexual fidelity is not demanded and a provision that either partner is free to seek out other relationships.

Adolescent Marriages

Current Census Bureau statistics indicate that more young people are delaying the age at which they marry than at any time since early in the century.[98] A trend appeared in the United States from 1900 to 1960 toward early marriages for both men and women. In 1900, for instance, men married for the first time on the average at 25 years and 9 months and women 21 years and 9 months. But in 1960, the average age of first marriage had dropped for men to 22 years, 5 months, and for women, to 20 years, 2 months. Today the downward trend has reversed itself and the average age for first marriage of men has climbed to 23 years and 3 months, the highest since 1948 and for women to 20 years, 9 months, the highest since 1940. In spite of the upward trend, however, many American young people marry at a relatively young age—nearly half of the women on the average, for example, are still teenagers on the occasion of their first marriage.

The benefits that marriage generally conveys, unfortunately, seldom accrue to those who seek early marriage. Marriage usually offers a pathway to adult responsibilities and roles; it is expected to promote social independence, attainment of social status, and expression of love. In early marriages, however, the dream apparently sours rather swiftly. The age group under 20 years has the highest incidence of divorce (43 per 1,000) followed by the age group 20 to 24 years (33 per 1,000).[99] Furthermore, the early marriages that survive appear in later years to be relatively unstable. According to the U.S. Census Bureau, couples who marry before the age of 21 relative to those who marry later, double their probability of divorce within 20 years.[100] The divorce rate is correlated with age at the time of marriage, and the older the couple is at marriage, the greater the likelihood that the marriage will succeed. The divorce rate declines for women with each year that they wait to marry until it levels off at about age 25; the divorce rate declines for men until about age 31, but it starts to level off around age 27.[101] De Lissovoy[102] and Reiner and Edwards,[103] have recently developed profiles of adolescent marriages. De Lissovoy studied 48 married high school age couples over a three-year period by means of self-rating scales, semi-structured interviews, knowledge tests, and clinical analyses. Reiner and Edwards reviewed 50 cases of couples who had married when both partners were under the age of 20 and who asked a Family Counseling Service for help with marital problems. The data derived from the investigations indicate why prospects for success are so gloomy among adolescent marriages. In de Lissovoy's study, the mean age of husbands and wives was 17.1 and 16.5, respectively, and their families of origin were predominantly rural working class. Neither husbands nor wives had had much previous dating experience. Approximately three-fourths of both sexes dropped out of school before graduation; pregnancy appeared to be the chief motivating factor for marriage since nearly all of the wives were expecting a child prior to the marriage. The couples in the Reiner and Edwards[104] study were predominantly white, from working class background, with incomes between $4,000 and $9,000. The researchers found that the young people were unable to describe their dissatisfactions—they were not sure what was reasonable to expect of a wife and husband. They were often depressed with respect to employment, lack of vocational prospects, and insufficient money. Frequent disagreements abounded between husbands and wives regarding sexual relations, and the young couples were unready and unprepared for the obligations of parenthood. Surprisingly, in spite of such problems, adolescent marriages do not appear to be the result of rash planning. De Lissovoy found that almost all of the couples in his study had known one another for an average of three years. And Reiner and Edwards reported that most of the couples in their investigation had gone together for several years—in only 12 cases had the couples dated less than one year.

The most difficult problem adolescents face in marriage is that of reconciling high expectations with typically low financial resources. De Lissovoy reported that many of the young couples in his study were receiving public assistance and surplus food. One-third of the couples had debts requiring regular payments and over one-half had borrowed from finance companies at exorbitant interest rates. Reiner and Edwards reported that the young couples they interviewed had had little preparation for handling money or contracts, and in many instances, were following in the pattern of ineffectual parental models. Car expenses, rent, and doctor's bills kept many of them from making ends meet. Lack of money tended to alienate them from former friends who were still single and a lack of a car, or being forced to live in a remote area to get a rental unit that they could afford, isolated many from former friends and family. Financial distress, however, sometimes was alleviated by parental assistance, for example, providing a place for the young couple to live (which usually meant moving in with relatives) or money for rent, a trailer, furniture, food, car payments, clothing, appliances, and extra spending.

Early marriages are often precipitated by unsatisfactory socializing experiences. The obstacles youth face in an early marriage, however, may be comparable in magnitude to those they left behind. Many young people find an early marriage is like jumping from the frying pan into the fire. Prospects for a relatively early marriage are enhanced when favorable marital opportunities are present, anticipated rewards appear promising, and alternative roles seem relatively unattractive and undesirable. Specifically, Elder[105] suggests that predisposition toward early marriage is strengthened in girls with (1) economic strain in the family, (2) unsupervised interaction with boys, and (3) emotionally distant or nonsupportive relations with parents (fathers especially). Elder says that "economic strain minimizes prospects for education beyond high school and enhances the appeal of marriage as an escape from family burdens; unsupervised interaction with boys provides opportunity for heterosexual involvement; and deprivation with respect to paternal affection and support is likely to increase dependence on boyfriends for the satisfaction of social and emotional needs."[106] The researcher investigated the process by which girls are oriented toward marriage at different ages by comparing 73 women who were participants in a long-term longitudinal study. The women were divided into three groups on the basis of their age at first marriage (relatively early, late, and average); indices of their independence, psychological state, and academic image were constructed from questionnaires and interview data. Elder found considerable support for his assumptions. Resistance to parental authority was fairly common among the girls who married early. They were inclined to talk back to their parents and to feel estranged from them, particularly their fathers. Indeed, only one-third of the women who married early expressed positive sentiments toward their fathers. The girls who married early also tended to be highly emotional, to desire social status early in adolescence, but in actuality to acquire lower social status than other girls of high school age. They were more likely than the other girls to have started dating at an early age and to have engaged in coitus during high school. Finally, the girls who married before the age of 20 scored appreciably lower on academic aptitude than girls who married later, and they were likely to favor domestic roles for themselves. Reiner and Edwards,[107] observing the wide range of family troubles young people often bring to an early marriage, suggest that many of them see it as an "escape hatch;" it is a matter of "any port in a storm."

Adolescent Marriages and School Policies.   The high school dropout rate is exceedingly high among youth who marry before graduation. De Lissovoy[108] reports that in his study of high school couples, 85 percent of the girls and 73 percent of the boys left school before graduation. The reasons youth have for leaving school are varied. On the one hand, pregnancy precipitates leaving school for young girls, and the necessity of earning a living often leads boys into full-time work. On the other hand, high schools have traditionally fostered irrelevant, even hostile environments for married adolescents. High schools have denied attendance privileges to married young people on the grounds that the schools are oriented primarily for serving unmarried, unemployed adolescents. Sometimes teachers and administrators believe that married students will either discuss sexual intimacies with other students, thus corrupting their morals, or will glamorize marriage, thus encouraging immature students to rush into matrimony. Officials may refuse to accept married or pregnant students in high school, believing acceptance to be equated with approval. In a survey of Minnesota school administrators, Anderson and Latts[109] reported that "a high percentage of the administrators claimed that married students discussed their marital sexual experiences with single students, had poor attendance records, were a bad influence, got pregnant again, neglected their studies, and encouraged other students to get married." During recent years, however, school boards throughout the country have become relatively lenient in permitting young people who marry to remain in school or to return to school whenever circumstances permit. School boards today may even be highly responsive to the needs of married students. They may provide a network of supportive learning activities—establishing special classes in maternity and child care, perhaps where the young pregnant wives or mothers and husbands can spend their mornings learning child care and homemaking and their afternoons in standard academic classes. A national assessment of the attitudes of school boards is unavailable, but Brown[110] has surveyed 765 Texas public school districts, and the results of his analyses are presented in Table 4. The data shown in Table 4 are based on 475 of the 765 districts that indicated that they had developed a policy regarding the supervision of married students (those that lacked any policy were the smaller districts for whom married students had not yet been a concern). The data encompassed more than two million students, and

Table 4

Types of Verbal and Written Policies in Effect on Married Students in 475 Participating School Districts

Content of Policy	Responding Schools	%
1. Married students are allowed to attend regular day school with no restrictions imposed solely because of their married status.	160	33.6
2. Married students are allowed to attend regular day school but are not allowed to participate in cocurricular activities.	398	83.8
3. Married students are allowed part-time attendance in the regular day school. Each case is considered by the board of education.	8	1.7
4. Married students must make application to the board of education through an authorized member of the administration to remain in the regular day school.	6	1.3
5. Each case will be judged on its own merits.	36	7.6
6. A special committee is appointed and makes a recommendation to the board. If the student is allowed to remain in the day school, there are no restrictions based solely upon his married status placed upon him.	4	0.8
7. Pregnancy brings immediate expulsion.	36	7.6
8. If both students are enrolled, one must withdraw, the choice being theirs.	3	0.6
9. Married students must make application through an authorized member of the administration. If the student is allowed to remain in the regular day school, his cocurricular activities are subject to regulation by either the board or by the administrative staff.	50	10.6
10. All married students are suspended from school for a prescribed period of time immediately after marriage.	7	1.5
11. Failure to report marriage immediately after marriage shall constitute justification for immediate suspension.	16	3.4

Source: B. B. Brown, married students in public high schools: a Texas study. *Family Coordinator,* 1972, **21,** 321–324. Reprinted by permission.

probably are fairly representative of school districts everywhere. They show that one-third of the Texas districts allow married youth to attend regular day school without academic restrictions; still, more than 80 percent do not permit married students to participate in co-curricular activities. Less than 2 percent of the districts currently suspend young people from school immediately after their marriage—a fact which reveals a dramatic change in attitude over the past decade. As recently as 1960, for example, a National Education Association poll indicated that more than one-half of the teachers polled believed that married boys and girls should be excluded from school.[111]

SUMMARY

Friendships offer adolescents opportunity for exploring and enlarging their sphere of interactions. Young people are attracted to one another in friendship patterns as a function of the rewards that a positive liking relationship brings to each of them. According to role theory, friendships develop between persons who share similar expectations of each other's performances, anticipate positive consequences of the relationship, and reinforce each other's patterns of behavior. Trust is a major dimension of friendship, but other ingredients like potential for intimacy, positive regard, admiration, and similarity also are important.

Popularity is an index of a person's desirability as a friend. Several traits have been empirically identified as components of popularity: kindness and sympathy, cheerful and carefree outlook, active participation in sports, above average intellectual capacity, physical attractiveness, and family social status. Good personal and social adjustment is the sine qua non of popularity. The ability of young people to process information about these traits increases throughout adolescence, which enables them to develop friendships of more and more sophistication. Physical attractiveness appears to be a particularly important correlate of popularity, and to some extent perceptions of physical attractiveness partially determine popularity. Physically attractive persons are assumed to possess more socially desirable personality traits than persons of lesser attractiveness and to lead happier and more successful lives. Peer status, another facet of interpersonal attraction and friendship formation, is also a function of popularity. It is either earned on the basis of capacity to act effectively in social settings or ascribed because of possession of the resources that facilitate peer interaction—money, car, clothes, impressive home, and so forth. On the whole, young people are likely to look to high-status youth for direction, and those who attain high status among their peers usually acquire an advantage in controlling their own destiny and that of others.

Prejudice serves to repulse interpersonal attraction. It occurs when stereotypical judgments are permitted to distort interpersonal involvement. Glock et al. advance a "cognitive theory of prejudice," in which they suggest that cognitively unsophisticated young people are more likely both to perpetuate stereotypes of others and to accept simpleminded notions when they are applied to themselves. The researchers propose such educational strategies to counteract prejudices as instruction in (1) the logic of inference, (2) the social, cultural, and historical bases of group differences, and (3) ways of avoiding overgeneralizations about group differences.

Boys and girls tend to demonstrate a developmental pattern in their opposite-sex friendship choices. According to Broderick's analysis, most 10 to 11 year olds disapprove of socializing with members of the opposite sex. The widest cleavage between the sexes occurs at age 12, but between 12 and 13 about half the young people have begun dating. Segregation of friendship choices by sex diminishes markedly among 14 to 15 year olds. By 16 or 17 years of age, negative feelings about the opposite sex have virtually disappeared.

Dating is one of the major social activities of adolescence. Dating facilitates mate selection because it enables adolescents to acquire a wide range of social skills. Dating may range from casual meetings to going steady and engagement for marriage. The most salient incentives for dating are companionship and mate selection, but sexual gratification, assertion of independence, status seeking, recreation, and courtship are also important.

Although the selection of partners for dating and courtship appears to be wide open, in fact, parents in many societies attempt to control and channel the direction of adolescent affection in order to preserve social stratification and lineage patterns. *Self-selection* is the custom in contemporary America; nonetheless, marriages tend to occur between partners of comparable social class, religion, racial, and educational levels. The mate-selection process also is strongly influenced by the phenomenon of romantic love, which often seduces young people into ignoring practical considerations and into making unwise choices. Marriage traditionally has been a means to achieve personal and social ends, for example, a means of meeting psychological expectations for intimacy, understanding, communication, and love, and of providing a stable environment for child-bearing and child-rearing. The majority of young people still hold conventional attitudes toward marriage, and see it as a crucial step in their identity formation, but a sizeable minority no longer look upon marriage as an institutional prerequisite to living together. Changing views about marriage are finding expression in new rituals regarding the marriage ceremony; these aim to celebrate the love and commitment of the couple in uniquely expressive ways.

Prospects for the success of an early marriage are especially poor when the young people are school dropouts, economically dependent on their parents, and burdened with a premarital pregnancy. The age group under 20 years has the highest incidence of divorce, and it is followed by the age group 20 to 24 years of age. The divorce rate is correlated with age at the time of marriage, and the older the average age of the couple the greater is the likelihood that the marriage will succeed. Research shows that neither husbands nor wives in early marriages have had much previous dating experience. The most difficult problem young people face in an early marriage is that of reconciling high expectations with typically low financial resources. Moreover, high schools have traditionally denied attendance privileges to married young people on the grounds that the schools primarily serve unmarried, unemployed adolescents. The traditional outlook is changing rapidly, however, and school boards are becoming responsive to the needs of married students and are beginning to provide a network of supportive learning activities.

REVIEW QUESTIONS

1. What are the major components of interpersonal attraction?
2. How are adolescent friendships interpreted in the context of psychoanalytic theory?
3. How do friendships emerge from interpersonal attraction?
4. What are the major ingredients of a friendship?
5. Which traits of popularity are valued highly by both children and adolescents?
6. Why is intelligence related to popularity?
7. What is the main advantage of physical attractiveness as a determinant of popularity?
8. What are the differences between achieved and ascribed popularity?
9. How do social experiences and cognitive unsophistication interact to produce ethnic prejudice?
10. Define the "cognitive theory of prejudice."
11. What instructional strategies would Glock and his colleagues develop to counter prejudicial thinking?
12. What are the main differences in friendship patterns among youth 10 to 11, 12 to 13, 14 to 15, and 16 to 17 years old?
13. Compare different types of dating by their structural elements.
14. What incentives make dating attractive?
15. What patterns have societies adopted to control mate selection?
16. How might social influences affect a couple's relationship during courtship?
17. Why is romantic love more a problem than a blessing during courtship?
18. What are the characteristics of the traditional view of marriage?
19. What are the trends that are altering contemporary youth's image of marriage?
20. Why are changes taking place in marriage ceremonies and in marriage contracts?
21. Why is success so unlikely among adolescent marriages?
22. What predisposes young people toward early marriage?
23. Why have high schools fostered hostile environments for married adolescents? Why are traditional views changing?

DISCUSSION QUESTIONS

1. Why is popularity among adolescents so closely related to peer status? What can an unpopular adolescent do to improve his or her peer standing?
2. How would you organize the extracurricular activities of a high school to reduce ethnic prejudice?

3. What are the critical social factors that affect the mate selection process in your community? What kinds of circumstances might overcome the influence of, respectively, social class, religion, ethnicity, and educational level?

4. Although most young people look upon marriage as a means to interpersonal growth, young people are increasingly looking for alternatives to conventional family life. What alternatives are emerging in your community? What recommendations regarding marriage would you make to an adolescent who asked for your advice?

5. Since adolescents often are unprepared to meet the obligations of an early marriage, what might high schools and community agencies do to ease their problems?

NOTES

1. E. Douvan and J. Adelson. *The adolescent experience.* New York: John Wiley, 1966.

2. Douvan and Adelson, *op. cit.,* p. 174.

3. J. T. Tedeschi. Attributions, liking, and power. In T. L. Huston (Ed.), *Foundations of interpersonal attraction.* New York: Academic Press, 1974, pp. 193–215.

4. G. S. Blum. *Psychoanalytic theories of personality.* New York: McGraw-Hill, 1953.

5. Douvan and Adelson, *op. cit.,* p. 179.

6. Douvan and Adelson, *op. cit.*

7. Tedeschi, *op. cit.*

8. Douvan and Adelson, *op. cit.*

9. Douvan and Adelson, *op. cit.,* p. 492.

10. Tedeschi, *op. cit.*

11. Tedeschi, *op. cit.,* p. 205.

12. Tedeschi, *op. cit.*

13. D. K. Wheeler. Popularity among adolescents in western Australia and in the United States of America. *School Review,* 1961, **69,** 67–81.

14. C. McC. Tryon. Evaluations of adolescent personality by adolescents. *Monographs of the Society for Research and Child Development,* 1939, **4,** 1–83.

15. N. Livson and W. C. Bronson. An exploration of patterns of impulse control in early adolescence. *Child Development,* 1961, **32,** 75–88.

16. W. Emmerich. Developmental trends in evaluations of single traits. *Child Development,* 1974, **45,** 172–183.

17. D. Elkins. Some factors related to the choice-status of ninety eighth-grade children in a school society. *Genetic Psychology Monographs,* 1958, **58,** 207–272.

18. R. F. Peck and C. Galliani. Intelligence, ethnicity and social roles in adolescent society. *Sociometry,* 1962, **25,** 64–72.

19. H. R. Marshall. Prediction of social acceptance in community youth groups. *Child Development,* 1958, **29,** 173–184.

20. H. Horowitz. Prediction of adolescent popularity and rejection from achievement and interest tests. *Journal of Educational Psychology,* 1967, **58,** 170–174.

21. J. S. Coleman. *The adolescent society.* New York: Free Press, 1961.

22. K. Dion, E. Berscheid, and E. Walster. What is beautiful is good. *Journal of Personality and Social Psychology,* 1972, **24,** 285–290.

23. D. Krebs and A. A. Adinolfi. Physical attractiveness, social relations, and personality style. *Journal of Personality and Social Psychology,* 1975, **31,** 245–253.

24. H. Sigall and D. Landy. Radiating beauty: effects of having a physically attractive partner on person perception. *Journal of Personality and Social Psychology,* 1973, **28,** 218–224.

25. Sigall and Landy, *op. cit.*

26. N. Cavior and P. R. Dokecki. Physical attractiveness, perceived attitude similarity, and academic achievement as contributors to interpersonal attraction among adolescents. *Development Psychology,* 1973, **9,** 44–54.

27. Krebs and Adinolfi, *op. cit.*

28. Krebs and Adinolfi, *op. cit.*

29. E. E. Snyder. High school student perceptions of prestige criteria. *Adolescence,* 1972, **6,** 129–136.

30. National Center for Health Statistics. *Health attitudes and behavior of youths 12–17 years: demographic and socioeconomic factors.* (DHEW, pub. no. [HRA] 76-1635.) Series 11, No. 153, 1975, p. 29.

31. N. D. Feshbach. Nonconformity to experimentally induced group norms of high-status versus low-status members. *Journal of Personality and Social Psychology,* 1967, **6,** 55–63.

32. O. J. Harvey and J. Rutherford. Status in the informal group: influence and influencibility at differing age levels. *Child Development,* 1960, **31,** 377–385.

33. M. Rokeach, P. W. Smith, and R. I. Evans. Two kinds of prejudice or one? In M. Rokeach (Ed.). *The open and closed mind.* New York: Basic Books, 1960.

34. E. A. Nelsen and N. P. Uhl. The influence of racial composition of desegregated secondary schools upon black students' perceptions of the school climates. Paper presented at the annual meeting of the American Education Research Association, San Francisco, 1976.

35. P. A. Cusick and R. J. Ayling. Biracial interaction in an urban, secondary school. *School Review,* 1974, **82,** 486–494.

36. Nelsen and Uhl, *op. cit.*

37. C. Y. Glock, R. Wuthnow, J. A. Piliavin, and M. Spencer. *Adolescent prejudice.* New York: Harper and Row, 1975.

38. Glock et al., *op. cit.,* p. 162.

39. Glock et al., *op. cit.,* p. 99.

40. Glock et al., *op. cit.,* pp. 176–177. Reprinted by permission.

41. L. E. Kanous, R. A. Daugherty, and T. S. Cohn. Relation between heterosexual friendship choices and socioeconomic level. *Child Development,* 1962, **33,** 251–255.

42. J. L. Moreno. *Who shall survive? A new approach to the problems of human interrelations.* Washington, D.C.: Nervous and Mental Disease Publishing Co., 1934.

43. C. B. Broderick. Socio-sexual development in a suburban community. *The Journal of Sex Research,* 1966, **2,** 1–24.

44. Kanous et al., *op. cit.*

45. W. J. Meyer. Relationships between social need strivings and the development of heterosexual affiliations. *Journal of Abnormal and Social Psychology,* 1959, **59,** 51–57.

46. C. B. Broderick and S. E. Fowler. New patterns of relationships between the sexes among preadolescents. *Marriage and Family Living,* 1961, **23,** 27–30.

47. Meyer, *op. cit.*

48. Broderick, *op. cit.*

49. Douvan and Adelson, *op. cit.*

50. Broderick, *op. cit.*

51. Broderick, *op. cit.*

52. Douvan and Adelson, *op. cit.*

53. Douvan and Adelson, *op. cit.*

54. E. L. Vockell and J. W. Asher. Dating frequency among high school seniors. *Psychological Reports,* 1972, **31,** 381–382.

55. J. Delora. Social systems of dating on a college campus. *Marriage and Family Living,* 1963, **25,** 81–84.

56. Delora, *op. cit.*

57. E. W. Burgess and H. J. Locke. *The family.* New York: American Book Co., 1940, pp. 382–393.

58. S. H. Lowrie. Dating theories and student responses. *American Sociological Review,* 1951, **16,** 334–340.

59. W. Waller. The rating and dating complex. *American Sociological Review,* 1937, **2,** 727–734.

60. G. Schwartz and D. Merten. The language of adolescence: an anthropological approach to the youth culture. *American Journal of Sociology,* 1967, **72,** 453–468.

61. R. H. Coombs and W. F. Kenkel. Sex differences in dating aspirations and satisfaction with computer-selected partners. *Journal of Marriage in the Family,* 1966, **28,** 62–66.

62. E. Walster, V. Aronson, D. Abrahams, and L. Rottmann. Importance of physical attractiveness in dating behavior. *Journal of Personality and Social Psychology,* 1966, **4,** 508–516.

63. J. W. Critelli. Physical attractiveness in dating couples. Paper presented at the annual meeting of the American Psychological Association, Chicago, 1975.

64. R. E. Grinder. Relations of social dating attractions to academic orientation and peer relations. *Journal of Educational Psychology,* 1966, **57,** 27–34.

65. Grinder, *op. cit.,* pp. 28–29.

66. J. K. Skipper, Jr. and G. Nass. Dating behavior: a framework for analysis and an illustration. *Journal of Marriage and the Family,* 1966, **28,** 412–420.

67. Douvan and Adelson, *op. cit.,* p. 205.

68. Douvan and Adelson, *op. cit.*, p. 206.

69. Douvan and Adelson, *op. cit.*, pp. 206–207.

70. Douvan and Adelson, *op. cit.*

71. W. J. Goode. The theoretical importance of love. *American Sociological Review,* 1959, **24,** 38–47.

72. Goode, *op. cit.*, pp. 43–45.

73. D. S. Smith. Parental power and marriage patterns: an analysis of historical trends in Hingham, Massachusetts. *Journal of Marriage and the Family,* 1973, **35,** 419–428, p. 426.

74. J. A. Bruce. The role of mothers in the social placement of daughters: marriage or work? *Journal of Marriage and the Family,* 1974, **36,** 492–497.

75. P. C. Rosenblatt and P. C. Cozby. Courtship patterns associated with freedom of choice of spouse. *Journal of Marriage and the Family,* 1972, **34,** 689–695.

76. Rosenblatt and Cozby, *op. cit.*, p. 691.

77. A. C. Kerckhoff. The social context of interpersonal attraction. In T. L. Huston (Ed.). *Foundations of interpersonal attraction.* New York: Academic Press, 1974, pp. 61–78.

78. R. H. Coombs. Reinforcement of values in the parental home as a factor in mate selection. *Marriage and Family Living,* 1962, **24,** 155–157; R. H. Coombs. Value consensus and partner satisfaction among dating couples. *Journal of Marriage and the Family,* 1966, **28,** 166–173.

79. J. R. Eshleman and C. L. Hunt. Social class influences on family adjustment patterns of young married college students. *Journal of Marriage and the Family,* 1967, **29,** 485–491.

80. B. I. Murstein. Person perception and courtship progress among premarital couples. *Journal of Marriage and the Family,* 1972, **34,** 621–626.

81. Goode, *op. cit.*, p. 45.

82. R. A. Lewis. Social influences on marital choice. In S. E. Dragastin, and G. H. Elder, Jr. (Eds.). *Adolescence in the life cycle.* New York: John Wiley, 1975, pp. 211–225.

83. Goode, *op. cit.*, p. 45.

84. Z. Rubin. From liking to loving: patterns of attraction in dating relationships. In T. L. Huston (Ed.). *Foundations of interpersonal attraction.* New York: Academic Press, 1974, pp. 383–402.

85. J. R. Udry, quoted in Rubin, op. cit., p. 163.

86. Rosenblatt and Cozby, *op. cit.*

87. P. H. Dreyer. Sex, sex roles, and marriage among youth in the 1970s. In R. J. Havighurst, and P. H. Dreyer (Eds.). *Youth–seventy-fourth yearbook of the National Society for the Study of Education.* Chicago: University of Chicago Press, 1975, pp. 194–223, p. 194.

88. Dreyer, *op. cit.*

89. Dreyer, *op. cit.*; G. H. Elder, Jr. Role orientations, marital age, and life patterns in adulthood. *Merrill-Palmer Quarterly of Behavior and Development,* 1972, **18,** 3–24.

90. Dreyer, *op. cit.*

91. E. D. Yost and R. J. Adamek. Parent-child interaction and changing family values: a multivariate analysis, *Journal of Marriage and the Family,* 1974, **36,** 115–121.

92. Yost and Adamek, *op. cit.*

93. Dreyer, *op. cit.*

94. Dreyer, *op. cit.*

95. Dreyer, *op. cit.,* p. 221.

96. M. Seligson. The new wedding. *Saturday Review of the Society,* 1973, **1,** 32–38.

97. Seligson, *op. cit.,* p. 32.

98. M. E. Lasswell. Is there a best age to marry?: an interpretation. *Family Coordinator,* 1974, **23,** 237–242.

99. P. Krishnan and A. K. Kayani. Estimates of age specific divorce rates for females in the United States, 1960–1969. *Journal of Marriage and the Family,* 1974, **36,** 72–75.

100. B. S. Reiner and R. L. Edwards. Adolescent marriage—social or therapeutic problem? *Family Coordinator,* 1974, **23,** 383–390.

101. Lasswell, *op. cit.*

102. V. de Lissovoy. High school marriages: a longitudinal study. *Journal of Marriage and the Family,* 1973, **35,** 245–255.

103. Reiner and Edwards, *op. cit.*

104. Reiner and Edwards, *op. cit.*

105. Elder, *op. cit.*

106. Elder, *op. cit.,* p. 10.

107. Reiner and Edwards, *op. cit.*

108. de Lissovoy, *op. cit.*

109. W. J. Anderson and S. M. Latts. High school marriages and school policies in Minnesota. *Journal of Marriage and the Family.* 1965, **27,** 266–270.

110. B. B. Brown. Married students in public high schools: a Texas study. *Family Coordinator,* 1972, **21,** 321–324.

111. G. C. Atkyns. Trends in the retention of married and pregnant students in American public schools. *Sociology of Education,* 1968, **4,** 57–65.

Chapter 11

Sexuality in Adolescence

CHAPTER HIGHLIGHTS

SEXUAL ATTITUDES AND BEHAVIOR IN THE
    UNITED STATES
SEXUAL PERMISSIVENESS
THE MEANING OF RECREATIONAL SEX
SEXUAL AGGRESSION IN ADOLESCENT BOYS
HOMOSEXUALITY
  THE SUPPORTING SUBCULTURE

SEXUAL STRUCTURE AND GENDER ROLE
SEXUAL DECISION MAKING
SUMMARY
REVIEW QUESTIONS
DISCUSSION QUESTIONS

ISSUES

American sexual norms have long been dominated by a double standard: procreational sex for women and recreational sex for men.

Sexual attitudes fostered by the double standard are incongruent with contemporary views of personality development.

Sigmund Freud and Havelock Ellis saw sexuality as a biological product of evolution and recognized its significance in personality development.

Alfred Kinsey established sexual expression as a domain of science, pointed to sharp incongruities between law and custom, and brought openness to discussion and conduct.

Sexual attitudes and conduct in America vary by age, sex, education, and social class.

The more dramatic shifts toward permissiveness in both attitudes and behavior are occurring today among young women.

Sexual values range from traditional to liberal.

The double standard often is invoked to justify physical agression in dating situations.

The view that homosexuality is a form of deviance is diminishing and legal reforms are removing criminal penalties.

A strong, supporting subculture facilitates the homosexual activity of young men.

Gender identity is acquired relatively early in childhood.

Sexual decision making leads to cumulative consequences.

Sexually permissive young people are relatively knowledgeable about contraceptive devices and techniques, but fail generally to take precautions.

Young people acquire sexual knowledge from peers, printed literature, school programs, and parents.

Attitudes in America toward sexuality have long been influenced by an all-pervasive ideal of sexual conduct—continence except for the purpose of pro-creation.[1] This dominant ethic of American sexual norms stems from a centuries-old, Judeo-Christian standard that stipulates sexual abstinence should be practiced before marriage. The social realities of short life spans and high rates of infant mortality made procreational sex at one time the first order of cultural survival. Lust, or anything akin to recreational sex, was to be subdued and regulated by conscience and laws.

Only a few years ago, official codes and laws prohibited any kind of sexual activity outside of marriage and placed taboos on public and scientific discussions of sex. Mouth-genital contact, for example, was thought to be indescribably lewd. Persons preferring sexual partners of their own gender lived under the constant threat of criminal prosecution and social ostracism. Ecclesiastical and medical authorities alike issued frightening warnings about masturbation to both sexes, but particularly to males, well into the twentieth century. Until the discovery of sexual hormones, medical opinion generally held that semen should be husbanded and reabsorbed in the body to ensure male virility. Masturbation, it was said, would cause illness and insanity, stunt physical growth, lead to unsatisfied sexual desires, and divert attention from constructive social activities in work, school, and mate selection. Consider, for example, the following plea for restraint from *The Family Physician*, a widely circulated medical book of the late nineteenth century.[2]

There is a vicious, degrading, and most destructive habit, destructive to both body and mind, indulged in frequently by young people of both sexes, but mostly by males which ought to be without a name. . . . Masturbation . . . It is worse than intemperance, worse than open lewdness, worse than all other vices in which young or old ever do or ever can indulge; more destructive to all the best interests of humanity, in this world and the world to come; destructive to body, mind and soul, and will, if persisted in, render existence a burden, a blank waste, and life a continued scene of wretchedness.

The ideal of sexual continence, however, has always applied more to women than to men. Codes of sexual conduct specify in reality a double standard: procreational sex for women, recreational sex for men. The tradition of two standards originated in the areas of the Eastern Mediterranean before biblical times.[3] The early books of the Old Testament show that marital life was originally polygamous. Wealthy men owned both private harems and slaves. Polygamy left many men of low station without wives, and these men were expected to frequent the prostitutes in the public harem. Later, if circumstances permitted, they might take private wives of their own, but only virgins could become private wives. Women in the public harem were deemed uneligible for marriage, and thus the double standard arose.

Peplau[4] identifies four products of the traditional double standard. First, a moral overtone is suggested in that more restrictive behavior is demanded of women than of men, for whom casual and premarital sex is acceptable. Women are categorized as "good girls" who "save themselves for marriage" and "bad girls" who do not. Chastity and sexual fidelity greatly enhance their desirability. Second, the assumption that men possess stronger sex drives than women bolster the double standard. Men are seen "as more interested in sex, as more easily aroused, as having a greater 'need' for sex." Women, in contrast, are said to regard sex as less urgent and more easily foregone. Thus, men are also presumed to be more knowledgeable and experienced sexually than women. Third, men are believed to be aggressive and women are thought to be passive during sexual interaction. Men are expected to initiate sexual activity, and women are expected to set limits on the magnitude of sexual intimacy the couple achieves. For men, seeing "'how far you could get' often serves to affirm masculinity, to acknowledge the woman's sexual attractiveness, and to test her virtue." A man might confirm his desirability by requesting more and more sexual satisfaction, and a woman may reassure herself of her desirability by simultaneously keeping him oriented while refusing his demands. The woman's role as limit-setter is "consistent with her presumed lesser interest in sex, and her greater stake in preserving a good reputation and avoiding pregnancy." Fourth, Peplau sees the double standard as a product of the belief that relationships between sex and love are stronger in women than in men. Whereas men learn to view sex as a way of demonstrating manhood, and of achieving status in the eyes of male peers, women are taught that love provides sexuality both justification and meaning. Sexual experimentation becomes more permissible for women as a relationship evolves from casual to close.

American sexual attitudes and practices even as recently as a decade ago were dominated by unspoken assumptions about the ideal of continence and the double standard. Calderone[5] has gathered together a variety of folk expressions that show how these assumptions affect the way sexuality is commonly viewed through the life span. The researcher's noteworthy aphorisms are presented below:

1. The child is presumed to be nonsexual or "innocent," that is, "pure in mind" regarding sexual thoughts, questions, and fantasies, and "void in body" of erotic feelings and actions. When such thoughts or feelings are

experienced by a child, they are simply dismissed by adults:

"You're too young to ask about such things."
"When you grow up you'll know."
"Don't ever mention that word to me again."
"Don't let me catch you doing that again."

2. The adolescent is socialized to inhibit sexual feelings and to be uninterested in sexual expression. Parents deal in moral overtones with questions of abstinence and the double standard:

"Playing with yourself is self-abuse."
"Don't let a boy near you."
"Don't get a nice girl into trouble."
"Nice girls aren't supposed to feel that way."
"Boys will be boys."
"When you get married you'll understand."
"Marriage is the beginning of true bliss."

3. The young adult is expected ideally to marry. Calderone points out that a few years ago it was inconceivable that anyone should not wish to be married; adults who remained single were believed to be involuntary victims of failure in the mate-selection process. And, except for the intrusion of the double standard, sexual bliss presumably arose in the context of marriage:

"If your wife 'comes' right from the beginning, it shows she's experienced."
"If your wife doesn't come it shows she's frigid."
"You won't know true ecstasy until you both come at the same time every time."
"The women's role is to satisfy the man."
"The man has a right to have his wife whenever he wants."

4. The older adult is viewed as disinterested in sexual expression. To be over 50 is to be too old for sex; to be over 65 is to be aged, and sex is no longer considered to exist:

"After the change, women lose their interest in sex."
"Men go downhill after 50."
"It's disgusting and perverted for old men and women over 60 to be still interested in sex."
"I tell my husband I'm 60 and through will all that foolishness."

The technology of the industrial society has increased life spans and decreased infant mortality, and as the pressure to maintain the population has eased and as birth control methodology has improved, the moral and legal condemnation of recreational sex has correspondingly waned. The beginning of twentieth-century efforts to lift human sexuality out of the dark ages appears in the earliest writings of Sigmund Freud and Havelock Ellis. The two sages moved sexuality "into the world of the noticed."[6] Both Freud and Ellis saw sexuality as a biological product of evolution and both recognized its implications in respect to personality development. Freud's 1905 essay on childhood sexuality initiated a significant shift in Western thought. Freud saw children's sexual attitudes and appetites as a prime source of motivation in shaping conventional lives, and he placed sexuality at the center of character formation. Psychosocial development ensued, according to psychoanalytic theory, as biological appetites and societal constraints channeled "libidinal" energy toward culturally approved modes of gratification. Freud assumed that the biological components of sexual development followed similar patterns of development in each individual and he centered attention more on the extent to which social forces inhibited sexual growth than on how they led to individual differences in sexual expression. He was preoccupied with the rise of human sexuality as a product of "irreducible conflicts between biological nature and cultural reality."[7] In contrast, Ellis rejected Freud's assumption of an inherent conflict between biological sexual impulse and societal constraint. He focused instead on the societal elements that he believed produced individual differences in sexual expression. Ellis emphasized educational factors as a means of dispelling ignorance and superstition about sexuality and of bringing sexual expression into harmony with cultural expectations.

Psychoanalytic theory, in offering a comprehensive view of sexual expression, provided cultural prescriptions for sexual conduct, and in its more radical forms, a rationale for sexual experimentation.[8] The theory gave rise to the viewpoint that tensions associated with sexuality would disappear when natural sexual energies were liberated. Conservative traditions, which specified that sexual instincts must be held in check, supplied a different outlook. Failure to control the "sexual beast," the conservatives said, would result eventually in the collapse of families, religious institutions, and even societies.[9] During the early years of the twentieth century, the persuasion of the conservatives routinely kept information and materials about birth control, venereal diseases, and literary accounts of sexuality out of general circulation. They invoked censorship "to protect those whom they saw as weaker and more corruptible than themselves—commonly the lower classes, women, and children—by preventing them from being exposed to sexually noxious ideas or materials."[10] The censorship, however, often attracted more controversy and public discussion than the offensive materials would have encountered had nothing been said, and it helped inadvertently to pave the way for more open discussion of human sexuality.

When Alfred Kinsey initiated his research in the 1940s very little information was available about either the actual history of sexual conduct or the current sexual activities of individuals. Psychoanalytic theory had provided insight into neither the distribution of sexual practices among youth and adults nor the extent to which these practices varied among them by age, sex, religion, social class, ethnic heritage, and educational level. Kinsey provided this information, and the publication of his two volumes, *Sexual Behavior in the Human Male,* in 1948, and *Sexual Behavior in the Human Female,* in 1953, had the impact of "a national event."[11] He established sexual expression as a researchable domain of science. The zoologist had applied objective and systematic research methods to an area that until then had been described largely in moralistic and impressionistic terms. Both of his studies were largely statistical compilations that described patterns of sexual behavior in quantitative terms. More importantly, his reports showed that many aspects of sexual behavior, which had long been viewed as criminal or deviant, were frequent occurrences in the general population. He revealed that the "normal" and the "perverse" are on a continuum in the realm of sexual expression, and his data pointed to sharp incongruities between law and custom in matters of sexual conduct.[12] Premarital intercourse, an activity Kinsey found to be characteristic of the majority of men and about 50 percent of the women, and adultery, which he learned was practiced by half of the men and a quarter of the women, had long been subject to social and criminal sanctions. Homosexuality he calculated to encompass between four and six million men and women, and each of them faced the danger of incarceration for allowing the course of their sexual development to deviate from the "normal."

A fundamental shift toward openness in both discussion of sexual attitudes and expression of sexual conduct has occurred since publication of the Kinsey studies. Gagnon points to the frankness that has emerged, for example, in the mass audience film and publishing industries. The decline in movies as family entertainment and the financial success of European cinema in depicting sexual activity has led the type of films that were shown only as "stag" movies in the late 1960s to become regular features today in major urban centers. A few years ago books containing photographs of coitus were available solely from peddlers of illicit materials, but best-selling, fully illustrated, sex-education books are routinely available now on the shelves of most book stores. Magazines in the 1940s were thought to be shocking when they showed women dressed in bathing suits with suggestively loosened tops, and *Playboy* in the 1960s was regarded as risque when it presented photographs of partially clad young women and cartoons suggestive of either mouth-genital contact or couples in simulated coital postures.[13] In contrast, magazines like *Hustler, Penthouse, Gallery,* and *Playgirl* serve both male and female readers, featuring pictures of nude men and women in modes of sexual expression once thought to be incredibly lascivious.

Perhaps, however, research is the most significant of the channels by which sexuality is being introduced into open social discourse. Masters and Johnson, for example, are among the social scientists who are advancing sexual research past that of the Kinsey era, when the emphasis was on listing kinds of behaviors, frequently of experiences, and number of partners.[14] Masters and Johnson are studying the emotional characteristics of sexual responsiveness. Couples may be "wired" in order to record their emotions and be videotaped to observe their actions while they go through routines of foreplay and coitus. Other social scientists are investigating, too, the effects of developmental and personality factors on sexual responsiveness, exclusivity or promiscuity in sexual relationships, and congruence between sexual attitudes and sexual satisfactions. It is this latter, developmental research that provides the framework for the discussion of adolescent sexuality in this chapter. The first section that follows presents normative data about contemporary sexual attitudes and behavior and compares these with the earlier Kinsey data. The subsequent six sections summarize current research in the following areas: sexual permissiveness, meaning of recreational sex, sexual aggression in adolescent boys, homosexuality, sexual structure and gender role, and sexual decision making.

SEXUAL ATTITUDES AND BEHAVIOR IN THE UNITED STATES

The first investigation comparable to Kinsey's surveys was carried out after a time span of nearly three decades, which is something of a tribute to the researcher's comprehensiveness. Wilson[15] conducted an extensive survey in 1970 of sexual attitudes and behaviors by randomly sampling 2,486 adults who were living in the contiguous 48 states, and his data provide a contemporary picture of American sexuality. He reports that a majority of adults (63 percent) believe that a sizeable difference exists between what people would like in their sexual experience and what they actually have. Men, whatever their education level, are more likely to believe this than are women, persons in their twenties are more likely to believe it than persons in other age groups, and women with less education are more likely to believe it than other women. Nonetheless, Wilson found that adults reject by a ratio of two to one the proposition that "first of all, sex is for fun." A substantial majority, on the other hand, rate their sexual attitudes as "conservative." Women rate themselves as more conservative than do men, persons with a high school or elementary education see themselves as more conservative than do those with a college education, and older adults rate themselves as more conservative than do young people. Males in their twenties are the least conservative of all, and women over 60 seem to be the most conservative.

Wilson's analyses of age at first masturbation and at first coitus are presented by sex in Table 1. The data pertaining to masturbation show that about half of the men first masturbated before age 15 and one-fifth started after age 15; about one-third either never masturbated or gave no answer. Higher proportions of the younger and more educated men, respectively, in 1970 reported an earlier age at first masturbation, and higher proportions of the older and least educated say that they never masturbated. Table 1 also shows that slightly more than one-tenth of the women first masturbated before age 15, and perhaps one-twentieth began after age 15; between one-half and two-thirds never masturbated, and one-fifth gave no answer. Although the proportion of women relative to men who masturbated is much lower, among those who have masturbated, the trends in the data parallel those for men, that is, both the younger and the better educated women, respectively, report having first masturbated at an earlier age than did either the older or the less educated women. In respect to coitus, Table 1 suggests that 98 percent of the adults in the United States have had coitus. Thirty-four percent of the men report their first coitus occurred at age 17 or younger, 27 percent from age 18 to 20, 19 percent at age 21 or older, 18 percent gave no answer, and 2 percent said "never" or

American sexual codes are dominated by unspoken assumptions about the way in which relationships are established.

Table 1
Age at First Masturbation and First Intercourse by Gender, Present Age, and Eduction (% Reporting Each Age Category)

| Behavior and Age at First Experience | Males (N = 911) | | | | | | | Females (N = 1,370) | | | | | | |
| | Total | Age | | | Educ. | | | Total | Age | | | Educ. | | |
		21–29	30–59	60+	Coll.	H.S.	Elem.		21–29	30–59	60+	Coll.	H.S.	Elem.
Masturbation:*														
12 & younger	23	31	22	17	29	22	16	8	15	7	3	11	7	3
13–14	25	26	28	16	30	27	13	5	7	5	3	7	5	2
15–17	18	19	19	15	18	18	17	4	6	3	4	5	4	4
18 & older	3	3	3	3	4	2	4	3	4	2	4	4	3	3
Never	14	12	12	20	8	13	27	57	53	60	55	54	59	54
Don't know	1	2	0	3	2	0	1	2	1	2	0	1	2	2
No answer	16	7	16	26	9	18	22	21	14	21	31	18	20	32
	100	100	100	100	100	100	100	100	100	100	100	100	100	100
Intercourse:†														
17 & younger	34	47	34	23	28	42	26	18	25	17	14	7	21	26
18–20	27	20	28	31	29	26	28	32	39	34	19	29	34	31
21 & older	19	16	10	19	25	15	19	28	19	30	31	43	23	18
Never	1	5	0	0	3	1	0	2	5	1	4	5	1	0
Don't know	1	0	0	1	1	1	1	0	0	0	0	0	0	0
No answer	18	12	18	26	15	15	26	20	12	18	32	16	21	25
	100	100	100	100	100	100	100	100	100	100	100	100	100	100

Source: W. C. Wilson, The distribution of selected sexual attitudes and behaviors among the adult population of the United States. *Journal of Sex Research*, 1975, **11**, 46–64. Reprinted by permission.

* The exact wording of the item is, "Thinking of when you were growing up, at what age did you first have the experience of masturbation?"

† The exact wording of the item is, "How old were you the first time you had sexual intercourse?"

"don't know." Women show later ages of first coitus than do men. Eighteen percent of the women report occurrence of first coitus at age 17 or younger, 32 percent from age 18 to 20, 28 percent at age 21 or older, 20 percent gave no answer, and 2 percent said "never." The younger men and women in 1970 experienced first coitus at an earlier age than did the older adults. Whereas members of both sexes who attended college indicated later experience of first coitus, the relationship appears to take on a U-shape for men—those with either elementary or college experience report an earlier age of first coitus than do men with only a high school education, but for women, later age of first coitus is a direct function of education, especially for those women who attend college.

Wilson's 1970 data compares favorably with the Kinsey data of 1948 and 1953, even though the two sets of data were collected approximately 25 years apart, sampling and collection procedures were different, and the manner varied by which the topics were defined. Table 2 shows, for example, the extent of congruence between the two studies for men relative to (1) the cumulative incidence

Table 2

Part 1: Cumulative Incidence of First Masturbation for Males by Education (% Reporting by Given Age)

Age	College		High School		Elementary	
	Kinsey	Wilson	Kinsey	Wilson	Kinsey	Wilson
12	28	32	23	26	16	21
14	72	67	78	61	60	38
17	87	86	93	82	87	60

Part 2: Cumulative Incidence of First Sexual Intercourse for Males by Education (% Reporting by Given Age)

Age	College		High School		Elementary	
	Kinsey	Wilson	Kinsey	Wilson	Kinsey	Wilson
17	23	33	66	50	68	36
20	46	67	80	81	86	74

Source: W. C. Wilson, The distribution of selected sexual attitudes and behaviors among the adult population of the United States. *Journal of Sex Research,* 1975, **11,** 46–64. Reprinted by permission.

of first masturbation from 12 to 17 years and (2) the cumulative incidence of first coitus from 17 to 20 years of age. The data regarding age at first masturbation are in close agreement for the men with some college experience and are in least agreement for those with only elementary school education. These differences may be a consequence of social changes that occurred across the 25 years separating the two studies, but Wilson speculates that in fact they are a result of a special methodological issue—he suggests that adults, especially older persons with only an elementary school education, are less able than the more educated persons to recall when they first masturbated. The differences between the two studies among men with only elementary school education may thus be a matter of the inability of lesser educated men to recall the exact age at which first masturbation occurred. The data presented in Table 2 regarding the cumulative incidence of first coitus for men follows a somewhat different pattern in that close agreement holds for those with a high school education, but not for those with either a college or elementary education. The discrepancies between the elementary age groups may be a product of the inability of the respondents to be any more precise in the area of coitus as they were in that of masturbation. The discrepancies among college youth in the two studies, however, may be a function of the fact that among educated young people, coitus is indeed being initiated earlier today than over a generation ago. But first coitus also is occurring earlier among all age groups, since educated youth report proportionately that their age of first coitus is later than that other age groups (See Table 1).

SEXUAL PERMISSIVENESS

We hear often that the American society is in the midst of a sexual renaissance or a sexual revolution because adherence to the Judeo-Christian ethic is giving way to sexual permissiveness. Nearly a half-century ago, for example, after investigating psychological factors associated with marital happiness, Lewis Terman, the distinguished principal author of intelligence tests, declared:

The trend toward premarital sex experience is proceeding with extraordinary rapidity. . . . If the drop should continue at the average rate shown for those born since 1890 virginity at marriage will be close to the vanishing point for males born after 1930 and for females born after 1940. . . . It will be of no small interest to see how long the cultural ideal of virgin marriage will survive as a moral code after its observance has passed into history.[16]

If Terman's prophecy had come to pass, American sexual conduct would have been wholly engulfed in a "fun morality" by around 1960. Terman obviously underestimated the holding power of traditional social customs, but three trends clearly are congruent with his expectations. (1) The proportion of persons holding permissive attitudes toward recreational sex has increased steadily over the past several decades. Further, the shift toward permissiveness has been greater in respect to attitudes than to behavior, and for both attitudes and behavior, the shift has been greater among women than men. (2) A selective weakening of the double standard has occurred. The American society is moving away from a standard of sexual abstinence for women to one of "permissiveness with affection."[17] (3) Both attitudes and behaviors of men and women toward sexual conduct are converging.

Social scientists are not in complete agreement regarding the trend toward sexual permissiveness. Offer,[18] for example, contends that there is no evidence to suggest that the attitudes of adolescents toward sexuality are changing. Over an eight-year period, Offer studied the attitudes of boys and girls aged 13 to 14 and 16 to 18 via psychiatric interviews, psychological tests, teacher ratings, and parent interviews. He found that young people, as they grow older, become less inhibited and more open about admitting that they think often about sex, but he also found lack of uniformity in their attitudes. Some were open and liberal and others felt that they were having difficulty handling their sexual feelings. Offer failed to discern any changes in the young people's attitudes toward sexuality that indicated a "sexual revolution" is underway. Another study over a three-year span, from 1970 to 1973, involving analyses of the sexual behavior of more than 4,000 young people of both sexes living in three different midwest communities, also revealed no evidence of a "major sexual revolution."[19] These data, which pertain primarily to premarital coitus, when compared to those of the Kinsey studies, suggest that the rate of incidence has remained stable since the 1940s. On the other hand, a burgeoning number of investigations report evidence of a trend toward greater permissiveness. Smigel and Seiden[20] noted a decade ago that a sexual revolution has occurred in terms of frankness and freedom of discussion. Godenne[21] insists that there is no doubt that we are in a climate of sexual permissiveness, but suggests that sexual attitudes are more permissive than sexual practices. Finger[22] has drawn a similar conclusion. He replicated several surveys over a period of years, using the same questionnaire in the same college course, and he found that the proportion of young men who have had premarital heterosexual experience rose from 45 percent in 1943–1944, to 61.8 percent in 1967–1968, and then, to 74.9 percent in 1969–1973. Finger also reports that the proportion of male youth now condoning premarital coitus has risen to over 90 percent, and he asks, as did Terman, "How long will it take for sexual behavior to catch up once again with the associated verbal behavior?"[23]

The more dramatic shifts toward permissiveness in both attitudes and behavior, however, are occurring primarily among young women. Croake and James,[24] for example, surveyed in 1968 and again in 1972 the attitudes of university students in three parts of the country toward permissive sexual behavior. Although both sexes liberalized their attitudes toward recreational sexual expression, the women's attitudes shifted more significantly in four years than did those of the men. Bauman and Wilson[25] also compared the attitudes of students in 1968 and 1972. The researchers concluded that in 1972 relative to 1968 students of both sexes (1) held more permissive attitudes toward premarital sexual behavior and (2) had converged in their attitudes toward recreational sex. Similarly, Perlman,[26] who compared the attitudes of two sets of college students toward various aspects of sexual permissiveness in 1959 and 1973, respectively, also affirms that youth of both sexes in 1973 were more liberal. Perlman reported, too, that a dramatic congruence has occurred in the views of the two sexes regarding premarital petting in the absence of strong affection. He found the standards of young men and women in respect to sexual conduct to be virtually identical. In 1959, for example, 44 percent of the male and 29 percent of the female respondents approved of premarital petting without great affection between the partners. But in 1973, 76 percent of the male and 74 percent of the female respondents looked approvingly on premarital petting. Perlman thus concluded that traditionally conservative standards of sexual conduct have changed over time more for women than for men, and that, further, permissiveness is moving away from standards that prescribe affection as a contingency for sexual conduct.

The traditional double standard seemed to prevail in the 1950s. Ehrmann[27] studied during that period the premarital sex behavior of approximately 1,000 youth as they moved through increasingly intense stages of intimacy, and he reported: "female sexual expression is primarily and profoundly related to being in love and going steady," while "male sexuality is more indirectly and less exclusively associated with romanticism and intimacy relationships." Smigel and Seiden,[28] however, describe the 1960s as having been a "transitional" period for the double standard, the idea that coitus is all right for men under any condition, but is acceptable for women only when they are in love. Bell and Chaskes[29] see the emergence of a new standard of "permissive with less affection." They compared the results of questionnaires pertaining to premarital sexual attitudes and behavior, which were administered in 1958 to 200 female students and in 1968 to 250 female students at the same large urban university. The two samples were comparable in terms of social class and religious background, mean age of first date (about 13), the number who had gone steady (about 75 percent), and the age at which they went steady (about 17). The percentage of girls who had premarital coitus while dating increased from 10 percent in 1958 to 23 percent in 1968; while going steady went from 15 percent to 28 percent; and engagement from 31 percent to 39 percent. There was a substantial increase in premarital coitus during the stages of dating and going steady. In 1958 it seemed that engagement, which provided a high degree of emotional and future commitment, was almost a prerequisite for a girl to have premarital intercourse. By contrast, it appeared that in 1968 engagement was much less important than the girl's assessment of the relationship. "No longer is the girl so apt to have her degree of sexual intimacy influenced by the level of the dating relationship."[30]

Nonetheless, the quality of a relationship still appears to be an important consideration in determining whether level of sexual intimacy will escalate. Peplau[31] points out that her study of university students showed that while most of the young people rejected the double standard—95 percent advocated identical standards for men and women in love relationships and 80 percent indicated that it was "completely acceptable" for couples who love each other to have coitus—only 20 percent of them fully endorsed casual sex. Vener, Stewart, and Hager[32] indicate that the attitudes of the two sexes begin to diverge today in terms of permissiveness at the point of light petting (caresses above the waist). The researchers report that light petting is the earliest stage at which girls now demonstrate inhibitions associated with the double standard. The developmental progression of girls toward permissiveness is similiar to that of boys through stages of sexual conduct involving holding hands, holding arm around another's waist or being held, kissing or being kissed, or necking (prolonged hugging and kissing), but girls become increasingly less permissive than boys through stages of sexual conduct ranging from light petting to coitus with more than one partner.

Young people meet social expectations in an enormous variety of contexts, and in the process of their socialization, they learn a plurality of cultural norms by which they prescribe their sexual conduct. One cannot, therefore, speak of a monolithic trend in society toward sexual permissiveness. On the contrary, the trend expresses itself unevenly across different sociocultural settings. For example, Alston and Tucker[33] found that farmers hold highly conservative attitudes toward sexuality, which suggests the trend toward permissiveness is more an urban than a rural phenomenon. Persons living in large urban areas, the researchers say, are likely to feel that premarital sex is "not wrong." And persons living in the West are more permissive than persons living in the North Atlantic states, who in turn, are more permissive than individuals living in the

South. Such regional differences in attitudes toward sexual permissiveness emerge rather clearly when comparisons are made across national boundaries. After surveying 2,230 college students of both sexes in five countries, for example, Luckey and Nass[34] found that Canadian and American students had more conservative sexual attitudes than Continental European, English, and Norwegian students. The women in each of the countries were more conservative than the men. About one-third of the girls and one-fifth of the boys in America and Canada, respectively, upheld the old double standard; these proportions exceeded those in the other countries. More European than North American women reported that men wanted to "go further on dates," and more European than North American men said that women were willing to go further. North American women, as contrasted with European women, indicated that their dates were generally content with a moderate degree of intimacy (such as petting and necking) and were less likely to be disappointed if they refused to go all the way. And European men, as contrasted with North American men, indicated that girls seemed to want to go all the way when the opportunity presented itself. The study also revealed that English men and women generally indulged in more genital petting, more frequent coitus, more patronage of prostitution, and more one night stands than those of other countries. Christensen and Carpenter[35] compared sexual permissiveness and premarital coitus in Denmark and America's Midwest and intermountain West. There was greater sexual permissiveness and more premarital coitus in Denmark, followed by America's Midwest and then the Intermountain West. The males also seemed to be more permissive and to engage in more coitus than the females; however, the differences between the sexes were smaller in Denmark than in the United States. Hobart[36] provides further international perspective on the double standard. He has recently conducted a study of the sexual attitudes of several hundred English and French Canadian students. The researcher found, relative to earlier studies, a "massive increase" in reported premarital coitus on the part of the women, and particularly on the part of the English-speaking women. Hobart interpreted his data as suggesting that the expectation of premarital virginity in women had greatly eroded, and therefore, that the double standard had relaxed considerably. Hobart explains the more conservative attitudes of the French relative to the English-speaking students by suggesting that the Church still sanctions traditional concepts of premarital sexual behavior for the former whereas among the more secularized English-speaking students, attitudes toward sexuality are increasingly derived from changing conceptions of conventional morality.

Permissiveness is accelerating more swifly among younger adolescents than any other age group, a fact which provides another source of variation in sexual attitudes. For example, Udry, Bauman, and Morris[37] conducted a study of trends in premarital coitus by age cohort, for four decades, of white and black women living in 16 cities across the United States. As Figure 1 shows, each successive age cohort experienced proportionately greater increases in premarital coitus between the ages of 15 and 20. Figure 1 also reveals that for both black and white young women, very rapid increases in sexual experience occurred for those who were between 15 and 19 in the late 1960s. Finally, Figure 1 suggests that black women have experienced premarital coitus at youthful ages in greater proportions than have white women. Indeed, the data show that the rate of premarital coitus among the earliest cohort of black women was higher than that of the latest cohort of white women. The evidence shown in Figure 1 affirming the increasing permissiveness of younger adolescents is supported by several other investigations. Jackson and Potkay,[38] for example, found that of 143 contemporary university students who reported having premarital coitus, 65 percent indi-

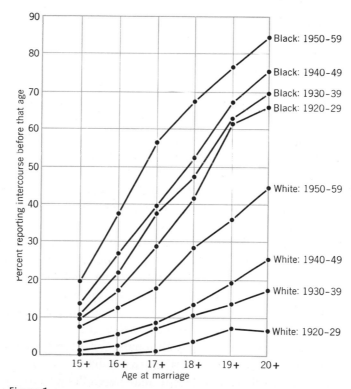

Figure 1

Percentage marrying at a given age or later who reported first intercourse at an earlier age by race and decade of birth. (From Udry et al., see text. Reprinted by permission.)

cated the initial experience had occurred before their eighteenth birthday, and 10 percent reported it as having occurred before their sixteenth birthday. And Alston and Tucker[39] have shown that persons born between 1940 and 1949 hold much more permissive attitudes toward premarital sexual behavior than those born before World War II. Finally, Vener et al.[40] have indicated that their 1973 findings show that by age 17 the double standard, at least on behavioral levels, has evaporated in that by this age both boys and girls report equivalent percentages of coital incidence.

THE MEANING OF RECREATIONAL SEX

Money[41] says that the twentieth-century discovery of methods of birth control ranks with the undated discovery of fire-making in its impact upon our personal lives. He says that our era may become better known as the birth-control age than either the atomic age or the space age. Cheap, mass-distributed, effective means of contraception have made it possible for the first time in history to separate procreational from recreational sex. The separation in times past meant little because life expectancy was so short. It was necessary for persons to marry and begin breeding soon after puberty in order to get their children reared to maturity before they themselves passed on. The rate of infant mortality was high, and the survivors needed to start their procreational sex lives early, with no prior time out for recreational sex.

Recreational sex now is evolving at every stage in the life span, but its effect is most dramatic in the premarital sexual conduct of young people. Adolescents of the current generation, more than those of any cohort before them, must accommodate their life styles to the conflicting expectations of traditional standards of procreational sex and the emerging standards of recreational sex. Every person, however, will balance the values of procreational and recreational sex somewhat differently. Peplau[42] has observed that sexuality is an expression of the kind of person one considers himself or herself to be; it is a means of self-presentation, a way of communicating information about one's character to others. The researcher has grouped the many ways in which young people integrate their sexual values into three categories—traditional, moderate, and liberal—and uses them to differentiate the meanings that young people express in their sexuality. The traditionals, for example, live by a single standard—abstinence from premarital coitus for both men and women except perhaps in the context of commitment to marriage. They feel that love alone is insufficient justification for premarital coitus. Sexual abstinence is taken to be a sign of integrity and maturity, even when they are deeply in love. Although traditional men relative to women may express greater interest in sex, generally they have had limited sexual experience. Traditional women are typically virgins. Moderates, on the other hand, may be expected to move gradually toward full sexual intimacy, which is a special activity to be shared exclusively with each other; it is a way of communicating emotional closeness and commitment. Since love is a prerequisite for premarital coitus, sexual intimacy may be impeded because the relationship is too new, one partner is not in love with the other, both are undecided about the depth of the love, or one or both may anticipate the relationship will end shortly. Coitus will be held in abeyance until the couple is sure that their love is real. Liberals, in contrast to the traditionals and moderates, are primarily interested in recreational sex. About the only restriction liberals place on premarital coitus is that the partner be physically attractive to them. Coitus may be preferred in a meaningful relationship, but it is acceptable without love or commitment. Liberals expect coitus to ensue as part of a dating relationship since they tend to see it as a sign that the relationship will continue for a time. They have much more interest in sexuality than either the traditionals or moderates, and they are more sexually experienced. Since they tend not to view premarital coitus as an expression of love, "liberals must provide their own answers to the question of what intercourse in a particular relationship means."

Peplau[43] also observes that a variety of attitudes and personality traits are associated with whether a person interprets sexuality as traditional, moderate, or liberal. For example, liberal women, but not men, are more likely to describe themselves as possessing "alternate" life styles. They report greater satisfaction and less guilt over their sexual conduct. Liberal women, relative to those who are more traditional, view themselves as less conventional, religious, and interested in being full-time housewives. They are more open to the possibility of being single, career women, and they appear to possess higher self-esteem, as reflected in relatively high self-ratings regarding intelligence, self-confidence, attractiveness, and desirability as a date. The traditionals and moderates of both sexes, who associate recreational sex with greater emotional intimacy, love, and future commitment, feel significantly closer than liberals to their partner, and a higher proportion of these young people believe that they are "in love." These couples reported that they knew their partner better and that their probability of marriage was greater. But contrary to what one might expect of the traditionals, assuming congruence in their values regarding love, commitment, and sexual expression, they reported less sexual satisfaction and rated their partners as less desirable marriage mates than did the liberals who engaged in premarital coitus early in their relationships.

Jessor and Jessor[44] also reported that patterns of personality attributes distinguish young people on the basis of their attitudes toward recreational sex. The researchers employed a wide variety of variables to assess the life styles of several hundred high school and college age young people who were subsequently compared on the basis of whether they were virgins or nonvirgins. The analyses focused on the youth's "transition-proneness" to "nontraditional behavior." The nonvirgins, and those virgins who were to have sexual experience within a year, were found to view independence as especially important. They experienced less parental control, and they had already loosened their ties to their families in favor of greater peer involvement. The young people also reflected less conventionality in their values and outlook, and they participated less in the activities of venerable institutions like the church. It appears, too, that the same conditions in the peer environment that provide support for transition to permissive forms of recreational sex also lead to relatively extensive drug and alcohol use. Jessor and Jessor show that among high school men, 61 percent of the nonvirgins reported using marijuana more than once whereas only 28 percent of the virgins used it more than once. Among high school women, 67 percent of the nonvirgins versus only 21 percent of the virgins had used marijuana more than once. The findings for drinking behavior follow similar patterns, that is, 96 percent of the nonvirgin men and 89 percent of the nonvirgin women used alcoholic beverages, but only 68 percent of the virgin men and 62 percent of the virgin women used them.

SEXUAL AGGRESSION IN ADOLESCENT BOYS

According to Schwartz and Merten,[45] adolescent girls see boys as "naturally" trying to "get all they can." When asked whose responsibility it is to control how far matters go on a date, one girl summed up her views as follows: "The girl's. I mean because guys can't help it. I mean they are born that way. . . ." Some girls thus tend to see the double standard in hereditary terms. They say that it is their responsibility both to satisfy the "inborn" male desire for sexual gratification and to keep the situation from getting out of hand. They acknowledge that they have strong sexual feelings but assert that only they are capable of setting rational limits. They say that boys are incapable of assessing the negative consequences of giving free reign to their sexual impulses, and nature literally has burdened girls with the responsibility of keeping sexual expression within prescribed limits. To achieve or retain an elite position in the adolescent social system, a girl must attract high-status boys and handle their sexual advances adeptly. She must "make out" without being "made;" she must allow herself to reach a relatively high level of sexual excitement without giving in to demands for greater sexual favors.

When the traditional double standard predominates in a dating relationship, the classic problem—aggressive boy versus reluctant girl may emerge. Aggression in the dating situation may turn on whether the girl is as seducible as the boy expects. Kanin[46] holds that the more the boy subscribes to the double standard, heightening the cleavage between male and female belief systems, the more he is likely to resort to physical aggression to get what he wants. For example, Kanin reports men generally believe that "'teasing' and 'golddigging' constitute norm-violative female behavior." A girl who acts like a "good girl" will be treated as one, but if she acts like a "bad girl," she will be expected to perform like one. Some men believe that a "teaser" or "golddigger" is breaching dating expectations; therefore, they justify their sexual aggression as punishment for her exploitation. "They [golddiggers] need to be slapped and put down. A lot of girls want to see how many guys they can go with or how many dances they can go to."[47] Further, when a boy believes that a girl is sexually promiscuous (whether or not she actually is) he can easily precipitate aggression. "The female of easy virtue, the 'loose' woman," fulfills a significant function for the double-standard boy and so he expects her to comply. To validate his double standard, a boy may consider those girls who are already "ruined" as legitimate sex outlets; therefore, he can simultaneously sanction sexual activities for men and feel that women should remain chaste. "By virtue of her indiscretions and the conferring upon her the role of 'easy make,' she has forfeited her right to accept or reject sexual partners. The role of 'easy' qualifies her, in some male groups, as public property; she is categorically deindividualized. . . . Her promiscuity, real or imagined, provokes her male companion to demand her sexual services."[48] As two of Kanin's subjects put it: "She had a bad reputation. I was able to neck and pet but I couldn't make her. I think I went too fast. What kept going through my mind was that I had a couple buddies who said she 'put out.' This frustrated me no end." "When a male doesn't respect a girl and he knows she is nothing but a whore anyway, I feel he is entitled to use force because he knows it isn't her first time."[49]

Kanin[50] observed that boys and girls believe that sex aggression is the "fault" of the female; girls are likely to report that they "let it get out of hand," and boys insist that "they [the girls] were asking for it." In a study of male sex aggression in the dating activities of high school girls, Kanin[51] found that 25 percent of the reported episodes beyond the level of necking involved abrupt sexual advances that were not preceded by consent. By including offensive necking episodes, about 60 percent of the abrupt sexual advances were not the result of prior sex play to which the female had consented. Kanin had questioned 262 first-year college girls. One hundred and sixty-three of them (62 percent)

Table 3
Offended Girls by Maximum of Erotic Intimacy

Maximum Level	No.	Percent
Necking	39	23.9
Petting above the waist	54	33.1
Petting below the waist	22	13.5
Attempted intercourse	34	20.9
Attempted intercourse with violence	14	8.6
Total	163	100.0

Source: E. J. Kanin. Male aggression in dating-courtship relations. *Journal of Sociology,* 1957, **63,** 197–204. Reprinted by permission.

reported offensive episodes at some level of erotic intimacy during their senior year of high school or the following summer. Table 3 shows the percentage of girls who were offended at each of five levels of erotic intimacy. Fewer than 70 percent of the episodes occurred when the boy was under the influence of alcohol, and more than 70 percent occurred in an automobile. Kanin's study showed that the more offensive episodes—attempts at intercourse with or without violence—were more heavily concentrated in the spring and summer months; it also showed that girls who had been warned and instructed by their parents experienced fewer aggressive episodes. Those girls who had older brothers also experienced fewer offensive sexual episodes. Possibly those with older brothers are more tolerant of male sexual aggression and thus less prone to view such episodes as offensive; however, it is more likely that those with older brothers have greater insight into boys' behavior and values that enable them to anticipate erotic aggression and tactics of exploitation. On the other hand, those girls with older sisters (who might relate untoward experiences and advise caution) experienced their full share of offensive encounters, as did those who attended church regularly.

Kanin's[52] findings contradict the generally held belief that when a girl continuously dates the same boy she is relatively safe from offensive erotic aggression. One might expect that most sexual aggression would occur during the first dates with a given boy, when misunderstanding and poor communication would probably be greatest. "In popular lore 'blind dates' and first dates are frequently portrayed as veritable wrestling contests."[53] However, he found that aggression at the more advanced levels of erotic intimacy were primarily associated with "the more durable and involved relationships," even after the girls were engaged. Kanin's study did not indicate whether the relationship ended or whether a mutual understanding was reached as a result of the boy's sexual aggression, but it did show that the offended girls refused to tolerate aggression however involved the relationship.

In spite of girls' low tolerance for such aggression, subsequent evidence has suggested that the sexually aggressive male succeeds rather well in gaining erotic gratification. In a comparative study of sexually aggressive and nonaggressive adolescent boys, Kanin[54] reported that the aggressive ones not only enjoyed more success but persistently sought new sexual involvements and frequently utilized surreptitious techniques to obtain their ends. The study included 400 undergraduate, unmarried boys at a large midwestern university who were asked to describe their sexual behavior anonymously. An episode was defined as offensively aggressive if the respondent said that he had made a forceful attempt at coitus, which he believed the girl perceived as disagreeable because of her crying, fighting, screaming, or pleading. The study revealed that forceful attempt at coitus was only one of the many erotic activities in which the aggressive male engaged. In contrast with less aggressive males, he utilized a variety of "seductive" approaches. After beginning to date in high school, he frequently tried to exploit girls for sexual gratification. Although he might not go so far as to promise marriage, he often tried to intoxicate a girl, falsely professed love, and threatened to dissolve their relationship unless she accommodated his sexual advances.

Although the aggressive boy employed a broad spectrum of deviant approaches to gain sexual gratification and attempted to engage in sexual play (and was indeed rather successful), ironically he tended to be more dissatisfied than the nonaggressive boy with his sexual activity. Probably the nonaggressive boy assesses his sexual needs less extravagantly than the aggressive one and thus feels little frustration at his lack of gratification. Kanin says that the different levels of sexual aspiration held by the two types of boys apparently reflect the different orientations of their respective friendship groups toward sexual conduct. Aggressive boys, for example, tended to report that their friends exerted a "great deal" of pressure on them to engage in sexual exploits. Under pressure to meet peer expectations, even a boy who is highly successful in his exploits may fail to live up to his goals and thus be dissatisfied. Perhaps much of the urgency with which adolescent boys seek premarital sexual outlets is due to pressure from their peer groups.[55]

HOMOSEXUALITY

Homosexual behavior is relatively common among both sexes in all cultures. Homosexuality, which refers to preference for sexual partners of one's own gender, is increasingly being recognized as "a variant form of sexual expression preferentially practiced as normative behavior by a minority of society."[56] A variety of "gay" organizations have been established in recent years, and homosexuals are currently seeking through them to have their sexuality recognized as a fully acceptable alternative to heterosexuality. The traditional view of homosexuality in the United States, however, is that it represents a pattern of sexual deviance (perversion). According to a recent representative sample involving over 3,000 adults, which was conducted by the National Opinion Research Center, nearly three-fourths of the adult population in the United States today holds stereotyped attitudes toward homosexuality and regards it as morally repugnant.[57] The average American adult, for example, would permit homosexual men to serve as beauticians, artists, musicians, and florists, but would not allow them to enter such responsible roles as court judges, school teachers, ministers, medical doctors, or government officials. It is especially dangerous to allow homosexuals to become teachers or youth leaders, it is said, because they might either corrupt children or seek them out for sexual purposes. The general public thus regards homosexuality as an illness from which its victims have only limited chance of recovery. One-third of the public view the majority of homosexuals as simply "born that way" and nearly half suppose that they are products of "how their parents raised them." Many persons believe that homosexuals could "stop being homosexuals if they want to," and from one-quarter to one-third of the public think that homosexuals could be turned into heterosexuals by sexually skilled members of the opposite sex. Lubin,[58] for example, relates that after he told his father of his gay tendencies, his father tried to make dates for him with prostitutes and tried to goad him into fights in order that he might prove his masculinity. Lubin reasoned: "I imagine he felt as many people do that, 'all this boy needs is a good lay and he'll be fine.'"

Although homosexuals have long been condemned as bad and deserving punishment or stigmatized as sick and requiring treatment, courts and legislatures have increasingly taken the position that consenting adult homosexuals have the right to express in private their sexuality as they wish. Legal reforms are emerging today that remove criminal penalties for homosexual activities. Geis, Wright, Garrett, and Wilson[59] recently surveyed police officials, prosecuting attorneys, and members of homosexual groups in seven states that have decriminalized private homosexual behavior between consenting adults (Colorado, Delaware, Oregon, Hawaii, Ohio, Illinois, and Connecticut). The survey revealed that involvement of homosexuals with minors, use of force by homosexuals, and amount of private homosexual behavior has not risen as a consequence of decriminalization. But it has eased problems of police harassment and it has allowed officials more time to concentrate on crimes against property and persons.

The Supporting Subculture

Homosexuals cannot be lumped together simply on the basis of their preference for a same-sex partner. They may differ on the bases of sexual arousability, preferred sexual techniques, characteristics of desired partners, intimacy required in a relationship, intensity with which they pursue sexual contacts, and locales in which they seek prospective partners. Since homosexuals are a highly diverse group, the task gay young people face in finding satisfactory mates never has been easy. But it has become easier today as a consequence of the rise of a strong, supporting subculture, at least for young men.

The individual who seeks sexual expression through homosexuality faces the major step of "coming out," of leaving the "closet" (ending isolation from other homosexuals). The hurdle is essentially one of learning of the ways in which gay people affiliate with one another. One frequently employed procedure gay people use to acquaint themselves with each other is the advertisement. Lee[60] indicates, for example, that personal ads that deal with sought-for partners constituted about 30 percent of the advertisements that appeared recently in three randomly selected issues of *The Advocate,* a biweekly gay newspaper with a circulation of 60,000 throughout the United States and Canada. Nearly all of the ads were placed by gay young men. Lee shows, too, how selective they may be in specifying the characteristics that they desire in partners. Seventeen different characteristics, for example, were specified in at least 10 percent of the advertisements. These are listed in rank order in Table 4. Acceptable age of partner is shown to be the most highly desirable characteristic (73 percent), followed by interest in a lasting relationship (53 percent), and straight or masculine appearance (45 percent). The emphases of the advertisers on "straight" appearance, other qualities of masculinity, and discretion probably is indicative of how carefully contemporary gays are to avoid the stigma that is generally attached to homosexual interaction in the American society.

Table 4 indicates that whether a prospective partner "frequents the bars" is of little significance to gay young men. The gay bar, in fact, dominates the gay scene today, and is more significant than advertisements in producing prospective homosexual acquaintances. Gay bars once were "clandestine hideaways where a few of the more brazen gay people sought one another out in secret."[61] As late as 1970 perhaps only one in ten gay persons had ever been to a gay bar, but greater openness about sex generally, gay liberation, and the recognition

Table 4
Desired Characteristics of Partners Specified in 248 Advocate Advertisements

Rank Order	Quality Desired in Partner	Percentage Seeking Desired Quality
1	Age within a special range	73%
2	Partner must want a faithful, lasting relationship	53%
3	Straight or masculine appearance	45%
4	Specific kind of physique (height, weight, build, musculature, etc.)	42%
5	Sincerity, honesty, seriousness	40%
6	Interest in specified social activities, hobbies, sports, arts, etc.	33%
7	Warm and/or affectionate	31%
8	Specified race	23%
9	Preferred sex role (e.g., butch, top man)	22%
10	Handsome, good-looking	20%
11	Qualities of character (sensitivity, stability, etc.) that are not listed above	19%
12	Not a drug user	18%
12	Not into sadomasochism (S & M)	18%
13	Intelligent and/or educated	16%
13	Not fat	16%
14	Size of penis or type of penis (e.g., "uncut")	15%
15	Discretion	14%
16	Smooth or hairy	12%
16	Socioeconomic status	12%
17	Not frequently at the bars	10%

Source: J. A. Lee. Forbidden colors of love: patterns of gay love and gay liberation. *Journal of Homosexuality,* 1976, **1,** 401–418. Reprinted by permission.

that homosexuality is not an illness has given rise within the past few years to at least 100 gay bars in New York City, more than 90 in Chicago, and over 4,000 throughout the United States. Gay bars vary tremendously in character, atmosphere, and clientele, but they overwhelmingly cater to adolescent and postadolescent young men. Bars catering to gay women are much fewer, and usually they are small places with quiet, intimate atmospheres. But for men, as Sage indicates, there are bars to chat in, dance in, cruise in, and have sex in. The most important function of the gay bar, however, is to provide young people with a way of meeting one another in an atmosphere of peer support. As one gay person said: "Gay people are raised in straight society and are taught its phobias as well as its values. They end up hating 'queers' just like everybody else does. They hopefully know those things [the myths] aren't true of themselves, but each thinks he's the only 'normal' person who feels that way, until he begins to find other gay people like himself."[62] Discretion is exceedingly important, and promiscuity as such often is absent in many gay bars. As the patron of one said: "There are places in the gay world for that, but not here. Guys are looking for someone. Sometimes a lover [a permanent or long-term mate], but always somebody they can relate to deeply both physically and emotionally."[63]

The patrons of gay bars put a high premium on youth, good looks, and in men, masculinity. "Those who don't measure up seem to get the message and stay away." The process of attraction and rejection in a gay bar follows a distinct pattern: masculine men are attracted to masculine men. The more masculine and handsome a man is, the more masculine or handsome must another man be to interest him. Gays also have developed an intricate communication system in the bars to express their sexual preference for the active or passive role in specific sex acts. The most generally recognized sign is the position of a metal ring of keys hooked to a man's belt. If the keys are worn on the right, he prefers to be passive, but if they are placed on the left, he prefers to be active. Many homosexuals, however, do not wear keys because their preferences are flexible.[64]

SEXUAL STRUCTURE AND GENDER ROLE

The anatomical structures that identify a boy or girl do not also determine whether that person will act in a masculine or feminine way. "There is no primary genetic or other innate mechanism to preordain the masculinity or feminity of psychosexual differentiation."[65] Indeed, it appears "possible for psychosexual differentiation to be contradictory of chromosomal sex, gonadal sex, hormonal sex, external genital sex, and internal genital sex, and to agree instead with assigned sex."[66] This means that children's image of their gender and the manner in which they anticipate how others expect them to develop sex-roles are affected by whether they learn to function as boys or girls. Questions about gender arise when parents make such statements as "She looks like a boy" or "He is pretty, like a girl." Parents may attract or frighten children into denying their anatomical sex and prepare them instead for the opposite sex role. Calderone[67] says that parental expectations of children early in their lives is critically important to their development of gender identity. Brown and

Lynn[68] have argued that sex-role differentiation is fairly well established by age five and that major realignment of gender during adolescence or later is rare. When children's early training has been dramatic and consistent, their early sex-role learning is likely to prevail even though it contradicts expectations derived from their anatomical features.

SEXUAL DECISION MAKING

The National Center for Health Statistics reports that in the United States there are about 400,000 unplanned births annually. About half of these births are to single adolescents between the ages of 15 and 19. Unplanned (out-of-wed-lock) births accounted in 1960 for about 15 percent of the births among adolescents, but the national rate has risen today to about 25 percent. It varies immensely, however, by ethnic, social class, and demographic factors. The New York City Health Department reports, for example, that whereas 28.6 percent of the births among adolescents were unplanned in 1960, the proportion had escalated to 53.6 percent in 1970, and 61.5 percent in 1973. One would expect that comparable trends hold for premarital pregnancies and abortions, respectively, but unfortunately, one can only speculate on these matters since reliable statistics in the two areas are unavailable.

The steep upward trend in unplanned births represents a very significant outcome of the sexual decision-making process. A minority of adolescents may regard birth control planning as irrelevant on the grounds that single parenthood would be acceptable to them as an acceptable role in society. An unplanned birth, for the majority, however, is a consequence of faulty decision making. As shown in Figure 2, the process of sexual decision making can be very complex.[69] The model presents a series of questions as a chain of sexual decision-making issues and describes the cumulative ramifications of sex-related decisions. Its decision points pertain to the following six questions:

Question	*Choice or Result*
1. Intercourse or no intercourse?	1. Intercourse
2. Children or no children?	2. Either
3. Birth control or no birth control?	3. Pregnancy
4. Delivery or abortion?	4. Delivery
5. Keep the child or give it up?	5. Either
6. Remain single or get married?	

The model identifies the critical questions young people must ask themselves in order to understand and analyze implications of their sexual conduct and to

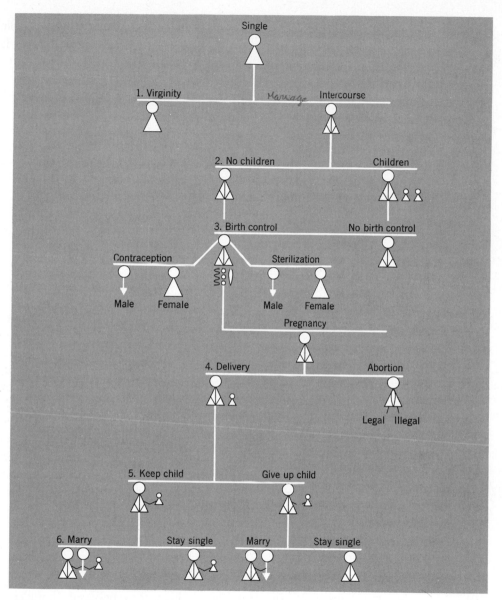

Figure 2

A model for sexual decision making. (From McCreary-Juhasz, see text. Reprinted by permission.)

cope calmly and rationally with issues as they arise. Whether to have coitus, bear a child, practice birth control, have an abortion, give up a child for adoption, and marry are among those issues that young people must face as they begin to assume responsibility for expression of sexual impulses. Each decision except for "no intercourse" leads to consideration of the next question. McCreary-Juhasz notes that unique aspects of every young person's life style will affect the way in which questions are answered. But the researcher maintains that there are today general factors and well-established facts that can be used as bases for a problem-solving approach to sexual decisions.

In general, sexually permissive persons, relative to those who restrict their sexuality, possess more knowledge of contraceptive devices and techniques.[70] This has been true for several years. A decade ago, Grinder and Schmitt[71] asked 304 single, white women students at a large midwestern university to classify several contraceptive techniques as either male- or female-controlled. The extent of the girls' knowledge appeared to be a function of their relationships with boys. For example, girls who dated at least once a week, who were in love, or who had coitus occasionally had more adequate information about contraceptives. Although sexually permissive young people are more knowledgeable, young people as a whole are relatively poorly informed about sexuality. McCreary-Juhasz[72] asked 893 young people at the University of British Columbia to take an examination on human sexuality and to rate the adequacy of their knowledge in this area. The questions were selected from those most frequently asked by young people who had attended a series of lectures on sexual behavior; the appropriateness of their answers was determined by a team of three medical doctors. It was found that the students did not really know much about sex and that they could not realistically evaluate their knowledge. McCreary-Juhasz[73] concluded that there was no relationship between their self-evaluation and their actual knowledge. Both sexes believed, for example, that they were well-informed about masturbation; however, only two-thirds of the boys and one-third of the girls actually were. On the subject of nocturnal emissions (or wet dreams)—a common physiological outlet for sexual tension in the male—most of the youth were confident of their knowledge, but about one-third of the boys and one-half of the girls were actually poorly informed. Neither boys nor girls knew as much as they believed about conception, and almost two-thirds of the girls had very little information. Finally, more than 30 percent of both sexes overestimated their knowledge of the structure and function of the sexual organs.

One significant indication of young people's dearth of sexual knowledge is their widespread neglect of contraceptives. Zelnick and Kantner,[74] for example, say that 75 percent of the nonvirginal 15- to 19-year-old girls in a nationwide sample revealed that they never or only sometimes used contraceptive protection. Sorensen's[75] representative investigation of 13 to 19 year olds also found that only about half of the girls and boys who engaged in coitus rarely made use of some kind of birth control methods. The methods that they most frequently reported using was birth control pills and withdrawal of the boy's penis before ejaculation. The study revealed that the girls virtually never used such birth control methods as the diaphragm, contraceptive jelly, contraceptive douche, and intrauterine device (IUD). Nearly 20 percent of the girls simply said, "I just trusted to luck that I wouldn't become pregnant," and another 10 percent indicated, "I didn't think about whether or not I might become pregnant."

Why do young people who are permissive in their recreational sex fail generally to take contraceptive precautions? Lindemann,[76] a birth control counselor, sought an answer to the question in the course of interviewing and counseling over 2,500 young women in public health clinics, high schools, and colleges throughout the Los Angeles metropolitan area. Lindemann found neglect of contraceptives to be related to two basic circumstances associated with patterns of premarital sexual expression. One, uncertainty regarding the occurrence of coitus, and two, low awareness of the need for birth control. On the matter of uncertainty, five features of premarital sexual expression may contribute to unpredictability and flux. First, the occurrence of coitus often is highly unpredictable, and hence need for contraception is difficult to anticipate, especially in respect to time, place, and sometimes, partner. Second, sexual conduct is influenced by the belief that sexual expression should be "natural;" contraception, however, requires forethought and anticipation. It imposes a rationale on sexuality that runs contrary to spontaneity. As one girl said: "Sex is better if it's natural. Birth control is artificial. Getting birth control would shatter romantic ideas. I didn't like the idea of birth control because sex should be spontaneous."[77] Third, occurrences of premarital coitus often are infrequent and sporadic. Although the overall chances of pregnancy are reduced when the pattern is irregular, young people often falsely assume that the likelihood of pregnancy occurring on any given occasion is reduced, too. Fourth, persons who engage actively in both heterosexual and homosexual conduct may give little thought to the circumstances (heterosexual) when protection would be appropriate. Fifth, sexual activity over a period of time, in the absence of pregnancy, may lead to the expectation that it is not going to occur. One might expect sexually active couples to adopt a birth control method, but nonuse may reinforce the belief that the danger of pregnancy is remote. One may hear, for example, "I don't think it could happen to me. I've been having sex for two years. So far it hasn't."[78]

The second basic circumstance Lindemann has identified as leading to nelgect of birth control devices, low awareness of need, suggests that the first prerequisite in using contraceptives is learning that there are ways to prevent conception. High awareness coupled with taking appropriate action would set aside concern generated by uncertainty and unpredictability in premarital sexual expression. Many adolescents, however, are wholly ignorant of birth control methods. Consider, for example, the following comments of three adolescent girls; each illustrates an instance of how remote the thought of pregnancy can be.[79]

"I don't remember if I thought about getting pregnant. I don't know why, but it just didn't bother me that much."

"It was just not possible for it to happen to me. I just didn't believe I could get pregnant."

"It just couldn't happen to me. I've read about birth control. I knew about contraceptives. I knew the statistics. I could have prepared for it. I knew it was easy to get pregnant, but not for me."

Socializing experiences must be favorable if young people are to acquire knowledge of birth control methods and to integrate them into their growing awareness of sexuality. Reiss, Banwart, and Foreman[80] say that given characteristics of the sexual life styles of young persons determine whether contraceptive devices will be used premaritally. The researchers note that stability of the sexual relationship is one of the best predictors as to whether contraception will be practiced. The life style most conducive to the use of contraception by a young woman thus is one involving a high degree of commitment to a particular heterosexual relationship, a view of sexuality stressing her right to make decisions about her own sex life, self-assurance concerning her body image, a history of early acquisition of sex information inside and outside her family, and a high degree of congruity between sexual attitudes and behavior. Reiss et al.,[81] in a study of 482 young women from the Midwest, found support for their beliefs that, on the one hand, young women fail to use contraceptives because they do not fully accept premarital coitus as proper and thus are unable to prepare rationally for it, and on the other hand, young women seek contraceptive information when they feel positively toward their own sexuality. The researchers found, for example, that adoption of a birth-control method was related to endorsing the right of persons to choose their own sexual life styles, to believing oneself to be attractive to men, and to having made a commitment to a relationship, for example, going steady, engagement, or planning to marry.

Since adolescents in general are not socialized in ways that would facilitate attainment of mature sexuality, the sizeable gaps and inconsistencies in their sexual knowledge and insights is not surprising. Most of their information comes from peers, followed in order by printed literature, school programs, and parents.[82] Peers, however, are usually a poor source of sexual information for young people who hold traditional attitudes about sex. There may be little open communication about sexuality among these young people in high school. Barriers to discussion may be imposed on topics such as masturbation and homosexuality, and sexual attitudes and appetites may be assumed to be private matters. The needs of these youth for adequate information and for sharing attitudes and feelings which are important in developing maturity may not be satisfied. On the other hand, young people holding permissive attitudes toward sexuality may communicate very effectively with one another. Lindemann[83] points out that a great deal of information about contraceptive methods is transmitted by word of mouth. One girl said, for example, "The first time I had sex I didn't use anything. The second time I used rhythm—found out about it from my girlfriend."

Next to peers, printed literature is the most useful source of information about sexual decision making. Whereas treatment of sexuality formerly dealt with superficial aspects of romantic love, magazines today like *Seventeen* and *Coed* regularly carry articles covering basic aspects of sexuality and contraception.

One might expect that sex education programs in the schools would be youth's primary source of information about sexuality, but only in a few instances have carefully planned, comprehensive programs been initiated. Sex education programs always seem to be engulfed in controversy, and opponents generally have been able to suppress proponents. Opponents of sex education in the schools see it in general as a threat to their personal values about sexuality, which usually are based on the traditional premises that (1) procreational sex is the sole purpose of sexuality and (2) recreational sex is to be damned. Proponents of sex education, in contrast, recognize that values associated with procreational and recreational sex are interrelated and that the school should teach young people how to reach decisions about sexual conduct. They maintain that explicit, value-oriented teaching about sexuality should be left to church and family. Proponents acknowledge that the family is ideally the best source of sexual information, but they insist that, like other school subjects, sexuality has become too complex to leave to the typical parent, who is either too uninformed or too bashful to share useful sexual information with young people. They also say that information furnished by school sex educators will liberate parents from the discomfort of revealing their own incomplete knowledge of the substance of sexual expression and allow them, instead, to concentrate on sharing with young people their values about sex.[84] To satisfy both factions, some schools have tried to initiate programs based on strict objectivity; for example, by teaching biology but not how to prevent pregnancy, or by including information in health courses on birth control methods and how they work, but not teaching where to obtain contraceptives or how to gain expert advice about them.[85]

Parents probably could be the most important source of information about sexual conduct, but for one reason or another, they are usually more of a hindrance than a help. Parents are often uninformed and may be ashamed of sexual topics; they may act shy, embarrassed, evasive or uncomfortable; and they may condemn adolescent inquisitiveness as a sign of temptation. Perhaps part of their reluctance to talk about sex with adolescents results from their fear that such discussion may reveal something of their own sexual experiences. As a consequence, few adolescents receive much sexual information at home. There is little communication about sex between father-son, father-daughter, or mother-son; although the mother is likely to tell her daughter about reproduction and menstruation, much of the information about reproduction is in response to childhood (not adolescent) questions. The average mother seems to think of menstruation as a distasteful topic and deals with it only because of necessity. Boys generally learn nothing from their fathers about contraception, prostitution, or coitus; however, a small proportion of boys may learn about menstruation from mothers. The conventional expectation that most boys will have a heart-to-heart talk about sexuality with their fathers seems to be a myth. Lindemann[86] points out, too, that an adolescent girl cannot readily ask her parents about birth control, since they are usually ambivalent or opposed to premarital sex. And parents may know very little about birth control when it comes to determining which method to use and where to obtain it. Parental reluctance to discuss sexual activity and contraception in concrete, here-and-now terms is common among both conservative and permissive families. In the former, premarital sex is judged to be unacceptable, and the daughter is expected to abstain from sexual activity until she is married. Under these conditions, there is no discussion, information about sexuality, and advice on birth control methods. In such families, if the daughter becomes pregnant, she may be forgiven for that one mistake, but she is expected to abstain from further sexual activity until she is married. She might be thrown out of the house, too, or she may elect to leave so that her parents do not discover her plight. Many permissive parents also hold back information on birth control, but often for different reasons. They do not wish to appear that they are sanctioning sexual activity. "They fear that this will be pushing the girl into premarital sex—that it will be a go-ahead sign."[87]

SUMMARY

American sexual norms have long been dominated by an ideal that sanctioned coitus only for the purpose of procreation, and then, only within the context of marriage. The actual codes of sexual conduct, however, specify a double standard: procreational sex for women and recreational sex for men. The double standard has for centuries restricted the sexual behavior of women more than that of men, for whom casual and premarital sex has always been acceptable.

Sigmund Freud and Havelock Ellis saw sexuality as a biological product of evolution and both recognized its significance in personality development. Alfred Kinsey established sexual expression as a researchable domain of science. Kinsey revealed that the "normal" and the "perverse" are on a continuum in the realm of sexual expression, and his data pointed to sharp incongruities between law and custom in matters of sexual conduct. Since publication of the Kinsey studies, a shift toward openness in both discussion of sexual attitudes and expression of sexual conduct has occurred. Research data show that 98 percent of the adults today have had coitus; one-third of the men and about 20 percent of the women report that their first coitus occurred at age 17 or younger.

Three trends are apparent in America in respect to sexual permissiveness: (1) the proportion of persons holding permissive attitudes toward recreational sex has increased steadily over the past few decades; (2) a weakening of the double standard has occurred; (3) the attitudes and behaviors of men and women in respect to sexual conduct are converging. The shift toward permissiveness is more dramatic among young women that it is among young men. Nonetheless, the quality of a relationship still is an important consideration in determining whether level of sexual intimacy will escalate. Although standards prescribing affection and love as prerequisites for coitus have become more permissive, only a small proportion of young people today fully endorse casual sex.

Peplau has grouped the ways in which young people integrate their sexual values into three categories: the *traditional*, which encompasses youth who believe that sexual abstinence is a sign of integrity and maturity; the *moderate*, which includes youth who may be expected to move gradually toward full sexual intimacy as a way of communcating emotional closeness and commitment; and the *liberal*, which characterizes youth who are primarily interested in recreational sex.

The reality of the double standard has led many adolescent boys to become highly aggressive in exploiting sexual opportunities. Both boys and girls believe that sexual aggression is the fault of the girl because she allowed a situation to get out of hand. Kanin reports that a girl who dates a boy steadily is no safer from aggression than a girl who dates a boy for the first time. Although girls seem to have little tolerance for male aggression, sexually aggressive boys appear to succeed in achieving their ends.

Homosexuality refers to preference for sexual partners of one's own gender. The traditional view of homosexuality in the United States holds that it is a form of sexual deviance. The majority of adults today still regard homosexuality as morally repugnant, but legal reforms are emerging that are removing criminal penalties for homosexual activity. A variety of "gay" organizations have been established in recent years, and homosexuals are currently seeking through them to have their sexuality recognized as a fully acceptable alternative to heterosexuality. The individual who seeks sexual expression through homosexuality faces the major step of "coming out," but as a consequence of the rise of a strong, supporting subculture, the task has become easy today, at least for young men.

Whether to have coitus, bear a child, practice birth control, have an abortion, give up a child for adoption, and marry are among the issues that young people must face as they begin to assume responsibility for their heterosexual behavior. McCreary-Juhasz notes that unique aspects of every young person's life style will affect the way in which the issues are faced.

In general, sexually permissive young people, relative to those who are more conservative, possess more knowledge of contraceptive devices and techniques. But young people who are permissive fail in general to take contraceptive precautions. Neglect of contraceptives may be related to two basic circumstances associated with premarital coitus: uncertainty regarding whether coitus will occur and belief that chance of pregnancy is remote. The sizeable gaps and inconsistencies in youth's sexual knowledge and insights are not surprising, since research shows that most of their information is learned unsystematically from peers, printed literature, school programs, and parents.

REVIEW QUESTIONS

1. What are the historical antecedents of the "ideal of sexual continence" and the double standard?
2. What sexual attitudes has the double standard produced?
3. How did Freud view sexuality as a conflict between biological nature and social constraints?
4. What effect have the Kinsey studies had upon American sexual attitudes?
5. What demographic variables are associated with sexual conservativeness?
6. In what ways are Wilson's 1970 findings about sexual behavior comparable to Kinsey's data?
7. What trends in America indicate a rise in sexual permissiveness?
8. What is the meaning of the phrase, "permissiveness with affection"?
9. How does the trend toward sexual permissiveness vary across sociocultural settings?
10. What bases did Peplau use to classify young people by their attitudes toward recreational sex?
11. Why do both boys and girls hold girls responsible when sexual aggression escalates?
12. What attitudes do adults conventionally hold toward homosexuality?
13. What are the characteristics of the subculture that supports homosexuality?
14. What are the six issues McCreary-Juhasz describes as important in sexual decision making?
15. Why do sexually permissive young people generally fail to take contraceptive precautions?
16. Describe the characteristics of the sources of youth's sexual knowledge.

DISCUSSION QUESTIONS

1. Evaluate the channels by which sexuality is being introduced into open social discourse. Which of these is likely to have the most impact on adolescence?

2. What grounds are there for believing that the impact of the double standard is diminishing?

3. Why should recreational sex be on the ascendance in contemporary society?

4. What do you think of Peplau's belief that sexuality is an expression of the kind of person one considers oneself to be?

5. What attitudes do persons with whom you are acquainted hold toward homosexuality? In what ways is the supporting subculture gaining legitimacy in your area?

6. How would you answer each of the sex-related questions McCreary-Juhasz raises? What reasons would you use in support of each of your decisions?

7. How would you evaluate the relative importance of peers, printed literature, school programs, and parents as sources of youth's sexual knowledge? How would you strengthen the significance of each?

NOTES

1. J. H. Gagnon. Sex research and social change. *Archives of Sexual Behavior,* 1975, **4,** 111–141.

2. W. R. Stokes. Modern view of masturbation. *Sexology,* 1961, **27,** 2–5, p. 2.

3. J. Money. The birth-control age. *The Chronicle of Higher Education,* 1973, **8,** No. 8, p. 20.

4. L. Λ. Peplau. Sex, love and the double standard. Paper presented at the meeting of the American Psychological Association, Washington, D.C., 1976.

5. M. S. Calderone. Eroticism as a norm. *The Family Coordinator,* 1974, **23,** 337–341.

6. Gagnon, *op. cit.*

7. Gagnon, *op. cit.,* p. 117.

8. Gagnon, *op. cit.*

9. Gagnon, *op. cit.*

10. Gagnon, *op. cit.,* p. 119.

11. Gagnon, *op. cit.,* p. 128.

12. Gagnon, *op. cit.*

13. Gagnon, *op. cit.*

14. W. Masters and V. Johnson. *Human sexual inadequacy.* Boston: Little, Brown, 1970.

15. W. C. Wilson. The distribution of selected sexual attitudes and behaviors among the adult population of the United States. *Journal of Sex Research,* 1975, **11,** 46–64.

16. L. M. Terman. *Psychological factors in marital happiness.* New York: McGraw-Hill, 1938, p. 323.

17. I. L. Reiss. *Premarital sexual standards in America.* New York: The Free Press, 1960.

18. D. Offer. Attitudes toward sexuality in a group of 1500 middle class teen-agers. *Journal of Youth and Adolescence,* 1972, **1,** 81–90.

19. A. M. Vener, C. S. Stewart, and D. L. Hager. The sexual behavior of adolescents in middle America: generational and American-British comparisons. *Journal of Marriage and the Family,* 1972, **34,** 696–705; A. M. Vener and C. S. Stewart. Adolescent sexual behavior in middle America revisited: 1970–1973. *Journal of Marriage and the Family,* 1974, **36,** 728–735.

20. E. O. Smigel and R. Seiden. The decline and fall of the double standard. *The Annals of the American Academy of Political and Social Science,* 1968, **36,** 6–17.

21. G. D. Godenne. Sex and today's youth. *Adolescence,* 1974, **9,** 67–72.

22. F. W. Finger. Changes in sex practices and beliefs of male college students: over 30 years. *Journal of Sex Research,* 1975, **11,** 304–317.

23. Finger, *op. cit.,* p. 314.

24. J. W. Croake and B. James. A four year comparison of premarital sexual attitudes. *Journal of Sex Research,* 1973, **9,** 91–96.

25. K. E. Bauman and R. R. Wilson. Premarital sexual attitudes of unmarried university students: 1968 vs. 1972. *Archives of Sexual Behavior,* 1976, **5,** 29–37.

26. D. Perlman. Self-esteem and sexual permissiveness. *Journal of Marriage and the Family,* 1974, **36,** 470–473.

27. W. W. Ehrmann. *Premarital dating behavior.* New York: Holt, 1959, p. 259.

28. Smigel and Seiden, *op. cit.*

29. R. R. Bell and J. B. Chaskes. Premarital sexual experience among coeds, 1958 and 1968. *Journal of Marriage and the Family,* 1970, **32,** 81–84.

30. Bell and Chaskes, *op. cit.,* p. 84.

31. Peplau, *op. cit.*

32. Vener et al., *op. cit.*

33. J. P. Alston and F. Tucker. The myth of sexual permissiveness. *Journal of Sex Research,* 1973, **9,** 34–40.

34. E. B. Luckey and G. D. Nass. A comparison of sexual attitudes and behaviors in an international sample. *Journal of Marriage and the Family,* 1969, **31,** 364–379.

35. H. T. Christensen and G. R. Carpenter. Value-behavior discrepancies regarding premarital coitus in three western cultures. *American Sociological Review,* 1962, **27,** 66–74.

36. C. W. Hobart. Sexual permissiveness in young English and French Canadians. *Journal of Marriage and the Family,* 1972, **34,** 292–303.

37. J. R. Udry, K. E. Bauman, and N. M. Morris. Changes in premarital coital experience of recent decade-of-birth cohorts of urban American women. *Journal of Marriage and the Family,* 1975, **37,** 783–787.

38. E. D. Jackson and C. R. Potkay. Precollege influences on sexual experiences of coeds. *Journal of Sex Research,* 1973, **9,** 143–149.

39. Alston and Tucker, *op. cit.*

40. Vener and Stewart, *op. cit.*

41. Money, *op. cit.*

42. Peplau, *op. cit.*

43. Peplau, *op. cit.*

44. S. L. Jessor and R. Jessor. Transition from virginity to nonvirginity among youth: a social-psychological study over time. *Developmental Psychology,* 1975, **11,** 473–484.

45. G. Schwartz and D. Merten. The language of adolescence: an anthropological approach to the youth culture. *American Journal of Sociology,* 1967, **72,** 453–468, p. 467.

46. E. J. Kanin. Selected dyadic aspects of male sex aggression. *Journal of Sex Research,* 1969, **5,** 12–28.

47. Kanin, *op. cit.,* p. 21.

48. Kanin, *op. cit.,* p. 23.

49. Kanin, *op. cit.,* p. 23.

50. E. J. Kanin. Male aggression in dating-courtship relations. *American Journal of Sociology,* 1957, **63,** 197–204, p. 201.

51. Kanin, Aggression in dating-courtship, *op. cit.*

52. Ibid.

53. Kanin, Aggression in dating-courtship, *op. cit.,* p. 200.

54. E. J. Kanin. An examination of sexual aggression as a response to sexual frustration. *Journal of Marriage and Family,* 1967, **29,** 428–433.

55. Kanin, Examination of sexual aggression, *op. cit.;* J. J. Teevan. Reference groups and premarital sexual behavior. *Journal of Marriage and the Family,* 1972, **34,** 283–291.

56. L. M. Roberts. Homosexuality: variance or deviance? *Forum of the Wisconsin Psychiatric Institute,* 1973, 4–7, p. 4.

57. E. E. Levitt and A. D. Klassen. Public attitudes toward homosexuality: part of the 1970 national survey by the Institute for Sex Research. *Journal of Homosexuality,* 1974, **1,** 29–43.

58. S. K. Lubin. On being a homosexual. *Forum of the Wisconsin Psychiatric Institute,* 1973, 35–36.

59. G. Geis, R. Wright, T. Garrett, and P. R. Wilson. Reported consequences of decriminalization of consensual adult homosexuality in seven American states. *Journal of Homosexuality,* 1976, **1,** 419–426.

60. J. A. Lee. Forbidden colors of love: patterns of gay love and gay liberation. *Journal of Homosexuality,* 1976, **1,** 401–418.

61. W. Sage. Inside the colossal closet. *Human Behavior,* 1975, **4,** 16–23, p. 16.

62. Sage, *op. cit.,* p. 19.

63. Sage, *op. cit.,* p. 22.

64. Sage, *op. cit.*

65. J. Money. Developmental differentiation of femininity and masculinity compared. In S. N.

Farber and R. H. L. Wilson (Eds.). *Man and civilization: the potential of woman.* New York: McGraw-Hill, 1963, pp. 51–65, p. 56.

66. Ibid.

67. Calderone, *op. cit.*

68. D. G. Brown and D. B. Lynn. Human sexual development: an outline of components and concepts. *Journal of Marriage and the Family,* 1966, **28,** 155–162.

69. A. McCreary-Juhasz. Sexual decision-making: the crux of the adolescent problem. In R. E. Grinder (Ed.). *Studies in Adolescence* (3rd ed). New York: Macmillan, 1975, pp. 340–352.

70. R. L. Delcampo, M. J. Sporakowski, and D. S. Delcampo. Premarital sexual permissiveness and contraceptive knowledge: a biracial comparison of college students. *Journal of Sex Research* 1976, **12,** 180–192.

71. R. E. Grinder and S. S. Schmitt. Coeds and contraceptive information. *Journal of Marriage and the Family,* 1966, **28,** 471–479.

72. A. McCreary-Juhasz. How accurate are student evaluations of the extent of their knowledge of human sexuality? *Journal of School Health,* 1967, **37,** 409–412.

73. McCreary-Juhasz, Knowledge of human sexuality, *op. cit.;* A. McCreary-Juhasz. Background factors, extent of sex knowledge and source of information. *Journal of School Health,* 1969, **39,** 32–39.

74. M. Zelnick and J. F. Kantner. The probability of premarital intercourse. *Social Science Research,* 1972, **1,** 335–341.

75. R. C. Sorensen. *Adolescent sexuality in contemporary America.* New York: World Publishing, 1973.

76. C. Lindemann. *Birth control and unmarried young women.* New York: Springer, 1974.

77. Lindemann, *op. cit.,* p. 15.

78. Lindemann, *op. cit.,* p. 17.

79. Lindemann, *op. cit.,* p. 20.

80. I. L. Reiss, A. Banwart, and H. Foreman. Premarital contraceptive usage: a study and some theoretical explorations. *Journal of Marriage and the Family,* 1975, **37,** 619–630.

81. Reiss, et al., *op. cit.*

82. H. D. Thornburg. Age and first sources of sex information as reported by 88 college women. *Journal of School Health,* 1970, **40,** 156–158.

83. Lindemann, *op. cit.,* p. 35.

84. J. Hottois and N. A. Milner. *The sex education controversy.* Lexington, Mass.: D.C. Heath, 1975.

85. Lindemann, *op. cit.*

86. Lindemann, *op. cit.*

87. Lindemann, *op. cit.,* p. 31.

Chapter 12

The Dynamics of the American High School

CHAPTER HIGHLIGHTS

ISSUES

The American high school today is expected to reinforce conflicting cultural values.

Optimal school size is related to the number of significant roles made available to students.

Young people's educational aspirations are likely to be influenced by the social-class values that predominate in their high school.

446

Teachers' attitudes toward youth in high school are often influenced more by personality than by intellectual traits.

Freedom of expression and due process in matters of suspensions and expulsions are key issues in current litigation pertaining to student rights.

Parental educational achievement, encouragement, and harmony positively affect youth's educational goals.

Youth's perceptions of classroom climate will influence their participation, motivation, and achievement.

Extensive youth-culture participation appears to be correlated negatively with educational achievement.

The image of the contemporary American high school is shaped in part by interscholastic athletics.

High school programs generally favor achievement-oriented students.

Underachievement may occur when youth's beliefs, values, and life styles conflict with traditional societal expectations.

School expectations and the academic needs of creative adolescents often conflict.

The aim of school discipline is to create an atmosphere in which students are motivated to learn.

Sex-role stereotyping in school programs and curricula leads adolescent girls to depress their educational aspirations and to fear success.

Compulsory attendance laws arose for humanitarian reasons but today they are largely coercive and custodial.

Adolescents may be discouraged from attending high school by their families, peers, academic skills, and school curricula.

The high school is today one of the most significant institutions in America. In suburban, small town, and rural areas the high school is often the most imposing structure around. It often constitutes the focal point for cultural events, community theater, and out-of-town speakers. And it consumes a major proportion of the local taxes. In most communities, the high school is a symbol of cultural continuity and, when its athletic teams are successful, a source of pride and solidarity. But the importance of the high school on the American scene is a relatively recent phenomena. Schools prior to the industrial era were voluntary. They focused mainly on literacy, and schooling was subsidiary to chores. The onset of the industrial revolution, however, required laborers who would be sufficiently mobile to work wherever they were needed. Migrations to industrial centers in search of high wages and marriage opportunities left enormous concentrations of young people free from adult supervision. Industrialism gave youth freedom to find their own way in society, and it simultaneously lessened the impact the family had in the eighteenth century on their choice of work roles and eventual transition to adulthood. The tempo of the revolution increased in the nineteenth century, and the attraction of young people to the urban areas, which was accompanied by compromises in conventional morality, increased delinquency, and a flow of immigrants, who were described by Elwood P. Cubberly as "largely illiterate, docile, lacking in initiative and almost wholly without the Anglo-Saxon conception of righteousness," led inevitably to a growing insistence that the state intercede in educating the young.[1] Political forces thus gradually maneuvered the school into a posture of *in loco parentis,* establishing in the nineteenth century a bureaucratic barrier between the family and the workplace. As demands grew to extend literacy training to all young people, the school began to supplant the family in training the young and to become a critically important conduit in their upward mobility. On the whole, the school was largely successful in carrying out the functions assigned to it by a society dominated by industrial capitalism. Child labor laws were enacted to keep young people out of the workplace, preventing their exploitation, but more importantly, to provide the school with opportunity to train a literate and enlightened workforce. Adolescent immigrants of European, Asian, and Latin descent were taught to speak English, and particularly, to adopt values associated with the achievement ethic. The functional value of the school to rising in the middle class was so prized that youthful immigrants learned willingly to be ashamed of their own faces, their family names, their parents and grandparents, and their class patterns, histories, and ethnicities.[2]

Public high schools were established as an upward extension of elementary schools in the latter half of the nineteenth century. They were to be coeducational, free from tuition charges, and accessible to both rural and urban youth.[3] The early public high schools were acutely conscious of their college-preparatory function; fewer than 15 percent of high school students in 1890–1891, for example, intended to go to college, but about half took college-preparatory courses. They were also highly selective. Some high schools required entrance examinations, making them beyond the reach of youngsters who had difficulty graduating from elementary school; moreover, the work often was so difficult that attrition rates were high among those who were admitted. Early in the twentieth century, however, the demands of industrialism transformed the high school from a college-preparatory institution for a few into one that was supposed to facilitate entry into adulthood for all. The number of white-collar jobs—clerks, salespersons, bookkeepers, office workers—expanded, but most required individuals with a high school education. At the same time, child labor and apprenticeship training waned and rural prosperity made the farm work of children less crucial. Suddenly, a large number of relatively immature youth were excused from work. Compulsory attendance laws thus were strengthened, and young people were assigned to school so they could be kept out from under foot and could acquire useful economic skills. The consequences have been startling. Rising enrollments have been accompanied by a continuous ferment about how to devise curricula for increasingly heterogeneous student bodies. The content, which formerly consisted of college-preparatory courses, had to be expanded for those heading for business and industry upon graduation. The proliferation of commercial, technical, and industrial schools, as well as the recognition that college-preparatory courses were not appropriate for all students, led the National Education Association to create a Commission on Reorganization of Secondary Education, which, in 1918, set forth seven "cardinal principles" as guidelines for future secondary education in America. They dealt with health, mental processes, quality of home life, vocational development, civic education, use of leisure time, and ethical character. According to Krug,[4] the diversification in aims led to more professionalism in the high school. Tests of intelligence, achievement, aptitude, and personality were developed, and guidance counseling became widespread. Compulsory attendance and student indifference about education led to problems of motivation and underachievement. Those who were sufficiently motivated and wanted to be in school became a minority in the high schools. To cope with the increased diversity, schools of education were founded to transform high school teachers from narrow academicians into sensitive, sympathetic persons well versed in educational psychology, human development, and group dynamics.

The American high school presently fulfills three different functions. First, it serves parents by providing them relief from child-care about six hours a day, 160 days per year. Second, the high school offers specific instruction in science, technology, fine arts, humanities, and so forth, which helps adolescents cope with complexities in the world beyond their families. Third, teachers and school administrators may serve as models in shaping the adolescent's personality, augmenting parental virtues, and reinforcing the cultural ethos. It is in fulfilling the third function that difficulties arise for the high school. For example, should the high school function (1) to sort individuals according to their abilities to achieve in the industrial world or (2) to show young people ways of changing society to overcome social inequities? The two purposes are largely incompatible; the former poses objectives of industrial competitiveness and the latter, those of social equality. The high school has traditionally served the ends of industrialism. It has provided opportunity for some to obtain more status than others in the social system. During elementary school, for example, children are expected to internalize the motivation to achieve and are selected for high school programs on the basis of that capacity.[5] In high school, further differentiation occurs as career aspirations, which partly stem from achievement motivation, lead youth to choose specific goals. The high school thus may function in part as a selecting agent in the American society. On the other hand, the high school is expected to serve today as an agent of socioeconomic equalization and ethnic integration and as a common meeting ground for youth from diverse social, economic, and religious backgrounds. The high school is asked to be an agency for conveying to young people the values, attitudes, and beliefs that underlie concepts of social justice. How can the high school simultaneously serve both ends? The solution evades us as we enter the twilight of the twentieth century. But the surge of the feminist movement for an educational system more responsive to women's needs and the rise in social consciousness associated with civil rights press us for answers.

America is committed to serving all adolescents in its schools, but the comprehensiveness of the task makes responsiveness and relevance difficult to achieve. The high school today is in transition and issues are being raised regarding the significance of its social-class composition, the role of athletics, student rights, sex-role biases and stereotyping, compulsory attendance laws, and so forth. The discussion in this chapter centers upon such critical issues as these. The chapter is divided into two major sections: one, the role of the high school in society, and, two, youth and the educational process. The ensuing discussion in Chapter 13 focuses on the manner in which youth are being prepared to enter the workforce. It considers the changing nature and significance of work to youth and reviews the kinds of changes in traditional programs that may be necessary if high schools are to serve both the economic ends and egalitarian objectives of society.

THE ROLE OF THE HIGH SCHOOL IN SOCIETY

School Size

McCowan, O'Reilly, and Illenberg[6] reviewed a number of studies that examined the impact of public school size; they reported that in terms of cost, number of offerings, guidance services, and breadth and comprehensiveness of programs, an enrollment of between 1,500 and 2,000 students was optimal. In larger schools, teachers appeared to be better prepared academically. Also the percentage of those who were required to teach in areas other than that of their major interest was lower than in smaller schools. The larger schools also appeared to be able to offer better preparation for college. On the other hand, in smaller schools there was more extensive and effective cooperation among teachers, teachers discussed students among themselves more often, and students were more inclined to confide in their teachers.

In perhaps the most extensive study of school size, Barker and Gump[7] concluded that, as a rule of thumb, a school should be small enough so that all students can fulfill significant roles. In a small school, for example, every member of the junior class may be able to participate in the class play, whereas in a large school perhaps only 15 percent of the class can do so. They compared a small school to a small engine or organism; it has the essential parts of a large entity, but less differentiation and fewer replications in its parts. Also the smaller school offers more versatile experiences, while the larger one offers more opportunity for specialization. To investigate adolescents' participation in school activities, Barker and Gump studied several eastern Kansas high schools, ranging in size from 35 to 2,287 pupils, which were homogeneous in terms of economic, cultural, and political factors. They found that the number of students who participated in music festivals, and in dramatic, journalistic, and student-government competitions was largest in high schools with enrollments between 61 and 150. The average number and kinds of extracurricular activities in which students participated during their high school career were twice as great in the small as in the large schools. Although those in the larger schools had more opportunities available—such as debate clinics, orchestra, chess clubs, and photographic rooms—those in the smaller schools participated more in the activities that were available. Moreover, a larger proportion of the students in the small schools (as compared with the large schools) held positions of importance and responsibility in extracurricular activities. Barker and Gump also reported that students in the smaller schools found greater satisfaction in being challenged, in engaging in important activities, and in being in group activities. Willems[8] also reported that students in smaller schools feel a greater sense of involvement. He compared the "sense of obligation" or level of commitment toward extracurricular activities of two groups: (1) potential dropouts—high school juniors with low IQs, low grades, non-professional fathers, and parents who had failed to complete high school, and (2) students with above average IQs, respectable grades, fathers in managerial or professional positions, and fathers and mothers who had graduated from high school. He found that in small schools, where there were relatively few students, marginal students reported a sense of obligation comparable to that of their schoolmates. But in the larger schools, marginal students felt left out and reported little, if any, sense of obligation. The more fortunate students, on the other hand, did not seem to be affected by the number of students competing for activities.

Thus, it appears that the large school offers both breadth and depth in curricula and faculty expertise, whereas the small school provides a network of social activities in which virtually everyone is expected to participate. One might suppose that socially mature adolescents would thrive in either school. One might also expect that less mature youth might be more comfortable in a smaller school setting where interpersonal interactions might help them acquire meaningful involvements. Although happy outcomes are indeed likely in small schools, such settings may also cause feelings of personal worth to deteriorate when students lack the abilities to respond effectively to perceived demands.[9] Students who might be overlooked in a large school for failing to make an athletic team, for example, might feel humiliated in a small school especially if alternative, status-seeking opportunities are also closed to them. Grabe[10] thus holds that high school students in the smaller schools sometimes experience considerable anxiety as they try to meet the expectations of significant others.

School Social-Class Composition and Educational Aspirations

A variety of studies have dealt with the effect high school social-class composition has on the educational plans of young people. Despite differences in the characteristics of samples, age levels of subjects, and measurement procedures, the findings show that (1) adolescents from higher social classes are more likely to aspire to higher educational goals, and (2) young people are likely to be influenced by the social-class values that predominate in their school. For example, youth will hold higher aspirations if they attend an upper- or middle-class school instead of a working-class school. In an earlier study of boys from eight San Francisco high schools, divergence was found among the schools in terms of the proportion of boys who wanted to go to college.[11] The schools were grouped into three categories—"upper white collar," "lower white collar," and "industrial." Only 10 percent of the boys in the upper white collar schools (as compared with 50 percent in the industrial schools) were sons of manual workers. About 65 percent of the fathers of boys in the upper white collar schools had some college education, but only 14 percent of the fathers of boys in the industrial schools had any college education. Wilson[12] found that 80 percent of the students in the upper white collar, 57 percent in the lower, and 38 percent in the industrial schools wanted to go to college, and concluded that the differences were largely a function of discrepancies in neighborhood reference-group norms. Wilson also reported that 93 percent of the sons of professional men and 50 percent of the sons of manual workers in the upper white collar schools hoped to attend college. By contrast, fewer than two-thirds of the sons of professional and one-third of the sons of manual workers attending the industrial schools wanted to go to college. And Boyle[13] studied senior girls in 70 high schools in western Canada. Of those attending the upper-class schools, 71 percent of the upper-class and 36 percent of the working-class girls planned to attend college, but of those attending working-class schools, only 48 percent of the upper-class and 11 percent of the working-class held college plans.

What is it about school social-class composition that raises or depresses the academic aspirations of young people? Perhaps the relationship is a product of parental design. For example, parents who are ambitious for their children may simply choose their place of residence so that the youth can attend enriched, upper-class schools. Hence, if these youth possess higher educational aspirations than youth of the same social class who attend lower-class schools, differences in aspiration levels among the young people at the two schools may be a function more of levels of initial desire than school social-class composition.[14] It is questionable, however, whether parental values toward education vary significantly within given social-class levels. It is more probable that youth's values toward education are homogeneous within a social class and that differential aspiration levels are produced as the student body gravitates toward the social-class-related opinions and values of the majority. For example, McDill, Meyers, and Rigsby[15] demonstrated that social pressures from peers at school may exert as much or more influence on a student's academic behavior as "home environment, scholastic ability, and academic value." They said that where "academic competition, intellectualism, and subject-matter competence are emphasized and rewarded by faculty and student bodies, individual students tend to conform to the scholastic norms of the majority and achieve at a higher level."

The relationship of social-class differentiation to academic aspirations may also be accounted for, in part, by the allocation of resources to programs. Bain and Anderson[16] suggest that features of educational programs in upper-class schools may be especially conducive to development of educational aspirations; these features include physical facilities and equipment, perpupil expenditures, adequacy of library, laboratory equipment, curricula organization and services, pupil-teacher ratio, and teacher abilities and attitudes. In contrast, Jencks and Brown[17] argue that such quality distinctions in high school programs contribute very little to differences in attainment and aspirations. They say: "high school quality accounts for only 1.0 to 3.4 percent of the variance in twelfth grade test scores, 0.2 to 2.4 percent of the variance in educational attainment, and 2.5 to 4.8 percent of the variance in occupational status and career plans." Heyns[18] suggests, however, that comparisons across high schools, such as Jencks and his colleagues have conducted, underestimate the effects of academic stratification within schools and the differential allocation of resources to the strata. The researcher observed, for example, that performance on achievement tests leads to academic tracking, and those students who attain the highest scores gain access to the resources. Since those who score highest also usually possess the highest educational aspirations, Heyns finds a high correlation between quality of high school programs and educational aspirations. Hence, it appears that comparisons across large, comprehensive schools may mask within-school differences, and may, then, indicate erroneously that high school quality and educational orientation are unrelated.

Alexander and Eckland[19] have explored how ability *and* school social-class composition interact to affect youth's goal-setting behavior. Let us consider how this may occur. The researchers note that youth often compare themselves with one another and that when the comparisons occur in high-ability contexts, the estimate each makes of his or her performance will be lower than when made in a low-ability context, which in turn, will tend to have a depressant effect on academic self-evaluation and educational aspirations. A high-ability context, then, may negatively affect educational plans, but since a high-status setting usually positively influences plans, the two factors would be offsetting. This reasoning led the researchers to suggest that educational aspirations would be heightened among youth in a social context characterized by a high-status, low-ability student body, and would be lowered in a setting characterized by a relatively low-status, high-ability student body. "A socially elite prep school with low academic standards would constitute the 'ideal' educationally enhancing environment."[20] Peer interaction would lead adolescents to raise their images of themselves as competent academically, even though they lacked the requisite skills to justify their self-evaluations. Further, as a result of sharing ideals with other high-status youth, they would develop strong educational aspirations. The problem of course, is that eventually, perhaps in college, these youth might become disillusioned as they mingled with high-ability youth who had participated in tough, competitive, high school programs and, hence, were in a better position to realize their goals.

Teacher Attitudes and Adolescent Educational Performance and Aspirations

Teachers develop differential perceptions of young people as they interact with them. These perceptions are based on their expectations of youth and their interpretations of their performance. Hecht[21] has shown that teacher perceptions often are distorted. She asked approximately 22,000 elementary school teachers how they viewed pupils who had been previously designated as either potential dropouts (significantly below average academically) or academically gifted (significantly above average academically). Her investigation revealed that teachers often confuse potential dropouts with young people who are intellectually impaired, fail to come to school regularly, or otherwise raise problems for them. And they frequently make classification as academically gifted contingent on being socially acceptable and nontroublesome. McCandless, Roberts, and Starnes[22] reported, too, that junior high teachers are inclined to mark the socially advantaged and white students according to how well socialized they are (by the teachers standards) and to mark the poor, particularly the black poor, according to their relative performance in the classroom. In a comparable study of teachers' attitudes, Laosa, Swartz, and Witzke[23] involved 49 high school teachers in a longitudinal study of relationships among students' cognitive, personality, and academic characteristics and teachers' perceptions of the students. The teachers had taught the students in the tenth, eleventh, and twelfth grades. The findings revealed that the rationale for teacher assessment shifted toward personality traits as relationships with the students lengthened. The teachers at first evaluated the youth on their intellectual ability and achievement as measured by standard intelligence tests. Later, as relationships evolved, those interpersonal traits and characteristics of the youth that were congruent with the teachers' goal expectations became the basis of their attitudes. At the tenth grade, for example, teachers were more favorably disposed toward the bright youth who possessed intellectual curiosity and accomplished difficult tasks. Two years later, when the youth were in the twelfth grade, teachers' positive ratings were especially influenced by their perceptions of the youth's ambition, industry, perseverance, and empathy.

Table 1 reveals the extent to which teachers' attitudes toward youth are influenced by their perception of youth's ability and socioeconomic status. The data presented in Table 1 are based on answers youth gave to one of the questions posed in a recent nationwide survey of the high school class of 1972: How much do teachers encourage or discourage young people's educational aspirations.[24] The data show that teachers seldom discourage any youth, whatever their ability and social class, from planning to attend college; however they especially encourage aspirations toward college among those of higher ability and of higher socioeconomic status. Moreover, teachers seldom discourage any youth from attending a vocational or trade school or from obtaining a job after school; yet with relatively high frequency, they encourage youth of low ability and of low socioeconomic status to choose one of these activities as an alternative to college.

Student Rights

Student rights expanded dramatically during the past decade. The civil rights movement and the demonstrations, confrontations, and boycotts of the 1960s heightened the political consciousness of youth and inspired demands that students be given opportunity to exercise their constitutional rights in school. The authority of the school to regulate student behavior derives from the premise of *in loco parentis*. Courts have long held that school authorities may develop comprehensive administrative regulations to enforce "appropriate" standards of behavior.[25] As a consequence of the unilateral power vested in their authority, schools have tended to operate rather arbitrarily on the basis of

Table 1

Percent of Youth in the High School Class of 1972 by Their Response to the Question: Have Your Teachers or Counselors Ever Tried to Influence Your Plans for after High School

	Ability			Socioeconomic Status		
	Low	Medium	High	Low	Medium	High
Response (weighted percentage of students)						
To go to college						
Discouraged me	6.4	1.8	0.4	3.7	2.7	1.0
Didn't try to influence me	42.4	35.1	19.3	36.2	33.4	25.9
Encouraged me	51.3	63.1	80.3	60.1	63.9	73.1
To go to vocational, technical, business, or trade school						
Discouraged me	6.4	4.9	7.9	5.3	5.4	8.7
Didn't try to influence me	46.6	62.2	80.0	50.6	62.8	78.1
Encouraged me	47.0	32.8	12.2	44.1	31.8	13.1
To get a job immediately after high school						
Discouraged me	12.7	12.9	17.2	11.3	13.6	17.7
Didn't try to influence me	58.5	73.7	78.2	64.7	71.9	76.6
Encouraged me	28.9	13.4	4.6	24.0	14.5	5.7

Source: W. B. Fetters. *National longitudinal study of the high school class of 1972.* National Center for Educational Statistics. (DHEW Pub. No. 76-235.) 1976. Reprinted by permission.

"uncodified traditions, administrative rulings, or school board policies."[26] Recent Supreme Court rulings have been aimed at protecting the rights of students, however, and have led to concentrated attempts at local levels to codify these rights. Nearly half the state school boards of education, for example, have promulgated written rulings, approximately 85 percent of the local school boards have adopted codes outlining student rights and responsibilities, several state legislatures have enacted statutes to protect student rights, and handbooks on student rights have proliferated.[27]

The two most important issues in current court cases regarding student rights pertain to freedom of expression and due process in matters of suspensions and expulsions. The United States Supreme Court, for example, ruled in 1969 that the First Amendment to the Constitution, which guarantees freedom of speech, is applicable to students in the public schools. The Court held in *Tinker v. Des Moines Independent School District* that it was unconstitutional for a school district to have suspended students for wearing black armbands to school as a protest against the war in Vietnam, since neither disruption nor interference with appropriate school discipline had occurred. The Court thus insisted that school authorities must regard students as more than "passive recipients" of what they believed the students should be taught, and the *Tinker* case has become a judicial precedent for striking down regulations restricting the political content of student speeches, newspapers, and handbills.[28]

Due process in suspensions and expulsions has long been a touchy issue. On the one hand, it is argued that the stability of the school and the safety of students can be maintained only when disruptive youth are removed swiftly from the scene. On the other, authority granted school administrators on arbitrary grounds often is abused. A school disciplinarian, for example, frequently acts on information gathered from others, who in turn may have learned of the incident indirectly. When facts are disputed and risk of error is high, victimized students can suffer considerably. Suspension or expulsion may jeopardize educational and employment opportunities because many colleges and employers specifically ask whether an applicant has ever been removed from school. Moreover, suspension or expulsion may make students' disciplinary problems worse by damaging their standing with peers and teachers and by retarding their academic progress. By a five to four vote, therefore, the United States Supreme Court, in *Goss v. Lopez* (1975), set forth basic procedural safeguards designed to guarantee students the right to due process in matters of discipline. The Court rulings stemmed from an incident in which black junior and senior high school students in Columbus, Ohio, had been suspended from several schools in massive numbers without reason or hearing following a period of racial tension in 1971. The action was justified on the basis of an Ohio statute authorizing suspension of students for up to 10 days without notice. The students challenged the statute on the grounds that it failed to provide due process as required by the Fourteenth Amendment to the Constitution. A three-judge United States District Court invalidated the suspension, and the United States Supreme Court subsequently upheld the lower court opinion. The courts held students had a "protected interest" in school attendance and that they must be given oral or written notices of charges against them in suspensions of up to 10 days. If they deny the charges, an explanation of the supporting evidence and an opportunity to present counterarguments must be provided. A hearing is thus required before students may be removed from school, except in instances where their presence might be judged dangerous or disruptive. But even if students are sent home immediately, a hearing is required as soon as possible.

The direction the courts have taken to resolve questions of freedom of expression and due process reflects judicial sentiment in other areas of student rights. The courts, for example, have consistently resisted efforts to regulate the appearance of students. As Haberman[29] states, "the growing legal consensus is definitely on the side of not permitting any such codes—not even when the student body has drawn up its own dress code and endorsed it by majority vote. Fashion and taste are not subject to regulation." Clothing that clearly is dangerous or disruptive of learning may, however, be disallowed. Few would disagree with rules prohibiting either metal cleats on shoes that might damage floors or long-haired sweaters in cooking and chemistry classes where open-flame gas burners may be used. But it becomes highly problematical when clothing is presumed to expose the body indecently and, thus, to be so distractive as to interfere with learning and teaching. But the courts have moved to protect students' privacy. They have asserted that school records should contain only educational data; reports relating to personality and attitudinal traits may be retained in temporary files, whose contents are to be systematically reviewed and eliminated. On matters of search and seizure, however, the courts have been relatively silent. A principal who believes a crime is being committed may today legally search students' lockers without their consent and without a valid warrant, and the contents may be turned over to the police for criminal prosecution. Concern regarding drug abuse has become the basis for most school search and seizure operations.[30]

The vigorous defense of student rights in the courts during the past decade has led many activist students to question whether society is as "oppressive and hypocritical" as their predecessors of the 1960s had proclaimed it to be.[31] The resolution of several critical issues in student rights, however, are far from settled. The *Tinker* decision notwithstanding, student expression still is curtailed by school authorities with the sanction of the lower courts even when conduct does not materially disrupt classwork. The lower courts, for example, have recently approved suspensions authorized by school administrators to punish the distribution of handouts on the grounds that the literature "'could conceivably cause an eruption,'" to censor a student for wearing an armband that had been the source of tension a year earlier, and to punish students who had been defiant of school officials.[32] On the whole, nonetheless, the courts have produced a series of useful guidelines, and we may anticipate that during the next decade a host of new judicial interpretations on student rights will be issued. The likely outcome of these new rulings is indicated in the excerpts from a sample student code presented below.[33] It was produced by the *Phi Delta Kappa* Commission on Administrative Behaviors Supportive of Human Rights. The Commission code stresses in brief that conduct rules should be in writing and well-distributed. Its contents specify that students shall have access to their personal school records and control over them, be given prior notification before general searches are initiated, be permitted to distribute and possess controversial material, and have the right to assemble in a nondisruptive time, place, and manner. It holds also that such factors as age, sex, race, religion, national origin, pregnancy, parenthood, and marriage shall not impede the rights of students to participate fully in classroom instruction and extracurricular activities. Further, the power of suspension is to be used only when circumstances are extraordinary; when it does appear to be warranted, a hearing shall be conducted before a panel, and students may have an attorney present, confront all adverse witnesses, and appeal the hearing panel's decision to the school board.

A SAMPLE STUDENT CODE

1.0 RULES GOVERNING STUDENT DISCIPLINE

1.1   This Code and any additional rules governing student discipline shall be distributed to students and their parent(s) or guardian(s) at the beginning of each school year and shall be posted in conspicuous places within each school throughout the school year. Changes in the rules shall not take effect until they are distributed to students and parents.

2.0 STUDENT RECORDS

2.1 Student records shall be defined as any material concerning individual students maintained in any form by the school board or its employees, except personal notes maintained by teachers and other school personnel solely for their own individual use and not communicated to any other person.

2.2 All records on a student, with the exception of personal evaluations submitted in confidentiality before the adoption of this section, shall be open to that student's parent(s) or guardian(s). Such records shall also be open to the student with the consent of one of his/her parents or guardians, except that consent is not required for any student in the tenth, eleventh, or twelfth grades. The school shall provide whatever assistance is necessary to enable the student and his/her parent(s) or guardian(s) to understand the material in the record.

3.0 SEARCHES OF STUDENTS

3.1 Searches of a student's person, his/her personal possessions, or his/her locker without a valid search warrant shall be prohibited unless the principal has a reasonable basis for believing that the student is concealing material the possession of which is prohibited by federal, state, or local law or the provisions of this Code.

4.0 POSSESSION AND DISTRIBUTION OF LITERATURE

4.1 Students shall have the right to distribute and possess any form of literature, including but not limited to newspapers, magazines, leaflets, and pamphlets; except that the principal may prohibit specific issue of a specific publication if there is a substantial factual basis for believing its possession or distribution will cause or is causing substantial disruption of school activities. This right of distribution shall extend to school grounds and buildings, absent the requisite finding of disruption.

5.0 FREEDOM OF EXPRESSION AND ASSEMBLY

5.1 Students shall have the right to express themselves by speaking, writing, wearing, or displaying symbols of ethnic, cultural, or political values such as buttons, badges, emblems, and armbands; or through any mode of dress or grooming style; or through any other medium or form of expression; except that the principal may regulate expression, provided there is a factual basis for believing a specific form of expression by a specific student will cause or is causing substantial disruption of school activities. Students shall also have the right to refrain from expressing themselves.

6.0 FREEDOM OF RELIGION

6.1 Students shall have the right to refuse to participate in or attend any form of religious activity, including but not limited to prayers, songs, readings, meditations, and seasonal programs.

7.0 EQUAL EDUCATIONAL OPPORTUNITY

7.1 The right of a student to participate fully in classroom instruction and extracurricular activities shall not be abridged or impaired because of age, sex, race, religion, national origin, pregnancy, parenthood, marriage, or for any other reason not related to his/her individual capabilities.

8.0 TEMPORARY SUSPENSION

8.1 A student may be temporarily suspended by the building principal only if the principal has reasonable cause to believe that:

   a. the physical safety of the student or of others is substantially endangered and will continue to be endangered; or

    b. the student is causing and will continue to cause substantial interference with classroom instruction.

Such temporary suspension shall be preceded by an informal conference between the student, the principal, and the teacher or supervisor who referred the student to the principal. At this conference the student shall be informed of the reason for the disciplinary action and shall be given the opportunity to persuade the principal that the temporary suspension is not warranted.

8.2 A temporary suspension shall terminate when it is reasonably determined that the student's presence in the school will not result in a situation warranting temporary suspension under Section 8.1, and in no case shall it last beyond the end of the school day following the day the temporary suspension began.

8.3 Within twenty-four (24) hours of the beginning of a temporary suspension, the principal shall mail a notice to the parent(s) or guardian(s) of the suspended student stating the specific act(s) for which the temporary suspension was ordered. On or before the day such notice is postmarked, the principal shall make a reasonable effort to contact the parent(s) or guardian(s) of the student by telephone to communicate directly the information contained in the written notice.

9.0 SUSPENSION

9.1 The principal shall not recommend suspension unless the student while on school grounds or during a school activity off school grounds:
    a. intentionally causes or attempts to cause substantial damage to school property or steals or attempts to steal school property of substantial value; or
    b. intentionally causes or attempts to cause substantial damage to private property or steals or attempts to steal valuable private property; or
    c. intentionally causes or attempts to cause physical injury to another person except in self-defense; or
    d. knowingly possesses or transmits any firearm, knife, explosive, or other dangerous object of no reasonable use to the student at school; or
    e. knowingly possesses, uses, transmits, or is under the influence of any narcotic drug, hallucinogenic drug, amphetamine, barbituate, marijuana, alcoholic beverage, or intoxicant of any kind; or
    f. knowingly uses or copies the academic work of another and presents it as his/her own without proper attribution; or
    g. repeatedly and intentionally defies the valid authority of supervisors, teachers, or administrators.

9.2 If the principal chooses to recommend a suspension not to exceed seven (7) school days, he/she shall mail a notice to the student and to the student's parent(s) or guardian(s) within twenty-four (24) hours of the alleged act(s) upon which the recommendation is based or within 24 hours of the time he/she learns of such alleged act(s). Such notice shall be in the language of the parent(s) or guardian(s) as well as in English and shall contain:

    a. a complete description of the school regulation(s) allegedly violated by the student;

    b. a full statement of the facts leading to the principal's recommendation for suspension;

    c. specific reference to the student's right to have a private hearing before an impartial hearing officer at which a tape recording will be made and at which the student and his/her parent(s), guardian(s), and adult representative, if any, shall be allowed to question adverse witnesses, contradict written statements of absent witnesses, and present evidence in the student's defense, including the presentation of live witnesses;

    d. the time and place of a hearing to be held no later than four (4) school days from the date the notice is postmarked; except the principal shall not schedule the hearing at a time prior to when he/she would reasonably expect the notice to arrive at the home of the parent(s) or guardian(s). The student shall be informed of his/her right to a reasonable postponement of the hearing date for the purpose of preparing his/her defense; and

    e. specific reference to the student's right to have access to his/her records as provided by Sections 2 of this Code.

10.0 EXPULSION AND INVOLUNTARY TRANSFER

10.1 The principal may recommend expulsion, which shall be defined as exclusion from regular classroom instruction for any period exceeding seven (7) school days, or involuntary transfer to the regular classroom program of another school during the school year only if the student persistently violates Section 9.1 of this Code in such a manner that his/her removal is necessary to protect the physical safety of others or to prevent substantial interference with the right of others to pursue an education.

11.0 INVOLUNTARY CLASSIFICATION

11.1 Before any student is involuntarily classified into special classes for mentally, emotionally, behaviorally, or physically impaired children, the student and his/her parent(s) or guardian(s) shall be entitled to all rights of notice, hearing, and appeal.

12.0 EDUCATION FOR EXCLUDED STUDENTS

12.1 Any student temporarily suspended, or expelled from regular classroom instruction shall be allowed full use of his/her regular textbooks and shall be provided with the assignments and tests for the classes from which he/she has been excluded. In addition, the student shall be allowed to participate at no cost in any alternative forms of instruction such as night school, tutoring, televised instruction, or correspondence courses provided to the public by the school board.

13.0 CORPORAL PUNISHMENT

13.1 Students shall not be subject to corporal punishment.

YOUTH AND THE EDUCATIONAL PROCESS

Family and Education

The effect of family background on the educational aspirations and attainment of adolescents is enduring and pervasive. It manifests itself in a mixture of genetic and socioeconomic variables. To some extent abilities and aptitudes are genetically determined; thus, there is an upper limit on every adolescent's potential academic achievements. Socioeconomic background may either inhibit or facilitate the adolescent's capacity to take advantage of existing opportunities. Parents who are socially advantaged, for example, may support the high school's role in facilitating social-class mobility and in assisting the educational and personal growth of their offspring. When these parents were young, the high school had served them well; therefore, they are likely to talk over school work with their children, discuss athletic and extracurricular activities, seek reasons for poor scholastic performance, help in taking corrective measures, encourage their children to have high aspirations and attend college, and importantly, express pleasure when their children receive high marks and perform well. Since adolescents are not economic assets to them, suburban, middle-class parents are likely to focus their attention on school work and long-range goals. Less advantaged parents, however, may feel differently about the high school. Many may not have a high school education themselves, and those who graduated may not have secured good jobs. These parents may view the school with suspicion, pessimism, and distrust. Because their experiences in school failed to pay off, they expect little from the school for their child. Although they may want teachers to enforce discipline, compel learning, and insist on quiet, conformity, obedience, and staying out of trouble, such parents seldom communicate a sense of excitement or urgency about school.[34] They are less likely than middle-class parents to provide a quiet place for their children to study or to discuss school with them. In economically disadvantaged homes sleep may be haphazard and meals may be little more than individual raids on the refrigerator. A crowded, noisy home makes serious study difficult. Often, too, vision, hearing, and other learning impairments may not be treated, thus hampering their children's ability to concentrate on school subjects.

Let us discuss briefly three parental characteristics—educational attainment, encouragement of learning, and parental role relationships—as they relate to the academic performance and aspirations of young people. First, Sewell and Shah[35] have shown that there is a strong relationship between the parents' educational achievement and adolescent aspirations. The data came from a questionnaire survey of all high school seniors in Wisconsin's public, private, and parochial schools in 1957, and a follow-up study conducted seven years later of college plans, attendance, and graduation. When the youth were classified in terms of their father's or mother's education, those with more highly educated parents were found more likely to seek higher levels of education. For example, when both parents had graduated from high school, the educational aspirations and attainment of the young people tended to match the achievement of the parents. Further, when the father, but not the mother, was the high-school graduate, adolescents of both sexes were more likely to become high school graduates. However, when the mother, but not the father, was the graduate, neither son nor daughter was likely to graduate from high school. In respect to college-level aspirations, among adolescents with one parent who did not finish high school and the other who had some college education, boys whose fathers and the girls whose mothers had attended college were likely to want to do so themselves. In general, the father's educational attainments had a more significant impact than the mother's on the high-level aspirations of the more intelligent boys and girls, perhaps because the father had more influence than the mother in terms of instrumental factors associated with prestige and earning power.

The extent to which parents encourage their son or daughter is also closely related to their achievement in school. Swift[36] said that "parents whose views of education are sympathetic and who see education as an important ladder for mobility, tend to have children who are successful in school. . . . A genuine, mutually reinforcing relationship between parental attitudes towards education and the child's 'ability' seems undeniable." Rehberg and Westby[37] said that parental encouragement functions as a mechanism that links "the social structure to the individual. It is a vehicle whereby the parents translate their achievement and mobility values into a role expectation comprehensible to the adolescent, i.e., the expectation that he is to continue his education beyond high school." Morrow and Wilson[38] summarized the results of several studies on the relationship between parental encouragement and school achievement. They found that the parents of high-achievers generally gave them more praise and approval, showed more interest and understanding, were closer to them, encouraged family belongingness, and emphasized parental identification. On the other hand, parents of underachievers appeared to be more domineering, restrictive, prone to use severe and frequent punishment, inclined to baby or push their offspring excessively, and insistent on either low or exceedingly high demands for achievement. Morrow and Wilson also compared high school boys of about equal socioeconomic status and high intelligence who were making good grades with those who were not. They found that family morale was important in fostering academic achievement, positive attitudes toward teachers and school, and an interest in intellectual activities.

Parental harmony has also been found to affect the educational aspirations of young people.[39] Myerhoff and Larson, for example, interviewed 73 adolescent boys and their parents and found that the greater the degree of family consensus, the greater the likelihood that the son will hold positive aspirations toward school. Boys who did not do very well in school tended to be from families with mid-range consensus, and aggressive boys tended to come from families with minimal consensus. The researchers suggested that family disorganization could lead to ineffective socialization and thus poor school adjustment. Parents may become upset if their son does not perform well academically; they may fail to understand his limitations; and thus they may disagree and bicker about how to resolve the problem. In a related investigation, Elder[40] interviewed approximately 1,000 people 18 years of age and older in the United States, Great Britain, West Germany, Italy, and Mexico to assess whether marital relationships of parents affected their child's self-confidence and scholastic progress. He found that in all five nations parental dominance was negatively associated with the probability of reaching secondary school—even when such factors as the size of birthplace, religion, and social class were held constant. Except in Italy, those who reported having had equalitarian relationships with their parents were more likely to have reached secondary school. Elder said that the likelihood of reaching secondary school in each of the countries was consistently low among persons with authoritarian parents, regardless of the parental decision-making pattern. Bowerman and Elder[41] also reported that a dominant mother, autocratic methods of child-rearing, or both, may hinder a youth's educational aspirations.

Peer Influences

Youth's Perception of the High School Classroom. A high school classroom is organized to carry on learning activities and to achieve instructional objectives. The psychosocial environment of the classroom is designed to support these aims. After spending months as an observer in a public high school of 1,100 students, Cusick[42] identified several mutually reinforcing characteristics that describe how learning and instructional aims are serviced in many high schools. He notes that teachers are expected to pass on particular specialities to students—the "passing on" is vertically organized and students are expected to obey their teachers and accept their authority; communication is largely downward, flowing from teachers to students; learning is "batch" processed, whereby a single teacher directs the activities of a large number of youth at a single setting; activities are routinized so that everyone knows where to go and what to do; and to ensure students conform to the system, governance is based on extensive rules and regulations. These characteristics appear in varying degrees and intensities in different classrooms, and thus affect instruction and learning as they relate to students' responsiveness in given classroom settings. Researchers during the past few years have begun to investigate youth's perception of classroom organization and activity. Trickett and Moos,[43] for example, have developed a Classroom Environment Scale (CES) which assesses nine classroom social-interaction dimensions. The CES may be used to make comparisons of classroom climate both within and between classes. The kind of information that may be derived from the scale is shown in Figure 1.[44] Two classroom profiles are superimposed for purposes of comparison. Classroom "8" represents a distributive education class of juniors in a rural high school; Classroom "14" represents a ninth-grade mathematics class in a suburban junior high school. Norms for the profiles were derived from 38 other high school classrooms; these are depicted by the horizontal line in Figure 1. The data reveal that both classes reported an equivalent emphasis on "competition" and "order and organization," both of which were about average in respect to the norms. Figure 1 also shows that students in Classroom "8" reported stronger affiliative relationships than those in Classroom "14." The former indicated that "students in this class get to know each other really well." They reported more involvement and innovation in their classwork, and looked forward to coming to class and getting to work. They saw their class offerings as more diverse, and "new ideas are always being tried out here." Further, students in Classroom "8" perceived themselves as having a more personal and supportive relationship with their teacher and were more likely to view the teacher as "taking a personal interest in students" and less likely to perceive the teacher as "talking down to students." On the other hand, the teacher in Classroom "8" was perceived by students as low in "task orientation," that is, as less demanding in terms of work and more prone to discussing irrelevant topics. The teacher also was ambiguous about the rules governing classroom behavior, low in "rule clarity," and more "laissez faire" (low "teacher control") regarding classroom management. In contrast, students in Classroom "14" indicated they were in a setting where (1) everyone sticks to classwork and seldom gets sidetracked (high "task orientation"); (2) the rules for behavior are clear and the consequences for breaking them generally unambiguous and consistent (high "rule clarity"); and (3) the teacher maintains control in the class and "runs a tight ship" (high "teacher control").

Walberg, House, and Steele[45] recently asked students in grades 6 through 12 to rate emphases given in the classroom to cognitive and affective processes. The researchers were interested in making comparisons across grade levels, and, in contrast to Trickett and Moos, they made no attempt to study what was happening within a given classroom. As the data presented in Figures 2 and 3 show, students' perceptions of classroom climate are very much affected by grade level. Figure 2 reveals that such lower-level cognitive processes as "memorizing" and "knowing the best answer" are seen as more significant in the upper grades, while the higher-level processes, application, comprehension, finding consequences, and discovering solutions, are viewed as more prominent in the earlier grades. The trends, however, are curvilinear; lower-level processes reach a peak and higher level processes, a trough in grades nine and ten. Figure 3 shows the relationship of affective dimensions to grade level. Class participation, inde-

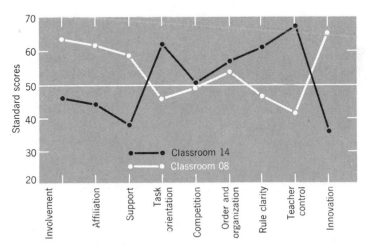

Figure 1
Comparison of sample profiles of students in two classes. (From Trickett and Moos, see text. Reprinted by permission.)

pendent activities, excitement and involvement are perceived as more prominent in grades six through eight than in the upper grades, while concern for grades is perceived as more pronounced in the latter years of high school. Several of the scales also reveal curvilinear properties; independent exploration, excitement and involvement, and opportunity to participate received less emphases in grades nine through eleven, whereas concern for grades peaked at grade ten. Walberg et al.[46] suggest that such changes in perceptions across grade levels indicate that high schools are failing to respond to student needs and abilities, especially in grades nine and ten. The researchers believe that changes in perception reflecting less interest in scholarship in the upper grades may be a function of pressure among achievement-oriented youth to get "right answers" for high grades and admission to college. The trends of noninvolvement in both the affective and

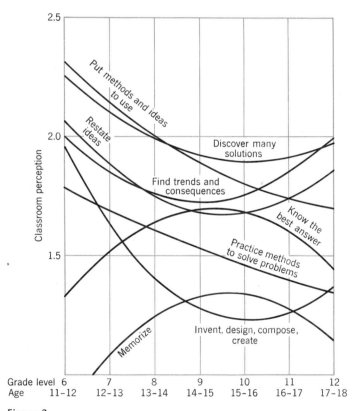

Figure 2
Cognitive criteria by grade level. (From Walberg et al., see text. Reprinted by permission.)

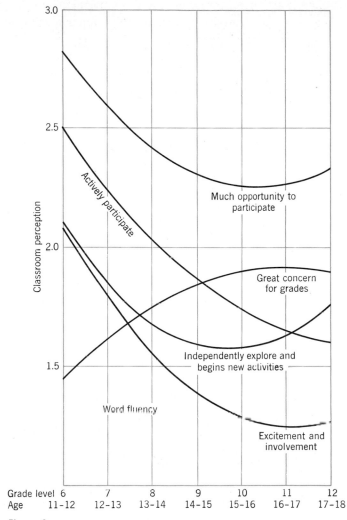

Figure 3
Affective criteria by grade level. (From Walberg et al., see text.
Reprinted by permission.)

cognitive areas suggest to the researchers that these "students may psychologically or physically withdraw from high school because their classes appear to
lack appropriate stimulation and intellectual challenge."[47]

Youth-Culture Participation and School Orientation. Cusick[48] notes
that young people are given impetus to affiliate with one another in high school

because they find the official structure of the school so impersonal. Youth-culture participation provides youth with affiliation, a communications network, social differentiation, and the immediate pleasure of participation in human interaction. In a study of young people in grades seven through twelve, Muma[49] found that students who were well liked by their peers tended to be more successful scholastically, while those who were clearly rejected by their peers tended to be less accessible than those of average acceptance. Muma investigated both "performance" classes (band, chorus, shop, physical education, and driver education) and academic classes (English, mathematics, and science), and reported that the relationship between achievement and peer acceptance was stronger in the academic than in the performance classes.

The fact that peer activities generate a "holding power" that helps the adolescent maintain educational objectives is part of the complex relationship between youth-culture involvement, especially at the "hedonistic" level, and educational attainment. A study of 10 schools made in the late 1950s showed that in each school scholastic achievement was valued less than youth-culture participation.[50] Boys valued athletic status and girls valued popularity and leadership in extracurricular activities. Boys who had done well in athletics tended to have a higher peer status than those who had done well scholastically; similarly, popular girls were more highly esteemed than those who had received higher grades. The "elites" (high-status youth) were less likely to choose the "brilliant student image" for themselves even though their socioeconomic backgrounds tended to be higher and they generally planned to go to college. Coleman concluded that adolescent social systems channel the energy of young people toward athletics and social activities and discourage scholastic achievement.

Grinder[51] investigated the assumption that participation in youth-culture activities (largely of the hedonistic sort) and commitment to academic goals involve two fundamentally incompatible reward systems. He reasoned that because every adolescent has only a fixed amount of time, immersion in the immediate, gratifying youth-culture reward system precludes participation in the delayed, uncertain satisfactions of academic achievement. He administered a Social Interest Inventory to more than 2,000 boys in seven high schools. The inventory was designed to tap interests in three incentive and four reference-group areas. The former comprised (1) *status-seeking*—a desire to associate with prestigious peers, receive invitations to parties, belong to an "in-group," and develop social etiquette, grace, and sophistication; (2) *independence-assertion*—a desire to achieve autonomy by extending oneself beyond the conventional standards of society (for example, seek shortcuts on a job, break city and school rules, ignore adult complaints about raucous behavior at a party or in a restaurant); (3) *sex-gratification*—a desire to have physical contact with members of the opposite sex and learn more about heterosexual behavior (for example, pulp magazines, talk about girls, crash all-girl parties, dance cheek-to-cheek, hold hands, stroll arm-in-arm, and caress or neck in a parked car). The four reference groups were (1) *solitariness*—actually a nongroup, but a means by which individuals participate in the youth culture; (2) *neighborhood friends*—a significant peer group that offers an alternate reward system to that of the family; (3) *cliques and crowds*—a means by which people are bound together by intimate face-to-face contacts; (4) *dating*—a situation in which couples pair off.

The investigation also included background information on the subjects who had taken the inventory. Their school records were examined to learn their age, number of absences, curricula, and aptitude test scores. Also, an "activity" inventory was administered to a random selection of more than 600 boys. It was made up of two parts: (1) self-report items, in which the subjects were asked to provide such information as the age at which they began dating, the frequency of dating, which nights they were permitted to go out each week, the number of close friends they had, the amount of contact they had with close friends, and the extent to which they participated in out-of-school sports and adult-sponsored activities; (2) peer-nomination items, in which the subjects were asked to name two boys in their class who were most likely and least likely, respectively, to participate in each of the four reference groups.

Comparing the Social Interests Inventory scales and the background information showed that there were strong and consistent relationships between a high commitment to youth-culture interests and a low commitment to high school objectives. Several of the relationships corroborated Coleman's[52] finding of peer solidarity and youth-culture divergence from adult values. High youth-culture interests correlated significantly with many absences, low aptitude test scores, early commencement of dating, high frequently of dating, many nights out per week, and frequent out-of-school, nonadult activities. By contrast, low youth-culture interests were correlated with significant participation in school clubs and government, school sports and adult-sponsored activities.

Weatherford and Horrocks[53] have said that interaction with peers and school achievement shows a curvilinear relationship—moderate interaction is positively related to school success but neither excessive nor infrequent socializing correlates with an academic orientation. Grinder[54] found, as noted above, that extensive youth-culture participation may be inimical to high school objectives. The researcher also found that moderate participation may support school objectives;

nonparticipation in the youth culture, like extensive participation, seems to be related to withdrawal from school aims. Self-reports of participation in school clubs, government, and sports correlated significantly with college-preparatory curricula, high aptitude, and peer reports of clique-crowd orientation. Also, those boys who reported having several friends scored high in extracurricular activities, adult-sponsored activities, and academic aspirations, but those who reported that they did not have any friends scored significantly low in both academic aspirations and clique-crowd visibility. Thus, it appears that school-sponsored activities reinforce school objectives by providing young people with "wholesome" activities, in which participation apparently does not diminish their peer visibility and status. The high school's socializing practices apparently fail to reach boys who are not interested in school or in their peers; these youth seem to be indifferent to both youth-culture interests and belonging to a reference group. Adolescents who have low academic aspirations, who participate in few extracurricular activities, and who have few friends have little to sustain them in either the high school or the youth culture, and their problems are compounded if they are older than average for their grade level. The older youth tended to begin dating at a later age, to have little participation in adult-sponsored activities or athletics, to have low visibility among their peers, and to have low academic standing. They were apparently out of step with their classmates, and perhaps, through exclusion, eventually became less perceptive and effective in their interpersonal relationships. They constituted the high school's losers, socially and academically, and for them, the youth culture was more irrelevant than subversive.

Coleman[55] had found, paradoxically, that high peer status in youth-culture activities was related to both a greater interest in going to college and a lesser interest in scholarly achievement. In a follow-up study, McDill and Coleman[56] both confirmed the original finding and added that the discrepancy between orientation toward college and scholastic achievement was likely to increase during high school. Participants in the follow-up study were seniors in high school but had been freshmen at the time of the initial investigation. The researchers found that youth with high youth-culture status were usually from "good" families who tended to send their children to college. Thus, nearly all the members of the "leading crowd" had expectations of going to college even before they became freshmen. However, the image of college held by these youth was of "campus social life, freedom from parental control, a shift to new friends, and all the other social attributes of college."[57] On the whole, these adolescents viewed college life as hedonistic rather than scholastic and saw college achievement as a sign of acquiescence to adult strictures rather than as an opportunity to prepare themselves for the future; "to teen-agers . . . scholastic achievement carries the connotation of acquiescence and subordination to adults." Since the adolescents expected college to be like their youth culture in high school, McDill and Coleman were able to explain the apparent paradox. Coleman's[58] data still support the finding that strong youth-culture participation in hedonistic-level activities is incompatible with academic objectives.

Interscholastic Athletics

The idea of physical education was borrowed from Germany and introduced to schools in Massachusetts in 1825.[59] Programs sanctioned by American schools in the nineteenth century included training primarily in gymnastics and in health concepts and practices. Although games and competitive team sports were played for enjoyment, such activities were for the most part conducted outside the auspices of the school. As intramural and extramural sports evolved, young people managed the teams and paid expenses themselves. Eventually, the sports activities were introduced as aspects of comprehensive physical education programs, and by the turn of the century, interscholastic athletics had so risen in prominence as to wholly dominate traditional dimensions of physical education in school budgets and programs. Management and control of teams were assumed by school administrations, coaching became a skilled profession, coaches were hired, fees began to be charged for admission to athletic events, athletic associations were formed, and "stars" among the athletes began to acquire recognition.[60]

Visitors to a typical high school today might wonder if they were at school or an athletic club. First of all, upon entering, they are likely to be confronted with a trophy case filled with more symbols of victory in athletic than scholastic contests. Wherever the visitors turn, they are likely to find considerable attention given to impending sports events. Most students bursting from their classrooms would probably be discussing Friday evening's football game and the top players; perhaps a few might be talking over history or science assignments.[61] The modern high school, moreover, has heightened its promotion of interscholastic athletics by creating several special statuses, symbols, and rituals: attractive cheerleaders, skilled baton twirlers, handsomely outfitted marching bands, all-star teams, halls of fame, school songs, athletic letters and sweaters, pep rallies, alumni booster clubs, and athletic banquets.

Why do adolescents and adults alike give interscholastic athletics priority among the functions of a high school? At first, athletics was touted as a cure to the problems of an increasingly urbanized, technological society. It was given credence as an educational function, and started its rapid expansion in secondary schools and American life as an antidote to the fractionation of social life, the monotony of work on the assembly lines, and the anxieties of urban living.[62] By the end of the nineteenth century, many persons believed that fresh air and athletics would morally rescue the urban masses. A report in New York City at the time stated that "crime in our large cities is to a great extent simply a question of athletics."[63] And the founder of the Playground and Recreation Association said: "Through the loyalty and self-sacrifice developed in team games . . . we are laying the foundations for wider loyalty and a more discerning self-devotion to the great national ideals on which democracy rests."[64] These reasons are advanced today essentially as before. More than any other school activity, athletics is compatible with adolescent energy, enthusiasm, and explosive spirit.[65] Athletic contests enable adolescents to share collective goals and develop a strong, positive identification with the high school. Sports transform disorganized, restless student bodies into close-knit communities with strong common goals. Adolescents will identify with their school, and think of the team and the student body as one by using the pronoun "we."[66] Athletics also introduces a democratizing factor in the status system by undercutting social class as a basis for status. And importantly, athletics provides collective goals for both students and local community. The high school is also an institution in the community, and Coleman[67] believes that communities, like schools, would have few common goals without interscholastic games. Athletic contests usually take place between different communities and are key events that bring people together, offering them a rare opportunity to feel and act like a community. The winning team provides its supporters with a sense of camaraderie and good will, and the spirits of all are lowered when the team loses.

Athletic prowess clearly is a major criterion for peer status. Athletic teams permit more intense and prolonged association than any other activity in high school. In his study of 10 schools, Coleman[68] found that every popular boy was going out for basketball or football. Since almost every adolescent wants to be successful, known, and recognized, and since athletics provides visibility, there is a strong motivation to participate in sports. From the beginning of the freshman year, athletics facilitates the creation of a cohesive, tightly knit group; during this crucial first year, the athletic crowd dominates. About six weeks after school opened, Coleman asked each boy in the 10 schools to name the boy he thought was the best student and the best athlete, respectively, in his grade. The best athletes turned out to be more visible than the best scholars.

Soon after school opened and again at the close of the year, Coleman[69] also asked the boys whether they would like to be remembered among their classmates as a brilliant student, an athletic star, or a very popular person. He speculated that since the school emphasized scholastic endeavors, during the course of the school year, the appeal of the brilliant student image would increase relative to that of the athletic star. The athletic star's image was found, as expected, to be considerably more attractive at the beginning of the school year, and surprisingly, to increase slightly over time in attractiveness, at the expense of the popularity image. The attractiveness of the brilliant student image, on the other hand, held steady in second place. Friesen,[70] however, felt that Coleman's attempt to contrast the "brilliant student," the "best athlete," and the "most popular" presented the student with unreal alternatives. He asked more than 10,000 Canadian boys and girls in Grades 10 through 12 the following question: "Which one of the following do you regard as most important for your future: academic achievement, popularity, or athletics and cheerleading?" He found that more than 80 percent of all students questioned believed that academic achievement was most important for their future. Fewer than 3 percent of the boys and 2 percent of the girls chose athletics and cheerleading. Friesen's data might suggest that when the alternatives are presented in terms of the future, the adolescent will readily acknowledge that athletics should be viewed in proper perspective.

It is apparent that the adolescent boy who succeeds in athletics enjoys more privileges in school than his less visible classmates, and such privileges probably will be accorded the adolescent girl as women's interscholastic athletics gains in popularity. Snyder,[71] for example, has identified several ways in which socialization favors the high school varsity athlete. For one thing, there is the degree of participation and the necessity of living up to the expectations of others. This far exceeds the pressures of regular physical education classes and offers the adolescent opportunity to adopt mature patterns of behavior. "The heavy investment of community recreational resources, parental and coaching involvement, pep talks to get 'psyched up,' admonitions by the spectators, and self-suggestions to 'get serious' indicate something more than a superficial degree of involvement.[72] Since participation is voluntary and varsity athletes willingly submits themselves to the rigors of practice, the coach and leading team members may acquire extensive prestige and power as models, especially in the skills of a given sport. Also the varsity player often develops a close, expressive relationship with the coach, not only in the matter of specific skills, but also with respect to general aspects of character building. Snyder,[73] for example, recently asked 175 coaches about the extent to which they gave advice and suggestions to athletes in such areas as personal and social behavior. More than 90 percent of the coaches proffered advice about whether to go to college; over 80 percent discussed swearing and hair styles; 60 percent got into personal problems, but less than 30 percent discussed how often to date, and only 11 percent told the athletes whom to date.

Rehberg[74] advanced several plausible reasons why athletic participation sometimes goes hand-in-hand with academic achievement. First, he suggested that the athlete is inclined to obtain higher grades and have higher educational expectations because the individual is more likely to belong to the "leading crowd," which, as Coleman[75] indicated, is both disproportionately middle class and college-oriented; this crowd views athletic competence as an extremely important criterion for membership. Second, sports emphasizes such achievement-related traits as "hard work, persistence, self-improvement, and preparation today for competition tomorrow"—all of which apply to other areas of life. Third, the extent to which an adolescent excels in sports will elicit a positive appraisal from significant others, thereby enhancing self-esteem. In setting high athletic goals, an athlete is likely to set high academic and career goals as well. Fourth, because the athlete is visible, he or she is under pressure to perform in a consistent, congruent manner, and thus strive for success in the classroom. Finally, because the athlete is visible, he or she is especially regarded as a representative of the school and community and thus tends to receive more encouragement and more scholastic and career counseling. "To the extent that the educational pursuits of grades and expectations are enhanced by such counseling and encouragement, and to the extent that the athlete is superior in this respect to nonathletes, this variable may account for a portion of the positive association between educational pursuits and participation in interscholastic athletics."[76] In a study of 785 male seniors from six urban high schools, Rehberg found that a greater proportion of athletes (as compared with nonathletes) expected to enroll in a four-year college, even when such factors as academic performance and parental encouragement varied extensively. Spreitzer and Pugh[77] also report a strong relationship between athletic participation and higher educational goals. The researchers found a definite association between athletic participation and number of close friends planning to attend college, which was especially apparent among "low endowment" athletes, that is, among boys in the lower socioeconomic strata, low IQ, and poor grades categories. Furthermore, the researchers also found that varsity athletes received more academic encouragement from teachers and counselors. Spreitzer and Pugh report, however, that the findings regarding athletic participation and educational expectations are affected by the school value climate toward athletics. In schools where the athletic specialist is highly regarded, the relationship is stronger; where the value climate rewards the "all-around boy," the relationship is weaker, and in schools where scholarship is a more significant source of peer status, there is virtually no relationship between athletic participation and educational expectations. Eitzen[78] has found, too, that enthusiasm for sports is highest in small high schools (less than 300 students) relative to larger schools (more than 1300 students), probably because the proportion of young people participating in interscholastic sports is higher in small schools. Eitzen also indicates that students from schools with winning traditions in football, basketball, and minor sports hold more favorable attitudes toward athletics than do youth from schools with average or poor athletic records.

Although athletes have many opportunities for success in high school, athletic privileges are reserved for only a few, especially in the larger urban schools. For example, Friesen[79] reported that half of the 10,000 Canadian boys and girls he investigated failed to participate in a single extracurricular activity in high school. Start[80] analyzed the athletic participation of 2,500 secondary school boys and girls, ranging in age from 11 to 15, and found that those who did not do well academically also did not participate extensively in sports. He suggested that those who function badly in school may not have enough self-esteem to engage in competitive sports. Yet these marginal students are the ones whose affiliation with school would be strengthened by an athletic program. Consider, for example, the impact on young people who fail to make the team of a highly selective interscholastic athletic program geared specifically to winning. Alley[81] points out that youngsters starting elementary school generally love to play at sports, regard recess as the best part of the day, and do not want to watch somebody else play. They want to be part of the action. But when they are told that they are not good enough to make "the" boys' tag football team or the girls' track squad or are cut from the program, what happens? What sort of adjustments do the young people make in their self-concepts when they are deprived of the social status and acclaim associated with athletic participation? Alley suggests that they may develop a "sour grapes mechanism" to convince themselves that they do not really care: "Anyhow, those jocks are all brawn and no brains. They've got strong backs and weak minds." Perhaps they will gain adequate personal status through academic prowess, but they may not have the skills to excel in scholarship. Alley thus calls for reviving the basic goals of physical education programs, coordinating them with interscholastic, intramural, and recreational sports, in order to provide *all* young people with opportunity to improve their physical fitness and to develop reasonable levels of athletic skills in recreational sports. Solberg[82] has called for replacing interscholastic sports with intramural programs. If this were done, a greater number of students could participate in athletics, the cost of sports could be reduced, and and teacher-coach could be replaced with recreational personnel. But because of the popularity and magnitude of interscholastic sports, the advantages that accrue to athletes, and the tendency of all who relish challenges to bring the best from far and near and pit them against each other, interscholastic athletics will probably not change in the near future.

The High School and the Talented Student

One of the basic purposes of high school is to provide opportunities for all students to develop their talents. Before World War II, much of the labor force was engaged in farming or in the various trades and jobs that required few highly intellectual or creative abilities. But during the war the country was hard-pressed for men and brains, and strenuous efforts were exerted to mobilize human resources. The war-time model demonstrated that organized research could be applied on a large scale to industrial problems when bright and creative persons set their minds to the task.[83] After the war, an acceleration occurred in demand for gifted persons who could manage complex organizations, advance the frontiers of knowledge, and promote economic growth. As the following discussion indicates, the move over the past decade or two to develop the abilities of highly gifted young people has led to provocative analyses of the characteristics of high-achieving and creative adolescents.

Personality Characteristics—The High School Achiever. High school achievers are those who perform at levels either above the average of their classmates or above expectations relative to their aptitudes.[84] The range of criteria for identifying successful achievers is obviously extensive, but it may include grades, sports, honors, student offices, social awards, and a good record in the college preparatory program.[85] Competition is so much a part of the school environment that many youth become totally infused with its values; they usually constitute the emotionally well-adjusted, high achievers. They have learned to fulfill the roles expected by their teachers; they are goal-directed; and they understand what is required for success and have developed reasonably strong expectations of succeeding.[86] America is a highly competitive society and probably will remain so for a long time; although competition may facilitate socialization within the society, competition in high school can exert a heavy toll. Anxiety about doing well may lead some youth to rationalize that they are not concerned about school on the ground that if school is not significant, their failure is also not significant.[87] Others may learn to perform well on tests and papers, viewing them as instrumental goals, but not acquire the capacity to enjoy learning for its own sake. Competition also breeds callousness, for one must know where one stands in the competitive order and then assess what one must do to maintain or improve one's position. Those at the top must jealously strengthen the attributes that will keep them there, and those lower down must strive to attain the skills that will enable them to climb up.

Although the competitive aspects of achievement may breed unwelcome side effects, high achievers usually are spoken of as relatively responsible, self-confident, independent, and autonomous. They are said to be motivated to do well academically, to be aggressive, to believe that they can achieve high standards, to be future-oriented, and to be committed to an instrumental work ethic. Hummel and Sprinthall[88] described typical superior achievers as mature, thoughtful, task-oriented, and willing to postpone immediate gratification in order to achieve distant goals. Similarly, Onoda[89] described third (Sansei) generation Japanese-American high-achieving boys and girls, relative to underachievers, as more self-controlled, serious, sober, responsible, obliging, and mannerly. The high achievers also described themselves as more intelligent, as possessing stronger determination to succeed, as more strong-willed, and as having greater confidence in themselves. And Gawronski and Mathis[90] reported that overachieving students tended to plan their study periods more effectively, show greater interest in school work, approach their work more systematically, persist in completing their assignments, and be more diligent in pursuing high academic standards. The overachievers also tended to accept authority, and to be more socially mature, cooperative, and sensitive about the rights and feelings of others.

Underachievers generally appear to be the opposite of high achievers. According to Hummel and Sprinthall, they are less task-oriented, less able to adopt meaningfully to school, less aware of long-range consequences, more inclined to value the immediate and practical results of academic work, and more likely to be fatalistic about the results of their personal effort. Roth and Puri[91] reported that underachievers have self-defeating attitudes about academic matters; and Silverman, Davids, and Andrews[92] found that they are easily distracted, not too accurate in their performance, and unable to concentrate very well. Gawronski and Mathis[93] reported that underachievers do not have efficient study habits, tend to emphasize pleasure and self-gain, do not try very hard to attain success-oriented goals, are more pessimistic about the future, and do not try to make a good impression on others. Carmical[94] pointed out that underachievers tend to oppose authority, have negative attitudes toward school, and seek excitement. Gawronski and Mathis also said that underachievers appear to be more adventurous and to reject customs and traditions when these interfered with their pursuits.

Overachievement is relatively easy to explain because, by definition, overachievers are fulfilling exacting role expectations. They have shown commitment to the established goals of schooling and they are being rewarded for living up to the expectations of their teachers and parents. Underachievement, on the other hand, may be explained as the opposite of overachievement, for example, as emotional handicaps related to achievement anxiety and personal disorganization. When personality deficiencies predominate, the underachiever may indeed be the opposite of the overachiever, but underachievement also may occur when youth's beliefs, values, and life styles conflict with the traditional goals and expectations of parents, teachers, and society at large. For example, reasons for the recently reported decline in high school achievement test scores probably have their origin in aspects of social change.[95] The details of the decline in average verbal and mathematical Scholastic Aptitude Test (SAT) scores, for college-bound seniors over the past decade, are shown in Table 2.

The SAT was first introduced in 1926, as a broad, objective, group-administered aptitude test, to be used as a criterion for college admission. It was the first widely used instrument to supplant the more cumbersome essay form of admission test, and is today the most extensively administered test in the country. More than one million college-bound high school juniors and seniors in the nation take the test each year.[96] As Table 2 indicates, the two SAT scores, verbal and mathematical, peaked in 1963, and both scores have declined steadily ever since. The verbal score decline shows three relatively large drops, 1966 to 1967, 1972 to 1973, and 1974 to 1975. Girls who once earned higher verbal scores than boys fell behind the average of boys in 1972, and their decline over the past decade is even more dramatic than that of boys. The loss in math SAT scores are about the same for boys and girls, but they are less extreme.

Harnischfeger and Wiley[97] suggest that several factors contribute to the decline, and thus, to the apparent underachievement of young people. The pupil absence rate, for example, has steadily increased over the past decade, resulting in smaller average years of schooling for many young people. On the other hand, a decline in the high school dropout rate over the past decade (see Table 3), while resulting perhaps in gains in general academic accomplishments, may be partially responsible for the manifest test score decline. That is, more dropout-prone young people may continue schooling until graduation, and if those who elect to take the SAT test are more heterogeneous in their academic skills, its average will be pulled downward. Harnischfeger and Wiley also suggest that reductions in enrollments in academic courses (high school youth are taking fewer courses in general English, mathematics, first-year foreign languages, and natural and physical sciences) may help account for the decline. The researchers note, too, that much learning occurs in out-of-school activities, and they point out that television, by decreasing time otherwise directed to homework and reading and by impoverishing family interaction, may play a role in the decline in SAT scores.

Table 2
Mean Scholastic Aptitude Test Scores for College-Bound Seniors, 1957–1976

Year	Verbal			Mathematical		
	Male	Female	Total	Male	Female	Total
1957			473			496
1958			472			496
1959			475			498
1960			477			498
1961			474			495
1962			473			498
1963			478			502
1964			475			498
1965			473			496
1966			471*			496*
1967	463	468	466	514	467	492
1968	464	466	466	512	470	492
1969	459	466	463	513	470	493
1970	459	461	460	507	465	488
1971	454	457	455	507	466	488
1972	454	452	453	505	461	484
1973	446	443	445	502	460	481
1974	447	442	444	501	459	480
1975	437	431	434	495	449	472
1976	433	430	431	497	446	472

Source: Adapted from A. Harnischfeger and D. E. Wiley, *Achievement test score decline: do we need to worry?* St. Louis, CEMREL, Inc., 1976, and report of the College Entrance Examination Board, 1976. Reprinted by permission.

* The figures from 1956–57 to 1965–66 are means of the total group that took the test, those for following years are for male and female high school seniors.

Personality Characteristics—The Creative Adolescent. MacKinnon[98] has suggested that there are two, perhaps three, types of creativity. One kind reflects the uniqueness of the creators; their products may represent their needs, perceptions, or evaluations, as in the case of the works of an artist, sculptor, poet, novelist, playwright, or composer. A second kind reflects an operation on some aspect of the environment that yields a novel product; however, the creative effort may be a scientific achievement and show very little of the creator's individuality in it. A third kind of creativity combines the other two: a product may both reflect the creator and meet the demands of some external problem, as, for example, in architecture.

Hitt[99] and Hitt and Stock[100] feel that originality and logical reasoning constitute the two main, but mutually dependent, dimensions of creativity. Original thinking requires intuition, imagination, and making guesses; logical reasoning is analytical, systematic, and critical. Thus, original thinking may produce an idea, but then it must be followed by logical evaluation to arrive at a new idea at a higher level. Complex ideas are formed in pyramid-like fashion: ideas must be screened initially, for if an individual is not critical, he or she may spend too much time and energy pursuing false leads; on the other hand, if he or she is not tolerant of guesses and hunches, there may be little to think about. Torrance[101] offered a similar definition of creativity: it is "the process of becoming sensitive to problems, deficiencies, gaps in knowledge, missing elements, disharmonies, and so on; identifying the difficulty; searching for solutions, making guesses, or formulating hypotheses about the deficiencies; testing and retesting these hypotheses and possibly modifying and retesting them; and finally communicating the results." Davis[102] has described creative adolescents in terms of four somewhat different, but complementary characteristics. First, creative young people are more independent and self-confident, which promotes risk-taking. Second, they possess high levels of energy and enthusiasm, which takes the form of strong curiosity, high need for novelty, and a keen attraction to new ventures. Third, they consciously consider themselves unconventional and original in many aspects of life, especially as they search for creative problem solutions and innovativeness in others. Fourth, they maintain a "child-like playfulness," which gives them a frame of reference for creating and exploring new possibilities.

As a psychological process, creativity appears to be made up of several elements. Guilford[103] thinks that more than 24 intellectual abilities may be involved in creative productions. He starts from three major elements—fluency, flexibility, and original thinking. Fluency may be subdivided into ideational fluency—the rate at which ideas are generated—and associational fluency—the completion of logical relationships (for example, when one reasons in novel ways, such as writing as many different four-word sentences as possible, with no word used more than once). Flexibility may be subdivided into "spontaneous" and adaptive categories. If an examinee is asked to list all the uses he or she can think of for a common brick and responds with "build a house, build a school, build a factory," he or she is demonstrating a high degree of spontaneous flexibility. Another subdivision of flexibility is adaptation. To succeed in school or in work, one may have to adapt to a task, devise a new approach or strategy, or plan alternative solutions. The third subdivision—original thinking—includes the "production of unusual, farfetched, remote or clever responses."

Guilford believes that fluency, flexibility, and originality together constitute "divergent" thinking—the production of novel and unknown solutions. The individual must examine alternatives, take intellectual risks, and adjust continuously to the data available. Divergent thinking takes place when a problem has not yet been defined or even identified and when there are no known solutions. Guilford feels that divergent thinking typifies the creative person. When an invention or new idea requires revising something that is already known, there is "convergent" thinking. Convergent thinkers are able to zero in on the most logical answer to given set of data. Thus, convergent thinkers are not especially prepared to rearrange their thoughts; by convincing themselves of the rightness of their views they may not be willing to make rapid, flexible changes in their intellectual orientations. Although convergent thinking is probably less likely to demonstrate creative potential, arriving at a convergent solution may require "creative" improvisation whereby the attributes of objects are redefined or transformed. For example, one of Guilford's tests of creativity asks which of five objects or their parts could be used to start a fire: fountain pen, onion, pocket watch, light bulb, or bowling ball. The "accepted" answer arrived at by transformation of use is pocket watch, since the cover of the watch face could be used as a lens to focus the light and generate heat.

Educational Settings and Creative Expression.   Research evidence suggests that young people in open classrooms, in which they spend relatively more time in interaction with both peers and concrete manipulable objects, tend to perform more creatively on figural and artistic tasks. Those in traditional classrooms, in contrast, where they spend large amounts of time either working alone on assignments or answering inquiries from the teacher, tend to perform more creatively on verbal tasks.[104] These tentative generalizations, however, emerge from complex interactions and are affected by teacher and parental attitudes toward creativity. On the one hand, many teachers seek primarily to preserve the classroom status quo. Many teachers have long placed a premium on conformity.[105] Over a period of several years, Torrance[106] asked several hundred teachers in the United States and elsewhere what kind of person they would like to see today's child become. He found that secondary school teachers generally valued conformity. Junior high teachers emphasized courteousness, sincerity, and getting work in on time; they did not stress curiosity, courageousness about one's convictions, self-confidence, self-sufficiency, and versatility. Junior high teachers also tended to punish inquisitive youth. Senior high teachers were more ambivalent: they hoped that adolescents would be independent in their thinking, self-confident, and ambitious, but they also insisted on considerateness, courtesy, promptness, and neither too much independence in judgment nor too much courageousness about convictions. Consequently, the pressures for conformity, under which many adolescents succeed scholastically, may comprise a straightjacket shackling the creativity of others and making them underachievers by conventional standards.

Parental values and expectations may also affect creative expression in the classroom. Parents of creative adolescents, for example, tend to expect less conforming behavior than parents of high achievers. They tend to prefer a complex and stimulating environment for themselves and for their children.[107] Getzels and Jackson[108] found that parents of youth who scored very well on intelligence tests but did poorly on measures of creativity tended to be more concerned about their children's academic performance; they emphasized cleanliness, good manners, and studiousness. In such families, on the whole, there was little individual divergence and risk-taking. By contrast, parents of youth who performed well on measures of creativity tended to be less critical of them and to encourage openness, enthusiasm, and interest in new experiences. In a study of 9,800 exceedingly talented adolescents, Holland[109] found that high academic performance was a function of a personal syndrome characterized by perseverance, self-control, popularity, and good citizenship. Creativity, on the other hand, was fostered by a conscious desire to be original, to pursue hobbies actively, and not to be concerned about good grades. Thus, the parents of the creative youth were more tolerant of unconventional ideas and encouraged critical evaluation; accordingly, they brought up their children to be intolerant of teachers' expectations about conforming, controlled, nonexploratory behavior.[110]

Creativity and Intelligence. Teachers have long been familiar with such conventional measures of intelligence as the Stanford-Binet, the Wechsler Intelligence Scales, and the California Test of Mental Maturity. Because these tests were designed in part to predict success in school learning, particularly in reading, arithmetic, and other academic courses, they tap mostly convergent thinking abilities. About 1960, investigations of divergent thinking led researchers to ask whether creativity might be a unique cognitive factor that was not reflected in intelligence tests. Later, empirical evidence showed that there was a difference between the attributes of divergent thinking and those embodied in traditional concepts of intelligence.[111] The most prominent investigation was conducted by Getzels and Jackson;[112] they administered conventional intelligence and Guilford-derived creativity measures to a large number of boys and girls from the sixth grade through high school. Not only did they find that creative behavior differed from general intelligence, but that the thinking of youth who possessed "high IQ without concomitantly high creativity" or "high creativity without concomitantly high IQ" resembled Guilford's factors of "convergent" and "divergent" thinking, respectively.[113]

Both Thorndike[114] and Wallach and Kogan[115] also have questioned the assumption that creativity and intelligence might be different attributes. The researchers independently found that correlations between creativity indices and measures of intelligence are about the same as the correlations among the creativity indices themselves. Since the various measures of creativity seem to be as equally related to general intelligence as to each other, it is reasonable to conclude that each is tapping a general aspect of intellect. Thus creativity indices could be incorporated within an intelligence test, and thereby, by establishing a broader concept of intelligence, the dubious distinction between them could be abolished.

Several researchers have suggested that intelligence and school achievement operate as a threshold for creativity.[116] Below a certain level of intelligence or school achievement, high scores on creativity tests are unlikely; at intermediate levels of intelligence, scores on creativity tests increase with IQ, but in persons with a very high IQ, such factors as school achievement may affect the range of creative expression. Dellas and Gaier[117] describe this possibility as the "fan-shaped" hypothesis, indicating that at very high IQ levels, a wide range in creativity will prevail, but that at lower IQ levels, the range in creativity will be greatly restricted.

Discipline

American adults have named "lack of discipline," in six of the seven annual Gallup Education Polls, as the most important problem facing the public schools.[118] Forty-five percent of the parents polled in 1975 said that, generally speaking, young people have "too many" rights and privileges whereas only 10 percent stated that they had too few. When the parents were asked where they would like to send their children to school, the majority said that they would send them to a "special school" that emphasized the three Rs and enforced strict discipline and a dress code.

Parental concern for law and order stems largely from the racial fighting, drug usage, vandalism, and assaults against teachers and administrators that have become commonplace in suburban and inner city high schools.[119] In 1975, for example, young people were responsible for 270,000 school burglaries and vandalized over $600,000,000 worth of school property.[120] Since 1970 assault and battery in schools has increased 58 percent; school robberies, 117 percent;

sex offenses, 62 percent; and drug problems, 81 percent. Serious crimes by girls under 18 have increased 306 percent since 1960, and the ratio of boy to girl involvement is now two to one whereas a short time ago it was six to one.[121] Consequently, a new industry promoting law and order is booming on the American high school scene. Walkie-talkies are being supplied to school security personnel, and closed circuit TV sentries and electronic alarm systems are being used to apprehend intruders. Other security features include special door alarms, key-control locks, stronger doors, fewer windows or none at all, outdoor floodlights, special interior lighting, vandal-resistant materials, and pen-sized personal alarms for teachers. These pen alarms or "panic buttons" allow teachers, by pressing a button, to send a signal to a master panel, which identifies for security officers the location of the trouble.[122]

Disciplinary Controls.   No one likes disciplinary controls. Administrators see them as a threat to order and efficiency, teachers resent the policing activities they impose, and students view them as sources of oppression.[123] Discipline, however, always suggests control in the interest of regulation, order, and rule. The need for such control would be negligible in an ideal situation. Here students would accept the authority and structure of the school, school administrators and teachers would respect student rights, and everyone would participate enthusiastically in the business of education. John Dewey once said that it is necessary to involve all constituencies in social governance to achieve a system in which all believe that it is wise and fair, that is, "It is not the will or desire of any person which establishes order but the moving spirit of the whole group."[124]

School discipline has its basis in self-discipline. The latter begins when external authority is imposed upon the young child. Cognitive growth during adolescence transforms the literal rules of childhood into general conduct guides and moral precepts. As control of conduct is displaced from socializing agents to personal, internalized standards, self-control emerges, and individuals begin to conduct themselves in terms of their responsibilities and obligations to society. Given the probability that the majority of students master the rudiments of self-control and are fully capable of disciplining themselves in high school, the question is how much the constitutional rights of the majority should be compromised, in the interest of institutional stability, to constrain the minority who are irresponsible and who engage in acts of misconduct? When controls are too loose, the less-disciplined may abuse the freedoms granted to them, and when controls are too restrictive, the well-disciplined young people may grow alienated, disrespectful, and rebellious. The dilemma is one that administrators and teachers everywhere have faced. Their solutions fall generally into one of the

School security personnel are becoming commonplace in American high schools.

three patterns, which we may describe roughly as (1) bureaucratic imposition, (2) penalities via punishment, and (3) authoritative control. Let us briefly review each pattern:

1. Bureaucratic imposition describes a view that calls for tight disciplinary controls to ensure order and conformity. It is an effort to institutionalize discipline to achieve a regulated atmosphere. The following account of a "typical" high school day in countless American high schools illustrates how passes, permission slips, tardy notes, bells, and buzzers are used to create an atmosphere of vigilance:[125]

At many schools the outer doors are not unlocked until a few minutes before school begins each morning; they are locked again shortly after school closes in the afternoon and students have left the building. Once admitted to the building, students are kept under close surveillance. They are carefully programed from one classroom to another. Throughout the day students move from one class to another according to a schedule planned by the administration. Little time is allowed for passing between classes. During such times teachers are stationed in the hallways to make certain the flow of students is continuous. A bell rings, signaling the start of a new period, and each student must be in his seat. Late arrivals are sent to the office to secure written permission to enter or are punished by being forced to remain late after school.

Throughout the day, the movement of students is carefully controlled. If a student leaves a class, he must have the permission of his teacher and an assigned pass that provides details about where he originates, where he is going, what time he left, and the reason for his trip—even if it is to the drinking fountain. A student apprehended without a pass is treated much as a citizen in an alien country without a passport. To check on passes, prevent vandalism, and to enforce school rules, some schools have established squads of senior boys and girls to act as agents for the administration. In return for special privileges, they sit at the ends of corridors acting as checkpoints, or they roam the corridors, restrooms, and parking lots searching for student offenders.

2. Penalties via punishment include such control techniques as verbal reprimands, fines, loss of privileges, and corporal punishment. Reprimands work best when they emanate from persons whom students respect. They arouse shame regarding failure to meet social expectations and serve to deflate social status, and perhaps, to redirect behavior. Fines, in contrast, involve material restitution, and are often imposed for damaging books or failing to return them to the library, but fines may be a meaningless punishment for youth who can readily afford them. Penalties involving loss of privileges include extra assignments, detention, suspensions, and expulsions. Extra assignments and detention ("staying after school") are often invoked for relatively minor misconducts. Suspension, although relatively drastic because it disrupts the academic process, is widely used for nonviolent offenses like smoking, rudeness, tardiness, and truancy. In instances of truancy, it may be irrelevant, since students may prefer to be outside rather than inside school anyway. Expulsion usually follows serious offenses related to property destruction, drug usage, and criminal activity. One of the severest of penalties, expulsion centers major responsibility for socializing transgressors upon either parents or juvenile correction agencies.

Corporal punishment is a physically painful penalty that follows as a consequence of performing forbidden behavior.[126] The right of educators to administer corporal punishment derives particularly from the doctrine of *in loco parentis,* in which the educator is presumed to stand in the place of the parent.

Teachers in all but three states—Maryland, Massachusetts, and New Jersey, which have banned physical punishment in the schools—today have the legal right to administer corporal punishment. Corporal punishment is a humiliating disciplinary practice which became widespread in the schools of Europe several centuries ago. American colonists, coming from a land where flogging and whipping had been common in schools, readily adopted the "spare the rod and spoil the child" mentality, and took it for granted that corporal punishment would be used to control young people in their schools.[127] Harsh, savage, and brutal treatments are prohibited today by either school policy or a communal sense of decency. Whipping posts and such corporal punishments as the following are largely outlawed: stuffing the mouth with paper tissue, washing out the mouth with soap, arm twisting, lifting by the hair, and exposure to extremes of temperature.[128] On the other hand, an observer in a school would encounter, in varying degrees of frequency, using masking tape as a gag, knuckle wraps on the head with the middle-finger or a ring, ear-pulling, throwing against the wall or floor, or requiring a youth to hold a stack of books in each hand at arms length for an indeterminate length of time, to sit on an imaginary stool, to stand in a corner, hands upraised, without touching the wall, or to do push-ups, usually 50 for girls and 100 for boys, under the threat of being swatted for failure. Above all, the tradition of the rod continues to thrive in the form of paddling, the most common form of corporal punishment.[129]

School officials contend that threat of corporal punishment is a necessary option for maintaining classroom control and ensuring order and efficiency, and generally they perceive it as one of their more effective disciplinary controls. The weight of empirical research, however, contradicts this outlook. Maurer's[130] exhaustive review of dozens of experimental investigations and theoretical treatises convincingly demonstrates that use of corporal punishment fails to control or redirect youths' disruptive behavior. Physical punishment, it is said, may divert attention from alternative, constructive responses, and in any event, may provide relatively few clues to the development of more functional behaviors and attitudes. And punishment usually intensifies the affective climate, engendering feelings of anger, frustration, dislike, and hostility. It strains social relationships between youth and teacher, and when embarrassment and shame ensue, young people may become socially ill at ease with their peers. Punishment may also engender aggression; students may be eager to "get even" with a teacher, administrator, or school environment. Perhaps worst of all, students may identify with punitive teachers, and adapt their style of handling social tensions.

3. Authoritative control aims to create a school climate in which students are motivated to want to learn. Authoritative teachers establish environments where

individuality is respected and where young people can pursue their interests free of distraction and without fear of abuse. A less authoritative teacher might invoke discipline by forcing the young people to sit quietly in rows with their hands folded on their desks, thus coercing them into a learning setting. Authoritative teachers, on the other hand, will convey to young people their expectations of them, showing the youth that they respect their ability to meet standards, and indicate to them that they want to help each develop pride in his or her abilities and school work. Authoritative teachers will rely on their status as models to establish in young people a motivation to learn. They will see bluffs, obscenities, and classroom disruptions as symptoms of status needs, and they will respond to the underlying needs as well as to the immediate problems.[131]

Sex-Role Stereotyping in the High School

Sexual Bias in Curriculum Materials and Programs. Title IX of the Educational Amendments, which were passed by Congress in 1972, forbids discrimination on the basis of sex in educational institutions receiving federal assistance. The publicity given to regulations pertaining to physical education and athletics has overshadowed the fact that Title IX also affects admission policies, financial aid, employment and compensation, counseling, extramural activities, and work-study.

According to the Department of Health, Education and Welfare, however, Title IX does not cover sexual bias in curriculum materials and textbooks.[132] To encompass curriculum would presumably transgress First Amendment guarantees of free speech. Consequently, the problem of sex-role stereotyping in curriculum is being dealt with today largely by textbook publishers and by school personnel at the district level. And the problems they face are relatively complex. Trecker's[133] analysis of widely used high school textbooks reveals that in mathematics, science, social studies, and American history, distinguished females were ignored and illustrative materials were consistently male-oriented. In the math books, for example, boys were shown involved in problems associated with gardening, building, sports, and painting; girls and women were restricted to examples related to sewing, cooking, and child care. Most of the science books depicted only males using scientific equipment or solving problems. Trecker also pointed out that few social studies tests have considered questions of "sex-role conditioning, women's current and historic legal status, social and philosophical attitudes toward women, or the connections between these attitudes and women's rights."[134] And in history textbooks, topics on "the evolution of the social and legal status of women, the importance of female and child labor in the industrial revolution, women's work in the wars and in social reforms, the women's movement, and the contributions of outstanding women are conspicuous by their absence." Moreover, most textbooks bury the female image by use of male pronouns and generic terms, for example, man, mankind, he or his.

The segregation of the sexes according to preconceived notions of appropriate curriculum activities reinforces sex role stereotyping in school programs.[135] Why should girls be channeled into homemaking courses and boys into industrial arts? In vocational-education programs, for example, more class slots are likely to be open to boys than to girls, a greater variety of courses will be open to the boys, and within a program, courses may be labeled as being appropriate for one sex or another.[136] The extent to which boys and girls are distributed according to traditional sex-role patterns is shown in the following statistics: "Ninety-three percent of all students registered in consumer and homemaking courses are female; eighty-five percent of those enrolled in home economics courses which lead to gainful employment are female, ninety-two percent of those registered in technical courses—metallurgy, engineering, oceanography, police science—are male, seventy-five percent in office occupations are female; and eighty-nine percent of all registered in trade and industrial courses are male."[137]

Effects of Sex-Role Stereotyping on the Educational Aspirations and Attainment of Adolescent Girls.

The socialization of sex-role stereotyping, which begins in the elementary school years, has led many girls by the time that they reach junior and senior high school to be reluctant to elect curricula in traditionally male areas, to lower their aspirations with regard to college and a career, and to achieve lower educational attainments. Alexander and Eckland,[138] for example, report that the educational attainment of girls, relative to boys, tends to be depressed, whatever their academic ability, curriculum enrollment, and the influence of significant others, including parents, teachers, and peers. Skipper[139] indicates that a lifetime of educational competition with highly intelligent peers especially affects adversely, relative to boys, the self-concept development of average-ability girls. And Campbell and McKain[140] showed that, relative to boys, high-school girls are more likely to express a slight loss in general intelligence (as tapped by group intelligence tests) during the high school years. Campbell and McKain divided the 290 girls in their study into those who declined (69) in intelligence, and those who did not decline (221), and found that the "decliners," relative to the "non-decliners," rated themselves as "less active," less interested in controlling others, and more interested in being included by others in activities. In brief, the researchers suggest that the young women who declined in general intelligence saw themselves as close to the ideal of the passive, nonassertive woman, who is no smarter than men. A current investigation of mathematically gifted young people has revealed that boys out-perform girls as early as grades seven and eight on very difficult precollege tests.[141] The intent of the study was to identify, counsel, and accelerate academically talented youth. The findings have shown that youth can be suc-cessfully accelerated by conducting experimental mathematical classes for them in a junior high school and on a university campus. However, it is much more difficult to foster precocious achievement and math acceleration among girls than boys.[142] Even the most mathematically able girls preferred social to theoretical activities and preferred to take a path toward "intellectual suicide" by remaining in classes too easy and boring for them. The girls apparently figured that acceleration would lead them to be labeled as different from their friends. They saw the advanced class meetings as dull, made references to the boys in the class as "little creeps," and overall, viewed the classes as socially unappealing and as having negative consequences for them in school.

Horner[143] has considerably enlarged our understanding of motivational dif-ferences between American males and females, and her findings have stimulated several subsequent investigations. Horner hypothesized that females more than males are inhibited by fear of success. Whereas men find success in achievement consistent with masculinity and self-esteem, capable women may experience negative or ambivalent motives when confronted with anticipation of success, especially when success entails aggression and competitiveness. To the extent that women depend on the approval of significant others, success in competition with others, especially men, may be viewed as evidence of lack of femininity and as leading eventually to social rejection and disapproval. Thus women face an unwelcome dilemma in competitive situations—to succeed means to appear unfeminine and to be feminine means to fail. To test the assumption that fear of success may underly major sex differences in achievement, Horner used a pro-jective measure with college students to assess presence or absence of the fear. Students were asked to write stories in response to the following verbal cue: "At the end of first-term finals, Anne (John) found herself (himself) on top of her (his) medical school class." The girls were given the cue about Anne and the boys received the cue about John. A majority of the girls (65 percent) portrayed Anne as anxious about success in medical school or predicted that it would have unpleasant consequences, but less than 10 percent of the boys responded with negative or avoidance stories. The data suggested, then, that females in our society have learned that success or competition in school is incompatible with prevailing images of femininity.

In her pioneering investigation, Horner[144] gave the Anne cue only to girls and the John cue only to boys, and consequently her study left a number of questions unanswered. For example, were the avoidance responses of subjects related to the sex of the respondents or to the sex of the protagonist in the story? If the latter were the case, it would suggest the possibility that the motive to fear success is less a fear common to women than a sex-role stereotype to which both sexes respond. Feather[145] thus asked female and male students in an Australian college and an American college to write stories to a verbal cue in which either a male or a female succeeded. Approximately half of the male and female subjects wrote to the male (John) cue, the other half to the female (Anne) cue. First, the researcher found that the proportion of fear of success stories written by females to the female cue was lower than that reported by Horner in her original study and the proportion of fear of success stories written by males to the male cue was higher. Horner's investigation was conducted several years ago, and perhaps men may now be less interested in being achievers and women may now be more willing to assert that achievement is female-appropriate.[146] Second, the evidence, especially from the Australian sample, suggested that Horner's methodology may indeed be tapping sex-role stereotypes, since both males and females reacted more negatively to Anne's success than to John's. The fact that the two sexes may be responding to a stereotype, depending on the cues presented to them, nonetheless, is not sufficient to reject Horner's assumption of a differential between males and females in the motive to avoid success. The issue is highly complex. Romer,[147] for example, has shown that the motive to avoid success changes developmentally. The researcher, in a study of boys and girls in the fifth through the eleventh grades, found that by the eleventh grade the boys' motive to avoid success had peaked and was decreasing in strength whereas the girls' motive to avoid success was still increasing in strength. Apparently, boys establish self-confidence in their achievement-oriented activities during the high school years while girls only acquire more fear of achievement. Another study has reported that high school girls who attended coed elementary and high schools experienced fear of success more than did those who had attended all-girls' schools, seemingly as if socialization in the presence of boys strengthened the girls' motive to avoid success.[148]

Compulsory Education and School Attendance

There are today compulsory attendance laws in every state except Mississippi. Massachusetts enacted the first attendance statute in 1852; half of the states and territories had followed by 1980 with similar statutes, and the remaining half had enacted them by 1918. Colonial America had committed itself to teaching basic skills, and by 1830 between 52 and 84 percent of the children in New England attended school. A century later public schooling was virtually universal for about 90 percent of the children between the ages of 8 and 11, except for those living in isolated rural areas and on the western frontier. Attendance at first was in private academies, but as each state became more and more involved in schooling, the public, tax-supported schools began to rise in prominence. When the "informal, loosely structured" educational process gave way to an increasingly centralized, bureaucratized public system, the administrative basis for regulating school attendance had arrived.[149]

Compulsory attendance laws arose in a context broader than that of merely providing young people with literacy skills. Horace Mann and his supporters in the Massachusetts State Legislature wanted the public school to serve "the general welfare of a democratic society, by assuring that the knowledge and understanding necessary to exercise the responsibilities of citizenship are not only made available but actively inculcated."[150] The efforts of those who struggled to enact coercive attendance laws as a means of perpetuating the democratic society redoubled during periods of nineteenth century industrial expansion and heavy immigration.[151] The immigrants were the particular victims of social disorganization during industrial expansion, and they soon became the target in the search for solutions to such problems as poverty, delinquency, and unemployment. Reformers believed that the children of poor, immigrant families might eventually create a burden for the American society, and to ensure themselves against the possibility, they advocated that the school become a surrogate parent. As schools adopted caretaking and custodial roles, child labor laws were enacted to protect the civil rights of young people, cut competition in the labor market, and train a literate workforce.

Bureau of the Census statistics show that with each succeeding decade since 1910, there has been an increasing number of adolescents enrolled in school. In 1910, fewer than six out of ten 14 to 17 year olds and fewer than two out of ten 18 to 19 year olds were enrolled in school, but in 1969, nine out of ten 14 to 17 year olds and five out of ten 18 to 19 year olds were enrolled in school. Current statistics show that today nearly 97 percent of the 12 to 17 year olds are presently in school.[152] A generalized nationwide attendance rate is difficult to establish, however, because it would vary in accordance with age, sex, ethnic background, social class, region, school climate, and so forth. Whereas nearly 100 percent of the 12 year olds may be enrolled in school, less than three-fourths of the 17 year olds may be enrolled. The National Education Association in 1975, for example, estimated the holding power of the school to be about 77.7% for those eligible to drop out, but for adolescents from migrant families, the holding power is estimated to be only 20 percent. One way of gaining perspective on the retention rate of schools is to consider members of each high school graduating class as a proportion of the cohort who had entered the fifth grade. Table 3 indicates these proportions for the even years, 1950 to 1972, and the odd year, 1973. As the data indicate, the holding power of high schools since 1968 is nearly twice what it was in the 1950s. The pupil dropout rate has stabilized today at about 25 percent of the fifth graders not graduating from high school. It is noteworthy that the data from 1973 provided in Table 3 correspond rather closely with the 1975 projection of the National Education Association (22.3 percent).

Although high schools have achieved unprecedented success in lowering the dropout rate, the fact remains that one-fourth of the high school age youth find school irrelevant. Many of them wholly ignore compulsory attendance requirements. Tyack[153] views the circumstances that we live in today as the midst of a

Table 3
School Retention Rates: High School Graduates per 1,000 Pupils Who Entered Fifth Grade

Year of Graduation	High School Graduates per 1,000 Pupils Who Entered Fifth Grade	Percent Dropout
1950	505	49.5
1952	522	47.8
1954	553	44.7
1956	581	41.9
1958	582	41.8
1960	621	37.9
1962	642	35.8
1964	676	32.4
1966	732	26.8
1968	749	25.1
1970	750	25.0
1972	750	25.0
1973	749	25.1

Source: Statistical Abstract of the United States 1974. U.S. Department of Commerce, Bureau of the Census. Washington, D.C.: U.S. Government Printing Office, 1974. Adapted from A. Harnischfeger and D. Wiley. *Achievement Test Score Decline: Do We Need to Worry?* Chicago: CEMREL, 1975. Reprinted by permission.

"post-compulsory phase" in the history of compulsory attendance. Schools have been stripped of much of their *in loco parentis* status, student-rights legislation has made enforcement of regulations more time-consuming than in the past, and the legitimacy of protecting the labor market is being questioned. Thus within the past decade hundreds of thousands of youth have become habitually absent from school, and authorities are making less than faint-hearted attempts to recruit them back. Johnson[154] indicates that enforcement problems are so severe at the secondary school level (beyond age 14) that "one can seriously question whether such enforcement can even be tried." He says the financial and social costs of enforcing compulsory attendance hardly seems worth the effort. Moreover, since he believes that it is unnecessary to enforce compulsory attendance beyond the age when most young people will have attained basic skills in reading, writing, and arithmetic, he advocates lowering the minimum age to 15 years. A 1973 report of the National Commission on Reform of Secondary Education takes an even more extreme position, urging that the compulsory attendance age be lowered to 14 years.[155] The report holds that young people cannot be brought up to understand citizenship and acquire respect for the law when the compulsory attendance laws are largely unenforcible and students everywhere flout them with full knowledge that nothing will happen to them. The report also disagrees with coercive attendance on ideological grounds. It asks "can the nation's high schools continue as custodial institutions and, at the same time, excel (or even survive) in the matter of teaching and learning?"[156] Johnson[157] wonders, too, once the custodial relationship implied by compulsory attendance has been removed, whether schools will be encouraged to provide more individualized opportunities for students and a wider variety of educational formats for those who voluntarily choose to further their education beyond the level of basic skills. Kiernan,[158] on the other hand, argues that the age of compulsory education should be extended to 18 years, not to foster the custodial role of secondary schools, but to ensure that the school will serve as a broker or planning agent in assisting as many youth as possible in making the transition to adulthood. Obviously, the question of compulsory attendance has yet to be resolved, but the attacks on its coercive and custodial features complement efforts to transform the high school from an institution centered on incarceration to one focused on learning opportunities.

Factors that Foster School Leaving

Adolescents who usually do well in school often feel that they can meet the expectations of their teachers, that their studies are relevant to their long-range objectives, and that the skills they acquire and rewards they obtain fit with their life styles. Many young people, however, find that such circumstances do not prevail in their lives and are precluded from making effective use of educational opportunities. Some adolescents may involuntarily be pulled out of school because of circumstances, such as illnesses or financial crises, over which they have no control, or be pushed out for disciplinary reasons. Others may lack the necessary intellectual or emotional attributes to do the work or perform the skills required of them. And still others may become disinterested in high school, perhaps because they failed to acquire the necessary skills earlier that would enable them to perform satisfactorily, because the life style they anticipate requires only limited education, or because they are unconvinced that the high school will lead them toward desirable goals. These factors arise as a consequence of a variety of experiences, and are grouped below for purposes of discussion in four comprehensive categories: family, peers, academic skills, and school custodianship.

Factors Related to the Family.   Parents of dropouts usually have not graduated from high school themselves. Bledsoe[159] found that parents who have between one and three years of high school education, who graduated from high school, or who attended one or more years of college, respectively, have proportionately more children who graduated from high school. Parents with only four to six years of schooling have the largest percentage of sons and daughters who drop out of school. A sizeable number of unschooled parents apparently feel that they have been reasonably successful in life and believe that their son or daughter can do as much without graduating from high school. In such families there is probably little parental encouragement to learn; the parents may not care what their children are doing in high school and they may feel that they should drop out. A few parents may even undercut the high school by saying "You don't need to know all that junk about triangles or the Romans to get along in this world," or "I told Jim that if that English teacher over at Junior High treated him the way she treated me, I wanted him to walk out."[160] Table 4 shows dramatically the degree to which family socioeconomic status is correlated with youth's orientation to school. Whereas differences by geographic region and type of community are relatively slight, the data reveal that number of grades repeated, rate of unusual absences, and academic rank, respectively, vary inversely with both parental income and education.

Perhaps the most significant difference between the parents of dropouts and those of nondropouts is the extent to which family members accept and respect each other.[161] The dropout's family is more likely to reside in an area of deteriorating homes or low-income housing developments where family conflicts may be high. Since young persons may not be able to resolve problems with

Table 4
Percent of Youth Aged 12–17 Years by Repeated Grades, Unusual Absences from School, and School Achievement by Selected Socioeconomic Variables: United States, 1966–70

Selected variables	Percent of Youths		Academic Achievement (Percent Distribution)			
	Grades Repeated	Unusual Absences	Upper Third in Class	Middle Third in Class	Lower Third in Class	Don't Know
Income						
Less than $3,000	30.4	19.8	15.1	36.4	44.0	4.5
$3,000–$5,000	23.0	16.7	16.9	39.7	37.7	5.6
$5,000–$7,000	19.3	14.0	20.9	38.4	33.6	7.0
$7,000–$10,000	14.1	11.7	26.8	40.7	25.9	6.5
$10,000–$15,000	9.1	8.8	35.7	39.1	20.8	4.4
$15,000 or more	5.1	7.0	39.8	40.2	16.3	3.7
Parents' Education						
Elementary	26.4	15.9	17.0	38.3	40.8	4.0
High school	14.7	13.0	24.0	41.7	27.8	6.6
Beyond high school	5.8	8.5	43.4	37.1	15.2	4.3

Source: National Center for Health Statistics. *Health attitudes and behavior of youths 12–17 years: demographic and socioeconomic factors.* (DHEW, pub. no. [HRA] 76-1635.) Series 11, No. 153, 1975, p. 36. Reprinted by permission.

their parents, they may carry the tensions to school; it may be easier for them to leave school and home than to deal with the basic problems.[162] The families of dropouts do not enjoy "mutual acceptance as total persons, deep intercommunication, and personal satisfaction derived from being in each other's company."[163] Cervantes matched 150 pairs of white adolescent boys in seven large cities; one member of each pair had dropped out of school and the other had completed the last semester of high school. The boys were matched according to age, number of siblings, scholastic ability, and high school attendance; the median family income was slightly less than $5,000 per year. Cervantes[164] found that four out of the five dropouts felt left out of their families, and nine times as many dropouts as graduates felt that their parents pushed "too much" by pressuring and nagging them, perhaps to contribute resources to the family or to attain unrealistic goals at school. Moreover, the parents of dropouts seldom talked to each other, and even the brothers and sisters spoke very little to each other. Companionship was conspicuously absent, little leisure time was spent together, and family members did not enjoy themselves too much in each other's company. The families of the dropouts never (or rarely ever) got together with relatives on big holidays.

Cervantes[165] also reported that the parents of the dropouts had fewer friends. They seemed to consider friendship in terms of either hedonism—"a friend is one you can get a lot of fun out of"—or utilitarianism—"a friend is one who will help you." They showed more spontaneity but less stability in their friendships; they appeared to latch on to anyone who happened to be close, useful, or available. The families of the high school graduates were more likely to think of friendship in terms of mutual understanding, to have meaningful intrafamily communication, and to enjoy being in each other's company. Cervantes found that there was a higher incidence of divorce, desertion, delinquency, and dropping out of high school within the families of the dropouts; the parents' friends also had more of these problems among their own children. By contrast, the families of the high school graduates had less friends with such problems as divorce, desertion, delinquency, alcoholism, or dropping out of school. These parents did not associate with couples or individuals whom they felt were out of harmony with the milieu that they had established for their children and themselves. Cervantes also observed that within the families of two out of three high school dropouts, the father had only limited authority; either the mother dominated family life or there was no control at all. In reply to the question, "If you needed help and advice to make a big decision, to whom would you go for that advice?" the majority of graduates went to both their fathers and mothers; the dropouts largely went to their mothers. When they decided to leave school, most of the dropouts did not seek help from anyone, but those who did generally went to their mothers. Because the fathers of the dropouts typically did not insist that their children finish high school, Cervantes[166] said that "the dropout is characteristically a mother's boy. . . ." In general, "if the father performs his full role in the family, the child will graduate from high school."[167]

Factors Related to Peers.   Disliking school and financial need are the two reasons typically given by boys for leaving school. Girls are most likely to say that they dropped out to get married. Disliking school reflects in part the dropout's sense of failure at not having achieved peer-group acceptance, and financial need reflects the dropout's desire to conform to the social expectations of the peer culture. Marriage may be an excuse for a girl who is lonely and not generally accepted by her peers. Marriage offers independence and an opportunity to escape from unhappy experiences at school.[168]

Most high school dropouts report that they felt they were poorly treated by other students. Girls especially said that they were sensitive about being snubbed, about not possessing the "right" clothes, and about being rejected by established cliques. Adolescent peer groups are likely to form according to socioeconomic background and a dropout may have been excluded from peer activities because of ethnicity or social class. Sometimes a potential dropout may succeed in a school-sponsored activity such as athletics, music, or art; and as Matthews[169] noted, the feeling of adequacy in just a single sphere of school life can counteract the negative effects of personal and social handicaps. Liddle[170] observed that the students who were successful in athletics or music usually graduate no matter what their level of scholastic ability.

Many dropouts said that they did not participate in school activities because they did not have enough money.[171] It takes money to go out on a date; to buy clothes for dances, class jewelry, snacks, and transportation; to buy materials, such as notebooks and supplies for courses; to pay required fees; to buy yearbooks and pictures; and to socialize with the crowd.[172] The potential dropout's family is often hard-pressed for funds; and because he or she cannot usually support himself or herself while in high school,[173] the potential dropout often is at a financial disadvantage. Consequently, the potential dropout may be motivated to take a job and thereby earn money and enjoy a sense of independence, especially if he or she does not find school particularly interesting or see much value in studying.

Since potential dropouts generally find little satisfaction in school, they will probably want to associate with those who share their feelings and participate mostly in activities outside of school. Elliott et al.[174] found that dropouts are usually friendly with youth who are already out of school. Adolescents who leave school frequently report that their best friend had already dropped out ahead of them. Association with other adolescents who have dropped out of school enables a prospective dropout to perceive the relative advantages of being out of school.[175]

Factors Related to Academic Skills. Fitzsimmons et al.[176] studied the academic histories of 270 youth from elementary school through high school, comparing the scholastic record of the dropouts with that of poorly performing graduates. Seventy-two youth dropped out and 198 eventually graduated. The researchers wanted to find out if future failure could be identified in elementary and secondary school and if the performance patterns of the dropouts could be distinguished from those of the youth who barely managed to graduate. Therefore, they posed eight questions.[177] First, "how early and in what subjects did initial failures occur among students who did poorly later in their academic careers?" They found that about 50 percent had begun to perform poorly by the second grade and 90 percent by the seventh grade; after junior high school, 97 out of 100 youth who were receiving low grades had a previous record of failure. Academic difficulties were mainly evident in English—reading, oral and written usage, and spelling—and in mathematics.

Second, "what were the dominant patterns of failure in terms of grade of onset, and by subject of origin?" The researchers hypothesized that five patterns of failure might emerge: (1) "spread patterns"—in which early poor performance in one or two areas expands to include other subjects, (2) "parallel patterns"—in which failure begins in three or more areas and continues in those areas, (3) "hourglass patterns"—in which early failure in three or more areas is followed by improvement and then by another failure in those areas, (4) "late failing patterns"—in which failure begins about the sixth grade, and (5) "random patterns"—in which no apparent pattern is clear. Fitzsimmons et al. found that about 40 percent of the 270 youth followed the spread pattern. English, especially reading, was the most frequent subject of initial failure, but occasionally it was mathematics. By the third grade, two-thirds of the students who would develop spread patterns in the future had experienced their first failure, and this was in English. There were no differences in the distribution of initial failures between the dropouts and the poorly performing graduates.

Third, "what were the patterns of failure among graduates and dropouts by year?" It was found that failure started early, rose quickly, and then increased slowly over the years. There were no significant "high points of failure," as, for example, in junior or senior high school. A significantly larger proportion of dropouts than graduates performed poorly in the ninth and tenth grades, suggesting that as the time neared for dropouts to leave school, they fell farther behind. A year-by-year comparison showed that graduates did relatively better than dropouts each year, and that by the fourth grade, the dropouts started doing progressively worse each year.

Fourth, "what were the patterns of failure among graduates and dropouts by subject?" The researchers found that English accounted for almost 30 percent of the total failures, mathematics and social studies each represented 18 percent, languages, 15 percent, and science, 13 percent. Shop and business indicated few failures. The patterns of failure among dropouts and graduates were similar, but the dropouts performed worse than the graduates in every subject, especially after the sixth grade.

Fifth, "what were the patterns of failure among graduates and dropouts by subject and year?" For Grades 1 through 3, low marks among graduates and dropouts were fairly evenly distributed in English, mathematics, science, and social studies. By Grades 4 through 6, the dropouts had received more failures in every subject. After the sixth grade, the discrepancy widened; the graduates leveled off in number of failures, but the dropouts gradually increased their number of failures.

Sixth, "in what grades did dropouts leave school?" Of the total of 72 youth who dropped out of school, 56 percent were boys: 4 percent in the ninth grade, 29 percent in the tenth, 36 percent in the eleventh, and 31 percent in the twelfth. Of the girls the largest percentage (20 percent) left in the twelfth grade. Boys were inclined to drop out because of a lack of interest in school and a desire to work; girls left for such personal reasons as marriage, pregnancy, or illness.

Seventh, "what were the interrelationships between early performance and midpoint performance?" Failure to pass reading in the fourth grade was related to failure in both social studies and English in the seventh grade; also, failure to pass mathematics in the fourth grade indicated an unlikelihood of passing English in junior high school.

Eighth, "what were the interrelationships between midpoint single and multiple failures at the seventh-grade level and graduation?" The data indicated that failure in seventh grade mathematics and, to a lesser extent, failure in English corresponded to dropping out at a later time.

Fitzsimmons et al. concluded that the majority of students in the sample who performed poorly in high school could have been identified early in elementary school. Although early failures may only appear in English or mathematics, a large percentage of the youth demonstrated a "downstream" spread pattern that encompassed social studies and science. "English language development appears to be a focal point of academic failures throughout the scholastic career. . . . Early general communication skills are vital to consequent success in other academic areas such as social studies and sciences."[178]

Factors Related to School Custodianship. A conventional, comprehensive high school probably will include four types of curricula: vocational/industrial, commercial/business, college prep, and general. The general curricula, which usually services attainment of minimal literacy and marketable skills, is the dumping ground for those youth whose prospects for continued education are judged dim by school authorities. The general curriculum thus appears to serve a custodial function. It holds low-achieving adolescents in school who had failed earlier to acquire the basic prerequisities in language, reading, mathematics, and science necessary for succeeding in high school. The academic skills of youth in the general curricula often decline progressively during junior and senior high school, but teachers "pass them along" nonetheless until they depart or accumulate sufficient credits to graduate. Combs and Cooley,[179] for example, have revealed the extent to which low-achieving students tend to be concentrated in the general curriculum. Upon analyzing the programs of several thousand youth, the researchers found that two groups, future dropouts and controls (adolescents comparable in academic grade-point average and socioeconomic status who graduated but did not continue their education) had been distributed fairly evenly in the ninth grade in terms of their plans to follow one of the high school curricula, including the college prep. Indeed, as the young people began the ninth grade, membership of future dropouts and controls in the general and college prep curricula was about the same. As the youth reached the upper grades, however, of those who left school before graduation, the proportion of boys in the general curriculum rose from 25 percent to 73 percent, and girls, from 25 percent to 67 percent. Among the controls (those who graduated), the proportion of boys in the general curriculum rose from 34 percent to 60 percent, and of girls, from 22 percent to 36 percent.

The custodial function may also distort the aspirations of ethnic minority youth, leading them to believe that they are succeeding in school when in fact they are learning very little. Obviously, such self-deception inhibits youth from taking corrective action before it is too late to reach career goals. A comparative study of chicano, white, black, and Asian youth showed recently that before entering high school, black and chicano youth obtained lower scores than white and Asian youth in tests of both math and verbal achievement; moreover, their relatively low standing persisted until their graduation.[180] But the black and chicano youth perceived themselves throughout as exerting more academic effort than the white and Asian young people saw themselves as expending. Moreover, about half of the black and chicano students, relative to about 30 percent of the higher achieving white and Asians, reported that they usually or always received teacher praise. The study indicated, however, that as many as a third of the blacks and chicanos of both sexes cut math, English, and social studies classes at least once a week. Lower grades did indeed tend to be assigned to students who cut school frequently, but those who came to class and participated minimally were likely to receive reasonably high grades. Fernandez et al.[181] suggest that "receiving praise for work that is not very creditable leads to distorted images of the level of effort and achievement each student believes he or she is putting forth." When youth are not given equal opportunity to compete with one another, the false images of academic skill and effort the custodial function engenders actually reinforce a pattern of "educational and occupational stratification." An even more basic problem is the fact that youth whose hopes and aspirations are aroused by their apparent school successes are likely to be disillusioned when they find themselves unprepared to achieve their future goals.

SUMMARY

Political forces maneuvered the school in the nineteenth century into a posture of *in loco parentis,* thus establishing a bureaucratic barrier between the family and the workplace. Public high schools were established as an upward extension of elementary schools in the latter half of the century, but they were largely college-preparatory and highly selective. The demands of technology for educated workers transformed the high school from a college-preparatory institution for a few into one that today is supposed to facilitate entry into adulthood for all. The American high school presently serves to provide (1) parents relief from child care, (2) instruction in science, technology, fine arts, humanities, and so forth, and (3) adult models who are expected to reinforce parental and cultural values. The comprehensiveness of the tasks makes responsiveness and relevance difficult to achieve. On the one hand, for example, the high school sorts individuals on the basis of ability to achieve competitively in the industrial world, and on the other, it urges young people to adopt the values, attitudes, and beliefs that underlie concepts of compassion, sharing, and egalitarianism.

The chapter is divided into two major sections. The first reviews the role of the high school in contemporary society and the second deals with factors affecting young people as they engage the educational process.

The first section considers the significance of school size, school social-class composition, teacher attitudes, and student rights. Optimal school size, for example, is related to the number of significant roles made available to students. Larger schools typically offer more opportunity for specialization, whereas smaller schools provide varied experiences. Marginal students may feel left out in larger schools and thus may feel little responsibility toward them. Research also suggests that (1) adolescents from higher social classes are more likely to aspire to higher educational goals, and (2) young people are likely to be influenced by the social-class values that predominate in their school. Teachers' attitudes are affected by social-class composition, too. McCandless et al., for example, report that teachers are inclined to mark socially advantaged and white students according to how well socialized they are and to mark economically poor, relatively socially disadvantaged young people according to their relative classroom performance. Teachers seldom discourage youth from planning to attend college, whatever their ability and social class, but they are inclined to encourage young people of relatively higher ability and socioeconomic status to continue their education.

Student rights expanded during the past decade as a consequence of the civil rights movement and the demonstrations, confrontations, and boycotts of the 1960s. The two most important issues in current litigation regarding student rights pertain to freedom of expression and to due process in matters of suspensions and expulsions. A series of useful guidelines have been produced by the courts, new judicial interpretations on student rights are likely to be forthcoming, and new conduct codes are evolving. A model for the codes of the future is suggested in the excerpts presented from a sample student code produced by the *Phi Delta Kappa* Commission on Administrative Behaviors Supportive of Human Rights.

The second section of the chapter considers a variety of relatively distinct issues that affect youth's interaction with educational processes, for example, family background, peer influences, interscholastic athletics, personality characteristics, discipline, sex-role stereotyping, compulsory education, and factors that foster school leaving.

Family background exerts an enduring and pervasive influence on youth's educational aspirations and attainment. Youth people with highly educated parents, for example, are more likely to seek higher levels of education. Further, parents help young people develop positive attitudes toward school when they hold high educational expectations and encourage success in school. Parental harmony, a well-organized home, and parental consensus on educational goals contribute to youth's success in school, too.

Relationships between peer pressures and school achievement are complex. Youth's responsiveness to their teachers and peers is related to their perceptions of classroom organization, structure, and activity. Youth perceive themselves as being less interested in scholarship in high school than they were in junior high school, maybe because in high school they feel pressure in respect to getting "right answers" for high grades and college admission. The interaction of peers and school involvement seems to be curvilinear, that is, moderate interaction positively relates to school success, but neither extensive nor infrequent participation correlates with academic orientation.

Adolescents and adults alike give high priority to athletic competition. Athletic contests enable young people to share collective goals and to develop strong, positive identification with the high school. Athletic prowess is a major criterion of peer status. In general, high school varsity athletes receive relatively more academic encouragement from teachers and counselors, and research suggests that there is a strong relationship between athletic participation and high educational aspirations. Unfortunately, athletic privileges are limited, especially in the large urban schools, and the question is whether interscholastic, intramural, and recreational sports can be coordinated in order to provide all young people with opportunity to improve their physical fitness and to develop reasonable levels of athletic skills.

One of the basic purposes of the high school is to provide opportunity for all students to develop their talents to their fullest. High-achieving students are usually described in laudatory terms. The high achievers are committed to the established goals of school and are rewarded for living up to the expectations of their teachers and parents. Underachievement may be a function of emotional handicaps, achievement anxiety, and personality disorganization; however, underachievement also may occur when youth's beliefs, values, and life styles conflict with the traditional goals and expectations of parents, teachers, and society at large. The pressures to conform, under which many adolescents succeed scholastically, may represent straitjackets for others, causing them to be underachievers by conventional standards.

American adults view "lack of discipline" as the most important problem facing the public schools. Discipline suggests control in the interest of regulation and order. School discipline has its basis in self-discipline. In general, solutions to discipline problems fall roughly into three categories: *bureaucratic imposition,* which calls for tight disciplinary measures to ensure order and conformity; *penalties via punishment,* which includes control techniques such as verbal reprimands, fines, loss of privileges, and corporal punishment, and *authoritative control,* which aims to create a school climate in which students are motivated to want to learn.

Many high school girls are reluctant to elect curricula in traditionally male areas and depress their college and career aspirations as a consequence of sex-role stereotyping, the socialization of which usually begins early in elementary school. The problem stems partly from sexual bias in curriculum materials and textbooks. Analyses of widely used high school textbooks reveal that in mathematics, science, social studies, and American history, distinguished women have been ignored and illustrative materials have been consistently male-oriented. Moreover, school programs have long segregated girls into homemaking courses and boys into industrial arts activities. Researchers thus hypothesize that women more than men are inhibited by fear of success. Whereas men find success and achievement consistent with masculinity and self-esteem, capable women may experience negative or ambivalent motives when confronted with anticipation of success, especially when success entails aggression and competitiveness.

Contemporary high schools have achieved unprecedented success in lowering the dropout rate, but the fact remains that one-fourth of the high school age youth find school irrelevant. Many young people thus wholly ignore compulsory attendance requirements. These laws arose at first to ensure that young people would obtain literacy skills, but they have been upheld over the years on the grounds that they are necessary to ensure that young people acquire the knowledge and understanding they need to function effectively in a democratic society. A recent report of the National Commission on Reform of Secondary Education, however, holds that young people cannot be brought up to understand citizenship and acquire respect for the law when the compulsory attendance laws are largely unenforceable and students everywhere flout them.

Factors that foster school leaving arise for a variety of reasons. Adolescents whose families do not encourage them to stay in school, who do not participate much in school activities, who cannot afford to match the expenditures of their classmates, who are two or three grades behind (and thus are older than their classmates), who attend school irregularly and are often late, who have poor reading ability, and who fail regularly in their school subjects show all the signs of becoming prospective dropouts. Youth whose prospects for continued education are judged dim by school authorities are often assigned to the "general curriculum," which performs a custodial function. It holds low-achieving adolescents in school (providing that they heed the compulsory attendance laws) after they fail to acquire the basic skills in language, reading, mathematics, science, and so forth, that they need to succeed in high school. The custodial function of the general curriculum thus may cause young people to inflate the real value of their accomplishments, leading them to believe that they are succeeding in school when in fact they are learning very little.

REVIEW QUESTIONS

1. What problems do American high schools encounter in fulfilling their functions?
2. What characterizes a school of optimal size?
3. Which aspects of social-class composition are associated with the academic aspirations of young people?
4. In what ways are teachers' perceptions influenced by the academic abilities and socioeconomic statuses of their students?
5. What are the issues in current litigation regarding student rights?
6. How does family background affect youth's educational aspirations and attainment?
7. What are some of the factors that influence youth's perception of classroom climate?
8. Why does active youth-culture participation inhibit educational achievement?
9. Why are interscholastic athletics given high priority among the functions of a high school?
10. Describe the personality characteristics of high school overachievers and underachievers, respectively.
11. How does Davis describe the personality of creative adolescents?
12. How have teachers generally related to creative adolescents?
13. Why is disciplinary control so disliked?
14. Describe three general patterns of disciplinary control.
15. How is corporal punishment likely to affect the learning climate of a high school?
16. What forms does sexual bias take in school programs and curricula?
17. Why is it difficult to foster achievement motivation in adolescent girls?
18. How are compulsory attendance laws out of phase with contemporary circumstances?
19. What are the differences between the families of dropouts and school-oriented youth?
20. How are peers likely to affect an adolescent's decision to stay in or dropout of school?

21. In what ways are the school performance patterns of dropouts different from those of nondropouts?

22. How does the general curriculum serve a custodial function for potential dropouts?

DISCUSSION QUESTIONS

1. What steps would you take to counter the effects of social-class composition on the educational aspirations of young people?

2. If you were asked to prepare a handbook on student rights, what key provisions would you include?

3. Since youth-culture participation is so meaningful to youth, how might its activities be oriented to facilitate scholastic achievement?

4. What adjustments are young people likely to make in their self-concepts when they are deprived of athletic participation?

5. On the assumption that intelligence and school achievement operate as a threshhold for creativity, in what ways might classroom activities be oriented to facilitate the creativity of capable young people?

6. What is the significance of the statement: "School discipline has its basis in self-discipline"?

7. Why do school personnel insist so strongly on the right to apply corporal punishment? What are the major disadvantages associated with its use?

8. How would you modify high school academic and social climates to equalize opportunities between boys and girls?

9. What is your position regarding compulsory attendance laws? What reasons would you advance, respectively, for keeping and abolishing them?

10. Would you attack the problem of school dropouts by reducing the age of compulsory attendance or by rehabilitating potential dropouts? What effects on society might ensue from the consequences of your decision?

NOTES

1. E. P. Cubberly. *Public education in the United States*. Boston: Houghton-Mifflin Co., 1919, p. 338.

2. W. Greenbaum. America in search of a new ideal: an essay on the rise of pluralism. *Harvard Educational Review*, 1974, **44,** 411–440.

3. E. A. Krug. *The secondary school curriculum*. New York: Harper, 1960.

4. Krug, *op. cit.*

5. T. Parsons. The school class as a social system: some of the functions in American society. *Harvard Educational Review*, 1959, **29,** 297–318.

6. R. J. McCowan, R. P. O'Reilly, and G. J. Illenberg. Relation of size of high school enrollment to educational effectiveness. *Child Center Study Center Bulletin*, 1968, **4,** 73–79.

7. R. G. Barker and P. B. Gump. *Big school, small school: high school size and student behavior.* Stanford, California: Stanford University Press, 1964.

8. E. P. Willems. Sense of obligation to high school activities as related to school size and marginality of students. *Child Development,* 1967, **38,** 1247–1260.

9. M. Grabe. Big school, small school: impact of the high school environment. Paper presented at the meeting of the American Educational Research Association, Washington, D.C., 1975.

10. Grabe, *op. cit.*

11. A. B. Wilson. Residential segregation of social classes and aspirations of high school boys. *American Sociological Review,* 1959, **24,** 836–845.

12. Wilson, *op. cit.*

13. R. P. Boyle. The effect of the high school on students' aspirations. *The American Journal of Sociology,* 1966, **71,** 628–639.

14. R. K. Bain and J. G. Anderson. School context and peer influences on educational plans of adolescents. *Review of Educational Research,* 1974, **44,** 429–445.

15. E. L. McDill, E. D. Meyers, Jr., and L. C. Rigsby. Institutional effects on the academic behavior of high school students. *Sociology of Education,* 1967, **40,** 181–199.

16. Bain and Anderson, *op. cit.*

17. C. S. Jencks and M. D. Brown. Effects of high schools on their students. *Harvard Educational Review,* 1975, **45,** 273–324, p. 323.

18. B. Heyns. Social selection and stratification within schools. *American Journal of Sociology,* 1974, **79,** 1434–1451.

19. K. Alexander and B. K. Eckland. Contextual effects in the high school attainment process. *American Sociological Review,* 1975, **40,** 402–416.

20. Alexander and Eckland, *op. cit.,* p. 414.

21. K. A. Hecht. Teacher ratings of potential dropouts and academically gifted children: are they related? *Journal of Teacher Education,* 1975, **26,** 172–175.

22. B. R. McCandless, A. Roberts, and T. Starnes. Teachers' marks, achievement test scores, and aptitude relations with respect to social class, race, and sex. *Journal of Educational Psychology,* 1972, **63,** 153–159.

23. L. M. Laosa, J. D. Swartz, and B. D. Witzke. Cognitive and personality characteristics of high school students as predictors of the way they are rated by their teachers: a longitudinal study. *Journal of Educational Psychology,* 1975, **67,** 866–872.

24. W. B. Fetters. *National longitudinal study of the high school class of 1972.* National Center for Educational Statistics. (DHEW Pub. No. 76-235.) 1976.

25. M. Haberman. *Students' rights: a guide to the rights of children, youth, and future teachers.* Washington, D.C.: Association of Teacher Educators, Bulletin 34, 1973.

26. Haberman, *op. cit.*

27. T. J. Flygare. Student rights. *Harvard Educational Review,* 1974, **44,** 172–177; R. F. Thorum. Codifying student rights and responsibilities. *NASSP Bulletin,* 1975, **59,** 9–13.

28. A. Goldstein. Students and the law: a changing relationship. *NASSP Bulletin,* 1974, **58,** 50–53.

29. Haberman, *op. cit.,* p. 11.

30. Haberman, *op. cit.*

31. Haberman, *op. cit.*

32. Flygare, *op. cit.*

33. Phi Delta Kappa Commission on Administrative Behaviors Supportive of Human Rights. A sample student code. *Phi Delta Kappan,* 1974, **56,** 236–242. Excerpts reprinted by permission.

34. G. P. Liddle and R. E. Rockwell. The role of parents and family life. *Journal of Negro Education,* 1964, **33,** 311–317.

35. W. H. Sewell and V. P. Shah. Parents' education and children's educational aspirations and achievements. *American Sociological Review,* 1968, **33,** 191–209.

36. D. F. Swift. Family Environment and 11+ success: some basic predictions. *British Journal of Educational Psychology,* 1967, **37,** 10–21.

37. R. A. Rehberg and D. L. Westby. Parental encouragement, occupation, education and family size: artifactual or independent determinants of adolescent educational expectations? *Social Forces,* 1967, **45,** 362–374, p. 371.

38. W. R. Morrow and R. C. Wilson. Family relations of bright high-achieving and underachieving high school boys. *Child Development,* 1961, **32,** 501–510.

39. D. P. Kramer and E. S. Fleming. Interparental differences of opinion and children's academic achievement. *Journal of Educational Research,* 1966, **60,** 1–3; B. G. Myerhoff and W. R. Larson. Primary and formal aspects of family organization: group consensus, problem perception, and adolescent school success. *Journal of Marriage and the Family,* 1965, **27,** 213–217.

40. G. H. Elder, Jr. Family structure and educational attainment, a cross-national analysis. *American Sociological Review,* 1965, **30,** 81–96.

41. C. E. Bowerman and G. H. Elder, Jr. Variations in adolescent perception of family power structure. *American Sociological Review,* 1964, **29,** 551–567.

42. P. A. Cusick. *Inside high school.* New York: Holt, Rinehart and Winston, 1973.

43. E. J. Trickett and R. H. Moos. Social environment of junior high and high school classrooms. *Journal of Educational Psychology,* 1973, **65,** 93–102.

44. Trickett and Moos, *op. cit.,* p. 99.

45. H. J. Walberg, E. R., House, and J. M. Steele. Grade level, cognition, and affect: a cross-section of classroom perceptions. *Journal of Educational Psychology,* 1973, **64,** 142–146; M. W. Apple, M. J. Subkoviak, and H. S. Luffler (Eds.). *Educational evaluation: analysis and responsibility.* Berkeley: McCutchan, 1974, pp. 237–268. Reprinted by permission.

46. Walberg et al., *op. cit.*

47. Walberg et al., *op. cit.,* p. 145.

48. P. A. Cusick. Adolescent groups and the school organization. *School Review,* 1973, **82,** 116–126.

49. J. R. Muma. Peer evaluation and academic achievement in performance classes. *Personnel and Guidance Journal,* 1968, **46,** 580–585.

50. J. S. Coleman. *The adolescent society.* New York: Free Press, 1961.

51. R. E. Grinder. Distinctiveness and thrust in the American youth culture. *Journal of Social Issues,* 1969, **25,** 7–18.

52. Coleman, *op. cit.*

53. R. R. Weatherford and J. E. Horrocks. Peer acceptance and under- and over-achievement in school. *Journal of Psychology,* 1967, **66,** 215–220.

54. Grinder, *op. cit.*

55. Coleman, *op. cit.*

56. E. L. McDill and J. S. Coleman. High school social status, college plans, and interest in academic achievement: a panel analysis. *American Sociological Review,* 1963, **28,** 905–918.

57. McDill and Coleman, *op. cit.,* p. 918.

58. Coleman, *op. cit.*

59. J. H. Spring. Mass culture and school sports. *History of Education Quarterly,* 1974, **14,** 483–499.

60. Spring, *op. cit.*

61. J. S. Coleman, *Adolescents and the schools.* New York: Basic Books, 1965.

62. Spring, *op. cit.*

63. Spring, *op. cit.*

64. Spring, *op. cit.*

65. Coleman, Adolescents and the schools, *op. cit.*

66. Coleman, Adolescents and the schools, *op. cit.*

67. Coleman, Adolescents and the schools, *op. cit.*

68. Coleman, Adolescent society, *op. cit.*

69. Coleman, Adolescent society, *op. cit.*

70. D. Friesen. Academic-athletic popularity syndrome in the Canadian high school society. *Adolescence,* 1968, **39–52.**

71. E. E. Snyder. Aspects of socialization in sports and physical education. *Quest,* 1970, **14,** 1–7.

72. Snyder, *op. cit.,* p. 2.

73. E. E. Snyder. Aspects of social and political values of high school coaches. *International Review of Sport Sociology,* 1973, **4,** 73–83.

74. R. A. Rehberg. Behavioral and attitudinal consequences of high school interscholastic sports: a speculative consideration. *Adolescence,* 1969, **4,** 70–88.

75. Coleman, Adolescent society, *op. cit.*

76. Rehberg, *op. cit.,* p. 79.

77. E. Spreitzer and M. Pugh. Interscholastic athletics and educational expectations. *Sociology of Education,* 1973, **46,** 171–182.

78. D. S. Eitzen. Athletics in the status system of male adolescents: a replication of Coleman's *The Adolescent Society. Adolescence,* 1975, **10,** 267–276.

79. Friesen, *op. cit.*

80. K. B. Start. Substitution of games performance for academic achievement as a means of achieving status among secondary school children. *British Journal of Sociology,* 1966, **17,** 300–305.

81. L. E. Alley, Athletics in education: the double-edged sword. *Phi Delta Kappan,* 1974, **56,** 102–105.

82. J. R. Solberg. Interscholastic athletics—tail that wags the dog? *Journal of Secondary Education,* 1970, **45,** 238–239.

83. D. Wolfle. Diversity of talent. *American Psychologist,* 1960, **15,** 535–545.

84. W. W. Farquhar and D. A. Payne. A classification and comparison of techniques used in selecting under- and over-achievers. *Personnel and Guidance Journal,* 1964, **43,** 874–884.

85. C. Weinberg. The price of competition. *Teachers College Record,* 1965, **67,** 106–114.

86. E. P. Torrance. Academic achievement as a factor in emotional adjustment in the secondary school. *The High School Journal,* 1968, **51,** 281–287; Weinberg, *op. cit.*

87. Weinberg, *op. cit.*

88. R. Hummel and N. Sprinthall. Underachievement related to interests, attitudes and values. *Personnel and Guidance Journal,* 1965, **44,** 388–395.

89. L. Onoda. Personality characteristics and attitudes toward achievement among mainland high achieving and underachieving Japanese-American Sanseis. *Journal of Educational Psychology,* 1976, **68,** 151–156.

90. D. A. Gawronski and C. Mathis. Differences between over-achieving, normal-achieving, and under-achieving high school students. *Psychology in the Schools,* 1965, **2,** 152–155.

91. R. M. Roth and P. Puri. Direction of aggression and the nonachievement syndrome. *Journal of Counseling Psychology,* 1967, **14,** 277–281.

92. M. Silverman, A. Davids, and J. M. Andrews. Powers of attention and academic achievement. *Perceptual and Motor Skills,* 1963, **17,** 243–249.

93. Gawronski and Mathis, *op. cit.*

94. L. Carmical. Characteristics of achievers and under-achievers of a large senior high school. *Personnel and Guidance Journal,* 1964, **43,** 390–395.

95. A. Harnischfeger and D. E. Wiley. *Achievement test score decline: do we need to worry?* St. Louis: CEMREL, Inc. 1976.

96. Harnischfeger and Wiley, *op. cit.*

97. Harnischfeger and Wiley, *op. cit.*

98. D. W. MacKinnon. Identifying and developing creativity. *Journal of Secondary Education,* 1963, **38,** 166–174.

99. W. D. Hitt. Toward a two-factor theory of creativity. *Psychological Record,* 1965, **15,** 127–132.

100. W. D. Hitt and J. R. Stock. The relation between psychological characteristics and creative behavior. *Psychological Record,* 1965, **15,** 133–140.

101. E. P. Torrance. Scientific views on creativity and factors affecting its growth. *Daedalus,* 1955, **94,** 663–681.

102. G. A. Davis. Care and feeding of creative adolescents. In R. E. Grinder (Ed.). *Studies in Adolescence.* New York: Macmillan, 1975, pp. 562–572.

103. J. P. Guilford. Factors that aid and hinder creativity. *Teachers College Record,* 1962, **63,** 380–392.

104. C. D. Ramey and V. Piper. Creativity in open and traditional classrooms. *Child Development,* 1974, **45,** 557–560.

105. Wolfle, *op. cit.*

106. E. P. Torrance. *Guiding creative talent.* Englewood Cliffs, New Jersey: Prentice-Hall, 1962; E. P. Torrance. The creative personality and the ideal pupil. *Teachers College Record,* 1963, **63,** 220–226; Torrance, Scientific views on creativity, *op. cit.*

107. K. Dewing and R. Taft. Some characteristics of the parents of creative twelve-year-olds. *Journal of Personality,* 1973, **41,** 71–85.

108. J. W. Getzels and P. W. Jackson. *Creativity and intelligence.* New York: John Wiley, 1962.

109. J. L. Holland. Creative and academic performance among talented adolescents. *Journal of Educational Psychology,* 1961, **52,** 136–147.

110. Holland, *op. cit.*

111. M. Dellas and E. L. Gaier. Identification of creativity: the individual. *Psychological Bulletin,* 1970, **73,** 55–73.

112. Getzels and Jackson, *op. cit.*

113. Getzels and Jackson, *op. cit.*

114. R. L. Thorndike. The measurement of creativity. *Teachers College Record,* 1963, **64,** 422–424.

115. M. A. Wallach and N. Kogan. A new look at the creativity-intelligence distinction. *Journal of Personality,* 1965, **33,** 348–369.

116. A. J. Cropley. Creativity: a new kind of intellect? *Australian Journal of Education,* 1967, **11,** 120–125; Dellas and Gaier, *op. cit.;* M. P. Edwards and L. E. Tyler. Intelligence, creativity, and achievement in a nonselective public junior high school. *Journal of Educational Psychology,* 1965, **56,** 96–99; Torrance, Guiding creative talent, *op. cit.*

117. Dellas and Gaier, *op. cit.*

118. G. H. Gallup. Seventh annual Gallup pole of public attitudes toward education. *Phi Delta Kappan,* 1975, **57,** 227–241.

119. J. Slater. Death of a high school. *Phi Delta Kappan,* 1974, **56,** 251–254.

120. National Education Association. Moving against school violence. *Education Daily,* January 29, 1976.

121. J. I. Grealy. Making schools more secure. Paper presented at the meeting of the American Association of School Administrators, Dallas, 1975.

122. Slater, *op. cit.*

123. J. F. Henning. Student rights and responsibilities and the curriculm. *Phi Delta Kappan,* 1974, **56,** 248–250.

124. Henning, *op. cit.,* p. 249.

125. G. W. Marker and H. D. Mehlinger. Schools, politics, rebellion, and other youthful interests. *Phi Delta Kappan,* 1974, **56,** 244–247.

126. A. Maurer. Corporal punishment. *American Psychologist,* 1974, **29,** 614–626.

127. D. Findley and H. M. O'Reilly. Secondary School Discipline. *American Secondary Education,* 1971, **2,** 26–31.

128. Maurer, *op. cit.*

129. Maurer, *op. cit.*

130. Maurer, *op. cit.*

131. R. W. Cole, Jr. Ribbin', Jivin', and playin' the dozens. *Phi Delta Kappan,* 1974, **56,** 171–175.

132. A. Fins. Sex and the school principal: a long look at Title IX. *NASSP Bulletin,* 1974, **58,** 53–62.

133. J. L. Trecker. Sex stereotyping in the secondary school curriculum. *Phi Delta Kappan,* 1973, **55,** 110–112.

134. Trecker, *op. cit.,* p. 110.

135. T. N. Saario, C. K. Tittle, and C. N. Jacklin. Sex role stereotyping in the public schools. *Harvard Educational Review,* 1973, **43,** 386–416.

136. Saario et al., *op. cit.*

137. Saario et al., *op. cit.,* p. 407.

138. K. L. Alexander and B. K. Eckland. Sex differences in the educational attainment process. *American Sociological Review,* 1974, **39,** 668–682.

139. C. E. Skipper. The personal development of adolescents with average intellectual ability in a high ability suburban school district. Paper presented at the meeting of the American Educational Research Association, Chicago, 1974.

140. P. B. Campbell and A. E. McKain. Intellectual decline and the adolescent woman. Paper presented at the annual meeting of the American Educational Research Association, Washington, D.C., 1975.

141. L. H. Fox. Mathematically precocious: male or female? Paper presented at the meeting of the American Educational Research Association, Chicago, 1974; L. H. Fox. Career interests and mathematical acceleration for girls. Paper presented at the meeting of the American Psychological Association, Chicago, 1975.

142. Fox, Career interests, *op. cit.*

143. M. S. Horner. Sex Differences in achievement motivation and performance in competitive and non-competitive situations. Unpublished doctoral dissertation, University of Michigan, 1968; M. S. Horner. The motive to avoid success and changing aspirations of women. In J.

M. Bardwick (Ed.). *Readings on the Psychology of Women.* New York: Harper and Row, 1972.

144. Horner, Sex differences in achievement motivation, *op. cit.*

145. N. T. Feather. Fear of success in Australian and American student groups: motive or sex-role stereotype? *Journal of Personality,* 1974, **42,** 190–203.

146. T. G. Alper. Achievement motivation in college women. *American Psychologist,* 1974, **29,** 194–203.

147. N. Romer. The motive to avoid success and its effects on performance in school-age males and females. *Developmental Psychology,* 1975, **11,** 689–699.

148. R. Winchel, D. Fenner, and P. Shaver. Impact of coeducation on "fear of success" imagery expressed by male and female high school students. *Journal of Educational Psychology,* 1974, **66,** 726–730.

149. R. B. Everhart. Some antecedents to compulsory school attendance. Paper presented at the meeting of the American Educational Research Association, Washington, D.C., 1975.

150. R. F. Butts. Assaults on a great idea. *Phi Delta Kappan,* 1973, **55,** 240.

151. D. B. Tyack. Some models for interpreting the history of compulsory schooling. Paper presented at the meeting of the American Educational Research Association, Washington, D.C., 1975.

152. National Center for Health Statistics. *Health attitudes and behavior of youths 12–17 years, United States.* (DHEW, Pub. No. [HRA] 76-1635.) Series 11, No. 153, 1975.

153. Tyack, *op. cit.*

154. H. M. Johnson. Are compulsory attendance laws outdated? *Phi Delta Kappan,* 1973, **55,** 226–232.

155. B. F. Brown. A defense for lowering compulsory education to age 14. *NASSP Bulletin,* 1975, **59,** 65–66.

156. Brown, *op. cit.*

157. Johnson, *op. cit.*

158. O. B. Kiernan. Compulsory Education. *NASSP Bulletin,* 1975, **59,** 61–64.

159. J. C. Bledsoe. An investigation of six correlates of student withdrawal from high school. *Journal of Educational Research,* 1959, **53,** 3–6.

160. G. P. Liddle. Psychological factors involved in dropping out of school. *High School Journal,* 1962, **45,** 276–280.

161. L. F. Cervantes. *The dropout: causes and cures.* Ann Arbor: University of Michigan Press, 1965; L. F. Cervantes. Family background, primary relationships, and the high school dropout. *Journal of Marriage and the Family,* 1965, **27,** 218–223; L. F. Cervantes. The isolated nuclear family and the dropout. *Sociological Quarterly,* 1965, **6,** 103–118; J. K. Tuel. Dropout dynamics. *California Journal of Educational Research,* 1966, **17,** 5–11.

162. C. E. Anduri. Identifying potential dropouts. *California Education,* 1965, **3,** 31.

163. Cervantes. Family background and the dropout, *op. cit.,* p. 218.

164. Cervantes. Family background on the dropout, *op. cit.*

165. Cervantes. Nuclear family and the dropout, *op. cit.*

166. Cervantes. Nuclear family and the dropout, *op. cit.,* p. 114.

167. Cervantes. Nuclear family and the dropout, *op. cit.,* p. 115.

168. Anduri, *op. cit.;* G. V. Campbell. A review of the dropout problem. *Peabody Journal of Education,* 1966, **44,** 102–109; R. L. Williams and J. W. Pickens. Contributing factors to school departures in Georgia. *Psychological Reports,* 1967, **20,** 693–694.

169. C. V. Matthews. The serious problem of the school dropout. *Illinois Education Association Discussion Topic,* 1962, **24,** No. 5.

170. Liddle, *op. cit.*

171. Tuel, *op. cit.*

172. Campbell, *op. cit.*

173. Matthews, *op. cit.*

174. D. S. Elliott, H. L. Voss, and A. Wendling. Dropout and the social milieu of the high school: a preliminary analysis. *American Journal of Orthopsychiatry,* 1966, **36,** 808–817.

175. Elliott et al., *op. cit.*

176. S. J. Fitzsimmons, J. Cheever, E. Leonard, and D. Macunovich. School failures: now and tomorrow. *Developmental Psychology,* 1969, **1,** 134–146.

177. Fitzsimmons et al., *op. cit.,* pp. 138–142.

178. Fitzsimmons et al., *op. cit.,* p. 144.

179. J. Combs and W. W. Cooley. Dropouts: in high school and after school. *American Educational Research Journal,* 1968, **5,** 343–363.

180. C. Fernandez, R. W. Espinosa, and S. M. Dornbusch. *Factors perpetuating the low academic status of Chicano high school students.* Stanford Center for Research and Development in Teaching, Stanford University, Memorandum No. 138, 1975.

181. Fernandez et al., *op. cit.*

Chapter 13

The Meaning of Work and Career Planning in an Industrial Society

CHAPTER HIGHLIGHTS

ISSUES

Few out-of-school youth obtain full-time work that leads directly into adult careers.

Young people are seeking work today that will have significance both to themselves and to society.

Adolescents' interests and career plans generally become more stable and consistent with increasing age.

Increasing numbers of adolescent girls believe that a career in work is equal or even more important to them than one as wife and mother.

Adolescent girls tend to believe that women have little hope of achieving positions of leadership and responsibility.

Rural youth tend to aspire relatively to lower levels of occupational achievement.

Youth's aspirations are influenced by the quality of their parents' occupations.

Youth view occupations that have significance and meaning as the most attractive and prestigious.

Career development theories generally integrate motivational, developmental, and social factors.

Career education aims to increase career options and facilitate career planning but it may also engender unrealistic hopes.

The emphasis on cognitive training in high schools tends to isolate youth from the workplace.

The occupational structure is having difficulty accommodating the number of young people who aspire to high-income, high-status, meaningful jobs.

Action-learning programs provide examples of experience-based alternatives to traditional classroom activities.

The circumstances of work preoccupy our lives for much of our life spans. Work affects most persons between the ages of 15 and 65, and the decisions adolescents make about their work, occupations, and careers will significantly affect their future social relationships, leisure-time activities, places of residence, material acquisitions, marital choice (or choices), and child-rearing practices. It has long been held in America that the willingness to work is a major component of character and maturity, and for nearly all persons the extent and significance of work is a prime determinant of standard of living, citizenship, and life style.

Before the Industrial Revolution, a son followed his father into farming or a trade; there was little change from generation to generation, and even an illiterate adolescent could learn enough in the way of basic skills to do productive work. After the Industrial Revolution, the demand for sophisticated skills accelerated swiftly, but still there was enough work for everyone. At the turn of the century young people were needed on farms, in local distribution and service trades, and in factories, stores, ships, and mines. Before World War II, the majority of young people had begun full-time employment or homemaking by the age of 20, and many of them had started in these activities as early as age 16.[1] After World War II the task of getting started as a young adult in the world of work grew increasingly complex. Urbanization restricted the involvement of youth in a wide variety of work activities formerly available to them; unskilled jobs became scarce, and child-labor prohibitions, certification standards, and apprenticeship requirements began to bar adolescents from simply getting jobs and working their way up into fulfilling and meaningful positions.

American youth generally make the transition from school to work between the ages of 16 and 24. Most 14 to 15 year olds are in school and are too young to move into full-time work, but nonetheless, approximately one-fourth of them are working part-time in unskilled occupations—delivering newspapers, bagging groceries, waitressing, babysitting, and so forth.[2] The 25 to 34 year olds have made the transition, since about 95 percent of the males and about 50 percent of the females have entered the labor force. The industries that engage young people 16 to 24 years of age, as they make the transition from school to work, is shown in Table 1.[3] The data are separated by sex and include school dropouts and high school graduates not in college. The breakdown reveals that more males than females, and more dropouts than graduates of high school are employed in agriculture. The majority of youth, however, are employed in manufacturing and trades, both wholesale and retail. The most significant difference among the two sexes shown in Table 1 appears in the "service and finance" area, where many more females than males are employed, probably as waitresses, housekeepers, and clerks. The data in Table 1 also reveal that youth's pattern of employment is approximately the same for graduates and dropouts. Apparently, high school graduation today no longer funnels youth toward jobs with any more promise than those available to dropouts. Havighurst and Gottlieb[4] indicate, for example, that relatively few adolescents now obtain full-time work that will lead them directly into adult careers. A characteristic difference between the pattern of the 1970s and that of earlier generations, they say, is the tentative and juvenile quality of work experience before age 20.

What are the prospects of youth finding full-time work that will lead to satisfying life-long careers? O'Toole[5] has observed that many jobs that look good (health paraprofessionals, teacher's aides, technicians with two-year associate arts degrees) lack career ladders—the X-ray technician may not progress up a ladder to become a radiologist, the health paraprofessional seldom becomes a nurse, and the teacher's aide seldom becomes a certified teacher. He notes that the proportion of jobs available in service-related activities increased from 15.9 percent in 1955 to over 20 percent in 1972. But O'Toole asks, what kinds of jobs are being created? Between 1960 and 1970, the number of orderlies and nurses aides increased by 420,000; the number of janitors by 530,000, and the number of busboys and dishwashers by 70,000. While they are not exactly leaf-raking, the new jobs are not of the nature, he says, that are likely to motivate a new generation of qualified workers. The jobs offer low salary and little in the way of career opportunities, and they appear "to have many of the worst characteristics of blue-collar work (the jobs are dull, repetitive, fractionated, and offer little challenge or personal autonomy). Also, these new jobs often lack the best characteristics of skilled, blue-collar jobs (relatively high salary, security, union protection, and the sense of mastery that comes from producing something tangible and needed by society)."[6]

The basic task facing the American society is that of ensuring that satisfying work is available to all youth who seek it. The workplace will move during the

Table 1

Industry Group and Class of Worker of Employed High School Graduates Not Enrolled in College and School Dropouts, by Sex. October 1972. (Percent distribution of persons 16 to 21 years of age)

Industry Group and Class of Worker	Graduates			Dropouts		
	Both Sexes	Male	Female	Both Sexes	Male	Female
All industry groups:						
Number (thousands)	4,830	2,316	2,514	1,504	1,027	477
Percent	100.0	100.0	100.0	100.0	100.0	100.0
Agriculture	3.3	5.5	1.2	8.0	8.9	6.1
Wage and salary workers	2.2	4.0	.6	6.8	8.1	4.0
Self-employed workers	.4	.6	.1	—	—	—
Unpaid family workers	.7	.9	.4	1.3	.9	2.1
Nonagricultural industries	96.7	94.5	98.8	92.0	91.1	93.9
Wage and salary workers	95.2	92.7	97.5	88.6	88.6	88.7
Mining	.6	1.1	.1	.5	.7	—
Construction	6.8	13.6	.6	12.7	18.6	—
Manufacturing	24.2	30.5	18.4	32.9	34.1	30.3
Durable goods	14.1	20.3	8.5	17.0	20.0	10.5
Nondurable goods	10.1	10.2	9.9	15.9	14.1	19.7
Transportation and public utilities	5.4	5.8	5.1	2.5	2.9	1.5
Wholesale and retail trade	26.2	26.2	26.2	21.6	20.2	24.6
Service and finance	29.1	13.6	43.4	17.8	11.2	32.1
Private households	1.3	.3	2.3	3.3	.6	9.0
Other service and finance	27.8	13.3	41.1	14.6	10.6	23.1
Public administration	2.8	1.9	3.6	.7	1.0	.2
Self-employed workers	1.3	1.5	1.2	2.7	1.8	4.6
Unpaid family workers	.2	.3	.2	.6	.6	.6

Source: A. M. Young. The high school class of 1972: more at work, fewer in college. Washington, D.C.: Bureau of Labor Statistics, *Special Labor Force Report 155,* 1973, Table J. Reprinted by permission.

next 20 years increasingly from a blue-collar industrial economy toward a white-collar service economy. The government will continue to be the fastest growing sector of the economy, and technology will continue to grow and machines will replace many persons in many jobs, which in turn, will increase the need for more and more persons to sell, deliver, and service the greater production automation has made possible. The number of young workers (16 to

24 years old) in the workforce will have risen from 20 million in 1970 to 23.8 million in 1980. The number is projected to decline by 350,000 a year during the 1980s to about 22.2 million by 1985 and 20.3 million by 1990—to about the same number in 1990 as in 1970.[7]

To deal with the complex issues facing youth in respect to the world of work, this chapter is divided into five relatively discrete sections: (1) the meaning of work to American youth, (2) the social factors that affect career choice, (3) major conceptual bases of career-development theory, (4) the career-education movement, and (5) beyond career education: a discussion of the probable alignments that schooling and work may forge in the decade ahead.

THE MEANING OF WORK TO YOUTH

Work has long been the principal source of self-esteem for Americans.[8] Men and women prize productive work, and during the nineteenth century and the first three-quarters of the twentieth century, the emphasis in America has been on the production of material goods. As Havighurst[9] puts it: "The most highly prized activities in American history have been instrumental. That is, they were means to an end beyond the activity. Americans broke the sod of the prairies and planted grain as a means of obtaining more food. They dug for coal, drilled for oil, harnessed the power of rivers, built railroads and factories, organized banks and corporations—all as instruments of greater material production. America became known for the instrumental activism of its life style." But the very abundance of a highly productive society has led people to revise their views toward affluence. "When there is enough food, comfortable housing, television, and automobiles for nearly every family, people who have these things come to take them for granted, and to value them less highly than when they were scarce and required much work and sacrifice to obtain."[10] Havighurst points out that Americans can now do the work necessary to maintain productivity in a four- or five-day work week, with several weeks of paid vacation every year. They have more free time than they had even a generation ago, and they have more options in the use of their time. They are no longer bound to a life style consisting mainly of work, and many are seeking in society an emphasis on quality of life rather than on quantity of material production.

The quest among the current generation for a better quality of life is being focused today in youth's emphasis on work having intrinsic meaning— challenge, responsibility, and achievement.[11] Many young people are saying their most important consideration in choosing a line of work is the need to obtain satisfaction. Gottlieb[12] says that a work ideology is emerging that stresses the *quality* of work. He says that young people are expecting that work can and should be of greater significance to the individual and of greater value to society. The 1960 Project TALENT survey of the interests of more than 400,000 students in a ramdon sample of all of the secondary schools in the United States, and its 1970 follow-up, for example, revealed that the most important factor influencing adolescent choice was "work which seems important to me."[13] These research findings are corroborated by answers made to one of the questions asked of members of a national sample of the high school class of 1972.[14] The participants were asked to indicate how important they believed a variety of expressive and instrumental factors would be to them in selecting a job or career. The data, summarized by sex, high school program, ethnicity, father's education, academic ability, socioeconomic status, and region, are presented in Table 2. They provide a valuable profile of contemporary youth's attitudes toward work, as the following interpretations of the findings suggest:

1. More females than males indicate preference for expressive factors—opportunities to be helpful to others or useful to society and work with people. The two sexes are equally interested in creativity, the world of ideas, steady progress, and avoidance of pressure, but more males view instrumental values as important—being looked up to by others, independence, making money, and leadership.

2. More youth in the academic relative to the general and vocational programs prefer expressive factors—to be helpful to others and useful to society, work with people, be creative, and able to live and work in the world of ideas. In contrast, the vocationally-oriented youth prefer to avoid extreme chance of success or failure, and they especially like such instrumental factors as a position looked up to by others and making a lot of money.

3. More black and Latin-American than white youth feel in general that both expressive and instrumental factors are important in selecting a job or a career.

4. More youth whose fathers graduated from college, relative to those whose fathers had not graduated, prefer the expressive factors. They also like jobs associated with avoidance of high pressure and limited supervision. Offspring of nongraduates are more likely to prefer opportunities for steady progress, a position looked up to by others, and making a lot of money.

5. Youth's values toward work are relatively similar across ability levels, except that high-ability youth tend to prefer expressive factors and low-ability youth are inclined to prefer positions that are looked up to by others, where they can make a lot of money, and where they have a chance to be a leader.

Table 2
How Important is Each of the Following to You in Selecting a Job or Career?

Response	All Students	Sex		High School Program			Ethnic Category		
		Male	Female	Acad	Gen'l	Voc	White	Black	Latin Amer
Weighted percentage of students who answered "very important"									
Opportunities to be helpful to others or useful to society	53.1	42.1	64.0	57.4	50.3	48.4	52.2	61.7	57.2
Opportunities to work with people rather than things	48.9	36.0	61.7	52.7	46.5	45.1	48.3	55.5	55.1
Opportunities to be original and creative	39.0	37.2	40.6	42.2	38.6	34.0	38.6	41.2	36.8
Living and working in the world of ideas	34.6	32.3	36.8	37.3	33.9	30.9	34.0	39.0	38.6
Opportunities for moderate but steady progress rather than the chance of extreme success or failure	33.7	32.0	35.4	30.7	34.9	37.9	33.4	38.9	36.3
Avoiding a high-pressure job that takes too much out of you	30.7	31.8	29.7	28.7	32.3	32.7	30.6	29.2	32.9
Having a position that is looked up to by others	25.4	28.6	22.3	22.7	28.4	26.5	23.1	41.4	35.2
Freedom from supervision in my work	23.4	29.1	17.7	22.2	26.2	22.3	22.6	26.7	27.0
Making a lot of money	22.2	28.5	15.9	17.0	26.5	26.1	19.9	39.6	25.6
The chance to be a leader	15.9	21.9	9.9	16.6	17.1	12.9	14.4	26.8	17.9

Source: W. B. Fetters. *National longitudinal study of the high school class of 1972.* National Center for Health Statistics, (DHEW) Nos. 208; 197; 1976. Reprinted by permission.

6. More youth of high relative to low socioeconomic status prefer expressive factors, but youth of low status prefer jobs with less risk, positions to which others look up, and opportunities to make a lot of money.
7. Regional differences in the relative importance of the work factors to youth are insignificant; it is noteworthy, however, that southern youth, relative to those from the other regions, are proportionately more interested in making a lot of money and having a chance to be a leader.

MAJOR INFLUENCES ON CAREER CHOICES
The Role of Realism in Occupational Decision Making

Planning for work requires a number of critical, sometimes irreversible, decisions. Adolescents move toward given occupations when the opportunities exist,

Father's Education				Ability				Socioeconomic Status			Region			
Not known	Not HS Grad	HS Grad	Coll Grad	Low	Med	High	Not Known	Low	Med	High	North-east	North-central	South	West
51.9	51.3	53.3	55.9	52.4	52.3	55.5	49.0	52.7	52.8	54.4	53.8	51.5	55.2	51.5
47.3	46.7	49.7	51.5	46.5	49.5	50.7	47.2	48.2	48.5	51.5	51.1	48.2	49.8	46.2
37.4	35.1	39.4	45.4	36.7	38.0	42.3	37.1	34.2	38.0	45.8	39.2	38.3	38.9	38.9
34.9	32.3	33.6	40.5	34.9	31.4	38.5	35.3	32.2	33.2	39.4	33.5	33.3	35.9	35.3
32.3	36.4	34.4	29.1	32.8	36.9	28.8	35.4	36.3	34.4	29.2	31.5	32.6	37.3	33.2
29.0	29.7	30.9	33.2	29.3	31.9	29.6	29.6	29.1	31.0	31.1	30.2	28.6	31.3	33.4
32.8	26.0	24.2	21.4	34.2	24.0	17.6	26.4	28.2	24.3	22.3	21.8	24.4	30.9	21.1
25.8	21.6	22.7	26.1	26.2	22.6	21.3	25.9	22.3	23.0	24.9	21.7	23.7	23.3	24.7
32.9	23.1	20.3	17.0	34.2	20.1	13.2	23.8	25.7	21.3	18.3	20.0	20.5	26.2	20.4
19.1	14.8	15.3	16.3	18.6	14.9	14.6	13.3	15.8	14.9	17.1	11.9	14.9	21.3	14.0

the training requirements can be met, the rewards will match or exceed their expectations, their reference groups approve, and the work-role demands are congruent with their personal values and life styles. Although the career-education model (to be discussed later) may make career education relevant at every grade level from kindergarten through postsecondary school, the educational system is presently structured in such a way that adolescents, if they are to take advantage of programs in the later grades, face critical choices about work during the transition from junior to senior high school and again from senior high school to college. According to Kelso,[15] young people who leave school before taking advantage of the opportunities it presents to develop their abilities and skills, relative to those who stay, tend to be lower in respect to both general intelligence and maturity of vocational decision making. But Kelso also showed that the boys in grade 9 who anticipated leaving school prior to grade 12 were as realistic as boys in grade 12 about their prospects, in respect to self-appraisals, aspirations, and perceptions of opportunities. Perhaps, when entry into the world of work is close at hand, self-examination and intense interest in work opportunities leads to early development of realistic attitudes toward work.

Planning for work is difficult for boys and girls in junior high school (or earlier) because it is hard for them to relate their values and interests to occupational goals. Their occupational aspirations tend to be idealistic and unrealistic, and consequently, their decisions about vocations are likely to be unstable. With increasing age, however, interests and career plans emerge and become more consistent as adolescents achieve greater insight into their own abilities and the demands of different occupations. In general, the youth who are strongest scholastically tend to raise their occupational ambitions whereas the less capable aspire to less intellectually demanding careers. Astin[16] noted, for example, that "career changes that take place during the high school years result partly from a greater self-awareness and recognition by the students of the aptitudes and skills that are necessary to educational and occupational success." Gribbons and Lohnes[17] initiated a "Career Development Study" in 1958 to follow the career plans of 110 boys and girls who had entered the eighth grade. Four extensive, structured interviews were conducted with all of the boys and girls in the eighth, tenth, and twelfth grades, and two years after high school. The researchers obtained information on curricular choices, career choices, and self-concept imagery, including the ability to verbalize personal strengths and weaknesses, make accurate self-appraisals, and be aware of interests, values, and independence of choices. In analyzing their data, Gribbons and Lohnes concluded that "perhaps the most noticeable trend is from 'idealism' in the eighth grade (*social service, personal goals, location and travel*) to 'realism' in the twelfth (*marriage and family, preparation and ability, advancement*)."[18] And Hollender,[19] who studied more than 4,500 youth from the sixth through the twelfth grades, found that while realistic occupational choices began to appear about the ninth grade there was a discernible trend for reality to take priority over subjective considerations as the youth became older.

Cooley[20] has said that the convergence of vocational interests and personal abilities probably occurs during high school. Since each person's career plans presumably originate in the commingling of work-role stereotypes with an awareness of one's abilities and motives, Cooley believes that career plans will change with one's educational experiences. On the one hand, as adolescents become more familiar with their own abilities and the demands of different occupations, their vocational interests should become more consistent with their abilities. On the other hand, early vocational interests may motivate adolescents to improve their abilities in pertinent areas. A youth with considerable interest in science, for example, might study harder in that field as well as in such related fields as mathematics. Cooley examined the relationship between interests and abilities by using the data obtained from 1,500 males and 1,500 females in the ninth and twelfth grades in the Project TALENT nationwide survey. He found that interests in grade 9 motivated the development of abilities between grades 9 and 12: "the ninth-grade boy who wanted to become a scientist produced greater gains in the mathematics areas during high school than would be expected from his grade 9 ability."[21] Moreover, abilities tended to determine vocational interests: "Thus some boys who did well on the grade 9 ability measures but planned nonprofessional careers tended to change to professional plans by grade 12, while some boys low on general ability yet with high expectations tended to lower their aspirations by twelfth grade."[22]

Flanagan has reported a trend toward greater realism in the career planning of high school boys and lesser realism in that of girls.[23] The study was part of a follow-up study of the 1960 national survey of 400,000 youth in Project TALENT. The researcher analyzed average scores on the same reading comprehension test administered to groups of eleventh grade students planning specific careers in 1960 and 1970. Flanagan found that the eleventh grade boys who planned careers in mathematics, the biological sciences, psychology or sociology, political science or economics, law, and pharmacology in 1970, for example, attained average reading scores that were comparable to those earned by youth in the 1960 Project TALENT survey who eventually entered these careers. The boys planning careers in these fields in 1960, in contrast, obtained average reading scores five to seven points lower than those who actually entered them. The lack of realism in the boys' choices in the 1960s may be due partly to (1) poorer vocational guidance counseling then and (2) the fact that proportionately more young men wanted to enter these fields in 1960 as a consequence of national efforts to bolster them following the Russian launch of Sputnik. The picture for girls was somewhat different. Girls in 1960 wanted to enter fewer fields, but their choices were relatively realistic. More girls in 1970 said that they planned to go to college, and instead of choosing the traditional female jobs such as nurse, secretary, and beautician, they indicated a trend toward a greater variety of professional jobs such as biological scientist, social worker, sociologist, or psychologist. However, the average reading scores of girls in 1970 who aspired to these careers were from six to ten points below the averages of the relatively few from the 1960 survey who had actually entered them. The relative lack of realism of girls in 1970 reveals a sharp discrepancy between desire, which probably was inspired by the growing demands by women for equal opportunity, and preparation to achieve occupational goals. Thus Flanagan[24] indicates that adolescent girls must obtain effective vocational guidance at an early stage of their secondary education if they are to plan and pursue a variety of careers successfully. They must either shift to lower levels of vocational aspirations or they must begin early to master the skills prerequisite to fulfilling professional-level jobs.

Ethnicity and Occupational Aspirations

Youth's career choices presumably become more realistic as they engage in the dynamics of occupational decision making. Preadolescents tend to express grandiose, idealistic career choices, but with increasing years, as the self-concept is brought into congruence with reality factors, that is, aptitudes, abilities, resources, and opportunities, occupational choices tend to become more realistic relative to prospects for actual attainment. The gradual attainment of realism is the conventional outcome of vocational decision making for most youth. One might expect, therefore, that low-income youth, especially from ethnic minorities, who generally encounter stiff barriers and resistance as they move toward status roles, would tend to lower their career aspirations and expectations as they proceed through high school. The research evidence shows, however, that disadvantaged youth tend over time to assume superficially high aspirations and expectations.[25] A recent tri-ethnic investigation of youth's occupational ambitions, for example, including black, Mexican-American, and white young people, has shown that ethnic minority youth perceive their future prospects for occupational attainment as brighter than do their white counterparts.[26] The data also showed that black and Mexican-American youth held occupational expectations that far exceeded the achieved status of their parents.

A variety of speculative reasons may be advanced to account for why ethnic minority youth develop unrealistically high occupational aspirations. First, the answer may lie, in part, in their efforts to conform to the American cultural emphasis on achieving occupational success and status.[27] Second, their high-level career choices may represent a compensation for failure to move ahead in a success-oriented society. Realistic choices might be ego-deflating. Cosby[28] points out that "the youth in high school with little opportunity for high level attainment can adjust to the high societal success values by planning, expecting, and projecting success into the future. He can accept past and present setbacks and accept failure to meet past choices by substituting new future-oriented projections." Third, the apparent magnitude of recent social and economic gains made by ethnic minorities have led these youth to exaggerate the level of their expectations. The American dream of upward mobility certainly has dominated the outlook of American youth and the civil rights movement has indeed opened up new horizons for ethnic minority youth. Perhaps, then, as barriers to occupational attainment are lifted, prospects of real opportunties being available to ethnic-minority youth will foster in them the development of more realistic aspirations. Attendance at integrated schools, for example, has at least enabled minority youth to gain access to information about employment opportunities that probably would not have been available to them in segregated schools.[29]

Feminism and the World of Work

The aspirations of women for as much access as men to self-fulfilling careers became a significant social issue in our times with the founding of the National Organization for Women (NOW). The organization was brought into existence in 1966 by 28 women who urged the federal government to enforce antidiscrimination laws. Feminism asserts that work ought to be as meaningful to women as it is to men—"that women as well as men need opportunities for achievement and fulfillment—with the recognition that in our society work is the chief source of those feelings for most people."[30] The ideology of the women's movement runs counter, however, to the way in which we have traditionally divided work between the two sexes. We generally assume, for example, that homemaking chores such as cooking, washing, and diapering are secondary issues to men in the labor force and that meaningful employment is of secondary concern to women, since they obtain satisfactions from homemaking responsibilities. American men, thus, are expected to place particular importance on job security, benefits, and advancement, whereas women are presumed to be interested mainly in short-term work or volunteer work, and relatively uninterested in developing long-range career plans.[31] One early investigation, which has since been corroborated on several occasions,[32] found, for example, that male high school seniors preferred jobs characterized by "independence, power, and high salaries, whereas female high school seniors desired jobs which were interesting and in which they could help others."[33] But women are recognizing today that life may hold more for them than homemaking, and as the feminist movement leads them to view their careers in work as equal or as even more important than their roles as wives and mothers, significant changes are likely to occur in employment practices, wage policies, and work patterns. Nonetheless, the current demands of the feminist movement for occupational and social equity and for rights to career opportunities open to men have had only limited impact on sex discrimination in the world of work. Datta[34] reports that women have come only a short way during the past 50 years in respect to work status and earnings. She cites Department of Labor data that show that, although women are entering the labor market in large numbers, their distribution in traditionally masculine, high-paying, high-status occupations is virtually unchanged. Also unchanged is the low proportion of men in occupations traditionally filled by women, such as, private household, clerical, sales, and service work.

Sexist myths regarding work roles are so persuasive in our society that they are already well-developed in childhood. An open-ended questionnaire administered to 61 second graders revealed that 97 percent of the children of both sexes said that they had thought about the occupations that they were likely to enter when they "grew up." However, the boys named twice the number of occupations as did the girls and all of them were male-oriented, for example, policeman, construction worker, or spaceman. In contrast, two-thirds of the girls selected either "teacher" or "nurse."[35] The sex-role attitudes of the boys and girls in grades one, two, three, and four was also examined by asking them a series of questions about work roles. The majority of the children agreed that men should be lawyers, astronauts, pilots, judges, farmers, police officers, and so forth, and they agreed that women should be nurses, secretaries, cooks, ballet dancers, baby sitters, and housecleaners.[36] As Siegel[37] suggests, by early in elementary school, children seem to have absorbed societal expectations of "sex-appropriate" work, are somewhat aware of their own sexual identity, and have elected accordingly the traditional cultural stereotype of their future work. Moreover, as the sexist stereotypes become firmly entrenched during the high school years, adolescent girls who hold them appear to anticipate achieving relatively low-status occupations.[38] Karmel,[39] for example, asked youth in grades 9, 11, and the first and third years of college (1) what their chances were of being employed in regular jobs when they were 40 years old and (2) what their chances were of earning more than the average person. The researcher found that males much more than females anticipated being employed and earning more than the average person. Similarly, Gottlieb and Bell[40] conducted a two-phase study in which graduating seniors were asked what they expected to earn upon leaving college, and then, one year later, were asked what they actually had earned. They found that the males fared better than the females in fulfilling postcollege career expectations and that the females came close to matching their expectations regarding earnings—"they anticipate less and they earn less."

What might be done to reduce the provincial attitudes of young girls toward work? Cole and Hanson[41] point out that only a short while ago young girls were socialized to anticipate that a very limited range of career prospects, options, and experiences would be available to them. Today, however, they say that we have a situation in which career options for girls are opening up so swiftly that early socializing experiences are lagging in preparing them to take advantage of the opportunities. Cole and Hanson,[42] therefore, suggest two different strategies that might be adopted to bring young women's occupational expectations and opportunities into congruence. The first emphasizes that change must be introduced early in socialization; the second stresses the importance of career exploration in adolescence:

1. *Hypothesis of Socialization Dominance.* Until the areas of socially accepted interest options become broadened during a person's development, the careers in which such people will be satisfied will not broaden.
2. *Hypothesis of Opportunity Dominance.* When career opportunities widen, people will find satisfaction in a wider range of careers in spite of limiting aspects of their earlier socialization.

Rossi[43] has said, in support of the first strategy, that "while the problem could be attacked at the college level, any significant change in the career choices men and women make must be attempted when they are young boys and girls. It is during the early years of elementary school education that young people develop the basic views of appropriate characteristics, activities, and goals for their sex." Harmon[44] has shown, too, that career choices of young women follow a developmental pattern. Harmon asked nearly 1,200 first-year college women to report, retrospectively, which of 135 occupational titles they had contemplated as careers during adolescence. Each girl was asked to indicate when in childhood a given occupation appealed to her, and if she subsequently lost interest in it, her age when interest was lost. The data, in brief, revealed that early choices do indeed persist into adolescence, and that, in general, adolescent girls believe that women need not aspire to positions of leadership and responsibility. Gaskell,[45] however, while agreeing that work-role stereotypes certainly influenced how girls plan their lives, says that success experiences in high school today can help them acquire confidence in their ability to hold their own in the world of careers. Gaskell thus supports both strategies, maintaining that sex-role myths can be defused during high school.

Surely it is important to implement both strategies simultaneously. It is important to correct maladaptive socializing practices as early as possible, and it is equally important for the current cohort of adolescent girls to take advantage of the opportunities the feminist movement is opening up for them. And there is evidence to suggest that contemporary high school girls are preparing themselves to respond to the range of work opportunities becoming available. The attitudes of young women, for example, appear to be expanding from a "work" to a "career" orientation. Richardson[46] has shown that many young women are becoming career-oriented—they are deviating "from the traditional feminine role in that they have long-term career goals which are central in their future plans." The "career-oriented" are directed toward a meaningful career rather than a particular occupational work role. This newly emerging group contrasts with the traditionally "work-oriented" women who consider work as something interesting to do but less intrinsically important than their homemaking roles and thus not central to their life style. Rand and Miller[47] report also that the cultural imperative that calls for the dominance of the marriage role is giving way to a new duality of marriage *and* career roles. Only a decade ago, Matthews and Tiedeman[48] reported that many women accepted the premise that a career in a field that competes with men is unwise. Women, they said, have generally been conditioned to believe that men view women who use their minds as unattractive and that is not advisable to enter a field requiring substantial intelligence, aggressiveness, and determination if they wish to marry. Matthews and Tiedeman observed that women whose childhood experiences taught them to devalue the use of their minds tend to feel inferior to men; therefore, they are likely to want to be homemakers and to reject the idea of a career even in conjunction with marriage. In a survey of more than 1,000 adolescent girls, Matthews and Tiedeman found that the girls were generally counseled by their parents to make themselves as marriageable as possible and not to become too competent in a career. But Rand and Miller[49] believe that today the cultural interdiction against work is disappearing; as young women begin to see that vocational and homemaking activities can be compatible, the marriage-career pattern will emerge as a new way of life. And current trends indicate that the new pattern is emerging very swiftly. A national survey, sponsored by the American Council on Education, of 1975 college freshmen indicates that the percentage of women pursuing the traditionally male-dominated careers of law, medicine, business and engineering has tripled in the last nine years. The number of women choosing a business career jumped from 3.3 percent in 1966 to 10 percent in 1975, while those choosing law increased from 0.7 percent to 2.5 percent and those picking medicine and engineering rose from 1.7 percent to 3.3 percent and from 0.2 percent to 1.1 percent, respectively. Apparently, the dramatic increase has occurred because the feminist movement has convinced a lot of girls that they can now pursue these occupations and that their productivity and that of men will be equitably assessed.

Rural versus Urban Opportunities for Adolescent Boys

Studies in Florida, Iowa, Kentucky, Washington, Utah, and Wisconsin have shown that youth from rural areas and smaller communities aspire to lower prestige and less well-paid occupations that those from urban areas.[50] Sewell[51] suggested that the lower educational level and socioeconomic status of rural families affect the aspirations of rural youth. To explore the relationship among intelligence, socioeconomic status, and community of residence relative to occupational aspirations, Sewell and Orenstein[52] utilized the responses of 10,000 youth who had been sampled in a 1957 survey of graduating seniors in all public, private, and parochial schools in Wisconsin. They found that with respect to community of residence, the differences in occupational aspirations were greatest among boys of relatively low intelligence and high socioeconomic status, respectively.

First, the influence of intelligence in relation to rural-urban life was not large, but its magnitude suggested that boys of lower intelligence may be more affected by their first-hand impressions of the local labor market, which is probably more restricted and depressed in a rural area, thus producing a large discrepancy between the aspirations of rural and urban youth. On the other hand, the more intelligent rural and urban boys may become aware of opportunities beyond their local community as a result of reading, counseling, and other sources of information, thus reducing the limitations of a given community for bright youth.

Second, the relationship between socioeconomic status and community size showed a significant difference in aspirations for youth of higher status. Earlier investigators believed that the relationship of community size and occupational aspirations would be greatest among working-class youth because in the smaller towns there would be less occupational stimulation than in urban areas, but Sewell and Orenstein[53] reported that the relationship was greatest among higher-status youth. They pointed out that the working-class boy can only have intimate contacts with adults who are in lower status occupations whether he lives in a small or a large community. These models do not have detailed knowledge of the work of high-status persons, do not have high aspirations for themselves, and probably recommend lower-status occupations to the youth. Thus, Sewell and Orenstein believe that a working-class boy encounters only limited stimulation whatever the size of his community. On the other hand, a high-status youth in a small community may have lower aspirations than a high-status youth in an urban area. First, he is exposed to a smaller range of occupations than his counterpart in a large city, and he can personally know only a few people in high-status positions. Second, the relevant adult models for small-town boys probably recommend occupations of lower status than would comparable adults in a large city who are better acquainted with job possibilities there. Third, the higher-status youth in the small community has only a limited number of contacts in his school and community; thus, he probably associates with peers who have low aspirations and is thereby influenced accordingly. Fourth, higher status rural parents may not be able to assist their children to obtain high-status urban positions because of their limited knowledge and influence, but urban families may have friends, relatives, and acquaintances who can assist a youth in the urban labor market.

One factor that may prevent rural youth from developing higher occupational ambitions is that their vocational training tends to be responsibility- and farm-oriented. Straus[54] noted that farm boys begin to work earlier than nonfarm boys, and few undertake any other jobs outside because most of their time is devoted to the family farm. In a study comparing the graduating seniors in a large urban community with those from a small rural community, Gaier and White[55] found that the rural youth were more likely to follow the "old-fashioned virtues, the principles, and philosophy of their parents." The rural youth tended to choose occupations and careers comparable to those of their parents and to reject, as their parents once did, post-high school education. Haller and Sewell[56] and Portes, Haller, and Sewell[57] said that when an adolescent boy plans a conventional career in farming, he is not likely to think of education as a means to attain a higher occupation. He will probably not be too receptive to new information and may lower the goals that significant others have for him. Rural youth may not try out various occupational opportunities that are available in large cities if they settle down to work in their own area and their friends and family encourage them to remain there.

Career Aspirations and Parental Occupations

Adolescents tend to aspire after the careers of their parents. For example, Hewer[58] showed that high school graduates whose fathers were in skilled trades tended to be interested in scientific and technical fields; those whose fathers were in business looked to business careers. A study of more than 350 seventh and eighth grade youngsters in an upper-middle-class school showed that boys' vocational preferences correlated with their fathers' but not their mothers' jobs; girls' preferences were related to the jobs of both parents, but especially to those of their mothers.[59] Werts[60] compared fathers' occupations with the career choices of more than 76,000 boys about to enter 246 institutions of higher education and found that the sons of physical scientists, social scientists, and medical men tended to "overchoose" the careers of their fathers. For example, 30 to 40 percent of the sons of physical scientists chose such careers as "engineer, chemist, physicist, architect, mathematician, biologist, and college scientist" as compared with 10 percent of the sons of medical men and 14 percent of the sons of social scientists. About 20 to 30 percent of the sons of social scientists chose such careers as "teacher, clergyman, college professor, social worker, and missionary" compared with 7 percent of the sons of physical scientists and 6 percent of the sons of men in medical fields. From 35 to 45 percent of the sons of medical men selected such careers as "veterinarian, pharmacist, dentist, and physician" compared with only 10 to 15 percent of the sons of physical and social scientists.

The quality of parental occupations has also been shown to exert considerable influence on youth's career-level aspirations. Smelser[61] found, for example, that boys from high-status, upwardly mobile families valued achievement, status, and mastery more than those from high-status, but stationary families. Smelser compared boys in the Berkeley growth study at 15½ years of age and again at 30 years of age from families that had revealed specific mobility strivings. He also found that those from high-status/upwardly mobile and low-status/upwardly mobile families made their occupational choices earlier, showed less variability in their job choices, and selected higher status jobs than did the boys from downwardly mobile families. And Viernstein and Hogan[62] have reported that highly talented young people vary in their career level aspirations as a function of their fathers' occupation and their parents' personality styles. In the study, youth who aspired to occupations one or more levels above those of their fathers were assumed to have high achievement aspirations and those who chose occupations at the same level or lower were assumed to have low achievement aspirations. The findings revealed that high-aspiring youth prefer activities in which they can understand and control physical, biological, and cultural phenomenon; the low-aspiring prefer activities that entail social, interpersonal, or human-relations skills. The data showed, too, that high-aspiring boys are positively influenced by both their mothers and their fathers. This was especially true where the mother was economically and socially ambitious and the family environment was fairly stable and characterized by low interpersonal tensions between the parents. On the other hand, high-aspiring girls model themselves after their fathers more than do low-aspiring. Girls "with high aspirations have profiles more similar to their fathers' profiles, whereas the low aspirers more closely resemble their mothers."[63]

Occupational Attractiveness

Adults may gauge whether they have chosen their occupations successfully in terms of income, recognition given by colleagues, standing in the community, attainment of objectives, or power and influence. They may assign each factor a different relative weight according to their particular life styles. Occupations that require extensive training, precise skills, and competition against relatively high standards usually receive the highest social ranking. A position acquires prestige if significant people evaluate it highly by bestowing respect, honor, and deference on its incumbent. The matter of occupational prestige is an important symbol of one's relative place in society.[64]

The prestige hierarchy of occupations is remarkably stable. First, rankings are stable when made across individuals at the same point in time. For example, Garbin[65] asked 490 persons, including freshmen college students, bankers, professors, secretaries, morticians, and manual workers, to rate the prestige of 30 occupations (including astrophysicist, physician, governor, factory operative, soldier, chauffeur, and garbage collector); he found only minor variations in the rankings. Garbin views the consensus as a form of "'stereotypical' judgments that are conveyed to societal members, irrespective of their positions in the social structure." Second, the prestige hierarchy of occupations is stable across time. Recent studies have shown that the rankings of occupations have remained stable for over 50 years—sex, age, socioeconomic status, ethnicity, and educational level, notwithstanding.[66] Bankers, physicians, and lawyers are ranked at the top of every list, for example, and janitors, hod carriers, and ditch diggers are listed at the bottom of all studies, beginning with one of the earliest in 1925.[67]

Although occupational prestige rankings are fairly stable in our society, they do tend to be affected by changes in perspective from childhood to adolescence. Lambert and Klineberg[68] investigated the vocational aspirations of 150 boys divided equally among 6 year olds, 10 year olds, and 14 year olds, half of whom were from lower-class families and half from middle-class families in 11 different countries, including France, Japan, Lebanon, and French Canada. The study revealed that boys of all ages were attracted to "glamorous and adventurous occupations (such as soldier, pilot, fireman, policeman and, particularly, truck driver)." However, there was "a progressive age trend from the more adventurous and glamorous occupations toward the more sober and mature occupational aspirations."[69] In a study aimed at analyzing age trends in ranking the prestige of various occupations, Gunn[70] asked 20 boys in each grade, from the first through the twelfth, to rank 11 jobs in order of their standing in the community. The typical boy in the first two grades was fairly egocentric, assigning a job top prestige if it also happened to be his father's job or if its requirements were of interest to him; for example, a "mechanic gets to 'jack up cars, oil them, stuff like that.'" Sometimes the boys rated jobs highly if they included activities that seemed to be dangerous, such as being a policeman or a butcher. In the first two grades, jobs tended to be ranked without reference to other jobs, but in grade 3, a status hierarchy started to emerge, and the typical boy began to list jobs in terms of their importance to the community. By the fourth, fifth, and sixth grades, almost no ranking was done in terms of a boy's personal interest in a job; now the physician (not the policeman) was given the highest prestige. In the seventh, eighth, and ninth grades, the boys increasingly used criteria like income, psychological rewards, and power—as well as community service—to assign prestige. Boys in the tenth, eleventh, and twelfth grades ranked occupations in essentially the same way as adults.

Nelson and McDonagh[71] conducted one of the most thorough studies of job attractiveness to adolescents. They started from the assumption that occupational status hierarchies are multidimensional and that the "image" of every occupation is a synthesis of several perspectives. They asked nearly 500 high school seniors to evaluate nine different professions in terms of 12 distinct characteristics of an "occupational man." From these evaluations, they obtained an image of each of the nine professions: business executive, clergyman, college professor, dentist, engineer, high school teacher, lawyer, physician, and social worker. The 12 components were divided into three groups: the *personal man*—general physical appearance, personality, intelligence, and honesty; the *receiving man*—prestige (admiration), power (influence), security (freedom from worry), and income; the *service man*—community activities, individual aid (helping other persons), altruism (sacrificing for others), and general value to the community. They found that adolescents hold two distinct images of these professions. The first image was a polar type, in which all or nearly all rankings clustered at one end or the other of the hierarchy. The business executive, for example, was at the low end; the clergyman and the physician were at the high end; the rankings for social worker, however, fell at both poles. The second image suggested a median type, in which the rankings were concentrated near the center. The college professor, high-school teacher, lawyer, engineer, and especially the dentist, tended to be in the center. Nelson and McDonagh's investigation thus showed how incumbents of these occupations would be regarded by youth as models. The following is a description of each of nine professions, as determined by the rankings:

Business executive: The business executive ranked in the upper third for general physical appearance, prestige, and income, and in the lower third for all of the other components except power, where the executive ranked sixth. The business person ranked last on honesty, security, and the four service variables.

Clergyman: The clergyman ranked in the upper third on all but three—general physical appearance (fifth), intelligence (seventh), and income (ninth). The profession ranked first on personality, honesty, power, individual aid, and altruism, respectively.

College professor: The college professor ranked in the middle third of the nine professions on six components. The professor was in the upper third on intelligence (first), honesty (second), and power (second), but was in the lower third on personality (eighth), individual aid (seventh), and general value to the community (seventh).

Dentist: The dentist was ranked in the middle third of the nine professions on eight components. The dentist was ranked first for security, but seventh for honesty, seventh for prestige, and ninth for power. Dentistry stood out from the other professions by virtue of the fact that security and power were at opposite extremes.

Engineer: The engineer rated in the upper third on general value to the community (third). The profession ranked in the middle third on six components, and in the lower third on power (eighth), individual aid (eighth), altruism (eighth), general physical appearance (ninth), and personality (ninth).

High school teacher: The high school teacher ranked in the upper third only for community activities (third). The teacher ranked in the middle third on eight components, and in the bottom third on prestige (eighth), general physical appearance (seventh), and income (seventh).

Lawyer: The lawyer ranked in the top third of the professions on four components, holding third place for general physical appearance, intelligence, power, and income, respectively. The lawyer ranked in the middle third on five components, and in the bottom third on honesty (eighth), community activities (eighth), and altruism (seventh).

Physician: The physician ranked in the top third on nine components, including first in prestige, income, and general value to the community, respectively. The profession rated in the middle third on power, and in the bottom third on security (eighth), and community activities (seventh).

Social worker: The social worker ranked in the top third on community activities (first), personality (second), altruism (second), and individual aid (third). The social worker ranked in the middle third on honesty, and in the bottom third on power (seventh), general physical appearance (eighth), income (eighth), general value to the community (eighth), prestige (ninth), and intelligence (ninth).

As the data Nelson and McDonagh[72] have compiled show, work that conveys the most significance and meaning is also the most attractive. Youth tend to evaluate as being highest in attractiveness those professions in which they can simultaneously realize several important considerations—helping others, working with people, expressing originality and creativity, being looked up to by others, making money, and being a leader.

CONCEPTUAL BASES OF CAREER DEVELOPMENT

For a long time, career specialists attempted mainly to match workers and occupations. Individuals wanted to know which occupations to enter, and vocational counselors tried to assess their aptitudes, skills, and interests and match them with the requirements of one or two occupations. Early career theorists assumed that persons developed traits in terms of their interests and abilities and that these traits tended to be both stable over time and susceptible to reliable measurement. They also assumed that individuals would be happiest when the demands and responsibilities of their chosen fields of work were commensurate with their trait profiles.[73] Consequently, a "matching method" arose, in which individuals were helped to better understand themselves in relation to opportunities and working conditions in different fields of work. The purpose of matching generally was to help a person find a job at some specific time—upon leaving school, changing a job, or being discharged from military service—and its appeal was in its "straight forward logic and relatively simple application."[74] The "matching method" has provided since the early 1900s a basis for career decision making that is still in widespread use, but it never has adequately accounted for developmental changes in motivation, interests, or skills. Indeed, the matching-method presents a developmentally *static* model of career decision making. One may have several jobs in one's lifetime, and the factors that make for a good match at one point in time may be quite different at another. An adolescent might be expected, for example, to develop a subservient role of his or her first job in a large corporation, and a healthy respect for authority might help the young person move into posts of increasing responsibility and stature, but in adulthood, where managerial demands might require initiative and boldness, the earlier subservience might be self-defeating.

The three relatively well-developed viewpoints presented below—self-concept development, cognitive-social growth, and life-style orientation—are representative of the emerging theories of career choice that take into account motivation and other developmental factors. The theories are speculative and lack extensive empircal verification, but as Borow[75] notes, they offer meaningful descriptions of occupational decision making as a developmental process, identify many of the personal, social, and economic factors that influence career decisions, indicate that the choice process is a multistage task in which evolving personal aspirations are linked with workforce considerations, and importantly, point to questions that may be framed as hypotheses and examined systematically.

Self-Concept Development—Super's Theory

In a very comprehensive review of career-development theories, Osipow[76] said that "no one has so intricately woven developmental hypotheses into career development as successfully as Super." Super holds that persons integrate various images of themselves into consistent self-concepts as they grow older. They will strive to preserve and enhance their self-concepts in all of their activities, including their occupations. Work-related choices constitute a sequence of developmental experiences that culminate not only in work roles but career patterns that will be consistent with the maturation of their self-images. Consequently, persons are motivated to select jobs that will enable them to fulfill roles and pursue interests that are commensurate with their evolving self-concepts. Every step in the career development process is an aspect of an individual's emotional, physical, and intellectual development. Super[77] believes that patterns of behavior become differentiated and integrated into habits and skills which, in childhood and adolescence, are manifested in the classroom, peer-group activities, athletics, community organizations, and part-time work. Aspirations are formulated, successes and failures are experienced, and increasingly realistic roles are performed, tested, and modified as the individual's self-concept develops and he or she achieves personality integration. Roles played out in childhood and adolescence foreshadow those an individual will seek in adulthood and are crucial to organizing a consistent concept of self.

Vocational choices are an important challenge to adolescents as they engage in the process of reality testing. "When the youth begins to look for a job, it is when he must demonstrate that his abilities, skills, and knowledge are worth paying for, and that his notions as to the kind of person he is and the kinds of things he can do are well-founded, that the crucial test is met."[78] One reason why an occupational choice represents a critical phase in the process of self-concept development is that it may encompass both strong commitment and involvement. Every vocational decision is a public declaration that "that is what I am;"[79] with deeper involvement, the adolescent has less freedom to determine the course of his or her life. The decision-making process is especially fraught with uncertainty since adolescents have no basis for even guessing if they will succeed in a chosen occupation. Galinsky and Fast point out that self-doubt, feelings of unworthiness, and fear of failure make it even more difficult to choose a job. Adolescents who believe that they cannot really do anything well or that they will inevitably fail are likely to change jobs frequently in the hope that "outer moorings might substitute for inner cohesion." These researchers suggest that occasionally people will accept a certain job in the belief that they will thereby take on the characteristics of successful persons in that field—as if they could put on a "magic cloak" and suddenly become what they have never been. Berger[80] has also observed that premature decisions, for example, announcing that one intends to be an engineer, architect, or nurse without knowing if one has the necessary talents, often turn out badly and are taken by the adolescent as a sign of failure. Berger suggested that high-school youth may not acquire a realistic understanding of their limitations if most of their schoolwork does not challenge them. They may develop a sense of omnipotence about their occupational future, believing that they can do well at just about anything if they try hard enough. Sometimes an adolescent will have an "either-or" attitude: "either I will be among the best in my field or I won't go into it—I refuse to be mediocre."[81]

The process of career planning ideally is made up of five activities that Super[82] calls vocational developmental tasks. The first of these—crystallization of a vocational preference—usually occurs between 14 and 18 years of age. Adolescents must develop ideas about work and concepts of themselves in order to make pertinent educational decisions. The second task—specification of a vocational program—Super said was characteristic of 18 to 21 year olds. Tentative vocational decisions made during the crystallization stage now become specific and, thus, the young person takes steps to acquire the necessary expertise; the prospective teacher, for example, will enroll in a teacher-training program. The third task—implementing the vocational preference—takes place when youth are about 21 to 24; by this time they are expected to have completed the initial phases of their training and to have obtained a beginning job. The fourth task—stabilization—usually occurs between 25 and 35; at this time individuals are expected to narrow their talents to particular fields of work and find personal satisfaction in fulfilling careers. Finally, the fifth task—consolidation—takes place after 35; at this time, individuals are expected to develop their expertise, strengthen their skills, and acquire status. It is assumed that they will gain seniority and respect as their careers advance.

Cognitive-Social Growth—Ginzberg's Theory

More than two decades ago, Ginzberg, Ginsburg, Axelrad, and Herma[83] advanced a still viable theory of the vocational decision-making process. It was developed at a time when psychoanalytic concepts dominated most theories of human development. Since it was widely believed that adolescence was a period of storm and stress, Ginzberg, et al. also assumed that stress inevitably affected vocational decision making. They believed that choosing an occupation was based on three key elements. First, every youth was required to make a series of decisions extending from perhaps age 11 or 12 to age 25. They divided the range in years into three major periods—*fantasy, tentative,* and *realistic* (each will be described below). Second, there was a strong element of irreversibility in the process. Every occupational decision was developmentally related to those that preceded it and those that would follow it. Since preparatory and educational experiences would be cumulative, options would narrow with increasing age, thus leading to irreversible occupational choices. Third, there was the matter of compromise. Every vocational decision required a balancing of aspirations, interests, and values with aptitudes, capacities, and work skills; the end result was inevitably a compromise.

Ginzberg[84] has reappraised each of the three original elements. His reformulated theory asserts that "occupational choice is a lifelong process of decision-making in which the individual seeks to find the optimal fit between his career preparation and goals and the realities of the world of work." At present, Ginzberg believes that the process of occupational decision making is "open-ended;" it may last as long as a working life and is not confined to the decade between adolescence and adulthood. Ginzberg realizes that many persons who decided early on a career and then dedicated themselves to it successfully for perhaps 20 years may, as a result of changes in their views or the work environment, seek another career. Three principal issues have affected his reasoning.

First there is the fact of personal feedback between the original choice and actual work experience. A person may want to begin a new career if his or her anticipated satisfactions in the first one fail to materialize or if he or she becomes aware of new job opportunities. Of course, the probability of starting a new career will depend on family circumstances, that is, if children are grown and if enough savings are available, and on whether there are pressures in the first job situation that compel looking for a new job.

Second, Ginzberg said that he and his colleagues were wrong to view the multiple educational and occupational decisions that a person makes between ages 15 and 25 as having an irreversible impact on his or her career. He now feels that decisions made before the age of 20 are not so crucial. Youth who graduate from high school may keep their options open by additional education and training. Those who do not graduate from high school may broaden their horizons and develop their skills through military service and subsequent qualification for the G.I. Bill, which will enable them to secure specialized training and reassess their occupational decisions. Ginzberg has also observed that the careers of noncollege youth are especially affected by whether they work for a large corporation that has training and promotional opportunities geared to seniority. Corporations have their own patterns of career development that supersede those made by individuals. On the matter of irreversibility, Ginzberg[85] asserted: "the principal challenge that young people face during their teens is to develop a strategy that will keep their options open, at least to the extent of assuring their admission to college or getting a job with a preferred employer."

Third, Ginzberg suggested that the term "optimization" is preferable to "compromise" in explaining how individuals arrive at a suitable balance between their preferences and the requirements of a job. He sees as continuous the search to find an occupation that will best meet changing desires and changing circumstances. As long as men and women want to change jobs, "they must consider a new balance in which they weigh the putative gains against the probable cost."

Although Ginzberg has revised his views in part, he still maintains his basic assumptions about vocational development in childhood and early adolescence. First, a period of *fantasy* appears to engulf the child until about 11 or 13 years of age. Although a child of four or five may state a specific choice when asked what it would like to be when it grows up, it makes little distinction between its desire and practical considerations. He or she may play at being a police officer, lawyer, or astronaut, but he or she has no conception of training requirements, availability of opportunities, or whether he or she has the necessary abilities and aptitudes. Sometime between 11 and 18 years of age, adolescents enter the *tentative* period, which has four distinct substages. The *interest* stage emerges around age 11 or 12; at this time, the youngster acquires the cognitive ability to have a reasoned interest in certain careers as well as specific likes and dislikes. The *capacity* stage follows around 12 to 14 years of age. At this point the adolescent raises questions about the required characteristics for various occupations and begins to evaluate his or her abilities accordingly. Between ages 15 and 16, the *value* stage appears. The adolescent now realizes that occupations offer different life styles and opportunities for self-fulfillment. At this time, the young person becomes cognizant of the socially relevant ways in which he or she may find self-expression; time takes on extended perspective, and work roles are seen as career patterns. Ginzberg's earlier views, based on psychoanalytic concepts, assumed that adolescents at the *value* stage would be filled with anxiety and urgency about making a career choice, sensing that any decision would be largely irreversible and that they were irrevocably committing themselves to a life-long career pattern. However, as pointed out, Ginzberg has disavowed irreversibility. The last substage in the tentative period is that of *transition,* occurring around 17 or 18 years of age. At this time, the adolescent faces the necessity of making relatively specific decisions about his or her occupational future, and he or she is likely to have increased freedom from the family to seek new surroundings in which to explore interests and test skills.

The *realistic* period follows the transition stage of the tentative period. Although Ginzberg originally held that the realistic period culminated before age 25, he now believes that options may be open for an individual throughout his or her working life.[86] His revised view is that this period is characterized by numerous cycles of exploration and crystallization. Ginzberg sees educational opportunities, work experiences, changes in aspirations, changes in financial resources, and the nature of the labor market as factors that constantly impel the individual to try to optimize the balance between his or her personal life style and the reality of the occupational world.

Life-Style Orientation—Holland's Typology

Whereas the self-concept development and cognitive-social growth theories attempt to explain how the process of vocational development occurs, Holland[87] has focused on analyses of the relationships between personality characteristics and vocational choice. Holland thus proposes a sophisticated version of the traditional practice of matching persons' personality attributes with the requirements of jobs. According to Holland, the choice of a vocation is an expression of personality; it is an attempt to implement personality style in the context of work. Every individual, he says, develops a hierarchy of orientations to cope with environmental tasks; he refers to the hierarchy as "the pattern of personal orientations." These personal coping styles or dispositions relate to six types of work orientation (see Table 3). Each type is made up of biological and cultural factors; habitual ways of coping with tasks; and certain abilities, aspirations, values, and self-concepts—a complex cluster of personal traits. Second, Holland believes that in making vocational choices individuals seek environments that are favorable to their personal orientations. Persons make changes in their vocational preferences, he says, because it leads to greater congruity, success, and satisfaction in their life styles. He holds, therefore, that it is possible to predict and understand decisions young people make regarding career options by relating their personality characteristics to the type of environment they prefer.

Table 3 lists six common personality types of Americans: realistic, intellectual, social, conventional, enterprising, and artistic.[88] The characteristics of each personality type are given together with several occupations chosen by persons representative of that type. Each description is called a model orientation; the model that an individual most closely resembles in his or her personality type. A "profile" can be prepared for an individual by measuring the extent to which that person resembles each of the six types.

Holland[89] has developed a vocational guidance instrument called "The Self-Directed Search (SDS) for Educational and Vocational Planning," which is self-administered and self-scoring. The SDS has two main purposes: "to provide a vocational counseling experience for people who do not have access to counselors or who cannot afford their services, and to multiply the number of people a

Table 3
The Personality Types and the Vocational Preferences Defining Each Type

Realistic. The model type is masculine, physically strong, unsociable, aggressive; has good motor coordination and skill; lacks verbal and interpersonal skills; prefers concrete to abstract problems; conceives of self as being aggressive and masculine and as having conventional political and economic values. Persons who choose or prefer the following occupations resemble this type: airplane mechanic, construction inspector, electrician, filling station attendant, fish and wildlife specialist, locomotive engineer, master plumber, photoengraver, power shovel operator, power station operator, radio operator, surveyor, tree surgeon, tool designer.

Intellectual. The model type is task-oriented, intraceptive, asocial; prefers to think through rather than act out problems; needs to understand; enjoys ambiguous work tasks; has unconventional values and attitudes; is anal as opposed to oral. Vocational preferences include aeronautical design engineer, anthropologist, astronomer, biologist, botanist, chemist, editor of a scientific journal, geologist, independent research scientist, meterologist, physicist, scientific research worker, writer of scientific or technical articles, zoologist.

Social. The model type is sociable, responsible, feminine, humanistic, religious; needs attention; has verbal and interpersonal skills; avoids intellectual problem solving, physical activity, and highly ordered activities; prefers to solve problems through feelings and interpersonal manipulations of others; is orally dependent. Vocational preferences include assistant city school superintendent, clinical psychologist, director of welfare agency, foreign missionary, high school teacher, juvenile delinquency expert, marriage counselor, personal counselor, physical education teacher, playground director, psychiatric case worker, social science teacher, speech therapist, vocational counselor.

Conventional. The model type prefers structured verbal and numerical activities and subordinate roles; is conforming (extraceptive); avoids ambiguous situations and problems involving interpersonal relationships and physical skills; is effective at well-structured tasks; identifies with power; values material possessions and status. Vocational preferences include: bank examiner, bank teller, bookkeeper, budget reviewer, cost estimator, court stenographer, financial analyst, IBM equipment operator, inventory controller, payroll clerk, quality control expert, statistician, tax expert, traffic manager.

Enterprising. The model type has verbal skills for selling, dominating, leading; conceives of himself or herself as a strong leader; avoids well-defined language or work situations requiring long periods of intellectual effort; is extraceptive; differs from the Conventional type in that he or she prefers ambiguous social tasks and has a greater concern with power, status, and leadership; is orally aggressive. Vocational preferences include business executive, buyer, hotel manager, industrial relations consultant, manufacturer's representative, master of ceremonies, political campaign manager, real-estate salesperson, restaurant worker, speculator, sports promoter, stock and bond salesperson, television producer, traveling salesperson.

Table 3 (Continued)

Artistic. The model type is asocial; avoids problems that are highly structured or require gross physical skills; resembles the Intellectual type in being intraceptive and asocial; but differs from that type in that he or she has a need for individualistic expression, has less ego strength, is more feminine, and suffers more frequently from emotional disturbances; prefers dealing with environmental problems through self-expression in artistic media. Vocational preferences include art dealer, author, cartoonist, commercial artist, composer, concert singer, dramatic coach, free-lance writer, musical arranger, musician, playwright, poet, stage director, symphony conductor.

Source: J. L. Holland. *The psychology of vocational choice.* Waltham, Mass.: Blaisdell, 1966. Reprinted by permission.

counselor can serve."[90] There are two booklets—one for self-assessment and one for occupational classifications. The assessment booklet includes checklists of preferred activities, competencies, occupational preferences, and self-ratings. The individual scores his or her responses and organizes his or her results into a profile, which shows the degree of resemblance to each of Holland's personality types. The letters of the three highest scale scores form a three-letter summary. An adolescent with the code RSC would resemble the realistic, social, and conventional personality types in that order. The occupational classification booklet lists 414 occupations which are organized according to the three-letter codes. The adolescent is asked to use his or her summary code to list the occupations in the classification booklet that exactly match his or her code, as well as those that correspond to all permutations of the letters in it. The validity of the SDS depends on Holland's theory of personality types; O'Connell and Sedlacek[91] reported that the SDS is highly reliable, and Zener[92] said that it can be of great assistance to guidance counselors in helping young people become better acquainted with educational opportunities and more aware of the relationships between their own personal attributes and those required for various occupations.

CAREER EDUCATION

Career education has spread to each of the 50 states; several have passed career-education laws; more than 25 state departments have promulgated policies on curricula; 5,000 school districts nationwide have formally introduced career education in their schools.[93] In Dallas, a $23 million Skyline Career

Development Center opened in 1971. Curriculum guides, testing materials, and books on the implementation of career education abound. A small allocation of discretionary funds in 1971 from the United States Office of Education launched the effort, and by 1974, $61 million in federal support had been appropriated. Congress probably will spend an additional $250 to $300 million on career education by 1980.

Career education received its current impetus in 1971 when Sidney P. Marland, then Commissioner of the United States Office of Education, declared: "If education is to serve properly its national purpose, then we must bridge the gulf between man and his work. . . . Our job is not done properly, in other words, until each and every one of those youngsters is capable of developing a clear sense of direction in life and enabled to make a responsible career choice."[94] Marland's concern stems from the widespread belief that young people often make career decisions on the basis of very little information. They

Providing career information at an appropriate level of understanding is an important component of career education.

may have limited understanding of their aptitudes, interests, values, and skills. They are thus uncertain about the meaning of the choices and decisions they make. The limited occupational and career information that they do obtain often is presented to them as isolated facts, and consequently, they find it void of psychological meaning and are unable to fit it into their developing life styles. Lacking information about available options, and unable to obtain access to role models as they go about their work activities, they make inappropriate and unrealistic career choices on the basis of glamorous and stereotypical images. Career education thus represents a call for educational reform. It seeks to correct such primary criticisms of the American educational system as:[95]

1. Many persons leave the system without the basic academic skills required to adapt to today's changing society.
2. Many students fail to see meaningful relationships between what they are being asked to learn in school and what they will do when they leave the system.
3. Many persons leave the system at both the secondary and collegiate levels unequipped with the vocational skills, the self-understanding and career decision-making skills, or the work attitudes essential for making a successful transition from school to work.

Programs in career education aim to change the educational system by increasing systematically the career options available to young people and by facilitating rational career planning. Marland[96] holds that young people will appreciate career education for its realism, educators will endorse its relevance, taxpapers will welcome its congruence with societal needs, and business and industry will respect its practicality and efficiency. He views career education as a wholly new concept and predicts that eventually its impact will be substantial. Career education will span the entire range of school programs—kindergarten, elementary, secondary, postsecondary, adult, and continuing education. The program would be sequenced to provide simultaneously self-understanding, career awareness, employable skills, and decision-making prowess. It would provide young people with two basic options at several points in their educational development: continue in education or enter the work force. According to the educational amendments passed by Congress in 1974, career education is an educational process designed:[97]

(1) to increase the relationship between schools and society as a whole;
(2) to provide opportunities for counseling; guidance and career development for all children;

(3) to relate the subject matter of the curricula of schools to the needs of persons to function in society;

(4) to extend the concept of the education process beyond the school into the area of employment and the community;

(5) to foster flexibility in attitudes, skills, and knowledge in order to enable persons to cope with accelerating change and obsolescence;

(6) to make education more relevant to employment and functioning in society; and

(7) to eliminate any distinction between education for vocational purposes and general or academic education.

Career education thus calls for placing the saving-and-work ethic high among the ideological priorities of public education and affirming that all phases of the curricula should be oriented toward the world of work. Students leaving school would be expected to possess immediately marketable skills and to be knowledgeable about the availability and requirements of jobs appropriate to their level of education. Children in the elementary school thus would be exposed to the general kinds of work available to adults and be taught an appreciation of work. Elementary teachers might introduce practical problems such as estimating product costs in arithmetic or simulating work experiences by actually producing a product. Young people in junior and secondary high schools would be directed toward choosing future work roles and acquiring specific skills. Grades 7 through 10 would be reserved for "career education," for example, experiences in which students would become familiar with groups of occupations—career clusters—and begin to make tentative choices about specialization. The last two grades of high school would be devoted to specialized training in the cluster chosen earlier. A cluster might consist of careers within a single industrial sector, and each high school graduate would learn a set of marketable skills in the one he or she has chosen. Career education would also be open to adults; those who wish to advance or change their careers or who had lost their jobs would have opportunity to become retrained for other work. Figure 1 illustrates a school-based career-education model.[98] It shows developmentally how career awareness leads to career exploration and career preparation. The plan for integrating the model into the school curricula is presented in Figure 2, which shows 12 basic career clusters. The design covers most occupations and it indicates how occupational experiences can be arranged in a developmental sequence.[99]

According to Figure 2, children from kindergarten through grade 3 would begin to explore occupations from two general perspectives—"goods" and "services"—while they develop skills in reading, writing, arithmetic, history,

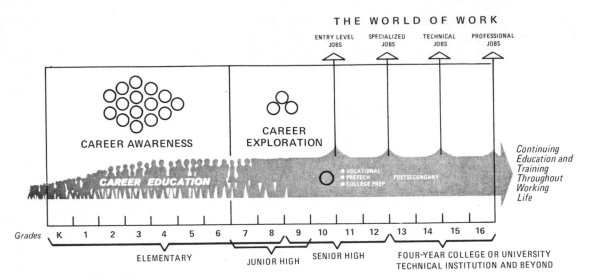

Figure 1
An example of a career education model. (From DHEW Publication No. (OE) 72-39.
Reprinted by permission.)

languages, and the physical and social sciences. From grades four through six,
the clusters would encompass industry, commerce, the arts, and so forth. By
grades seven, eight, and nine, the student is expected to be developmentally
ready for exposure to career-exploratory experiences in all 12 clusters. For
example, in the "transportation occupations" cluster, young people would
become aware of such diverse occupational areas as aerospace, pipeline, road,
and water transportation. They would be made aware of the hundreds of jobs
available in each area, relationships among the jobs, and how the jobs would
relate to themselves as well as to other members of society. The same exposure
would be provided in the "health occupations" cluster, with possibilities in
accident prevention, pharmacology, and medical and dental sciences. In grades
seven through nine, young people would examine those clusters in which they
are most interested. By the end of the tenth grade, they would have developed
elementary job entry skills—as typists, construction helpers, social work aides,
service station attendants, or environmental technician aides—skills that they
can pursue if they do not complete the twelfth grade. If they complete the
twelfth grade, they are prepared to enter the world of work or to continue their
education at a college or vocational school.

The idea of organizing the occupational world in terms of career clusters,
conceptualizing occupational experiences as a developmental sequence, and

introducing an education-for-work ideology into the school curricula is intriguing, especially if one believes that schools have indeed isolated young people from work, thus making it into an abstraction for them. But the model may prove difficult to implement. Swanson[100] points out that relatively small schools would encounter practical problems in attempting to cover each of the occupational clusters and in providing opportunities for a wide range of work experiences. He suggests also that it may be unrealistic to presume that children will move in any meaningful way through the career clusters by the time they reach sixth grade. If the concept of careers proves to be too remote for elementary school-age children, a great deal of superficiality may result. Moreover, since the youngsters must shift at the sixth grade from emphasis on career awareness to career exploration experiences, the middle school plays a key role in the success of the entire career-education effort, and a herculean implementation effort at this time would be necessary.

Career education has also been severely criticized on the grounds that it aims primarily to match potential workers with existing jobs, taking the economic structure and corporate order for granted.[101] On the one hand, American educators are urged to accept, "as an unquestioned social ideal," an image of the industrial society that emphasizes personal achievement, upward mobility,

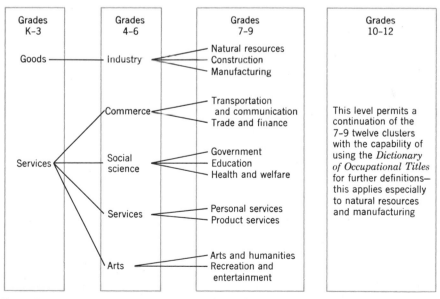

Figure 2
Occupational clusters for delivering CCEM objectives by grade level. (From Miller, see text. Reprinted by permission.)

increasing economic growth, and technical resolutions of social problems. But many young people, Nash and Agne note, question whether a career couched in terms of the expectations of an advanced industrial society is for them, and they ask for opportunities to explore alternative life styles.[102] The researchers contend that career education promotes "a view of life superficially utilitarian," which would lead, first, to "specialism," by filtering knowledge through the clusters and by neglecting aspects of growth associated with the arts, humanities, and religion; second, to preoccupation with marketable skills, by overlooking the value of skills "which may be probing, questioning, noninstrumental, and confrontive;" and third, to a tyranny of credentials, by emphasizing product-oriented, system-serving, adult-imposed performance criteria.

Grubb and Lazerson[103] point to the disturbing prospect that career education will foster false hopes about upward mobility. They note that career education is designed explicitly to prepare students for entry-level jobs and that it cannot prepare them for an upward progression of jobs. Grubb and Lazerson argue that relatively few jobs are arranged in career ladders of any length and contend that the declaration that career education will prepare individuals more for careers than dead-end jobs is based on a misconception of the world of work. The researchers observe that most workers encounter short career ladders and that mobility is more horizontal than vertical—to different jobs that require about the same level of skill and responsibility. Therefore, they assert, "career education is not directed at resolving social problems, developing avenues of upward mobility, or making school and work more satisfying experiences. It is aimed at reducing expectations, limiting aspirations, and increasing commitments to the existing social structure."[104] Many minority parents, consequently, fear that career education might become a device to limit rather than to enhance the upward mobility of their children by relegating them to programs oriented vocationally rather than academically.

Grubb and Lazerson also point out that while most persons value work in the abstract, they are aware that many available jobs lack the moral qualities attributed to work generally. Most work is viewed as boring. It is characterized by unvaried routine, simplicity of tasks, and constant supervision. Many workers fail to develop feelings of competence, responsibility, and accomplishment. Their relations are mediated by impersonal market relationships and their isolation from one another denies them a sense of connectedness with their fellow workers and the rest of the economy. Hence, "given the negative aspects of most jobs, the introduction of 'real work' in the schools might have just the opposite effect from that intended: feelings of alienation, anomie, and disconnectedness, or physical manifestations such as hypertension, high blood pressure, and poor mental health might begin earlier."[105]

The conceptual problems associated with a work-oriented view of career education, in which personal success or failure is tied to economic success or failure, has led a growing body of career educators to advocate a career pedagogy that fosters adolescent growth not only toward work but throughout life. According to O'Toole,[106] "career education can deal with the unemployed self by encouraging learning through experience." Schools, thus, might prepare youth to look, as they grow older, for stimulation and rewards in any experience—both in their leisure and in their work. O'Toole would equip young people to find educational experiences even in the poorest of jobs. He would not try to lower the expectations of young people through teaching them that bad jobs are their assigned lot in life, but he would seek to instill *realistic* expectations. Feingold[107] adds that career education should provide "entrances, more convenient exits, stopouts, and recreation routes as interests, conditions, abilities, and potential change." Career education, he says, must recognize alternative styles of learning—open schools, home study, and credit for experiences in work, travel, and leisure. Such breadth can make both study and work more meaningful, for school can become the real world, not something merely akin to it. Both Feingold and O'Toole view career education as a way of enabling persons to participate in life-long patterns of education.

The basis for conceptualizing career education as a life-long process has been outlined by Hoyt[108] who starts from the assumption that both one's career and one's education extend from the preschool through the retirement years. Career education and education in general would be for all persons—young and old, mentally handicapped and intellectually gifted, poor and wealthy, male and female, elementary school pupil and college student. Hoyt believes that the cosmopolitan nature of society demands that career education embrace a multiplicity of work values rather than a single work ethic. Work thus would include paid employment and unpaid activities in which one engages as part of leisure and/or recreational time. A career-education program would help all individuals become motivated toward work, acquire the skills necessary for work, and find ways of engaging in work that is both beneficial to society and personally satisfying. The career-education programs of the future, then, would be designed primarily to reduce distinctions between work and leisure and to deemphasize the "marketability" of a career in favor of stressing its potential for self-realization.

Beyond Career Education: The Integration of Schooling and Work

During the eighteenth century the family had major responsibility for opening social roles to youth and dominated the influences that affected their transition to work status. When the family was influential in youth's transition, acquisition of work roles was more a matter of ascription than achievement, and the family's status largely conditioned the range of available opportunities. Schooling at the time was an option, and one engaged in formal schooling to augment the competencies demanded by living and doing. But as demands grew in the nineteenth century to extend literacy training and to make schooling compulsory, the school began to supplant the family in socializing the young; first, in training them for citizenship, and later, in preparing them for work. The history of the American high school has been marked by an accumulation of responsibilities, and as a consequence, it now holds youth in a dependent status and shields them from productive work.[109] The school has replaced the experiential learning that once took place in the family and workplace with the "student role" in which adolescents wait to be taught. The school has kept the classroom as its main mode of teaching, and as it has changed emphases in socialization from learning through experience to learning via instruction; it has reduced the student role to a passive one in which the adolescents are always in preparation for active work but never actually engaged in it. One consequence of separating learning from action and experience has been to segregate youth from adults. They have been removed from the labor market and their contacts with adult models in working situations has become highly limited. Moreover, the contacts that they do have with adults ensue from highly specialized relationships, and they meet them less as persons than as technicians or specific subject-matter experts—as teachers, dentists, lawyers, doctors, garage mechanics, and so forth.[110]

Because the functions of the high school are largely isolated from the workplace, youth interested in work generally must find out about the availability of jobs on their own. One would hope that the process would involve talking with parents, school counselors, teachers, workers, and local employers in their community. However, a national sample of 32,000 eighth, ninth, and eleventh grade youth from 200 schools and 33 states shows that half of the eleventh graders said that they had received little or no help in career planning from their counselors or schools, 37 percent said that they received some help, and only 13 percent said that they had received "a lot of help."[111] More than 90 percent of the eleventh graders indicated that they had discussed their work plans with a parent, relative, or guardian, but over 40 percent said that they never had talked with workers in the jobs that interested them and never had discussed with a counselor or teacher relationships between the jobs that they were considering and their personal goals, interests, and aptitudes. Further, over two-thirds had never taken a survey course about the world of work or attended a "job fair" or "career day." On the whole, eighth and ninth graders had received even less help than eleventh graders, and girls had obtained less help than boys. A substantial number of young people apparently have little involvement with career planning activities at a time when career-related decisions acquire critical importance.[112]

Youth still in high school may look to work for a variety of reasons. Many of them seek part-time work, not because it will necessarily complement their academic goals, but perhaps to achieve a measure of economic independence from their families, develop disciplined work habits, acquire sophistication in job-hunting methods, and learn about the workplace. Other in-school youth look for work hoping to find activities that will directly relate to their ambitions, for example, clerking in a law office in anticipation of law school, serving as a hospital orderly in preparation for a pre-med program, or selling as a salesperson in a retail store before beginning one's own business.

Whether youth approach the workforce in school or out of school, its structure has given rise to two serious problems that they must confront—unemployment and underemployment. On the one hand, unemployment among youth has become widespread, especially for minority youth in urban ghettos. Wirtz[113] has observed that during any particular month in the mid-1970s between a million and a half and two million young people were looking for work and were unable to find it. The youth unemployment rate was about 20 percent in 1975, about three times as high as the rate for adults. But the unemployment rate was

Socialization is facilitated when business enterprises offer young people part-time work.

even higher among black, Mexican-American, Puerto Rican, and native-American youth—where it soared to approximately 40 percent. On the other hand, youth who prolong their education, aspiring to better jobs and more satisfying careers, are likely to become disenchanted and frustrated when they find that opportunities in the workplace lead mainly to underemployment—to jobs for which they have been overtrained. Where, Berger[114] asks, "is the occupational structure to take care of the large number of young people with aspirations for high-income, high-status, and high-'meaning' jobs." O'Toole describes the dilemma as follows:[115]

The rub is that no industrialized nation has been able to produce an adequate number of jobs that provide the status and require the skills and educational levels that their workforces are achieving. By way of analogy, the situation is nearly Malthusian in its proportions: Levels of educational attainment have tended to grow in almost geometric progression while the number of jobs that require higher levels of education has tended to grow at a much slower pace. . . . There simply are not enough good jobs to go around to everyone who thinks he deserves one.

The basic labor problem in the American society is a shortage of jobs—skilled and unskilled—rather than a shortage of skilled individuals. One fact is inescapably clear—there is no single or easy solution to contemporary workforce problems. But one may attack the problem from two fundamentally different perspectives: either (1) alter the structure of demand for labor, thus bringing opportunities in the workforce in line with occupational expectations, or (2) realign occupational aspirations through education to fit the realities of the labor market, on the assumption that its structure is largely fixed. The two perspectives obviously interrelate in that it is possible to modify both the demand and supply characteristics of the labor market; however, for purpose of discussion here, each is discussed separately below:

Changing the Structure of the Workforce. A "functional rationality" has long governed the forces that control the labor market, but as Berger[116] observes, "a basic fissure" lies between the enterprises promoted by industrial economics and the rising ethos of young people who are seeking meaning and self-realization in the work they perform. Many knowledgeable analysts of present public policies and economic practices believe that it will be necessary to "humanize and democratize the workplace and the institutions which prepare people for work" to resolve the problem.[117] The ideology of meaningfulness presumes that even in apparently tedious tasks, worker participation can be enhanced by helping persons who are interested learn the rationale behind their activities. The theory behind industrial practices, for example, may be made accessible to those on the assembly line as well as to those in management. Consider the following illustration of a way in which relations within the labor market may be restructured to broaden the base of job meaningfulness.[118]

It is recognized that the maker of light bulbs will quickly learn everything that there is to know about his actual job. Therefore, a system of continuing learning has been established, the goal of which is to permit the worker to learn the theory behind industrial practices. The curious light bulb maker might thus be given the resources to learn the physics of light and electricity, about the sources and chemistry of tungsten, manganese, and neon, and about the engineering principles on which the machines that make the light bulb were designed. In short, there is no limit to how deep or how broad the worker might pursue knowledge about his work. . . . Each worker should be given the tools to find all that is interesting and ennobling about his work. And, unlike job redesign, the dull or unwilling worker is not forced into accepting a challenge that he doesn't want or is incapable of handling—there is no coercion to learn or accept responsibility.

Another approach to changing the workforce structure would be to realign relationships among traditional work roles by creating new types of employment. Berger[119] calls for governmental intervention to open up a large number of new jobs that would bridge the human relations gap between individuals and the institutions of society. Berger advocates creating "people work"—"to serve the more subtle—but nonetheless real—interpersonal and psychological needs of groups and individuals." The possibilities include new social services for the very young and the very old, new therapeutic services for every age, new agencies for community development, political participation, intergroup conflict resolution, and new super agencies to coordinate programs and resolve jurisdictional disputes between agencies.

Whether the workforce is democratized, whether its responsiveness to personal fulfillment is heightened, or whether other alternatives evolve, the issue is clear: Can the structure of the workforce in contemporary America adapt itself to the waiting adolescents who aspire to meaningful employment?

Realigning Occupational Aspirations through Education. The structure of the workforce appears to be moving to accommodate an ideology of meaningfulness, but the transition will not be dramatically swift; most adolescents in the twentieth century will encounter a relatively fixed workforce structure, and they will have to find meaningfulness pretty much in the forms that it is presently available in the job market. A coordination of work opportunities and educational systems simultaneously at national, state, and community levels, therefore, is necessary to ensure that their aspirations align with the realities of the job market. The aim of such coordination would be to develop a national labor policy that would enable all American youth, on the basis of their aspirations and abilities, to find a niche for themselves in the existing workforce structure. One might introduce a totalitarian system whereby the government regulates both schooling and job market so that only those who can be absorbed into the system are educated. This model would abandon all young people to their own devices except those that the state chooses to utilize. Such a solution, however, is patently undemocratic in a society that prides itself on the options it provides young people. One might also attempt to reduce the disparity between the expectations of youth and the reality of the workforce by introducing a system of compulsory vocational education of sufficient breadth and magnitude to parallel the current emphasis on general and preprofessional curricula, but this would create a dual-track system, leading to sharp distinctions between the middle and the lower classes. It is undemocratic, too, for it disregards developmental differences in motivation and aspiration levels, and it foreordains the occupational future of children to the extent that they are assigned to one or the other track at an early age.

Two recent projections of labor policy for youth are more in keeping with democratic principles, and each is receiving a great deal of attention. The first is contained in a report made by a subcommittee, Panel on Youth, of the President's Science Advisory Committee,[120] and the second is based on education-work policy developed for the National Manpower Institute.[121] The proponents of both models share a common interest in removing barriers related to youth employment in present child labor laws, compulsory attendance regulations, prohibitions against youth working in hazardous occupations, and statutory measures regarding minimum wages. Child labor laws were enacted early in the century to keep young people out of the workplace, preventing their exploitation, but more importantly, to provide the school with opportunity to train a literate and enlightened workforce for burgeoning industry. The problem is that these laws operate today to deny forms of work experience that might, in fact, be valuable to young people. Many aspects of jobs for the young are no longer hazardous. Although only 5 percent of all employment is foreclosed to 16 and 17 year olds by federal and state legislation, many employers are concerned about violating the laws and are consequently reluctant to hire anybody under 18. And when competition for work is particularly keen, a lower minimum wage in selected areas might help some youth gain access to work that would otherwise be denied them.

The Panel on Youth report starts from the assumption that schools emphasize cognitive training primarily and that alternative modes of experiential learning must be provided youth through work and in other social contexts. The report advanced policy recommendations in six areas: (1) to change the structure of the high school to provide more options; (2) to integrate part-time work and part-time schooling (3) to establish residential youth communities; (4) to eradicate such legal barriers as minimum wages that impede youth from taking advantage of work opportunities; (5) to support education after age 16 with a voucher plan; and (6) to develop federally funded public service programs. The National Manpower Institute report starts from the assumption that work and education must be coordinated by governmental agencies. It would establish education-work councils in 25 cities and rural communities, through which local school officials, employers, members of labor unions, and members of the public could develop and administer programs that integrate education and work. The councils would also maintain a comprehensive recording system to provide both long-term and medium-term projections of workforce needs. The report advocates, too, that all high schools offer every adolescent a minimum of five hours per year of career guidance and counseling, opportunity for a minimum of 500 hours of work or service experience, and the right to work for at least a year between the ages of 16 and 20. Finally, it recommends that adults be entitled to attend secondary schools, that individuals in training programs be eligible for unemployment insurance, and that work institutes be established to assist persons achieve maximum satisfaction from their work.

The two reports are noteworthy for the national attention they focus on the necessity of integrating the schooling adolescents receive in formal instruction and in society at large. Whether education-work councils or something akin to them are established, a great deal of collaborative effort will be required before the rhetoric can be translated into action. A commitment to change and willingness to share programs and control of resources for a common good must be the basis of education/work integration. This means that individuals who work in educational institutions and the social bureaucracies (community agencies, businesses, and industries) would have to find common bases on which to share their contributions and responsibilities. Fortunately, cooperative programs have been implemented on a small scale in several parts of the country, and these may serve as excellent models for future planning. The programs have usually been thought of as examples of *action-learning,* and they have been designed to provide youth with realistic, experience-based alternatives (in community agencies, businesses, and industries) to traditional classroom activities. Action-learning is defined as "learning from experience and associated study that is or could be accredited by an educational institution."[122] It provides youth with planned, school-organized activities that offer a chance to learn by doing.[123] According to Graham, action-learning encompasses the experiential learning components of such programs as work-study, cooperative education, work-service, service-learning, career education, and most forms of internship, on-the-job training, and self-directed work and study. Action-learning, therefore, may include tutoring young children, learning activities associated with work in retail stores and mental health clinics, studies of municipal and civic problems, and paraprofessional assignments in classrooms, city government agencies, union headquarters, and welfare agencies. Youth who participate in school-supervised action-learning programs apparently are more satisfied with their jobs and the meaning the experiences hold for them than are youth who obtain part-time jobs on their own. Silberman[124] surveyed nearly 2,000 high-school youth, about two-thirds of whom participated in 50 action-learning programs and about one-third who simply held part-time jobs. The youth who participated in the action-learning programs were significantly more satisfied with their work. The greater satisfaction of these youth was derived from social climates that facilitated teamwork, the availability of adult role models, the meaningfulness of work, and the feedback that the youth obtained regarding their performances.

Action-learning programs up to the present have been conducted at the local school district level. But they point to the kinds of alternatives to traditional schooling that eventually may become available to youth on a comprehensive, perhaps national scale. The variety of programs in service is vast indeed, yet they generally fall into one of three distinct types relative to whether they provide remuneration and/or academic credit. The three types are illustrated below. Features of each may be readily implemented on a nationwide scale.

1. Remuneration *and* academic credit. The work-study framework provides a contemporary prototype for programs that offer students both remuneration and academic credit. These programs flourish today in several forms, ranging from high school cooperative education programs, in which youth may spend half of each day at work on a job and half at school, to industry-sponsored educational programs, for which participating workers may be given released time. A school advisor generally is assigned to assist work-study youth find jobs in which they can develop their work skills and to help them plan their academic programs to accommodate their work schedules.[125] Although academic credit is often given for the work experience, school officials usually are reluctant to treat it as a substitute for requirements in the academic program. Viewing work-study as an academic elective protects students who

change their goals as they progress through high school.[126] Remunerative work in a setting with adults engaged in similar work, however, frequently facilitates youth's transition to the work force, and when work experience is the final course in a program of study, it sometimes is allowed wide latitude as an alternative for graduation requirements.

2. Academic credit—no remuneration. Whereas work-study programs integrate school and work largely to prepare young people for entering into the workforce, a new form of experiential learning is emerging that enables youth to obtain first-hand information about careers. These are the school-supervised voluntary service programs; they are managed much like work-study, and today they are part of a new educational idea called human services education.[127] Work-for-pay situations are limited, especially in professional fields, but volunteerism in human services education provides access to a limitless variety of careers. When services are free, youth are able to investigate roles in the workforce that especially interest them, for example, teaching, law, medicine, fine arts, and business management. A human services education program is likely to encompass a tremendous heterogeneity of service opportunities, and to maintain program integrity, most schools stipulate that each student draw a contract that specifies (1) his or her obligations, (2) the expectations of those in the service agencies, (3) the school's supervisory role, and (4) the amount of academic credit to be granted for the voluntary service. The contract first is reviewed by the student's advisor to ensure that it is consistent with the student's future educational plans. It is then signed by the student, his or her parents, the cooperating agency, and the program director. Each contract usually covers one semester, with option for renewal, and may specify that a semester hour credit will be granted for between 40 and 100 hours of service performed. On-site visits by school personnel may serve to check attendance and performance quality. A participating student will probably be asked to maintain anecdotal records of experiences and perhaps will write a final report summarizing his or her experiences.

3. No remuneration—no academic credit. The Census Bureau estimates that 20 percent of the total youth population, 14 to 24 years of age, participate informally in part-time volunteer work, involving religious, educational, health, recreational, and community activities. From 1965 to 1975 the rate of participation among adolescents in volunteer activities nearly doubled. There are today nearly as many volunteers as job holders among 14 to 17 year olds and the volunteers average about eight hours per week of service.[128] Hedin and Conrad[129] indicate that high schools might facilitate the development of informal, voluntary service programs by organizing them around students'

free time. Sometimes the voluntary service may be arranged during either unscheduled periods or study hall sessions, especially if it can be placed near lunch or at the end of the day. The investigators described a program in which the students themselves developed a catalog of service opportunities. It became the basis for a "volunteer's bureau," which the youth operated during the school year without pay. The bureau served as a central clearing house for a number of voluntary school-community interactions; the youth who had the time and interest came into the bureau to find out what was available, and if they found an interesting opportunity, after checking it out personally, they signed a "contract" to carry out the volunteer service. Although both the quality of the service and meaningfulness of the experience were reviewed, no grades or credit were given for the work.

SUMMARY

A national survey shows that more males than females and more dropouts than graduates of high school are employed in agriculture; however, the majority of youth out of school are employed in manufacturing and trades. The quality of youth's work experience today, however, appears more tentative and juvenile than it did during earlier generations.

A work ideology is emerging that stresses the quality of the activity. Young people are emphasizing that work should have intrinsic meaning—challenge, responsibility, accomplishment, and value to society. Young men see instrumental values (being looked up to by others, independence, making money, and leadership) as especially important factors in their selection of a job or career, and young women prefer expressive values (opportunities to be helpful to others, useful to society, and work with people), but the two sexes are equally interested in creativity, the world of ideas, steady progress, and avoidance of pressure.

Career planning is difficult because few younger adolescents possess well-conceptualized values or significant understanding of different occupations. Any match between life style and career planning during the early years of high school is likely to be quite unstable, but with increasing age, interest and career plans emerge and become more internally consistent as adolescents achieve greater insight into their own abilities and the demands of different occupations.

The realism of career planning is affected by a number of factors. Low-income youth, especially from ethnic minorities, tend to assume superficially high aspirations and expectations, perhaps because they seek to conform to cultural emphases on achievement or to avoid acceptance of the constraints reality imposes. Young women are beginning to recognize that life may hold more for them than homemaking, and the feminist movement is leading them to view a career in work as equal or as even more important than those of wife and mother. Research suggests, however, that adolescent girls generally believe that women have little hope of achieving positions of leadership and responsibility. Two strategies are thus suggested for bringing into congruence the occupational expectations of young women and the work opportunities available to them. The first emphasizes that change must be introduced early in socialization, and the second stresses the importance of career exploration during adolescence. Further, studies suggest that youth from rural areas and smaller communities aspire to lower prestige and less well-paid occupations that those from urban areas. Another important factor in occupational choice is the father's occupation. A father who holds a prestigious, instrumental, highly paid position is likely to be viewed favorably by both sons and daughters. Egocentrism may affect the criteria by which young people rank occupations in attractiveness. Children are likely to be attracted to occupations on the basis of glamorous and adventurous features whereas adolescents probably will be interested in them in terms of income, psychological rewards, power, and community service.

The socializing experiences that lead adolescents to make career commitments are made up of many factors, and several theories have emerged to explain how career planning takes place. According to Osipow, these theories assume that vocational planning is a systematic, developmental process; career preferences start from a very shallow, broad basis in childhood and become more crystallized, yet still changeable, in adolescence. Three relatively distinct views on occupational choice are reviewed: *self-concept development* emphasizes vocational choice as a series of developmental tasks that evolve as the self-concept gains maturity; *cognitive-social growth* views occupational choice as a matter of lifelong decision making in which individuals optimize a balance between their preferences and the requirements of jobs; *life-style orientation* sees occupational choice as an attempt to implement personality style in the context of work.

Because young people often make career decisions on the basis of little information, have limited understanding of their aptitudes, interests, values, and skills, and are thus uncertain about the meaning of the choices and decisions they make, programs in career education have evolved to change the educational system. Career education aims to (1) increase systematically the career options available to young people and (2) facilitate rational career planning. Children in elementary school would be exposed to the general kinds of work available to adults and be taught an appreciation of work. Young people in grades seven through ten would become familiar with groups of occupations—career clusters—and begin to make tentative choices about specialization. The last two grades of high school would be given over to specialized training in a cluster chosen earlier. Career education has been severely criticized, however, on the grounds that it aims primarily to match potential workers with existing jobs, takes the economic structure and corporate order for granted, and fosters false hopes about upward mobility.

The contemporary structure of the American work force has given rise to two serious problems that young people must confront—unemployment and underemployment. On the one hand, unemployment among youth has become widespread, especially for minority youth in urban ghettos, and on the other, meaningful work is hard to find, and youth who prolong their education, aspiring to better jobs and more satisfying careers, may become disenchanted and frustrated when they find that they are overtrained for the kind of work that is open to them. One may increase opportunities for personal fulfillment in two ways. One, change the structure of the workforce, that is, create new types of employment and realign relationships among traditional work roles. Two, co-ordinate existing work opportunities and educational preparation simultaneously at national, state, and community levels. Examples of cooperation already may be found in *action-learning* programs. These have been designed to provide youth with realistic, experience-based alternatives (in community agencies, businesses, and industries) to traditional classroom activities. Action-learning programs point to innovative new approaches to traditional schooling that eventually may become available to youth on a comprehensive, perhaps national scale.

REVIEW QUESTIONS

1. In what types of work are the majority of youth who are out of school employed?
2. What are the characteristics of the work youth generally find?
3. What does the national sample of the high school class of 1972 show youth's attitudes toward work to be?
4. What are some of the factors that promote realism in career planning?
5. Why do so many young girls believe that avenues to leadership and responsibility are closed to them?
6. Why do rural youth aspire relatively to lower levels of occupational achievement?
7. What are the circumstances that lead youth to aspire to the careers of their parents?
8. What are the features of occupations that youth employ to evaluate their prestige?
9. Outline Super's self-concept theory of career development.
10. What is the meaning of the fantasy, tentative, and realistic period, respectively, in career development theory?
11. What are the characteristics of the six model orientations that Holland proposes?
12. What are the primary objectives of career education?
13. Why do proponents of career education believe it should be implemented?
14. What are the general characteristics of a career education program?
15. What are the major objections to career education?
16. How do youth generally learn about the availability of jobs?
17. Why are unemployment and underemployment, respectively, problems youth must confront?
18. What workforce policies does the Panel on Youth and the National Manpower Institute advocate, respectively, to remove barriers related to youth employment?
19. What are the characteristics of action-learning?
20. Describe the types of programs action-learning encompasses.

DISCUSSION QUESTIONS

1. What strategy would you adopt to fit the educational aspirations of young girls to the opportunities open to them?

2. Which occupations in your community are likely to be most attractive to youth? What career ladders do these occupations offer?

3. Let us assume that you are asked to chart a young person's career development. Which theory would you use as a model for your analyses? Why?

4. What objectives would you prescribe for a high school career education program? How would you ensure that your program conveys to youth more than simply an acquaintance with careers?

5. What is the status of action-learning programs in the high schools of your community? What programs would you recommend be strengthened and/or developed?

NOTES

1. R. J. Havighurst and D. Gottlieb. Youth and the meaning of work. In R. J. Havighurst and P. H. Dreyer (Eds.). *Youth—seventy-fourth yearbook of the National Society for the Study of Education*. Chicago: University of Chicago Press, 1975, pp. 145–160.

2. Havighurst and Gottlieb, *op. cit.*

3. A. M. Young. The high school class of 1972: more at work, fewer in college. Washington, D.C.: Bureau of Labor Statistics, *Special Labor Force Report 155*, 1973, Table J.

4. Havighurst and Gottlieb, *op. cit.*

5. J. O'Toole. The reserve army of the underemployed. Washington, D.C.: U.S. Department of Health, Education, and Welfare. *Monographs on Career Education Series, 1975*.

6. O'Toole, *op. cit.*, p. 10.

7. O'Toole, *op. cit.*

8. R. J. Havighurst. Youth in social institutions. In R. J. Havighurst and P. H. Dreyer (Eds.), *Youth—seventy-fourth yearbook of the National Society for the Study of Education*. Chicago: University of Chicago Press, 1975, pp. 115–144.

9. Havighurst, *op. cit.*, p. 119.

10. Havighurst, *op. cit.*, p. 118.

11. Havighurst and Gottlieb, *op. cit.*

12. D. Gottlieb. College youth and the meaning of work. *Vocational Guidance Quarterly*, 1975, **24,** 116–124.

13. J. M. Chick. Implications for counselor education. *Vocational Guidance Quarterly,* **22,** 1973, 108–111; J. C. Flanagan. Some pertinent findings of Project TALENT. *Vocational Guidance Quarterly,* 1973, **22,** 92–96.

14. W. B. Fetters. *National longitudinal study of the high school class of 1972*. National Center for Health Statistics, (DHEW) Numbers 208; 235; 1975; 1976.

15. G. I. Kelso. The influences of stage of leaving school on vocational maturity and realism of vocational choice. *Journal of Vocational Behavior*, 1975, **7,** 29–39.

16. H. S. Astin. Stability and change in the career plans of ninth grade girls. *Personnel and Guidance Journal*, 1968, **46,** 961–966.

17. W. D. Gribbons and P. R. Lohnes. Predicting five years of development in adolescents from readiness for vocational planning scales. *Journal of Educational Psychology,* 1965, **56,** 244–253.

18. W. D. Gribbons and P. R. Lohnes. Shifts in adolescents' vocational values. *Personnel and Guidance Journal,* 1965, **43,** 248–252, p. 251.

19. J. W. Hollender. Development of a realistic vocational choice. *Journal of Counseling Psychology,* 1967, **14,** 314–318.

20. W. W. Cooley. Vocational interests. Paper read at the annual meeting of the American Educational Research Association, 1967; W. W. Cooley. Interactions among interests, abilities, and career plans. *Journal of Applied Psychology,* 1967, **51,** 1–16.

21. Cooley, Vocational interests, *op. cit.,* p. 9.

22. Cooley, Vocational interests, *op. cit.,* p. 7.

23. Flanagan, *op. cit.*

24. Flanagan, *op. cit.*

25. A. G. Cosby, Occupational expectations and the hypothesis of increasing realism of choice. *Journal of Vocational Behavior,* 1974, **5,** 53–65; J. S. Picou, A. G. Cosby, J. W. Lemke, and H. T. Azuma. Occupational choice and perception of attainment blockage: a study of lower-class delinquent and non-delinquent black males. *Adolescence,* 1974, **9,** 289–298; E. J. Smith. Profile of the black individual in vocational literature. *Journal of Vocational Behavior,* 1975, **6,** 41–59.

26. W. P. Kuvlesky, D. E. Wright, and R. Z. Juarez. Status projections and ethnicity: a comparison of mexican-american, negro, and anglo youth. *Journal of Vocational Behavior,* 1971, **1,** 137–151.

27. Picou et al., *op. cit.*

28. Cosby, *op. cit.,* p. 65.

29. Smith, *op. cit.*

30. L. Komisar. Where feminism will lead: an impetus for social change. *Civil Rights Digest,* 1974, **6,** 2–9, p. 2.

31. J. N. Singer. Sex differences-similarities in job preference factors. *Journal of Vocational Behavior,* 1974, **5,** 357–365.

32. S. L. Singer and B. Stefflre. Sex differences in job values and desires. *Personnel and Guidance Journal,* 1954, **32,** 483–484.

33. Singer, *op. cit.,* p. 358.

34. L-E. Datta. Foreword. In E. E. Diamond (Ed.). *Issues of sex bias and sex fairness in career interest measurements.* Washington, D.C.: Department of Health, Education, and Welfare, 1975.

35. S-L. Tibbetts. Sex role stereotyping in the lower grades: part of the solution. *Journal of Vocational Behavior,* 1975, **6,** 255–261.

36. Tibbetts, *op. cit.*

37. C. L. Siegel. Sex differences in the occupational choices of second graders. *Journal of Vocational Behavior,* 1973, **3,** 15–19.

38. Siegel, *op. cit.*

39. B. Karmel. Education and employment aspirations of students: a probabilistic approach. *Journal of Educational Psychology,* 1975, **67,** 57–63.

40. D. Gottlieb and M. L. Bell. Work expectations and work realities: a study of graduating college seniors. *Youth and Society,* 1975, **7,** 69–83.

41. N. S. Cole and G. R. Hanson. Impact of interest inventories on career choice. In E. E. Diamond (Ed.). *Issues of sex bias and sex fairness in career interest measurement.* Washington, D.C.: Department of Health, Education and Welfare, 1975, pp. 1–17.

42. Cole and Hanson, *op. cit.,* p. 10.

43. A. S. Rossi. Equality between the sexes: an immodest proposal. In M. H. Garskoff (Ed.). *Roles women play: readings toward women's liberation.* Belmont, California: Brooks Cole, 1971.

44. L. W. Harmon. The childhood and adolescent career plans of college women. *Journal of Vocational Behavior,* 1971, **1,** 45–56.

45. J. Gaskell. Explaining the aspirations of working class girls. Paper presented at the annual meeting of the American Educational Research Association, Chicago, 1975.

46. M. S. Richardson. The dimensions of career and work orientation in college women. *Journal of Vocational Behavior,* 1974, **5,** 161–172.

47. L. M. Rand and A. L. Miller. A developmental cross-sectioning of women's careers and marriage attitudes and life plans. *Journal of Vocational Behavior,* 1972, **2,** 317–331.

48. E. Matthews and D. V. Tiedeman. Attitudes toward career and marriage and the development of life style in young women. *Journal of Counseling Psychology,* 1964, **11,** 375–384.

49. Rand and Miller, *op. cit.*

50. W. H. Sewell and A. M. Orenstein. Community of residence and occupational choice. *American Journal of Sociology,* 1965, **70,** 551–563,

51. W. H. Sewell. The educational and occupational perspectives of rural youth. Paper prepared for the National Conference on Problems of Rural Youth in a Changing Environment, 1963.

52. Sewell and Orenstein, *op. cit.*

53. Sewell and Orenstein, *op. cit.*

54. M. Straus. Work roles and financial responsibility in the socialization of farm, fringe, and town boys. *Rural Sociology,* 1962, **27,** 257–274.

55. E. L. Gaier and W. F. White. Modes of conformity and career selection of rural and urban high-school seniors. *Journal of Social Psychology,* 1965, **67,** 379–391.

56. A. O. Haller and W. H. Sewell. Occupational choices of Wisconsin farm boys. *Rural Sociology,* 1967, **32,** 37–55.

57. A. Portes, A. O. Haller, and W. H. Sewell. Professional—executive vs. farming as unique occupational roles. *Rural Sociology,* 1968, **33,** 153–159.

58. V. H. Hewer. Vocational interests of college freshmen and their social origin. *Journal of Applied Psychology,* 1965, **49,** 407–411.

59. S. Krippner. Junior high school students' vocational preferences and their parents' occupational levels. *Personnel and Guidance Journal*, 1963, **41,** 590–595.

60. C. E. Werts. Maternal influence on career choice. *Journal of Counseling Psychology*, 1968, **15,** 48–52.

61. W. T. Smelser. Adolescent and adult occupational choice as a function of family socioeconomic history. *Sociometry*, 1963, **26,** 393–409.

62. M. C. Viernstein and R. Hogan. Parental personality factors and achievement motivation in talented adolescents. *Journal of Youth and Adolescence*, 1975, **4,** 183–190.

63. Viernstein and Hogan, *op. cit.*

64. R. H. Hall. *Occupations and the social structure* (2nd ed.). Englewood Cliffs, N.J.: Prentice-Hall, 1975.

65. A. P. Garbin. Occupational choice and the multidimensional rankings of occupations. *Vocational Guidance Quarterly*, 1967, **15,** 17–25.

66. J. A. Fossum and M. L. Moore. The stability of longitudinal and cross-sectional occupational prestige rankings. *Journal of Vocational Behavior*, 1975, **7,** 305–311; M. Plata. Stability and change in the prestige rankings of occupations over 49 years. *Journal of Vocational Behavior*, 1975, **6,** 95–99.

67. G. S. Counts. Social status of occupations. *School Review*, 1925, **33,** 16–17.

68. W. E. Lambert and O. Klineberg. Cultural comparisons of boys' occupational aspirations. *British Journal of Social and Clinical Psychology*, 1963, **2,** 56–65.

69. Lambert and Klineberg, *op. cit.*, p. 58.

70. B. Gunn. Children's conceptions of occupational prestige. *Personnel and Guidance Journal*, 1964, **42,** 558–563.

71. H. A. Nelson and E. C. McDonagh. Perception of statuses and images of selected professions. *Sociology and Social Research*, 1961, **46,** 1–14.

72. Nelson and McDonagh, *op. cit.*

73. H. Borow. Career development. In J. F. Adams (Ed.). *Understanding adolescence* (3rd ed.). Boston: Allyn & Bacon, 1976.

74. Borow, *op. cit.*

75. Borow, *op. cit.*

76. S. H. Osipow. *Theories of career development.* New York: Appleton-Century-Crofts, 1968, p. 117.

77. D. E. Super. *The psychology of careers.* New York: Harper and Row, 1957.

78. Super, *op. cit.*, p. 101.

79. M. D. Galinsky and I. Fast. Vocational choice as a focus of the identity search. *Journal of Counseling Psychology*, 1966, **13,** 89–92, p. 92.

80. E. M. Berger. Vocational choices in college. *Personnel and Guidance Journal*, 1967, 45, 888–894.

81. Berger, *op. cit.*, p. 892.

82. D. E. Super. Vocational development in adolescence and early childhood: tasks and

behaviors. In D. E. Super, R. E. Starishevsky, N. Matlin, and J. P. Jordaan (Eds.). *Career development: self-concept theory.* New York: College Entrance Examination Board, 1963.

83. E. Ginzberg, S. W. Ginsburg, S. Axelrad, and J. L. Herma. *Occupational choice: an approach to a general theory.* New York: Columbia University Press, 1951.

84. E. Ginzberg. Toward a theory of occupational choice: a restatement. *Vocational Guidance Quarterly,* 1972, **20,** 169–176.

85. Ginzberg, *op. cit.,* p. 171.

86. Ginzberg, *op. cit.*

87. J. L. Holland. *The psychology of vocational choice.* Waltham: Blaisdell, 1966; J. L. Holland. *Making vocational choices: a theory of careers.* Englewood Cliffs: Prentice Hall, 1973.

88. Holland, Psychology of vocational choice, *op. cit.,* pp. 16–17.

89. J. L. Holland. *A counselor's guide for use with the self-directed search for educational and vocational planning.* Palo Alto: Consulting Psychologists Press, 1971.

90. Holland, Counselor's guide, *op. cit.,* p. 3.

91. T. J. O'Connell and W. E. Sedlacek. *The reliability of Holland's self-directed search for educational and vocational planning.* College Park, Md: University of Maryland, 1972, 1–8.

92. T. B. Zener. An evaluation of the self-directed search: a guide to educational and vocational planning. Paper presented at the meeting of the American Educational Research Association, Chicago, 1972.

93. W. N. Grubb and M. Lazerson. Rally 'round the workplace: continuities and fallacies in career education. *Harvard Educational Review,* 1975, **45,** 451–474.

94. S. P. Marland. Career education: more than a name. In K. Goldhammer and R. E. Taylor (Eds.). *Career education: perspective and promise.* Columbus, Ohio. Charles E. Merrill, 1972, pp. 43–52.

95. Report of the United States General Accounting Office to the Secretary of Health, Education and Welfare. *Career education: status and needed improvements.* Washington, D.C.: Department of Health, Education and Welfare, 1976, p. 1.

96. S. P. Marland. *Career education: a proposal for reform.* New York: McGraw-Hill, 1974, p. 185.

97. Report of General Accounting Office, *op. cit.,* p. 2.

98. DHEW—U.S. Department of Health, Education and Welfare. *Career education.* Washington, D.C.: DHEW Pub. No. (OE) 72-39, 1–10.

99. A. J. Miller. *The emerging school-based comprehensive education model.* Columbus: The Center for Vocational and Technical Education, Ohio State University, 1972, 1–29.

100. G. I. Swanson. Career education. In K. Goldhammer and R. E. Taylor (Eds.). *Career education: perspective and promise.* Columbus, Ohio: Charles E. Merrill, 1975. pp. 107–119.

101. R. J. Nash and R. M. Agne. *Phi Delta Kappan,* 1973, **54,** 373–378.

102. Nash and Agne, *op. cit.,* p. 377.

103. Grubb and Lazerson, *op. cit.*

104. Grubb and Lazerson, *op. cit.,* p. 473.

105. Grubb and Lazerson, *op. cit.,* p. 466.

106. O'Toole, *op. cit.,* p. 19.

107. S. N. Feingold. Perspectives on career guidance: an administrator's view. *Peabody Journal of Education,* 1974, **52,** 5–13, p. 6.

108. K. B. Hoyt, R. N. Evans, E. F. Mackin, and G. L. Mangum. *Career education: what it is and how to do it.* Salt Lake City, Utah: Olympus Publishing Company, 1974.

109. J. S. Coleman. How do the young become adults? *Review of Educational Research,* 1972, **42,** 431–439.

110. Coleman, *op. cit.*

111. R. J. Noeth, J. D. Roth, and D. J. Prediger. Student career development: where do we stand? *Vocational Guidance Quarterly,* 1975, **23,** 210–218.

112. Noeth et al., *op. cit.*

113. W. Wirtz. *The boundless resource: a perspectus for an education-work policy.* Washington, D.C.: New Republic Book Co., 1975.

114. B. Berger. "People Work"—the youth culture and the labor market. *The Public Interest,* 1974, No. 35, 55–56.

115. O'Toole, *op. cit.,* p. 3.

116. B. Berger. The coming age of people work. *Change,* 1976, **8,** 24–30.

117. W. H. Behn, M. Carnoy, M. A. Carter, J. C. Crain, and H. M. Levin. School is bad; work is worse. *School Review,* 1974, **82,** 49–68, p. 67.

118. O'Toole, *op. cit.,* pp. 23–24.

119. Berger, People work, *op. cit.;* Berger, Coming age, *op. cit.*

120. J. S. Coleman. *Youth: transition to adulthood.* Chicago: University of Chicago Press, 1974.

121. Wirtz, *op. cit.*

122. R. Graham. Youth and experiential learning. In R. J. Havighurst and P. H. Dreyer (Eds.). *Youth—seventy-fourth yearbook of the National Society for the Study of Education.* Chicago: University of Chicago Press, 1975, pp. 161–193, p. 162.

123. G. H. Deutschlander. Action-learning—the curriculum beyond the school. *Bulletin of the National Association of Secondary School Principals,* 1974, **58,** 33–38.

124. H. F. Silberman. Job satisfaction among students in work education programs. *Journal of Vocational Behavior,* 1974, **5,** 261–268.

125. Coleman, Youth, *op. cit.,* p. 139.

126. H. L. Walen. America's high school dilemma, *Bulletin of the National Association of Secondary School Principals,* 1972, **56,** 79–85.

127. F. K. Heussenstamm. Human services education: promises and problems. *Bulletin of the National Association of Secondary School Principals,* 1975, **59,** 55–63.

128. D. J. Eberly. Patterns of volunteer service by young people 1965 and 1974. Paper read at the annual meeting of the American Educational Research Association, San Francisco, 1976.

129. D. Hedin and D. Conrad. Some action-learning models. *Bulletin of the National Association of Secondary School Principals,* 1974, **58,** 22–28.

Photo Credit List

Chapter One
Page 4: Jim Anderson/Woodfin Camp. Page 15: The Granger Collection.
Page 21: Culver Pictures.

Chapter Two
Page 59: Courtesy J. M. Tanner, University of London, From *Daedalus*, 1971,
pp. 907–930.

Chapter Three
Page 91 & 95: Bob Johnstone/Scottsdale Progress.

Chapter Four
Page 110: Nancy Hays/Monkmeyer. Page 116: Charles Gatewood. Page 127:
Andy Mercado/Jeroboam.

Chapter Five
Page 142: Jim Anderson/Woodfin Camp. Page 160: George Cohen/Stock,
Boston.

Chapter Six
Page 187: Sybil Shackman/Monkmeyer.

Chapter Seven
Page 218: Peter Southwick/Stock, Boston. Page 240: Richard Kalvar/
Magnum. Page 253: Frank Siteman/Stock, Boston. Page 257: Charles
Gatewood.

Chapter Eight
Page 298: Rohn Engh/Photo Researchers. Page 302: Erika Stone/Photo
Researchers.

Chapter Nine
Page 339: Yan Lukas/Rapho-Photo Researchers. Page 348: Alex Webb/
Magnum.

Chapter Ten
Page 364: Jim Anderson/Woodfin Camp. Page 366: John Launois/Black Star.
Page 371: Jim Anderson/Woodfin Camp. Page 392: Bruce Roberts/Photo
Researchers.

Chapter Eleven
Page 413: Jim Anderson/Woodfin Camp.

Chapter Twelve
Page 487: Jim Anderson/Woodfin Camp.

Chapter Thirteen
Page 547: Mimi Forsyth/Monkmeyer. Page 555: Sepp Seitz/Magnum.

Glossary

Abstract thinking   The capacity to reason without reference to direct experience; to deal with words, symbols, and concepts; to synthesize several factors into one idea and to manipulate symbols in novel ways.

Accommodation   (Piaget) A change in existing cognitive structures in reponse to new information from the environment.

Achievement test   A standardized test intended to determine how effectively a person has learned a particular area or school subject.

Acquired characters   The concept that new habits or characteristics, acquired as adaptations to environmental conditions, may alter physical structures, which, in turn, are inherited by offspring.

Addiction   Physiological dependence on cigarettes, alcohol, or drugs; associated with a compulsion to continue consumption and withdrawal symptoms.

Affect   A feeling, emotion, or mood that becomes a factor in behavior.

Amphetamines   Drugs that stimulate the central nervous system to suppress sleep and appetite, increase expenditures of energy, check fatigue, and produce feelings of alertness.

Anal stage   (Freud) The second psychosexual period of development; from one to three years of age the child acquires mobility and control of toilet functions. Traits of autonomy, creativity, obstinacy, and stinginess are believed to arise at this time.

Androgynous   A term employed to describe a cultural role for which neither male nor female characteristics are prerequisite.

Anthropometric changes   Changes in such physical characteristics as height and weight and skeletal, muscular, and reproductive structures.

Aptitude test   A standardized test designed to measure how well a person may learn a new subject, skill, or task.

Assimilation   (Piaget) The incorporation of new information into existing cognitive structures.

Authoritarian control   (Baumrind) A pattern of child rearing whereby the child's behavior and conduct are evaluated and controlled firmly in accordance with a set standard of conduct.

Authoritative control   (Baumrind) A pattern of child rearing whereby the child's behavior is guided by reason and justification. An authoritative agent of socialization values both autonomy and conformity.

Autism   A condition in which thinking is governed by personal needs or desires and fantasies, instead of by reality.

Autonomy   Independence; capacity for self-regulation. Moral autonomy refers to the capacity to make decisions that transcend self-interest and promote humankind.

Barbiturates   Central nervous system depressants or sedatives that tranquilize the activity of the heart, nervous system, and skeletal muscles and lead to relaxation and drowsiness.

Body image   An individual's concept of how his or her body appears to others. Relates to standards of beauty learned early in life and contributes to self-concept.

Centration   (Piaget) A tendency in cognitive reasoning to focus on personal actions and viewpoints.

Cognitive development   Growth in intellectual capacity to engage objectively in logical analyses and make symbolic representations.

Concrete operational stage   (Piaget) The third stage of cognitive development, roughly from about seven to eleven years,

during which children acquire the capacity to reason effectively about things, but not yet about verbal propositions.

Conservation   (Piaget) The ability to recognize that the essential features of an object or situation remain invariant or constant, despite a general context of change.

Convergent thinking   (Guilford) The ability to examine data and reduce alternatives in order to arrive at the most logical but not necessarily the most creative answer.

Cross-sectional method   Systematic comparisons of individuals of different ages at the same point in time.

Deductive process   The logical process by which a previously established principle is used to derive a specific conclusion.

Depressant   A mood-altering drug that decreases alertness and diminishes impact of the outer environment on thoughts and feelings.

Descriptive approach   Research procedure by which data are reported numerically or biographically. Descriptive data do not lend themselves to causal inferences.

Designed approach   The process of collecting data either by making systematic observations without disturbing the environment or by contriving to elicit specific behaviors.

Diagnostic tests   Tests designed to identify specific deficiencies and areas that require improvement.

Divergent thinking   (Guilford) A process whereby alternatives are examined, intellectual risks are taken, and data are continuously analyzed in order to arrive at creative solutions.

Ego   (Freud) The personality component that involves reality perception and control of cognitive functions.

Empirical research   A methodology based on observation and experimentation

Equilibration   (Piaget) A self-regulating mechanism whereby balance is achieved between accommodation and assimilation as a child moves through stages of cognitive growth.

Fear of success   Negative or ambivalent feelings that arise when an individual anticipates success, especially when the success requires expression of aggression and competiveness.

Formal operational stage   (Piaget) The final stage of cognitive development, which begins at about 12 years of age. It encompasses the ability to generate all possible combinations within a logical system.

Generational unit model   (Mannheim) The explanation that countercultures arise because young people, as they coalesce as a generational unit, develop a new social consciousness and exert pressure on the relatively stable structures of society for new forms of social organization.

Genetic psychology   A viewpoint about human development in which hereditary rather than social aspects of growth are stressed.

Growth spurt   The rapid growth in bodily dimensions that occurs for most children between the ages of about nine and fifteen; called the "adolescent growth spurt."

Habituation   Psychological dependence on cigarettes, alcohol, or drugs; associated with a compulsion to continue consumption but not with consistent withdrawal symptoms.

Hallucinogen   A drug that produces perceptions which may lack a basis in reality.

Heredity   The transmission of characteristics from parent to offspring.

High achiever   (overachiever) A student who performs in school above expectations relative to his or her aptitude.

Hypothesis   A theory or proposition accepted either as a tentative explanation or as a basis for further investigation.

Id   (Freud) The biological component of personality, which is governed by the pleasure principle and is the source of instinctual drives.

Identification   The process by which an individual acquires particular behavioral characteristics and attitudes of significant persons.

Identity formation   The acquisition of an integrated self-concept or self-image that is autonomous of the values and standards of others.

Inductive process   The logical process by which particular observations are used to infer a principle or generalization.

Instinct   An inborn, unlearned tendency to behave in a certain characteristic way.

Intelligence test   A standardized test designed to either assess or predict functioning in a wide variety of situations.

Lamarckianism   See *Acquired characters*.

Latency period   (Freud) A period of psychosexual development, from about age five to the onset of puberty, during which sexuality is dormant and aspects of cognitive, affective, and physical growth acquire salience.

Libido   (Freud) The source of psychic energy; the driving force behind sexual impulses.

Longitudinal method   Systematic comparisons based on the same person or group of persons at periodic intervals.

Manipulative procedure   A *designed approach* in which specific conditions are contrived in the laboratory or natural environment to elicit specific behaviors.

Mastery test   A test used to analyze deficiencies, but more importantly, to establish either how much an individual knows or the extent to which he or she can perform a task.

Maturation   Progressive development of physical and cognitive functions; largely a function of genetic predispositions.

Menarche   The onset of menstruation; occurrence of the first menstrual period.

Model   An individual whom another admires and seeks to emulate.

Motive   An inner drive or impulse that arouses, maintains, and directs behavior toward an incentive or goal.

Narcotic   A drug derived from opium or its chemical equivalent; originally used as pain reliever; now primarly as a *psychoactive drug*.

Naturalistic procedure   Data collection based on systematic observations in the natural environment. Care is taken to avoid disturbing the environment under study.

Norm A representative standard of a group, often the numerical median or average, against which the performance of an individual may be compared.

Nubility The capacity of an adolescent girl to ovulate, become pregnant, carry a fetus to term, and manage childbirth.

Nuclear family Family unit comprised of mother, father, and their children living independently of relatives.

Operation (Piaget) Cognitive coordination of perceptions and motor behaviors that leads to logical systems and generalizable actions.

Oral stage (Freud) The first psychosexual period, about the first year of life, during which the infant focuses on erogenous sensations derived from sucking, biting, chewing. Emotional dependency and feelings of love and hate are believed to be engendered at this time.

Peer A person equal to another in terms of such characteristics as age and social class.

Perception The process of translating sensory stimuli into awareness and knowledge of objects and events.

Permissive control (Baumrind) A pattern of child rearing whereby the child's behavior is guided in a nonpunitive, acceptant, and affirmative manner.

Phallic stage (Freud) The third psychosexual stage of childhood; from three to five or six years of age, sexual and aggressive feelings are focused on the sexual organs. The oedipal conflict occurs during this period.

Preoperational stage (Piaget) Roughly the second stage of cognitive development, from age two to about seven years, during which children acquire language and symbolic functions and begin to recognize perspectives other than their own.

Primary sex characteristics The genitals and accessory organs, encompassing the penis, testes, and scrotum in males and the uterus, ovaries, vagina, labia, and clitoris in females.

Psychedelic drugs Drugs used to alter the intensity of sensory perceptions that may have no direct environmental basis.

Psychoactive drugs Drugs that affect moods, perceptions, and levels of consciousness.

Puberty The stage in physical development when an individual becomes capable of sexual reproduction.

Recapitulation, theory of (Hall) The concept that each individual retraces the historical record of his or her species (phylogeny) in his or her own growth (ontogeny).

Reflex A simple, stimulus-response sequence. Innate reflexes are usually regarded as involuntary actions.

Retrospective approach A research method by which present behavior is analyzed in terms of past events. Includes both *longitudinal* and *cross-sectional* methods of data collection.

Rite of passage A ritual that marks the transition of an individual from one stage of life to another.

Role The behavior and attitudes that a person who holds a social position is expected to perform and express.

Schema (Piaget) The basic unit of cognitive organization which continuously changes as perceptions and motor behavior become coordinated.

Secondary sex characteristics Bodily features correlated with development of reproductive capacity; for example; in males, facial hair and deepening voice; in females, breast and hip development; in both, pubic and axillary (armpit) hair.

Self-concept Perceptions an individual has about himself or herself formed through inferences drawn from experiences.

Sensorimotor stage (Piaget) Roughly the first stage of cognitive development, from birth to about two years, during which children integrate mental imagery, motor activity, and physical experiences.

Sex-role learning The acquisition of the role performances and attitudes that coincide with cultural expectations of either masculinity or femininity.

Sex-role stereotyping The belief that males and females should be socialized to conform to cultural expectations regarding masculinity and femininity, respectively.

Social class A classification by which individuals are grouped as a consequence of income, family background, education, and occupational status. Persons in different classifications are believed to be distinguishable on the basis of their conceptions of social reality.

Socialization The process by which individuals learn the values, attitudes, skills, and motivations that enable them to function in the settings in which they live.

Socioeconomic status See *Social class*.

Sociometry A technique for describing social preferences in a group; results in a sociogram; a composite diagram that represents each member's feelings about others in the group.

Stimulant A drug that pushes expenditures of energy, enhances reaction to stimuli, and fosters feelings of exhileration.

Structural-functionist model (Eisenstadt) The explanation that countercultures arise, not because youth reject adult society, but because they believe that they have only limited opportunity to obtain its rewards and are reacting against the social forces that impede them.

Superego (Freud) The social-conscience component of personality that encompasses internalized values and standards. Self-control supersedes parental control in the mature superego.

Syllogism A form of logical reasoning in which a conclusion is drawn from two statements or premises.

Transitivity The capacity to arrange elements in a series; for example, from shortest to longest or from smallest to biggest.

Underachiever A student who performs in school below expectations relative to his or her aptitude.

Underemployment The concept that the work tasks required of an individual are elementary relative to his or her work skills.

Variable Any property or characteristic that may change from one situation to another. An independent variable is controlled and varied systematically; a dependent variable is expected to change as a consequence of the manipulation of the independent variable.

Venereal disease A contagious infection such as gonorrhea or syphilis, which is usually communicated through sexual intercourse.

Youth culture A common repertoire of language, slang, grooming, clothing, music, and so forth that a cohort of young people adopt collectively to express distinctiveness.

Author Index

Subject Index

597